Yearbook of International Humanitarian Law

Volume 17

More information about this series at http://www.springer.com/series/8912

Terry D. Gill
General Editor

Yearbook of International Humanitarian Law Volume 17, 2014

ASSER PRESS

Springer

General Editor
Terry D. Gill
University of Amsterdam and Netherlands
Defence Academy
Amsterdam/Breda
The Netherlands

Cover picture: Bucy-le-Long, district of Soissons, Aisne, France, 1917. Section of gunners, 4 soldiers in ruins, pulling. Reproduced with permission, www.worldwaronecolorphotos.com.

ISSN 1389-1359 ISSN 1574-096X (electronic)
Yearbook of International Humanitarian Law
ISBN 978-94-6265-089-3 ISBN 978-94-6265-091-6 (eBook)
DOI 10.1007/978-94-6265-091-6

Library of Congress Control Number: 2015950975

Published by T.M.C. ASSER PRESS, The Hague, The Netherlands www.asserpress.nl
Produced and distributed for T.M.C. ASSER PRESS by Springer-Verlag Berlin Heidelberg

Printed on acid-free paper

Springer Science+Business Media B.V. Dordrecht is part of Springer Science+Business Media
(www.springer.com)

Contents

1914–2014: WWI Centenary 100 Years of Warfare Evolution

Chapter 1
The Evolution in the Legal Protection of Victims of Armed Conflict

Peter Maurer

Abstract As the means, methods and strategy of warfare have evolved over centuries, so have the effects of war on its victims. The changing nature of armed conflict, evolving means and methods of combat, and the definition of who is considered a war victim under the law are inextricably linked to the relatively new concept of legal protection of victims of armed conflict, which emerged only at the end of the nineteenth century. Both the definition of victims of conflict and the scope of legal protection may have to be revised as modern warfare changes the conditions and consequences of conflict. To date, the Geneva Conventions have lent themselves to reinterpretation as the nature of conflict has evolved, providing progressively extensive legal protection in different types and situations of conflict. However, it cannot be excluded that a revision or extension of the very foundations of IHL may be necessary at some point in the near future, further expanding the legal protection of victims of armed conflict. It is the duty of the ICRC as the guardian of IHL to consider and propose changes to this body of law to ensure that future victims of conflict will have the necessary legal protection.

Keywords International Committee of the Red Cross · ICRC · Geneva Conventions · Victims of armed conflict · Interpretation of international humanitarian law

---

Peter Maurer is President of the International Committee of the Red Cross.

P. Maurer (✉)
International Committee of the Red Cross, Geneva, Switzerland

T.D. Gill et al. (eds.), *Yearbook of International Humanitarian Law 2014*,
Yearbook of International Humanitarian Law 17,
DOI 10.1007/978-94-6265-091-6_1

1.3 IHL and the ICRC

The fundamental aim of international humanitarian law can be summarised as protecting and assisting those who are not or no longer participating in hostilities: civilians; sick and wounded members of armed forces; and prisoners of war. Whenever the parties to a conflict do not respect this body of law, they can be held accountable. As IHL has evolved over the years, the standards of what is considered acceptable within conflict have also evolved. The distinction between collateral damage, regrettable side effects, unacceptable violations and outright atrocities is largely due to the principles underpinning IHL.

The ICRC performs a particular role as the guardian of IHL. It also provides aid and other support to civilians and other non-combatants when the authorities are unwilling or unable to do so themselves. As a neutral, impartial and independent humanitarian organisation, it acts exclusively to protect the lives and dignity of victims of conflict. In order to fulfil its mandate, the forms of assistance and protection it offers to victims of armed conflict have developed in parallel with the changing nature and methods of conflict.

The ICRC's wide array of activities in situations of armed conflict can be divided into three main categories: preventive, operational and post-conflict. The ICRC works with authorities and all arms carriers to make them aware of their legal obligations under IHL, in an effort to prevent suffering by strengthening respect for this body of law. Efforts to protect and assist victims of armed conflict can take various forms, including providing for basic needs like food, water, shelter, medical attention and other essential items. Particularly vulnerable people such as detainees may receive special assistance. When communications are cut off or families are separated by conflict, the ICRC seeks to restore contact and reunite families, often long after the fighting ends.

In its capacity as a neutral, impartial and independent organisation, the ICRC maintains contact with all parties to a conflict and works tirelessly to gain access to conflict zones. However, humanitarian workers themselves—including ICRC staff—are at times specifically targeted by weapon bearers, which can ultimately jeopardise operations by creating unacceptable security risks. In such cases the legal protection of victims of armed conflict reaches an impasse: when those whose task it is to protect the victims are prevented from doing so by life-threatening dangers, legal protection becomes an abstraction; and this despite States' responsibility to respect and ensure respect for the law.

Any analysis of the legal protection for victims of armed conflict and how it has changed over time must consider the evolution of on-the-ground assistance operations. Irrespective of advances, or the lack thereof, in the legal sphere, unparalleled financial and operational means and a global network of humanitarian actors have revolutionised the effective protection of victims of armed conflict. The law may have an all-encompassing ambition and claim, but in reality the feasibility and extent of operations often determine the actual implementation of the law.

During the First World War, for instance, 41 ICRC delegates carried out only 524 visits to detainees. During the Second World War, 11,000 detention visits by 150 delegates took place. And in 2013 alone, 750,000 detainees received ICRC visits. Greater operational and financial capacity today simply allow for a much broader implementation of the protection enshrined in IHL.

Throughout its 150-year history, the ICRC has shown its mastery of its unique status as an organisation whose mandate encompasses both developing the law and operating on the ground. When operational expansion makes sense within the legal framework, the ICRC expands on the ground. When the legal framework needs elaboration, the organisation pushes for that. Be it in the legal or operational sphere, the ICRC pursues its mandate to protect and assist the victims of conflict.

1.4 The Changing Nature of Conflict

Since the end of the Cold War, the world has seen an increasing number of asymmetric conflicts in a multipolar world. Non-State armed groups, which themselves are often fragmented, together with the constant emergence of new armed groups raise new hurdles for IHL and related assistance and protection efforts.

During the First World War, countries declared war on each other, and each of the warring parties was clearly delineated. One hundred years later, the majority of conflicts are waged by non-State armed groups that do not necessarily accept their legal responsibilities under IHL. Indeed, these groups may not even be aware of their obligations, posing a new challenge to the ICRC, which in turn seeks to inform and educate all weapon bearers about their responsibilities under the law.

State armies function as the extension of States that have ratified the Geneva Conventions; non-State armed groups, operating in the vacuum left by weak States, may not recognise or know their duties under IHL. A current example is the public propaganda of ISIS, which deliberately calls for attacks on both soldiers and civilians.

This new paradigm forces the ICRC to rethink its approach to informing and educating all weapon bearers of their responsibilities under IHL.

1.5 Developments in Means and Methods of Warfare

The evolving nature of warfare is not limited to changes in the parties engaging in armed conflict but also encompasses the means and methods of warfare. Warfare no longer looks much like the First World War, when opposing armies faced off bearing traditional weapons, and much of this is due to technological advances.

The focus of hostilities, for example, has shifted from battlefields to urban centres over the past century. Fighting that targets military objectives located in densely populated areas or takes place in urban settings where civilian homes and infrastructure are destroyed rarely complies with the IHL principles of distinction, proportionality and precaution.

Some new technologies may actually have a positive impact by reducing the numbers of potential victims of armed conflict. For instance, the use of targeted drones can minimise the effects on the civilian population compared to large-scale bombardments. However, technological advances, even when ushering in apparently positive consequences, pose a challenge as they may require the existing law to be reinterpreted, or even adapted.

New actors and methods within conflict raise new challenges for IHL. But the legal framework has always been and continues to be a living body of norms. While adapting IHL to the constantly shifting sands of conflict, we must take care to preserve what has been achieved and to safeguard the standards of protection that have stood the test of time.

IHL will be continually adapted to keep up with changes in warfare. The ICRC in turn will, in accordance with its mandate, continue to do what it has done for the past 150 years: serve as the guardian of IHL, upholding its current form and seeking to further develop and expand this body of law in the future.

1.6 The Way Forward

As the reality of warfare is constantly changing, new questions regularly arise for the interpretation and advancement of IHL.

One striking example is the legal vacuum exposed by the plight and status of the tens of thousands of people every year who risk their lives trying to cross the Mediterranean Sea to reach Europe. Their reasons vary; some are fleeing conflict in their home countries, while others are economic migrants trying to build new lives abroad. On those ramshackle boats crammed with people, we see a situation of grave humanitarian need where neither the security nor the dignity of the passengers is ensured. Government authorities, human rights organisations and the humanitarian sector have to face up to this new form of humanitarian crisis: a crisis that is temporary in nature for the victims; that is the culmination of a multitude of factors; and that features some of the same needs as conflict-related humanitarian crises. Humanitarian groups are being forced to consider whether their mission is keeping pace with a changing reality.

Both the definition of victims of conflict and the scope of legal protection may have to be revised as modern warfare changes the conditions and consequences of conflict. To date, the Geneva Conventions have lent themselves to reinterpretation as the nature of conflict has evolved, providing progressively extensive legal protection in different types and situations of conflict.

However, it cannot be excluded that a revision or extension of the very foundations of IHL may be necessary at some point in the near future, further expanding the legal protection of victims of armed conflict. It is the duty of the ICRC as the guardian of IHL to consider and propose changes to this body of law to ensure that future victims of conflict will have the necessary legal protection.

Chapter 2
One Hundred Years of Chemical Warfare and Disarmament: Then and Now

Ahmet Üzümcü

Abstract On 22 April 2015, we commemorate the turning of a tragic page in human history—the 100th anniversary of the first large-scale use of chemical weapons near Ieper in Belgium. In the wake of this attack and for the remainder of World War I, both sides unleashed similar weapons, as well as developed new and deadlier ones to inflict more than a million casualties. What made these events all the more tragic was the fact that an international legal instrument banning the use of poisonous gases in warfare was in place well before the outbreak of World War I. This was The Hague Convention of 1899. Now, as we contemplate what we have achieved in chemical disarmament since that time, it is worth asking what has contributed to our success, and what we need to do in order to secure the durability of this success into the future. As we commemorate the centenary of the chemical attacks in Ieper, we need to draw inspiration not only from the success of the Chemical Weapons Convention as a unique multilateral accord, but also from the political will that has driven its implementation. These form the axis of a comprehensive and effective regime, driven by close partnership with science and industry—a regime that will continue to address new and emerging challenges to make our hard-won disarmament gains permanent.

Keywords Organisation for the prohibition of chemical weapons · OPCW · Chemical warfare · Biological Weapons Convention · Chemical Weapons Convention

---

Ahmet Üzümcü is Director-General of the Organisation for the Prohibition of Chemical Weapons.

A. Üzümcü (✉)
Organisation for the Prohibition of Chemical Weapons, The Hague, The Netherlands

T.D. Gill et al. (eds.), *Yearbook of International Humanitarian Law 2014*,
Yearbook of International Humanitarian Law 17,
DOI 10.1007/978-94-6265-091-6_2

On 22 April 2015, we commemorate the turning of a tragic page in human history—the 100th anniversary of the first large-scale use of chemical weapons near Ieper in Belgium. In the wake of this attack and for the remainder of World War I, both sides unleashed similar weapons, as well as developed new and deadlier ones to inflict more than a million casualties. The widespread use of chemical weapons stands as one of the First World War's most haunting legacies. For many, it marked the conflict as 'the chemists' war'.

What made these events all the more tragic was the fact that an international legal instrument banning the use of poisonous gases in warfare was in place well before the outbreak of World War I. This was The Hague Convention of 1899. Now, as we contemplate what we have achieved in chemical disarmament since that time, it is worth asking what has contributed to our success, and what we need to do in order to secure the durability of this success into the future.

Unusually in the history of multilateral arms control, the 1899 Hague Convention had anticipated the brutal impact of chemical weapons before it came to be experienced. It was an uncommon instance of diplomats and lawyers successfully defining inhumane weapons, and seeking to prevent them from being used, before they had actually made their debut on the scale that they did.

Failure to enforce this instrument in the course of World War I marked the beginning of an almost century-long effort to arrive at a comprehensive global ban against chemical weapons. This finally came in the form of the Chemical Weapons Convention, which was concluded in 1992 and entered into force 5 years later in 1997.

This was a difficult process. For unlike other types of weapons of mass destruction, chemical weapons were used with brutal regularity over the course of the twentieth century, from Africa to Asia. What is more, their use was not limited to the battlefield. The place names of Halabja in Iraq and Sardasht in Iran have become synonymous with the human misery resulting from peaceful civilians being attacked with these terrible weapons.

After the chemical horrors of the First World War, the 1925 Geneva Protocol sought to address ambiguities in The Hague Convention. But its shortcomings soon became apparent, when several signatories submitted reservations that left open the possibility of retaliating against chemical weapon attacks in kind. Further, while banning the use of chemical weapons, the Protocol failed to curb production, development and stockpiling of such weapons. In the absence of provisions for this, more than 70,000 metric tonnes of chemical agent—mainly deadly nerve gases such as sarin—had been stockpiled by the 1980s.

The next breakthrough came much later, when talks on a chemical weapons treaty began in the wake of the conclusion of the Biological Weapons Convention in 1972. If there was any consolation to be had from the brutal excesses of chemical weapons use during the Iran-Iraq War, it was that it focused minds in the course of negotiations on a global chemical weapons ban at the Conference on Disarmament in Geneva. These negotiations, assisted also by a new spirit of cooperation between the superpowers in the twilight of the Cold War, rendered a treaty with a uniquely comprehensive scope.

More than two decades since it was concluded, the Chemical Weapons Convention remains the most comprehensive disarmament and non-proliferation treaty in the history of multilateral arms control.

The Convention prohibits not only the use of chemical weapons, but also their development, production, stockpiling, transfer and retention—something that was missing in the chemical disarmament treaties preceding it. And, unlike the Nuclear Non-Proliferation Treaty, it is non-discriminatory. There are no haves and have-nots, given that no member is permitted to possess chemical weapons: those that do are obliged to destroy them, while those that do not are obliged never to acquire them. Finally, to hold the 190 members of the Convention to shared obligations, all are subject to an international verification regime administered by the Convention's implementing body, the Organisation for the Prohibition of Chemical Weapons (OPCW).

In short, the Chemical Weapons Convention is the only international treaty that not only bans an entire class of weapons of mass destruction, but also has the authority and mechanisms for policing this ban through international verification.

Diplomats and lawyers did not have a monopoly on the successful negotiation of this landmark treaty. Its extensive provisions were the product of participation in the Geneva negotiations by scientists and industry representatives on the basis of a simple but key fact: states' confidence in the Convention would depend on the effectiveness of its verification methods and on the integrity of its confidentiality arrangements. Given that many of the materials and technologies relevant to the development of chemical weapons also have legitimate commercial applications, scientists and industry were, and continue to be, key partners in global chemical disarmament.

These foundations have made the Chemical Weapons Convention the remarkable success that it is. In only 17 years, we have seen our membership swell to 190 States Parties, and the OPCW has verified the destruction of some 86 % of all declared chemical weapons and conducted more than 2500 inspections of industrial facilities in more than 80 countries. It is this record of achievement that in 2013 earned the OPCW the award of the Nobel Peace Prize.

Most recently, the unprecedented mission to eliminate Syria's chemical weapons has amply demonstrated the resilience of the Convention. Syria's accession to the Convention meant that there was no need for a specially mandated ad hoc arrangement to oversee the removal and destruction process—the Convention came into play as a ready-made, tried-and-tested vehicle for achieving Syria's complete chemical demilitarisation.

Nonetheless, the confirmed use of chemical weapons in Syria last year had made clear that our success can only be as broad as our reach. That is why one of our most immediate priorities is to persuade the six countries—Angola, Egypt, Israel, Myanmar, North Korea and South Sudan—that still remain outside the Convention to join it, without delay and without conditions. There should be no doubt in anyone's mind that, despite its not yet being universally adhered to, the Convention is a long-standing global norm which the international community has shown itself only too willing to enforce.

More also needs to be done to strengthen implementation of the Convention at the national level. Seventeen years since the Convention's entry into force, many States Parties have still not established mechanisms for meeting their obligations or, in some cases, even adopted implementing legislation. This is a serious shortcoming, as we ultimately can only be as strong as our weakest link. However comprehensive the Convention is, its effectiveness derives from actions, not mere words on paper.

Looking into the future, the challenge for the Convention will be to maintain its relevance and effectiveness in the face of new advances in science and technology that could test its integrity and implementation. Thankfully, it was to avoid any ambiguity over what constitutes a chemical weapon that the Convention included a general-purpose criterion that defines chemical weapons in terms of their function rather than lethality. This should not, nonetheless, prevent the Convention from hosting informed discussion between stakeholders to make sure that practice keeps up with theory—something that we at the OPCW do through various formal and informal mechanisms.

In this regard, a decisive moment is looming for us as we rapidly approach complete destruction of declared chemical weapon stocks and begin to recalibrate our priorities to prevent the re-emergence of such weapons. The activities of non-state actors, especially terrorist groups in regions of instability and conflict, present an especially daunting challenge in this regard, given their often stated interest in acquiring and using such weapons. How to deal with players whose actions are not deterred by traditional disincentives presents a quandary for the international community that goes well beyond global non-proliferation norms. Part of our approach must be informed by the holistic nature of the mission that the Chemical Weapons Convention charges us with: while we are not an anti-terrorist organisation, we do have responsibility for ensuring chemical weapons do not spread in any form or in any guise.

As we prepare to commemorate the centenary of the chemical attacks in Ieper, we need to draw inspiration not only from the success of the Chemical Weapons Convention as a unique multilateral accord, but also from the political will that has driven its implementation. These form the axis of a comprehensive and effective regime, driven by close partnership with science and industry—a regime that will continue to address new and emerging challenges to make our hard-won disarmament gains permanent.

Chapter 3
Warfare 1914–2014: The Most Violent Century in Human History

Wim Klinkert

Abstract In the Spring of 1915 the French literary critic, journalist and theatre director Alphonse Séché (1876–1964) published a book on the Great War which was about six months old at the time. He called his extensive analysis *Les guerres d' enfer* (Wars of Hell) and this unlikely expert displayed a remarkable insight into the fundamental shift that warfare had experienced in the previous months. War is very multifaceted today. We have great difficulty to come to terms with it in a conceptual way. So many names have come and gone to describe the framework in which violence is used: peacekeeping, counterinsurgency, responsibility to protect, peace enforcing, low intensity conflict, ethnical or religious conflict, postmodern war, hybrid war, third-generation warfare, etc. Some terms are legal, others political or historical. The great diversity shows the confusion in how to interpret the influence of modern (digital) technology and new ideas on how and when to use violence.

Keywords World War I · World War II · Violence · Séché · Total War

---

W. Klinkert (✉)
Netherlands Defence Academy, Breda, The Netherlands
University of Amsterdam, Amsterdam, The Netherlands
e-mail: w.klinkert@uva.nl

T.D. Gill et al. (eds.), *Yearbook of International Humanitarian Law 2014*,
Yearbook of International Humanitarian Law 17,
DOI 10.1007/978-94-6265-091-6_3

In the Spring of 1915 the French literary critic, journalist and theatre director Alphonse Séché (1876–1964) published a book on the Great War which was about six months old at the time. He called his extensive analysis *Les guerres d' enfer* (Wars of Hell) and this unlikely expert displayed a remarkable insight into the fundamental shift that warfare had experienced in the previous months. War had lost all its romantic and chivalric connotations like courage and sacrifice, bravery and exemplary leadership and the moral qualities associated with the will to win for a greater good. War in the year 1915 was about technology, about indiscriminate violence against soldiers and civilians alike, it was about mass destruction—especially from the air—and it meant the end of any optimistic idea that rules of law could reduce random destruction in any way. In short, Séché saw industrial mass warfare and mass destruction of cities, not hindered by legal restraints, as the consequence of the modern age he lived in. He did not condemn this, but accepted it as the way of warfare befitting the industrial age. In practice it meant countries as a whole—military and civilians together—had to prepare economically, militarily and morally for this future in order to survive.

Séché was one of the first, but certainly not the only one, who concluded in 1915 that warfare had undergone a dramatic change. It was only months after the 'rape of Belgium' by the German army, it was the year poison gas, hand grenades, modern mortars and many new mass-produced weapons entered the battlefield. And it was the year airplanes were first used to deliberately attack cultural landmarks, when the Austrian army attacked Venetian church domes and that year both Germans and Allied bombed civilian centres in enemy territories from the air. For many contemporaries it seemed as if the war had shredded the whole structure of humanitarian and international law, as if the Nobel Peace Prize and the recently opened Hague Peace Palace had outlived their short existence already.

Séché did not use the term yet—it was only coined in 1918—but war had become 'total'. Societies as a whole attacked their opponents not only on the battlefield but also inland, either from the air or through naval blockades. Hunger and the tenacity of the civilian population to withstand all this became as important as battlefield victories. The French Prime Minister Georges Clemenceau (1841–1929) declared in parliament on 20 November 1917: *Nous nous présentons devant vous dans l'unique pensée d'une guerre intégrale.* (We come before you in the one thought of an integrated war), by which he meant that the struggle of France was a struggle of all its citizens, in factories, in universities and in the military. At the same time the German generals more or less turned the country into a military dictatorship in order to peruse their war aims. The general's attempts to control all aspects of society failed, but the experience of *Totale Mobilmachung* (the title of the 1930 book by Ernst Jünger) would resound for decades.

Turning the battlefield experience into a 'production line of death' was one of the strong images that dominated Europe after 1918, as well as the idea that modern war meant destruction of population centres and cultural landmarks, as well as deportations and hunger. The purifying role of warfare, a popular notion at the end of the nineteenth century and the liberal optimism that globalisation and rational international juridical agreements between 'civilised' (which meant white) nations promised a more peaceful future lay shattered in pieces. Radical ideologies of the right and the left, unleashed by years of massive brutality in Europa also seemed to predict a violent future. The Wilsonian appeals "to end all wars" and "to make the world safe for democracy" found less resonance than the fears of future aerial bombing of civilians with gas and ideologies that celebrated antagonism, notwithstanding the pacifism among many veterans of the trenches and the lofty ideals of the League of Nations. But the legacy of the more than ten million dead of the First World War was multifaceted.

On the one hand, international negotiations led to reductions in weaponry like at the Washington Conference (1921–1922) that prevented a new naval arms race and the Geneva Protocol banning the use of chemical and biological weapons (1925). Also, many powers reduced their defence spending considerably. Moreover, any war memoirs, which were published in huge numbers in all former belligerents, had a distinct anti-war message, the most famous being *Le Feu* by Henri Barbusse (1916) and *Im Westen Nichts Neues* (1929) by Erich Maria Remarque.

On the other hand, violence in many forms was rife in the 1920s and 1930s. The First World War had unleashed the airplane as a weapon and the British army in Somalia and Iraq made the first post-war use of it in 1919–1921. Encouraged by Winston Churchill, the Royal Air Force was deployed to bomb civilians in order to uphold British authority in these distant corners of the Empire. In Europe the combination of an aerial attack with bombs and gas against cities was the gloom-and-doom scenario, vividly portrayed in many anti-war publications. In the colonies things were different and both the Spanish and the Italians did not shy away from using airplanes to throw gas bombs on targets in Morocco and Ethiopia respectively.

In Europe itself, ideologically inspired violence was everywhere: from the Russian civil war, and the Russian-Polish War to the Irish struggle for independence and the Italian strife between fascists and socialists, which brought the country to the brink of civil war. In the new Turkish Republic the Greeks fought a war that, in the end, dislodged them from their ancestral homeland. All in all, violence and warfare had become very diverse in appearance and the ideological context it was used.

What was the real lesson of 1914–1918? Again, the answers varied considerably, but one thing was more or less certain to many observers: the Versailles Peace Treaty would not lead to a peaceful world. To a greater or lesser extent all European powers agreed on this. The League of Nations was not strong enough to solve fundamental differences; it had enough trouble with containing smaller disputes. The first time it established a multinational peacekeeping force was in 1920 to Vilnius, a city disputed by Lithuanians, Poles and Russians. This was no great success, but the League did prove its worth when it organised plebiscites and even administrated former German territories like Danzig (Gdansk) and Saar (Sarre).

Of a more fundamental nature were lessons drawn by the major belligerents. The French, for instance, thought a new war would be a long drawn out 'total war', to be fought by the entire population, either in the army or in the factory.

Also, the enemy was not to enter French territory again and destroy precious parts of it, like in 1914–1918. As trench warfare had been a French victory ('the line had held') but a very costly one, a new, well-prepared, modern trench line directly at the border had to be created: the Maginot Line, simultaneously stressing the 'Frenchness' of the returned provinces of Alsace and Lorraine. The French army invested in concrete, guns and strong defence lines.

The dominant British lesson was a completely different one. The impact and shock the war had had on the British Isles was such that support for the 'continental commitment' disappeared. To avoid future mass deaths, British strategic thinkers emphasised the role of the navy and, even more that of the air force to protect and to deter. Furthermore, the concepts of 'total war' and conscription ware alien to most British, which gave free reign to ideas that focused on technology and professionalism in the armed forces, as most loathed the WWI mass army. Ironically, for this reason, well-known British military thinkers like Basil Liddell Hart (1895–1970) and John Fuller (1878–1966) stimulated ideas of modern technological warfare, thereby influencing Germans and Russians in their development of the modern mechanised battlefield.

It was the Germans and Russians—the two pariahs of 1918—that during the interwar years brought military thinking substantially many steps further. Ideologically opposed, but both interested in building a strong modern army based on modern technology, they even collaborated successfully in the 1920s. The German officers were driven by both a tradition of military scholarship of the highest level and by a desire to win the next war. Violating the limitations set by the allies in the 1919 Versailles peace treaty, the German *Reichswehr* analysed and experimented, both technologically and with army doctrine. When Hitler provided them with the money and goods to put ideas into practice, a modern army and air force were built up quickly. This did not mean the German military spoke with one voice on future warfare; they themselves were probably the most thunderstruck by their own victory over France in 1940, but by developing armoured armies based on speed and mobility they set a new standard in warfare.

The Russian contribution is twofold. First, the Russian officers thought it was possible to have a mass low-tech infantry army based on conscription together with a huge, modern armoured tank force, and combined with a huge air fleet with paratroopers and fast modern mechanised units on the ground. No other country had the potential to create an army like this on such a scale, using standardised modern armoured technology. Second, the Russians were extremely innovative in creating their army doctrine. They developed a new level between tactics and strategy: the operational level, theoretically defined by its intellectual father Alexander Svechin (1878–1938) as "the art of combining preparations for war and the grouping of operations for achieving the goal for the armed forces set by the war". It meant 'strategy' got a new meaning, having lost its classic connotation with major military campaigns. It is on these main developments in Germany and Russia that the American army would build its theoretical basis during and after the Cold War.

In the late 1930s the world drifted to another global conflict. The League of Nations could not live up to its promises and aggression paid off, be it by Japan in Asia or Italy in Africa. But war is never unavoidable, human choice is always involved. History is not deterministic. That the world had to live through another world war, many times more atrocious, deadly and boundless than the one fought by the previous generation was no 'law of nature'. Hitler's coming to power and the fact that he could employ the power of the German state in order to realise megalomaniac and extreme ideological war aims, put the world in flames yet again. Warfare reached unimaginable extremes in the largest land war seen in history, the battle between Germany and the Soviet Union (1941–1945). Mechanised warfare was waged in gigantic battles, from which military theorists—Americans and Israelis especially—drew their own ideas until far into the twentieth century. But by far the most radical feature of the eastern front of World War II was the openly declared ideological character of the struggle. War and genocide, war and racism were intertwined in an unprecedented manner. Hitler declared all laws of war null and void, as far as the Eastern Front was concerned, giving carte blanche for crimes against humanity on a massive scale. Stalin in turn fought a ruthless, massive battle for survival. How many millions died will never be known.

War and ideology were not only combined in the East. In the West the United Stated and Great Britain countered the Nazi-'faith' with the Atlantic Charter, a pivotal policy statement issued on 14 August 1941. The Charter stated the goals of the war in idealistic terms: no territorial aggrandisement; no territorial changes made against the wishes of the people; restoration of self-government to those deprived of it; reduction of trade restrictions; global cooperation to secure better economic and social conditions for all; freedom from fear and want; freedom of the seas; and abandonment of the use of force, as well as disarmament of aggressor nations. It was an extended version of the famous Fourteen Points of President Wilson dating from 1918. But now two major belligerents supported it. It is always difficult to ascertain how these ideological statements and ideas influenced the course of the war, or were even essential for its outcome. The fact is, between 1939 and 1945, as never before, fundamentally opposed ideological views on a future world order characterised war aims.

When we look closer at 'why the Allies won'—to quote the title of Richard Overy's famous 1995 book—ideology is only part of the story. As in World War I, victory has to do with economic stamina, technological innovation, organisation of command structures and ways to keep the morale of fighting men high. Overy convincingly shows that tactical mastery on the battlefield and even technological innovative weaponry—both German strengths—do not win a modern war. Standardisation of mass production, be it by force in a communist society or by pursuit of profit in a capitalist society, proved to be much more decisive. Also, the way Britain and the United Stated cooperated in command structures and on major projects like combating U-boats was a vital component for victory. This Allied military cooperation, unprecedented in history, would form one of the foundation stones for NATO.

The Second World War was, militarily speaking, less fundamentally innovative than the First World War. Nevertheless some major developments have to be mentioned: the computer, developed by Alan Turing (1912–1954), radar and sonar, the jet engine, the rocket and, the most fundamental of all, the nuclear bomb. It was only the last that really changed the face of war fundamentally. The other perfected ways of war that were, in essence, practised or developed during the First World War, submarine warfare and major bombing raids on cities, were brought to an extreme level of destruction and technological innovation.

The bombing of Hiroshima and Nagasaki in August 1945, using atomic bombs for the first time, formed a watershed in the history of warfare and in the thinking about strategy and war. One could argue aerial warfare had won WWII with the fulfilment of the air theorists' dream that a major air attack on population centres would make costly lands warfare obsolete. Or one could argue it was a logical next step in making carpet-bombing cheaper and more efficient, but the real meaning was seen already in 1946 by a professor at Yale, Bernard Brodie (1910–1978), who wrote the famous words: "Thus far the chief purpose of our military establishment has been to win wars. From now on its chief purpose must be to avert them. It can have almost no other useful purpose". The book was *The Absolute Weapon: Atomic Power and World Order,* analysing one of the most fundamental new insights into the waging of war since Clausewitz. The road to the atomic bomb had started only seven years earlier when three Hungarian scientists, Eugene Wigner (1902–1995), Leo Szilárd (1898–1964) and Edward Teller (1908–2003) had convinced President Roosevelt to start the Manhattan Project. Brodie realised the outcome of this project had a fundamental impact on the way we look at war and how we conduct war. Nuclear bombs were political weapons, too dangerous to be controlled by the military alone and only their non-use meant victory.

The Cold War which developed from around 1947 onwards not only brought deterrence as an important concept to the forefront, it also led to the most peculiar strategic theories, sometimes bordering on the bizarre, explaining how nuclear armament led to stability and maybe even safety and security. Mutual Assured Destruction—the acronym MAD was first used by the Hungarian mathematician and physicist John von Neumann (1903–1957)—aptly describes this dangerous equilibrium the world lived on during more than four decades. For present generations it is hard to imagine how thinking of war and absolute destruction were part and parcel of any discussion of war and peace. Maybe Stanley Kubrick's black-comedy masterpiece *Dr. Strangelove or How I Learned to Stop Worrying and Love the Bomb* from 1964 summarises the Cold War thinking better than anything else. War was no longer something to be done on the battlefield, but it was the work of (rocket) scientists, strategic theorists and politicians. It was stability for a price and it gave us the space age. But the Cold War also led to protests against nuclear war already from the 1950s onwards, starting in Japan, the UK and the US. Pioneer was the American peace activist Norman Cousins (1915–1990). *Ban the Bomb* became a worldwide slogan for decades from the late 1950s. Never in history had anti-war movements been so massive, on all continents and over such a long period of time.

Nuclear armament shifted 'real war' to the periphery: some were 'classic' interstate wars like in Korea, the Middle East and between India and Pakistan, the majority were wars of decolonisation or national liberation. These 'counter-insurgency' wars resembled the colonial wars of the past—never taken seriously by Western military thinkers—and now showed Western impotence to fight entire populations, who claimed their right to self-determination. All these wars were called 'limited' meaning that the major powers did not fight among themselves, but only fought 'by proxy'. But 'limited' in this sense is an euphemism if there ever were one: the Nigerian civil (1967–1970) war, the Cambodian tragedy (1975–1979), the Soviet invasion in Afghanistan (1979–1988) and the Iran-Iraq war (1980–1988) all rank among the most deadly conflicts of recent centuries.

The one Cold War-era conflict that has most profoundly influenced our perception of war is the Vietnam conflict (1946–1975). The impotence of first France and later of nuclear superpower US to crash a 'people's army' that possessed comparatively inferior weaponry remains intriguing to say the least. Not only did Vietnam show the restraints the Cold War put on super powers, it also showed that advanced technology was not in all instances superior, and that technological solutions and kinetic escalation could not bring the desired results. As the European colonial powers had experienced earlier, a motivated people, given the right amount of external material support, can withstand a superior military opponent. In Vietnam the US lost more than just a battle, it lost faith in itself. For the first time, the US could not present itself as bearer of freedom and democracy. The world witnessed horrific suffering by the Vietnamese people and even war crimes committed by American soldiers. Symbolic is the news of November 1969: the American public was proudly informed on the Apollo 12 moon flight, while simultaneously on national television lieutenant William Calley (1943–) confessed the war crimes he had committed in My Lai 20 months before. Brutality and technological achievement are two faces of war. Vietnam also brought the world's largest fighting force to a deep crisis, which it took two decades to overcome and it made war a media event, to be followed closely by the entire world. From Walter Cronkite (1916–2009) to Peter Arnett (1934–) to the video of the US marine killing an Iraqi in a mosque in Fallujah (2004), modern war can reach every home on the planet within days or even hours.

1989 was a watershed year in the history of warfare, as 1945, but in a very different way. With the end of the Cold War, the world seems to have said goodbye to large-scale interstate warfare. From Napoleon, so for almost two centuries, the benchmark for warfare has been massive land operations conducted by major powers. Although the Cold War prevented wars between major powers for the first time in history, the thinking of 'war' in its ideal form, still remained, on the operational level at least, the classic Western patron. Wars in the (former) colonies were looked down upon as not being 'the real thing'. The end of the Cold War did not mean a return to major power military conflicts, as had been the case before 1945, in fact in meant confusion on what 'war' in the so-called post modern era is or should be. Even the word 'war' itself receded to the background in many countries, to be replaced by a variety of euphemisms.

At the close of the most violent age in the history of mankind, war is in crisis again. As the First World War led to new and very diverse ideas on what war in the modern age is, the end of the Cold War and the revolution in information technology, digitalisation and integration of all kinds of activities through electronic networks again brings us to a crossroads. In my opinion a fundamental one, because change is not only technological, but the whole idea of how and why violence can be used, on its juridical legitimacy, on the aims for which it can be used and on the role of people practicing violence, is shifting.

War since 1989 still has ‘classic’ characteristics in the sense that throughout history we can trace similar features: asymmetric warfare is as old as mankind, logistic support by civilian contractors was common in early modern times, combat as a human activity has always been stressful, religion and war are closely linked at all times and modern armies still have many features that date from nineteenth and twentieth century warfare, but on the other hand we see: network centric warfare, created by modern electronics, which revolutionised concepts of both time and space as well as of command and control and we see man as the carrier of arms moving to the background as machines are replacing him. It was the Vietnam War, in the early 1970s that triggered the idea of unmanned weapons. From the work of the Association for Unmanned Systems International (1972) came the Unmanned Air Vehicles (UAVs) now known as drones and part of modern war since November 2002 when a moving car occupied by four terrorists in Yemen suspected of bombing the USS *Cole* was destroyed by a Hellfire missile ejected from a UAV. Also, on the ground robotic warfare has become a ‘normal’ phenomenon. And ‘war’ has become more and more an array of different kinds of (semi) permanent interventions all with their own cultural, legal and military characteristics. We can see this diversity when we look at the ‘belt of violence’ that stretches from Mali via Somalia and the Middle East to Afghanistan. In this area, hugely important strategically and because of its resources, a variety of ‘wars’ and interventions from twenty-first century warfare will develop: highly technological and restrained in manpower on the one hand, extremely cruel and ideological on the other, in need of new concepts in international and humanitarian law as modern multinational coalitions engage in tribal warfare and structures alien to Western armies.

War is very multifaceted today. We have great difficulty to come to terms with it in a conceptual way. So many names have come and gone to describe the framework in which violence is used: peacekeeping, counterinsurgency, responsibility to protect, peace enforcing, low intensity conflict, ethnical or religious conflict, postmodern war, hybrid war, third-generation warfare, etc. Some terms are legal, others political or historical. The great diversity shows the confusion in how to interpret the influence of modern (digital) technology and new ideas on how and when to use violence. Stephen Metz (1956–), a prominent American thinker on future warfare has given us some guidelines, stressing the importance of psychological, ethical and cultural aspects that in cooperation with dedicated modern technology should make armies effective against a wide array of opponents. But maybe, to grab the essence of war, we should also look at the non-academic, more visionary views on war. H.G. Wells' *War of the Worlds* (1898) predicted, and inspired, modern technological warfare at the start of the century and Isaac Asimov gave us, already in 1950, a view in the future of a robotic world in *I, Robot.* I started this short overview with the French writer Séché as an astute critic of war in 1915. Who is our present day Séché? Is it Tom Clancy (1947–2013) in books like *Against All Enemies* (2011) or is it the raw reality of a Sebastian Junger's 2010 impressive documentary *Restrepo*? Or is it both?

Recommended Books on the Evolution of Modern Warfare

S. Biddle, *Military Power: Explaining Victory and Defeat in Modern Battle* (2004)
I. Duyvestein (ed.), *Rethinking the Nature of War* (2005)
A. Gat, *War in Human Civilisation* (2006)
J. Turrito, 'Understanding warfare in the 21st Century' 18(3) *International Affairs Review* (Winter 2010)
R. Smith, *Utility of Force. The Art of War in the Modern World* (2006)

Part II
The Law of Weaponry 1914–2014

Chapter 4
The Prohibition to Use Chemical Weapons

Thilo Marauhn

Abstract A century ago, chemical weapons were used in World War I, with their use during the second battle of Ypres, in particular on 22 April 1915, demonstrating their nature as weapons of mass destruction. On 21 August 2013, during the Syrian civil war, sarin-filled rockets hit the Ghouta suburbs of Damascus, killing a large number of civilians. It is against the background of the indeed limited use of chemical weapons over the last century that the steps towards a nearly universal prohibition thereof are analysed. The starting point is early steps towards only prohibiting the use of chemical weapons (primarily focusing upon the 1899/1907 Hague Regulations and the 1925 Geneva Protocol) and their emerging customary law nature. With the adoption of the 1993 Chemical Weapons Convention, the prohibition of use was strengthened not only in scope but also by linking it to pertinent disarmament and arms control provisions. The latest steps address individual criminal accountability for using chemical weapons as a means of warfare, based upon the 1998 Rome Statute and the 2010 Kampala amendments thereto. As the concluding section illustrates, the effectiveness of a century of pertinent international law making depends on the universality of the prohibition to use chemical weapons and the common efforts of all stakeholders to ensure the integrity of the regime established by these various layers of international law.

Keywords Chemical weapons · Chemical warfare · Disarmament · International criminal law · Means and methods of warfare · Geneva protocol 1925 · Hague regulations 1899/1907 · Chemical weapons convention 1993 · Rome statute 1998 · Kampala amendments 2010

T. Marauhn (✉)
Faculty of Law, Justus Liebig University, Licher Strasse 76, 35394 Giessen, Germany
e-mail: thilo.marauhn@recht.uni-giessen.de

T.D. Gill et al. (eds.), *Yearbook of International Humanitarian Law 2014*,
Yearbook of International Humanitarian Law 17,
DOI 10.1007/978-94-6265-091-6_4

Contents

4.1 The Use of Chemical Weapons

Looking back at the use of chemical weapons over the last century, one notes a history of suffering. During the (second) battle of Ypres, on 22 April 1915, the German armed forces released more than 150 tons of chlorine gas over a frontline of more than 6 km.[1] While this was not the first use of chemical weapons during World War I,[2] it was the first such use that demonstrated their nature as weapons of mass destruction.[3] The attack resulted in an estimated 6,000 victims.[4] Altogether, the use of chemical weapons during World War I caused more than 1,300,000 casualties, thereof 100,000 fatalities.[5]

Unfortunately, neither the number of victims and their suffering nor the continuously declining effectiveness of chemical weapons prevented states from using chemical weapons after World War I. The United Kingdom employed toxic gas against Russian revolutionaries in 1919, and allegedly against Iraqi insurgents in 1920[6]; Spain used chemical weapons against Rif tribes in the 1920s[7]; Italy, both in Libya in 1930 and in Ethiopia in 1936, relied upon chemical warfare[8]; further-

[1]Zanders 1997, pp. 197–198; Solis 2010, pp. 600–601.

[2]Heller 1984, pp. 4–7.

[3]On the notion of weapons of mass destruction see Strydom 2013, paras 1–2.

[4]Heller 1984, p. 10.

[5]UN Doc. A/7575/Rev. 1 (= UN Doc. S/9292/Rev. 1), para 3.

[6]In contrast to the use of irritants on Bolshevik troops (Jones 2009), the use of chemical warfare in Iraq has been questioned recently (Douglas 2009).

[7]Balfour 2002, pp. 123–156.

[8]Grip and Hart 2009.

more, there are claims that Japan employed chemical weapons in the course of its military intervention in Manchukuo in 1937/1938.[9]

Before and during World War II, the Axis and the Allied powers had established large stockpiles of chemical weapons. Nevertheless, no major use of chemical weapons as a weapon of warfare occurred during World War II.[10] However, many of the victims of the Holocaust were murdered using poisonous gases.

Two major uses of chemical weapons in the second half of the twentieth century have to be mentioned: the Egyptian use in the North Yemen civil war (1962–1970), with numerous incidents of chemical weapons use and related casualties of approximately 1,500 fatalities and a similar number of injuries[11]; and the war between Iran and Iraq from 1980 to 1988, which saw Iraqi chemical attacks against the Iranian armed forces with between 50,000 and 100,000 casualties,[12] as well as a chemical weapons massacre against the Kurdish people in the city of Halabja, on 16 March 1988.[13]

A serious terrorist use of chemical weapons caused deaths and injuries in Tokyo on 20 March 1995.[14] In response to the taking of hostages by armed Chechens in Moscow on 23 October 2002, Russian special forces, on 26 October 2002, applied an incapacitating agent in the course of their raid.[15]

The latest use of chemical weapons occurred during the Syrian civil war. On 21 August 2013, sarin-filled rockets hit the Ghouta suburbs of Damascus, killing a large number of civilians.[16] The parties to the conflict blamed each other, but none admitted the attack.

Overall, it should be borne in mind that merely listing the events of chemical weapons use over the past century does not in the least adequately illustrate the sufferings of individuals, whether combatants or civilians. In many respects, the effects of chemical warfare are recordable but inexpressible.

To date, three distinct steps have been taken to outlaw chemical weapons: first, states negotiated a prohibition of chemical weapons use, which further developed over time; second, states agreed upon chemical disarmament; and third, states established individual criminal liability for chemical warfare not only at the national level, but also at the international. Each of these three steps will be analysed and discussed below, leading to the concluding question what needs to be done to maintain the integrity of the existing regime(s) directed against chemical weapons and warfare.

---

[9]Tanaka 1988.

[10]Robinson and Leitenberg 1971, pp. 294–335; Price 1995, pp. 74–79.

[11]Terrill 1991.

[12]UN Doc. S/17911; Dunn 1987.

[13]Kelly 2008, pp. 33–40.

[14]Smithson 2000.

[15]Dolnik and Pilch 2003.

[16]UN Doc. A/67/997 (= UN Doc. S/2013/553).

4.2 The Prohibition of the Use of Chemical Weapons

4.2.1 Early Limitations upon the Use of Chemical Weapons

Not only the history of chemical weapons use can be traced back to antiquity, but also efforts at prohibiting such use. Greek and Roman lawyers already argued that war must be waged with weapons, not with poison: "Armis bella, non venenis, geri".[17] However, efforts to ban chemical warfare were rather singular and only increased during the second half of the nineteenth century. The 1868 St. Petersburg Declaration[18] while not expressly addressing chemical or poisonous weapons includes a prohibition of "arms which uselessly aggravate the sufferings of disabled men, or render their death inevitable". This prohibition, as well as the Martens clause,[19] may be read to indirectly outlaw chemical or poisonous weapons.[20]

The 1874 Project of an International Declaration concerning the Laws and Customs of War,[21] which due to the lack of comprehensive ratification did not enter into force, in its Article 13 expressly forbids the "(e)mployment of poison or poisoned weapons". This prohibition eventually found its way into the 1899/1907 Regulations concerning the Laws and Customs of War on Land, annexed to The Hague Convention (IV) respecting the Laws and Customs of War on Land.[22] Article 23 lit. a of The Hague Regulations reads "In addition to the prohibitions provided by special Conventions, it is especially forbidden (a) To employ poison or poisoned weapons; ...". This instrument was preceded by the 1899 Hague Declaration (IV, 2) concerning Asphyxiating Gases,[23] stating "The Contracting Powers agree to abstain from the use of projectiles the sole object of which is the diffusion of asphyxiating or deleterious gases". The weakness of this latter Declaration was its restrictive wording, focusing only upon "projectiles", and not

[17]Translation: "War is waged with weapons, not with poison" (Valerius Maximus, Factorum et Dictorum Memorabilium, Liber VI:5.1). For other sources and additional constraints over time, see Zanders 2003, pp. 392–394.

[18](1907) AJIL Supplement 1:95–96.

[19]Included in the Preamble of The Hague Convention (IV) respecting the Laws and Customs of War on Land (205 CTS 277): "Until a more complete code of the laws of war has been issued, the High Contracting Parties deem it expedient to declare that, in cases not included in the Regulations adopted by them, the inhabitants and the belligerents remain under the protection and the rule of the principles of the law of nations, as they result from the usages established among civilized peoples, from the laws of humanity, and the dictates of the public conscience" Zanders 2003, p. 394 rightly labels this as a "milestone".

[20]Koplow 1990, p. 16.

[21](1907) AJIL Supplement 1:96–103.

[22]205 CTS 277.

[23](1907) AJIL Supplement 1:157–159.

on other means of delivery—more specifically: Germany argued that the release of Chlorine at the battle of Ypres was not in violation of international law as it did not result from the use of projectiles.[24]

4.2.2 The 1899/1907 Hague Regulations

As far as Article 23 lit. a of The Hague Regulations is concerned, many arguments limited its scope.[25] First, it was questioned whether this provision covered chemical weapons at all; in respect of gases, some considered The Hague Declaration as *lex specialis*, thus limiting the scope of Article 23 lit. a to "poison or poisoned weapons" other than "asphyxiating or deleterious gases".[26] Second, some limited their reading of the scope of Article 23 lit. a to known or existing poison.[27] Third, others argued that the prohibition only covered perfidious use of poison.[28]

While it is admitted that the a different wording of these instruments invites distinguishing interpretations, the object and purpose of The Hague Regulations as it can be taken from the preamble of the Convention should be borne in mind: "to serve … the interests of humanity and the ever progressive needs of civilization", and "inspired by the desire to diminish the evils of war, as far as military requirements permit". Given a treaty—according to customary international law—is to be interpreted not only "in accordance with the ordinary meaning to be given to the terms of the treaty in their context" but also "in the light of its object and purpose" (as codified by Article 31, para 1, Vienna Convention on the Law of Treaties, hereinafter VCLT), it can be argued that Article 23 lit. a of The Hague Regulations should not be read in a restrictive but rather in a broad manner, at least not more restrictive than the ordinary meaning of its wording.[29] Furthermore, it is submitted, in light of another customary rule of treaty interpretation (as codified by Article 31, para 4, VCLT), that a special meaning can be given to Article 23 lit. a of The Hague Regulations only if there are indications that the parties indeed sought such interpretation; but there is no evidence to this end.[30] Finally, Article 23 lit. b of The Hague Regulations explicitly outlaws perfidy; the context of lit. a thus speaks against only prohibiting perfidious use of poison.[31]

---

[24]Tucker 2006, pp. 11–12.

[25]For an overview of pertinent arguments see Bothe 1973, p. 5.

[26]Pillet 1918, p. 218.

[27]O'Brien 1962/63, p. 21; on the background see Zanders 2003, p. 405.

[28]Castren 1954, p. 194.

[29]Bothe 1973, p. 8; more cautious in respect of the ordinary meaning: Thomas and Thomas 1970, p. 49.

[30]Bothe 1973, pp. 6–7.

[31]Thomas and Thomas 1970, p. 56; Bothe 1973, p. 9.

Whether anti-materiel agents are excluded from the scope of Article 23 lit. a Hague Regulations is debatable; the exclusion of anti-plant agents, however, is difficult to argue.[32] Claims towards a derogation of this provision by the conduct of hostilities during World War I can be rejected in light of State practice and case law (as an expression of *opinio iuris*).[33]

4.2.3 The 1925 Geneva Protocol

In the context of the inter-war arms control and disarmament efforts, the 1925 Geneva Protocol for the Prohibition of the Use of Asphyxiating, Poisonous or Other Gases, and of Bacteriological Methods of Warfare[34] was agreed upon. The Protocol, which builds on the wording of Article 171 of the Versailles Peace Treaty,[35] applies to "the use in war of asphyxiating, poisonous or other gases, and of all analogous liquids materials or devices". First, this means that it is only applicable during an armed conflict, and, in light of the doctrine of inter-temporal law,[36] only during international armed conflict.[37] Second, in terms of substances it goes beyond The Hague Declaration and The Hague Regulations[38]; it comprehensively covers all chemical substances,[39] including irritants, defoliants and psycho-chemical agents.[40] It is noteworthy that States Parties do not only "accept this prohibition" but also "agree to extend this prohibition to the use of bacteriological methods of warfare". The main limitation concerning the Geneva Protocol was that in light of the many reservations made, the Protocol-based prohibition was largely reduced to a prohibition of "no first use" of chemical weapons.[41]

This limitation of the Protocol's prohibition of chemical warfare today, arguably, is of only limited relevance, first, since it is doubtful whether and to what extent these reservations did at all affect the parallel prohibition of chemical warfare in

---

[32]Thomas and Thomas 1970, p. 52; Bothe 1973, p. 16.

[33]Bothe 1973, pp. 9–11.

[34]94 LNTS 65.

[35]225 CTS 188; the first paragraph of Article 171 reads: "The use of asphyxiating, poisonous or other gases and all analogous liquids, materials or devices being prohibited, their manufacture and importation are strictly forbidden in Germany".

[36]Kotzur 2008, paras 11–12.

[37]Baxter and Buergenthal 1970, pp. 868–869; Blake and Mahmud 2013, p. 251.

[38]Thomas and Thomas 1970, p. 73.

[39]It is noteworthy that the minor differences between the English and the French authentic texts were not meant to reduce the prohibition in scope: the French text refers to "gaz … similaires", the English text to "other gases".

[40]This is, among others, the conclusion arrived at by Baxter and Buergenthal 1970, p. 867.

[41]Boothby 2009, pp. 124–125.

customary international law,[42] and, second, since Article I of the Chemical Weapons Convention[43] (hereinafter CWC), which opened for signature on 13 January 1993 in Paris, has established a comprehensive prohibition on chemical weapons use.

4.2.4 The 1993 Chemical Weapons Convention

Article I CWC not only prohibits the development, production, acquisition, stockpiling, retaining or transfer of chemical weapons (Article I, para 1, lit. a), but also their use (Article I, para 1, lit. b). It is noteworthy that agreement on the inclusion of a prohibition of use could only be reached at a relatively late point in the long-lasting negotiations leading to the CWC.[44]

The intricate relationship between the CWC and the Geneva Protocol may best be illustrated in respect of three problems: first, the situations to which the respective instruments apply; second, the agents covered; and third, the effect of the CWC on the reservations made to the Geneva Protocol.

4.2.4.1 Situations Covered

As to the situations covered, it has already been pointed out that the Geneva Protocol only applies to international armed conflicts. In contrast, it is debatable whether the parallel prohibition of chemical warfare in customary international law was and is applicable to non-international armed conflicts.[45] Today, States Parties to the CWC clearly state that they will "never under any circumstances" use chemical weapons. This not only includes international and non-international armed conflicts, but it goes far beyond these situations. Rather, the only situations excluded from the prohibition are situations of "law enforcement including domestic riot control purposes", as mentioned in Article II, para 9, CWC. This provision only applies to riot control agents, which—as can be taken from Article I, para 5, CWC—are explicitly outlawed as "a method of warfare". Thus, the prohibition of use is comprehensive in terms of situations covered, with the only exception of the use of riot control agents for purposes of law enforcement (including riot control).

---

[42]While treaty reservations as such do not affect existing customary international law, the content of the customary international law prohibition of chemical warfare is not necessarily identical in scope to the Geneva Protocol.

[43]1974 UNTS 45.

[44]Krutzsch 2014a, p. 66.

[45]The question of the customary law status of the 1925 Protocol has been relevant in the context of the Halabja attacks on the Kurdish population by Iraqi armed forces in 1988 (McCormack 1990/1991) and in the context of Syrian civil war in 2013 (Blake and Mahmud 2013, pp. 255–257).

A debate emerged on whether or not "law enforcement" and "domestic riot control" are alternatives.[46] However, applying the customary rules on treaty interpretation as reflected in Article 31 VCLT and bearing in mind the "types and quantities" criterion of Article II, para 1, lit. a CWC[47] leads to the conclusion that Article II, para 9, CWC requires "enforcement measures pertaining to cases of severe disturbance of public order",[48] and that the two terms describe a single category of purposes.[49]

In light of UN peace operations, the further question has been put forward whether UN peacekeeping forces (and possibly UN authorized forces) may use chemical agents. In addition to the UN's commitment to comply with the law of armed conflict,[50] the CWC only seems to allow the use of riot control agents by UN forces when acting as a domestic police force.[51]

4.2.4.2 Substances Covered

The exception for riot control purposes already illustrates the overlap between situations and chemical substances, and points to the second critical issue: the agents covered by the CWC prohibition on chemical weapons use. Article II, para 1, CWC defines chemical weapons. The definition includes toxic and precursor chemicals, munitions and devices specifically designed for chemical weapons purposes, as well as equipment specifically designed for uses directly related to the employment of such munitions and devices. Toxic chemicals and their precursors are ultimately defined on the basis of their intended purpose (general-purpose criterion),[52] i.e. they are generally covered by the CWC "except where intended for purposes not prohibited under this Convention, as long as the types and quantities are consistent with such purposes" (Article II, para 1, lit. a CWC). Defining "purposes not prohibited" (Article II, para 9, CWC) thus is essential. While lit. a and b of Article II, para 9, CWC do not provide major interpretative challenges, this is different for lit. c and even more so for lit. d.

Lit. c excludes chemicals used for "(m)ilitary purposes not connected with the use of chemical weapons and not dependent on the use of the toxic properties of chemicals as a method of warfare". This was meant to exclude from the definition

[46]Krutzsch and Trapp 2014, p. 94: This "is needed to overcome any ambiguity and to identify the dividing line, agreed by the negotiators, that separates the chemicals designed for these non-prohibited purposes from chemical weapons".

[47]"as long as the types and quantities are consistent with such purposes".

[48]Krutzsch and Trapp 2014, p. 97.

[49]Id., referring to the French and Spanish authentic texts.

[50]UN Doc. ST/SGB/1999/13 (observance by United Nations forces of international humanitarian law).

[51]Krutzsch and Trapp 2014, pp. 101–102.

[52]Krutzsch and Trapp 2014, pp. 77–80.

of chemical weapons such chemicals, the predominant effect of which is not toxicity against humans or animals, such as explosive chemicals, fuels, incendiaries and related compounds.[53]

The most difficult issue arising from the general-purpose criterion in respect of chemicals is the interpretation of Article II, para 9, lit. d, CWC referring to "law enforcement including riot control purposes". This provision, read together with Article I, para 5, CWC, is the compromise output of the negotiations on whether or not to include riot control agents in the Convention.[54] Article II, para 7, CWC adds to this compromise by clarifying that only non-listed chemicals can be used as riot control agents, and, as can be taken from Article II, para 1, lit. a, CWC, only in "types and quantities … consistent with such purposes" (the types and quantities criterion).[55]

In order to better unfold the complexities of these provisions, it is useful to take a look at the CWC negotiations: Initially, a number of states were opposed to the inclusion of riot control agents.[56] The rolling text of 20 January 1992[57] then included a definition of toxic chemicals, meaning, among others to "any chemical which through its chemical action on life processes can cause death, temporary incapacitation or permanent harm to humans and animals". A footnote attached indicated that "problems related to irritants used for law enforcement and riot control … could be handled outside the definitions of chemical weapons if this will result in a more clear and understandable definition".[58] The final text only refers to incapacitating agents in two provisions: "temporary incapacitation" in Article II, para 2, CWC and "disabling physical effects which disappear within a short time following termination of exposure" in Article II, para 7, CWC. This has given rise to a debate on whether incapacitating agents can be used for riot control purposes.[59] Already in light of the "types and quantities" criterion, it may be argued that most incapacitating agents will not be compatible with the CWC; however, even better arguments result from human rights law.[60]

Herbicides are not covered by the CWC.[61] This follows from Article II, para 2, CWC, which does not include anti-plant agents and from the preamble, which only recognizes "the prohibition, embodied in the pertinent agreements and relevant principles of international law, of the use of herbicides as a method of

---

[53]Marauhn 1994, pp. 54–55, referring to CCD/PV.557 (United Kingdom), CCD/PV.635 (Sweden), CCD/505 (Yugoslavia).

[54]Marauhn 1994, p. 55; Krutzsch 2014a, p. 69.

[55]Krutzsch and Trapp 2014, pp. 96–97.

[56]CD/500 (USA), CD/1143 (Australia); both documents explain the positions of these countries.

[57]CD/1116.

[58]CD/1116, p. 14.

[59]Krutzsch and Trapp 2014, pp. 97–99.

[60]ICRC 2013.

[61]Krutzsch 2014b, pp. 55–56; Krutzsch and Trapp 2014, p. 83.

warfare", thereby pointing to, among others, Articles 35 and 55 of the 1977 Protocol Additional to the Geneva Conventions of 12 August 1949, and relating to the Protection of Victims of International Armed Conflicts (Protocol I)[62] and to the 1976 Convention on the prohibition of military or any hostile use of environmental modification techniques.[63] It should, however, be stressed that neither the said provisions of Protocol I nor those of the 1976 Convention prohibit the use of herbicides as such.

4.2.4.3 The CWC and Reservations to the Geneva Protocol

Addressing finally the reservations made to the 1925 Protocol, the CWC prevails as *lex posterior* as between the parties to both instruments.[64] No other conclusion can be drawn from Article XIII CWC, which explicitly states that

> "(n)othing in this Convention shall be interpreted as in any way limiting or detracting from the obligations assumed by any State under the Protocol for the Prohibition of the Use in War of Asphyxiating, Poisonous or Other Gases, and of Bacteriological Methods of Warfare, signed at Geneva on 17 June 1925".

Even though some States had hoped that this provision could serve to uphold the validity of their reservations, the wording clearly points to the opposite: "limiting or detracting" only refers to less protection against chemical weapons use, not to more.[65]

4.3 Linking the Prohibition of Use to Disarmament

As early as the Versailles Peace Treaty, the prohibition of chemical warfare was linked to arms control and disarmament.[66] However, the Treaty's Article 171 only imposed limitations upon Germany. The disarmament and arms control efforts of the League of Nations only generated the 1925 Protocol, but no distinct arms control or disarmament obligations. After World War II, the Federal Republic of Germany and Austria renounced the possession of chemical weapons on the basis of the 1954 Paris Protocol III to the Brussels Treaty[67] and the 1955 Austrian State Treaty.[68]

As already explained, the 1993 CWC prohibits the development, production, acquisition, stockpiling, retention, transfer and use of chemical weapons (Article I,

[62] 1125 UNTS 3.

[63] 1108 UNTS 151.

[64] On the *lex posterior* rule Matz-Lück 2010, paras 14–17.

[65] Krutzsch 2014c, pp. 383–385.

[66] Zanders 2003, p. 398.

[67] 211 UNTS 304.

[68] 347 UNTS 3.

para 1, lit. a and b). It adds obligations to destroy chemical weapons and their production facilities[69] and sets up the Organization for the Prohibition of Chemical Weapons (hereinafter OPCW) in The Hague to oversee the Convention's implementation.[70] The fairly strong verification regime has gained model status.[71]

Routine verification[72] is the primary means to ensure compliance with the provisions of the Convention. It is based on initial and annual declarations, submitted by States Parties according to Articles III and VI CWC, among others, on past and present chemical weapons programmes, on old and abandoned chemical weapons, and on past and anticipated industrial activities and the ex- and import of scheduled chemicals. The OPCW has the power to verify the accuracy of information declared by a broad variety of means. On top of these routine procedures, the OPCW may conduct challenge inspections in order to clarify and resolve any questions of possible non-compliance (Article IX, paras 8–25 CWC).[73]

The Convention requires States Parties possessing chemical weapons to destroy their stocks within a period of ten years, with the possibility to apply for extensions, and ensures that all possessor States destroy their stockpiles at approximately the same rate, subject to verification.[74] Due to technical, environmental and financial problems, the time limits originally envisaged for the destruction of chemical weapons under the CWC have not been fully met, but overall destruction has been rather successful[75]—and the OPCW has proved enormous flexibility in the context of Syria's accession to the Convention.[76]

In the absence of the Convention's full universality and in view of non-state actors seeking to acquire chemical weapons capabilities, States have long adopted counter-proliferation measures.[77] Early steps had already been taken in the 1980s, both at the national level and by way of international co-ordination, such as the export controls organized through the so-called Australia group.[78] The effectiveness of such controls is doubtful, notwithstanding other multilateral efforts such as UN Security Council Resolution 1540 of 28 April 2004 on the non-proliferation of weapons of mass destruction.[79]

---

[69] Article I, para 2; Article IV, para 4, CWC.

[70] Article VIII CWC; for an analysis of the organization, see Tabassi 2001.

[71] Feakes 2002.

[72] Van Heck and Marauhn 1998.

[73] Kurzidem 1998.

[74] Trapp and Walker 2014, pp. 126–138.

[75] Asada 2014.

[76] Zanders and Trapp 2013; Krutzsch et al. 2014.

[77] Zanders 1993; Zanders 2013.

[78] Lak and Faraday 2014, pp. 358–359.

[79] Asada 2008; Lak and Faraday 2014, p. 359.

4.4 Ensuring Accountability: Rome and Kampala

4.4.1 The Obligation Under the CWC to Adopt Penal Legislation

Unfortunately, none of the prohibitions of chemical weapons use have been labelled as a grave breach according to the Geneva Conventions nor the Additional Protocols. Nevertheless, there have been pertinent characterizations in national legislation.

Paying tribute to the special significance of the obligations included in Article I CWC, Article VII, lit. a, CWC requires States Parties to "(p)rohibit natural and legal persons anywhere on its territory or in any other place under its jurisdiction as recognized by international law from undertaking any activity prohibited to a State Party under this Convention, including enacting penal legislation with respect to such activity". Lit. c strengthens this obligation by requiring states parties to extend their "penal legislation enacted under subparagraph (a) to any activity prohibited to a State Party under this Convention undertaken anywhere by natural persons, possessing (their) nationality, in conformity with international law". Given the prohibition on chemical weapons use included in Article I CWC, this does not only strengthen the Convention's preventive efforts, but it also ensures accountability.[80]

4.4.2 Accountability Before the International Criminal Court

On top of these requirements, Article 8 of the Rome Statute establishing the International Criminal Court[81] includes chemical warfare as war crime, albeit with a number of restrictions. Article 8, para 2, lit. b, Rome Statute refers to "serious violations of the laws and customs applicable in international armed conflict", and includes subparagraphs (xvii) and (xviii) referring to "(xvii) Employing poison or poisoned weapons; (xviii) Employing asphyxiating, poisonous or other gases, and all analogous liquids, materials or devices". Apart from only addressing international armed conflicts, this provision is only applicable if the war crimes were "committed as part of a plan or policy or as part of a large-scale commission of such crimes".

No parallel provision was included in the original version of the provisions on war crimes in non-international armed conflicts.[82] It was only by adopting Annex I to Resolution RC/Res.5 at the Kampala Conference in 2010 that pertinent

[80]Tabassi and Dhavle 2014, p. 200 state: "Consistent with para 6 of the Preamble, the *use of chemical weapons* would be the gravest offence" (italics in the original).

[81]2187 UNTS 90.

[82]On the negotiations, see Zimmermann and Şener 2014, pp. 440–441.

subparagraphs were added as part of Article 8, para 2, lit. e, of the Rome Statute, ensuring that the possibility for criminal prosecutions will be the same for international as for non-international armed conflicts: "(xiii) Employing poison or poisoned weapons; (xiv) Employing asphyxiating, poisonous or other gases, and all analogous liquids, materials or devices".

4.4.3 Substances Covered by the Rome Statute's Provisions

The war crimes included in the Rome Statute build upon the old provisions of The Hague Regulations and the Geneva Protocol, referring to "poison or poisoned weapons" and "asphyxiating, poisonous or other gases, and all analogous liquids, materials or devices". Neither does the Statute include a specific war crime on the basis of Article I CWC nor does Article 8, para 2, lit. b, subpara xx, Rome Statute add to the above crimes. The latter provision takes up the pertinent provision of The Hague Regulations on superfluous injuries and makes it a war crime to employ "weapons, projectiles and Materials and methods of warfare which are of a nature to cause superfluous injury or unnecessary suffering or which are inherently indiscriminate in violation of the international law of armed conflict". It is, however, only applicable in respect of weapons which are subject to a comprehensive prohibition and included in an Annex to the Statute; no Annex to this provision has yet been agreed upon.[83]

The question arises whether—and if so, why—the Rome Statute's criminal law provisions on chemical weapons lag behind pertinent law of armed conflict.[84] This necessitates a glance at the drafting history of Article 8 of the Statute. While it had originally been proposed to include explicit provisions on chemical warfare, pertinent provisions were removed from the final draft.[85] Obviously, the removal of an explicit reference to chemical warfare from the Statute "was a compromise designed to appease some non-nuclear states, who felt that excluding nuclear weapons alone smacked of hypocrisy".[86] Whether this negotiating history necessarily limits the scope of the Statute's provisions on chemical weapons to the old Hague and Geneva law is debatable.[87] Once again, the customary rules on treaty interpretation as codified in Article 31 VCLT serve as a useful starting point for interpreting Article 8, para 2, Rome Statute.

A literal interpretation of the terms "poison or poisoned weapons" and "asphyxiating, poisonous or other gases, and all analogous liquids, materials or devices" suggests that this covers chemical weapons.

[83] Cottier 2008, pp. 423–425.

[84] For pertinent discussions, see Zimmermann and Şener 2014, pp. 438–439; Schabas 2010, p. 198.

[85] Zimmermann and Şener 2014, pp. 438–439.

[86] Schabas 2013.

[87] See Alamuddin and Webb 2010, pp. 1227–1228; but see Akande 2013.

Looking at context, the parallels to The Hague Regulations and to the Geneva Protocol as well as the differences to the CWC must be taken into account. As demonstrated above, the CWC's definition aims at being comprehensive, focusing on arms control, but at the same time making the 1925 prohibition on use more extensive for all parties to the CWC. In so far the CWC can be read as subsequent treaty practice,[88] with pertinent consequences for the interpretation of the Rome Statute: along these lines, the terms of the Rome Statute may be interpreted in light of the 1993 Convention for all States Parties to the CWC; only in respect of the small number of non-parties to the ICC Statute, a more limited interpretation may be required.

However, the Statute is not an arms control agreement but it sets up an international body, which has the power to prosecute individuals. In the context of international criminal law and in the absence of the CWC's universality, therefore, the 1993 terminology cannot be relied upon. First, it is not possible to establish uneven standards for the purposes of criminal prosecutions depending on which state party the accused belongs to; international criminal law only permits an even interpretation of its terms (taking into account Articles 2 and 26 of the International Covenant on Civil and Political Rights[89]). Second, international criminal law must provide for legal certainty on the basis of the rule of "nulla poena sine lege certa"; an interpretation contrasting with the wording and to the disadvantage of a possible offender is not permissible.[90]

As a consequence, the Rome Statute's provisions on chemical weapons, in terms of the substances covered, cannot be read in light of the CWC's definition but remain limited along the lines of The Hague Regulations and the Geneva Protocol[91] even though the elements of crime in respect of Article 8, para 2, lit. b, subpara (xviii), state that "(n)othing in this element shall be interpreted as limiting or prejudicing in any way existing or developing rules of international law with respect to the development, production, stockpiling and use of chemical weapons". [92]

4.4.4 Situations Covered

As already indicated, the original Rome Statute limited war crime criminal accountability for use of "poison or poisoned weapons" and "asphyxiating, poisonous or other gases, and all analogous liquids, materials or devices" to international armed

[88]Akande 2013.

[89]999 UNTS 171.

[90]In addition, reference may be made to Article 22, para 2, Rome Statute, stipulating that the "definition of a crime shall be strictly construed" and that any such "definition shall be interpreted in favour of the person being investigated, prosecuted or convicted". Whether this only applies after other interpretative methods have failed to clarify ambiguities is debatable; see Broomhall 2010, p. 726.

[91]For a slightly broader view, see Zimmermann and Şener 2014, p. 440.

[92]ICC Doc. ICC-PIDS-LT-03-002/11_Eng (2011), p. 26 note 48.

conflicts. No parallel provision was included for such use in non-international armed conflicts. This is not just surprising against the background of the CWC's comprehensive prohibition on use but even more in light of the jurisprudence of the Appeals Chamber of the International Criminal Tribunal for the Former Yugoslavia (ICTY)—at least *prima facie*.

The Chamber, in its Decision on the Defence Motion for Interlocutory Appeal on Jurisdiction in the *Tadić* case, not only stated that international law prohibits the use of chemical weapons in internal armed conflicts but also included this prohibition in international criminal law. Referring to the "general principle … limiting the right of the parties to conflicts 'to adopt means of injuring the enemy'",[93] and to the Turku Declaration of Minimum Humanitarian Standards of 1990,[94] arguably endorsed by the Conference on Security and Cooperation in Europe in its Budapest Document of 1994,[95] the Chamber submitted that "(w)hat is inhumane, and consequently proscribed, in international wars, cannot but be inhumane and inadmissible in civil strife", and it subsequently turned, "(b)y way of illustration", to chemical weapons.[96] Analysing and discussing pertinent state practice and expressions of *opinio iuris* the Chamber concluded "there undisputedly emerged a general consensus in the international community on the principle that the use of those weapons is also prohibited in internal armed conflicts".[97] Having pointed out several limitations on the general application of rules on means and methods of warfare in non-international armed conflict, the Chamber stated that "it cannot be denied that customary rules have developed to govern internal strife. These rules … cover such areas as … prohibition of means of warfare proscribed in international armed conflicts and ban of certain methods of conducting hostilities".[98]

While the Chamber's conclusions on the general prohibition of chemical warfare in non-international armed conflict are convincing and in line with the ICRC's customary international law study, the Chamber fails to present equally convincing arguments on the inclusion of such a prohibition in international criminal law.[99]

In 2010, the Rome Statute's limitations in respect of the use of chemical weapons were overcome during the Kampala Review Conference. The parties to the ICC Statute adopted an amendment to Article 8, para 2, lit. e, which extends the list of war crimes in non-international armed conflicts to include "employing poison or poisoned weapons" and "employing asphyxiating, poisonous or other gases, and all analogous liquids, materials or devices".[100]

---

[93]Prosecutor v. Tadić, Case No. IT-94-1-AR72, Appeal on Jurisdiction, para 119.

[94]Reprinted in UN Doc. E/CN.4/1995/116.

[95]Conference on Security and Cooperation in Europe, Budapest Document 1994: Towards Genuine Partnership in a New Era, para 34 (1994).

[96]Prosecutor v. Tadić, Case No. IT-94-1-AR72, Appeal on Jurisdiction, para 120.

[97]Ibid., para 124.

[98]Ibid., para 127.

[99]But see Zimmermann and Şener 2014, p. 438.

[100]Annex I to ICC Doc. RC/Res.5.

According to Article 121, para 5, of the Statute, this amendment enters into force for each State Party that ratifies it. However, Article 121, para 5, also limits the jurisdiction of the Court in respect of states parties not accepting the amendment; as a consequence, it is debatable whether the Court's jurisdiction is likewise limited in the case of a Security Council referral. Arguably, the purpose of Security Council referrals to the ICC is to expand the Court's jurisdiction "to cover acts by nationals of non-parties or on the territory of non-parties".[101] Along these lines it is submitted that, at least after the amendment's entry into force as such, the Court's jurisdiction in case of a Security Council referral would also include the new crimes. A parallel reasoning may be drawn from the inclusion of the crime of aggression, which the Court can rule upon in the case of a Security Council referral irrespective of a State Party having ratified the amendment—as long as the conditions set out in the aggression amendments are met. Indeed, the ICC Review Conference "confirm(ed) its understanding that in respect to this amendment the same principle that applies in respect of a State Party which has not accepted the amendment applies also in respect of States that are not parties to the Statute".[102] The purpose of this understanding obviously was to ensure equal treatment of non-parties and of parties that do not ratify the amendment. Article 121, para 5, of the Statute is thus limited to referrals based on State consent.

It follows that, were the Security Council to refer a situation to the ICC, the Court would have jurisdiction to prosecute specifically for use of chemical weapons in both international and non-international armed conflicts.

4.5 Beyond Regime-Building: Maintaining Regime Integrity

As can be taken from the above analysis, the efforts to outlaw chemical weapons as a means of warfare have been rather successful when looking at existing agreements. Indeed, States have gradually agreed upon a fairly comprehensive prohibition of use since 1868. The current treaty regime, emerging from The Hague Regulations, the Geneva Protocol and the CWC, can be considered a success. This is even more true if looking at the two important elements, supporting the prohibition of use: the (preventive) arms control and disarmament provisions of the CWC, coupled with a strong verification regime, and the (repressive) criminal law provisions included in the Rome Statute. Even though built step-by-step, the current regime against chemical weapons use is a solid basis for winning the war on chemical weapons.

Some deficiencies, however, remain: first, the regime is not yet fully universal; second, the dispute on incapacitating agents weakens the prohibition; third, the

[101] Akande 2013.

[102] ICC Doc. RC/Res.5, second preambular paragraph.

integrity of the regime will best be preserved by eventually including a comprehensive provision in the Rome Statute.

The use of chemical weapons in the Syrian civil war has illustrated the most serious weakness of the current regime: the absence of full universality. It has always been the intention of States Parties to the CWC to aim at universality.[103] Indeed, even treaty provisions (among others those on export controls) serve that purpose. Syria has now become a State Party to the CWC—even though, arguably, only as a result of coercive diplomacy. The remaining non-parties should indeed join the regime. But, unfortunately, in some cases the nexus to the nuclear weapons issue remains a problem. Whether the current efforts to clarify the substance of Article VI of the Treaty on the Non-Proliferation of Nuclear Weapons will eventually contribute to the CWC's universality is an open question.

As has been demonstrated above, the CWC arguably can be interpreted as excluding incapacitating agents from its definition of riot control agents. However, as academic, judicial and political discourse in the aftermath of the 2002 Moscow theatre event has shown, the illegality of incapacitating agents can be better argued on the basis of anti-drug law and human rights law.[104] Given the difficulty to ensure precise quantities and qualities of incapacitating agents in view of the varying physical and mental capacities of humans potentially exposed to such agents in a law enforcement scenario, the use of such agents risks to run counter to the right to life. Ensuring the integrity of the CW regime necessarily invites States to avoid any possible loophole or weakening of the regime, even by way of interpretation. Thus, the ICRC[105] and others rightly argue in favour of adopting a policy statement to exclude incapacitating agents from the CWC's riot control agent definition.[106]

Whether international law really works can only be ascertained after regimes have been built. Making treaties work is the responsibility of governmental actors and of civil society alike. Apart from mechanisms ensuring compliance with such treaties, the integrity of the regime against use of chemical weapons in warfare requires regular and unambiguous affirmations of the regime's obligations. While the CWC includes a strong verification regime, the law of armed conflict currently lacks a working compliance control mechanism. There is hope that the Swiss ICRC initiative to strengthen compliance with international humanitarian law,[107] based upon Resolution 1 of the 31st International Conference of the Red Cross

[103]Zanders 2002.

[104]Doswald-Beck 2013; Vandova 2013. Criticism may raised against the ruling of the European Court of Human Rights in the case of Finogenov and Others v. Russia, Applications nos. 18299/03 and 27311/03 (Judgment of 20 December 2011) on the account that the Court did not sufficiently address the quantities and qualities of the incapacitating agent applied.

[105]OPCW Doc. RC-3/NAT.72.

[106]Dunworth 2013.

[107]Pertinent documents are available at https://www.icrc.org/eng/what-we-do/other-activities/development-ihl/strengthening-legal-protection-compliance.htm.

and Red Crescent,[108] will lead to a first agreed document in 2015. This will support *bona fide* behaviour of States participating in the regime against chemical weapons use, and will contribute to winning the war on chemical weapons, eventually establishing a chemical weapons-free world.

References

Akande D (2013) Can the ICC prosecute for use of chemical weapons in Syria? EJIL: Talk!. http://www.ejiltalk.org/can-the-icc-prosecute-for-use-of-chemical-weapons-in-syria/

Alamuddin A, Webb P (2010) Expanding jurisdiction over war crimes under Article 8 of the ICC Statute. J Int Crim Justice 8(5):1219

Asada M (2008) Security Council Resolution 1540 to combat WMD terrorism. J Confl Secur Law 13(3):303

Asada M (2014) The OPCW's arrangement for missed destruction deadlines under the Chemical Weapons Convention. Am J Int Law 108(3):448

Balfour S (2002) Deadly Embrace: Morocco and the road to the Spanish Civil War. OUP, Oxford

Baxter RR, Buergenthal T (1970) Legal aspects of the Geneva Protocol of 1925. Am J Int Law 64(5):868

Blake J, Mahmud A (2013) A legal "Red Line"? Syria and the use of chemical weapons in civil conflict. UCLA Law Rev Disc 61:244

Boothby WH (2009) Weapons and the law of armed conflict. Oxford University Press, Oxford

Bothe M (1973) Das völkerrechtliche Verbot des Einsatzes chemischer und biologischer Waffen. Carl Heymanns, Cologne

Broomhall B (2010) Nullum crimen sine lege—article 22. In: Triffterer O (ed) Commentary on the Rome statute of the International Criminal Court, 2nd edn. Beck, Munich, p 713

Castren E (1954) The present law of war and neutrality. Suomalaisen Kirjallisuuden Seuran Kirjapainon Oy, Helsinki

Cottier M (2008) War crimes—Article 8 para. 2 (b) (xx). In: Triffterer O (ed) Commentary on the Rome statute of the International Criminal Court, 2nd edn. Beck, Munich, p 423

Dolnik A, Pilch R (2003) The Moscow theater hostage crisis: the perpetrators, their tactics, and the Russian response. Int Negot 8(3):577

Doswald-Beck L (2013) Assessing "incapacitating chemicals agents" under human rights law. In: ICRC, "Incapacitating chemical agents": law enforcement, human rights law and policy perspectives. Expert meeting, Montreux, Switzerland, 24–26 April 2012, p 39. https://www.icrc.org/eng/assets/files/publications/icrc-002-4121.pdf

Douglas RM (2009) Did Britain use chemical weapons in mandatory Iraq? J Mod Hist 81(4):859

Dunn P (1987) Chemical aspects of the Gulf War, 1984–1987. Investigations by the United Nations, Maribyrnong

Dunworth T (2013) The silent killer: toxic chemicals for law enforcement and the Chemical Weapons Convention. N Z Yearb Int Law 2012(10):3

Feakes D (2002) Evaluating the CWC verification system. Disarmament forum 2002(4):11

Grip L, Hart J (2009) The use of chemical weapons in the 1935-36 Italo-Ethiopian War. SIPRI Arms Control and Non-proliferation Programme. www.sipri.org/research/disarmament/chemical/publications/ethiopiapaper/

Van Heck H, Marauhn T (1998) Routine verification under the Chemical Weapons Convention. In: Bothe M, Ronzitti N, Rosas A (eds) The new Chemical Weapons Convention—implementation and prospects. Kluwer, The Hague, p 219

[108] https://www.icrc.org/eng/resources/documents/resolution/31-international-conference-resolution-1-2011.htm.

Heller CE (1984) Chemical warfare in World War I: the American experience, 1917–1918. Leavenworth Papers No. 10, Fort Leavenworth
ICRC (2013) "Incapacitating chemical agents": law enforcement, human rights law and policy perspectives. Expert meeting, Montreux, Switzerland. https://www.icrc.org/eng/assets/files/publications/icrc-002-4121.pdf. Accessed 24–26 April 2012
Jones S (2009) "The right medicine for the Bolshevist": British air-dropped chemical weapons in North Russia, 1919. Imperial War Museum Rev 12:78
Kelly MJ (2008) Ghosts of Halabja: Saddam Hussein and the Kurdish genocide. Praeger Security International, Westport
Koplow DA (1990) Long arms and chemical arms: Extraterritoriality and the Draft Chemical Weapons Convention. Yale J Int'l L 15:1 et seq
Kotzur M (2008) Intertemporal law. In: Wolfrum R (ed) The Max Planck encyclopedia of public international law, Max Planck Institute for Comparative Public Law and International Law (online edn). http://opil.ouplaw.com/home/epil
Krutzsch W (2014a) Article I: general obligations. In: Krutzsch W, Myjer E, Trapp R (eds) The Chemical Weapons Convention—a commentary. Oxford University Press, Oxford, p 61
Krutzsch W (2014b) Preamble. In: Krutzsch W, Myjer E, Trapp R (eds) The Chemical Weapons Convention—a commentary. Oxford University Press, Oxford, p 51
Krutzsch W (2014c) Article XIII: relation to other international agreements. In: Krutzsch W, Myjer E, Trapp R (eds) The Chemical Weapons Convention—a commentary. Oxford University Press, Oxford, p 383
Krutzsch W, Myjer E, Trapp R (2014) Issues raised by the accession of Syria to the Chemical Weapons Convention. In: Krutzsch W, Myjer E, Trapp R (eds) The Chemical Weapons Convention—a commentary. Oxford University Press, Oxford, p 689
Krutzsch W, Trapp R (2014) Article II: definitions and criteria. In: Krutzsch W, Myjer E, Trapp R (eds) The Chemical Weapons Convention—a commentary. Oxford University Press, Oxford, p 73
Kurzidem T (1998) Challenge inspections and investigations of alleged use. In: Bothe M, Ronzitti N, Rosas A (eds) The new Chemical Weapons Convention—implementation and prospects. Kluwer, The Hague, p 249
Lak M, Faraday D (2014) Article XI: economic and technological development. In: Krutzsch W, Myjer E, Trapp R (eds) The Chemical Weapons Convention—a commentary. Oxford University Press, Oxford, p 351
Marauhn T (1994) Der deutsche Chemiewaffen-Verzicht. Springer, Berlin
Matz-Lück N (2010) Treaties, conflicts between. In: Wolfrum R (ed) The Max Planck encyclopedia of public international law, Max Planck Institute for Comparative Public Law and International Law (online edn). http://opil.ouplaw.com/home/epil>
McCormack TLH (1990/1991) International law and the use of chemical weapons in the Gulf War. Calif W Int Law J 21(1):1
O'Brien WV (1962/63) Biological/chemical warfare and the international law of war. Georgetown Law J 51(1):1
Pillet A (1918) Les Conventions de la Haye du 29 juillet 1899 et du 18 octobre 1907. Pedone, Paris
Price R (1995) A genealogy of the chemical weapons taboo. Int Org 49(1):73
Robinson JP, Leitenberg M (1971) The rise of CB weapons. Almquest & Wiksell, Stockholm
Schabas WA (2010) The International Criminal Court. Oxford University Press, Oxford
Schabas WA (2013) Chemical weapons: is it a crime? http://humanrightsdoctorate.blogspot.co.uk/2013/04/chemical-weapons-is-it-crime.html
Smithson AE (2000) Rethinking the lessons of Tokyo. In: Smithson AE, Levy L-A, Ataxia: The chemical and biological terrorism threat and the US response, Stimson Report No. 35. Stimson Centre, Washington, p 71
Solis GD (2010) The law of armed conflict. Cambridge University Press, Cambridge
Strydom HA (2013) Weapons of Mass Destruction. In: Wolfrum R (ed) The Max Planck encyclopedia of public international law, Max Planck Institute for Comparative Public Law and International Law (online edn). http://opil.ouplaw.com/home/epil

Tabassi L, Dhavle A (2014) Article VII: national implementation measures. In: Krutzsch W, Myjer E, Trapp R (eds) The Chemical Weapons Convention—a commentary. Oxford University Press, Oxford, p 195

Tabassi LW (2001) The OPCW: model or anomaly? Hague Yearb Int Law 14:55

Tanaka Y (1988) Poison gas: the story Japan would like to forget. Bull At Scientists 44:10

Terrill WA (1991) The chemical warfare legacy of the Yemen War. Comp Strategy 10(2):109

AvW Thomas, Thomas AJ (1970) Legal limits on the use of chemical and biological weapons. Southern Methodist University Press, Dallas

Trapp R, Walker P (2014) Article IV: chemical weapons. In: Krutzsch W, Myjer E, Trapp R (eds) The Chemical Weapons Convention—a commentary. Oxford University Press, Oxford, p 119

Tucker JB (2006) War of nerves: chemical warfare from World War I to Al-Qaeda. Pantheon Books, New York

Vandova V (2013) The European Court of Human Right's judgment in the case of Finogenov and Others v. Russia. In: ICRC, "Incapacitating chemical agents": law enforcement, human rights law and policy perspectives. Expert meeting, Montreux, Switzerland, p 46. https://www.icrc.org/eng/assets/files/publications/icrc-002-4121.pdf. Accessed 24–26 April 2012

Zanders JP (1993) Chemical-weapons deproliferation and the chemical weapons convention. Revue Belge de Droit International 26(1):264

Zanders JP (1997) The destruction of old chemical munitions in Belgium. In: Stock T, Lohs K (eds) The challenge of old chemical munitions and toxic armament wastes, SIPRI Chemical & Biological Warfare Studies No. 16. Oxford University Press, Oxford, p 197

Zanders JP (2002) The Chemical Weapons Convention and universality. Disarmament Forum 2002(4):23

Zanders JP (2003) International norms against chemical and biological warfare: an ambiguous legacy. JCSL 8(2):391

Zanders JP (2013) Chemical Weapons Convention (CWC) article XI and the future of the CWC. In: Meier O (ed) Technology transfers and non-proliferation: between control and cooperation. Routledge, London, p 176

Zanders JP, Trapp R (2013) Ridding Syria of chemical weapons: next steps. Arms Control Today 43(9):8

Zimmermann A, Şener M (2014) Chemical weapons and the International Criminal Court. Am J Int Law 108(3):440

Chapter 5
The Evolution of Legal Approaches to Controlling Nuclear and Radiological Weapons and Combating the Threat of Nuclear Terrorism

Jonathan Herbach

Abstract This chapter traces the evolution of international law related to the weaponization of nuclear and other radioactive materials, focusing in particular on the law pertaining to preventing acts of nuclear terrorism. International efforts to control atomic energy have evolved substantially since the only use of nuclear weapons, against Japan, in 1945. Unlike for chemical and biological weapons, whose legal regimes are centred on total bans of such weapons, the legal regime for nuclear weapons founded in the Treaty on the Non-Proliferation of Nuclear Weapons codifies a situation in which certain States retain weapons, pledging to negotiate toward disarmament, while others forego them and submit to a system of verification to ensure no diversion of nuclear energy from peaceful uses to nuclear weapons or other nuclear explosive devices. The recognition that physical protection of nuclear material and nuclear facilities from acts such as theft and sabotage was also highly important to both non-proliferation and radiation safety, but was not provided for under the safeguards system set up to detect and deter diversion by States of nuclear material to non-peaceful purposes, precipitated the nuclear security framework, starting with physical protection recommendations developed under the auspices of the International Atomic Energy Agency and the Convention on the Physical Protection of Nuclear Material. Subsequent developments related to nuclear security have been driven primarily by two issues: first, concerns regarding vulnerability of a significant amount of nuclear and other radioactive material, not necessarily part of weapons programmes, particularly following the end of the Cold War; and second, the threat that terrorists would obtain and

J. Herbach (✉)
Faculty of Law, Centre for Conflict and Security Law, Utrecht University,
Achter Sint Pieter 200, 3512 HT Utrecht, The Netherlands
e-mail: j.d.herbach@uu.nl

T.D. Gill et al. (eds.), *Yearbook of International Humanitarian Law 2014*,
Yearbook of International Humanitarian Law 17,
DOI 10.1007/978-94-6265-091-6_5

use such materials. The latter issue came to the fore in the wake of the terrorist attacks on 11 September 2001, displaying a new strain of mass-casualty international terrorism. These attacks were a transformative event for the area of nuclear security, leading to a number of actions aimed at strengthening the international legal framework. However, from the beginning, nuclear security has been formulated as fundamentally a national responsibility of States pursuant, where applicable, to certain international obligations. National sensitivities continue to affect the extent to which States are willing to enter into legally binding agreements. With that in mind, the present chapter looks at methods by which the law evolves and considers how they have been put into practice with respect to nuclear security in light of said national sensitivities and in response to perceived threats.

Keywords Nuclear security · Non-proliferation · Nuclear weapons · Radiological weapons · Nuclear terrorism · International organizations · Dual-use · Arms control law

Contents

5.1 Introduction

In the summer of 2014, the group known as the Islamic State of Iraq and the Levant (ISIL) or, alternatively, the Islamic State took control of Iraq's second largest city, Mosul. This concerning turn of events was compounded by later reports of the militants seizing nearly 40 kg of nuclear material, namely uranium, from a research facility at the city's university. Though it turned out that the form of the material taken—"low-grade" according to a spokesman of the International Atomic Energy Agency (IAEA)[1]—meant that it posed no real threat of being used in a weapon, the scenario of a terrorist group obtaining unsecured nuclear material is enough to give anyone pause. In fact, nearly 70 years after the first test of a

[1]See statement by Gill Tudor, IAEA spokeswoman, in Dahl 2014.

nuclear weapon, codenamed Trinity, the prospect of nuclear terrorism has been called "the most immediate and extreme threat to global security".[2]

International efforts to control nuclear energy have evolved substantially since the only use of nuclear weapons, against Japan, in 1945. The devastation wrought by relatively small bombs, in terms of the nuclear material employed,[3] shocked the conscience of the international community and led to immediate attempts to prevent such weapons from ever being used again. The intervening years, however, have seen eight more States develop nuclear weapons capabilities, with a number of others embarking upon and then rethinking nuclear weapons programmes, or remaining causes for concern. In addition, three major accidents involving nuclear power plants—Three Mile Island in the U.S. (1979), Chernobyl in the Soviet Union (1986), and Fukushima Daiichi in Japan (2011)—have prompted a range of responses, including the adoption of new nuclear safety treaties in the wake of the Chernobyl accident.[4]

Regardless of such issues, the technology to develop and make use of atomic energy has spread, and the number of peaceful uses for the materials has continued to increase, and with it so too has the potential for catastrophic events. In assessing possible international legal responses to controlling nuclear energy, States realized early on that it was neither possible nor desirable to attempt to withhold or deny others the benefits of atomic energy. For this reason, the right to peaceful use has been made a cornerstone of the system devised for controlling atomic energy and has meant that potentially dangerous materials and facilities are globally prevalent and are likely to become even more so going forward. Unfortunately, it was inevitable that nefarious actors would eventually seek to misuse these materials and facilities. The terrorist attacks of 11 September 2001 proved to be an important catalyst for action in the area of nuclear security. The attacks did not involve nuclear or other radioactive material nor were they directed at nuclear facilities. However, the intent of the perpetrators to cause casualties and damage indiscriminately on such a massive scale raised the specter that such actors would seek to employ the most destructive weapon known to man to achieve their aims. This coupled with the knowledge that a number of terrorist organizations—Al Qaeda, Chechen separatists, Lashkar-e-Taiba and Aum Shinrikyo among them—have demonstrated interest in obtaining nuclear weapons led to increased international activity to address this threat.

---

[2]This quote is from the famous speech on nuclear weapons given by U.S. President Barack Obama in Prague (5 April 2009) in which he announced the Nuclear Security Summit initiative. He prefaced his remarks by observing, "In a strange turn of history, the threat of global nuclear war has gone down, but the risk of a nuclear attack has gone up".

[3]According to the World Nuclear Association, around 60 kg of highly enriched uranium was used in the bomb that was dropped on Hiroshima, and the explosive charge of the bomb dropped on Nagasaki three days later came from 8 kg of plutonium, available at www.world-nuclear.org. The explosive yields were roughly 15 and 21 kt, respectively. An estimated 135,000 people were killed in Hiroshima, and 50,000 were killed in Nagasaki.

[4]Namely the Convention on Early Notification of a Nuclear Accident and the Convention on Assistance in Case of a Nuclear Accident or Radiological Emergency, both adopted in 1986. See IAEA Board of Governors Decision GOV/OR.649, adopted on 21 May 1986.

This chapter is focused on the evolution of international legal approaches to nuclear security—those rules, principles and norms aimed at preventing, detecting and responding to terrorist or other criminal activities involving nuclear or other radioactive materials and related facilities. It is important from the outset to make clear that this is closely related to, but not the same as, nuclear non-proliferation, which deals with the diversion by States of nuclear energy from peaceful uses to nuclear weapons. In other words, nuclear security is focused on non-State actors, and the existing international legal framework mainly applies to peaceful use materials, while non-proliferation primarily concerns States and military programmes. This said, the continued existence of nuclear weapons in State arsenals has a significant bearing on nuclear security, with the vast majority of nuclear materials being used for military purposes. It would therefore be an artificial construct to attempt to completely separate non-proliferation from nuclear security, as the latter was originally an outgrowth of the former. Thus, by necessity, this chapter will discuss aspects of the non-proliferation regime as well. One reason for the specific focus of this chapter is that several studies have already examined the nuclear non-proliferation regime in some detail,[5] while there is a dearth of international legal analysis of the nuclear security regime.

The other main reason for focusing on nuclear security here is that when it comes to evolution, the threat of nuclear terrorism has been a major driving force behind most recent developments in this area, a trend that has continued with the increased attention to nuclear security under the U.S. presidency of Barack Obama. In 2009, President Obama initiated the Nuclear Security Summit (NSS) process, which originally aimed at securing all vulnerable nuclear material—military and peaceful use[6]—within a period of 4 years. The scope has since expanded to consider other radioactive material besides nuclear material, as well as the interface between nuclear safety and nuclear security. The NSS process has brought together a significant number of States at the level of heads of State or government, representing a fairly broad cross section of the international community,[7] and sharing in the commitment to strengthen nuclear security and reduce the threat of nuclear terrorism by means of, *inter alia*, "sustained and effective international cooperation".[8] By its nature, the NSS process is of limited duration[9] and limited participation. Though the international legal framework has played a central role

---

[5]See, *inter alia*, Shaker 1980; Joyner 2011; Coppen 2012; Njølstad 2011; Lodgaard 2011.

[6]For the purposes of this article, and for the sake of clarity, the dichotomy of peaceful use versus military use will be maintained. However, it is worth noting that the category "military-use" is not monolithic and work has been and continues to be carried out to get a better grasp of the types of materials that fall within this category. See, for instance, the NTI Nuclear Materials Security Index (second edition, Jan. 2014), available at http://ntiindex.org/.

[7]47 States participated in the first Summit in Washington in 2010, a number that increased to 53 for the two subsequent gatherings (in Seoul, South Korea, in 2012 and The Hague, the Netherlands, in 2014).

[8]Preamble to the Communiqué of the Washington Nuclear Security Summit.

[9]The final Summit, in its current form, is scheduled to take place in 2016 in the U.S. Notably, Russia has indicated that it will not be participating.

in the process as part of the "global nuclear security architecture" outlined in the consensus Summit documents, the advent of the NSS is itself an implicit acknowledgment that the framework as it now stands, or as it is currently applied, is insufficient to effectively combat the threat of nuclear terrorism.

5.2 The Evolution of Legal Rules Under the International Law of Arms Control

Before tracing the evolution of legal rules aimed at controlling nuclear and radiological weapons, it is worthwhile to consider briefly the general ways in which such rules evolve. Ipsen pointed to three categories of methods that are contained in arms control treaty regimes: review conferences, amendment or modification clauses and obligations to continue negotiations.[10] Specific review conference provisions are a common feature of treaty regimes concerning weapons of mass destruction (WMD).[11] The wording of the review conference provisions is fairly consistent across the WMD-related treaties, the aim being to review the operation of the treaties with a view to ensuring that the purposes of the treaty are realized. The purview of review conferences is not explicitly amendment or modification of the treaty itself, though review could be a catalyst for such processes or new instruments, as will be seen below. Instead, the evolutionary impact has to do with their role in clarification, development of common understandings or illustration of subsequent practice that can have a bearing on treaty interpretation.[12] Amendment or modification, on the other hand, refers to procedures for altering provisions of the treaty with respect to all parties or to two or more parties as between themselves, respectively. Processes for amendment contained in WMD-related treaties vary in terms of procedural requirements for introduction, adoption and entry into force.[13] When it comes to obligations to continue negotiations,

---

[10]Ipsen 1991.

[11]The term weapons of mass destruction was defined in 1948 by the Commission on Conventional Armaments as "atomic explosive weapons, radioactive material weapons, lethal chemical and biological weapons, and any weapons developed in the future which have characteristics comparable in destructive effect to those of the atomic bomb or other weapons mentioned above" (Resolution of the Commission for Conventional Armaments, August 12, 1948). This commission was established by the Security Council in 1947 (Resolution 18) to consider the regulation and reduction of conventional armaments and armed forces.

[12]See, for instance, Article VIII, para 22 of the Chemical Weapons Convention (CWC). For the CWC, with its supervisory organization the Organization for the Prohibition of Chemical Weapons (OPCW), the review conference mechanism is embedded in the powers and functions of the OPCW, namely in the role of the plenary body, the Conference of States Parties. Treaties without such supervisory bodies will be reviewed by the States Parties, see Article XII of the Biological and Toxin Weapons Convention (BTWC).

[13]Compare Article VIII of the NPT, pursuant to which at least certain States (namely nuclear weapon States) must approve the amendment, with Article XV of the CWC, which differentiates between amendments to the Convention and changes to the Annexes. By contrast, Article XI of the BTWC is highly simplistic.

the Treaty on the Non-Proliferation of Nuclear Weapons (NPT) is a prime example. Under the NPT, certain States—those recognized as nuclear weapon States—must negotiate in good faith on effective measures relating, *inter alia*, to nuclear disarmament. The International Court of Justice has deemed this not only an obligation of conduct, but also one in which there is an obligation to achieve a specific result.[14]

Evolution of a legal regime, of course, is not limited to employing mechanisms under existing treaties. Changing circumstances, such as the rise of terrorist groups with the desire and means to inflict harm on a global scale and recognition of the vulnerability of new categories of materials, sometimes dictate the need for new law, or additional instruments aimed at dealing with specific issues. Moreover, and of particular relevance when it comes to nuclear security, one must consider the role played by a supranational institution, in this case the IAEA, in standard-setting and norm creation that impacts State behaviour. For nuclear security, the institutional process involved in developing non-legally binding guidelines, namely the *Nuclear Security Series* documents, contributes to the overall acceptance of these documents as indicative of standards of or commitments to certain conduct. The process entails drafting of the documents by the IAEA Secretariat in cooperation with Member State experts, followed by review and approval by the Nuclear Security Guidance Committee, to which each IAEA Member State may nominate a member, and culminating in a 120-day formal review by Member States. Put another way, the broad acceptance of these instruments can serve to legitimize conduct foreseen therein and make it more difficult to maintain the legality of opposing positions.[15] The central role of these documents in the nuclear security regime stems from the fact that, while each State has a strong interest in the highest possible standards being met in other States, the national security sensitivities surrounding the relevant materials and facilities impact the extent to which States are willing to enter into legally binding agreements.[16]

[14]Legality of the Threat or Use of Nuclear Weapons, Advisory Opinion, I.C.J. Reports 1996, p. 226, International Court of Justice (ICJ), 8 July 1996, para 99. It is outside the scope of the present chapter, but it bears mentioning that the Marshall Islands recently submitted three applications to institute proceedings before the International Court of Justice against the United Kingdom, Pakistan and India regarding the obligation to negotiate toward nuclear disarmament. The United Kingdom is bound by Article VI of the NPT pursuant to which States Parties undertake "to pursue negotiations in good faith on effective measures relating to cessation of the nuclear arms race at an early date and to nuclear disarmament, and on a treaty on general and complete disarmament under strict and effective international control". Pakistan and India are not parties to the NPT.

[15]See Boyle and Chinkin 2007, pp. 211–212.

[16]See Kellman 2000.

5.3 Devising an International Legal Framework to Control Atomic Energy

In its first-ever resolution, the UN General Assembly established a Commission to "deal with the problems raised by the discovery of atomic energy", called the Atomic Energy Commission (UNAEC).[17] The UNAEC was tasked with making proposals, *inter alia*, to control atomic energy in order to limit its use to peaceful purposes and for the "elimination from national armaments of atomic weapons and of all other major weapons adaptable to mass destruction". The General Assembly subsequently requested that the Security Council expedite its consideration of conventions providing for "the creation of an international system of control and inspection" and including prohibition of "atomic and all other major weapons adaptable now and in the future to mass destruction and the control of atomic energy to the extent necessary to ensure its use only for peaceful purposes".[18]

The UNAEC, in its first report to the Security Council, noted "the intimate relation between the activities required for peaceful purposes and those leading to the production of atomic weapons; most of the stages which are needed for the former are also needed for the latter",[19] a situation often referred to as the dual-use dilemma. The concern at the time, of course, was State-centric and had to do with diversion of materials to use for military purposes, not accounting for the later phenomenon of nuclear terrorism. Nonetheless, it is worth noting that the UNAEC concluded from its preliminary findings that an "international control agency" must be responsible for a system of safeguards and control. Among other things, this international control agency "should control the storage and shipment of [nuclear] materials to the degree necessary for security purposes" and "should itself store and handle all enriched or pure nuclear fuel in transit".[20]

It was at the first meeting of the UNAEC on 14 June 1946 that U.S. delegate Bernard Baruch put forward what came to be known as the "Baruch Plan". The Baruch Plan conceived of an international organization to be "entrusted [with] all phases of the development and use of atomic energy".[21] The Plan entailed a system for control of atomic energy, assigning to the international authority, *inter alia*, managerial control or ownership of all atomic energy activities of potential danger to world security and the power to control, inspect and license *all other* atomic activities. The authority would also be the seat of atomic knowledge in

---

[17]A/RES/1(I) (24 January 1946).

[18]A/RES/41(I) (14 December 1946).

[19]First Report of the Atomic Energy Commission to the Security Council, December 30, 1946, 1947 International Organization, no. 2, p. 389.

[20]*Ibid*, p. 392.

[21]Baruch Plan, Presented to the United Nations Atomic Energy Commission on June 14, 1946, available at http://www.atomicarchive.com/Docs/Deterrence/BaruchPlan.shtml.

order to comprehend, and thus be able to detect, any misuse of atomic energy. Once an adequate system of control was in place, including but not limited to renunciation of atomic bombs as weapons, along with establishing violations of the system of control as "international crimes", only then would production of atomic bombs cease and existing bombs be disposed of. This course of action—first a system of control and then disposal of existing weapons—favoured the U.S., which at the time had a monopoly on the possession of nuclear weapons.

The Soviet Union countered five days later with a draft convention, referred to as the Gromyko Plan,[22] which reversed the steps, starting rather with the prohibition of manufacturing and use of nuclear weapons and the destruction of existing weapons. Only once the prohibition was in place and the destruction of existing weapons had occurred, which was to take place within a period of three months, would a system to ensure compliance with the terms of the convention be established. The system of control, in other words, would follow later, the focus being in the first instance on disarmament, thereby rebutting the Baruch Plan. The Soviet Union also insisted on making control consistent with the UN Charter, meaning maintaining the veto powers for permanent members of the Security Council, which is something the Baruch Plan argued against in the case of the control of atomic energy.

Even with these disagreements, the UNAEC tried to continue its work, focusing on attempts to reach a compromise between the divergent points of view. However, by the time of the third report of the UNAEC to the Security Council, it had reached an impasse. The UN General Assembly dissolved the UNAEC in 1952, by which point the Soviet Union and the UK had each also developed nuclear weapons and established the United Nations Disarmament Commission under the Security Council with the same membership and rules of procedure as the UNAEC.[23] The UNAEC, for all its deficiencies, did foreshadow the repercussions of technological advancements in research and development and the potential for natural persons to misuse nuclear material and processes for malicious ends, thereby prescribing prohibition of both "nations and *individuals* from using the nuclear fuel for the perfecting, production or assembly of any atomic weapon whatsoever".[24]

---

[22]See the address by the Soviet Representative, Andrei Gromyko, to the United Nations Atomic Energy Commission, June 19, 1946, available at http://fissilematerials.org/library/GromykoPlan1946.pdf.

[23]A/RES/502 (VI) (11 January 1952). This Disarmament Commission met inconsistently until 1978 when it was replaced by a successor Disarmament Commission under the General Assembly, composed of all Member States.

[24]Second Report of the Atomic Energy Commission to the Security Council [emphasis added], September 11, 1947, A Decade of American Foreign Policy 1941–1949, Avalon Project, Yale Law School.

5.3.1 Overcoming "Narrow Sovereignty": The International Atomic Energy Agency

With the entry of the Soviet Union and the UK into the club of nuclear-armed States, along with nuclear programmes being initiated by a number of other States, there was increased concern about the further spread of nuclear weapons.[25] At the same time, the American approach to nuclear issues characterized by secrecy and denial gave way to a nuclear policy centred on safeguarded assistance and cooperation.[26] Secrecy and denial had proved incapable of preventing the spread of information and technology, and there was a growing interest in developing the peaceful commercial applications of atomic energy.[27]

This change in approach was articulated by U.S. President Eisenhower in his 1953 "Atoms for Peace" speech to the UN General Assembly.[28] Acknowledging fears of the destructive power and spread of nuclear weapons but also the promise of atomic energy used for peaceful purposes, while proclaiming that "if a danger exists in the world, it is a danger shared by all", Eisenhower outlined the establishment of an international atomic energy agency under the aegis of the United Nations. Joint contributions of fissile material would be made by possessor States to the new agency, which would then be in charge of the holding, storage and protection thereof. The agency would be assigned the role of allocating material from this bank to peaceful uses. This fissile material bank proposal was put forward partially as a way to avoid, at least from the outset, contentious discussions aimed at setting up "a completely acceptable system of world-wide inspection and control".

The "Atoms for Peace" proposal eventually led to the establishment of the IAEA in 1957,[29] with the objective to "accelerate and enlarge the contribution of atomic energy to peace, health and prosperity throughout the world", while at the same time ensuring that atomic energy will not be misused for military purposes.[30] The central tenet of the Eisenhower plan, however—that the Agency would act as a fissile material pool or bank thereby gradually reducing the material possessed by nuclear weapon States and working toward nuclear disarmament—has never come to pass, though plans continue to establish a multinational nuclear fuel bank under IAEA ownership in Kazakhstan.

The IAEA became the first specialized international organization that was directly tasked with supervision of compliance with multilateral arms control

---

[25]In introducing the Baruch Plan, Bernard Baruch lauded States that are "unwilling to be fobbed off by mouthings about narrow sovereignty, which is today's phrase for yesterday's isolation".

[26]Scheinman 1987, pp. 56–59.

[27]*Ibid.*

[28]Text available at http://ifpafletcherconference.com/pdf/eisenhower_speech.pdf.

[29]It is outside the scope of this chapter to get into the details of the IAEA Statute negotiations. For a good overview, see Scheinman 1987 and Fischer 1997.

[30]IAEA Statute 1957, Article II.

obligations upon entry into force of the Treaty on the Non-Proliferation of Nuclear Weapons (NPT).[31] Additionally, primarily by way of its statutory functions, namely providing training and technical advice, providing equipment or supplies and facilitating exchange of information and related services,[32] the IAEA has played a central role in fostering international cooperation in nuclear security as a way of ensuring peaceful uses of nuclear technology.[33]

5.3.2 From Non-Proliferation to Physical Protection

Unlike the Biological Weapons Convention and the Chemical Weapons Convention that comprise total bans on entire categories of weapons (the latter under strict international control), the NPT codifies a stratified system in which certain States—those that had manufactured and exploded a nuclear weapon or other nuclear explosive device prior to 1 January 1967[34]—retain their nuclear weapons while others commit to foregoing such weapons. The NPT, which entered into force in 1970, is based on a so-called "grand bargain" by which non-nuclear weapon States (NNWS) give up nuclear weapons ambitions, and submit to a system of verification (founded in the IAEA's safeguards system[35]) to ensure no diversion of peaceful-use nuclear material to nuclear weapons, in exchange for the recognized right to peaceful uses of nuclear energy and a commitment by nuclear weapon States (NWS) to negotiate towards nuclear disarmament. While it remains the cornerstone of the legal regime concerning nuclear weapons, the NPT does not account for the acquisition of weapons or weaponization of nuclear or other

[31]Goldblat 1994, p. 227. The establishment of the IAEA predates and is separate from the entry into force of the NPT, with respect to which it has been tasked with supervisory responsibilities. Compare this to the Organization for the Prohibition of Chemical Weapons specifically established under the Chemical Weapons Convention "to achieve the object and purpose of this Convention, to ensure the implementation of its provisions, including those for international verification of compliance with it, and to provide a forum for consultation and cooperation among States Parties" (Article VII, para 1).

[32]IAEA Statute, Articles III.A.4, III.A.1 and 2, and Articles III.A.3 and VIII, respectively. See also, IAEA International Law Series no. 4: The International Legal Framework for Nuclear Security.

[33]See 2010 Review Conference of the Treaty on the Non-Proliferation of Nuclear Weapons, Final Doc. Vol I, para 28.

[34]NPT, Article IX(3).

[35]The safeguards system comprises the provisions of the IAEA Statute and safeguards agreements modelled on INFCIRC/153 (corrected), as well as the Model Additional Protocol (INFCIRC/540) which extends the power of the IAEA with respect, *inter alia*, to gathering information and having site access. The objective of the safeguards system is to detect and deter the diversion of significant quantities of nuclear material from peaceful nuclear activities to the production of nuclear weapons or of other nuclear explosive devices or for purposes unknown, see INFCIRC/153 (corrected), para 28.

radioactive materials by non-State actors.[36] It is this element that is the focus of the law related to nuclear security.

Nuclear security began in the form of measures aimed at the physical protection of nuclear material and was an extension of the non-proliferation regime.[37] Pursuant to Article III of the NPT, non-nuclear weapon States Parties are obligated to conclude an agreement with the IAEA under the Agency's safeguards system with a view to preventing diversion of nuclear energy from peaceful uses to nuclear weapons or other nuclear explosive devices. The IAEA consequently developed INFCIRC/153,[38] which is formatted as the model agreement for States to fulfil their NPT Article III obligations and is based on the concept of nuclear material accountancy. While the safeguards system was set up to focus on detecting and deterring diversion by States of nuclear material to non-peaceful purposes, it was recognized that physical protection of nuclear material and nuclear facilities from acts such as theft and sabotage was also highly important to both non-proliferation and radiation safety, though such measures were not obligatory under the safeguards agreements, and the Agency was given no responsibility with respect to a State's physical protection system.

Acknowledging the need for some guidance to assist States in developing physical protection systems, a series of meetings was held between 1971 and 1972 which resulted in the document "Recommendations for the Physical Protection of Nuclear Material", which was subsequently revised in 1975 and published under the INFCIRC series as INFCIRC/225.[39] These original guidelines, along with subsequent revisions, have been of fundamental importance to the development of the international legal framework for nuclear security, prompting further consideration of ways to support international cooperation in addressing physical protection issues.[40] Following the formulation of the INFCIRC/225 guidelines, provisions related to physical protection began to be included, and thereby made legally binding, in a number of bilateral and trilateral agreements involving the application of Agency safeguards to material and/or equipment pursuant to Article III.A.5 of the IAEA Statute.[41]

Under the auspices of the 1975 NPT Review Conference, the Conference of States Parties called upon all States to "enter into such international agreements

[36]Garvey 2008, p. 344. Garvey considers the fact that the NPT does not address the proliferation concern of nuclear terrorism as a sign of its collapse.

[37]See Goldblat 1994, p. 85.

[38]IAEA, "The Structure and Content of Agreements between the Agency and States Required in Connection with the Treaty on the Non-Proliferation of Nuclear Weapons", INFCIRC/153 (corrected).

[39]Entitled: *The Physical Protection of Nuclear Material*. The 1972 Recommendations were revised upon review by a group of experts in order to reflect progress in physical protection as well as challenges posed by increasing use of nuclear material for peaceful purposes.

[40]IAEA 1975, General Conference *Resolution adopted during the 183rd plenary meeting on 26 September 1975*, Physical Protection of Nuclear Material, GC(XIX)/RES/328.

[41]Morawiecki 1978.

and arrangements as may be necessary to ensure" the physical protection of nuclear material in use, storage and transit.[42] Further consultations with IAEA Member States as well as the work of an Advisory Group on Physical Protection of Nuclear Material indicated a growing recognition that there was a need for an international legally binding instrument on physical protection. Following the circulation, in June 1977, of a draft "Convention on Physical Protection of Nuclear Facilities, Material and Transports" prepared by the U.S., the IAEA General Conference endorsed efforts by the Director-General to facilitate development of a legal instrument to provide for international cooperation in ensuring adequate physical protection of nuclear material, while taking into account that physical protection is primarily a national responsibility.[43] This clearly represents a significant moment in the development of the international approach to the physical protection of nuclear material, particularly when one compares the General Conference Resolution on the same topic adopted two years prior[44] in which reference is made only generally to the need to consider ways and means of facilitating international cooperation on physical protection without any additional specification as to the form such cooperation should take.

While States, and the European Atomic Energy Community, participating in the negotiations on what would become the Convention on the Physical Protection of Nuclear Material (CPPNM) agreed on the necessity of adopting legally binding obligations with respect to physical protection, there was substantial disagreement as to the scope of the eventual treaty. The objectives of the draft convention included obtaining commitment from States to implement adequate physical protection for civilian nuclear material *domestically*; providing for physical protection of civilian nuclear material during international transit; setting up a framework for international cooperation comprising mechanisms for prompt detection of, rapid reaction to, and rapid recovery of lost or stolen nuclear material; and establishing a framework for punishment of perpetrators meant to deter theft and threats relating to nuclear material, facilities and transports.[45] While a number of States shared the opinion that the scope should be comprehensive, extending to domestic use, storage and transport of nuclear material and even to the protection of nuclear facilities, several other States expressed the viewpoint that the scope should be limited to nuclear material in international transport, invoking the claim that legal, security, and technical differences from State to State would cause serious difficulties in applying standardized rules at the national level.

[42]Final Declaration of the Review Conference of the Parties to the Treaty on the Non-Proliferation of Nuclear Weapons, NPT/CONF/35/I, Annex I.

[43]IAEA 1977, General Conference Resolution adopted during the 199th plenary meeting on 30 September 1977, The Physical Protection of Nuclear Facilities, Materials and Transports, GC(XXI)/RES/350.

[44]GC(XIX)/RES/328.

[45]IAEA 1979, Convention on the Physical Protection of Nuclear Material, Legal Series, no. 12. See U.S. Statement, CPNM/15.

As the negotiations continued, the discussion became more about the comprehensiveness of the scope versus attaining the broadest reach among States, thereby underlining the dilemma that often arises in multilateral treaty negotiations between developing far-reaching and detailed obligations and aiming for consensus to achieve, to the greatest possible extent, universality. With that in mind, it was decided that physical protection of nuclear material in international transport was the most urgent issue and therefore should be the focus of the convention, though physical protection during domestic use, storage and transport was undoubtedly important and would thus be referenced in the preamble. Various States expressed their agreement with the limitation on the scope, some with the caveat that a review procedure should leave room for extending the Convention's aims. Others cautioned that the Convention should not be considered a first step toward a broader treaty aimed at physical protection of national facilities.

Another issue raised was whether the scope should be confined to nuclear material for *peaceful uses*, with a number of States advocating for extending the physical protection requirements to nuclear material used for military purposes, which represents the majority of nuclear material in the world. It was pointed out that the dangers stemming from non-State actor misuse of nuclear materials and facilities are the same whether those materials and facilities are used for military or peaceful activities. Therefore, it was questioned why there should be a difference in treatment.[46] One gathers from the record of negotiations that the U.S. prevented the inclusion of military-use materials in the operative text, stating that restricting the scope to peaceful uses was "critical" for its delegation.[47] In the end, the importance of securing nuclear materials used for military purposes was recognized in the preamble, with the added assurance that this material already was and would continue to be afforded strict physical protection.[48] The inclusion of this preambular paragraph does, however, bring the issue of physical protection of military-use materials within the purview of CPPNM review conferences, which are discussed below.

The CPPNM, which was opened for signature in 1980 and which entered into force in 1987, reflects a three-pronged approach[49] that characterizes the international law related to nuclear security: prevention of nuclear terrorism through

[46]*Ibid*, see the preliminary national statement of Germany, CPNM/6. Even the Soviet Union advocated for a convention covering all nuclear materials, see CPNM/18.

[47]*Ibid*, statement of the U.S. delegation regarding Article 2 (scope) of the draft convention, CPNM/77.

[48]The adequacy of this statement has been brought into question on several occasions, perhaps most notably in the 2012 incident at the Y-12 National Security Complex in the U.S. See Broad and Wald 2012.

[49]The three-pronged approach is explicitly stated in Article 1A of the amendment to the CPPNM, adopted in 2005 though not yet entered into force (see below).

protection[50] of materials and facilities, criminalization of certain acts in domestic legislations (including the principle of *aut dedere aut judicare*)[51] and international cooperation. The CPPNM requires States Parties to implement benchmark levels of physical protection measures, as laid down in the annexes, with respect to nuclear material used for peaceful purposes while in international transport. In addition, the CPPNM obliges States Parties to make the commission, the threat or attempt to commit and participation in certain offences punishable under national law, making punishment commensurate with the grave nature of said offences.[52] Third, the CPPNM contains provisions for international cooperation involving, *inter alia*, information exchange on national central authorities or points of contact with responsibility for physical protection of nuclear material and for coordinating recovery and response operations; cooperation and assistance on recovery and protection of nuclear material in the case of theft, robbery or other unlawful taking, or threat thereof, of such material; and cooperation and consultation as appropriate with respect to design, maintenance and improvement of systems of physical protection of nuclear material in international transport.[53] The CPPNM remains the only multilateral treaty dealing with the physical protection of nuclear material.[54]

In 1992, five years after the CPPNM entered into force, a review conference was held in accordance with Article 16 of the Convention. The purpose of the conference as foreseen in that Article was to review implementation of the Convention, as well as its adequacy "as concerns the preamble, the whole of the operative part and the annexes in light of the then prevailing situation". Using

---

[50]The objectives of physical protection are to "establish and maintain conditions to:

- protect against unauthorized removal of nuclear material in use and storage, and during transport;
- ensure the implementation of rapid and comprehensive measures by the State to locate and recover missing or stolen nuclear material;
- protect against sabotage of nuclear facilities and sabotage of nuclear material in use and storage and during transport; and
- mitigate or minimize the radiological consequences of sabotage".

IAEA Board of Governors 2001, Nuclear Verification and Security of Material: Physical Protection Objectives and Fundamental Principles, GOV/2001/41, Attachment p. 2.

[51]This is a common element of the body of counter-terrorism conventions.

[52]CPPNM, Article 7. The offences are not confined to activities involving nuclear material in international transport, but rather also extend to nuclear material used for peaceful purposes in domestic use, storage and transport.

[53]CPPNM, Article 5. Besides para 3, this Article also pertains to nuclear material also used for peaceful purposes in domestic use, storage and transport.

[54]Other instruments, such as the African Nuclear-Weapon-Free Zone Treaty (Treaty of Pelindaba), have provisions on physical protection of nuclear material referring back to the CPPNM and/or IAEA guidelines, namely INFCIRC/225. Similarly, physical protection is a fundamental principle in guidelines for nuclear transfers under the auspices of the Nuclear Suppliers Group (NSG), which state that "all nuclear materials and facilities identified by the agreed trigger list should be placed under effective physical protection levels (…) consistent with the relevant IAEA recommendations, in particular those set out in INFCIRC/225".

the phrase "the then prevailing situation" would seem to indicate an implicit acknowledgement that changing circumstances could impact the adequacy of the Convention as a whole and ostensibly necessitate amendment. The prevailing situation could entail technological or scientific developments, or even reflect changing dynamics among States. One would expect that the need to test the adequacy of the Convention against the current circumstances would indicate a concern that the Convention might no longer be suitable to fulfil its object and purpose. Perhaps presupposing inadequacy of the elements of the Convention at the time of review[55] and harking back to the disagreements regarding the scope of the Convention, a proposal had been made to combine the review and amendment processes into an overall evaluation conference. It was eventually determined that the processes should be kept separate, however, to allow for amendment proposals and related amendment conferences at any time.

At the 1992 Review Conference, the conference of States Parties to the CPPNM found the Convention to be adequate.[56] In particular, the conference of States Parties expressed agreement that the Convention provided an appropriate framework for cooperation with regard to protection, recovery and return of stolen nuclear material and for international cooperation in the application of criminal sanctions against persons who may commit illegal acts involving nuclear material. The short Final Statement also illustrates the close relationship among legally binding and non-legally binding physical protection instruments concluded under the aegis of the IAEA. Though only one review conference is required under the Convention, Article 16(2), in a provision nearly identical to that of Article VIII(3) of the NPT, provides for a majority of CPPNM States Parties to obtain the convening of further Review Conferences, at intervals of at least five years. This provision has not yet been invoked, but it represents an opportunity for taking up certain issues, namely the security of military-use materials.

Not long after the review conference, a number of States began to express a concern that the CPPNM was incomplete. The IAEA Director-General convened an Expert Meeting in 1999 to examine whether the CPPNM should be revised. The Expert Meeting established an open-ended Working Group to assess the relevant issues, and in 2001 the Working Group's Final Report identified a need to strengthen the international physical protection regime by means of, *inter alia*, an amendment to the CPPNM pursuant to Article 20. Shortly thereafter, the terrorist attacks of 11 September 2001 in the U.S. underlined the urgency of securing nuclear and other radioactive materials. Following requests to convene an amendment conference by a majority of CPPNM States Parties, as required under

[55]Toward the end of negotiation in 1979, in reference to a proposed text in CPNM/77, the German delegation noted that possible changes could foreseeably be made in the transport of nuclear material in the near future that would necessitate the Annexes, and maybe other clauses, being brought up to date.

[56]IAEA 1992, Final Statement of the Review Conference of Parties to the Convention on the Physical Protection of Nuclear Material.

Article 20, the conference was held in 2005. While even States that had been hesitant to support the development of international legal obligations covering domestic use, storage and transit of nuclear material and nuclear facilities recognized the need to strengthen the legal framework to prevent malicious acts involving said material and facilities, there remained significant aversion to certain measures such as requiring regular reports by States Parties on the implementation of the Convention or including provisions for mandatory peer review of the level of physical protection applied in a State Party.[57]

The resulting Amendment (CPPNM Amendment) has not yet gained the ratification, acceptance or approval of two-thirds of the CPPNM States Parties necessary to enter into force. When it does so, it will comprise a general broadening of the scope of the CPPNM. This includes the commitment to apply physical protection measures to nuclear material in domestic use, storage or transport and to nuclear facilities, thereby laying out fundamental principles of physical protection, increased international cooperation and the added criminal offence of sabotage of nuclear material or a nuclear facility. While the CPPNM Amendment does represent a substantial strengthening of the Convention, the focus remains on nuclear material and facilities used for peaceful purposes thereby leaving around 85 percent of nuclear material, used for military purposes, outside of the Convention's scope.[58] However, pursuant to the CPPNM Amendment, a review conference must be convened five years after its entry into force, which will, as mentioned before, offer the chance to consider the physical protection of military-use materials.

5.3.3 Other Radioactive Materials: Little Battlefield Utility, High Terrorist Attractiveness

To this point, the chapter has focused on nuclear materials, namely highly enriched uranium and plutonium. However, radioactive materials other than nuclear materials are considered to be particularly attractive to terrorists due to their portability, dispersibility and often relatively weak physical protection, as well as their global prevalence given that every country makes use of radioactive sources to some extent in medicine, agriculture, industry and/or research.[59]

[57]IAEA 2006, Summary Record of the First Meeting, Plenary, CPPNM/AC/Plen/SR.1., Amendment to the Convention on the Physical Protection of Nuclear Material, IAEA international law series, no. 2. On the concept of peer review, namely the IAEA advisory activities such as International Physical Protection Advisory Service (IPPAS) and International Nuclear Security Advisory Service (INSServ) missions, and how it is playing a central role in discussions on strengthening the nuclear security regime, see Herbach 2014.

[58]For a breakdown of the uses of nuclear material for military purposes, see the NTI Nuclear Materials Security Index, supra note 6.

[59]See Ferguson et al. 2003, p. v, in which it is stated that "several tens of thousands [of commercial radioactive sources], pose inherently high security risks because of their portability, dispersibility, and higher levels of radioactivity".

Radiological weapons could come in many forms. The one most often discussed is a so-called "dirty bomb" in which a conventional explosive is used to disperse radiation from a radioactive source.

Though no State has been known to produce such weapons for use on the battlefield, a discussion on banning radiological weapons has been on the agenda of the Conference on Disarmament (CD) for many years. Based on the inclusion of "radioactive material weapons" in the 1948 definition of WMD, the issue of radiological weapons was taken up in 1979 in the Committee on Disarmament, which became the Conference on Disarmament, as part of the discussion on "new types of weapons of mass destruction and new systems of such weapons; radiological weapons". This followed from the introduction of an "Agreed joint USSR-United States proposal on major elements of a treaty prohibiting the development, production, stockpiling and use of radiological weapons".[60] Under the proposal, radiological weapons were defined specifically to be distinct from nuclear weapons, namely as any device other than a nuclear explosive device that is designed to disseminate radioactive material to cause destruction, damage or injury through radiation produced by the material's decay, as well as radioactive material, other than that produced by a nuclear explosive device, specifically designed for that use.[61] In other words, the destruction, damage and injury would be caused by the emission of radiation from the radioactive material in the radiological weapon, instead of by the results of the nuclear explosion process (heat, blast, radioactive fallout) as created by a nuclear weapon. An ad hoc committee on radiological weapons was thereafter established on an annual basis to further consider the issue, and it was maintained until 1992.

Progress on the radiological weapons convention has persistently been thwarted by two main issues. First, disagreements regarding the definition of such weapons have been unable to be resolved. Some States, for instance, felt excluding nuclear explosive devices from the definition would legitimize the use of nuclear weapons.[62] The second issue had to do with the scope of the convention. A proposal was advanced to include in the prohibitions attacks on nuclear reactors and other nuclear facilities that could cause damage through the release of radiation. The question of precisely which facilities would be included, however, remained open.[63]

---

[60]See Report of the Committee on Disarmament, A/RES/34/27 (9 October 1979), p. 17.

[61]See Goldblat 1994, pp. 115–117.

[62]*Ibid.*

[63]Report of the Conference on Disarmament, Official Records of the Forty-Seventh Session of the General Assembly, Supplement No. 27, A/47/27. It is worth mentioning that under the law of armed conflict, "nuclear electrical generating stations (…) shall not be made the object of attack" if the attack may cause the release of radiation causing civilian deaths (Protocol Additional to the Geneva Conventions of 12 August 1949, and relating to the Protection of Victims of International Armed Conflicts (Protocol I), 8 June 1977, Article 56).

Though the work of the ad hoc committee on radiological weapons stopped in 1992, there was an attempt to revive the issue in the CD, again following the terrorist attacks of 11 September 2001. At its thirty-eighth session in 2002, the UN Advisory Board on Disarmament Matters[64] advised that the issue of radiological weapons should be revived by the CD, but this time with the focus on the potential terrorist use of such weapons.[65] This topic has remained on the agenda of the CD, discussions having taken place as recently as 2006 in the plenary and thereafter in informal settings. However, the discussions have remained inconclusive.

5.3.4 Elaboration of a Nuclear Terrorism Convention

The concern that terrorists could obtain and seek to use radioactive materials, particularly in the wake of the end of the Cold War and subsequent reports of unaccounted radioactive material, has also been considered in the UN General Assembly. In 1994, the General Assembly refocused its efforts on international terrorism by means of a declaration on measures to eliminate international terrorism.[66] The declaration was supplemented in 1996 with another resolution[67] that, *inter alia*, established an Ad Hoc Committee to elaborate an international convention on terrorist bombings, and subsequently an international convention for the suppression of acts of nuclear terrorism. In 1998, the Russian Federation introduced a draft Convention on the Suppression of Acts of Nuclear Terrorism under the auspices of the Ad Hoc Committee. In terms of the contribution to the evolution of the international legal framework for nuclear security, this draft contained, among other provisions, a wider obligation to take physical protection measures going beyond the CPPNM to include generally *all* nuclear and other radioactive material, used for military or peaceful purposes, and related installations. Subsequent proposals even added combating illicit trafficking to the scope of requisite measures under the same Article.

However, the text of the convention that was finally adopted, the 2005 International Convention for the Suppression of Acts of Nuclear Terrorism (ICSANT), while maintaining the reference to all radioactive material, contains language requiring States Parties to "make every effort to adopt appropriate measures" with respect to physical protection, leaving substantial State discretion when

[64]The Board is tasked with, among other things, advising the Secretary-General on matters within the area of arms limitation and disarmament, including on studies and research under the auspices of the United Nations or institutions within the United Nations system.

[65]Work of the Advisory Board on Disarmament Matters 2002, Report of the Secretary-General, A/57/335.

[66]UN General Assembly, Measures to eliminate international terrorism, A/RES/49/60 (9 December 1994).

[67]A/RES/51/210 (17 December 1996).

it comes to the adequacy of actions taken. There was much discussion in the context of negotiating ICSANT about ensuring that there would be no conflict or significant overlap with the CPPNM. Some delegations proposed formulating ICSANT as a protocol or amendment to the CPPNM in order to prevent derogation from or duplication of the CPPNM, while the authors of the draft ICSANT emphasized its strictly anti-terrorism object and purpose. The suggestion was also made that only counter-terrorist provisions should be included with no incorporation of provisions related to the protection of nuclear material.[68] In the end, though, the due diligence formulation regarding physical protection measures was adopted.

In terms of criminalization, ICSANT adds offences involving activities with radioactive material other than nuclear material to the list of international crimes, as long as they are accompanied by the requisite intent to cause death or serious bodily injury or substantial damage to property or to the environment.[69] ICSANT also lays out rules for handling radioactive material that is seized or taken control of by States following commission of one of the offences, referring to physical protection recommendations of the IAEA and including provisions related to cooperation among States and with the IAEA.

5.3.5 The Collective Security Approach: Nuclear Terrorism and the UN Security Council

In the wake of the Cold War, the Security Council made a general statement[70] labelling for the first time the proliferation of WMD as a threat to international peace and security, the trigger phrase for legally binding action under Chapter VII of the UN Charter. This followed revelations of clandestine WMD activity in Iraq. As an extension of this approach, and reflecting the changing dimensions of the perceived terrorist threat following the 9/11 attacks, the UN collective security system has taken a leading role in addressing the issue of WMD terrorism, namely through Resolution 1540, which was unanimously adopted in 2004.

Resolution 1540 labels, *inter alia*, the proliferation of nuclear weapons and their means of delivery, as well as illicit trafficking in nuclear weapons, their means of delivery and related materials, as a threat to international peace and security. Adopted under Chapter VII of the UN Charter, Resolution 1540 is binding on all Member States of the UN. Pursuant to the resolution, Member States are obliged to adopt and enforce laws prohibiting non-State actors from developing,

---

[68] United Nations, Report of the Ad Hoc Committee established by General Assembly resolution 51/210 of 17 December 1996, A/53/37.

[69] This element of intent plus the scope related to all radioactive materials differentiates the criminalization provisions of ICSANT from those contained in the CPPNM.

[70] Note by the President of the Security Council 2002, UN Doc. S/23500.

acquiring, using and transferring nuclear, biological or chemical weapons. It also requires States to develop and maintain appropriate and effective measures to account for and secure relevant items in production, use and storage as well as appropriate and effective physical protection measures, border controls and export controls.[71] The scope covers nuclear, chemical and biological weapons, their means of delivery and "materials, equipment and technology covered by relevant multilateral treaties and arrangements, or included on national control lists, which could be used for the design, development, production or use of nuclear, chemical and biological weapons and their means of delivery" ("related materials").

The adoption of this Resolution was recognition of both the gaps in the existing relevant treaty regimes impeding the ability to deal with contemporary issues, namely WMD terrorism, as well as the time-consuming nature of multilateral law-making that makes it difficult to respond appropriately to emerging threats. In the years following the adoption of Resolution 1540, the Security Council has reaffirmed on a number of occasions the measures foreseen therein.[72] All States are thus bound to take nuclear security-related measures. However, what it means to take "appropriate effective" action is not further described. Judging by the tools developed by the 1540 Committee,[73] which is tasked with monitoring and facilitating implementation of the resolution, "appropriate effective" means, at least in part, adhering to the relevant treaties, including the CPPNM and its Amendment. This, of course, does not mean that Resolution 1540 automatically binds States to these treaties. It does mean, though, that in the context of the overall legal framework there is more pressure on States to become party to the relevant instruments.

5.4 Conclusion

The evolution of the international law related to nuclear security has been driven primarily by two inter-related issues: the recognized vulnerability of a significant amount of nuclear and other radioactive material worldwide, in both military and peaceful use, and the demonstrated desire to obtain and expected willingness to use such materials on the part of terrorists. The former stems in large part from the fall of the Soviet Union and end of the Cold War, leading to significant amounts of unaccounted for and unsecured materials and facilities, as well as from increased demand for nuclear energy and the extensive global use of radioactive materials in peaceful activities, leading to the spread of the materials, technologies and

[71]Asada has pointed out, for instance, that "no treaties can obligate States to establish such a national export control system so extensively, so quickly and so effectively," see Asada 2008, p. 318.

[72]S/RES/1673 (27 April 2006), S/RES/1810 (25 April 2008) and S/RES/1977 (20 April 2011).

[73]See the 1540 Matrix Template, available at http://www.un.org/en/sc/1540/national-implementation/pdf/Matrix%20Template%202013%20(E).pdf.

capabilities. The latter issue came to the fore in the wake of the terrorist attacks on 11 September 2001, displaying a new strain of mass-casualty international terrorism, and has been considered the primary catalyst in the development of the nuclear security framework, much in the same way as Chernobyl was for nuclear safety and Iraq in the 1990s was for nuclear safeguards.[74]

The international law that has developed for nuclear security is composed of a mix of treaties, which concern physical protection of materials and facilities, criminalization of certain offences in domestic jurisdictions[75] and international cooperation; non-legally binding guidelines and principles developed under the auspices of the IAEA that supplement and complement the treaty law; and resolutions adopted by the UN Security Council under Chapter VII of the UN Charter, namely Resolution 1540. The fact that the legal framework for nuclear security remains founded in treaties of restricted scope and non-legally binding documents has to do with the fact that nuclear security is seen by many States as the sole responsibility of the State, as it touches upon domestic law enforcement, national defence and intelligence activities and energy production, among other sensitive sectors, meaning that it impacts fundamental aspects of national sovereignty. Therefore, issues certainly still remain, and the extent of continued evolution of the international law in this area will be determined by the confluence of national interests and motivations. For instance, while nuclear security is a high priority for the States that have participated in the NSS process, a number of them have singled out the existence of nuclear weapons and insufficient progress in terms of nuclear disarmament as the main issues that need to be resolved in realizing an effective global regime.[76] In other words, physically protecting materials and related facilities is not the main problem. It has, in fact, been proposed that, going forward, any such discussion on nuclear security should expand in focus to include disarmament and non-proliferation.[77] From an institutional perspective, this would seem to imply that the issue of nuclear security should be absorbed into the NPT process. However, nuclear security as such is not part of the NPT. The bitter irony is

---

[74]This assertion was made by Laura Rockwood, former Section Head for Non-Proliferation and Policy Making in the Office of Legal Affairs of the IAEA, during a panel discussion focused on "How the Evolving Domestic, Regional, and IAEA Safeguards Requirements and Practices are Influencing Safeguards Implementation and Culture", at the 55th Annual Meeting of the Institute of Nuclear Materials Management, 22 July 2014.

[75]Other instruments of relevance to nuclear security and focused on criminalization of certain offences include the 1997 International Convention for the Suppression of Terrorist Bombings, the 2005 Protocol to the Convention for the Suppression of Unlawful Acts against the Safety of Maritime Navigation, the 2005 Protocol to the 1988 Protocol for the Suppression of Unlawful Acts against the Safety of Fixed Platforms Located on the Continental Shelf and the 2010 Beijing Convention on the Suppression of Unlawful Acts Relating to International Civil Aviation.

[76]See the National Progress Reports submitted for the 2014 NSS in The Hague by, for example, Indonesia, New Zealand and Japan, available at https://www.nss2014.com/en.

[77]See National Statement of Switzerland presented at the 2014 NSS in The Hague. Chile made a similar statement.

that in the wake of a nuclear terrorist attack, the obstacles that prevent further strengthening of the international legal framework today will melt away, necessary action will be taken and States will be forced to reflect on what more could have been done.

References

Asada M (2008) Security Council Resolution 1540 to combat WMD terrorism: effectiveness and legitimacy in international legislation. J Confl Secur Law 13:303–332

Boyle A, Chinkin C (2007) The making of international law. Oxford University Press, Oxford

Broad W, Wald M (2012) Security questions are raised by break-in at a nuclear site. The New York Times

Coppen T (2012) The role and rationale of the nuclear non-proliferation treaty in the twenty-first century. Rom J Soc Polit 2:95–119. http://conflictandsecuritylaw.org/web_documents/tom_coppen_rjsp.pdf. Accessed 7 Jan 2015

Dahl F (2014) UPDATE 4-seized nuclear material in Iraq "low grade"—UN agency. Reuters

Ferguson C et al (2003) Commercial radioactive sources: surveying the security risks. Monterey Institute of International Studies, Occasional Paper No. 11

Fischer D (1997) History of the International Atomic Energy Agency: the first forty years. International Atomic Energy Agency, Vienna

Garvey J (2008) A new architecture for the non-proliferation of nuclear weapons. J Confl Secur Law 12:339–357

Goldblat J (1994) Arms control: a guide to negotiations and agreements. Sage Publications Ltd, London

Herbach J (2014) The Nuclear Security Implementation Initiative: a catalyst for needed action. Arms Control Today 44:8–12

Ipsen K (1991) Explicit methods of arms control treaty evolution. In: Dahlitz J, Dicke D (eds) The international law of arms control and disarmament: proceedings of the symposium, Geneva, 28 February–2 March 1991. United Nations, New York, pp 75–93

Joyner D (2011) Interpreting the nuclear non-proliferation treaty. Oxford University Press, Oxford

Kellman B (2000) Protection of nuclear materials. In: Shelton D (ed) Commitment and compliance: the role of non-binding norms in the international legal system. Oxford University Press, Oxford, pp 486–505

Lodgaard S (2011) Nuclear disarmament and Non-Proliferation, 1st edn. Routledge, New York

Morawiecki W (1978) The IAEA's role in promoting physical protection of nuclear material and facilities. Int At Energy Agency Bull 20:39–45

Njølstad N (2011) Nuclear proliferation and international order: challenges to the Non-Proliferation Treaty. Routledge, New York

Scheinman L (1987) The International Atomic Energy Agency and world nuclear order. Resources for the Future Inc, Washington

Shaker M (1980) The nuclear non-proliferation treaty: origin and implementation 1959–1979 (Volume 1). Oceana Publications, London

Part III
The Methods of Warfare 1914–2014

Chapter 6
The Development of the Law of Naval Warfare from the Nineteenth to the Twenty-First Century—Some Select Issues

Wolff Heintschel von Heinegg

Abstract This chapter highlights some developments of the law of naval warfare that have resulted either in the continuing validity of traditional concepts, principles and rules or in a modification of the 'old rules'. Those modifications were not necessarily agreed upon because of the evolution of weapons technology but rather with a view to enhance the legal protection of victims at sea. The overall assessment of the development of the law of naval warfare is positive because it has indeed produced a higher degree of legal clarity. This certainly holds true for the categories of lawful targets and for methods and means of naval warfare. Nevertheless, there are some issues that are in need of further clarification. While the traditional rule, according to which only warships are entitled to exercise belligerent rights, has survived, the emergence of unmanned maritime systems has created new problems insofar as their legal status is far from clear. Similar questions relate to submarine communications cables, which, despite their overall importance, have so far been neglected. Another aspect that deserves some attention relates to protected vessels, in particular hospital ships, and to protected persons. The latter is of high importance because the status of neutral nationals in times of naval war is not yet fully settled.

Keywords Law of naval warfare · Warships · Submarines · Unmanned maritime systems · Submarine communications cables · Hospital ships · Merchant vessels · Methods and means of naval warfare · Naval mines · Torpedoes · Blockade · Exclusion zones · Naval bombardment · Protected persons

---

W. Heintschel von Heinegg (✉)
Europa-Universität Viadrina, Frankfurt (Oder), Germany
e-mail: heinegg@europa-uni.de

T.D. Gill et al. (eds.), *Yearbook of International Humanitarian Law 2014*,
Yearbook of International Humanitarian Law 17,
DOI 10.1007/978-94-6265-091-6_6

Contents

6.1 Introduction

A comprehensive description and assessment of the development of the law of naval warfare, including the law of maritime neutrality and prize law, from its origins to its current state would certainly go beyond the scope reserved for the present chapter. Accordingly, neither the law of prize nor the law of maritime neutrality will be dealt with here.[1] The important aerial element will be disregarded as well because the traditional law of naval warfare is characterized by a strong focus on ships and because the law governing air and missile warfare, including air operations in a naval context, has matured into a separate branch of the law of armed conflict.[2] Finally, the practice of States during the international armed conflicts of the twentieth and twenty-first centuries can be addressed marginally only.

This chapter will focus on some aspects of the traditional law of naval warfare and pursue the question whether and to what extent the respective traditional rules and principles continue to apply in the twenty-first century. By necessity the approach is selective and is does not provide an answer to every question that may arise with a view to the legality of the conduct of hostilities at sea.

[1]For the current law of maritime neutrality see Helsinki Principles 1998; Heintschel von Heinegg 2007, p. 543 et seq. For the development and current state of prize law see Kraska 2012, p. 480 et seq; Heintschel von Heinegg 1991 and 1992.

[2]See AMW Manual 2013. It may be added that the provisions of the San Remo Manual on naval air operations have been overtaken by the AMW Manual.

6.2 Exercise of Belligerent Rights Exclusively by Warships

Prior to 1856, the exercise of belligerent rights at sea—i.e. attacks against enemy warships and merchant vessels as well as visit, search, capture and under exceptional circumstances, destruction of merchant vessels under prize law—was not limited to warships. Rather, sovereigns/States were free to authorize private actors to exercise belligerent rights on their behalf (or to engage in 'privateering'), although the legality of that practice was a contentious issue.[3] In view of the authorization, the respective private actors could not be considered pirates, and the requirement of the just war theory, according to which resort to war must be based on the decision of a sovereign/government, was satisfied. At the same time, the sovereign was relieved from considerable financial investments that are always involved in the commissioning of warships. From the perspective of neutral trade, the use of private actors was most unfortunate because the authorized ships could not be identified as acting in pursuance of governmental ends, unless they had the opportunity of taking notice of the respective authorization that was contained in a so-called letter of marque. In particular in situations of war, it was, however, crucial for neutral merchantmen to clearly distinguish between State ships/warships and private ships/merchant vessels since, under the law of naval warfare as it then stood (and as it continues to stand today), they were obliged to obey orders given to them by belligerent warships only.

6.2.1 Surface Warships and Converted Merchant Vessels

In 1856, 51 States agreed, in the Paris Declaration 1856, on the abolishment of privateering.[4] Although there was no treaty either expressly limiting the exercise of belligerent rights to warships proper or providing for a definition of warships, the delegates to the 1907 Hague Peace Conference seemingly agreed that, with the abolishment of privateering, the exercise of belligerent rights at sea had become exclusively limited to warships. Hague Convention VII (1907) contains the requirements merchant vessels converted into warships must comply with, which are almost identical with those laid down today in the generally accepted definition of the term 'warship' in Article 29 UNCLOS (1982) and corresponding customary international law.[5]

In this context, it is important to emphasize that the permission of the conversion of merchant vessels into warships cannot be considered a revival of

[3]Colombos 1967, p. 513 et seq; Oppenheim 1952, p. 261 et seq.

[4]Paris Declaration: "1. Privateering is, and remains, abolished".

[5]Venturini 1988, p. 120 et seq; Tucker 1955, p. 40; Colombos, p. 517 et seq; Heintschel von Heinegg 2012a, p. 791 et seq.

'privateering'.[6] First, Hague Convention VII (1907) "in no way abrogated the rule of the Declaration of Paris that privateering is and remains abolished".[7] Second, the converted ship is no longer under the command of a private master but of a commissioned officer, it is part of the respective State's naval forces and marked as such, and the crew is under regular military discipline. While it is true that, with the conversion, "a weak naval power hopes to compensate for its weakness in much the same manner that weak naval powers in the past compensated for their weakness by the use of privateers",[8] the strict requirements a converted merchant vessel must comply with do not justify the claims of a revival of privateering 'through the backdoor' of Hague Convention VII.

However, two issues remained unresolved: the location of the conversion and the legality of a re-conversion during an on-going war.[9] While some States did not accept a conversion on the high seas, others took the position that the location of conversion was irrelevant as long as the requirements of Hague Convention VII were met. A similar divergence of opinions existed as to the question whether a merchant vessel converted into a warship could be re-converted into a merchant vessel in the course of the war.

6.2.2 Submarines

During the 1907 Hague Peace Conference, it also became clear that submarines, if operated by the armed forces, marked as such, commanded by a commissioned officer and manned by a crew under regular military discipline, qualify as warships and, thus, as lawful means of warfare at sea. In particular, the British Government had tried to outlaw the submarine because it considered it a threat to its surface forces, but other States were not prepared to accept the British proposal because they wished to preserve the option of challenging a superior surface force by the use of submarines.[10] In view of the practice of the First World War, it became necessary to clarify the applicability of the law of naval warfare, in particular of prize law, to submarines. Although submarines were extremely vulnerable when surfaced (e.g. by enemy merchant vessels trying to ram them, or by the weapons of enemy warships and armed enemy merchant vessels) and although there was not sufficient space on board for the crews and passengers of merchant vessels that were to be destroyed under prize law, Article 22 of the 1930 London Naval Treaty, which was reaffirmed by the London Protocol 1936, provides inter alia that "in their action with regard to merchant ships, submarines must conform

[6] See, however, Stone 1959, p 576.

[7] Oppenheim 1952, p. 265.

[8] Tucker 1955, p. 40.

[9] Venturini 1988, p. 122 et seq.

[10] See the references in von Heinegg 2009, p. 331 et seq.

to the rules of international law to which surface vessels are subject". Today, there is general agreement that the law of naval warfare applies to all submarine operations during an international armed conflict.[11]

It follows from the foregoing that, under the traditional law of naval warfare, "[o]nly the naval forces of a belligerent are permitted to conduct offensive operations against the enemy" and, "the traditional rules governing neutral-belligerent relations in naval war presuppose throughout the possibility of distinguishing between the naval forces of belligerent and belligerent merchant vessels".[12] In other words, the exercise of belligerent rights is reserved to warships, including converted merchant vessels and submarines. Whether they are armed or not is irrelevant.[13] Other State ships, in particular auxiliary, police and customs vessels, are not entitled to exercise belligerent rights.[14]

6.2.3 Continuing Validity of the Traditional Approach

The traditional law seems to be overly formalistic with regard to offensive operations. Indeed, one may ask whether the right to attack lawful enemy targets is still limited to warships as defined under international law because an attack by an armed merchant vessel (or by a State ship other than a warship) against a lawful target will deprive the attacking vessel of its protection against attack but would not necessarily render the attack as such illegal. Still, during the international armed conflicts of the twentieth century, States only employed vessels that complied with the requirements of the definition, i.e. warships by design and merchant vessels converted into warships in accordance with Hague Convention VII (1907). The fact that, during the First World War, England and France made use of so-called 'Q ships'[15] and that England armed its merchant vessels during both World Wars provides no sufficient evidence that offensive operations may be conducted by other than warships. The arming of British merchant vessels was justified by reference to the right of enemy merchant vessels (not of neutral merchant vessels!) to actively resist visit, search and capture.[16] It was not meant to confer upon them the right to engage in hostilities against any enemy warship or to engage in the

---

[11] San Remo Manual 1995, para 45; NWP 1–14 M 2007, para 8.7; German Manual 2013, para 1054; UK Manual 2004, para 13.31; Canadian Manual 2001, para 826.

[12] Tucker 1955, p. 38.

[13] Tucker 1955, p. 39. See, however, Hyde 1945, p. 1920, who maintains an unarmed warship "should not be dealt with as though it were a dreadnought".

[14] German Manual 2013, para 1020; Colombos 1967, p. 515 et seq; Oppenheim 1952, p. 467: "But only a man-of-war is competent to attack either men-of-war or merchantmen".

[15] Q ships were heavily armed merchant vessels that were to trap enemy submarines. Today, the use of Q ships would be considered unlawful. See San Remo Manual, Explanations 1995, para 111.2.

[16] Oppenheim 1952, p. 467; Colombos 1967, p. 521 et seq.

exercise of belligerent rights against merchant vessels. In the armed conflicts since 1945, States only used ships operated by the armed forces or by armed groups integrated into, or assimilated to, the regular armed forces.[17] Moreover, it may not be left out of sight that naval warfare will regularly not be limited to belligerent national waters but will be conducted in high seas areas. It will have an impact on neutral shipping (and neutral aviation). Because the law of naval warfare so strongly focuses on military operations in international waters, which continue to be used by belligerents and neutrals at the same time, the formal approach of the traditional law is still valid today: the exercise of belligerent rights, whether directed against enemy or neutral vessels (and aircraft), whether qualifying as attacks or as an exercise of prize measures, is limited to warships.[18]

This finding does not provide a solution with regard to the legal status of unmanned maritime systems that are increasingly used by the naval forces for a variety of purposes. While there are convincing reasons to consider them lawful means of warfare, if designed or used for attack purposes, they probably do not qualify as warships *strictu* sensu. Accordingly, it would not be permissible to employ them for the exercise of belligerent rights other than offensive operations against lawful enemy targets. Moreover, they would not enjoy independent passage rights, including transit passage and archipelagic sea lanes passage in normal mode, in neutral waters.[19] It remains to be seen whether States are prepared to either consider certain unmanned maritime systems as, or to assimilate them to, warships proper, and to grant them the same rights warships enjoy under the law of naval warfare and of maritime neutrality.

6.3 Protected Vessels and Persons

During the nineteenth and the beginning of the twentieth centuries, States formally agreed on the protection of certain categories of enemy vessels from capture (and, thus, from attack) and on the special protection of hospital ships. Whereas the former continue to apply in their original form, the latter have undergone an

---

[17]Tucker 1955, p. 38 et seq; Oppenheim 1952, p. 467 et seq; Colombos 1967, p. 507 et seq.; Heintschel von Heinegg 2012a.

[18]German Manual 2013, para 1019.

[19]For a claim to that effect see The Commander's Handbook on the Law of Naval Operations, NWP 1–14 M 2007, para 2.5.2.5: "Customary international law as reflected in the 1982 LOS Convention gives vessels of all nations the right to engage in innocent passage as well as in transit passage and archipelagic sea lanes passage. The size, purpose, or type of cargo is irrelevant. The same rules apply to USV and UUV transit and navigation. USVs and UUVs retain independent navigation rights and may be deployed by larger vessels as long as their employment complies with the navigational regimes of innocent passage, transit passage, archipelagic sea lanes passage as applicable." With regard to the legality of autonomous systems see, inter alia, the papers available at: https://www.usnwc.edu/Publications/International-Law-Studies-(1).aspx (accessed 15 December 2014).

impressive development by subsequent treaties and State practice. Likewise, the category of protected persons has been extended considerably.

6.3.1 Hague Conventions VI and XI

The traditional law, as codified in The Hague Conventions VI (1907) and XI (1907), exempts certain categories of enemy vessels from capture and confiscation.[20] While the customary character of Hague Convention VI(1907)has been doubted by some,[21] it is safe to hold that, today, it is generally considered as declaratory of customary international law.[22] The same holds true for the categories of enemy vessels exempt from capture under Hague Convention XI (1907).[23] Those vessels are protected from capture because they serve either humanitarian (in particular supply of the local coastal population with goods essential for their survival) or other purposes (e.g. scientific or religious) that have no bearing on the conduct of hostilities at sea. This special protection accorded to the said enemy vessels is limited to capture under prize law and it is without prejudice to their liability to attack if they qualify as lawful targets, e.g. by effectively contributing to the enemy's war effort. Of course, if they do not qualify as lawful military objectives, their exemption from capture *a fortiori* includes their protection from attack.

6.3.2 Hospital Ships

Hague Conventions VI (1907) and XI (1907), although the latter also protects "vessels on philanthropic missions", do not apply to hospital ships, whose special protection was laid down in other treaties. During the eighteenth and nineteenth centuries, naval forces were regularly accompanied by ships that were to collect, treat and transport the wounded members of the armed forces, including casualties from land warfare, and there was general agreement on their protection against attack and capture.[24] That protection was first codified in the Additional Articles (1868), which were never formally adopted. Still, at the first Hague Peace Conference (1899), the Additional Articles were "considered as capable of constituting the best basis" for adapting "to maritime wars the stipulations of the Geneva

[20] Tucker 1955, p. 87 et seq; Shearer 1988, p. 184 et seq; de Guttry 1988, p. 103 et seq.

[21] Tucker 1955, p. 87.

[22] German Manual 2013, para 1028; de Guttry 1988, p. 108.

[23] San Remo Manual 1995, para 47, 136; UK Manual 2004, paras 13.33, 13.100; Canadian Manual 2001, paras 828, 864; German Manual 2013, para 1040.

[24] Mossop 1947, p. 399. For the practice of States during the eighteenth and nineteenth centuries see Grandclément 1938, p. 396 et seq. For the use of vessels transporting the wounded in antique times see the references by Pictet 1960, p. 154.

Convention of 1864".[25] Accordingly, Article 1(1) Hague Convention III (1899) provided that military hospital ships shall "be respected and cannot be captured while hostilities last". Under Articles 2 and 3, the same protection was accorded to private hospital ships of enemy or neutral character.[26] At the Second Hague Peace Conference (1907), the delegates did not consider it necessary to substantially modify the 1899 provisions.[27] However, during the two World Wars, the provisions agreed upon in 1899 and 1907 proved to be insufficient.[28] In particular, the lack of an agreed upon minimum tonnage had proven to be one of the reasons why the protection of hospital ships was less effective than envisaged by the drafters of The Hague Conventions.[29] Many of those problems were solved by Geneva Convention II (1949), which has without doubt improved the special protection of hospital ships.[30] However, the technological development since then as well as new threats, in particular by actors who do not respect the special protection of hospital ships, have created some uncertainties as to whether the 1949 rules, as progressively developed by the Additional Protocol I (1977),[31] continue to apply in an unmodified manner.

6.3.2.1 Means of Communication

One issue relates to the use of a hospital ship's means of communication. The first rule providing for the permissibility of the "presence of a wireless telegraphy apparatus" on board hospital ships was Article 8(2) of Hague Convention X (1907), although there were some doubts as to whether a provision to that effect was advisable.[32] During the two World Wars, the presence of means of communication on board hospital ships, in particular of a wireless, continued to be met with suspicion and hospital ships were captured and condemned because they had been

[25]See the summary of the 2nd meeting of the First Sub-Commission of the Second Commission of the 1899 Hague Conference, in: Conference Report 1899, p. 444.

[26]These are "hospital ships, equipped wholly or in part at the cost of private individuals or officially recognized societies" of either belligerent or neutral countries.

[27]See Conference Report 1907 Hague Conference, p. 63.

[28]See Oppenheim 1952, p. 505; Colombos 1967, p. 602 et seq.; Battle 1921, p. 15 et seq; Fenrick 1991, p. 247 et seq.

[29]See Report on the Work of the Preliminary Conference of National Red Cross Societies for the Study of the Conventions and of Various Problems relative to the Red Cross (Geneva, July 26—August 3, 1946), p. 58: "In their Report to the Conference, the International Committee stated that during the recent War, controversy had arisen between belligerents with regard to the minimum tonnage of hospital-ships. Some belligerents refused to recognize certain hospital-ships as such, on the grounds of insufficient tonnage."

[30]See Articles 22 to 35 Geneva Convention II (1949).

[31]Articles 22 and 23 Additional Protocol I (1977).

[32]The President of the Third Commission believed that the presence of such apparatus was "of a nature to beget suspicions". See Conference Report 1907, p. 300. This Report is also known as the 'Renault Report' and is reprinted in: 2 AJIL 295-306 (1908).

used as signalling ships for military purposes.[33] Still, Article 35(2) Geneva Convention II (1949), like its 1907 predecessor, provides that the "presence on board of apparatus exclusively intended to facilitate [...] communication" shall "not be considered as depriving hospital ships [...] of the protection due to them". At the same time, Article 34(2) explicitly prohibits hospital ships "to possess or use a secret code for their wireless or other means of communication". Interestingly, the equally authentic English and French[34] versions of para 2, as finally adopted, differ considerably. [35].

The prohibition according to the authentic English text seems to apply to any use of the means of communication, whether for transmitting or receiving messages, whereas the equally authentic French version is limited to a prohibition of possessing or using a secret code for transmitting messages via the wireless or other means of communication. In this context, it is important to note that at the time of the adoption of the Second Geneva Convention there was no wireless (or other means of communication) that could be used for both transmitting and receiving messages. Hence, a distinction between those apparatuses certainly reflected the practice of States as well as the state of technology at the time Geneva Convention II (1949) was adopted. Moreover, it may not be left out of consideration that hospital ships must be able to receive timely information about their area of operation. If that information were transmitted in clear, the enemy could become aware of a planned operation. Therefore, the equally authentic French text that merely prohibits the possession and use of a secret code for the purpose of transmitting messages—as distinguished from receiving them—seems to better capture the drafters' true intention.

The communications technology used on board ships has changed considerably. Most ships, including hospital ships, communicate via satellites. Therefore, the US has taken the following position:

> "[...] subsequent technological advances in encryption and satellite navigation, while recognized as problematic, have not been specifically addressed by treaty. As a practical matter, modern navigational technology requires that the traditional rule prohibiting 'secret codes' be understood to not include modern encryption communications systems. However, such systems must not be used for military purposes in any way harmful to a potential adversary".[36]

The use of modern satellite communication technology that is based on some form of encryption has not been challenged by other High Contracting Parties as

[33]For the case of German hospital ship *Ophelia* that was captured and condemned by the British Prize Court because she was also up as a signalling ship for military purposes, see Colombos 1967, p. 591; Garner 1927, p. 244 et seq.

[34]See Article 54(1) Hague Regulations (1907).

[35]The French text reads as follows: "En particulier, les navires-hôpitaux ne pourront posséder ni utiliser de code secret pour leurs émissions par T.S.F. ou par tout autre moyen de communication." 'T.S.F.' stands for 'transmission sans fil', i.e. 'wireless', and 'émissions' for 'transmission' or 'broadcast'.

[36]NWP 1–14 M 2007, para 8.6.3.

being in violation of Article 34(2) GC II.[37] Interestingly, a 'very narrow majority' of the experts drafting the San Remo Manual has taken the view that "present law still prohibits the use of such equipment and that this law has not fallen into desuetude".[38] Hence, according to the San Remo Manual, hospital ships are not explicitly allowed to use cryptographic equipment. The respective paragraph merely contains a recommendation *de lege ferenda*.[39] In view of State practice it is, however, doubtful whether the use of satellite communications is still considered a violation of Article 34(2) GC II.[40]

6.3.2.2 Arming of Hospital Ships

The right of the crews of hospital ships to carry arms and use them, if necessary, for the maintenance of order, for their own defence or that of the sick and wounded is well-established. It has been recognized since 1907,[41] and it has been reaffirmed by Article 35(1) Geneva Convention II (1949). According to Article 35(3) the same holds true for "portable arms and ammunition taken from the wounded, sick and shipwrecked and not yet handed to the proper service". At the same time, the equipment of hospital ships with heavy arms, i.e. in excess of those permitted by Article 35(1) and (2), has been generally considered as depriving them of their special protection under international humanitarian law.

Therefore, the US practice of arming hospital ships seems to be highly problematic.[42] That practice is justified as follows:

> "[…] due to the changing threat environment in which the red cross symbol is not recognized by various hostile groups and actors as indicating protected status, the United States views the manning of hospital ships with defensive weapons systems, such as anti-missile defence systems or crew-served weapons to defend against small boat threats as prudent AT/TP[43] measures, analogous to arming crew members with small arms, and consistent

---

[37]See Grunawalt 2005, p. 106 et seq.

[38]San Remo Manual, Explanations 1995, para 171.5.

[39]San Remo Manual 1995, para 171: "In order to fulfil most effectively their humanitarian mission, hospital ships should be permitted to use cryptographic equipment. The equipment shall not be used in any circumstances to transmit intelligence data nor in any other way to acquire any military advantage."

[40]Grunawalt 2005, p. 109, takes the view that "the likelihood that a hospital ship would be employed to collect and promulgate military intelligence in this age of satellite sensors, over-the-horizon radar, and fixed and mobile long-range hydrophones is extremely remote; it strains the imagination to conjure up a scenario where it would have any utility whatsoever."

[41]Hague Convention X (1907), Article 8(2).

[42]According to media reports, the hospital ship USNS *Comfort*, prior to her deployment in the course of the 2003 international armed conflict between Iraq and the United States, was equipped with "weapons like .30-cal. and .50-cal machine guns […], exclusively for defence, to fend off attacks by swarming, heavily armed speed boats or suicide craft"; see Sirak 2003.

[43]This is a typographical error. It should read: 'AT/FP', which stands for 'Anti-Terrorism/Force Protection'.

with the humanitarian purpose of hospital ships and duty to safeguard the wounded and sick".[44]

Indeed, if there are reasonable grounds for suspicion that hospital ships will be attacked by actors who intentionally disregard their protection under international humanitarian law, it would be difficult to deny them the right of defending themselves against such illegal attacks.[45] On the other hand, it is unlikely that the Parties to the conflict will continue to respect and protect hospital ships, if they are "armed to an extent that they could inflict damage to a warship" because that could be considered an 'act harmful to the enemy' under Article 34(1) of the Geneva Convention II (1949).[46] The United Kingdom, during the 1990 Iraq-Kuwait conflict, arrived at the conclusion that it was impossible to effectively protect hospital ships against illegal attacks and at the same time preserving their specially protected status under the Second Geneva Convention.[47] Moreover, it is difficult, if not impossible, to clearly distinguish between the defensive and (potentially) offensive nature of arms other than light/portable individual weapons. Therefore, it is doubtful whether hospital ships may be equipped with other than light individual weapons and "purely deflective means of defence, such as chaff and flares".[48]

6.3.3 Protected Persons

As regards the protection of victims in an international armed conflict at sea, it is necessary to first recapitulate the gradual extension of the category of protected persons and then to distinguish between the general obligation to rescue wounded, sick and shipwrecked and the more specific obligations of hospital ships to provide assistance.

6.3.3.1 Categories of Protected Persons

Members of the Armed Forces

Hague Convention III (1899) and Hague Convention X (1907) were focused on the protection of sick, wounded and shipwrecked members of belligerent armed forces, without distinguishing between land and naval forces. This has been reaffirmed by Articles 12(1) and 13(1) Geneva Convention II (1949). According to

---

[44]NWP 1–14 M 2007, para 8.6.3.

[45]See Heintschel von Heinegg 2006, p. 222 et seq; Grunawalt 2005, p. 109 et seq.

[46]San Remo Manual 1995, para 60(f).

[47]Hence, RFA *Argus*, which was equipped with light air defence systems, was no longer deployed as a hospital ships but as a 'casualty receiving ship' that also transported troops. The United Kingdom did not claim protected status for her. See Foxwell and Jolly 1991; Bouvier 1992.

[48]San Remo Manual 1995, para 170.

Article 13(2) GC II the protection has been extended to members of militias, volunteer corps and organized resistance movements, provided they fulfil the four conditions set out in that provision. In particular during the Second World War, some belligerents were unwilling to consider pilots shot down over the seas as protected.[49] Under Geneva Convention II (1949) such a narrow interpretation of the term 'shipwrecked' is no longer tenable because, according to Article 12(1) GC II, the term 'shipwreck' means "shipwreck from any cause and includes forced landings at sea by or from aircraft". Hence, regardless of the cause, members of the regular armed forces of a belligerent or of groups assimilated to such forces who find themselves in distress or in a helpless situation at sea are to be considered shipwrecked personnel entitled to protection.[50]

Crews and Passengers of Merchant Vessels

The Hague Conventions were silent on the crews and passengers of enemy or neutral merchant vessels. The London Protocol (1936) provides that they have to be taken to a place of safety before a merchant vessel is destroyed in accordance with prize law. Hence, the law of naval warfare, until 1949, lacked a provision on whether and to what extent the crews and passengers of merchant vessels qualify as protected persons. Rather, their protection depended upon the respective domestic law of the flag State. Only if enemy merchant seamen were embodied in the armed forces, were they protected as combatants.[51] However, enemy merchant vessels had become increasingly involved in the belligerents' war efforts.[52] By that conduct they had become military objectives and liable to attack.[53] Therefore, the masters and the crews of merchant vessels had to be assimilated, to a certain extent, to the members of the regular armed forces. According to Article 13(5) Geneva Convention II (1949), the wounded, sick and shipwrecked masters and crews of "the merchant marine" of the Parties to the conflict who do not benefit by more favourable provisions of international law are protected persons.[54]

Geneva Convention II (1949) is silent on the protection of the crews and passengers of neutral merchant vessels that have been attacked.[55] Article 13(5) GC II

[49]For instance, in 1940 the British Government "adopted a narrow construction of the Convention and argued that on no view of its meaning could an airman who was shot down into the sea unwounded be regarded as 'shipwrecked'"; Mossop 1947, p. 403.

[50]Tucker 1955, p. 126 n 96.

[51]Mossop 1947, p. 400.

[52]For State practice during the two World Wars see O'Connell 1975, p. 46 et seq.; Tucker 1955, p. 64 et seq.

[53]In the case of Admiral Dönitz, the International Military Tribunal held that British merchant vessels that had been armed or integrated into the war effort had lost their protection. See also San Remo Manual 1995, para 60.

[54]Tucker 1955, p. 119.

[55]San Remo Manual 1995, paras 67 and 70; Helsinki Principles 1998, para 5.1.2; AMW Manual 2013, Rule 174.

explicitly only refers to the crews of the merchant marine and to the crews of civil aircraft *of the Parties to the conflict*. Since neutral merchant vessels contributing to the enemy's military action are sometimes considered to have acquired enemy status,[56] one might be inclined to extend the protective scope to the crews (and passengers) of such vessels. The dictates of humanity would clearly justify such an extension. Still, the wording of Article 13(5) GC II is clear and it is, therefore, doubtful whether the crews and passengers of neutral merchant vessels that have been attacked as lawful military objectives belong to the persons protected by the Convention. It may, however, not be forgotten that Geneva Convention II (1949) indirectly extends its protection to such persons, provided they are sick, wounded or shipwrecked. According to Article 34(4), hospital ships and sick-bays as well as their crews do not lose their protection if they render assistance to wounded, sick or shipwrecked civilians.[57]

Civilians

Civilians at sea who do not belong to any of the aforementioned categories, even if wounded, sick or shipwrecked, were not protected under The Hague Conventions[58] and they are only indirectly protected by Geneva Convention II (1949) and Additional Protocol I (1977). Still, there is general agreement that they must receive the same protection when found at sea.[59] Whether this also holds true for civilians in port or on land who are neither wounded nor sick is unsettled. Of course, women, children and the elderly are, in principle, considered as vulnerable and, thus, entitled to respect and protection[60] but they cannot be considered as wounded or sick, unless they are "in need of immediate medical assistance or care".[61] The same applies to civilians who may find themselves in a desperate situation (e.g. refugees on land). Since their status under the law of naval warfare is unclear, the best way of providing them the necessary assistance is an agreement with the respective enemy allowing for their transportation on a cartel vessel.

---

[56]NWP 1–14 M 2007, para 7.5.

[57]According to Article 22(1) Additional Protocol I (1977), hospital ships are allowed to extend their assistance to wounded, sick and shipwrecked civilians "who do not belong to any of the categories mentioned in Article 13 of the Second Convention".

[58]Mossop 1947, p. 399: "[T]he consequences of warfare at sea were confined to the combatants on either side; they—and they alone—needed the protection conferred by the Convention. … In 1907 civilians stood safely outside the arena and required neither consideration nor protection in a Convention expressly stated to be intended as an adaptation to maritime warfare of the principles of the Geneva Convention relating to warfare on land."

[59]See also Article 16(2) Geneva Convention IV (1949) and Article 98 UNCLOS (1982) for a general obligation in the law of the sea. For the opposing view see Tucker 1955, p. 120 n. 76.

[60]For this argument see Mossop 1947, p. 400.

[61]See Article 8(a) Additional Protocol I (1977), which expressly includes "the infirm or expectant mothers".

6.3.3.2 General Obligation to Rescue Survivors

The general obligation of the Parties to the conflict to search for and rescue the shipwrecked, wounded and sick is laid down in Article 18 Geneva Convention II (1949).[62] Article 18 may not be interpreted as obliging naval commanders to search for and rescue survivors "at all times". Such an obligation only exists for land warfare.[63] In naval warfare, the obligation comes into operation "after each engagement" only. The duration of such an engagement will depend upon the circumstances ruling at the time but it is quite obvious that an engagement is not necessarily terminated as soon as a vessel has been sunk. Moreover, belligerents are obliged only to take all "possible" measures. This is of specific relevance for submarines, which are vulnerable when surfaced and which often do not have sufficient space.[64] Hence, submarine commanders are not obliged to engage in search and rescue operations, if that would imply an unreasonable risk for their ship. This does not mean that they are relieved of any obligation whatsoever. If available, the survivors must be provided with the means necessary to enable them to await rescue or to reach the coast.[65] Whether there also is an obligation to contact a hospital ship, rescue craft, or other ship in the vicinity will, again, depend upon the circumstances ruling at the time.[66]

In view of the fact that certain military considerations have been recognized in Article 18 GC II there is no room for further exceptions. In the light of Article 16 Hague Convention X (1907), the same holds true for the situation prior to 1949. Of course, the International Military Tribunal "refused to hold Admiral Dönitz guilty of deliberately ordering the killing of shipwrecked survivors" because it found the so-called Laconia Order, which was issued on September 17, 1942, ambiguous.[67] Although the Order might be interpreted as providing an exception from the obligation to rescue survivors only for reasons of operational necessity, it was clearly unlawful insofar as it expressly stated that "rescue runs counter to the rudimentary demands of warfare".[68]

---

[62] See also Article 16 Hague Convention X (1907).

[63] For instance, Article 15(1) Geneva Convention I (1949) provides: "At all times, and particularly after an engagement [...]."

[64] Pictet 1960, p. 131: "Of course, one cannot always require certain fighting ships, such as fast torpedo-boats and submarines, to collect in all circumstances the crews of ships which they have sunk, for they will often have inadequate equipment and insufficient accommodation. Submarines stay at sea for a long time and sometimes they neither wish nor are able to put in at a port where they could land the persons whom they have collected. Generally speaking, one cannot lay down an absolute rule that the commander of a warship must engage in rescue operations if, by doing so, he would expose his vessel to attack."

[65] Pictet 1960, p. 131. See also Heintschel von Heinegg 2009, p. 353 et seq.

[66] Heintschel von Heinegg 2009, p. 355.

[67] See Tucker 1955, p. 73.

[68] For the English translation see Tucker 1955, p. 72.

6.3.3.3 Obligations of Hospital Ships

The categories of protected persons are comparatively limited. This may have an impact on whether and to what extent hospital ships are allowed to render assistance to persons who are not expressly included. Of course, according to Article 35(4) Geneva Convention II (1949) and according to Article 22(1) Additional Protocol I (1977), hospital ships are allowed to render assistance to sick, wounded and shipwrecked civilians. Civilians in port or on land who are not wounded, sick or "in need of immediate medical assistance or care"[69] do not belong to the category of persons hospital ships may assist. Unfortunate as this is, the law does not justify the conclusion that hospital ships are entitled to rescue refugees.[70]

There is yet another important exception with regard to the crews (and passengers) of merchant vessels captured as prize and that are, as an exceptional measure, destroyed at sea.[71] Insofar, it has been rightly stated that the "duty of a hospital ship is to take on board wounded, sick and shipwrecked persons, and it does not come within her functions to provide accommodation for injured passengers and crews taken from destroyed merchant vessels, thereby rendering valuable assistance to the warship from which they are received".[72] Therefore, hospital ships may not be abused to relieve the capturing warship of the burden of transporting crews and passengers to a place of safety. If a hospital ship were allowed to receive the merchant vessel's crew (and passengers), this would result in an almost unlimited destruction of merchant vessels captured as prize. The exceptional character of the right to destroy merchant vessels under prize law would be vitiated. If, however, individual crew members or passengers of such a merchant vessel are in need of immediate life-sustaining treatment and are taken on board a hospital ship, this does not relieve the commander of the warship of the obligation to provide for the safety of the remaining crews and passengers of a merchant vessel to be destroyed as prize.

6.4 Lawful Targets

6.4.1 Enemy Warships and Auxiliaries

The traditional law of naval warfare does not provide a definition of lawful military objectives. It was, however, generally agreed that enemy warships and enemy auxiliaries were lawful targets by nature.[73] This has been reaffirmed by the contempo-

[69]See Article 8 (a) Additional Protocol I (1977).

[70]When the "German Government wanted to evacuate refugees from the Baltic States in 1939 in a hospital ship, they removed its markings and operated it as an ordinary liner." See Mossop 1947, p. 399.

[71]San Remo Manual 1995, paras 139, 140. For the continuing validity of prize law see also Helsinki Principles 1998, para 5.2; NWP 1-14 M 2007, paras 7.4 et seq; Kraska 2012, p. 477 et seq.

[72]Pearce Higgins 1910, p. 414. See also Colombos 1967, p. 591.

[73]See only Tucker 1955, p. 39.

rary law of naval warfare.[74] The definition of lawful military objectives in Article 52(2) Additional Protocol I (1977) is considered customary in character and as applicable to naval warfare.[75] Claims according to which unarmed warships should be treated differently from armed warships[76] have never become part of the law.

6.4.2 Merchant Vessels

Under the traditional law, enemy and neutral merchant vessels were dealt with only in the context of prize law. According to customary international law, enemy merchant vessels were liable to capture, unless specially exempted by the provisions of Hague Conventions VI (1907) and XI (1907). The London Declaration (1909) provided that neutral merchant vessels were liable to condemnation, if more than half of their cargoes consisted of contraband—Article 40, if they engaged in 'unneutral service'—Articles 45 and 46—or if they forcibly resisted "to the legitimate exercise of the right of stoppage, search, and capture—Article 63". The acts of 'unneutral service' included the vessel's direct participation in hostilities—Article 46(1), the "transportation of enemy troops and the transmission of intelligence in the interest of the enemy"—Article 46(4). If a neutral merchant vessel was liable to condemnation, it could, as an exceptional measure, be destroyed—Article 49, provided that all persons on board have been "placed in safety" and all relevant documents have been taken on board the warship—Article 50. Later, these provisions were declared applicable to all merchant vessels, whether neutral or enemy in character.[77]

Although the belligerents of the two World Wars justified the sinking of merchant vessels by reference to belligerent reprisals, the aforementioned rules were relied upon by the International Military Tribunal in the case against Admiral Dönitz. The Tribunal held, inter alia, that the

> "argument of the Defense is that the security of the submarine is, as the first rule of the sea, paramount to rescue, and that the development of aircraft made rescue impossible. This may be so, but the Protocol is explicit. If the commander cannot rescue, then under its terms he cannot sink a merchant vessel and should allow it to pass harmless before his periscope. These orders, then, prove Dönitz is guilty of a violation of the Protocol".[78]

This passage and the provisions of the London Declaration 1909 and of the London Protocol (1936) have often been misunderstood as excluding merchant

---

74 German Manual 2013, para 1024; NWP 1–14 M 2007, para 8.2.1.

75 San Remo Manual 1995, para 40; UK Manual 2004, para 13.26; Canadian Manual 2001, para 825; NWP 1–14 M 2007, para 8.2; German Manual 2013, paras 1024 et seq. See also Robertson (1998).

76 Hyde 1945 Vol 3, p. 1920.

77 London Protocol 1936.

78 1 IMT 313.

vessels from the category of lawful targets in naval warfare and as only allowing for the exceptional right of destroying those vessels, which are liable to condemnation under the law of prize. Such a view is, however, inconsistent with the traditional law and the contemporary law of naval warfare. First, the London Protocol (1936) does not apply "in case of persistent refusal to stop on being duly summoned, or of active resistance to visit or search". Second, it was generally understood that the Protocol does not apply to merchant vessels that have become lawful military objectives. After adoption of the draft Submarine Treaty by the 1921–1922 Washington Conference the Italian delegate stated that the term 'merchant ship' was to be understood as referring to "unarmed merchant vessels" only.[79] During the 1930 London Naval Conference a commission of lawyers stated that "the expression 'merchant vessel', where it is employed in the declaration, is not to be understood as including a merchant vessel which is at the moment participating in hostilities in such a manner as to cause her to lose her right to the immunities of a merchant vessel".[80] Finally, the Nuremberg Tribunal was "not prepared to hold Dönitz guilty for his conduct of submarine warfare against British armed merchant ships".[81] The Tribunal also explicitly referred to the British convoy system, to the integration of "merchant vessels into the warning network of naval intelligence", and to the announcement of the British Admiralty of 1 October 1939 "that British merchant ships had been ordered to ram U-boats if possible"[82].

Today, the law is clear. Merchant vessels, whether neutral or enemy, are liable to attack, if, by use or purpose, they make an effective contribution to the enemy's military action, and if their destruction offers a definite military advantage.[83] However, a more cautious approach is taken with regard to armed merchant vessels. According to the San Remo Manual, they qualify as lawful military objectives only, if they are "armed to an extent that they could inflict damage to a warship".[84]

In this context, it is important to briefly refer to the case of Captain Fryatt, the master of the British merchant vessel The Brussels, which, in 1915, had tried to ram the German submarine U23. In its judgment of July 27, 1916, the German War Council held Fryatt guilty of having committed an "act of 'franc-tireur', which the law of war punishes with death".[85] At first glance, the German decision would seem to be in accordance with the contemporary international humanitarian

[79]See the references by Mallison 1968, p. 42 n 84.

[80]Documents of the London Naval Conference 1930 p. 443.

[81]1 IMT 312.

[82]1 IMT 312.

[83]San Remo Manual 1995, paras 60, 67; UK Manual 2004, paras 13.41, 13.47; Canadian Manual 2001, paras 834, 835; NWP 1–14 M 2007, paras 7.5.1, 8.6.2; German Manual 2013, para 1029. See also Mallison 1968, p. 32 et seq; Tucker 1955, p. 319 et seq; Colombos 1967, p. 526 et seq.

[84]San Remo Manual, para 60(f). This "excludes light individual weapons for the defence of personnel, e.g., against pirates, and purely deflective systems such as 'chaff'".

[85]See Colombos 1967, p. 526 et seq; Oppenheim 1952, p. 468.

law, because the ramming of an enemy submarine by a civilian could be considered an act of 'direct participation in hostilities' depriving the civilian of his/her protection under international humanitarian law.[86] In case of capture the aggrieved belligerent would be allowed to apply its domestic criminal law. It may, however, not be forgotten that Article 51(3) Additional Protocol I (1977) is inapplicable to "sea warfare", which does not "affect the civilian population, individual civilians or civilian objects on land".[87] Moreover, under the law of naval warfare, enemy merchant vessels (not: neutral merchant vessels!) are not obliged to submit to belligerent orders or to refrain from rendering active resistance to visit, search or capture. While they become liable to attack, the law does not consider the responsible master to have engaged in some form of direct participation in hostilities that would be punishable under the respective domestic criminal law. Finally, as regards the case of Captain Fryatt, it has been rightly stated that, in view of the "unrestricted German practice of sinking merchant vessels at sight [...], there is every reason to hold Captain Fryatt justified in his efforts to ram the German submarine [...] as it afforded him the only chance of saving his ship and the lives of his crew".[88]

6.4.3 Submarine Communications Cables

According to Article 54 of The Hague Regulations (1907), "submarine cables connecting an occupied territory with a neutral territory shall not be seized or destroyed except in case of absolute necessity". This means that, under the traditional law, submarine communications cables are not protected from destruction if they connect enemy territory with the territory of an ally of the enemy or if they connect enemy territory, which is not occupied, with neutral territory.[89] Moreover, Article 54 is limited to land warfare and, therefore, does not necessarily provide for interference with submarine communications cables in sea areas beyond the outer limit of the territorial sea. The San Remo Manual has not necessarily contributed to an improvement of the protection of submarine communications cables, it merely provides that "belligerents shall take care to avoid damage to cables [...] laid on the sea-bed which do not exclusively serve the belligerents".[90]

Today, submarine communications cables are the backbone of international data traffic. Submarine cables "carry over 95 % of the world's international voice, data, and video traffic, including almost 100 % of transoceanic Internet ocean

[86]See only ICRC 2009, p. 70 et seq.

[87]Article 49(3) Additional Protocol I 1977.

[88]Colombos 1967, p. 526 et seq. See also Oppenheim 1952, p. 469.

[89]Colombos 1967, p. 535 et seq.

[90]San Remo Manual 1995, para 37. See also UK Manual 2004, para 13.23; Canadian Manual 2001, para 824; German Manual 2013, para 1043.

traffic"[91] and because of their bandwidth, the "lower cost and longer lifespan [they] have surpassed satellites as the principal means of delivering international telecommunications traffic".[92] According to other sources, "99 percent of the world's long-distance communications travel through fiber links. The remaining 1 percent are […] satellite-based".[93]

In view of the overall importance of submarine communications cables, it is doubtful whether their wide exclusion from the categories of protected objects in the law of naval warfare may still be considered as properly reflecting the current legal situation. Unfortunately, States have neglected this issue not only in the context of the law of armed conflict but also in the context of the international law of the sea. Therefore, any allegation of an extended protection cannot be based on State practice.

6.5 Methods and Means of Warfare

The principle of distinction applies to naval warfare qua customary international law.[94] Accordingly, belligerents are under an obligation to only apply those methods and means of naval warfare, which are in compliance with that cardinal principle of the law of armed conflict. However, naval warfare is characterized by some special features that have had an impact on the rules specifically applying to the conduct of hostilities at sea. Despite their considerable age, many of those rules continue to be valid today or they are indicative of general principles that also govern methods and means of naval warfare that were not envisaged more than a century ago.

6.5.1 Mines and Torpedoes

Despite some efforts to outlaw or to at least restrict the use of naval mines they have always been considered lawful means of warfare.[95] The same holds true for torpedoes.[96] Hague Convention VIII (1907) only applies to submarine automatic

[91] Wrathall 2010–2011, p. 228.

[92] Wrathall 2010–2011, p. 228.

[93] Sechrist 2010, p. 16, citing Jim Hayes, President of the California-based Fiber Optic Assocation.

[94] San Remo Manual 1995, para 39; NWP 1–14 M 2007, para 8.1; UK Manual 2004, para 13.25; Canadian Manual 2001, para 825; German Manual 2013, para 1021.

[95] For proposals aimed at a prohibition or restriction of the use of naval mines see Levie 1992, p. 23 et seq.

[96] San Remo Manual 1995, para 79; German Manual 2013, para 1052; UK Manual 2004, para 13.51; NWP 1–14 M 2007, para 9.4.

contact mines (and to torpedoes) and, as such, not to modern mines, which engage a target by reacting to magnetic or acoustic signatures or pressure. Still, it is safe to hold that Hague Convention VIII contains a set of general principles that apply to modern naval mines.[97]

6.5.2 *Naval Blockade*

The rules of the Paris Declaration (1856) and the London Declaration (1909)[98] on naval blockades have more or less survived, although the modern weapons technology has made the establishment and enforcement of a close blockade virtually impossible. Military manuals and contemporary State practice provide ample proof of the continuing validity of the traditional rules.[99]

6.5.3 *Zones*

The most remarkable development of the law regarding methods of naval warfare seems to have occurred with regard to the legality of maritime exclusion zones.[100] Under the traditional law, such zones were unlawful.[101] Today, they seem to have become a recognized and lawful method of naval warfare, provided the restrictions laid down in the San Remo Manual are observed.[102] Accordingly, an exclusion

---

[97]San Remo Manual 1995, paras 80–92; NWP 1–14 M 2007, para 9.2; Canadian Manual 2001, paras 836–843; UK Manual 2004, paras 13.52–13.64; German Manual 2013, para 1045–1051. For a legal analysis of the said principles see Heintschel von Heinegg 1993, p. 56 et seq.

[98]London Declaration (1909), Articles 1–21.

[99]San Remo Manual 1995, paras 93-104; NWP 1–14 M 2007, para 7.7; UK Manual 2004, paras 13.65–13.76; Canadian Manual 2001, paras 844–851; German Manual 2013, paras 1060–1063; Helsinki Principles 1998, para 5.2.10. See also Tucker 1955, p. 283 et seq.; Heintschel von Heinegg 2012c, p. 960 et seq.

[100]For the various zones of the two World Wars see Tucker 1955, p. 296 et seq.

[101]The IMT, in its judgment against Admiral Dönitz, held that "the proclamation of operational zones and the sinking of neutral merchant vessels which enter those zones presents a different question. This practice was employed in the War of 1914-18 by Germany and adopted in retaliation by Great Britain. The Washington conference of 1922, the London Naval Agreement of 1930, and the Protocol of 1936, were entered into with full knowledge that such zones had been employed in the First World War. Yet the Protocol made no exception for operational zones. The order of Doenitz to sink neutral ships without warning when found within these zones was, therefore, in the opinion of the Tribunal, a violation of the Protocol", 22 IMT 635 et seq. It may be added that Admiral Dönitz was not sentenced for 'unrestricted submarine warfare' because Great Britain, in the Skagerrak, and the U.S., in the Pacific, had resorted to a similar method.

[102]San Remo Manual 1995, paras 105-108; UK Manual 2004, paras 13.77–13.80; Canadian Manual 2001, paras 852–855; NWP 1–14 M 2007, para 7.9.

zone may be established and enforced with a view to protecting high-value targets, to containing the geographic area of the conflict or to keeping neutral shipping at a safe distance from areas of actual or potential hostilities. An exclusion zone may not be established with the sole purpose of facilitating the difficult target identification process or of establishing a zone of unrestricted (submarine) warfare.[103]

6.5.4 Naval Bombardment

Although Hague Convention IX (1907) seems to be recognized as declaratory of customary international law,[104] its current relevance is but minor. Attacks by naval forces against targets on land will in most cases have to be assessed in the light of the Additional Protocol I (1977). According to Article 49(3) AP I, Articles 48-67 apply to "any sea warfare which may affect the civilian population, individual civilians or civilian objects on land. They further apply to all attacks from the sea […] against objectives on land". The famous dispute between Rauch and Meyrowitz on the applicability of Additional Protocol I (1977) to naval warfare should have become obsolete.[105] For those States that have not (yet) become parties to AP I customary international law applies. Accordingly, it is prohibited to launch attacks against the civilian population as such and the parties to the conflict are obliged to distinguish between legitimate military targets and civilians or civilian objects. Moreover, the prohibition of indiscriminate attacks and the obligation to take all feasible precautionary measures are binding on all naval forces, irrespective of the area they are targeting.[106]

6.6 Concluding Remarks

Many of the traditional rules of naval warfare have not become obsolete but they either continue to apply or they are declaratory of a variety of customary principles governing the contemporary conduct of hostilities at sea. The current law of naval warfare is still characterized by a rather formal approach with regard to the entitlement to exercise belligerent rights at sea. However, States will increasingly make use of unmanned maritime systems, including offensive operations, and it is therefore necessary to clarify their legal status.

---

[103]For the legal issues involved see also Heintschel von Heinegg 2012b, p. 773 et seq.

[104]*See*, inter alia, Robertson 1988, p. 161 et seq.

[105]Rauch 1984, p. 57 et seq; Meyrowitz 1985, p. 243 et seq.

[106]For the applicability of these principles and rules NWP 1–14 2007, paras 5.3.2, 5.3.3; UK Manual 2004, paras 13.24–13.31. See also Roach 2002, p. 375 et seq; Tucker 1955, p. 143 et seq.

The traditional rules on protected vessels and persons have been progressively developed but the current law of naval warfare still does not provide satisfactory answers to all questions. This certainly holds true for hospital ships, the use of their means of communication and of their arming. Since only a small number of States (e.g. the U.S., the PR China, and the Russian Federation) continue to operate military hospital ships and since international armed conflicts at sea do not occur all too often one might be inclined to consider the ensuing issues of minor relevance. However, there is a realistic potential of future international armed conflicts at sea and, should they come into existence, the protection of hospital ships may again become a contentious issue, if there is a lack of legal clarity. The same holds true with regard to the category of protected persons, whether they are to receive assistance by hospital ships or whether they are to be respected and protected according to the other rules of the law of naval warfare.

With regard to those objects qualifying as lawful military objectives under the law of naval warfare, there seems to be no need for a further clarification. The law is both specific and flexible enough to provide answers also for objects that do not necessarily belong to the established categories of lawful targets at sea. Still, one should not be overly optimistic. In particular the silence of the law regarding the status of submarine communications cables may be the source for future disputes. In view of their overall importance for international data traffic, there is an undeniable need for a progressive development of the law of naval warfare.

Finally, the rules and principles governing the conduct of hostilities at sea seem to have been sufficiently developed to adequately regulate the use of methods and means of naval warfare. Again, this finding does not necessarily mean that there are no contentious issues left. In this context it suffices to merely mention exclusion zones, whose purpose is far from clear.

Despite the above findings the necessary clarification of the modern law of naval warfare should not be the task of an inter-governmental codification conference. At present, the chances of such a conference producing a meaningful and operable product are but minor because too many irreconcilable positions exist. Probably, the best way of arriving at a progressive development of the law of naval warfare is an update of the San Remo Manual, which will then hopefully be received in the same positive manner as the original.

References

Treaties and Documents

Paris Declaration (1856) Declaration respecting maritime law, Paris. Am J Int Law 1(Suppl):89–90 (1907)

Additional Articles (1868) Additional Articles relating to the Condition of the Wounded in War, Geneva. www.ircr.org/ihl.nsf/WebPrint/125-FULL?OpenDocument. Accessed 20 Oct 1868

Conference Report (1899) The proceedings of the Hague conferences. The conference of 1899. Prepared in the division of international law of the carnegie endowment for international peace under the supervision of James Brown Scott. Oxford University Press, New York 1920

Hague Convention III (1899) Convention (III) for the adaptation to maritime warfare of the principles of the Geneva Convention of 22 August 1864, The Hague. www.ircr.org/ihl.nsf/WebPrint/155-FULL?OpenDocument. Accessed 29 July 1899
Hague Regulations (1907) Convention (IV) respecting the laws and customs of war on Land, annex to the convention, regulations respecting the laws and customs of war on Land, The Hague. Am J Int Law 2(Suppl):90–117 (1908)
Hague Convention VI (1907) Convention (VI) relative to the status of enemy merchant ships at the outbreak of hostilities, The Hague. In: Conference Report (1907) pp 640–642, 18 Oct 1907
Hague Convention VII (1907) Convention (VII) relating to the conversion of merchant ships into war-ships, The Hague. Am J Int Law 2(Suppl):133–138 (1908)
Hague Convention IX (1907) Convention (IX) concerning bombardment by Naval forces in time of war, The Hague. Am J Int Law 2(Suppl):146–153 (1908)
Hague Convention XI (1907) Convention (XI) relative to certain restrictions with regard to the exercise of capture in Naval war, The Hague. Am J Int Law 2(Suppl):167–174 (1908)
Conference Report (1907) Report to the 1907 Hague conference. The proceedings of the Hague conferences. The conference of 1907 Vol. I. Prepared in the division of international law of the carnegie endowment for international peace under the supervision of James Brown Scott. Oxford University Press, New York 1921
London Declaration (1909). Declaration concerning the laws of maritime war, signed at London. In: Brown JS (ed) The declaration of London February 26, 1909. Oxford University Press, New York 1919
London Protocol (1936) Procès-verbal relating to the rules of submarine warfare set forth in Part IV of the treaty of London of April 22, 1930, London, 6 November 1936, LNTS 173:353–357 (1936–1937). Am J Int Law 31(Suppl):137–139 (1937)
Geneva Convention II (1949) Geneva Convention for the amelioration of the condition of wounded, sick and shipwrecked members of armed forces at sea, Geneva, 12 August 1949, 75 UNTS 85–133 (1950)
Additional Protocol I (1977) Protocol Additional to the Geneva Conventions of 12 August 1949, and relating to the protection of victims of international armed conflicts (Protocol I), Geneva, 8 June 1977, 1125 UNTS 3–608 (1979)
UNCLOS (1982) United Nations Convention on the Law of the Sea, 10 December 1982. UN Doc. A/CONF.62/122 and Corr
San Remo Manual (1995) San Remo Manual on International Law Applicable to Armed Conflicts at Sea, IRRC 595–637 (Nov–Dec 1995)
Helsinki Principles (1998) International Law Association, Helsinki principles on the law of maritime neutrality. Final Report of the Committee on Maritime Neutrality, Report of the 68th Conference, 496–516. Taipei 1998
Canadian Manual (2001) Canada, Office of the Judge Advocate General, Law of Armed Conflict at the Operational and Tactical Levels
UK Manual (2004) UK Ministry of Defence, The Manual of the Law of Armed Conflict. Oxford University Press, Oxford
NWP 1–14 M (2007) Office of the Chief of Naval Operations, U.S. Dept. of the Navy, The Commander's Handbook on the Law of Naval Operations. Naval Warfare Pub. No. NWP 1–14 M
Manual AMW (2013) Program on humanitarian policy and conflict research. Manual on International Law Applicable to Air and Missile Warfare. Cambridge University Press, Cambridge
German Manual (2013) Bundesministerium der Verteidigung, Humanitäres Völkerrecht in bewaffneten Konflikten—Handbuch—ZDv 15/2

Books and Articles

Battle G (1921) The trials before the Leipsic (sic!) Supreme Court of Germans accused of war crimes. Va Law Rev 8:1–26

Bouvier A (1992) Fighting hospital ships. Int Defense Rev 3:246–247

Colombos CJ (1967) The international law of the sea, 6th edn. Longmans, London

Fenrick WJ (1991) Legal aspects of targeting in the law of naval warfare. Can Yearb Int Law 29:238–282

Foxwell D, Jolly R (1991) The RFA Argus – a gas-tight, floating field hospital. Int Defense Rev 2:116–117

Garner JW (1927) Prize law during the world war. Macmillan, New York

Grandclément (1938) Les navires hôpitaux. IRRC 20:395–427

Grunawalt RJ (2005) Hospital ships in the war on terror. Naval War Coll Rev 58:89–119

de Guttry A (1988) Commentary on Hague Convention VI. In: Ronzitti N (ed) The law of naval warfare. Martinus Nijhoff, Dordrecht, pp 102–110

Heintschel von Heinegg W (1991) Visit, search, diversion, and capture in naval warfare: part I, the traditional law. Can Yearb Int Law 29:283–329

Heintschel von Heinegg W (1992) Visit, search, diversion and capture in naval warfare- conditions of applicability: part II, developments since 1945. Can Yearb Int Law 30:89–136

Heintschel von Heinegg W (1993) The international law of mine warfare at sea. Isr Yearb Hum Rights 23:53–76

Heintschel von Heinegg W (2006) Current legal issues in maritime operations: maritime interception operations in the global war on terrorism, exclusion zones, hospital ships and maritime neutrality. In: Jaques R (ed) Issues in international law and military operations, U.S. Naval War College, Newport, pp 207–233

Heintschel von Heinegg W (2007) "Benevolent" third States during international armed conflicts: the myth of the irrelevance of the law of neutrality. In: Schmitt MN, Pejic J (eds) International law and armed conflict: exploring the faultlines, essays in honour of Yoram Dinstein, Martinus Nijhoff, Leiden, pp 543–568

Heintschel von Heinegg W (2009) The international legal framework of submarine operations. Isr Yearb Hum Rights 39:331–356

Heintschel von Heinegg W (2012a) War ships. In: Wolfrum R (gen ed) Max Planck Encyclopedia of international law vol X. Oxford University Press, Oxford, pp 790–802

Heintschel von Heinegg W (2012b) War zones. In: Wolfrum R (gen ed) Max Planck Encyclopedia of international law vol VIII. Oxford University Press, Oxford pp 763–771

Heintschel von Heinegg W (2012c) Blockade. In: Wolfrum R (gen ed) Max Planck Encyclopedia of international law vol I. Oxford University Press, Oxford, pp 960–972

Hyde CC (1945) International law chiefly as interpreted and applied by the United States. 2nd rev ed, Little, Brown & Co, Boston

ICRC (2009) Interpretive guidance on the notion of direct participation in hostilities under international humanitarian law. International Committee of the Red Cross, Geneva

Kraska J (2012) Prize Law. In: Wolfrum R (gen ed) Max Planck Encyclopedia of International Law Vol VIII, Oxford University Press, Oxford pp 477–484

Levie (1992) Mine warfare at sea. Martinus Nijhoff, Dordrecht

Mallison WT Jr (1968) Submarines in general and limited wars. Government Printing Office, Washington D.C

Meyrowitz H (1985) Le protocole additionnel I aux Conventions de Genève de 1949 et le droit de la guerre maritime. Revue Générale de Droit International Public 89:243–298

Mossop JC (1947) Hospital ships in the Second World War. BYIL 24:398–406

O'Connell DP (1975) The influence of law on seapower. Manchester University Press, Manchester

Oppenheim L (1952) International law vol. II. 7th edn. In: Lauterpacht H (ed) Longmans, London

Pearce Higgins A (1910) Hospital ships and the carriage of passengers and crews of destroyed prizes LQR 26:408–414
Pictet J (1960) II Geneva Convention Commentary. International Committee of the Red Cross, Geneva
Rauch E (1984) The protocol additional to the Geneva Conventions for the protection of victims of international armed conflicts and the united nations convention on the law of the sea: repercussions on the law of naval warfare. Duncker & Humblot, Berlin
Roach JA (2002) Legal aspects of submarine warfare. 6 Max Planck Yearbook of United Nations Law 6:367–385
Robertson HB Jr (1988) Commentary on Hague Convention IX. In: Ronzitti N (ed) The law of naval warfare. Martinus Nijhoff, Dordrecht, pp 161–171
Robertson HB Jr (1998) The principle of the military objective in the law of armed conflict. In. Schmitt MN (ed) The law of military operations, U.S. Naval War College, Newport, pp 197–223
San Remo Manual, Explanations (1995) San Remo Manual on international law applicable to armed conflicts at sea. In: Doswald-Beck L (ed) Cambridge University Press, Cambridge
Sechrist M (2010) Cyberspace in deep water: protecting undersea communication cables by creating an international public-private partnership. Harvard Kennedy School March 23, 2010
Shearer IA (1988) Commentary on Hague Convention XI. In: Ronzitti N (ed) The law of naval warfare. Martinus Nijhoff, Dordrecht, pp 183–191
Sirak M (2003) U.S. Navy seeks to revise laws of war on hospital ships. Jane's Defence Weekly 19 August 2003
Stone J (1959) Legal controls of international conflict. A treatise on the dynamics of disputes- and war-law. Stevens & Sons, New York
Tucker RW (1955) The law of war and neutrality at sea. Government Printing Office, Washington D.C, U.S
Venturini G (1988) Commentary on Hague Convention VII. In: Ronzitti N (ed) The law of Naval Warfare. Martinus Nijhoff, Dordrecht, pp 120–128
Wrathall LR (2010–2011) The vulnerability of subsea infrastructure to underwater attack: legal shortcomings and the way forward. San Diego Int Law J 12:223–261

Other Consulted Source

Hague Rules (1923) Rules of aerial warfare, The Hague. Am J Int Law 32(Suppl):12–56 (1938)

Chapter 7
From Inter-state and Symmetric to Intra-state and Asymmetric: Changing Methods of Warfare and the Law of Armed Conflict in the 100 Years Since World War One

Emily Crawford

Abstract This chapter examines the changing methods of warfare over the last 100 years, how the law has adapted to respond to these changing methods, and whether the law as it exists in 2014 is still consonant with armed conflict as it exists in 2014. Over the last century, the preponderant type of armed conflict—international armed conflict—has given way to non-international, transnational, and internal armed conflicts. These newly predominant types of armed conflict have also brought with them new participants, new tactics, and new targets. The law of armed conflict has attempted to keep pace with these developments, adopting new comprehensive treaties in 1949 and 1977 (along with a raft of treaties governing permissible means and methods). However, as these new participants employ new or irregular methods to fight their wars, pressures are brought to bear on the existing law of armed conflict. This chapter will use the First World War and its centennial in 2014 as 'bookends' with which to frame the discussion of just how wars have changed over the last 100 years, how the law has responded to such changes, and whether the law needs to continue to change in response to altered methods of armed conflict.

Keywords Law of armed conflict · International armed conflict · Non-international armed conflict · Asymmetric warfare · Guerrilla warfare · Soft law

---

E. Crawford (✉)
Sydney Law School, University of Sydney, Sydney, Australia
e-mail: emily.crawford@sydney.edu.au

T.D. Gill et al. (eds.), *Yearbook of International Humanitarian Law 2014*,
Yearbook of International Humanitarian Law 17,
DOI 10.1007/978-94-6265-091-6_7

Contents

7.1 Introduction

One hundred years ago, two powerful alliances faced one another along a trench system that spanned the breadth of Europe. Both sides were essentially matched in terms of capabilities—equipped with machine guns, heavy artillery and, eventually, air craft and tanks—they fired on each other and were fired upon, until the 4 years of attrition warfare proved too much, and the hostilities were ended.[1] One hundred years later and powerful alliances continue to face one another in combat.[2] This time, however, the combatants do not share the same geographical space, and the sides employ vastly different methods to inflict damage, with the 'weaker' of the parties often employing methods which give them strategic advantages, but violate the rules on warfare that have existed in written form for over 150 years.

This chapter examines the changing methods of warfare over the last 100 years, how the law has adapted to respond to these changing methods, and whether the law as it exists in 2014 is still consonant with armed conflict as it exists in 2014. Over the last century, the preponderant type of armed conflict—international armed conflict—has given way to non-international, transnational, and internal armed conflicts. These newly predominant types of armed conflict have also brought with them new participants, new tactics, and new targets.[3] The law of armed conflict has attempted to keep pace with these developments, adopting new

[1]The First World War lasted from 1914–1918 and was marked by brutal attrition trench warfare, and culminated in the later years in tank warfare and aerial bombardment. Much has been written on the conflict, but for an introductory perspective, see further Robson 2007; Tooley 2003; Bourne 2005.

[2]The ongoing conflicts against al-Qaeda and affiliates spans Pakistan, Afghanistan, Yemen, and Somalia—for a general introduction to the conflict, see further Scahill 2013.

[3]For further analysis and exploration of these changes, see further Vité 2009; Browning 2002 and the International Committee of the Red Cross 2011.

comprehensive treaties in 1949 and 1977 (along with a raft of treaties governing permissible means and methods).[4] However, as these new participants employ new or irregular methods to fight their wars, pressures are brought to bear on the existing law of armed conflict—just how far can and should the law adapt to cover behaviours that flout over a century's worth of established and accepted behaviour in wartime?

The first part of this chapter will look at the kind of armed conflict that the law was originally designed to regulate—international armed conflicts between two (or more) States. This section will also examine some of the political and technological pressures that began to push against the narrow concept of war and its lawful participants under international law, leading to the second part of this chapter, and the examination of the legal recognition of non-international armed conflicts in the mid-twentieth century. An examination of the political pressures on that category will lead to the third part of this chapter, which explores the emergence of what has been termed 'asymmetric warfare', and how this 'new' warfare is challenging traditional understandings of the role of the law of armed conflict in regulating the conduct of armed conflict. This chapter will use the First World War and its centennial in 2014 as 'bookends' with which to frame the discussion and analysis, and to examine just how wars have changed over the last 100 years, how the law has responded to such changes, and whether the law needs to continue to change in response to altered methods of armed conflict.

7.2 Armed Conflict and International Law at the Start of the First World War

When the First World War broke out in 1914, the law in place to govern its conduct was already decades old—the Geneva Convention of 1864[5] was the first of a number of instruments, both binding and non-binding,[6] which sought to govern the conduct of hostilities by parties to an armed conflict. These documents all were predicated on warfare as an endeavour which was the sole domain of the State,

[4]Including the 1954 Hague Convention for the Protection of Cultural Property in the Event of Armed Conflict (249 UNTS 240); the 1972 Convention on the Prohibition of the Development, Production and Stockpiling of Bacteriological (Biological) and Toxin Weapons and on their Destruction (1015 UNTS 163); and the 1980 Convention on the Prohibition or Restriction on the Use of Certain Conventional Weapons which may be deemed to be Excessively Injurious or Have Indiscriminate Effects (1342 UNTS 137).

[5]1864 Geneva Convention for the Amelioration of the Wounded (129 CTS 361).

[6]Including the 1868 Declaration Renouncing the Use, in Time of War, of Explosive Projectiles Under 400 Grammes Weight; the 1874 Project of an International Declaration concerning the Laws and Customs of War; the 1880 Manual of the Laws of War on Land; the 1899 and 1907 Hague Regulations and their conventions and declarations; and the 1906 Convention for the Amelioration of the Condition of the Wounded and Sick in Armies in the Field.

and "thus essentially involving conventional armies".[7] In most of these instruments, little attention was paid to who might be lawfully allowed to fight those wars. It was taken as a given that, according to Rousseau's maxim, "war, then, is not a relationship between man and man, but between State and State … each State can have for enemies only other States, and not men; for between things disparate in nature there can be no real relation".[8] As such, there seemed to be no need to consider how the law should address individual participants in armed conflict.

This understanding of war as an organised State endeavour is reflected in the substantive provisions of the law in the early decades of the twentieth century—for example, the opening provision of the (non-binding) Oxford Manual on the Laws of War outlined that "the state of war does not admit of acts of violence, save between the armed forces of belligerent States", defining the armed forces of the State as:

1. The army properly so called, including the militia;
2. The national guards, *landsturm*, free corps, and other bodies which fulfil the three following conditions:
   (a) That they are under the direction of a responsible chief;
   (b) That they must have a uniform, or a fixed distinctive emblem recognisable at a distance, and worn by individuals composing such corps;
   (c) That they carry arms openly;
3. The crews of men-of-war and other military boats;
4. The inhabitants of non-occupied territory, who, on the approach of the enemy, take up arms spontaneously and openly to resist the invading troops, even if they have not had time to organise themselves.[9]

Warfare, as conceptualised in the law of armed conflict in the early twentieth century, was meant only for the State. Irregulars who were not part of the armed forces prior to the outbreak of hostilities had to 'regularise' their participation through submission to responsible command and through the wearing of uniforms. Only in one very narrow circumstance (that of the *levée en masse*—the uprising of civilians in non-occupied territory), could the use of force in armed conflict be legitimately waged by anyone other than the State.

This entrenchment of the State monopoly on the use of force was further solidified by the means with which wars were fought; as Showalter notes, "well before 1914 the instruments of war had evolved from hand tools into machines, whose increasing and interfacing complexities had changed essentially the nature of military operations".[10] The State monopoly on warfare necessarily resulted in a State monopoly on the *means* of warfare—the technology with which wars were fought,

[7]Bassiouni 2008, p. 715.

[8]Rousseau 1762, Book I, Chap. 4.

[9]Article 2, Oxford Manual on the Laws of War.

[10]Showalter 2000, p. 73.

like tanks, thus tended to be kept in the hands of the State. However, this technology—advanced though it was—came with limitations, which themselves shaped the ambit of the law. The majority of the weapons of the First World War, such as machine guns, required adverse parties to be in reasonably close proximity to one another. The technology did not allow for remote or long-distance warfare.[11] Taken together, the political emphasis on warfare being the sole domain of the State, the essential State monopoly on the means of warfare, and the geographical limitations of the technology, account for how the law of armed conflict was structured when war broke out in 1914. As Brooks notes, "the paradigmatic battle imagined by the framers of the [first written laws of armed conflict] … was one fought by opposing armies on a large plain, with civilians tucked away safely far behind the front lines".[12]

However, the technological limitations that dictated military strategy in the First World War were soon overcome, with advancements in means of waging war beginning to shape the methods of waging war. As the range of the weapons increased, there was no need to remain in visual proximity to the opposing side. Opposing sides were no longer restricted to trenches, or limited to specifically demarcated battlefields.[13] Long range artillery and tanks made ground-assaults lead by foot-soldiers armed with bayonets inefficient. The traditional method of trench warfare that typified the First World War was now an obsolete method for defending a border or advancing a front.[14] In addition, aircraft and advances in naval technology regarding submarines and battleships opened up the seas and airspace as expanded or entirely new theatres of war.[15] With these new weapons, destruction could be effected in a shorter time, and from a greater distance. Opposing sides could wage war from thousands of miles away from one another.[16] As Best notes, "science put hitherto unimagined weapons and capabilities into the hands of war-makers, and the scale of the war presented them with hitherto unimagined needs or opportunities for their use".[17]

---

[11]For more detailed explorations of the interrelationship between technology and warfare, and how technological developments have shaped military strategies and tactics, see further the writings of Martin van Creveld 1989, especially Chaps. 11–15 on technology and warfare between 1830 and 1945.

[12]Brooks 2004–2005, p. 730. See also Kinsella 2011, p. 115—"recall that the development of the distinction between combatant and civilian in the late nineteenth century assumed the existence of professionalised standing armies engaged in set-piece battles with one another… identifiable through their military regalia or presence in specific formations of war".

[13]McCormack 1997, pp. 627–628.

[14]See Black 2002, pp. 24–41, for a general discussion of some of the technological advancements of the late nineteenth and early twentieth centuries, and how these advancements altered military tactics.

[15]See Best 1997, pp. 47–55.

[16]See Best 1980, pp. 301–305.

[17]Best 1997, p. 48.

Despite these changes in means and tactics, wars remained essentially State-based affairs.[18] This was reflected in the law of the time; the Geneva Conventions of 1929, adopted to address the deficiencies of The Hague Regulations with regards the treatment of prisoners of war (POWs) and the wounded and sick in armies in the field made clear during the First World War,[19] reaffirmed the legal presumption of armed conflict as a State-based endeavour. The wars of the early twentieth century also indicated a general symmetry of military capabilities. Both sides of these early twentieth conflicts tended to be equipped (or able to be equipped) with the same means of combat—tanks, machine guns, aircraft, naval vessels. The law made no concessions for disparity of arms or men—the rules were to be applied and observed regardless of whether one had a standing army of 1000 or 100,000, and whether one standing army had the latest military technology or archaic or obsolete weaponry. Indeed, as Banks notes, "the laws of war … [were] developed from Clausewitz's Eurocentric conception of war based on symmetric conflicts between state armies of roughly equal military strength and of comparable organisational structures".[20]

7.3 The Second World War and the Law of International and Non-international Armed Conflicts

Following the First World War, and in the lead up to the Second World War, international armed conflicts were infrequent events. In their place, non-international armed conflicts became the norm, with wars in Russia, Spain, China, Nicaragua, and Afghanistan a few of the considerable number of civil, internal and independence wars that beset the interwar period.[21] These wars were soon eclipsed by the scope and brutality of the Second World War, which lasted 6 years and resulted in casualties of between 50 and 70 million dead, military and civilian, on both sides of the conflict.[22] In response to the horrors of the conflict, the community of nations convened to reaffirm and develop the law of armed conflict, in order to address some of the shortcomings of the law that the conflict had highlighted.[23] As with the 1899, 1907, and 1929 laws before them, the Geneva Conventions of 1949 were based on the idea of war as a state of affairs between sovereign nations. As

[18]See Haines 2012, pp. 16–17.

[19]See Bugnion 2003, pp. 118–125.

[20]Banks 2011, p. 5.

[21]See Sivakumaran 2012b, pp. 32–39 on the civil wars during the inter-war period.

[22]See generally Bourke 2001.

[23]Draper notes of WWII: "the tide of inhumanity by man to man reached a level more shocking than the world ever had the misfortune to witness" (Draper 1988, p. 67).

outlined in Common Article 2 to the Geneva Conventions, "the present Convention shall apply to all cases of declared war or of any other armed conflict which may arise between two or more of the High Contracting Parties, even if the state of war is not recognized by one of them".[24] Indeed, even the extension of combatant status to partisan and resistance fighters in occupied territory was still premised on the idea of such resistance being offered by State loyalists against the invasion of their territory by another State.[25]

However, States were not ignorant of the changes in types of armed conflict, and, more specifically, that non-international armed conflicts were causing the kinds of "unrelieved suffering"[26] that was experienced in international armed conflicts. Advocacy work undertaken by the Red Cross prior to and after the Second World War made it clear to States convening to debate the 1949 Geneva Conventions that "in civil war the great humanitarian principles which are the soul of the Red Cross should be increasingly applied, not only to the wounded, sick and prisoners of war, but also to non-combatants, and to children in particular"[27] and that there was value in "laying down definite rules … for the application of the principles of Geneva"[28] in non-international armed conflicts. Thus, when the Diplomatic Conference convened in Geneva to adopt the 1949 Conventions, it was agreed that "in the case of armed conflict not of an international character occurring in the territory of one of the High Contracting Parties, each Party to the conflict shall be bound to apply, as a minimum"[29] certain fundamental principles for the protection of all "persons taking no active part in the hostilities, including members of armed forces who have laid down their arms and those placed 'hors de combat' by sickness, wounds, detention, or any other cause".[30] Despite the significant advancements made by the law in 1949, the law of armed conflict would soon be placed under considerable stresses, as the kind of war envisaged by the Geneva Conventions—international armed conflicts—would soon be surpassed in frequency by non-international armed conflicts.

[24] High Contracting Parties to the Geneva Conventions could only be States.

[25] In Article 4A of Geneva Convention III, partisan and resistance fighters were granted POW protections and combatant status, similar to regular armed forces, providing they were commanded by a person responsible for his subordinates, wore a fixed distinctive sign recognisable at a distance, carried their arms openly, and conducted their operations in accordance with the laws and customs of war. As such, partisan and resistance fighters were 'regularised' much like members of the regular State armed forces.

[26] Resolution XIV on Civil War, Tenth International Red Cross Conference (1921).

[27] Report of the Sixteenth Annual Red Cross Conference (1938), p. 83.

[28] *Ibid* at 82–83.

[29] Common Article 3 to the Geneva Conventions of 1949.

[30] *Ibid.*

7.4 The Post-Second World War Rise of Non-international Armed Conflicts and Wars of National Liberation, and the Move Away from Symmetric/International Armed Conflicts

The Geneva Conventions of 1949 went a considerable way towards addressing some of the lacunae in the law regarding armed conflict in the first half of the 20th century. However, the Convention's own shortcomings were soon apparent. Within a matter of years following the adoption of the Geneva Conventions, internal armed conflicts surged in frequency: between 1945 and 1970, there were 42 internal armed conflicts[31] which took place on nearly every continent of the globe, and resulted in casualties estimated at between 2.5 million and 4 million combatants and civilians.[32] During that same time, only 11 armed conflicts were categorised as international.[33] The Geneva Conventions, which contained only one generally worded article which specifically dealt with internal armed conflicts,[34] seemed to be regulating a kind of conflict that was rapidly becoming the exception rather than the rule—as Bassiouni notes, the Geneva Conventions were "premised on certain assumptions about the methods and means of warfare in existence at the time that the norms were formulated, namely: that conflicts are between regularly constituted armed forces that share mutuality of interests".[35] Indeed, the shortcomings of the Conventions were acknowledged by the ICRC itself in 1969, when it published its general study on the laws of armed conflict. In that report, the ICRC noted that while "international wars involving the application of the Conventions have been few since 1945, non-international wars have been frequent and

[31]This number includes armed conflicts fought between insurgent groups against a government; armed opposition groups in conflict amongst themselves; and secessionist groups fighting against the State. The statistics for these numbers come from studies undertaken by James Fearon and David Laitin, in the Political Science Department at Stanford University in 2003, and from statistics collated by the Correlates of War Project (COW), hosted by Pennsylvania State University. The Fearon/Laitin figures put the number of internal armed conflicts at 42; the Correlates of War Intra-State War Data, 1816–1997 (v 3.0) (COW), put the number at 40, as they do not include the UK-IRA conflict, or the conflicts which took place in the USSR in the immediate post-WWII period involving Latvia, Estonia, Lithuania, and the Ukraine. The COW also included some conflicts, like the Buganda Tribe conflict with Uganda, which the Fearon/Laitin study did not. See further Fearon and Laitin 2003; Reid Sarkees 2000.

[32]The high figure comes from the Fearon/Laitin Study; the lower from the COW (version 3.0) study. The discrepancies are due to the different conflicts that have been included. The datasets from which the Fearon/Laitin figures are drawn can be found in Lacina and Gleditsch 2007. The COW (v 3.0) figures are drawn from Sarkees, "The Correlates of War Data on War: An Update to 1997".

[33]These figures come from the COW Inter-State War Data, 1816–1997 (v 3.0); see further the COW website at http://cow2.la.psu.edu/.

[34]That one article being Common Article 3.

[35]Bassiouni 2008, p. 759.

deadly".[36] Furthermore, the ICRC noted that while Common Article 3 "was a veritable victory in 1949, succeeding internal conflicts have demonstrated that it [is] inadequate to ensure the human person all the necessary protection".[37]

Part of the surge in frequency of non-international armed conflict was due to the rise of so-called 'wars of national liberation' in colonial countries in Africa and Asia. The post-Second World War era saw a notable surge in organised groups under colonial rule actively resisting such colonial rule. Emergent nationalism in a number of colonies frequently lead to outright armed resistance to colonial rule.[38] By the 1970s, international attention increasingly focused on these conflicts; these wars of national liberation were becoming so pervasive that the UN General Assembly adopted a number of influential declarations regarding self-determination and national liberation wars,[39] essentially recognising wars of national liberation as being international in character, and those who fought national liberation wars deserving of combatant and prisoner-of-war status.[40] With the UN giving increasing recognition to organised groups asserting their right to self-determination,[41] there was a push towards giving concomitant recognition in international humanitarian law to participants in such struggles.[42] The relative inadequacy of the Geneva Conventions to deal with these new participants was a common refrain.[43]

Also a common refrain was that the Geneva Conventions were ill-equipped to regulate the *methods* with which wars of national liberation were being fought.[44] The employment of guerrilla tactics was a hallmark of wars of national liberation.[45] Guerrilla tactics are, in practical terms, almost opposite to the military tac-

---

[36] XXIst International Conference of the Red Cross 1969, p. 8.

[37] *Ibid.*

[38] On national liberation wars generally see further Wilson 1988; Cassese 1984.

[39] The UN had adopted a number of declarations and resolutions regarding self-determination and national liberation movements. See further Schwebel 1974.

[40] As noted in UN General Assembly Resolution 3103 (XXVIII) on the Basic Principles of the Legal Status of the Combatants Struggling Against Colonial and Alien Domination and Racist Regimes, in 1973, armed conflicts "involving the struggle of peoples against colonial and alien domination and racist regimes are to be regarded as international armed conflicts in the sense of the 1949 Geneva Conventions". Furthermore, the resolution states that "the legal status envisaged to apply to the combatants in the 1949 Geneva Conventions and other international instruments is to apply to the persons engaged in armed struggle against colonial and alien domination and racist regimes" (UN Doc. A/9030, 12 December 1973).

[41] See generally Pomerance 1982; Cassese 1995.

[42] McCoubrey 1998, p. 82.

[43] See debates regarding the shortcomings of the provisions for dealing with resistance fighters, both generally and in the context of national liberation wars, in the *Report of the Conference of Government Experts 1971* at 68, and the *Report on the Conference of Government Experts 1972*, Vol. I, at 133–135.

[44] Rosenblad 1978, pp. 87–89; see also Draper 1971, p. 214, where he bluntly states "an 'open' guerrilla is a dead guerrilla".

[45] Suter 1984, pp. 1–4; Best 1980, pp. 326–328.

tics employed by States with large-scale standing regular armies. Indeed, the word 'guerrilla', Spanish for 'little war',[46] demonstrates the difference between conventional military tactics and guerrilla tactics. Guerrilla strategy aims to wage many 'little wars' against the much larger and better-equipped enemy, attacking supply lines, armouries, and smaller bases, rather than large military installations. Guerrillas will manipulate the conflict to ensure that the battles are fought in situations that favour their techniques. Therefore, the geographical locations chosen will be those where large armies in conventional deployments cannot easily venture, or where their supply lines will be restricted, such as mountainous regions or jungle areas. Guerrillas usually wear no uniform or insignia to distinguish themselves from the civilian population; indeed, guerrilla groups will frequently locate their bases within a civilian population, so as to remain undetected (or to use the civilian population as a shield against the State's forces). Furthermore, crucial to the guerrilla tactic of stealth and concealment, guerrillas will traditionally conceal their weaponry, only producing arms immediately prior to use in combat. The guerrilla bears little in appearance to the regular State soldier, who wears a uniform and carries his firearm openly.[47]

The disjuncture between wars as they were being fought, and wars as they were conceptualised in the law, was stark. For example, under the Geneva Conventions of 1949, Article 4A(2) of the POWs Convention grants combatant status to irregular fighters. However, such status is dependent on irregulars carrying their arms openly and wearing a fixed, distinctive insignia, recognisable at a distance. Such provisions are at odds with the way wars of national liberation were generally fought—through guerrilla tactics, the hallmark of which is stealth and secrecy. The requirement of wearing a fixed visible insignia seemed an unfeasible provision to include in a treaty concerning guerrilla warfare.[48] The absurdity of such a provision is noted by Greenwood, who argues that if, as the British Military Manual requires, all irregulars "standing against the skyline should be at once distinguishable from the outline of a peaceful inhabitant, and this by the naked eye of an ordinary individual at a distance from which the form of an individual can be determined"[49]; it is likely that "the life expectancy of such an irregular would be short".[50]

[46]Rosenblad 1978, pp. 75–76.

[47]For a more thorough analysis of guerrilla tactics and ideology, see Taber 1970, specifically Chap. 10, "Principles of Guerrilla Strategy and Tactics".

[48]For the debate at the Diplomatic Conference regarding the exact meaning of insignia that is "visible at a distance", see CDDH/III/SR.55-56, from 22 April 1977; also, the comments from the French delegation in Committee III at the 2nd Session of the Diplomatic Conference, regarding the unrealistic nature of distinction requirements for resistance fighters as outlined in the Article 4A(2) of GC III at 14 CDDH 537, 538 (CDDH/III/SR.33-SR.36). Similar comments were made by Norway (CDDH/III/SR.33-36; CDDH at 400, 537). See also commentary by Mallison and Mallison 1978, pp. 22–25 regarding the shortcomings of provisions on the open carrying of arms by resistance fighters. See also Bothe et al. 1982, p. 245.

[49]*British Manual of Military Law* (1958) Part III at para 92.

[50]Greenwood 2003, p. 795.

In response to the increased political attention being given to national liberation wars, and to non-international armed conflicts more generally, the ICRC proposed that States re-examine and develop the existing treaty law of armed conflict, ultimately convening diplomatic conferences in Geneva in 1974, which would culminate in the adoption of the 1977 Protocols Additional to the Geneva Conventions.[51] One of the major issues placed on the agenda for consideration was that of whether the law should take into account guerrilla and resistance fighters, and whether the requirements for combatant status needed re-evaluation. That existing rules on combatant status seemed ill-equipped to deal with guerrilla fighters was obvious. Indeed, as noted in the Commentary to Additional Protocol I, it was "recognised early"[52] at the Diplomatic Conferences that it was virtually impossible for guerrillas to abide by the Article 4A(2) obligations of fixed visible insignia and open carriage of arms. In order for guerrilla and national liberation fighters to have any chance of success in their struggles, they "must work secretly, wear no uniform or distinguishing sign, and withhold their identity prior to their attack".[53] As such, it was evident to the Diplomatic Conference that if the new Protocols were to have any impact, then it was incumbent on States to "relax or abolish the 1949 Geneva Conventions standards for 'freedom fighters'".[54]

With this in mind, the international community adopted Additional Protocol I, recognising 'wars of national liberation' as international armed conflicts,[55] and acknowledging the methods by which such wars were usually waged, that is, through guerrilla tactics. Guerrilla fighters are thus granted combatant status[56] and are to be granted full combatants rights and responsibilities, and concomitant POW rights, if captured.[57]

Additional Protocol I makes a considerable concession for guerrilla fighters in Article 44, by eliminating the conventional combatant requirements of wearing a fixed, distinctive emblem and the open carrying of arms.[58] This development creates an exemption to the general rule of distinction—that combatants are required to distinguish themselves from the civilian population.[59] However, this exception does not extend to regular armed forces: as outlined in Article 44(7) of Protocol I, this provision is "not intended to change the generally accepted practice of States

[51]See Bugnion 2003, pp. 320–322.

[52]Bothe et al. 1982, p. 245.

[53]*Ibid.*

[54]*Ibid.*

[55]Cullen 2005, p. 89.

[56]See generally Aldrich 1982.

[57]Under Article 43 of Protocol I, the armed forces of a Party to the conflict include all organised armed forces, groups and units participating in the conflict, who are under responsible command, subject to an internal disciplinary system, and who operate in compliance with the laws of armed conflict.

[58]Article 44(3), API.

[59]Bothe et al. 1982, p. 246.

with respect to the wearing of the uniform by combatants assigned to the regular, uniformed armed units of a Party to the conflict".[60] By creating this general exception to the rule for one particular group involved in armed conflicts, the law began to evidence an asymmetry of application that had not been seen in the law to date. The Additional Protocols also reflected the changing character of armed conflict, in that Protocol II's adoption recognised that the bulk of armed conflicts taking place internationally were generally non-international or internal in character—even above those conflicts that were eventually classified international wars of national liberation.[61] Protocol II significantly develops the law of internal armed conflict,[62] including provisions on methods of armed conflict, detailed provisions regarding the protection of the wounded, sick and shipwrecked,[63] and protections for persons deprived of their liberty.[64]

Together, the Additional Protocols of 1977 reflected the changing character and methods of armed conflict that were prevalent during that period—non-international and internal armed conflicts, often fought using guerrilla or other unconventional tactics. The adoption of the Additional Protocols was an attempt to better reflect the new realities of warfare. However, both of the Protocols demonstrated certain fundamental underpinnings that were common to the 1949 Geneva Conventions and, indeed, the 1899 Hague Regulations. Aside from the exception outlined in Article 44 regarding combatant status, Additional Protocol I *still* privileges international armed conflict as the exemplar of armed conflict. The limited provisions contained Additional Protocol II is reflective of the resistance to international regulation of non-international armed conflict—there are only a few articles, which provide general instruction on non-international armed conflict, but nowhere near the kind of comprehensive regulation contained in either the Geneva Conventions, Hague Regulations, or indeed Additional Protocol I.[65]

[60]See Sandoz et al. 1987, p. 542.

[61]Article 1(1) of Additional Protocol II provides that the Protocol applies in armed conflicts which take place "in the territory of a High Contracting Party between its armed forces and dissident armed forces or other organized armed groups which, under responsible command, exercise such control over a part of its territory as to enable them to carry out sustained and concerted military operations and to implement this Protocol".

[62]As noted by UN Ambassador at Large for War Crimes, David Scheffer, "if the provisions of Protocol II were followed by rebel and government forces through the world, many of the most horrific human tragedies the world has documented within the past decade could have been avoided". See Murphy 2002, p. 370.

[63]Articles 7–12.

[64]Articles 4–6.

[65]Disappointingly, both instruments also enjoyed limited success in practice—in the decades following the adoption of the Protocols, national liberation wars dwindled in frequency and while non-international armed conflicts continued to occur, the few rules in place were often ignored. See further Banks 2011, p. 8; see also Clapham 2006, p. 494.

7.5 The Predominance of Asymmetric Warfare in the Post-Protocols Era—From the End of the Cold War, to 9/11 and Beyond

In the 100 years following the outbreak of World War I, warfare—both in practice, and how that practice is reflected in the law—has evolved from predominantly State-based symmetric events into predominantly non-international armed conflicts, fought by non-State actors, often employing unconventional methods and tactics in order to achieve their aims. The prevalence of these kinds of conflicts in the last decades has led to such conflicts being termed 'asymmetric' wars.

While there is no accepted international law definition of the term 'asymmetric warfare' (for, indeed, it is a term of descriptive art, rather than one bearing any legal consequences) a useful working definition has been proposed by Metz and Johnson, who describe asymmetric warfare as "acting, organising, and thinking differently than opponents in order to maximise one's own advantages, exploit an opponent's weaknesses, attain the initiative, or gain greater freedom of action … it can entail different methods, technologies, values, organisations, time perspectives, or some combination of these".[66] Asymmetric conflicts have also frequently been described as 'new wars',[67] as the tactics and techniques employed seem so different from conventional conceptualisations of armed conflicts.

The whole idea of 'asymmetry in war', and that asymmetric wars are somehow profoundly 'new' or 'different' from all other wars in history, is conceptually problematic in a number of ways. Firstly, the broad definition of 'asymmetric warfare' is somewhat superficial, for, as Strachan points out, "much of the debate about asymmetry in war is historically naïve: all enemies try to get under the other side's guard by using responses that are unpredictable".[68] Indeed, the very term 'asymmetric' implies that 'symmetric' conflicts are precisely that—conflicts involving equally matched sides, perfectly corresponding in equipment, personnel, tactics and strategies. If this were the case, no conflict would ever be won, as both sides would never be able to overpower their equally matched opponent.[69] Furthermore, the idea that these wars are 'new' is something of a misnomer; there is nothing particularly 'new' in practice regarding these conflicts. Guerrilla strategies and irregular fighters have been involved in armed conflicts as long as such conflicts have taken place.[70]

---

[66]Metz and Johnson 2001, pdf available at http://www.strategicstudiesinstitute.army.mil/pdffiles/pub223.pdf.

[67]See, for example, Banks 2011; Bassiouni 2008; Kaldor 1999.

[68]Strachan 2011, p. 14.

[69]As Geiß notes, "perfect symmetries have rarely been present in war" (Geiß 2006, p. 758).

[70]See Goulding 2000–2001, p. 21, where he argues that asymmetric warfare is "a concept as old as warfare itself. For centuries, even millennia, weaker opponents have sought to neutralise their enemy's technological or numerical superiority by fighting in ways or on battlefield that nullify it".

However, there is utility in the term 'asymmetric conflict', in that it serves as a general summary of certain trends in armed conflict witnessed in the past 25 years.[71] It does not mean that conventional 'symmetric' armed conflicts no longer take place, or that States no longer go to war with one another, but rather that the conflicts of the last decades seem to display more marked, significant asymmetries. Moreover, the idea of asymmetric war as 'new war' is accurate in one respect—these conflicts are comparatively 'new' to international law, and international legal regulation. Since the origins of the written law of armed conflict, international armed conflicts between sovereign States who observe (or at least profess to observe) the laws of armed conflict have been the exemplar. One hundred and 50 years later and armed conflicts are now "mostly characterised by the participation of non-state actors as the core combatants ... who are not subject to the discipline of effective command and control. Maybe more significantly, they feel that to abide by IHL would put them at a disadvantage with the state-actor opponents because of the asymmetry of power between the protagonists".[72] Asymmetric wars are thus perhaps less a "revolution in military affairs",[73] more a revolution in military *legal* affairs.

Regarding the mechanics of asymmetric warfare, theorists have identified certain behaviours or traits as being typical in asymmetric conflicts, conflicts where there is no equality of arms, but rather where the 'stronger' of the parties to the conflict has access to superior (in both quality and quantity) military matériel and personnel and is more likely to abide by, or profess to abide by, the existing laws of armed conflict in their prosecution of the conflict. In contrast, the 'weaker' party to an asymmetric armed conflict will likely have limited access to technologically advanced matériel and will likely have fewer well-trained personnel available to engage in hostilities. As such, the 'weaker' party often seeks to counter this structural disadvantage by engaging in prohibited practices such as direct attacks against enemy civilians, using human-shields, hostage-taking, and using protected sites, like schools and religious buildings, as military bases. In doing so, the 'weaker' party is depending on the 'stronger' party to comply with IHL and not attack such protected sites, for fear of violating principles on indiscriminate attack, distinction, and proportionality.[74] However, such practices by the 'weaker' party often prompt the 'stronger' party to engage in their own violations of international law, through practices such as extraordinary rendition, targeted killings, and

[71]Indeed, one could argue that these trends have been evident since the Second World War.

[72]Bassiouni 2008, pp. 762–763.

[73]The idea of a "revolution in military affairs" (RMA) is a central topic in strategic studies in the last quarter century—one that posits that technological advances require a complete rethink of military strategy. For an overview of the concept see further Williamson and Knox 2001; Singh 1998. For an assessment of the interaction between RMA and asymmetric warfare, see further Benbow 2009.

[74]Geiß 2006, p. 758; see also Arreguín-Toft 2001, pp. 96–104; Mack 1975; Benvenisti 2010, pp. 342–344.

so-called 'enhanced interrogation' in order to combat their enemy.[75] Thus, the term 'asymmetric conflict' is a useful blanket phrase to describe a raft of behaviours whereby seemingly weaker parties in armed conflicts are able to successfully combat an adverse party who is stronger or better equipped in terms of matériel, personnel, and training.

The ongoing conflict between Israel and the Palestinians in Gaza is an exemplar of asymmetry in action.[76] While conflict in the region has been a part of the political and social landscape for decades, for the purposes of this chapter the period in question that will serve as a short case study is known as Operation Cast Lead, an Israeli offensive launched against Gaza between December 2008 and January 2009. It is something of an understatement to say that the background to the period in question is notoriously complex;[77] however, a few key events are useful to know. Operation Cast Lead was undertaken by Israel in December 2008, when an official six-month ceasefire between Israel and the authorities in Gaza ended.[78] That ceasefire, announced on 18 June 2008, had been brokered by Egypt in an attempt to put an end to ongoing rocket attacks that were being launched into Israel from Hamas-controlled Gaza.[79] However, the ceasefire was soon broken when, on 23 June 2008, Israeli troops fired on Palestinians collecting firewood near the border.[80] This was soon followed by numerous violations of the ceasefire, from both sides; rockets were routinely fired into Israel,[81] prompting return action by Israel.[82] When the ceasefire came to an official end on 18 December 2008, Hamas declared that they would not seek to renew the truce on the grounds that

---

[75]Geiß 2006, p. 758.

[76]As Laurie Blank notes, Israel's conflicts in Gaza "offer perhaps the most searing commentary about the nature of asymmetrical war" (Blank 2010, p. 288).

[77]For further analyses of the background to that period see Scobbie 2012, pp. 280–316; the background given in the *Report of the United Nations Fact-Finding Mission on the Gaza Conflict on Human Rights in Palestine and Other Occupied Arab Territories* 2009, pp. 46–62 (hereinafter *Goldstone Report*); and Volume 38(3) of the Journal of Palestine Studies, which devotes a significant portion of the edition on Operation Cast Lead, the conflict in Gaza between 2008–2009.

[78]Nidal al-Mughrabi, "Hamas declares end to ceasefire with Israel in Gaza", *Reuters*, 18 December 2008, available at http://www.reuters.com/article/2008/12/18/us-palestinians-israel-ceasefire-idUSLI756232200812l8.

[79]Isabel Kirshner, "Israel Agrees to Truce with Hamas on Gaza", *The New York Times*, 18 June 2008, available at http://www.nytimes.com/2008/06/18/world/middleeast/18mideast.html?fta=y&_r=0.

[80]*Goldstone Report*, p. 63; see also the United Nations Office for the Coordination of Humanitarian Affairs, *Protection of Civilians Weekly Report*, 18–24 June 2008, available at http:/ /www.ochaopt.org/documents/weekly_briefing_notes_265_english.pdf.

[81]*Goldstone Report*, pp. 64–69.

[82]*Ibid.*

Israel has not abided by its obligations under the agreement,[83] a charge that was likewise levelled at Hamas by Israel.[84]

Operation Cast Lead was launched by Israel on 27 December 2008.[85] From the outset, obvious asymmetries between the adversaries were evident. Israel deployed its navy to shell the Gaza coast from the Mediterranean Sea,[86] and used its air force to provide cover for ground forces, which entered Gaza on 3 January 2009.[87] Reports and analysis put the number of Israeli air sorties during Cast Lead at between 2300 and 3000;[88] with the number of strikes launched against targets in the first week numbering between 300 and 526.[89] During the 'ground phase' of the conflict, Israel deployed five Armoured Corps Brigades[90] and an additional three brigades, comprising upwards of nine battalions.[91] Unmanned aerial vehicles (UAVs) were also deployed during the conflict, both for surveillance and attack purposes,[92] as well as tanks and other armoured vehicles.[93] Of the reported casual-

[83]Nidal al-Mughrabi, "Hamas declares end to ceasefire with Israel in Gaza", quoting Hamas official Ayman Taha, who said that the ceasefire would not be renewed "because the enemy did not abide by its obligations" to ease the blockade on Gaza.

[84]See comments made by Gabriela Shalev, Permanent Representative of Israel to the United Nations, at the 6061st meeting of the Security Council, UN Doc S/PV.6061, 6 January 2009, where she said "we also agreed 6 months ago to an Egyptian-brokered *tahadiya*—a situation of calm. Hamas violated this arrangement on a daily basis. Over 365 rockets and mortar shells were fired during this period".

[85]*Goldstone Report*, p. 71; see also Jenny Percival, "Israel launches deadly Gaza attacks", *The Guardian*, 27 December 2008, available at http://www.theguardian.com/world/2008/dec/27/israelandthepalestinians.

[86]See the Israeli Ministry of Foreign Affairs, "IDF Operation in Gaza: Cast Lead", a daily summary of IDF operations during Cast Lead, available at http://mfa.gov.il/MFA/ForeignPolicy/Terrorism/Palestinian/Pages/Aerial_strike_weapon_development_center%20_Gaza_28-Dec-2008.aspx.

[87]Chris McGreal, "Israeli ground forces cross border into Gaza", *The Guardian*, 3 January 2009, available at http://www.theguardian.com/world/2009/jan/03/middleeast-israelandthepalestinians.

[88]*Goldstone Report*, p. 87.

[89]*Ibid.*

[90]*Goldstone Report*, p. 86.

[91]*Ibid.* The Golani, Givati, and Paratrooper Brigades were reportedly involved in the ground invasion of Gaza—estimates place the number of individual troops involved in the ground phase at 20,000—see further Jason Koutsoukis, "Israeli troops enter Gaza", *The Sydney Morning Herald*, 4 January 2009, available at http://www.smh.com.au/news/world/israeli-troops-enter-gaza/2009/01/04/1231003816897.html. For a more detailed overview of the Israeli side of the conflict, specifically the amounts and types of weapons deployed, see "The Israeli Arsenal Deployed Against Gaza During Operation Cast Lead" 2009.

[92]*Ibid*, pp. 176, 182.

[93]*Ibid*, pp. 180–182.

ties inflicted by Israel, sources place the number of Palestinians killed during the three-week war at between 1166[94] and 1444.[95]

In comparison, the Palestinian side of the conflict had no air force or navy, no tanks or UAVs; they mainly used rockets and mortars with limited range,[96] and used personal hand weapons, grenades, and some shoulder-launched weapons during the land war, as well as improvised explosive devices (IEDs) and other anti-personnel mines and booby-traps.[97] The groups fighting against Israel were a mixed lot of Hamas and Hamas-affiliated groups.[98] Israeli estimates put Palestinian forces during Operation Cast Lead at around 15,000–20,000;[99] however, some have argued that the bulk of these fighters were not actively involved in hostilities.[100] The numbers of Israeli casualties as a result of the three-week conflict was reported as 13, of which three were civilians, and four were the result of friendly fire.[101] In addition to these structural asymmetries of personnel and matériel, asymmetries in methods of warfare also typified Operation Cast Lead. The Palestinian side of the conflict engaged in a number of archetypal behaviours usually employed by the weaker party in asymmetric conflicts, such as launching attacks from densely populated civilian areas,[102] and there were allegations (though contested) that the Palestinians used mosques, schools, and hospitals as sites for storing munitions.[103]

---

[94]This figure comes from the Israeli Defence Force (IDF)—see further Yaakov Lappin, "IDF releases Cast Lead casualty numbers", *The Jerusalem Post*, 26 March 2009, available at http://www.jpost.com/Israel/IDF-releases-Cast-Lead-casualty-numbers; and a statement by the IDF, "Vast majority of Palestinians killed in Operation Cast Lead terror operatives", 26 March 2009, available at http://mfa.gov.il/MFA/ForeignPolicy/Terrorism/Pages/Vast_majority_Palestinians_killed_Operation_Cast_Lead_terror_operatives_26-Mar-2009.aspx.

[95]This figure was submitted to the Goldstone Report by the Gaza Authorities' Ministry of Justice Central Commission for Documentation and Pursuit of Israeli War Criminals (TAWTHEQ)—see the *Goldstone Report* at 90. Other non-governmental organisations such as B'Tselem and the Palestinian Centre for Human Rights put the figures at 1387 and 1417 respectively (*ibid*).

[96]See "Palestinian Weapons Deployed Against Israel During Operation Cast Lead" (2009) Journal of Palestine Studies XXXVIII (3): 193–197.

[97]*Ibid*, pp. 197–199.

[98]*Goldstone Report*, p. 86.

[99]"Palestinian Weapons Deployed Against Israel During Operation Cast Lead", p. 192; see also Tim Butcher, "Hamas fighters now a well-organised force", *The Telegraph*, 5 January 2009, available at http://www.telegraph.co.uk/news/worldnews/middleeast/israel/4127074/Hamas-fighters-now-a-well-organised-force.html.

[100]*Ibid.*

[101]See *Goldstone Report*, citing reports by the IDF and B'Tselem, p. 92.

[102]*Goldstone Report,* p. 113; see also reports from Amnesty International 2009, pp. 74–75; International Crisis Group 2009, p. 3; Human Rights Watch 2009, p. 21.

[103]These claims were made by Israel to the *Goldstone Report*, pp. 117–119; the *Goldstone Report* could not definitively state that such activities took place (p. 122). However, for arguments against the Goldstone findings, see further Blank 2010, p. 284; Cordesman 2009, p. 24.

7.6 New Laws for 'New Wars'? Responding to the Challenge of Asymmetric Conflict

As the conflict in Gaza illustrates, asymmetric conflicts are marked by a number of imbalances, such as in means and methods. However, one significant additional element, seems to be a disregard for the law of armed conflict, with the weaker party often ignoring the law as they feel that it disadvantages them against a stronger foe—as Geiß outlines, "direct attacks against civilians, hostage-taking and the use of human shields—practices that have long been outlawed in armed conflicts—have seen a revival in recent conflicts in which the far weaker party has often sought to gain a comparative advantage over the militarily superior enemy by resorting to such practice as a matter of strategy".[104] This denial of the applicability of the law of armed conflict is evidenced by the 'stronger party' also, who frequently argue that these 'new' wars fall outside the scope of the existing law of armed conflict, thus allowing them to engage in tactics such as targeted killing, extraordinary rendition, indefinite detention, and 'enhanced interrogation'.[105] This refusal to observe the laws of armed conflict by both sides has prompted debate as to whether the existing law needs to be amended, to better reflect the more prevalent forms of conflict.[106] Should there be new laws to better account for 'weaker' parties in asymmetric conflict, and/or to take into account the tactics employed by the 'stronger' parties?

There is precedent for such an approach. The law of armed conflict has, in the past, made concessions for the 'weaker' party in armed conflicts—namely, by allowing for exceptions to strict combatant rules for guerrilla fighters in national liberation wars, allowing such fighters to forego the wearing of a fixed distinctive emblem or the open carrying of arms at all times.[107] However, whether an entirely new treaty should be adopted to specifically address asymmetric warfare seems untenable and unlikely—as Dinstein points out, "a decade into the twenty-first century, states are shying away from any proposal to re-examine the current law lest the process would open a Pandora's Box of toil and trouble. This is quote unfortunate, inasmuch as new international armed conflicts always subject the legal system to novel strains and disruptions".[108] Indeed, one would have to question whether, in situations where parties seem to already be ignoring the existing laws, the solution is to introduce more laws. However, this leaves unanswered the question of how to deal with these conflicts, and how to ensure that the existing rules are observed by all.

---

[104]Geiß 2006, p. 758.

[105]*Ibid.* For a comprehensive assessment of the different kinds of asymmetry that exist in contemporary armed conflicts, see further Schmitt (2008), who examines asymmetry between the parties to contemporary armed conflicts in terms of technology, strategy and tactics, and in the applicable law governing such participants.

[106]See arguments outlined by Paulus and Vashakmadze 2009, pp. 108–111; Münkler 2003, p. 7; Schmitt 2008, pp. 33–38.

[107]See *infra*.

[108]Dinstein 2010, p. 296.

Given the purported unconventional nature of many of these conflicts, a possible solution might be found in unconventional sources of law; that is, not through binding treaties, but through 'soft law' instruments. Soft law instruments, such as interpretive documents[109] and international expert manuals of instruction,[110] are those instruments which "have been articulated in non-binding form according to traditional modes of law-making",[111] which "emanate from bodies lacking international law-making authority";[112] which are often directed at or designed to include "non-state actors who practice cannot constitute customary international law";[113] and which are usually based on "voluntary adherence, or rely upon non-juridical means of enforcement".[114] These instruments can serve as useful, context-specific explanations of the relevant applicable law, and may assist in guiding the conduct of both States and non-State actors in situations, like asymmetric armed conflicts, where the applicability of the law is contested or unclear. By adopting manuals of instruction or codes of conduct, States and non-State groups alike can agree on the applicable rules, and affirm their commitment to humanitarian principles—indeed, there are a considerable number of examples of non-State groups as well as States issuing unilateral declarations, adopting codes of conduct, or agreeing to bilateral and multilateral instruments affirming their commitment to the law of armed conflict, even where such rules may not have, at first, seemed applicable.[115] Codes of conduct or expert manuals in situations of asymmetric warfare may well provide ample opportunity for States and non-State groups to affirm and develop the law of armed conflict.

It may seem counterintuitive to suggest that non-binding documents will improve compliance with a set of rules that already appear to be systematically ignored or violated. However, research into soft law instruments indicates that soft law offers the potential for both States and non-State groups to engage with international law in a cooperative and flexible manner, and can effectively promote "some change in behaviour without producing the harsh and possible

[109]Such as the ICRC's Interpretive Guidance on the Notion of Direct Participation in Hostilities Under International Humanitarian Law (2009), the ICRC Study into Customary International Humanitarian Law (2006), and the Montreux Document on Pertinent International Legal Obligations and Good Practices for States related to Operations of Private Military and Security Companies during Armed Conflict of 17 September 2008.

[110]Such as the Tallinn Manual on the International Law Applicable to Cyber Warfare (2013).

[111]Chinkin 2000, p. 30.

[112]*Ibid.*

[113]*Ibid.*

[114]*Ibid.* For an assessment of the differing approaches to and definitions of soft law, see further Baxter 1980; Ellis 2012, pp. 315–323; Guzman and Meyer 2015, pp. 4–6. Note, however, some theorists reject the notion of soft law outright, arguing that a particular rule or norm is either binding or not, and if it is not binding, it cannot be law, soft or otherwise. For this approach, see generally Klabbers 1996; d'Aspremont 2011; Schachter 1977.

[115]See further Sivakumaran 2012b, pp. 430–445, for an exploration of these methods of implementation and enforcement of the law of armed conflict in non-international armed conflicts.

counterproductive consequences of breach".[116] Soft law also offers the promise of increased normative pull for actors who have been intentionally excluded from conventional norm generation. That is to say, research indicates that non-State armed groups are more inclined to comply with rules they feel 'ownership'[117] over—i.e., rules that they themselves were involved in developing and codifying. As noted above, armed groups have sometimes repudiated the applicability of IHL norms, stating that due to their own exclusion from the creation and adoption of such norms, they feel no compulsion to observe them—for example, in interviews with Human Rights Watch, some Colombian non-State groups argued that Additional Protocol II did not apply to their conflict as the instrument had not been "negotiated directly with them".[118] However, research undertaken by the International Council on Human Rights Policy suggests that when armed groups have been involved in the development of codes of conduct, there is an increased probability of compliance.[119] Preliminary research undertaken into the effectiveness of Geneva Call's Deeds of Commitment[120] for non-State actors also supports the contention that collaboration and cooperation with non-State groups in norm-generation (rather than 'top-down' imposition of rules) fosters a culture of compliance.[121] There is also evidence to suggest that State compliance with IHL norms increases when non-State actors participate in norm generation and norm adherence.[122] As such, soft law instruments may well provide at least part of the solution to better address the problems raised by asymmetric warfare.

7.7 Conclusion

The last 100 years has proven immensely challenging for the law of armed conflict. Technology has profoundly changed the means and methods of warfare, and international law has become increasingly involved in regulating non-international armed conflicts. The bulk of the written law of armed conflict, structured as it is

[116]Chinkin 2000, p. 34.

[117]The idea of 'ownership' of IHL norms is central to much of the literature on non-State groups and compliance with IHL, and is often argued as being pivotal to whether non-State groups comply with IHL norms; see further See for example, Sivakumaran 2012a; Bongard and Somer 2011, p. 681; Maurer 2014; Clapham 2010, p. 19.

[118]Human Rights Watch 1998. See also Roberts and Sivakumaran 2012, p. 127.

[119]The International Council on Human Rights Policy 2000, p. 52.

[120]Including the Deed of Commitment for Adherence to a Total Ban on Anti-Personnel Mines and for Cooperation in Mine Action, the Deed of Commitment for the Prohibition of Sexual Violence in Situations of Armed Conflict and towards the Elimination of Gender Discrimination, and the Deed of Commitment under Geneva Call for the Protection of Children from the Effects of Armed Conflict—see further http://www.genevacall.org.

[121]See comments by Decrey Warner 2013.

[122]See Roberts and Sivakumaran 2012, pp. 129–130.

around conventional armed forces belonging to States, has come under immense pressures as unconventional and irregular participants have begun to dominate the landscape of armed conflict, employing means and methods that the law did not, and could not, have envisaged in 1899, 1949, or 1977. States have made some attempts to address these challenges, through the introduction of some rules regarding conduct in non-international armed conflicts, through expanding the categories of those entitled to combatant and prisoner-of-war status, and through modifying the law to better reflect the means and methods employed by irregular fighters.

However, as means and methods continue to change, and more civilians and irregulars participate in armed conflicts, the law may be seen as out of step with the situations it seeks to regulate. The challenge for all those who teach, discuss, debate, and apply the laws of armed conflict is clear: how can laws that have their genesis in the time of cavalry and bayonets adapt to deal with drones, cyber-attacks, autonomous weaponry, and suicide bombers? These questions and the issues they raise is something that is of interest to all those involved in the implementation and development of the law of armed conflict, and will no doubt set the stage for practitioners and academics for the next 100 years.

References

Aldrich G (1982) Guerrilla combatants and prisoner of war status. Am Univ Law Rev 31:871–882

Amnesty International (2009) Israel/Gaza: operation 'cast lead': 22 days of death and destruction. http://www.amnesty.org/en/library/asset/MDE15/015/2009/en/8f299083-9a74-4853-860f-0563725e633a/mde150152009en.pdf. Accessed 11 April 2015

Arreguín-Toft I (2001) How the weak win wars: a theory of asymmetric conflict. Int Secur 26:93–128

Banks W (2011) Towards an adaptive international humanitarian law. In: Banks W (ed) New battlefields, old laws: critical debates on asymmetric warfare. Columbia University Press, New York, pp 1–22

Bassiouni MC (2008) The new laws and the crisis of compliance with the law of armed conflict by non-state actors. J Crim Law Criminol 98:711–810

Baxter R (1980) International law in 'her infinite variety'. Int Comp Law Q 29:549–566

Benbow T (2009) Irresistible force or immovable object? The 'revolution in military affairs' and asymmetric warfare. Defense Secur Anal 25:21–36

Benvenisti E (2010) The legal battle to define the law on transnational asymmetric warfare. Duke J Comp Int Law 20:339–359

Best G (1980) Humanity in warfare: the modern history of the international law of armed conflicts. Weidenfeld and Nicolson, London

Best G (1997) War and law since 1945. Clarendon, Oxford

Black J (2002) Warfare in the western world, 1882–1975. Indiana University Press, Bloomington and Indianapolis

Blank L (2010) Finding facts but missing the law: the Goldstone report, Gaza and lawfare. Case West Reserve J Int Law 43:279–305

Bongard P, Somer J (2011) Monitoring armed non-state actor compliance with humanitarian norms: a look at international mechanisms and the Geneva call deed of commitment. Int Rev Red Cross 93:673–706

Bothe M, Partsch KJ, Solf W (eds) (1982) New rules for victims of armed conflicts: commentary on the two 1977 protocols additional to the Geneva Conventions of 1949. Martinus Nijhoff, The Hague

Bourke J (2001) The second world war: a people's history. OUP, Oxford

Bourne J (2005) Total war I: the great war. In: Townshend C (ed) The Oxford history of modern war. OUP, Oxford, pp 117–137

Brooks RE (2004) War everywhere: rights, national security law, and the law of armed conflict in the age of terror. Univ PA Law Rev 153:675–761

Browning P (2002) The changing nature of warfare: the development of land warfare from 1792–1945. CUP, Cambridge

Bugnion F (2003) The ICRC and the protection of war victims. ICRC, Geneva

Cassese A (1984) Wars of national liberation and humanitarian law. In: Swinarski C (ed) Studies and essays on international humanitarian law and Red Cross principles in honour of Jean Pictet. ICRC, Geneva, pp 313–324

Cassese A (1995) Self-determination of peoples: a legal reappraisal. CUP, Cambridge

Chinkin C (2000) Normative development in the international legal system. In: Shelton S (ed) Commitment and compliance: the role of non-binding norms in the international legal system. OUP, Oxford, pp 21–44

Clapham A (2006) Human rights obligations of non-state actors in conflict situations. Int Rev Red Cross 88:491–523

Clapham A (2010) The rights and responsibilities of armed non-state actors: the legal landscape and issues surrounding engagement. Draft for comment available on SSRN at http://ssrn.com/abstract=1569636. Accessed 15 April 2015

Cordesman, A (2009) The 'Gaza war': a strategic analysis. Centre for strategic and international studies. http://csis.org/files/media/csis/pubs/090202_gaza_war.pdf. Accessed 11 April 2015

Cullen A (2005) Key developments affecting the scope of internal armed conflict in international humanitarian law. Mil Law Rev 183:66–109

D'Aspremont J (2011) Formalism and the sources of international law: a theory of the ascertainment of legal rules. OUP, Oxford

Decrey Warner E (2013) Engaging with non-state armed groups: lessons learned. 36th round table on current issues of international humanitarian law, respecting IHL: challenges and perspectives. Institute of international humanitarian law, San Remo, 5–7 Sept 2013. http://www.iihl.org/iihl/Documents/DECREY-WARNER.pdf. Accessed 11 April 2013

Dinstein Y (2010) The conduct of hostilities under the law of international armed conflict, 2nd edn. CUP, Cambridge

Draper G (1971) The status of combatants and the question of guerrilla warfare. Br Yearb Int Law 45:173–218

Draper G (1988) The development of international humanitarian law. In: International dimensions of humanitarian law. UNESCO/Henri Dunant Institute/Martinus Nijhoff, Paris/Geneva/Dordrecht/Boston/London, pp 67–90

Ellis J (2012) Shades of grey: soft law and the validity of public international law. Leiden J Int Law 25:313–334

Fearon J, Laitin D (2003) Ethnicity, insurgency and civil war. Am Polit Sci Rev 97:75–90

Geiß R (2006) Asymmetric conflict structures. Int Rev Red Cross 88:757–777

Goulding Jr V (2000–2001) Back to the future with asymmetric warfare. Parameters 30:21–30

Greenwood C (2003) The laws of war (international humanitarian law). In: Evans M (ed) International law. OUP, Oxford, pp 789–824

Guzman A and Meyer T (2015) Soft law. In: Kontorovich E (ed) The research handbook on the economics of public international law. Elgar, forthcoming, paper available on SSRN at http://papers.ssrn.com/sol3/papers.cfm?abstract_id=2437956

Haines S (2012) The nature of war and the character of contemporary armed conflict. In: Wilmshurst E (ed) International law and the classification of conflicts. OUP, Oxford, pp 9–31

Human Rights Watch (1998) War without quarter: Colombia and international humanitarian law. http://www.hrw.org/legacy/reports98/colombia/Colom989-03.htm#P457_59724. Accessed 14 April 2015

Human Rights Watch (2009) Rockets from Gaza: harm to civilians from Palestinian armed groups' rocket attacks. http://www.hrw.org/reports/2009/08/06/rockets-gaza-0
International Committee of the Red Cross (1969) Reaffirmation and development of the laws and customs applicable in armed conflicts. ICRC, Geneva
International Committee of the Red Cross (2011) Report of the XXXIst international conference of the Red Cross and Red Crescent, international humanitarian law and the challenges of contemporary armed conflicts, Document No. EN 31IC/11/5.1.2. https://www.icrc.org/eng/assets/files/red-cross-crescent-movement/31st-international-conference/31-int-conference-ihl-challenges-report-11-5-1-2-en.pdf. Accessed 11 April 2015
International Council on Human Rights Policy (2000), Ends and means: human rights approaches to armed groups. http://www.ichrp.org/files/reports/6/105_report_en.pdf. Accessed 11 April 2015
International Crisis Group (2009) Middle East report no.85, Gaza's unfinished business. http://www.crisisgroup.org/~/media/Files/Middle%20East%20North%20Africa/Israel%20Palestine/85%20Gazas%20Unfinished%20Business.pdf
Kaldor M (1999) New and old wars: organized violence in a global era. Polity Press, Oxford
Kinsella H (2011) The image before the weapon: a critical history of the distinction between combatant and civilian. Cornell University Press, Ithaca and London
Klabbers J (1996) The redundancy of soft law. Nord J Int Law 65:167–182
Lacina B, Gleditsch NP (2007) Monitoring trends in global combat: a new dataset of battle deaths. Eur J Popul 21:145–166
Mack A (1975) Why big nations lose small wars: the politics of asymmetric conflict. World Polit 27:175–200
Mallison WT, Mallison S (1978) Juridical status of privileged combatants under the Geneva protocol of 1977 concerning international conflicts. Law Contemp Probl 42:4–35
Maurer P (2014) Establishing a dedicated IHL compliance system. Opening speech at the third meeting of states on strengthening compliance with international humanitarian law, Geneva, 30 June–1 July 2014. https://www.icrc.org/eng/resources/documents/statement/2014/06-30-compliance-ihl-maurer.htm. Accessed 15 April 2015
McCormack T (1997) From Solferino to Sarajevo: a continuing role for international humanitarian law? Melbourne Univ Law Rev 21:621–649
McCoubrey H (1998) International humanitarian law: modern developments in the limitation of warfare, 2nd edn. Ashgate, Dartmouth
Metz S and Johnson D (2001) Asymmetry and US military strategy: definition, background, and strategic concepts. Strategic Studies Institute. http://www.strategicstudiesinstitute.army.mil/pdffiles/PUB223.pdf. Accessed 11 April 2014
Münkler H (2003) The wars of the 21st century. Int Rev Red Cross 849:7–22
Murphy S (ed) (2002) United States practice in international law. CUP, Cambridge
Palestinian weapons deployed against Israel during operation cast lead (2009) J Palestine Stud 39:192–200
Paulus A, Vashakmadze M (2009) Asymmetrical war and the notion of armed conflict—a tentative conceptualisation. Int Rev Red Cross 91:95–125
Pomerance M (1982) Self-determination in law and practice: the new doctrine of the United Nations. Martinus Nijhoff, The Hague
Reid Sarkees M (2000) The correlates of war data on war: an update to 1997. Confl Manage Peace Sci 18:123–144
Roberts A, Sivakumaran S (2012) Lawmaking by nonstate actors: engaging armed groups in the creation of international humanitarian law. Yale J Int Law 37:107–152
Robson S (2007) The first world war, 2nd edn. Pearson, Harlow
Rosenblad E (1978) International humanitarian law of armed conflict: some aspects of the principle of distinction and related problems. Henry Dunant Institute, Geneva
Rousseau J (1762) Du contrat social. http://www.constitution.org/jjr/socon.htm. Accessed 13 April 2015
Sandoz Y, Swinarski C, Zimmerman B (eds) (1987) Commentary on the additional protocols of 8 June 1977 to the Geneva Conventions of 12 August 1949. ICRC/Martinus Nijhoff, Geneva

Scahill J (2013) Dirty wars: the world is a battlefield. Serpent's Tail, London
Schachter O (1977) The twilight existence of nonbinding agreements. Am J Int Law 71:296–304
Schmitt M (2008) Asymmetrical warfare and international humanitarian law. Air Force Law Rev 62:1–42
Schwebel S (1974) Wars of liberation—as Fought in UN organs. In: Norton Moore J (ed) Law and civil war in the modern world. Johns Hopkins Press, Baltimore, pp 446–457
Scobbie I (2012) Gaza. In: Wilmshurst E (ed) International law and the classification of conflicts. OUP, Oxford, pp 280–316
Showalter D (2000) Mass warfare and the impact of technology. In: Chickering R, Forster S (eds) Great war, total war: combat and mobilization on the western front, 1914–1918. CUP, Cambridge, pp 73–94
Singh A (1998) The revolution in military affairs: 4-dimensional warfare. Strateg Anal 22:169–179
Sivakumaran S (2012a) The ownership of international humanitarian law: non-state armed groups and the formation of enforcement of IHL rules. In: Perrin B (ed) Modern warfare: armed groups, private militaries, humanitarian organisations, and the law. UBC Press, Vancouver, pp 87–101
Sivakumaran S (2012b) The law of non-international armed conflict. OUP, Oxford
Strachan H (2011) The changing character of war. In: Haug KE, Maaø OJ (eds) Conceptualising modern war. Columbia University Press, New York, pp 1–28
Suter K (1984) An international law of guerrilla warfare. St Martins Press, New York
Taber R (1970) The war of the flea: a study of guerrilla warfare theory and practice. Paladin, London
The Israeli arsenal deployed against Gaza during operation cast lead (2009) J PA Stud 8:175–191
Tooley H (2003) The western front: battle ground and home front in the first world war. Palgrave, New York
United Nations fact-finding mission on the Gaza conflict (2009) Report on human rights in Palestine and other occupied Arab territories (2009) UN Doc A/HRC/12/48
Van Creveld M (1989) Technology and war: from 2000 BC to the present. Free Press, New York
Vité S (2009) Typology of armed conflicts in international humanitarian law: legal concepts and actual situations. Int Rev Red Cross 91:69–94
Williamson W, Knox M (eds) (2001) The dynamics of military revolution, 1300–2050. CUP, Cambridge
Wilson H (1988) International law and the use of force by national liberation movements. Clarendon, Oxford

Part IV
Challenges to Humanitarian Assistance and Protection

Chapter 8
Humanitarian Activities Carried Out Across Borders in Times of Armed Conflict in the Light of State Sovereignty and International Humanitarian Law

Keiichiro Okimoto

Abstract The purpose of this chapter is to clarify the extent to which a State may exercise its discretion to decide whether to allow humanitarian organizations to carry out humanitarian activities across borders in times of armed conflict in the light of the principle of State sovereignty and international humanitarian law. In particular, this chapter discusses the interplay between the principle of sovereignty and international humanitarian law and clarifies the extent to which the applicable rules of international humanitarian law limit the exercise of the sovereign right to control the entry of humanitarian organizations into a State's territory. The chapter concludes that, in times of armed conflict, the consent of the State is required in order to carry out humanitarian activities in the territory of that State, including in those parts that are controlled by the enemy State or an armed group, but that the State's discretion to withhold consent is limited by specific rules of international humanitarian law as well as by binding decisions of the Security Council.

Keywords Sovereignty · International humanitarian law · Humanitarian activities · Armed conflict · Consent

The views expressed herein are those of the author and do not necessarily reflect the views of the United Nations.

K. Okimoto (✉)
Office of the Legal Counsel, Office of Legal Affairs, Secretariat of the United Nations, New York, USA
e-mail: okeiichiro4@hotmail.com

T.D. Gill et al. (eds.), *Yearbook of International Humanitarian Law 2014*,
Yearbook of International Humanitarian Law 17,
DOI 10.1007/978-94-6265-091-6_8

Contents

8.1 Introduction

Humanitarian activities carried out by humanitarian organizations across borders and into a State's territory during armed conflict are not a new phenomenon. While pragmatism has often played an important role in reaching those in need and delivering the help they need, legal aspects of such humanitarian activities have, on occasion, become contentious particularly when State sovereignty and its associated rights and obligations appear to be the source of obstacle for humanitarian organizations to cross the border and reach those who are in need of help.[1]

This chapter revisits these issues from the perspective of both general international law, particularly the principle of sovereignty, and international humanitarian law (IHL). This chapter will first discuss the extent to which a State may exercise its discretion to allow, or not to allow, humanitarian organizations to carry out humanitarian activities on its territory during armed conflict, in the light of the principle of State sovereignty. It will then discuss the extent to which IHL limits the exercise of the sovereign right of a State to control the entry of humanitarian organizations into that State's territory to carry out humanitarian activities. It will also discuss the legal consequences in case a party to an armed conflict withholds consent to external humanitarian activities in violation of IHL, and the role of binding decisions of the Security Council.

This chapter deals with humanitarian activities in general and is not confined to the narrower activity of humanitarian assistance or relief actions, such as the delivery of foodstuffs and medical supplies. Whatever the humanitarian activity, such as visits to prisoners of war or medical care for the wounded and sick, external humanitarian organizations are required to cross the border of a State. Therefore, State sovereignty is relevant in all cases of humanitarian activities carried out across borders.

In addition, it is also noted that this chapter mainly deals with humanitarian activities carried out by international organizations, particularly by the United Nations.

[1]See generally, Meyer 1989; Kalshoven (ed) 1989; Plattner 1992; Torrelli 1992; Schindler 1994; Dinstein 2000; Bugnion 2003; Stoffels 2004; Barber 2009; Schwendimann 2011; Gillard 2013; Ryngaert 2013 and the International Committee of the Red Cross (ICRC) 2014.

8.2 Sovereignty of States

When an international organization contemplates a humanitarian activity across the border and into a territory of a State in times of armed conflict, two sets of rules of international law become particularly relevant: the principle of sovereignty and IHL. These sets of rules constitute a two-pronged test to assess not only the legality of the humanitarian activity but also the legality of the State's reaction to the offer of such humanitarian activity, particularly the refusal of or the lack of response to such offer.

As far as the principle of sovereignty is concerned, unlike IHL, which specifically applies in times of armed conflict and contains specific rules concerning humanitarian activities, it is of general application and therefore is applicable to various situations where an international organization enters a territory of a State.[2] Humanitarian activities carried out across borders in times of armed conflict are just one of such situations.

Humanitarian activities may be carried out in various ways, such as by land, air or sea; in various types of territory, such as in a territory of a State occupied by another State or controlled by an armed group, or a State without a government; and for various types of persons who do not or no longer take a direct part in hostilities, such as civilians, the wounded and sick, prisoners of war, internees, and other detainees. Whatever the form a humanitarian activity takes, the fact that an international organization takes action in a territory of a State gives rise to the question of whether it has been carried out with full respect of that State's sovereignty.

The rights and obligations that derive from the principle of sovereignty that are most relevant to cross-border humanitarian activities are the inviolability of the territorial integrity and political independence of the State concerned,[3] the right of that State to exercise jurisdiction over their territory and over all persons and things therein,[4] and the duty not to intervene in matters within the domestic jurisdiction of that State, including their internal and external affairs (principle of nonintervention).[5]

---

[2]E.g., the principle of nonintervention, which derives from State sovereignty, was applied in the *Nicaragua* case in relation to the legality of a use of force and the principle of sovereignty was applied in the *Jurisdictional Immunities of the State* case in relation to the immunity of State from the jurisdiction of another State. See, International Court of Justice (ICJ), *Case concerning Military and Paramilitary Activities in and against Nicaragua (Merits)*, 27 June 1986, para 251; *Jurisdictional Immunities of the State (Merits)*, 3 February 2012, para 57.

[3]Declaration on Principles of International Law concerning Friendly Relations and Cooperation among States in accordance with the Charter of the United Nations, General Assembly resolution 2625 (XXV) of 24 October 1970 (1970 Friendly Relations Declaration).

[4]Article 2, Draft Declaration on Rights and Duties of States, General Assembly resolution 375 (IV) of 6 December 1949, Annex (1949 Draft Declaration).

[5]1970 Friendly Relations Declaration. See also, Article 3, 1949 Draft Declaration; para 1, Declaration on the Inadmissibility of Intervention in the Domestic Affairs of States and Protection of Their Independence and Sovereignty, General Assembly resolution 2131 (XX) of 21 December 1965.

While the duty to respect these rights and obligations was traditionally incumbent upon States, international organizations, as subjects of international law, are also bound by it. For example, Article 2 of the Charter of the United Nations provides that "[t]he Organization [the Untied Nations] and its Members…shall act in accordance with the following Principles" including "the principle of the sovereign equality of all its Members" and the prohibition on "the United Nations to intervene in matters which are essentially within the domestic jurisdiction of any state" except where enforcement measures are taken under Chapter VII of the Charter.

With respect to the question of whether cross-border humanitarian activities are consistent with the principle of nonintervention, the International Court of Justice stated in the *Nicaragua* case that "[t]here can be no doubt that the provision of strictly humanitarian aid to persons or forces in another country, whatever their political affiliations or objectives, cannot be regarded as unlawful intervention, or as in any other way contrary to international law."[6] However, at the same time, the State on whose territory humanitarian activities are carried out still retains the right to exercise jurisdiction over their territory and over all persons and things therein.[7] In practical terms, one of the clearest reflections of this right is the right of the territorial State to give or not to give consent to a humanitarian activity carried out by an outside entity on its own territory.[8]

Consent of the territorial State as a requirement in case of cross-border humanitarian assistance was subsequently confirmed by the General Assembly, thereby clarifying the role of State sovereignty specifically in the context of humanitarian assistance. In its guiding principles on emergency humanitarian assistance, the General Assembly explicitly stated that "[t]he sovereignty, territorial integrity and national unity of States must be fully respected in accordance with the Charter of the United Nations. In this context, humanitarian assistance should be provided with the consent of the affected country."[9] The guiding principles were adopted by the General Assembly by consensus, which reflects the general agreement of the

[6] *Nicaragua* case, para 242.

[7] Schindler 1994, p. 699.

[8] Kalshoven 1989, pp. 22–23; Torrelli, p. 232.

[9] General Assembly resolution 46/182 of 19 December 1991, Annex, para 3. See also, General Assembly resolution 2675 (XXV) of 9 December 1970 entitled "Basic principles for the protection of civilian populations in armed conflicts" which provides, in operative para 8, that "[t]he provision of international relief to civilian populations is in conformity with the humanitarian principles of the Charter of the United Nations" and further provides that "[t]he Declaration of Principles for International Humanitarian Relief to the Civilian Population in Disaster Situations, as laid down in resolution XXVI adopted by the twenty-first International Conference of the Red Cross, shall apply in situations of armed conflict, and all parties to a conflict should make every effort to facilitate the application." The Declaration in question provides that "[r]elief by impartial international humanitarian organisations for civilian population in natural or other disaster situations…should be so organised as to avoid prejudicing sovereign and other legal rights." See ICRC 1969, p. 632.

membership of the United Nations.[10] Although the guiding principles do not specify whether they also apply during armed conflict, subsequent practice of the Security Council shows that they also apply with respect to situations of armed conflict.[11] Therefore, the General Assembly and the Security Council clearly confirmed that the principle of sovereignty requires the consent of the State in whose territory humanitarian assistance is to take place in order for that assistance to be lawful under international law in times of armed conflict.[12]

However, the principle of sovereignty does not provide detailed guidance on the specific circumstances in which the right to give or not to give consent to a humanitarian activity may be exercised. This is where IHL complements the principle of sovereignty, and provides for specific rules that set out the conditions under which the right to give or not to give consent may be exercised.

At the same time, IHL, on occasion, does not fully clarify whether the territorial State may exercise the right to give or not to give consent. In particular, it has been argued that, when the territorial State loses control of a portion of its territory, IHL only requires that the humanitarian activity destined for that portion be authorized by the entity which is actually controlling that portion, and the consent of the territorial State is not necessary. In such instances, the principle of sovereignty could complement IHL and provide greater clarity as to whether the territorial State may exercise the right to give or not to give consent.[13]

The following section discusses these aspects in greater detail.

8.3 International Humanitarian Law

A number of IHL rules deal with humanitarian activities carried out by humanitarian organizations during armed conflict, including across the frontiers of States. Each rule contains different conditions for humanitarian organizations to lawfully carry out humanitarian activities in a State's territory, and grounds which may be invoked by a State not to accept humanitarian activities. These rules will be individually examined below.

---

[10] A/46/PV.78, p. 41. See also, *United Nations Juridical Yearbook, 2003*, p. 533.

[11] See, e.g., Security Council resolution 2126 (2013), para 20, on Abyei; Security Council resolution 2127 (2013), para 52, on the Central African Republic; Security Council resolution 2139 (2014), para 4, on Syria.

[12] See also, Article IV(2), Institute of International Law's resolution on "Humanitarian Assistance" of 2 September 2003; Article 14(1), International Law Commission's draft articles on protection of persons in the event of disasters, adopted on its first reading, A/69/10, para 55.

[13] As Article 31(3)(c) of the 1969 Vienna Convention on the Law of Treaties provides, "any relevant rules of international law applicable in the relations between the parties" should be taken into account in interpreting treaties.

8.3.1 International Armed Conflict (General)

8.3.1.1 Conditions Attached to Entities and Persons Carrying Out Humanitarian Activities

IHL contains specific provisions that require entities carrying out humanitarian activities to obtain consent of the parties to an international armed conflict, thereby confirming the principle of sovereignty and its associated rights and obligations under general international law. Thus, humanitarian organizations should be "duly authorized by the respective Parties to the conflict" to carry out humanitarian activities under the 1949 Geneva Conventions and 1977 Protocol I.[14] Similarly, "the consent of the Parties to the conflict concerned" is required to carry out humanitarian activities beyond those specified in the Geneva Conventions and Protocol I.[15] The Protecting Powers, although they are not an institution frequently employed in international armed conflict, may carry out certain humanitarian activities, but their delegates are "subject to the approval of the Power with which they are to carry out their duties."[16] These provisions clearly require the consent or authorization of the State in whose territory humanitarian activities will be carried out, including with respect to humanitarian activities to be carried out in a territory over which that State has lost control.

The International Committee of the Red Cross (ICRC) is in a different category, as Article 81(1) of Protocol I specifically requires the parties to a conflict to grant the ICRC "all facilities within their power so as to enable it to carry out the humanitarian functions assigned to it by the Conventions and this Protocol." Therefore, while States parties to the conflict retain the authority to grant facilities to the ICRC, the sovereign right of those States to decide whether to allow or not to allow such facilities is strictly limited. However, with respect to humanitarian activities other than those specified in the Geneva Conventions and Protocol I, the ICRC's actions are "subject to the consent of the Parties to the conflict concerned."[17]

Apart from the provisions concerning specific entities, Protocol I specifically deals with relief personnel and provides that their participation in relief actions "shall be subject to the approval of the Party in whose territory they will carry out their duties" pursuant to Article 71(1). A commentary to this provision argues that

---

[14]Article 81(4), Protocol Additional to the Geneva Conventions of 12 August 1949, and Relating to the Protection of Victims of International Armed Conflicts (Protocol I).

[15]Article 9, Geneva Convention for the Amelioration of the Condition of the Wounded and Sick in Armed Forces in the Field (GC/I); Article 9, Geneva Convention for the Amelioration of the Condition of Wounded, Sick and Shipwrecked Members of Armed Forces at Sea (GC/II); Article 9, Geneva Convention Relative to the Treatment of Prisoners of War (GC/III); Article 10, Geneva Convention Relative to the Protection of Civilian Persons in Time of War (GC/IV).

[16]Article 8, GC/I; Article 8, GC/II; Article 8, GC/III; Article 9, GC/IV.

[17]See also Article 9, GC I; Article 9, GC/II; Article 9, GC/III; Article 10, GC/IV.

the party from which the approval should be obtained is "the Party which exercises control over this territory [in which relief action is carried out], e.g., in the case of occupied territories, the Occupying Power, and not the Party whose territory is occupied."[18] While this position may be valid from a very narrow perspective of IHL, under general international law, even if a part of the State's territory is occupied, the occupied State still exercises sovereignty over the occupied territory.[19] Hence, for example, if relief personnel of an international organization enter that occupied territory without the approval of the occupied State, it could be a breach of the sovereignty of that State. An indicative example in this regard is the occupation of Jersey and Guernsey by Germany during the Second World War, when the ICRC obtained consent not only from the occupying power, Germany, but also from the United Kingdom, the State which had sovereignty over the territory, to deliver relief supplies to the two islands.[20]

Moreover, Article 71(1) deliberately uses the phrase "the Party in whose territory," while it could have been worded more specifically if it was to indicate "the Party which exercises control over the territory." For example, Article 47(2)(d) of Protocol I employs the expression "territory controlled by a Party to the conflict."[21] Following this formulation, Article 71(1) could have been drafted as "subject to the approval of the Party to the conflict controlling the territory." The negotiating history of Article 71(1) also does not contain any indication supporting the commentary's interpretation.[22] Therefore, Article 71(1) seems to require the consent of the State that has sovereignty over the territory in which relief action takes place.[23] However, as a practical matter, the consent of the enemy State that has actual control over the territory may be necessary to gain access to the civilian population in need.

The consent of both the occupied State and the occupying power is particularly required when occupation is partial, and when the central government of the occupied State is still functioning alongside the authorities of the occupying power. An indicative example is when the ICRC obtained the consent of both France and Germany, when it delivered relief supplies to civilians trapped in French cities still occupied by Germany in the summer of 1944.[24] However, a case of total occupation, such as that by the United States and the United Kingdom from 2003 to

[18]Sandoz et al. (eds) 1987, para 2881.

[19]See e.g. Brownlie 1998, p. 107.

[20]Bugnion 2003, p. 226.

[21]In addition, the following expressions are employed in Protocol I: Articles 42(2)—"in territory controlled by an adverse Party"; Article 46(2)—"in territory controlled by an adverse Party"; Article 47(2)(d)—"of territory controlled by a Party to the conflict"; Article 49(2)—"the national territory belonging to a Party to the conflict but under the control of an adverse Party"; Article 70(1)—"any territory under the control of a Party to the conflict."

[22]See the references in Sandoz et al. (eds) 1987, p. 831.

[23]See Meyer 1989, p. 218.

[24]Bugnion 2003, p. 226.

2004, presents different issues, as there may be no functioning central government of the occupied State. This issue is dealt with in more depth in Sect. 8.4 below.

8.3.1.2 Conditions Attached to Humanitarian Activities for Specific Categories of Persons

With respect to humanitarian activities in favor of prisoners of war (POWs) and civilian internees, international relief societies may distribute relief supplies and material for educational, recreational or religious purposes, including across borders. However, the Detaining Power has the authority to (1) subject those societies to the measures it may consider essential to ensure their security or to meet any other reasonable need, and (2) limit the number of societies and supervise their activities, so long as it does not hinder the supply of effective and adequate relief to POWs and internees.[25] The discretion of the Detaining Power not to allow such societies to carry out humanitarian activities is very broad, and even if they are allowed, it may subject relief societies to measures that meet "any other reasonable need" of the Detaining Power.

The discretion of the parties to the conflict to decide whether to allow humanitarian activities is significantly limited with respect to access by the Protecting Powers and the ICRC to POWs and civilian internees. Thus, their delegates "shall" have access to all places where POWs and civilian internees are present, be able to interview them, and have full liberty to determine the places they wish to visit and the duration and frequency of such visits.[26] The consent of the Detaining Power is clearly required to access POWs and civilian internees. In case the Detaining Power is holding POWs and civilian internees in the territory of an enemy State, the consent of that enemy State is also required as that State continues to exercise sovereignty over the territory in question. However, the parties to the conflict may prohibit their visits only on one ground: "reasons of imperative military necessity, and then only as an exceptional and temporary measure." Therefore, States involved in allowing the Protecting Powers and the ICRC to gain access to POWs and internees have very limited scope of discretion to prohibit such access. In practice, the ICRC was not able to access POWs for an extended period of time during the Iran–Iraq War,[27] and the Eritrea–Ethiopia Claims Commission concluded that refusal to permit the ICRC to have access to POWs for more than 2 years during the Eritrea-Ethiopia Conflict was unlawful under IHL.[28]

With respect to relief actions for the civilian population, Article 23 of the Fourth Convention requires each State party to allow the free passage of limited types of objects, namely "all consignments of medical and hospital stores and

[25] Article 125, GC/III; Article 142, GC/IV.

[26] Article 126, GC/III; Article 143, GC/IV.

[27] ICRC 1983, p. 221; ICRC 1984, p. 114.

[28] Eritrea-Ethiopia Claims Commission, *Prisoners of War, Ethiopia's Claim 4*, 1 July 2003, para 62.

objects necessary for religious worship intended only for civilians of another High Contracting Party," and additionally, "all consignments of essential foodstuffs, clothing and tonics intended for children under fifteen, expectant mothers and maternity cases." However, any party to the Fourth Convention may refuse the passage of such relief consignments if it has serious reasons for fearing:

(1) that the consignments may be diverted from their destination;
(2) that the supervision may not be effective, or
(3) that the consignments may offer a definite military advantage to the military efforts or economy of the enemy.

The drafters of this provision, based on their experience during the Second World War, included these grounds, which potentially provide a broad discretion to refuse passage of relief consignments, mainly to prevent a situation where relief actions compromise the effectiveness of a blockade imposed on an enemy State.[29]

Article 70(1) of Protocol I went beyond the mind-set of blockade and required that "[i]f the civilian population of any territory under the control of a Party to the conflict…is not adequately provided with the supplies mentioned in Article 69, relief actions which are humanitarian and impartial in character and conducted without any adverse distinction shall be undertaken, subject to the agreement of the Parties concerned in such relief actions."[30] The phrase "agreement of the Parties concerned in such relief actions" has been interpreted in different ways.

On the one hand, the drafters of the provision seemed to have envisaged an agreement concluded between the parties to the conflict. The report of Committee II of the 1974–1977 Diplomatic Conference, which drafted Article 70, to the Plenary states that the draft article "should be reworded to state that relief actions shall be carried out in accordance with agreements concluded between the Parties."[31] Committee II therefore adopted the draft with the phrase "subject to the agreement of the Parties concerned in such relief actions." This indicates that relief actions under Article 70(1) are to be undertaken only if the parties to the conflict have come to an agreement between them, which is different from consent given by each party to the conflict to humanitarian organizations. However, this does not exclude the possibility that subsequent practice has given a different meaning to the phrase in question.[32]

In this connection, it has been argued that Article 70(1) primarily requires the agreement of the parties from which the relief is to come and the parties for which the relief is intended.[33] Therefore, if, for example, relief actions are destined for a territory controlled by an invading State, the agreement of that invading State

[29]Switzerland 1949, Vol II A, pp. 819–820.

[30]This rule has become part of customary international law. See rule 55, Henckaerts and Doswald-Beck 2005, p. 193.

[31]Switzerland 1978, Vol. XIII, p. 379.

[32]See Article 31(3) (b), 1969 Vienna Convention on the Law of Treaties. See also, Plattner 1992, p. 258; Spieker 2011, p. 13; Gillard 2013, pp. 363–364.

[33]Sandoz et al. (eds) 1987, para 2807.

suffices and that of the invaded State is not required. However, this interpretation is hardly consistent with the principles of sovereignty and nonintervention as the invaded State still has sovereignty over the territory controlled by the invading State.[34] The interpretation above is also prone to challenge in the light of the more specific languages used in other parts of Protocol I. As noted earlier, for example, Article 47(2) (d) employs the expression "territory controlled by a Party to the conflict." Following this wording, the phrase in question in Article 70(1) could have been drafted as "subject to the agreement of the Party controlling the territory" to indicate that only the party exercising actual control over a territory may allow or refuse relief actions.

A relevant case in this regard is the conflict in the former Yugoslavia in the early 1990s during which Bosnia and Herzegovina and the Bosnian Serb forces, which were acting on behalf of the Federal Republic of Yugoslavia,[35] concluded agreements that provided for free flow of humanitarian supplies into Srebrenica and Zepa.[36] In this case, the Bosnian Serb forces had control over areas around the two towns, but Bosnia and Herzegovina had sovereignty over those areas. Therefore, in this particular case, both the entity that had actual control over the areas concerned and the territorial State gave their agreement to the provision of humanitarian supplies.

The conflict in the former Yugoslavia is also relevant in the sense that, in a few cases, the International Tribunal for the former Yugoslavia (ICTY) examined the legality of a specific justification to restrict relief actions, namely the alleged lack of impartiality of relief actions. A case in point is the *Popović* et al. case. In this case, the Trial Chamber concluded that Radivoje Miletić, a general of the Bosnian Serb forces, was guilty of crimes against humanity, partly because his involvement in, and use of the convoy approval and notification procedure restricted humanitarian aid to Srebrenica and Zepa, which created the conditions for forcible transfer of the population.[37] However, at the Appeals Chamber, he argued that a portion of the humanitarian aid was used to supply the Bosnia and Herzegovina armed forces, which "constituted an independent justification for the restrictions placed upon some of the convoys."[38] The Appeals Chamber admitted "the applicable international humanitarian law did not oblige the VRS [Bosnian Serb forces] to allow passage of consignments of humanitarian aid for the benefit of the ABiH [Army of Bosnia and Herzegovina], or of military equipment under the guise of humanitarian aid. Such consignments were deprived of their impartial character."[39]

---

[34]Meyer 1989, p. 215; Ryngaert 2013, p. 6.

[35]*Prosecutor v. Tadić* (Judgment, Appeals Chamber) ICTY-IT-94-1-A, para 162. ICTY concluded that "even after 19 May 1992 the armed conflict in Bosnia and Herzegovina between the Bosnian Serbs and the central authorities of Bosnia and Herzegovina must be classified as an *international* armed conflict" (emphasis in original).

[36]S/25700, Annex II and A/54/549, para 65.

[37]*Prosecutor v. Popović* et al. (Judgment, Trial Chamber), IT-05-88-T, para 1710.

[38]*Prosecutor v. Popović* et al. (Judgment, Appeals Chamber), IT-05-88-A, para 608.

[39]Ibid, para 615.

However, the Appeals Chamber rejected the accused's argument, partly because there was no indication that the blocked humanitarian convoys contained military articles.[40]

Similarly, in the *Tolimir* case, the Trial Chamber concluded that Zdravko Tolimir, a military commander of the Bosnian Serb forces, was guilty of crimes against humanity, partly because he participated in the restrictions of convoys entering Srebrenica and Zepa, which led to the forcible removal of the Bosnian Muslim population of Eastern Bosnia and Herzegovina.[41] However, at the Appeals Chamber, he argued "impeding the passage of prohibited convoys could not contribute to a criminal enterprise, because it is the right of a warring party under international humanitarian law to approve or reject such convoys."[42] The Appeals Chamber admitted that "while Additional Protocol I allows a party to a conflict to prescribe technical requirements for the passage of convoys, it also prohibits any interference with humanitarian relief consignments" and held that the accused's argument that the Bosnian Serb forces had limitless discretion in deciding humanitarian convoys to allow into Srebrenica and Zepa was not correct under IHL.[43] The Appeals Chamber also referred to the *Popović et al.* case and concluded that Tolimir "[did] not point to any evidence and [did] not even allege that the unauthorised humanitarian aid convoys were essentially dispatches of military equipment or other aid to the ABiH and were thus not impartial."[44] It therefore rejected this portion of appeal by Tolimir.

These cases were useful in highlighting that IHL imposes limitations on the discretion of the conflicting parties not to allow humanitarian activities, and that the grounds that may be invoked to withhold consent to such activities are specifically set out in the relevant rules of IHL.

8.3.2 International Armed Conflict (Occupation)

The key provision dealing with relief actions for the civilian population in an occupied territory is Article 59 of the Fourth Convention.[45] Unlike Article 23 of that Convention, Article 59 requires the occupying power to agree to relief schemes for the civilian population,[46] and does not restrict the type of relief consignments. However, the obligation to agree to relief schemes applies only "[i]f the whole or part of the population of an occupied territory is inadequately supplied."

---

[40]Ibid, para 616.

[41]*Prosecutor v. Tolimir* (Judgment, Trial Chamber) IT-05-88/2-T, paras 1093–1095.

[42]*Prosecutor v. Tolimir* (Judgment, Appeals Chamber) IT-05-88/2-A, para 323.

[43]Ibid, para 329.

[44]Ibid.

[45]See also Article 69, Protocol I.

[46]Schwendimann 2011, p. 1002; Gillard 2013, pp. 357–358.

While the obligation of the occupying power to allow relief actions in an occupied territory is peremptory, it still retains the authority to grant its agreement to those relief actions. The occupying power does not exercise sovereignty over the occupied territory so its authority to grant agreement to relief actions does not derive from the sovereignty, but rather from its temporary obligation to "take all the measures in his power to restore and ensure, as far as possible, public order and safety."[47] However, the only ground the occupying power may invoke to withhold its agreement to relief schemes is the adequate provision of supplies to the population of the occupied territory. No other ground may be invoked.

With respect to the State whose territory has been occupied by the enemy State, under Article 59, it is required to permit the free passage of relief consignments destined for the population in the occupied territory. At the same time, because it still has the sovereignty over the occupied territory, it still retains the power to consent to the passage of such consignments. However, that power is limited by the Fourth Convention since it only allows the occupied State to refuse the passage of such consignments on three grounds: (1) if a humanitarian organization refuses the search of the consignments by the occupied State when requested; (2) if a humanitarian organization declines the time and routes prescribed by the occupied States; or (3) if it has concrete evidence that the consignments are to be used for the benefit of the occupying power.

8.3.3 Non-international Armed Conflict

Article 3 common to the Geneva Conventions provides that "[a]n impartial humanitarian body, such as the International Committee of the Red Cross, may offer its services to the Parties to the conflict." In the absence of any specific mention, it cannot be presumed that the parties are obliged to accept the offer.[48] Rather, the parties have a broad discretion to decide whether to accept the offer or not.

However, if a government refuses the offer but the armed group opposing it accepts it, is an impartial humanitarian body permitted to carry out humanitarian activities in the territory controlled by the armed group, without the consent of the government? An argument has been made that "[w]hen the situation of the victims so demands and they can be reached without crossing territory controlled by the party that claims to be the legitimate government, the International Committee [of the Red Cross] is therefore entitled to perform its humanitarian activities in areas outside that party's control without necessarily having to obtain its [the legitimate government's] consent."[49] However, because common Article 3 does not explicitly

---

[47] Article 43, 1907 Regulations concerning the Laws and Customs of War on Land.

[48] Pictet et al. 1952 (GC/IV), p. 41; ICRC 1971, Vol V, p. 73; Barber 2009, p. 385.

[49] Bugnion 2003, p. 450.

permit humanitarian activities without the consent of the government concerned, States that have become parties to the Geneva Conventions cannot be deemed to have renounced their sovereign right to control the entry of humanitarian organizations into their territory, even if those organizations are directly destined for an area controlled by an armed group.

Protocol II is more explicit with respect to the sovereignty of States as its Article 3 provides that "[n]othing in this Protocol shall be invoked for the purpose of affecting the sovereignty of a State" and that "[n]othing in this Protocol shall be invoked as a justification for intervening, directly or indirectly, for any reason whatever, in the armed conflict or in the internal or external affairs of the High Contracting Party in the territory of which that conflict occurs." These provisions clearly preserve the sovereignty of States and the associated rights and obligations under general international law.[50]

Other provisions in Protocol II should be seen in the light of Article 3 of that Protocol.[51] Article 18(2) of the Protocol, in particular, provides that "[i]f the civilian population is suffering undue hardship owing to a lack of the supplies essential for its survival, such as foodstuffs and medical supplies, relief actions for the civilian population which are of an exclusively humanitarian and impartial in nature and which are conducted without any adverse distinction shall be undertaken subject to the consent of the High Contracting Party concerned."[52]

The phrase "the High Contracting Party concerned" has been interpreted by some experts as meaning the government in power,[53] whereas others have interpreted it as meaning the party which has actual control over the territory. According to the latter view, "the consent of the established government of a country is required only where a relief action has to pass over territory which is effectively controlled by that government…where the territory controlled by the insurgents is accessible from the sea or directly from another country, it seems to be a reasonable interpretation of Article 18 not to require the consent of the established government."[54] A similar argument was made in relation to the situation in Syria in 2014.[55]

In the light of Article 3 of Protocol II, Article 18(2) may not be invoked to disregard sovereignty of a State. Therefore, a State has the right to decide whether to consent to relief actions on its territory, even if part of the territory may currently

---

[50]Kalshoven 1989, p. 23.

[51]As Article 31(2) of the 1969 Vienna Convention on the Law of Treaties provides, the "context" should be taken into account in interpreting a treaty, including the text of the treaty concerned.

[52]This rule has become part of customary international law. See rule 55, Henckaerts and Doswald-Beck 2005, p. 193.

[53]Sandoz et al. (eds) 1987, para 4884; Meyer 1989, p. 221; Plattner 1992, p. 260; Stoffels 2004, pp. 534–535.

[54]Bothe 1989, p. 94.

[55]Akhavan et al. 2014.

be under the control of an armed group.[56] In this regard, a commentary to Article 3 makes reference to Article 18(2) and states "there is no obligation to accept assistance from such an organization [humanitarian organization]. Parties remain free to accept or refuse assistance offered them, precisely in order to retain their complete freedom of judgment and so as not be exposed to external interventions."[57] The only circumstance precluding a breach of sovereignty is the consent given by the State in question. In this sense, neither Article 3 to the Geneva Conventions nor Protocol II derogate from the principle of State sovereignty.[58]

However, Protocol II contains obligations that have the effect of limiting the scope of a State party's discretion whether to grant or not to grant consent to relief actions. First, when "the civilian population is suffering undue hardship owing to a lack of the supplies essential for its survival," the State party concerned will automatically be required to allow humanitarian organizations to enter its territory and carry out relief actions.[59] The consent of the State party required by Article 18(2) becomes a mere formality. The only grounds that the State party may invoke to withhold consent are the following: (1) the civilian population is not suffering undue hardship or (2) the relief actions are not of an exclusively humanitarian and impartial nature, and are carried out with adverse distinction.

Furthermore, Article 14 of Protocol II prohibits "[s]tarvation of civilians as a method of combat." A breach of this provision, for example by systematically taking foodstuffs away from civilians which eventually leads to the starvation of civilians, would inevitably lead to a situation where "the civilian population is suffering undue hardship owing to a lack of the supplies essential for its survival", which then requires the State party to allow external relief actions.

Moreover, Article 4(1) of Protocol II prohibits any order to the effect that there shall be no survivors. If a party to a non-international armed conflict orders a siege for a specific village with a view to starving the entire civilian population to death,

---

[56]ICRC 1971, Vol V, p. 74; ICRC 1972 Vol I, p. 89; Switzerland 1978 Vol IV, p. 106; Vol VII, pp. 146–147, 163; Vol XII, pp. 348, 351–53, 406, 407, and 410; Spieker 2011, p. 15; Gillard 2013, p. 366; Ryngaert 2013, p. 17. However, for slightly different views, see, Switzerland 1978 Vol VII, pp. 147, 156, and 157.

[57]Sandoz et al. (eds) 1987, para 4505. See also, Barber 2009, p. 386.

[58]See, however, the ICRC practice in the conflicts in Biafra, Nigeria, and Cambodia. In 1968, during the conflict in Biafra, the ICRC negotiated with the Government of Nigeria with a view to placing a landing strip in Biafra under ICRC control for the purpose of delivering relief consignments in Biafra. However, it appears that, after failing to obtain the consent of the Government, the ICRC nevertheless placed the landing strip under its control. See, ICRC 1968, pp. 460–461. Furthermore, the ICRC and the United Nations Children's Fund (UNICEF) negotiated with the authorities of the People's Republic of Kampuchea in 1979 in order to deliver relief consignments to displaced persons on the Cambodian side of the Thai–Cambodia border. The authorities protested such proposal, but it seems that the ICRC and UNICEF nevertheless carried out such cross-border humanitarian assistance. See, Bugnion 2003, pp. 811–812 and ICRC 1979, pp. 323–324.

[59]Plattner 1992, p. 260; Henckaerts and Doswald-Beck 2005, p. 197. See, however, Dinstein 2000, pp. 85–86.

and if that order is implemented, this would lead to a breach of Article 4(1) as well as Article 14 mentioned above. Such a situation would simultaneously require the State party concerned to allow external relief actions pursuant to Article 18(2).

8.4 Legal Consequences of Unlawfully Preventing Humanitarian Activities

When a State exercises its rights deriving from sovereignty and prevents a humanitarian organization from carrying out its humanitarian activities in a manner that is inconsistent with the limits imposed by the relevant rules of IHL, this would be a breach of an international obligation.[60] Two main legal consequences follow such a breach: (1) individual criminal responsibility[61] and (2) State responsibility.

First, in an international armed conflict, intentionally using starvation of civilians as a method of warfare by depriving them of objects indispensable to their survival, including wilfully impeding relief supplies as provided for under the Geneva Conventions, is a war crime.[62] Thus, for example, an individual who internationally withholds consent to relief actions to be carried out by external humanitarian organizations for the civilian population, while they are suffering from the lack of supplies, may amount to a war crime.

Furthermore, "extermination" is an act that constitutes a crime against humanity in the Rome Statute of the International Criminal Court.[63] According to the Statute, "extermination" includes "the intentional infliction of conditions of life, *inter alia* the deprivation of access to food and medicine, calculated to bring about the destruction of part of a population." Therefore, as long as the other requirements are met, the obstruction of humanitarian assistance could amount to a crime against humanity.

In the *Popović* et al. and *Tolimir* cases, ICTY found the accused guilty of crimes against humanity partly because of their involvement in the restriction on humanitarian assistance to Srebrenica and Zepa. In those cases, ICTY found that

---

[60]It has been said that such action by a State to prevent humanitarian activities constitutes an "arbitrary" denial of consent to humanitarian activities, but the test of arbitrariness does not yet exist in the lex lata. Withholding of consent to humanitarian activities is either lawful or unlawful, rather than arbitrary or not, by assessing it in the light of the existing rules of international law in force. It is, however, noted that some instruments refer to the test of arbitrariness in giving consent to humanitarian activities, although none of these is binding under international law: Article 5, Resolution of the Institute of International Law on the protection of human rights and the principles of nonintervention in internal affairs of States (1989); Article VIII(1), Resolution of the Institute of International Law on humanitarian assistance (2003); Principle 25(2), Guiding principles on internal displacement (E/CN.4/1998/53/Add.2).

[61]See generally Rottensteiner 1999.

[62]Article 8(2)(b)(xxv), Rome Statute of the International Criminal Court.

[63]Article 7(1)(b), Rome Statute of the International Criminal Court.

such restriction contributed to the forcible transfer of Bosnian Muslims.[64] That forcible transfer was considered an inhumane act which was an act constituting crimes against humanity under Article 5(i) of the ICTY Statute.[65]

Furthermore, in the *Prlić* et al. case, ICTY found five out of the six accused guilty of grave breaches of the Geneva Conventions, violations of the laws or customs of war, and crimes against humanity partly on the basis that they had blocked the delivery of humanitarian aid to East Mostar.[66]

Apart from the individual criminal responsibility, when there is a breach of an international obligation, a State becomes immediately under the obligation to cease the breach and make full reparation for the injury caused by such breach.[67] The obligations to bear responsibility and make full reparation, including compensation, for breaches of IHL are explicitly provided for in the 1907 Hague Convention,[68] Geneva Conventions[69] and Protocol I,[70] which have also now become part of customary international law applicable to both international and non-international armed conflict.[71]

Whether withholding of consent by a State in whose territory humanitarian activities are intended to take place amounts to a breach of IHL depends on the applicable rule. In the case of Article 3 common of the Geneva Conventions, there is no restriction on the discretion of the parties to the conflict whether to accept an offer of service by a humanitarian organization. Therefore, the mere fact that a State does not accept the offer of service does not give rise to State responsibility.

On the other hand, the only ground which a State may invoke to withhold permission to the Protecting Powers and the ICRC to visit POWs and civilians internees is "imperative military necessity," which may only be invoked as an "exceptional and temporary measure."[72] If a Detaining Power cannot justify the withholding of such permission for reasons of "imperative military necessity," it will be in breach of the Third and Fourth Geneva Conventions and will be under an obligation to cease such breach and immediately grant permission. In addition, if POWs and internees are held in a territory other than that of the Detaining Power, such as an occupied territory, the State whose territory was occupied may only prohibit the entry into its territory and access to POWs and internees by the

---

[64] *Popović* et al. case (Trial), para 1710; *Tolimir* case (Trial), paras 1093–1095.

[65] *Popović* et al. case (Trial), para 2108; *Tolimir* case (Trial), para 1197.

[66] *Prosecutor v. Prlić* et al. (Judgment, Trial Chamber), IT-04-74-T, Vol 4, pp. 96, 142–143, 253–254, 316–317, and 380–381.

[67] Articles 30 and 31, draft articles on responsibility of States for internationally wrongful acts, General Assembly resolution 56/83 of 12 December 2001, Annex.

[68] Article 3, 1907 Convention (IV) Respecting the Laws and Customs of War on Land.

[69] Article 51, GC/I; Article 52, GC/II; Article 131, GC/III; Article 148, GC/IV.

[70] Article 91.

[71] Rule 150, Henckaerts and Doswald-Beck 2005, p. 537.

[72] Article 126, GC/III; Article 143, GC/IV.

Protecting Powers and the ICRC for "imperative military necessity," or otherwise that State will be in breach of the Third and Fourth Conventions.

On the other hand, there are provisions that allow a State to withhold consent in broader circumstances. Thus, under Article 18(2) of 1977 Protocol II, a State in which a non-international armed conflict is taking place may withhold consent to relief actions, but only if the civilian population is not suffering undue hardship, or the relief actions are not of an exclusively humanitarian and impartial nature and are conducted with adverse distinction. If, for example, humanitarian organizations are providing adequate supplies to the civilian population, the State concerned may withhold consent to relief actions newly offered by other humanitarian organizations without breaching Article 18(2). Conversely, if the consent is withheld while the civilian population is still suffering undue hardship, the State is in breach of Article 18(2). The State is then under an obligation to cease that breach and to allow relief actions by humanitarian organizations.

In this context, it has been argued that when a State unlawfully prevents humanitarian activities, countermeasures and necessity may possibly be invoked to preclude wrongfulness of entering a State's territory to carry out humanitarian activities without the consent of that State.[73] However, so far as countermeasures are concerned, Article 22(2) (b) of the Draft articles on the responsibility of international organizations adopted by the International Law Commission (ILC) provides that they may not be invoked unless "the countermeasures are not inconsistent with the rules of the organization."[74] The term "rules of the organization" includes "the constituent instruments, decisions, resolutions and other acts of the international organization adopted in accordance with those instruments, and established practice of the organization."[75] With respect to the United Nations, among other instruments, General Assembly resolution 46/182 of 19 December 1991 containing the guiding principles on emergency humanitarian assistance provides that "humanitarian assistance should be provided with the consent of the affected country."[76] Therefore, at least the United Nations would not be able to invoke countermeasures as a ground to preclude wrongfulness of entering a State's territory to provide humanitarian assistance. In this connection, a prior breach of an international obligation by a State, for example by withholding consent on grounds that are not permitted under a specific rule of IHL, does not entitle an international organization to breach its international obligations by entering a State's territory without its consent.

Moreover, the aim of countermeasures is to induce a State that is responsible for an internationally wrongful act to comply with its international obligations. In

---

[73]Schindler 1994, p. 699; Stoffels 2004, 537; Gillard 2013, pp. 371–373.

[74]Draft articles on the responsibility of international organizations, General Assembly resolution 66/100 of 9 December 2011, Annex.

[75]Ibid, Article 2(b).

[76]General Assembly resolution 46/182 of 19 December 1991, Annex, para 3.

this regard, it is highly doubtful whether the delivery of humanitarian assistance across the border qualifies as an action of such a kind.[77]

With respect to the argument based on necessity, Article 25(2) (a) of the Draft articles on the responsibility of international organizations provides that "necessity may not be invoked by an international organization…if…the international obligation in question excludes the possibility of invoking necessity." As discussed above, consent of the States concerned is the method adopted in IHL rules in order for humanitarian activities to be carried out lawfully across borders.[78] Moreover, at least with respect to the United Nations, General Assembly resolution 46/182 mentioned above requires the United Nations to obtain the consent of the affected country to provide humanitarian assistance. The resolution specifically refers to the consent of the affected country as the ground precluding wrongfulness of entering a State's territory to provide humanitarian assistance, and does not refer to necessity. Therefore, the argument based on necessity does not seem to be appropriate in justifying humanitarian assistance provided across the border without the consent of the State.

However, particular difficulties arise in instances where a government does not exist. The mere absence of a government does not signify that the sovereignty of the State concerned has ceased to exist. Therefore, international organizations continue to be bound by the obligations to respect it. At the same time, if there is no government from which consent could be obtained, a question arises as to how international organizations could carry out humanitarian activities in the territory of the State concerned.

Such a case may arguably fall in a situation where a fundamental change of circumstances may be invoked as a ground for suspending the operation of a treaty. In this regard, the Vienna Conventions on the Law of Treaties of 1969 and 1986 provide, in Article 62(1), that "[a] fundamental change of circumstances which has occurred with regard to those existing at the time of the conclusion of a treaty, and which was not foreseen by the parties, may not be invoked as a ground for terminating or withdrawing from [or suspending, as indicated in Article 62(4)], the treaty unless: (a) the existence of those circumstances constituted an essential basis of the consent of the parties to be bound by the treaty; and (b) the effect of the change is radically to transform the extent of obligations still to be performed under the treaty."

For example, "the consent of the High Contracting Party concerned" is an essential part of Article 18(2) of Protocol II. The absence of a government may constitute a fundamental change of circumstances in the context of this Article. In such a case, the requirement of consent in that Article may arguably be suspended

---

[77]Stoffels 2004, p. 536. See, however, Ryngaert 2013, p. 15.

[78]Consent is, in fact, one of the circumstances precluding wrongfulness provided for in Article 20 of the ILC's draft articles on the responsibility of international organizations. In this connection, the commentary to the ILC's draft articles on State responsibility also specifically refers to "humanitarian relief and rescue operations" as "[e]xamples of consent given by a State which has the effect of rendering certain conduct lawful." See A/56/10, p. 176.

temporarily for the duration of the absence of the government.[79] However, even if a provision in IHL can be considered temporarily suspended, the principle of State sovereignty under general international law still needs to be respected. As far as international organizations like the United Nations are concerned, in instances where a government from which consent should be obtained does not exist, it would seem more appropriate to obtain an authorization of the Security Council pursuant to its binding decision. Moreover, from an operational point of view, the consent of those who have the actual control over the territory in which a humanitarian activity is intended to be carried out, or through which a humanitarian organization needs to transit, should be obtained.

8.5 Binding Decisions of the Security Council

Binding decisions of the Security Council within the meaning of Article 25 of the Charter of the United Nations can have consequences on the sovereignty of a State in the sense that they could limit the right of the State to control the entry of international organizations into its territory for the purpose of carrying out humanitarian activities.[80]

For example, when the Security Council demands the parties to the conflict facilitate humanitarian assistance carried out by external actors, particularly by a decision taken under Chapter VII of the Charter, it may have the effect of limiting the right of a State to control the entry of external actors providing humanitarian assistance into its territory. One of the first resolutions adopted under Chapter VII that contained such a decision was Security Council resolution 859 (1993), which demanded that "all concerned facilitate the unhindered flow of humanitarian assistance…in particular to the safe areas in Bosnia and Herzegovina." Such a decision has subsequently been taken on a number of occasions. These decisions do not seem to go as far as to suspend the right of a State to control the entry of humanitarian organizations into its own territory. However, unlike, for example, Article 18(2) of 1977 Protocol II, such demands of the Security Council to allow relief actions by external humanitarian organizations are not normally limited to a situation where "the civilian population is suffering undue hardship owing to a lack of the supplies essential for its survival." Therefore, the scope of the discretion of a State to withhold consent to relief actions by external actors may be more limited than that under Protocol II.

In some cases, the Security Council may decide to suspend the right of a State to control the entry of humanitarian organizations into its own territory. A recent

[79]On the question of whether certain clauses in a treaty may be suspended, as opposed to the entire treaty, see Article 44 of the 1969 and 1986 Vienna Conventions on the Law of Treaties.

[80]See, Principle 7, International Institute of Humanitarian Law 1993; Article VIII(3), Institute of International Law's resolution on "Humanitarian Assistance" of 2 September 2003; Dinstein 2000, p. 86.

example is resolution 2165 (2014) concerning the situation in Syria by which the Security Council determined that "the deteriorating humanitarian situation in Syria constitutes a threat to peace and security in the region," emphasized Member States' obligation under Article 25 of the Charter, and decided that "the United Nations humanitarian agencies and their implementing partners are authorized to use routes across conflict lines and the border crossings of Bab al-Salam, Bab al-Hawa, Al Yarubiyah and Al-Ramtha, in addition to those already in use, in order to ensure that humanitarian assistance, including medical and surgical supplies, reaches people in need throughout Syria through the most direct routes." This binding decision of the Security Council effectively suspended the right of Syria to control the entry of certain humanitarian organizations into its territory through border crossings.

Another way of limiting the right of a State to control relief actions by external actors has been to authorize, under Chapter VII of the Charter, United Nations peacekeeping operations to facilitate humanitarian assistance through, where necessary, the use of force. Thus, United Nations Operation in Somalia II (UNOSOM II) was authorized to "secure or maintain security at all ports, airports and lines of communications required for the delivery of humanitarian assistance" by resolution 814 (1993), which was partly adopted under Chapter VII. Furthermore, the United Nations Protection Force (UNPROFOR) in Bosnia and Herzegovina was authorized by resolution 836 (1993) adopted under Chapter VII "to take the necessary measures, including the use of force…in the event of any deliberated obstruction…to the freedom of movement of…protected humanitarian convoys." These mandates allowed UNOSOM II and UNPROFOR to facilitate humanitarian assistance by external actors without necessarily obtaining prior consent of the State in whose territory the assistance was to be carried out.

8.6 Conclusions

The main theme of this chapter was to clarify the extent to which a State may exercise its discretion to withhold consent to humanitarian activities to be carried out on its territory during armed conflict, in the light of the principle of State sovereignty under general international law, and IHL. It also addressed the interplay between the principle of sovereignty and IHL and clarified the extent to which IHL limits the exercise of the sovereign right of a State to control the entry of external actors into that State's territory.

So far as international organizations, particularly the United Nations, are concerned, State sovereignty is not limited by international law, including IHL, to such an extent that international organizations are allowed to enter a State's territory without the prior consent of that State. This conclusion also applies in instances where an international organization intends to carry out humanitarian activities in a territory over which the territorial State has lost control, for example, because the enemy State or an armed group has taken control of that territory.

However, the circumstances in which a State may withhold consent to a particular humanitarian activity on its territory are determined by specific rules of IHL and by binding Security Council decisions. These circumstances are not the same in all cases. Whether a State has lawfully withheld consent to a humanitarian activity can only be assessed by looking at the specific rules of IHL that apply in the specific situation.

In limited cases, the State's right to control the entry of humanitarian organizations into its territory may be suspended, particularly when the Security Council adopts binding decisions to that effect.

References

Akhavan P et al (2014) There is no legal barrier to UN cross-border operations in Syria. The Guardian, 28 April 2014. http://www.theguardian.com/world/2014/apr/28/no-legal-barrier-un-cross-border-syria

Barber R (2009) Facilitating humanitarian assistance in international humanitarian and human rights law. Int Rev Red Cross 874:371–397

Bothe M (1989) Relief actions: the position of the recipient state. In: Kalshoven F (ed) Assisting the victims of armed conflict and other disasters. Martinus Nijhoff Publishers, Dordrecht, pp 91–97

Brownlile I (1998) Principle of public international law. Oxford University Press, Oxford

Bugnion F (2003) The International Committee of the Red Cross and the protection of war victims. Macmillan Education, Oxford

Dinstein Y (2000) The right to humanitarian assistance. Naval War College Review LIII, pp 77–91

Final Record of the Diplomatic Conference of Geneva of 1949 Vols I–III. Swiss Federal Political Department, Berne

Gillard E-C (2013) The law regulating cross-border relief operations. Int Rev Red Cross 890:351–382

Henckaerts J-M, Doswald-Beck L (2005) Customary international humanitarian law, vols I, II. International Committee of the Red Cross, Geneva and Cambridge University Press, Cambridge

International Committee of the Red Cross (1968) Help to war victims in Nigeria. International Review of the Red Cross 90:455–462

International Committee of the Red Cross (1969) Declaration of principles for international humanitarian relief to the civilian population in disaster situations. Int Rev Red Cross 104:632–633

International Committee of the Red Cross (1971) Conference of government experts on the reaffirmation and development of international humanitarian law applicable in armed conflicts (Geneva, 24 May–12 June 1971), vols I–VIII. International Committee of the Red Cross, Geneva

International Committee of the Red Cross (1972) Conference of government experts on the reaffirmation and development of international humanitarian law applicable in armed conflicts (Geneva, 3 May–3 June 1972): Report on the Work of the Conference, vols I–II. International Committee of the Red Cross, Geneva

International Committee of the Red Cross (1983) Conflict between Iraq and Iran. Int Rev the Red Cross 235:220–222

International Committee of the Red Cross (1984) Conflict between Iran and Iraq. Int Rev Red Cross 239:113–116

International Committee of the Red Cross (2014) ICRC Q & A and lexicon on humanitarian access. International Committee of the Red Cross, Geneva
International Institute of Humanitarian law (1993) Guiding principles on the right to humanitarian assistance. Int Rev Red Cross 297:519–525
Kalshoven F (ed) (1989) Assisting the victims of armed conflict and other disasters. Martinus Nijhoff Publishers, Dordrecht
Meyer M (1989) Development of the law governing relief operations. In: Meyer M (ed) Armed conflict and the new law: aspects of the 1977 Geneva Protocols and the 1981 UN Weapons Convention. British Institute of International and Comparative Law, London, pp 209–223
Official Records of the Diplomatic Conference on the Reaffirmation and Development of International Humanitarian Law Applicable in Armed Conflicts, Geneva 1974–1977 (1978), vols I–XVII. Swiss Federal Political Department, Bern
Pictet J et al (1952) Commentary on the Geneva Conventions of 12 August 1949, vols I–IV. International Committee of the Red Cross, Geneva
Plattner D (1992) Assistance to the civilian population: the development and present state of international humanitarian law. Int Rev Red Cross 288:249–263
Rottensteiner C (1999) The denial of humanitarian assistance as a crime under international law. Int Rev Red Cross 835:555–582
Ryngaert C (2013) Humanitarian assistance and the conundrum of consent: a legal perspective. Amsterdam Law Forum 5–2:5–19
Sandoz Y et al (eds) (1987) Commentary on the additional protocols of 8 June 1977 to the Geneva Conventions of 12 August 1949. International Committee of the Red Cross, Geneva
Schindler D (1994) Humanitarian assistance, humanitarian interference and international law. In: Macdonald R (ed) Essays in honour of Wang Tieya. Nijhoff, Dordrecht, pp 689–701
Schwendimann F (2011) The legal framework of humanitarian access in armed conflict. Int Rev Red Cross 884:993–1008
Spieker H (2011) The right to give and receive humanitarian assistance. In: Heintz H-J, Zwitter A (eds) International law and humanitarian assistance: a cross cut through legal issues pertaining to humanitarianism. Springer, Heidelberg, pp 7–31
Stoffels RA (2004) Legal regulation of humanitarian assistance in armed conflict: achievements and gaps. Int Rev Red Cross 855:515–546
Torrelli M (1992) From humanitarian assistance to "intervention on humanitarian grounds"? Int Rev Red Cross 288:228–248

Other Consulted Sources

Allen CA (1989) Civilian starvation and relief during armed conflict: the modern humanitarian law. Georgia J Int Comp Law 19:1–85
Arnison N (1993) International law and non-intervention: when do humanitarian concerns supersede sovereignty? Fletcher Forum World Aff 17:199–211
Beigbeder Y (1991) The role and status of international humanitarian volunteers and organizations: the right and duty to humanitarian assistance. Martinus Nijhoff Publishers, Dordrecht
Dailler P, Forteau M, Pellet A (2009) Droit international public. L.G.D.J, Paris
Domestici-Met M-J (1989) Aspects juridiques récents de l'assistance humanitaire. Annuaire Français de Droit International 35:117–148
Gottlieb G (1972) The United Nations and emergency humanitarian assistance in India-Pakistan. Am J Int Law 66:362–365
Helton A (1992) The legality of providing humanitarian assistance without the consent of the sovereign. Int J Refugee Law 4:373–375
Jakovljević B (1987) The right to humanitarian assistance: legal aspects. Int Rev Red Cross 260:469–484

Jennings R, Watts A (ed) (1996) Oppenheim's international law, vol I, 9th edn. Longman, London

Luopajärvi K (2003) Is there an obligation on states to accept international humanitarian assistance to internally displaced persons under international law? Int J Refugee Law 15:678–714

Naqvi and Pabst (2004) Humanitarian assistance in armed conflict, Conference of the Luxemburg Group 24–25 May 2004. Int Rev Red Cross 856:879–916

Sommaruga C (1992) Assistance to victims of war in international humanitarian law and humanitarian practice. Int Rev Red Cross 289:373–382

Stopford M (1993) Humanitarian assistance in the wake of the Persian Gulf War. Va J Int Law 33:491–502

Usmani M (2007) Restrictions on humanitarian aid in Darfur: The role of the International Criminal Court. Georgia J Int Comp Law 36:257–289

Chapter 9
Legal Challenges in the Provision of Humanitarian Assistance: The Case of Non-international Armed Conflicts

Emilie E. Kuijt

Abstract In the twenty-first century, non-international armed conflicts have become increasingly common. Such conflicts are often characterized by large-scale humanitarian crises, leading to calls by the international community for the provision of assistance. Yet, the factual provision of assistance in such conflicts is not without legal challenges, in particular related to the role of both the state sovereign and that of non-state actors. Obstruction of access to emergency aid by parties to the conflict, depriving those in need of assistance, may lead to legal enforcement issues. This chapter will address such current issues and offer some solutions in existing international law to ensure protection for those in need.

Keywords Humanitarian assistance · Non-international armed conflict · Human rights law · Humanitarian law · Enforcement

Contents

Emilie E. Kuijt is a PhD Fellow and Lecturer at the Grotius Centre for International Legal Studies, University of Leiden. She would like to thank Dr. Daniëlla Dam-de Jong and Dr. Myriam Feinberg for their valuable comments. Any errors or omissions of course remain the author's own.

E.E. Kuijt (✉)
Grotius Centre for International Legal Studies, University of Leiden, Leiden, The Netherlands
e-mail: e.e.kuijt@law.leidenuniv.nl

T.D. Gill et al. (eds.), *Yearbook of International Humanitarian Law 2014*, Yearbook of International Humanitarian Law 17,
DOI 10.1007/978-94-6265-091-6_9

9.1 Introduction

An evolution in warfare over the past century has coincided with a change in the nature of conflicts. Whereas, the first half of the twentieth century was characterized by international armed conflicts and circumstances of occupation, over the last few decades the nature of 'war' has increasingly been that of non-international armed conflicts (NIAC). Despite the non-international character of such conflicts, the need for the provision of humanitarian assistance remains equally high, if not higher. Examples like the current conflict in Syria portray issues such as the creation of (often large) groups of internally displaced persons (IDPs) and challenges in identifying duty-bearers amongst various parties involved in the conflict. Moreover, these crises are exacerbated by a lack of access for external parties to provide aid when certain territory is no longer under the control of the sovereign, or a sovereign's and/or armed groups' refusal of access to provide assistance. As is well known, this is often for political reasons related to the conflict at hand.

The law pertaining to armed conflict, i.e. international humanitarian law, and its regulation of the provision of humanitarian assistance as we know it today, has been mostly developed in the aftermath of World War II. Thus, its provisions concerning the delivery of emergency aid are most specifically tailored to circumstances of international armed conflict and occupation. NIACs and natural disasters, or a combination thereof resulting in complex emergencies, are today however the most common circumstances in which the provision of aid is needed. The recent conflicts in Syria and Iraq, including the role of 'ISIS', clearly reflect a need for international assistance to the civilian population, as well as conflicting interests of the state sovereigns in charge. Moreover, these emergencies evidence the difficulties of the UN Security Council in addressing and determining adequate action.

This chapter discusses the legal issues faced in the provision of humanitarian assistance in times of NIAC and offers some solutions to the current issues with the law. First, the boundaries of the current legal framework in time of NIAC are addressed, and a perspective on the *lex specialis* doctrine is offered in this regard. Second, issues pertaining to the various rights and duties under humanitarian law and human rights law are discussed, prior to a discussion of enforcement challenges. The last part of this chapter then provides solutions to obtaining access, amongst others through Security Council action, for the purpose of aid delivery.

9.1.1 Boundaries of the Framework for the Provision of Humanitarian Assistance

A central issue in ascertaining the problems pertaining to the delivery of assistance is the determination of the *legal boundaries* of the framework within which such provision operates. International law does not provide a definition of the notion of 'humanitarian assistance', although a proper delimitation would enhance clarity regarding the substance and circumstances of its provision. Given the circumstances in which humanitarian aid is needed, it is proposed to be: 'assistance consisting of food, medicine, shelter and logistics for its provision; for urgent purposes and which is indispensable to the survival of the people at which it is aimed'.[1]

Furthermore and particularly relevant in time of conflict, the *providers* of assistance must be distinguished from those intervening and *using* force (for example by way of the Security Council in the creation of a stable environment in which aid can be delivered). To be considered 'humanitarian assistance', such aid must therefore be provided according to the principles of humanity, neutrality and impartiality.[2]

One of the great challenges in the current law concerning humanitarian assistance is the fact that the level of protection the law offers is dependent on the specific characterization of the circumstance as an international armed conflict, a NIAC or a crisis following a (natural) disaster. In other words, rather than being dependent on the *needs* of the persons in crisis, the level of protection provided is dependent on the *circumstances* proper. For example, those needing emergency aid following a tsunami would be lacking the protection available to those in need of aid in time of an international armed conflict, whilst the need for food or water remains essentially equal. Furthermore, the law pertaining to the delivery of assistance in NIACs in particular is dependent on factors relating to the *type* of such a non-international armed conflict, as well as to *which party* holds international legal responsibility for the *determination* that a territory may be in need of emergency aid.

---

[1]Kuijt 2015, p. 55.

[2]Statutes of the International Red Cross and Red Crescent Movement, adopted by the 25th International Conference of the Red Cross at Geneva in 1986, amended in 1995 and 2006, Preamble; UNGA Resolution 2675 (XXV) 9 December 1970 para 8; UN Doc. A/RES/2717 (XXV), 15 December 1970 Preambular para 4; UN Doc. A/RES/43/131, 8 December 1988 Preambular para 12; UN Doc. A/RES/46/182, 19 December 1991, para 2. As of 2004, the UN has also included 'independence' as a principle in the provision of humanitarian aid: UN Doc. A/RES/58/114, 5 February 2004, Preambular paras 4 and 5.

9.1.2 Typology of Non-international Armed Conflicts and Humanitarian Assistance

For the purpose of this chapter, a brief differentiation is necessary of the types of NIACs, given that such typology may directly influence the potential provision of aid. A distinction can be made between NIACs governed by Common Article 3 of the Geneva Conventions and those NIACs falling within the scope of Additional Protocol II (AP II). Common Article 3 is applicable to situations of armed conflict 'not of an international character' in the territory of a state party to the convention, for 'each party' to the conflict.[3] The regime of AP II requires a higher threshold, and is applicable only to those NIACs taking place between a state party and 'dissident armed forces or other organized armed groups which, under responsible command, exercise such control over a part of its territory as to enable them to carry out sustained and concerted military operations and to implement this Protocol'.[4] Thus, this second category of NIAC requires the state to be party to AP II, as well as a certain threshold of 'control' and organization by armed groups.

Whilst on the one hand AP II grants more protection to civilians by means of the provision of assistance (discussed below) in circumstances when its threshold is met, on the other hand not as many states are party to the Protocol as to the Geneva Conventions, nor does it have customary status like Common Article 3.[5] However, in the well-known *Tadic*-judgment, the ICTY concluded that once its threshold is met, AP II should not be restricted to the 'actual hostilities' nor should it be limited geographically in scope.[6] With regard to the provision of humanitarian assistance, it can then be concluded that once the threshold set by AP II regarding a NIAC is met, *all* people *affected* by the conflict are to be protected by the provisions of AP II, for the purposes of the delivery of humanitarian aid.

Yet for the application of humanitarian law, an armed conflict must be present. The establishment of 'what' entails an armed conflict remains a factual determination. In such instances, the degree of control of non-state actors will need to be determined, to assess whether the NIAC is governed by Common Article 3 or AP II, should the affected state be a Party to the Protocol. Indeed, a common defence for the non-application of international humanitarian law is the argument that no armed conflict exists, or that no acting responsible sovereign may be in place, due to the loss of control over a territory. The on-going clashes in the Ukraine reflect both these difficulties, and the struggles of the international community therewith. Such circumstances, regardless of their classification, however may warrant the provision of

[3]The Commentary to common Article 3 argues that it should be widely applicable, submitting potential (non-exhaustive) circumstances that may indeed fall within this scope: Commentary Geneva Convention IV (1958), pp. 35–36.

[4]Article 1 AP II.

[5]Sandoz et al. 1987, p. 1348. See also ILA Hague Conference, Final Report on the Meaning of Armed Conflict in International Law, Committee on the Use of Force (2010), p. 12.

[6]ICTY *Tadic* Appeals Chamber Decision 2 October 1995, Decision on the Defence motion for Interlocutory Appeal on Jurisdiction, para 69.

assistance, as a crisis for a civilian population may be taking place.[7] Indeed, although internal disturbances may not amount to an armed conflict and therefore fall outside the scope of international humanitarian law, they can be distinguished according to a level of organization and intensity.[8] Yet, even when the NIAC can be classified, struggles remain with regard to the provision of assistance, as set out below. It is therefore proposed that the notion of a *humanitarian crisis* should be adhered to, defined as 'a situation deriving from a variety of origins, including natural or man-made disaster, armed conflict and occupation; causing grave damages of a personal or material nature to persons, where (national/external) assistance is needed as the local capacity is either overwhelmed, unable or sometimes unwilling to manage the circumstances'.[9] Through such an approach, persons finding themselves in need of aid in those circumstances that cannot be classified as a NIAC will not be left without the protection of humanitarian assistance. Indeed, in such circumstances, should difficulties exist in applying humanitarian law, recourse can be had to human rights law.

9.1.3 The Lex Specialis Doctrine and the Provision of Humanitarian Assistance

A conflict of norms may occur regarding the law applicable to the delivery of humanitarian assistance in time of NIAC. Whilst the provision of humanitarian assistance in time of a NIAC is framed specifically within humanitarian law, it has long been established and accepted that both international humanitarian law and human rights law aim to protect the basics of human dignity and humanity.[10] Resulting from the greater interaction over the past decades of both *corpora juris*, as well as established acceptance of the continued application of human rights law in times of armed conflict, a simultaneous application of the two fields of law exists in time of armed conflict.[11] In particular, those provisions in human rights

[7]Kuijt 2015, pp. 65–66.

[8]ICTY *Prosecutor v Tadic* Trial Chamber, 7 May 1997, para 562. See also ILA Hague Conference (2010), p. 28.

[9]Kuijt 2015, pp. 71–72.

[10]See with regard to the notion of a 'common minimum standard of humanity' amongst others the 1990 Turku Abo Declaration.

[11]ICJ (Advisory Opinion) Legality of the threat or use of nuclear weapons, 8 July 1996, para 25. See also ICJ (Advisory Opinion) Legal consequences of the construction of a wall in the occupied Palestinian Territory, 9 July 2004, para 106; ICJ *Armed Activities on the Territory of the Congo (Democratic Republic of the Congo* v. *Uganda), I.C.J. Reports 2005* (*Congo* v. *Uganda*), Judgment, 19 December 2005, ICJ Rep. 2005, 1 at para 216. ECtHR Case of Isayeva, Yusupova and Bazayeva v. Russia (Applications nos. 57947/00, 57948/00 and 57949/00) Judgment 24 February 2005; the Inter-American Court on Human Rights, Bamaca Velásquez v Guatamala Judgment 25 November 2000 para 207. See in relation to the applicability of human rights in time of armed conflict and their derogability, Human Rights Committee UN Doc. CCPR/C/21/Rev.1/ Add.11 General Comment 29 pursuant to Article 4 'States of Emergency', paras 3, 9 and 11 (2001).

law tailored to the provision of humanitarian assistance do not contain derogation clauses, ensuring their continued applicability in emergency circumstances.[12] Whereas the *lex specialis* doctrine as a concept in itself is an accepted principle through which to determine the applicable provision of law, its content remains disputed. To determine upon what law the protection of persons in need of assistance in time of a NIAC is based, a specific application of the *lex specialis* doctrine must be ascertained. International humanitarian law, as a body of law, is often argued as the *lex specialis* in time of conflict, but this may not hold true for the provision of assistance in time of NIAC, as human rights law plays a significant and relevant role for those in need of aid, the state sovereign and armed groups.

Various approaches exist regarding the determination of the relationship between humanitarian law and human rights law, which are of relevance to the law protecting persons in need of humanitarian aid. The ICJ's approach that 'some rights may be exclusively matters of international humanitarian law; others may be exclusively matters of human rights law; yet others may be matters of both these branches of international law' is well known today.[13] Alternatively, the HRC has argued with regard to the ICCPR that whilst 'more specific rules' of humanitarian law can be particularly relevant for the interpretation of certain rights within the treaty, 'both spheres of law are complementary, not mutually exclusive'.[14] Moreover, Sassòli argues for an approach to the 'lex specialis' doctrine in which each specific circumstance or rule is regarded individually, to make an assessment.[15] Such an approach leads to the situation in which either human rights law or humanitarian law may be found the *lex specialis*, depending on the particular instance, whilst the general law remains present in the background. The ILC's Report of the 'Study group on the fragmentation of international law' has concurred with this approach and argued the relational character of the special and the general rule.[16] In particular, regarding protection in time of NIACs, Krieger has noted that human rights law is often more specific than provisions in humanitarian law, thus going against the argument that humanitarian law *as a body* should be the prevalent *lex specialis*.[17] Interchangeable gap-filling thereby appears more appropriate, as also considered by the European Court for Human Rights in circumstances of NIAC.[18]

[12]See however Article 2 ICESCR regarding 'progressive development'.

[13]ICJ, Legal Consequences of the Construction of a Wall in the Occupied Palestinian Territory, Advisory Opinion of 9 July 2004, ICJ Rep. 2004, para 106 and Armed Activities on the Territory of the Congo (Democratic Republic of the Congo v. Uganda), I.C.J. Reports 2005, para 216 (Congo v. Uganda).

[14]HRC UN Doc. CCPR/C/21/Rev.1/Add.13 (2004), General Comment No. 31 (Article 2), para 11.

[15]Sassòli and Olson 2008, pp. 603–604.

[16]UN Doc. A/CN.4/L.682 (2006) ILC Study Fragmentation of the Law, paras 104 and 112.

[17]Krieger 2006, p. 273.

[18]ECtHR *Isayeva, Yusupova and Bazayeva v. Russia* (Isayeva I) Case Nos. 57947/00, 57948/00, 57949/00, [2005] ECHR 129, 24 February 2005, paras 167 and 169; ECtHR *Isayeva v. Russia* (Isayeva II) Case No. 57950/00, [2005] ECHR 128, 24 February 2005, para 173; and ECtHR *Ilascu and others v. Moldova and Russia* Case No. 48787/99, [2004] ECHR 318, 8 July 2004. The debate whether or not (regional) human rights courts or other bodies *should* be applying humanitarian law remains outside the scope of this contribution.

Krieger has in this regard suggested the 'most favourable principle' as a method of interpretation, which would grant that norm the 'specialis' character which provides the *greatest protection to individuals*.[19] Indeed, both human rights law and humanitarian law can be seen to have a common goal: the protection of persons and the preservation of their dignity. This in itself is precisely the goal of the provision of humanitarian assistance. Such a harmonious and protective approach to the *lex specialis* principle therefore falls in line with both the goals of human rights law and humanitarian law as well as with the enhancement of the delivery of humanitarian assistance, which contributes precisely thereto. Such an interpretation method would also align with the approach in international humanitarian law to interpret provisions 'protectively', i.e. to err on the side of caution. Furthermore, it follows Article 31(3)(c) of the Vienna Convention on the Law of Treaties, stating that as a basic interpretative rule, together with the object, purpose and context of a treaty, also the other relevant applicable rules of international law must be considered.[20]

Thus, given the joint evolution of human rights law and humanitarian law over the past decades with an enhanced focus on the protection of persons both in time of conflict and peace, a proper interpretation of provisions in either field of law relating to the provision of humanitarian assistance should be interpreted with the *other* body of law in mind also. Indeed, as the following Sections demonstrate, the continued applicability of human rights law is key to the greater protection of persons in need of aid in time of NIACs. Such has also been argued in particular concerning the protection of life of civilians in time of NIAC by Doswald-Beck.[21] The provision of assistance can thus function as fulfillment of various human rights. Indeed, the enhancement of the protection of persons in need of assistance is aided by human rights law functioning as *lex specialis* in certain circumstances where humanitarian law is lacking in specific provisions and furthermore pursues the common 'humanitarian' denominator of both fields of law.[22]

It is submitted therefore with regard to the *lex specialis* doctrine, for the purpose of the provision of humanitarian assistance, that the applicable law must be sought in those provisions of humanitarian law and human rights law that provide the utmost *protection* in a given circumstance. Such a comprehensive approach assists in the joint interpretation of human rights law and humanitarian law, especially in the event of doubt as to the preferred application of either. In adhering to such a 'most protective clause' approach, persons in need of assistance will be guaranteed the greatest protection at all times, regardless of which of the *corpora juris* the provision stems from. The following section takes a closer look at the specific rights and duties in both these bodies of law available for the protection of persons in need of aid.

---

[19]Krieger 2006, p. 274.

[20]Articles 31(1) and (3)(c) Vienna Convention.

[21]Doswald-Beck 2006, p. 882 onwards.

[22]Such has also been argued by UN Special Rapporteur Eduardo Valencia Ospina for the ILC Study on the 'Protection of Persons in the Event of Disaster' regarding the interdependency of these fields of law, UN Doc A/CN.4/598 (2008), para 52.

9.2 The Current Legal Framework for the Provision of Humanitarian Assistance in a Non-international Armed Conflict

The current legal framework regarding humanitarian assistance in NIAC has been subjected to a proliferation of actors. It comprises rights and duties for the affected persons, the affected state, armed groups involved in the conflict and external third parties wishing to contribute assistance, the latter of which include both states and international organizations. Both the Security Council and General Assembly have frequently asserted their recognition of the fact that the affected state has a *primary* duty to protect civilians within its jurisdiction.[23] The Security Council has furthermore on multiple occasions called upon states to allow for rapid passage of humanitarian assistance, whilst simultaneously referring to the notion of state sovereignty.[24] The Council is thus fully aware of the potential international legal barriers that might exist in a NIAC when considering the potential obligation of the affected states or non-state actors to allow full freedom of movement to humanitarian personnel and humanitarian access.

9.2.1 Rights and Duties in the Provision of Humanitarian Assistance Under International Humanitarian Law During a NIAC

International humanitarian law provides for certain specific regulations both for the affected state, the armed group as non-state actor, and for third parties, pertaining to the delivery of humanitarian assistance. Humanitarian law does not however recognize a 'general duty' of the sovereign or other parties to provide assistance in a NIAC.

---

[23]See amongst others UN Doc. S/RES/1674 (2006), para 13; S/RES/1894 (2009) preamble and para 15. See also amongst others: S/RES/13255 (31 October 2000); S/RES/1430 (14 August 2002); S/RES/1906 preamble (23 December 2009); and S/1861 preamble (14 January 2009); S/RES/1970 preamble and S/RES/1973 preamble and para 3 (2011); Sec Council 1975 preamble; UN Doc S/RES/1996 (2011) Security Council Resolution Reports of the Secretary-General on the Sudan 8 July 2011, para 3(b)(iv); UN Doc S/RES/2014, 21 October 2011, preamble; UN Doc. S/RES/2016, 27 October 2011, para 3; UN Doc. S/RES/2040, 12 March 2012, para 4 as well as UN Doc. A/RES/58/114, 5 February 2004, para 12; A/RES/59/141, 25 February 2005, para 15; A/RES/60/124, 8 March 2006, para 3; A/RES/62/94, 25 January 2008, para 19; A/RES/63/139, 5 March 2009, para 21; A/RES/64/76, 2 February 2010, para 22; A/RES/65/133, 3 March 2011, para 23; A/RES/66/119, 7 March 2012, para 29.

[24]See amongst others UN Doc. S/RES/1769 (2007) 31 July 2007; S/RES 1794 (2007) 21 December 2007 and S/RES/1906 (2009) 23 December 2009.

Common Article 3 of the Geneva Conventions merely calls upon the 'humane treatment' of those caught in the conflict by all involved parties. By referring explicitly to *all* parties, Common Article 3 makes it absolutely clear that this obligation also rests upon armed groups. This assertion has been affirmed on numerous occasions by the Security Council as it calls upon armed groups to abide by their duties under humanitarian law.[25]

The principle formulated in Common Article 3 in fact entails the obligation to not intentionally, through an act or omission cause 'serious mental or physical suffering or injury or constitute[s] a serious attack on human dignity'.[26] Thus, it may be argued that a duty exists for parties to the conflict to provide a minimum of assistance based upon Common Article 3, despite a lacking specific codified obligation thereto. Furthermore Article 3(2) supplies that an 'impartial humanitarian body' may offer services to parties to the NIAC. The stipulation that offers of humanitarian assistance *may* be done is an indication that the drafters envisioned a supplementary role for any outside party, with a responsibility resting first and foremost on the parties to the conflict.[27] No *duty* for third parties to provide assistance as such exists under Article 3 and Pictet argues in the Commentary that parties to the conflict may 'decline the offer if they can do without it'.[28] Yet this determination pinpoints a crucial difficulty within the delivery of assistance: identifying *who* shall *determine* whether or not the sovereign or non-state actor is sufficiently capable and willing to provide assistance to a needy population, or whether assistance from abroad is necessary due to the *inadequate* supply of the affected territory.

Additional Protocol II—although applicable with a threshold of control for armed groups—attempts to supplement these provisions and elaborates in Article 14 that the starvation of civilians 'as a method of combat' is prohibited.[29] The civilian objects 'indispensible to the survival of the population' must be respected, regardless of who in fact controls a part of the territory. Subsequently, concerning the provision of relief through external sources, Article 18 AP II provides that:

> 1. Relief societies located in the territory of the High Contracting Party, such as Red Cross (Red Crescent, Red Lion and Sun) organizations, may offer their services for the performance of their traditional functions in relation to the victims of the armed conflict […] 2.

---

[25]See for example UN Doc. S/RES/1265 (1999), para 4; S/RES/1863 (2009), para 19 and S/RES/2036 (2012), para 16.

[26]ICTY, the Prosecutor v. Zejnil Delalic et al., Case No IT-96-21-T, Judgment, 16 November 1998, para 543.

[27]Pictet 1958, p. 41.

[28]Ibid.

[29]The full text of Article 14 AP II reads: "Starvation of civilians as a method of combat is prohibited. It is therefore prohibited to attack, destroy, remove or render useless, for that purpose, objects indispensable to the survival of the civilian population, such as foodstuffs, agricultural areas for the production of foodstuffs, crops, livestock, drinking water installations and supplies and irrigation works".

> If the civilian population is suffering undue hardship owing to a lack of the supplies essential for its survival, such as foodstuffs and medical supplies, relief actions for the civilian population which are of an exclusively humanitarian and impartial nature and which are conducted without any adverse distinction *shall* be undertaken *subject to the consent of the High Contracting Party concerned.*[30]

Similar to Common Article 3 therefore, relief societies 'may' offer assistance. Only in the situation that civilians are experiencing 'undue hardship', does such a right to offer become an *obligation* through the wording of 'shall', as stipulated in the second paragraph.

Whilst such wording implies an obligation that might be construed as a limitation of the notion of State sovereignty, consent of the affected State continues to be required. This Article reflects the continuous struggle faced in balancing the age-old notion of sovereignty versus the needs of a population facing a humanitarian crisis as the Article does not clarify upon which actor the obligation lies to determine this 'undue hardship'. Article 18 AP II must be read in conjunction with Article 14 prohibiting starvation, and the provision of assistance must thus be authorized when the population is threatened therewith. Together, these two provisions do not allow for parties to a NIAC to use the argument of 'military necessity' as failure to provide for the civilian population when a civilian population is at risk of starvation, despite the leeway allowed for State sovereignty.[31]

Yet again, the authorization of aid rests with the sovereign or other parties controlling areas of conflict as often the case in a NIAC, resulting in practical difficulties such as faced in Syria in recent years. In this regard, Security Council Resolution 2165 of 2014, for the provision of aid to Syria without the specific consent of the Syrian authorities, has been a novel approach, although it has yet to be repeated (see Sect. 9.3.2). Indeed, Article 18(2) AP II solely addresses the need for consent from the 'concerned' 'High Contracting Party'. In reality on the ground, a non-state actor exercising a certain level of *de facto* control could also be a 'concerned party' within the meaning of Article 18(2) and therefore not allowed to arbitrarily refuse consent.[32] Problematic in this respect is the difficulty in establishing contact with such entities, as contact may be interpreted as a manner of (legal) recognition which states may wish to avoid and which should therefore be specifically addressed in their contact. Such discussions arose amongst others in the recognition of the Libyan 'Transitional Council' in 2011 and in practice is easier for NGOs.[33] According to the official Commentary, in the event it is unclear

---

[30]Emphasis added.

[31]Sandoz et al. 1987 p. 1457.

[32]Dungel 2004, para 2.3.1.2 and Rynaert 2013, pp. 17–18.

[33]See amongst others regarding the recognition by France: http://www.nytimes.com/2011/03/11/world/europe/11france.html?_r=0 (last retrieved 21 March 2015) and the US: http://www.washingtonpost.com/world/middle-east/western-arab-leaders-meet-in-turkey-on-libyas-future/2011/07/15/gIQAZLbjFI_story.html (last retrieved 21 March 2015).

who the authorities are, consent must be presupposed so as to prevent the prolongation of suffering from the affected population.[34] Although the Commentary is widely recognized, such an assertion cannot be said to be commonly supported in practice as the recent discussions relating to the UN decision to bring aid to Syria without state consent demonstrate.[35] This absence of an explicit obligation resting upon non-state actors results in a barrier in the provision of assistance on the ground.

The formulation of Article 18 AP II has led to various discussions. Amongst others Dinstein argues that declining an offer of assistance is permissible and that states shall always find plausible arguments to suit them,[36] whilst Plattner suggests that an offer which meets the terms of Article 18 AP II cannot be considered an unlawful interference and may not be arbitrarily refused.[37] The latter has also been held by the ICJ in its well-known Nicaragua judgment, in which the ICJ argued that an offer of actual humanitarian assistance cannot be construed as an 'intervention in the internal affairs' of a state.[38]

Outside the realm of armed conflict, the International Law Commission has more recently argued in its study on the Protection of persons in the event of disasters that such a determination must be made on a 'case-by-case basis', without elaborating as to whom should be the determinant in such circumstances.[39] Yet, whilst the 'arbitrariness' of the refusal of an offer may eventually be determined by an authoritative legal body such as the ICJ, in practice such an initial argument in time of a NIAC shall always be made by the sovereign of an affected territory, or the controlling non-state actor. Indeed, in response hereto, third-party action may be warranted upon determination by the Security Council as authoritative body with more *ad hoc* possibilities of enforcement than the ICJ.

Regardless of the typology of the NIAC and therefore the applicability of humanitarian law, human rights law continues to apply in time of armed conflict as well as those circumstances not meeting such thresholds, warranting a further discussion.

---

[34]Sandoz et al. 1987 p. 1479.

[35]Note in this regard: http://www.nytimes.com/2014/07/25/world/middleeast/defying-syria-united-nations-sends-in-trucks-carrying-aid.html?_r=0 (last retrieved 28 August 2014) and http://www.reuters.com/article/2014/07/24/us-syria-crisis-un-aid-idUSKBN0FT25G20140724 (last retrieved 28 August 2014).

[36]Dinstein 2000, p. 9.

[37]Plattner 1996, p. 177.

[38]Military and Paramilitary Activities in and against Nicaragua (Nicaragua vs. United States), Merits 1986 ICJ REP. 14 (Judgment of 27 June 1986), para 243.

[39]UN Doc. A/CN.4/643, ILC, Fourth report of the Special Rapporteur, Mr. Eduardo Valencia-Ospina (63rd session of the ILC (2011)) on the protection of persons in the event of disasters, para 72.

9.2.2 Rights and Duties in the Provision of Humanitarian Assistance Under Human Rights Law During a NIAC

As has become increasingly accepted in international law, human rights obligations also rest upon non-state actors or armed groups in time of NIAC.[40] With regard to the on-going hostilities in Syria, the Security Council has for example demanded that 'all parties' desist from 'violations and abuses of human rights'.[41] Given that the content of humanitarian assistance is *emergency* aid, the most relevant human rights are the rights to life, food and health, for which the delivery of aid functions as a vehicle in their fulfillment. This perspective has also been taken by the CESCR, declaring in its General Comment pertaining to Article 11 ICESCR that

> Violations of the right to food can occur through the direct action of States or other entities insufficiently regulated by States. These include: (…) prevention of access to humanitarian food aid in internal conflicts or other emergency situations.[42]

Thus, the CESCR argues that parties to a NIAC are obliged to fulfill the right to food through humanitarian assistance. This obligation, through which the state should provide in food for those under its jurisdiction, can also be found in various other treaties.[43] Furthermore, the right to life in a NIAC continues to entail a right to not be 'arbitrarily deprived' of one's life as codified in Articles 3 UDHR, 6 ICCPR, 2 ECHR, 4 ACHR, 4 ACHPR as well as Articles 6 & 22 CRC. The non-provision of aid, as a result of which death may incur, would then be categorized as such an arbitrary deprivation. The right to health, in particular Article 12(2)(c) ICESCR with regard to the prevention of diseases, provides for a right of the population in time of conflict to request assistance from the affected state. Although with a less homogenous codification, it is also found in Articles 25 UDHR, 5(e)(iv) ICERD and various other conventions.[44] With regard to the rights to food and health, Article 2(1) ICESCR calls upon *international* cooperation in their fulfillment. As such, the affected state is obliged to seek international 'assistance and

[40]See amongst others Clapham 2006, p. 522; Tomuschat 2004, p. 586; Steiner et al. 2008, pp. 675 and 1420. See also for example UN Doc. S/RES/1265 (1999) para 4 and S/RES/1863 (2009), para 19; and Articles 9 and 10 ARSIWA.

[41]UN Doc. S/RES/2139 (2014) para 2.

[42]CESCR E/C/12/1999/5 (1999) General Comment No. 12 (Article 11), para 19.

[43]See in this regard Article 24(2)(c) CRC, Article 12(2) CEDAW, Article 28 CRPD, Article 12 of the Additional Protocol to the ACHR in the Area of Economic, Social and Cultural Rights and Article 15 of the Additional Protocol to the ACHPR on the Rights of Women in Africa and Article 25 UDHR.

[44]See Articles 24 CRC, 11 European Social Charter, 10 of the Additional Protocol to the ACHR in the area of Economic, Social and Cultural Rights, 16 ACHPR, 14 of the African Charter on the Rights and Welfare of the Child and 14 of the Protocol to the ACHPR on the Rights of Women in Africa.

cooperation' in the realization of such rights, but Article 2 falls short in creating an international obligation on the part of third states.

Whilst the ICESCR does not contain a derogation clause, Article 2 does differentiate between 'progressive development' and 'minimum core obligations' to be fulfilled by the state party. In relation to the provision of humanitarian assistance, such provision has been argued to form part of these 'minimum core obligations' and as such must be ensured at all times.[45] However, it must be acknowledged that the rights as enshrined in the ICESCR remain obligations of conduct, as opposed to obligations of result, thereby focusing on the *means* to achieving an end, resulting in less readily available enforcement of the 'result' *stricto sensu*. Conversely to humanitarian law, therefore, human rights law *does* contain various more general obligations for parties to a conflict in the protection of human rights, and the provision of emergency aid can function as the fulfillment thereof. These general duties however do also not include an obligation of third parties to provide aid.

This protection furthermore reaches greater depths on the African continent through the Kampala Convention. Article 3(1)(j) codifies generally the obligation for State Parties to provide assistance to IDPs by meeting their basic needs and respecting their rights, whilst Article 4 states the obligation to prevent conditions that may lead to arbitrary displacement and, 'where necessary, provide immediate protection and assistance to internally displaced persons'. More specifically concerning the primary obligation and responsibility of a sovereign in the provision of humanitarian assistance to all IDPs within a territory or jurisdiction, Article 5 specifies a duty to 'take necessary steps to effectively organize relief action that is humanitarian, and impartial in character'. The Kampala Convention deals with the prohibition for armed groups of hampering the provision of protection and assistance to IDPs under any circumstances and denying IDPs the right to live in satisfactory conditions of dignity, security, sanitation, food, water, health and shelter in Article 7(5)(b) and (c). Finally Articles 9(1), 9(2)(b) and (c) and 9(2)(k) entails a duty to provide IDPs to the fullest extent practicable and with the least possible delay, with adequate humanitarian assistance, which shall include food, water, shelter, medical care and other health services, sanitation, education and any other necessary social services.

The Convention therefore lays detailed obligations upon State Parties with regard to the provision of humanitarian assistance, in particular concerning IDPs. Whilst it is innovative in its explicit recognition of the role and obligation that it asserts for armed groups, its recent entry into force does not yet amount to practical changes in time of existing conflicts. Furthermore, this Convention merely operates on the African continent that, although prone to conflicts, would therefore result in more fragmented protection for IDPs under international law. The UN Guiding Principles for IDPs in this sense provide a more general standard in Principles 3(2) and 25, although they are soft law.[46]

---

[45] CESCR E/1991/23 (1990) General Comment No. 3 (Article 2), para 10.

[46] Principle 3(2) asserts a right to request and receive assistance from authorities, and Principle 25 addresses a corresponding duty to provide.

The explicit address of armed groups in the Kampala Convention furthermore highlights the fact that, while it is increasingly accepted that such actors must abide by human rights norms, these norms are traditionally not tailored towards them, rather focusing on the state sovereign as duty-bearer. In practice, it is often seen that states and non-state actors come to agreements in the provision of humanitarian assistance. This results in non-state actors often taking certain human rights obligations voluntarily upon themselves, regardless of potential existing legal obligations as asserted by amongst others the Security Council. Problematic however remains the notion of legal enforcement of human rights law. Given the fact that in most treaties, the affected state is the explicit duty-bearer, human rights bodies, courts and other enforcement mechanisms are tailored towards the adjudication of disputes regarding alleged violations by the state party.

9.3 Enforcement Challenges in the Provision of Humanitarian Assistance

The above discussion has highlighted some distinct challenges in the provision of assistance in time of non-international armed conflicts. Throughout the discussion of the various rights and duties involved in the provision of assistance, the role of the 'authority' in the affected territory has been addressed as one of these challenges. Indeed, in a NIAC either the state sovereign or the non-state actor involved in the conflict is the designated duty-bearer of the obligation to provide assistance, based upon humanitarian law and/or human rights law. However, in the event both the state sovereign and the non-state actor involved in NIAC do not provide assistance, enforcement hereof is necessary.

Such enforcement would then occur through third parties obtaining *access* should the affected authorities be unwilling or unable to provide assistance themselves, as discussed in the following Section. Enforcement *ex post facto* through, for example, adjudication by human rights bodies, the International Court of Justice or International Criminal Court remains an option, but falls outside the scope of this Chapter.

9.3.1 Access for the Provision of Humanitarian Assistance

In the face of a humanitarian crisis, often the case in time of NIAC, action must be taken to aid the civilian population in need of food, medicine and shelter. Human rights law does not however distinctly address a possibility for third parties to gain access to a territory. Equally in humanitarian law, a right to access by third parties is distinctly not incorporated in AP II. Although having been part of draft versions of the Article, this right was removed in the final acceptance thereof.[47] This act by the drafting States Parties to AP II is reflected today in the fact that States do not generally exercise a right to access independently. The ICRC has argued in its Customary International Humanitarian Law study that access is a 'conditio sine qua non' for the provision of relief and that the obligation to ensure freedom of movement for humanitarian personnel, consequential to the obligation to allow access to civilians, holds customary international legal status also concerning NIACs.[48] However, with the underlying obligation absent both from AP II and state practice, arguing a customary legal norm *derived* from an obligation which in itself has not unequivocally crystallized appears somewhat premature.

International law on the contrary formulates a *duty* for the affected authorities to embrace international aid. This duty can be read in Article 2(1) ICESCR concerning international assistance, as well as the formulation in AP II that an offer of assistance may not be 'arbitrarily' refused. Such duties have frequently been reiterated by the Security Council acting under Chapter VII through wording as 'demanding' compliance with international humanitarian and human rights law and 'allowing unimpeded, safe passage' for those providing assistance, such as amongst others in the conflicts in the Côte d'Ivoire, the Republic of South Sudan, the DRC and Somalia.[49] Thus, the *action* problematically lies in the hands of the controlling authorities. Indeed, this is acknowledged both in human rights law (the act to seek international aid) and humanitarian law (the refusal of an offer of assistance using various arguments such as visa requirements or taxes to forego arbitrariness).

Problematic is in particular the determination of 'arbitrariness' in the refusal of an offer of assistance. Such a determination should be made by an authoritative (legal) body, for the purpose or assessing whether or not access might be obtained (forcefully) following an arbitrary refusal. In the midst of a humanitarian crisis such as a NIAC, quick decisions must be made. In the current international legal domain, international judicial bodies would then benefit from concepts such as 'summary proceedings' or 'interlocutory judgments' as often found in national courts. With an ongoing crisis and need for immediate action however, in practice the Security Council—through action based upon Chapter VII UN Charter—is the designated body with the opportunity to take action for access in the provision of humanitarian aid.

---

[47]See Article 33 of the Draft Additional Protocol II submitted by the ICRC to the Diplomatic Conference (CDDH).

[48]ICRC Customary International Humanitarian Law Study (2005), Rules 55 and 56.

[49]UN Doc S/RES/1975 (2011) preamble and para 10; S/RES/1996 (2011) para 8; S/RES/2046 (2012) para 4; S/RES/2076 (2012) para 11; S/RES/2127 (2013) paras 51 and 52.

9.3.2 Security Council Action, Inaction and Potential Solutions for the Provision of Assistance

The opportunity for the international community to take action can arguably at times be considered a legal *obligation* under Articles 25 and 42 UN Charter, should the non-provision of assistance amount to war crimes, crimes against humanity, racial discrimination or genocide.

Of these four crimes, only the first requires a nexus to an armed conflict and as such the latter may occur in circumstances that do not meet particular thresholds of AP II or of the Geneva Conventions in general, allowing a broad mandate for the Security Council, which needs to establish the more political 'threat to the peace' according to Article 39 UN Charter.[50] Furthermore, all four crimes amount to violations of norms which are currently accepted in international law as *jus cogens*, whereas the well-known Martens Clause that reflects the principle of humanity is considered to constitute an 'intransgressible' principle of international law.[51] Indeed, the deprivation of a population of food, water, shelter and medicine may amount to a violation of *jus cogens* norms by the responsible state or armed group should its actions or omissions reach that threshold. When a breach of norms of *jus cogens* takes place (regardless of the actor involved), the ARSIWA declare a duty upon third parties to 'cooperate to bring to an end through lawful means' such a violation.[52] This provision envisages a *positive* obligation that may be executed either through an institution such as the UN, or in a non-institutionalized manner.[53]

---

[50] Article 1 Genocide Convention, and regarding crimes against humanity: The Prosecutor v. Duško Tadić (Appeals Chamber), (*Decision on the Defence Motion for Interlocutory Appeal on Jurisdiction*), No IT-94-1-AR72, para 141 (ICTY 1995) on the development thereto in customary law. See concurring also the Human Rights Commission UN Doc. E/CN.4/1999/92, "Commission on Human Rights, "*Promotion and Protection of Human Rights: Fundamental Standards of Humanity*", para 12 (1998) and the Statute of the International Criminal Court, Article 7.

[51] See amongst others ICJ East Timor case (Portugal v. Australia), Judgment 30 June 1005, I.C.J. Reports 1995, para 29 concerning the right to self-determination; ICJ Case Concerning Armed Activities On The Territory Of The Congo (New Application: 2002) (Democratic Republic Of The Congo v. Rwanda) Jurisdiction Of The Court And Admissibility Of The Application Judgment Of 3 February 2006, para 64 concerning the prohibition of genocide; ICJ 'Questions Relating To The Obligation To Prosecute Or Extradite' (Belgium v. Senegal) Judgment 20 July 2012 para 99 concerning the prohibition of torture; somewhat more generally concerning *erga omnes* obligations the ICJ *Barcelona Traction, Light and Power Company Limited (Belgium v. Spain)* case *ICJ Reports 1970*, paras 33–34 regarding the prohibition of aggression and genocide, as well as 'basic human rights' such as the protection from slavery and racial discrimination. See also concerning war crimes and crimes against humanity the ICTY Prosecutor v. Furundzija, 10 December 1998, IT-95-17/1-T paras 153–157; Prosecutor v. Delalic, 20 February 2001, para 172; Prosecutor v. Krstic, 2 August 2001, para 541. Regarding the Martens Clause, see ICJ *Legality of the Threat or Use of Nuclear Weapons,* Advisory Opinion 1996, paras 78–79.

[52] See Articles 40–41 ARSIWA.

[53] UN Doc. A/56/10 (2001) ILC Commentary to the ARSIWA pp. 286–287.

The UN recognizes in Article 1(3) as a purpose of the Organization to 'achieve international cooperation in promoting and encouraging respect for human rights and fundamental freedoms for all'. Such was reaffirmed early on in the work of the UN General Assembly through the 'Declaration on Principles of International Law concerning Friendly Relations and Cooperation among States in accordance with the Charter of the United Nations' that formulated the 'duty of States to cooperate with one another in accordance with the Charter'.[54] Furthermore, the notion of the Responsibility to Protect (despite on-going discussion on the acceptance of the doctrine) as embraced by the UN with its four core crimes, warrants Security Council action in the event genocide, war crimes, ethnic cleansing or crimes against humanity take place.[55] The ICJ has also provided its perspective on cooperation in its 2007 *Bosnia v Serbia* judgment, where the Court argued that 'an obligation of conduct' exists for state parties to the Genocide Convention to prevent the occurrence of genocide *and* acknowledged that the Genocide Convention is certainly not the only international legal instrument that provides for a duty of states parties to take steps in the prevention of acts the instrument attempts to prohibit.[56] Indeed, the Court recognizes a duty of conduct that may itself result in a responsibility for *third* states should they 'manifestly fail to take all measures' and asserts that this responsibility is both joint and individual.[57] Compare in this regard also Article 89 AP I that recognizes such a duty to cooperate in the face of serious violations in time of an *international* armed conflict. Indeed, it can be concluded that the international community is called upon in both human rights law and humanitarian law to assist in the provision of aid or the fulfillment of certain rights, from which a duty can be deduced to refrain from performing an opposite act: reinforcing the crisis.

International law and doctrine therefore provide ample opportunity for the Security Council to take lawful measures through Chapter VII of the UN Charter and upon establishing a threat to the peace, should the deprivation of humanitarian assistance reach the threshold that the circumstance amounts to potential war crimes, crimes against humanity, genocide or racial discrimination as this determination leads to international obligations for third states to provide aid. Such a determination under current international law rests with the Security Council itself, which has unfortunately shown varying degrees of willingness hereto in recent years. Whilst the Council has affirmed the *possibility* of the use of force for the sole purpose of delivering humanitarian aid, as for example regarding Chad, it has often fallen short of actually using force.[58] As is well-known, the decision is ultimately determined by those states within the Council and their political agenda.

---

[54]UN Doc. A/RES/25/2625 (1970).

[55]2005 UN World Summit Outcome Document paras 138–139.

[56]ICJ Case Concerning Application Of The Convention On The Prevention and Punishment Of The Crime Of Genocide (Bosnia And Herzegovina v. Serbia And Montenegro), Judgment Of 26 February 2007, para 429.

[57]Ibid, para 430.

[58]UN Doc. S/RES/1861 (2009) para 7.

In its Resolution 1973 regarding the situation in Libya in 2011, the Council has proceeded to indeed recognize and take this legal responsibility.[59] However, in subsequent circumstances such as in Syria and Mali, the Council has remained mute with regard to the use of force. However, in a novel approach, the Security Council asserted in Resolution 2165 the possibility of entering the Syrian territory without specifically acknowledging the sovereign's consent, to enable the provision of humanitarian assistance 'across conflict lines'.[60] This call has subsequently been reaffirmed in Resolution 2191, but has yet to be applied to other circumstances.[61] However, the Council does appear to be approaching the delivery of humanitarian assistance in novel manners. In 2013 it for example created an 'Intervention Brigade' (part of its MONUSCO mission in the DRC) that for the first time enhanced a peacekeeping mission with the task to 'carry out targeted offensive operations' to neutralize armed groups in the protection of civilians, as well as ensure the protection of civilians and humanitarian personnel.[62] The notions of 'sovereignty' and 'consent' as a barrier in relation to the provision of assistance thus seem to be slowly wavering as the Council attempts to find new approaches to the delivery of aid.

Whilst the option to use force *to enable the provision of humanitarian assistance* is in fact 'on the table', in practice the greatest challenge to the current law regulating the provision of humanitarian assistance in a NIAC is perhaps not legal, but political. The absence of a 'standard' situation or formulation to entice the Security Council into action painfully reveals the distinct political perspectives it brings into its decision-making. However, its crucial lack of action in some circumstances should not be interpreted as a demonstration of a lacking *potential to act* in others.

9.4 Conclusion

Several legal challenges can be highlighted from the above discussion on the legal framework regarding the provision of humanitarian assistance in a NIAC. The protective approach to the 'lex specialis' issues between humanitarian law and human rights law attempts to provide some answers to these existing legal challenges. This approach furthermore assists those facing a 'humanitarian crisis' that falls outside the scope of humanitarian law.

Factually, the law differentiates amongst those in a NIAC protected by Common Article 3, versus those protected by AP II. In both instances however, the *external* provision of aid is dependent on the determination that a territory is

[59]UN Doc. S/RES/1973 (2011), preamble and paras 4, 7.

[60]UN Doc. S/RES/2165 (2014) paras 2, 6 and 7.

[61]UN Doc. S/RES/2191 (2014) para 2.

[62]UN Doc. S/RES/2098 paras 9 and 12.

inadequately supplied, as well as on the consent of the concerned party. In particular with regard to Article 18 AP II, questions are raised as to the possibility to consider the armed group exercising control over a territory as the 'concerned party' of a particular territory. Consent may not be withheld *arbitrarily* in any circumstance under Article 18 AP II, but this concept remains undefined and is furthermore lacking from those NIACs that merely have Common Article 3 of the Geneva Conventions to fall back on. Human rights law however remains applicable throughout various types of NIACs, as well as those humanitarian crises that do not meet the threshold of an armed conflict. A duty of the affected state to seek international assistance can be sought in this body of law also.

Indeed, the *law* concerning the provision of humanitarian assistance in time of a NIAC is not necessarily lacking, in particular if the 'most protective' approach is taken. The *enforcement* of this law, however, forms the greatest challenge today. In particular, the authoritative determination that a territory is inadequately supplied and persons are warranting assistance through external sources, is often lacking. The international legal judiciary bodies are challenged in their ability to provide *ad hoc* solutions of enforcement, whilst the Security Council—which does have these possibilities through the use of force—is challenged by its political composition and course of action. A solution combining both methods of enforcement might provide a way forward: a judiciary body or committee to advise the Security Council in those instances that a humanitarian crisis unfolds. This committee would be able to provide more neutral, judicial backing to the political decision-making process of the Council.

Case Law

PCIJ

S.S. Lotus (Fr. v. Turk.), 1927 P.C.I.J. (ser. A) No. 10 (Sept. 7), The Case of the S.S. Lotus France v. Turkey Judgment, 7 September 1927

ICJ

Barcelona Traction, Light and Power Company Limited (Belgium v. Spain) case ICJ Reports 1970

Military and Paramilitary Activities in and against Nicaragua (Nicaragua vs. United States), Merits 1986 ICJ REP. 14 (Judgment of 27 June 1986)

ICJ East Timor case (Portugal v. Australia), Judgment 30 June 1995, I.C.J. Reports 1995

ICJ (Advisory Opinion) Legality of the threat or use of nuclear weapons, 8 July 1996. See also ICJ (Advisory Opinion) Legal consequences of the construction of a wall in the occupied Palestinian Territory, 9 July 2004

ICJ Armed Activities on the Territory of the Congo (Democratic Republic of the Congo v. Uganda), I.C.J. Reports 2005 (Congo v. Uganda), Judgment, 19 December 2005, ICJ Rep. 2005, 1

Case Concerning Armed Activities on the Territory of the Congo (New Application: 2002) (Democratic Republic of the Congo v. Rwanda) Jurisdiction of the Court and Admissibility of the Application Judgment Of 3 February 2006

Case Concerning Application of the Convention on the Prevention and Punishment of the Crime of Genocide (Bosnia and Herzegovina v. Serbia and Montenegro), Judgment of 26 February 2007

'Questions Relating to the Obligation to Prosecute or Extradite' (Belgium v. Senegal) Judgment 20 July 2012

ICTY

The Prosecutor v. Duško Tadić (Appeals Chamber), 2 October 1995 (*Decision on the Defence Motion for Interlocutory Appeal on Jurisdiction*), No IT-94-1-AR72 (ICTY 1995)
The *Prosecutor v Tadic* Trial Chamber, IT-94-1-T 7 May 1997
The Prosecutor v. Zejnil Delalic et al., Case No IT-96-21-T, Judgment, 16 November 1998
The Prosecutor v. Furundzija (Trial Judgment), No. IT-95-17/1-T, 10 December 1998, (ICTY 1998)
The Prosecutor v. Delalić et. al. (Celebici - Case) (Appeals Chamber), No. IT-96-21-A, 20 February 2001 (ICTY 2001)
Prosecutor v. Krstic, (Trial Chamber) IT-98-33-T, 2 August 2001

ECtHR

Ilascu and others v. Moldova and Russia Case No. 48787/99, [2004] ECHR 318, 8 July 2004.
Isayeva, Yusupova and Bazayeva v. Russia (Isayeva I) Case No. 57947/00, 57948/00, 57949/00, [2005] ECHR 129, 24 February 2005
Isayeva v. Russia (Isayeva II) Case No. 57950/00, [2005] ECHR 128, 24 February 2005

IACtHR

Bamaca Velásquez v Guatamala Judgment 25 November 2000

UN Documents

2005 UN World Summit Outcome Document

Security Council Resolutions

UN Doc. S/RES/1265 (1999)
UN Doc. S/RES/13255 (31 October 2000)
UN Doc. S/RES/1430 (14 August 2002)
UN Doc. S/RES/1674 (2006)
UN Doc. S/RES/1769 31 July 2007
UN Doc. S/RES 1794 (21 December 2007)
UN Doc. S/1861 (14 January 2009)
UN Doc. S/RES/1863 (2009)
UN Doc. S/RES/1894 (2009)
UN Doc. S/RES/1906 (23 December 2009)
UN Doc. S/RES/1970 (2011)
UN Doc. S/RES/1973 (17 March 2011)
UN Doc. S/RES/1975 (2011)
UN Doc. S/RES/1996 (2011)
UN Doc. S/RES/2014 (21 October 2011)
UN Doc. S/RES/2016 (27 October 2011)
UN Doc. S/RES/2040 (12 March 2012)
UN Doc. S/RES/2098 (2013)
UN Doc. S/RES/2165 (2014)
UN Doc. S/RES/2191 (2014)
Security Council Resolution Reports of the Secretary-General on the Sudan 8 July 2011

General Assembly Resolutions

UN Doc. A/RES/25/2625, 24 October 1970
UNGA Resolution 2675 (XXV) 9 December 1970
UN Doc. A/RES/2717 (XXV), 15 December 1970
UN Doc. A/RES/43/131, 8 December 1988
UN Doc. A/RES/46/182, 19 December 1991
UN Doc. A/RES/58/114, 5 February 2004
UN Doc. A/RES/59/141, 25 February 2005
UN Doc. A/RES/60/124, 8 March 2006
UN Doc. A/RES/62/94, 25 January 2008
UN Doc. A/RES/63/139, 5 March 2009
UN Doc. A/RES/64/76, 2 February 2010
UN Doc. A/RES/65/133, 3 March 2011
UN Doc. A/RES/66/119, 7 March 2012

Human Rights Bodies

Human Rights Commission UN Doc. E/CN.4/1999/92, "Commission on Human Rights, "Promotion and Protection of Human Rights: Fundamental Standards of Humanity" (1998)
CESCR E/1991/23 (1990) General Comment No. 3 (Article 2), 14 December 1990
CESCR E/C/12/1999/5 (1999) General Comment No. 12 (Article 11) 12 May 1999
Human Rights Committee UN Doc. CCPR/C/21/Rev.1/Add.11 General Comment 29 pursuant to Article 4 'States of Emergency' (2001)
HRC UN Doc. CCPR/C/21/Rev.1/Add.13 (2004), General Comment No. 31 (Article 2) (26 May 2004)

Other UN Bodies

UN Doc. A/56/10 (2001) ILC Commentary to the ARSIWA
UN Doc. A/CN.4/L.682 (ILC Study Fragmentation of the Law) 16 April 2006
UN Special Rapporteur Eduardo Valencia Ospina for the ILC Study on the 'Protectionn of Persons in the Event of Disaster', UN Doc A/CN.4/598 Preliminary Report, February 2008
UN Doc. A/CN.4/643, ILC, Fourth report of the Special Rapporteur, Mr. Eduardo Valencia-Ospina (63rd session of the ILC (2011)) on the protection of persons in the event of disasters

Other

Commentary to the Vienna Convention, Yearbook of the International Law Commission, 1966, Vol. II
Statutes of the International Red Cross and Red Crescent Movement, adopted by the 25th International Conference of the Red Cross at Geneva in 1986, amended in 1995 and 2006
Turku/Åbo Declaration Of Minimum Humanitarian Standards (1990)
ICRC Customary International Humanitarian Law Study (2005)
ILA Hague Conference, Final Report on the Meaning of Armed Conflict in International Law, Committee on the Use of Force 2010

http://www.nytimes.com/2014/07/25/world/middleeast/defying-syria-united-nations-sends-in-trucks-carrying-aid.html?_r=0 (last retrieved 28 August 2014)
http://www.reuters.com/article/2014/07/24/us-syria-crisis-un-aid-idUSKBN-0FT25G20140724 (last retrieved 28 August 2014)
http://www.nytimes.com/2011/03/11/world/europe/11france.html?_r=0 (last retrieved 21 March 2015)
http://www.washingtonpost.com/world/middle-east/western-arab-leaders-meet-in-turkey-on-libyas-future/2011/07/15/gIQAZLbjFI_story.html (last retrieved 21 March 2015)

References

Clapham A (2006) Human rights obligations of non-state actors in conflict situations. IRRC 88(863):491–523
Dinstein Y (2000) The right to humanitarian assistance. Nav War Coll Rev Autumn 2000:77–92
Doswald-Beck L (2006) The right to life in armed conflict: does international humanitarian law provide all the answers? IRRC 88(864):881–904
Dungel J (2004) A Right to humanitarian assistance in internal armed conflicts respecting sovereignty, neutrality and legitimacy: practical proposals to practical problems. J Humanitarian Assistance, May 2004
Krieger H (2006) A conflict of norms: the relationship between humanitarian law and human rights law in the ICRC customary law study. J Conflict Secur Law 11(2):265–291
Kuijt E (2015) A humanitarian crisis: reframing the legal framework on humanitarian assistance. In: Zwitter A et al (eds) Humanitarian action: global regional and domestic legal responses. Cambridge University Press, Cambridge
Pictet J S (ed) (1958) Commentary to the Geneva Conventions of 12 August 1949
Plattner D (1996) ICRC neutrality and neutrality in humanitarian assistance. IRRC 311
Rynaert C (2013) Humanitarian assistance and the conundrum of consent: a legal perspective. Amsterdam Law Forum 5(2):5–19
Sandoz Y et al. (eds.) (1987) Commentary to the additional protocols to the Geneva Conventions of 12 August 1949
Sassòli M, Olson LM (2008) The relationship between international humanitarian and human rights law where it matters: admissible killing and internment of fighters in non-international armed conflicts. IRRC 90(871):599–627
Steiner J et al (2008) International human rights in context. Oxford University Press, Oxford
Tomuschat C (2004) The applicability of human rights law to insurgent movements. In: Fischer H et al (eds) Krisensicherung und humanitärer schutz—crisis management and humanitarian protection. Berliner Wissenschafts-Verlag, Berlin, pp 573–591

Other Consulted Sources

Bellamy A (2009) Responsibility to protect: the global effort to end mass atrocities. Polity Press, Cambridge
Hoffmann J, Nollkaemper A (eds) (2012) Responsibility to protect: from principle to practice. Pallas Publications, Amsterdam
Schrijver NJ (1999) The changing nature of state sovereignty. Br YearB Int Law 70:65–98
Thakur R (2006) The United Nations, peace and security: from collective security to responsibility to protect. Cambridge University Press, Cambridge

Part V
Other Fields of Law

Chapter 10
A Century of the Law of Occupation

Yaël Ronen

Abstract The law of occupation, which was first codified around the turn of the twentieth century, has not often been applied in the century that followed. States have always been reluctant to constrain themselves by its rules, and political, social and economic changes that have taken place through the years have gradually made such constraints difficult even with the best of intentions. As a result, the law of occupation developed largely through doctrine and little through practice. The present chapter examines how these factors have affected the law of occupation from within and without. From within, it traces the development of the definition of occupation and the legitimate scope of intervention by an occupant in the administration of the territory. From without, it addresses the relationship between the law of occupation and other bodies of law, principally the right to self-determination and international human right law; and their impact on the development of criteria for determining the legality of occupation.

Keywords Law of occupation · Geneva Conventions · Hague regulations · International human rights law · Self-determination · Transformative occupation

---

Yaël Ronen is Professor of International Law, Sha'arei Mishpat Academic Center, Hod Hasharon, and the Minerva Center for Human Rights, Hebrew University in Jerusalem.

Y. Ronen (✉)
Minerva Center for Human Rights, Hebrew University, Jerusalem, Israel
e-mail: yael.ronen@mail.huji.ac.il

T.D. Gill et al. (eds.), *Yearbook of International Humanitarian Law 2014*,
Yearbook of International Humanitarian Law 17,
DOI 10.1007/978-94-6265-091-6_10

Contents

10.1 Introduction

The international legal regime of occupation in the modern sense has its roots in the second half of the nineteenth century. It became part of positive international law through The Hague regulations of 1899 and later those of 1907.[1] Yet the enormous changes in the conduct of war and in political thought during the first half of the twentieth century have rendered the provisions of The Hague Regulations inadequate almost as soon as they were formulated. The exploitation and brutal treatment of civilians in occupied Allied territories during World War II, together with a systematic attempt by occupants to use the gaps in The Hague Regulations, highlighted the urgent need for reform of the law.[2] The latter was carried out in 1949 when the Fourth Geneva Convention (GC IV) was adopted. In addition to reformulating the interests which the law of occupation sought to accommodate, the Convention contains specific provisions on the treatment of civilians based on the experience of the previous years, regarding matters such as deportation, protection of property, collective punishment and procedures in occupation courts.[3] Important issues nonetheless remained under-regulated due to the inability to reach consensus, such as the economic exploitation of occupied territory.[4]

[1]Hague Convention (IV) respecting the Laws and Customs of War on Land and its Annex: Regulations concerning the Laws and Customs of War on Land, Oct. 18, 1907, Martens Nouveau Recueil (ser 3) 461 [hereinafter Hague Regulations].

[2]Von Glahn 1957, p. 16.

[3]Convention (IV) relative to the Protection of Civilian Persons in Time of War, Aug. 12, 1949, 75 U.N.T.S. 287 [hereinafter GCIV]; Protocol Additional to the Geneva Conventions of 12 August 1949, and relating to the Protection of Victims of International Armed Conflicts (Protocol I), June 8, 1977, 1125 U.N.T.S. 3 [hereinafter Additional Protocol I] addresses the law of occupation only briefly.

[4]Which is only briefly regulated, e.g. Hague Convention (IV) respecting the Laws and Customs of War on Land and its annex: Regulation concerning the Laws and Customs of War on Land, Martens Nouveau Recueil (ser 3) 461 Article 55; Von Glahn 1957, p. 20.

The 1949 revision did not, however, succeed in bringing states to acknowledge their status as occupants and to apply the law of occupation. Despite numerous instances in which effective control was established by state forces in foreign territory,[5] between World War II and the early 1990s only one state (Israel) regarded itself as occupant in territories in which it has established control.[6]

Since the 1990s the law of occupation has had a revival, when its applicability was acknowledged by coalition partners in Iraq (1991), Afghanistan (2001) and again in Iraq (2003). These incidents have both revived the interest in old questions (such the powers of the occupant to exploit resources of the occupied territory) and created new ones (such as the transformative role of occupation). The status of the law of occupation as positive international law is undisputed. In 1939, the International Military Tribunal in Nuremberg declared that the 1907 Hague Regulations had become customary international law.[7] It may already have constituted customary law at the time, as the antecedent principles of The Hague Regulations had been incorporated into the military manuals of many states.[8] While only 43 states are parties to The Hague Regulations, and only seven of them have acceded since World War II,[9] the Geneva Conventions have been universally accepted. Some go so far as to argue that at least certain provisions of the law of occupation are peremptory.[10] Given the denial by most occupants of their status as such,[11] state practice implementing the law of occupation from World War II until

---

[5]E.g. the Gaza Strip by Egypt (1948–1967), the West Bank by Jordan (1948–1967), West Sahara by Morocco (1975–), East Timor by Indonesia (1975–99), Northern Cyprus by Turkey (1974–) Afghanistan by the USSR (1978–88), Cambodia by Vietnam (1979–89), Grenada by the US (1983–4), Panama by the US (1989), Kuwait by Iraq (1990), Iraq by the US-led coalition (1991), Uganda by the DRC (1998-2003), Afghanistan by the US-led coalition (2001–2), Georgia by Russia (2008). For analyses of these cases see Benvenisti 2012.

[6]Israel acknowledges its status in the West Bank (and previously also in the Gaza Strip) as occupant de jure under The Hague Regulations. As for GC IV, Israel maintains that it is not applicable to territory taken from a non-sovereign, but has declared its commitment to apply de facto the humanitarian provisions of the Convention. Ajuri and ors v Israeli Defence Force Commander in West Bank and ors, Original Petition to the High Court of Justice, Case No HCJ 7015/02, 56(6) PD 352, [2002] Isr L Rep 1, (2003) 97 AJIL 173, ILDC 14 (IL 2002), para, 13, 3rd September 2002; Shamgar 1982, pp. 38–40. Israel also recognised its status as occupant in Lebanon from 1982 to 2000.

[7]International Military Tribunal at Nuremberg, Case of the Major War Criminals, Judgment, 1 October 1946, Official Documents, Vol. I, pp. 253–254.

[8]Von Glahn 1957, p. 11; citing Garner 1925, p. 20. Given the limited space of this contribution, secondary sources are at times substitute for aggregation of primary sources. However, throughout the text secondary sources are cited from the period discussed, to reflect contemporary views rather than historical reflection and hindsight wisdom.

[9]Dutch Government depositary information, https://treatydatabase.overheid.nl/en/Verdrag/Details/003319.

[10]Ferraro 2012, p. 71.

[11]Most recently by the Russian Federation with respect to the Crimean Peninsula, which it has annexed in March 2014. Address by President of the Russian Federation, 18 March 2014, http://eng.kremlin.ru/news/6889.

the 1990s was limited to one state, Israel,[12] but the continuous doctrinal engagement with the topic for over a century[13] has brought about radical changes to the law.

The present chapter examines selected issues in the development of the law of occupation since World War I. It examines changes within the law of occupation itself, regarding its applicability and the scope of the occupant's authority to administer the territory. It also examines the applicability of bodies other than the law of occupation and their impact on the legal status of the occupation.

To appreciate the causes of these changes and their effect, it is first necessary to be familiar with the law of occupation as originally conceived. This is the purpose of the next section.

10.2 The Law of Occupation as Originally Conceived

The drafters of The Hague Regulations conceived occupation as a transient situation, for the short period in which one state established effective control over the territory of another. This regime would characteristically come to an end with the conclusion of a peace treaty under which the territory would be ceded to the victor or if the defeated state recovers the advantage and drives the occupant away.[14] This conception was part of a more general theory of war in the nineteenth century, in which use of force was a legitimate means for achieving national goals, including acquisition of territory.

War was seen as a match between governments and their armies. The Hague Regulations were drafted with a view to protecting sovereignty, which at the time inhered in the government. The law of occupation thus regulated the relations between state elites—the government in effective control and the ousted sovereign one—rather than between an occupying government and population in occupied territory. States were not only the only subjects of law,[15] but also its beneficiaries.[16]

This conception of war combined with the *laissez faire* philosophy, which prevailed in political and economic thought at the time, namely minimalised

---

[12]For a discussion of the application of the law of occupation in Iraq in 1991 see Roberts 1993, pp. 134, 173–174.

[13]A non-exhaustive list of monographs includes (in chronological order) Olivier 1913; Braas, 1918; Graziani 1928; Pauly 1930, Graber 1949; Von Glahn 1957; Debbasch and Maurice 1962; Feilchenfeld 1971' Benvenisti 1993; Arai-Takahashi 2009; Kolb and Vité 2009. There have been waves of shorter pieces and case studies following major relevant events, such as World War I, the Israeli occupation of the West Bank and Gaza Strip, the 1990–1991 occupation of Kuwait by Iraq, and the 2003 occupation of Iraq by the Coalition Provisional Authority. The Israeli occupation has dominated the literature in the last decades of the twentieth century.

[14]Robin 1913, pp. 5–6; Oppenheim 1917, pp. 363, 364.

[15]Oppenheim 1917, pp. 363, 367.

[16]Benvenisti 2012, pp. 70–71.

intervention of the government in economic life.[17] Accordingly, little interaction was expected to take place between the inhabitants of the occupied territory and the occupying government and there was little to regulate. Yet around the turn of the twentieth century, the *laissez faire* doctrine was already on the decline, replaced by an increasing involvement of the state in economic and social life.[18] At the same time, the centrality of the state as the locus of sovereignty began to loosen. The interests of the population distinctly from those of the government, embodied in the principle of self-determination, gained a foothold in international relations,[19] gradually leading to a weakening of the government's prerogative in determining the future of territory. Furthermore, the centrality of the individual as beneficiary of the law began to emerge. Rather than the relations between two actors, the occupant and the ousted government, the law of occupation now had to contend with a third actor: the local population. The modified conception of occupation is reflected in the definition of occupation and in the delineation of the occupant's authority to intervene in the administration of the territory. The next section examines those.

10.3 Development of the Law of Occupation

10.3.1 What Constitutes Occupation?

The Hague Regulations envisage occupation as a situation in which the military forces of one state gain effective control over territory of another state without its consent, through engagement in war. Yet as early as during World War I, phenomena occurred which were similar to this scenario but not identical to it. These included the invasion of neutral states;[20] the assumption of effective control without any military resistance;[21] and, in the aftermath of the War, treaty-based effective control without sovereignty.[22] World War II saw annexation and the setting up of puppet regimes in occupied territory,[23] and concluded with the occupation-to-

[17]Ibid, p. 70.

[18]Friedmann 1956, pp. 475, 475–478.

[19]Fourteen Points, (Jan. 8, 1918), declaration by U.S. President Woodrow Wilson during World War I.

[20]E.g. the occupation of neutral China's Manchuria by Japan during the Russo-Japanese War. Judge Advocate General's School 1945, 3–5, and the occupation of Luxembourg by Germany in World War I. Kautsky 1922, p. 136 Doc No 637.

[21]E.g. Neutral Luxembourg did not offer military resistance to German forces. Kautsky, ibid.

[22]E.g. France's occupation of the Ruhr in claimed application of the Treaty of Versailles, Part VIII, Annex 2, Articles 17–18 (1919) American Journal of International Law Supplement 13, pp. 151, 385 (1919). For a debate on the lawfulness of that action see Allemés and Schuster 1924.

[23]For a detailed account see Lemkin 1944.

extinction of Germany. New phenomena since World War II included the entry of military forces into foreign territory not previously under internationally recognised sovereignty[24] and administration by international organisations.[25]

The qualification of every instance of alleged occupation has been a matter of debate. In some cases, controversy revolved over the interpretation of the facts, such as whether the entry of forces was by invitation (in which case they were not 'hostile'),[26] or whether they had established effective control.[27] A separate set of arguments have challenged the interpretation of the law. Thus, following World War I the Allies contended that the armistice occupation of the Rhineland was outside the scope of The Hague Regulations because of its consensual origin,[28] which according to conservative views rendered it subject only to constitutional law.[29] Following World War II, the Allies claimed that the law of occupation did not apply in the case of Germany because it had become extinct.[30] Another major challenge to the applicability of the law was put forward by Israel soon after the 1967 Six-Day War. Although Israel does not deny that it was an occupying power as defined by The Hague Regulations, its official position is that GC IV does not apply to territory taken from a non-sovereign.[31] In all of these cases, the denial of the applicability of the law of occupation has served to allow the alleged occupants to carry out significant changes in the political and economic structure of the regions that were patently unlawful under the law of occupation. Perhaps the boldest assertion in this context was put forward with respect to the occupation in US–UK occupation of Iraq in 2003 (although both states have actually acknowledged

[24]Israel in the West Bank and Gaza Strip and Indonesia in Timor Leste.

[25]UN operations worldwide, the US-led coalitions in Afghanistan and Iraq.

[26]E.g. the entry of Syrian forces into Lebanon in 1976, see Beirut Radio and Voice of Palestine Radio Report of Lebanese-Syrian-Palestinian Agreement, 22 January 1976, in Foreign Affairs and National Defence Division, Congressional Research Service, Library of Congress, *The Search for peace in the Middle East :documents and statements, 1967–79: report prepared for the Subcommittee on Europe and the Middle East of the Committee on Foreign Affairs, US House of Representatives* (US Government Printing Office 1979), p. 329 Doc No 113; the Soviet intervention in Afghanistan in 1979, Conversation of the chief of the Soviet military advisory group in Afghanistan, Lt. Gen. Gorelov, with H. Amin, 11 August 1979, in Cold War International History Project Woodrow Wilson International Center for Scholars (2001) Documents on the Soviet Invasion of Afghanistan, Washington DC, p. 153.

[27]*Prosecutor* v *Naletilić & Martinović*, Case No. IT-98-34, ICTY Trial Chamber Judgment 31 March 2003, para 587 [hereinafter Naletilić] Armed Activities on the Territory of the Congo, Judgment, 2005 I.C.J. 168, 190, paras 168–169 (Dec. 19) [hereinafter Congo v. Uganda].

[28]Benvenisti 2012, pp. 129–30.

[29]Colby 1925, pp. 904, 904–907.

[30]Benvenisti 2012, p. 160.

[31]A doctrine developed in Blum 1968, pp. 293–294; Israel's View on the Convening of the UN Emergency Special Session July 1997 (Communicated by the Israel Foreign Ministry 14 July 1997; Legal Consequence of the Construction of a Wall in the Occupied Palestinian Territory, Advisory Opinion, 2004 I.C.J. 136, para 90 (July 9) [hereinafter Wall Advisory Opinion]. http://mfa.gov.il/MFA/InternatlOrgs/Issues/Pages/Israel-s%20View%20on%20UN%20Emergency%20Special%20Session%20July.aspx.

their status as occupants). It was contended that since the law of occupation prohibited state transformation, it should not apply to that occupation, or apply only in part.[32]

Some of these apparent loopholes were redressed by the reform in GC IV. Thus the Convention provides that territory would be regarded as occupied even if it was taken over without resistance,[33] and implicitly also covers occupation following an armistice or capitulation, so long as the state of war continues.[34] In addition, international law has grown less formalistic, for example, by abandoning the strict differentiation of legal regimes between peace, war and neutrality; and by dismissing recognition of belligerence as a condition for the applicability of the laws of armed conflict. Consequently, the particularities of the various situations have become less significant.[35]

But most important for the interpretation of the applicability of the law of occupation is the shift of emphasis from the protection of an ousted sovereign's rights to the protection of the population in the occupied territory. The appreciation that the existence of a temporary, non-sovereign regime is a situation which inherently breeds a conflict of interests between the occupant and the population,[36] and that it is therefore crucial to impose limitations on the authority of the occupant, has given rise to a more liberal view of occupation, which largely dismisses the significance of the various circumstances in which non-sovereign effective control has been established. This shift is reflected in the broadening of the definition of occupation under GC IV.[37] In the same vein, the International Court of Justice (ICJ) has held that GC IV applies in the West Bank despite not having previously been under sovereign rule,[38] and by the Eritrea-Ethiopia Commission, which held generally that the international law of occupation does not suggest that 'only territory the title to which is clear and uncontested can be occupied territory'.[39]

---

[32]E.g. Scheffer 2003, pp. 842, 848–49.

[33]GC IV, Article 2(2).

[34]Commentary on the Geneva Convention of 12 August 1949: GC IV (Oscar M. Uhler & Henri Coursier eds., 1958) p. 22.

[35]This deformalisation was reflected in the drafting of the Hague Regulations themselves. The definition of the beginning of occupation as the time in territory 'is actually placed under the authority of the hostile army and the latter's 'authority has been established and can be exercised' (Hague Regulations Article 42) was a compromise between those who held that the occupation began upon publication of notice anywhere within an administrative unit, and those who held that what was required was the ability to use immediate force. Hall 1895, pp. 1895, 500–504 para 161.

[36]Jones 1923, pp. 149, 159; Judge Advocate General's School 1945, p. 1; Roberts 1984, pp. 249, 300–301; Benvenisti 2012, p. 318.

[37]Without abrogating the definition under The Hague Regulations, Naletilić, *supra* note 27, para 215.

[38]Wall Advisory Opinion, *supra* note 30, para 95.

[39]Central Front (Eritrea v. Ethiopia), Ethiopia's claim 2, Partial Awards, Eritrea Ethiopia Claims Commission, April 28, 2004, para 29.

The more liberal perception of occupation has also informed the engagement with new challenges, such as novel types of occupants. In 1907, the law of occupation applied strictly to the armed forces of individual states. Through time, effective control over territory has been exercised jointly by allied states,[40] and by states acting on behalf of the UN[41] or of other international organisations.[42] As the emphasis in the law of occupation moves towards the conflict of interests between the governing authorities and the population, irrespective of the circumstances which have brought about the situation, there appears to be little justification to deprive peaceful civilians from protection against the hardships of conflict to only because the entity in control of the territory is multi-national.[43] At the same time, particular challenges arise, such as attribution and sharing of responsibility,[44] as well as the need for a nuanced approach to the issue of consent, when nominal consent by the government does not reflect the sentiments of the population or large sections thereof.[45] Another question arising with respect to UN operations is the relationship between the law of occupation and Security Council resolution mandates on territorial administration, which grant the administering authorities powers to support and facilitate political reforms, which may be in excess of what the law of occupation permits.[46]

As the law of occupation increasingly focuses on the protection of the population rather than regulating an inter-state relationship, the different phenomena coalesce into a minimalist definition of 'occupation' as a situation in which foreign forces state exercise effective control over non-sovereign territory. Such a regime is temporary, and accordingly, the occupant's authority is limited.

Notably, despite the growing convergence of the laws of international armed conflict and those of non-international armed conflict, the distinction persists with respect to the law of occupation, which has not been extended to situations of internal conflict.[47] This is particularly interesting in view of the fact that much of the early law of occupation originated in the US Civil War, which, notwithstanding

---

[40]In Italy and in Germany following World War II.

[41]UNMIK in Kosovo and UNTAET in Timor Leste (1999–2002), UNITAF in Somalia (1992–1993).

[42]NATO's KFOR (1995–1996) and SFOR (1996–2005) in Bosnia-Herzegovina.

[43]As the notion of concerted international action emerged, von Glahn contemplated whether the fact that such action is by definition taken against aggressor states should affect the applicability of the laws of war, including law of occupation. Von Glahn 1957, p. 23. However, not only does the distinction between *ius ad bellum* and *ius in bello* cotintue to be relevant, but experience since von Glahn has put forward this proposition demonstrates that international intervention is not limited to action against aggressor states.

[44]Scheffer 2003, pp. 842, 846; Ferraro 2012, pp. 34–35; Wilde 2010, pp. 354–56.

[45]Ratner 2005, p. 698.

[46]E.g. UN SCR 1244, UN Doc S/RES/1244 (1999) 10 June 1999 para 11; SCR 1483, UN Doc S/RES/1483 (2003) 22 May 2003 para 8; Wills 2009 chap IV; Ferraro 2012, pp. 33–34.

[47]Note that the term 'internal' is used to designate an armed conflict within the territory of a single state, between the government and a non-state actor; and not any non-international conflict, which may include an armed conflict across borders between a government and a non-state actor.

the recognition by the federal government of Confederacy forces as belligerents, was essentially a non-international conflict. Arguably, beyond the general reluctance of states to allow international law to penetrate the domestic scene, there is less need to apply the law of occupation in such situations to ensure the provisional character of the situation. So long as international law remains state-centric, effective control by a non-state actor is inherently a temporary situation; effective control by the state, even if the government is in conflict with its population, vindicates the continuing sovereignty of the state and needs no qualification.

The expansive definition of occupation on the one hand ensures that no vacuum would exist in the legal protection of civilians; at the same time, it demands flexibility to enable effective accommodation of a growing range of circumstances, needs and interests.[48] The next section examines the manner in which the occupant's scope of intervention in the administration of the occupied territory has developed in light of this expansion.

10.3.2 The Legitimate Scope of Intervention by the Occupant in the Administration of the Territory

Article 43 of the Hague Regulations, sometimes referred to as the constitutional norm of the law of occupation, provides that '[t]he authority of the legitimate power having in fact passed into the hands of the occupant, the latter shall take all the measures in his power to restore, and ensure, as far as possible, public order and safety, while respecting, unless absolutely prevented, the laws in force in the country'. The authority of the occupant rests only on the fact of effective control.[49] Accordingly, the occupant may not perform acts which depend on the quality of sovereignty, such as annexation or interference in the ousted power's legislative and institutional system. It must nonetheless substitute the ousted government in restoring and ensuring the continued administration of affairs.[50] Under the early view, military necessity was the sole relevant consideration that could 'absolutely prevent' an occupant from maintaining the prevailing order in the occupied territory.[51]

The almost complete separation between governmental and private activity on which the Hague Regulations were premised, which viewed the occupant as a disinterested invader, soon proved inadequate. The broadening of state involvement in the economic activities of its citizens was mirrored in situations of occupation, as occupants sought to intervene in the affairs of the territories under their control.[52]

[48] Roberts 1984, pp. 249, 271.

[49] Hague Regulations, Article 42.

[50] Hague Regulations, Article 43.

[51] Schwenk 1945, pp. 393–395.

[52] Benvenisti 2012, pp. 71–72.

The economy of the occupation was also altered by the totality of war. The latter was no longer financed solely by funds available when it broke out, but by continued production sustaining the military effort. The overall increase in the amount of material and human resources which occupants had to dedicate to war created pressure to exploit local resources in the occupied territory and put a strain on the previously assumed neat distinction between public and private property.[53] Conversely, the rise of the welfare state led to a greater expectation of administrative undertakings for the socio-economic benefit of the civilian population.[54]

These changes were manifest in the German occupation of Belgium during World War I and in the subsequent occupation of the Rhineland; both rested on the interests of the occupants not only to maintain their military advantage but to control the resources of the occupied territory;[55] yet none of the major parties was keen to acknowledge the inadequacy of the rules. Instead, Germany contended that it was acting within the limits of Article 43,[56] while the allied powers altogether denied the applicability of the law of occupation to their territorial holdings.[57] The gap between doctrine and practice thus persisted unaddressed through World War II.[58]

In an attempt to redress the situation, GC IV revised the scope of the occupant's permissible intervention in the administration of the territory. The Convention imposes duties on the occupant in order to ensure the humane treatment of protected persons, irrespective of military necessity. GC IV Article 64, therefore, provides that the occupant may subject the population of the occupied territory to 'provisions which are essential to enable the Occupying Power to fulfil its obligations under the present Convention' in addition to provisions that are essential for it 'to maintain the orderly government of the territory, and to ensure the security of the Occupying Power' as The Hague Regulations already did.[59] Thus, the 'necessity' guiding the occupant was no longer viewed as exclusively military, but also legal and material.[60] This broader authority naturally introduces a greater element of discretion for the occupant, but not an unlimited one. Various tests have been suggested to gauge the legitimacy of such changes, such as through comparison

[53]Stone 1959, pp. 728-29.

[54]Benvenisti 2012, pp. 78–79.

[55]Ibid, pp. 122–126.

[56]E.g. the German Governments' reply to the formal representations of the United States Government concerning the deportation of Belgians, cited in (1917) Diplomatic Correspondence Between the United States and Belligerent Governments Relating to Neutral Rights and Commerce. The American Journal of International Law Supplement vol. 11:249–269, p. 253, and more generally Bisschop 1918.

[57]Benvenisti 1993, p. 57.

[58]Potter 1949, pp. 323, 324.

[59]Benvenisti 2012, p. 78.

[60]Ferraro 2012, p. 57.

with the law in the occupant's sovereignty territory[61] or with the evolving law of the ousted sovereign's,[62] or by reference to international human right law (IHRL).[63]

One of the elements affecting the evaluation of necessity is the prolongation of occupation, which The Hague Regulations did not envisage. GC IV contains a contingency provision in Article 6, which stipulates that in the case of occupied territory, the Convention shall cease to apply one year after the general close of military operations, except for enumerated provisions which would continue in force for the duration of the occupation. Relying on the experience in Germany and Japan,[64] the drafters assumed that even if the occupation were to continue long after the general cessation of hostilities, a time would doubtlessly come when the application of the Convention was no longer justified, especially if most of the governmental and administrative duties had been handed over to the authorities of the occupied territory. Since World War II numerous occupations have continued for decades, although, as noted above, only in the case of the Israeli occupation have the implications of prolongation for delimiting the occupant's freedom of action been examined *in cocreto*, since other occupants had not acknowledged their status as such. It has been argued that during a prolonged occupation, the occupant must be permitted greater freedom of action, including adoption of long-term measures, so as not to deprive the population in the territory from the benefits of technological, social and cultural developments.[65] At the same time, particular vigilance is necessary to thwart the danger that such leeway inherently creates of the occupied territory becoming permanently bound to the occupant.[66] Once the occupant is enjoined to take positive measures for the benefit of the population, the distinction between its conduct as sovereign in its own territory and its conduct in the occupied territory may be all too easily blurred, particularly if the territories are adjacent. The inextricability of the occupied territory and its population from the occupant may take various forms, affecting both individuals and the community as a whole.[67]

Probably, the greatest challenge to the law of occupation at the beginning of the twenty-first century, if only because it dominates the two instances in which occupation has been acknowledged by the states in control of the territory, is 'transformative occupation', namely an operation whose main objective is to overhaul

---

[61]Dinstein 2009, pp. 121–122.

[62]Benvenisti 2012, pp. 104–105.

[63]Ferraro 2012, p. 58.

[64]ICRC Commentary to GC IV 62.

[65]Jam'iat Iscan Al-Ma'almoun v. Commander of the IDF Forces in the Area of Judea and Samaria, HCJ393/82; IsrSC 37(4) 785, para 22, 1983. For discussion see Ferraro 2012, pp. 72–74.

[66]Roberts 1990, pp. 44, 87.

[67]Ronen 2014, pp. 429–431.

the institutional and political structures of the occupied territory, often to make them accord with the occupant's own preferences.[68] The phenomenon is not entirely new: At the end of World War II, one of the objectives of the occupation in Germany and Japan was to modify the economic, political and social setup of the country in view of considerations deemed important to the occupants.[69] This was viewed as clearly in excess of the powers of an occupant.[70] Some attempted to obviate this conflict by holding that the law of occupation was inapplicable to the Allied occupation in Germany, on the ground that the law of occupation protected the interests of a sovereign, and was thus inapplicable when the sovereign had abandoned governmental authority altogether.[71] Others held that this expanded scope of intervention, while not anticipated, was not unlawful,[72] and proposed to designate it an 'occupation of intervention'.[73] The transformative operations in Afghanistan and Iraq brought the question back to the centre of attention. The former approach, according to which abdication of sovereign authority excludes the law of occupation, is no longer persuasive, as the law of occupation is perceived as protecting the indigenous population directly, not merely as resources of the ousted elite.[74]

Various doctrines have been proposed to justify transformations during occupation: respect for human rights law; the consent of the local population; the characteristics of prolonged occupation; the case of occupied failed states; and the fulfilment of Security Council resolutions.[75] All of these may justify the introduction by the occupant of certain changes to local administration, because compliance with the obligation to restore and maintain public order and civil life in occupied territory could, in fact, oblige the occupant to engage in important reforms, when the local laws in force prevent the occupying power from fulfilling its duties under the law of occupation.[76] However, the occupant may not model the governmental structure of the occupied territory according to its own needs or perceptions in disregard the intrinsic characteristics of the occupied society.[77]

The question nonetheless remains as to transformative operations which, notwithstanding the limits imposed by the law of occupation, are also subject to Security Council resolutions. This is but one example of a wilder issue, discussed in the next section, namely the relations between the law of occupation and other legal regimes.

[68] Ferraro 2012, p. 67.

[69] Potter 1949, pp. 323–324.

[70] Kunz 1950, pp. 538, 556.

[71] Fahy 1948, pp. 11, 13.

[72] Potter 1949, pp. 323–324.

[73] Arndt 1948, p. 3.

[74] Benvenisti 2012, p. 73.

[75] Ferraro 2012, pp. 68–71.

[76] Ibid, p. 68.

[77] Ibid, p. 67.

10.4 Relations Between the Law of Occupation and Other Legal Regimes

10.4.1 Legal Regimes Applicable in Occupied Territory

For many years the scope of the occupant's authority was gauged exclusively by the law of occupation, the interpretation of which was informed by political, economic and other perceptions. Towards the end of the twentieth century, new sources of law developed which may affect that authority.[78]

10.4.1.1 Ius Ad Bellum

The law of occupation belongs to *ius in bello*, and is thus apparently insulated from *ius ad bellum*. For example, when a proposal arose to exempt forces acting under UN authority from the law of occupation on the ground that they would be acting against an aggressor state,[79] the discriminatory application of the law of occupation on the basis of *ius ad bellum* considerations was rejected.[80] However, the division between *ius ad bellum* and *ius in bello* is not entirely impermeable. As discussed in the next section, *ius ad bellum* serves as a normative standard by which to examine the legality of an occupation.

Specific norms that are adjacent to *ius ad bellum* have also impacted on the law of occupation. One is the impermissibility of unilateral acquisition of territory through use of force.[81] The basic tenet of the law of occupation, namely the preservation of sovereignty, preceded the emergence of this norm but agrees with it. If originally the inability to acquire territory followed from the factual volatility of the situation on the ground, it now rests on normative constraints. The prohibition on the unilateral acquisition of territory through use of force, or more generally the need to obtain consent (ordinarily of the sovereign) for territorial changes, also contributes to the prolongation of occupation, a phenomenon which, as noted above, affects the scope of discretion of the occupant.

---

[78]The discussion in this section is not exhaustive. One may also mention international criminal law and the emerging jus post bellum.

[79]Stone 1959, p. 695.

[80]Additional Protocol I, preamble. For a historical overview of the debate see Orakhelashvili 2007.

[81]Declaration on Principles of International Law concerning Friendly Relations and Co-operation among States in accordance with the Charter of the United Nations annexed to UN General Assembly Resolution 2625 (XXV), UN Doc A/RES/2625 (1970) 24 October 1970.

10.4.1.2 Self-determination

The concept of the law of occupation as a relationship between states did not leave room for, not require, resort to the principle, later the right, to self-determination, which accrues to peoples. As the laws of self-determination and of occupation evolved, points of overlap emerged. For example, in both the occupation of the West Bank and Gaza Strip by Israel and the occupation of Timor Leste by Indonesia, a situation of effective control by a hostile army occurred in territory which was not lawfully claimed by any sovereign,[82] but the population of which has been recognised as having the right to self-determination.[83] Thus it has been argued that Israel's dismissal of the applicability of GC IV on the ground that the territory has not previously been under sovereign rule has been rejected not only on the basis of the language of GC IV,[84] but also on the ground that the Convention protects not only sovereignty but also the realisation of the right to self-determination.[85]

Another point of overlap is when a state establishes control over the territory of another purportedly in order to realise the right of the local population to self-determination. International reaction to military intervention and occupation in support or 'remedial secession'[86] (India's intervention in Bangladesh in 1971) has been tolerant, but it has rejected those as illegal when it did not consider the local population to have been deprived of political participation rights (e.g. Turkey's intervention in Cyprus in 1974).[87] Similarly, the UN General Assembly expressed reservations with respect to the intervention of the Russian Federation in Crimea in early 2014,[88] where the population of Crimea, although largely in favour of the Russian intervention, has not been systematically deprived of rights in a manner which might justify secession[89] (and later incorporation in the Russian Federation).[90]

---

[82]Timor Leste was a non-self-governing territory under Portuguese rule. The West Bank was under purported sovereignty of Jordan which was not recognised internationally, while the Gaza Strip was under Egyptian non-sovereign rule. In 1988 Jordan renounced its claims to the West Bank.

[83]UN Security Council Resolution 384(1975) UN Doc S/RES/384 (1975) 22 December 1975 para 1; Wall Advisory Opinion, *supra* note 32, paras 88, 122.

[84]Wall Advisory Opinion, *supra* note 32, paras 91–101.

[85]Imseis 2003, p. 97.

[86]*Reference Re Secession of Quebec*, [1998] 2 S.C.R. 217, paras 134–35.

[87]UN Security Council Resolution 541(1983) UN Doc S/RES/541 (1975) 18 November 1983.

[88]UN General Assembly Resolution 68/262 UN Doc A/RES/68/262 1 April 2014.

[89]Chatham House, The Ukraine Crisis: An International Law Perspective, 11 July 2014, http://www.chathamhouse.org/sites/files/chathamhouse/field/field_document/20140711Ukraine Law_0.pdf.

[90]Treaty between the Russian Federation and the Republic of Crimea on the adoption of the Russian Federation Republic of Crimea and education in the Russian Federation of new subjects, official version at http://kremlin.ru/news/20605, unofficial translation and commentary by Anatoliy Pronin at https://www.academia.edu/6481091/A_treaty_on_accession_of_the_Republic_of_Crimea_and_Sebastopol_to_the_Russian_Federation._Unofficial_English_translation_with_little_commentary.

10.4.1.3 International Human Rights Law (IHRL)

The consolidation of the protection of the individual as an objective of international law is reflected also in the law of occupation. It has been suggested that the obligation of the occupant under GC IV Article 64 included compliance with international law more generally, including IHRL.[91] This calls for applying a human rights paradigm in interpreting the occupant's scope of action, particularly in situations of prolonged occupation.[92]

A different basis for the applicability of IHRL in occupied territory, which has taken over the discourse at the turn of the twenty-first century, is directly under the terms of IHRL itself. Such applicability involves two distinct, if factually related, notions. One is the applicability of IHRL in situations of armed conflict,[93] and the other is the extraterritorial applicability of IHRL. Both notions have acquired broad-brush confirmation[94] although the precise requisites for the applicability of IHRL remain controversial. It is nonetheless the least controversial in situations of occupation, where the government exercises effective control[95] and is therefore in a position to ensure human rights despite their extraterritoriality, and where the situation, while formally falling within the laws of war, is one of calm rather than hostilities which justify special exceptions to the universality of human right law. It is also with respect to occupation that the concurrent applicability of the law of occupation and of IHRL has received the endorsement of the ICJ, the Human Rights Committee (HRC) and the European Court of Human Rights (ECtHR).[96] In view of their mandates, the HRC and ECtHR have not directly address the relationship between the law of occupation and IHRL but have only considered the applicability of IHRL in situations where occupation was a given fact. The ICJ, for its part, has laconically stated that the two could apply concurrently.[97]

[91] E.g. Roberts 1987. For a discussion the relevance of GC IV Article 64 see Ferraro 2012, p. 68.

[92] Falk 1989, pp. 40, 46.

[93] Legality of the Threat or Use of Nuclear Weapons Advisory Opinion, 1996 I.C.J. 226, paras 24–25 (July 8) [hereinafter Nuclear Weapons Advisory Opinion].

[94] E.g. including Additional Protocol 1, *supra* note 2, Article 1(2); Nuclear Weapons Advisory Opinion, *supra* note 74, para 25; Human Rights committee, *Sophie Vidal Martins v Uruguay*, Communication No R.13/57, UN Doc Supp No 40 (A/37/40) 157 (1982); *Mabel Pereira Montero v Uruguay*, Communication No 106/1981, UN Doc CCPR/C/OP/2 136 (1990); Human Rights Committee, General Comment No. 26, Continuity of Obligations, UN doc. CCPR/C/21/Rev.1/Add.8/Rev.2 (* December 1997) para 4.

[95] E.g. Loizidou v Turkey (Merits) 1996–VI ECHR (18 December 1996), paras 52, 56.

[96] Wall Advisory Opinion, *supra* note 30, para 112; Congo v Uganda, *supra* note 22, para 216; Human Rights Committee, Concluding Comments on Israel, 29 July 2010, CCPR/C/ISR/CO/3, para 5; ECtHR: Al-Skeini and ors, Bar Human Rights Committee (intervening) and ors (intervening) v United Kingdom, Merits and just satisfaction, App No 55721/07, [2011] ECHR 1093, (2011) 53 EHRR 18, 30 BHRC 561, IHRL 207 (ECHR 2011), 7th July 2011, European Court of Human Rights [ECtHR, Grand Chamber], para 169.

[97] Wall Advisory Opinion, *supra* note 32, para 112; Congo v Uganda, *supra* note 22, para 216.

Nonetheless, opinions differ as to whether in circumstances of occupation IHRL should apply without modification. For example, the extent to which an occupant may engage in fulfilling rights may be affected by the limits of its powers under the law of occupation.[98]

10.4.2 Occupation as a Normative Phenomenon

Occupation was originally viewed as 'wholly a matter of fact, and not a legal situation'.[99] As a factual situation only, there was no question of its lawfulness or otherwise, merely of its existence. This view changed somewhat once occupation was expanded to post-surrender arrangements, such as the post-World War I occupation of the Rhineland.[100] The administration of the occupied territory could then be evaluated by reference not only to the law of occupation itself but also to the undertakings by the parties to the Treaty of Versailles. The existence of occupation nonetheless remained a matter of fact.

Once norms emerged which regulated the threat or use of force (by which occupation is commonly if not inevitably comes to exist), the normative framework affecting occupation broadened. It became possible to query whether the occupation had come to exist in a lawful manner. For example, the month-long Italian occupation of Corfu in 1923 was a contravention of Italy's commitments under the League of Nations.[101] But so long as the governing norms were applicable only *inter partes*, their violation did not render the occupation unlawful as a matter of objective status, but only as against specific states to whom the violated obligation was owed.

The notion of occupation being objectively unlawful arose with the emergence of norms operating *erga omnes*. Violations of such norms are opposable to all states, and thus may create an objective status. Of particular importance in the present context is the prohibition on the use of force and the obligation to respect the right to self-determination. A violation of these norms creates an objectively unlawful situation.[102] Accordingly, although the law of occupation applies irrespective of the state's responsibility under *ius ad bellum*, the lawfulness of the

[98]Ferraro 2012, pp. 63–65.

[99]Robin 1913, p. 8.

[100]Jones 1923, p. 149.

[101]Ibid, pp. 149, 157–58.

[102]ILC, Draft Articles on Responsibility of States for Internationally Wrongful Acts, with commentaries, UN Doc A/56/10 (2001) art 40 commentary paras 4, 5; Barcelona Traction, Light and Power Company Limited (Belgium v. Spain) 1970 I.C.J. 3, paras 33–34 (Feb. 5); Military and Paramilitary Activities in and Against Nicaragua (Nicaragua v. U.S.), Preliminary Objections, Judgment, 1984 I.C.J. 392, para 188 (Nov. 26); East Timor (Portugal v. Australia) 1995 I.CJ. Rep 90, para 31 (June 30).

occupation itself may be compromised by the violation of either of these bodies of law. Moreover, the prohibition on the use of force and the obligation to respect the right to self-determination are also widely viewed as peremptory norms.[103] Under the law of state responsibility, an occupation created by a serious breach of these may not be recognised as lawful.[104]

This does not mean, however, that any belligerent occupation is necessarily unlawful, because neither of the norms is absolute. An occupation created through an act of self-defence would not, in itself, be a breach of the prohibition on the use of force.[105] Nor would it, in itself, be a violation of the right to self-determination. Thus, an occupation created in self-defence would not be inherently unlawful. However, it has been suggested that an occupation may become unlawful if the occupant refuses to negotiate a withdrawal, or acts in a manner which undermines the temporary character of the occupation.[106]

10.5 Conclusion

The laws of armed conflict reflect a compromise: instead of pursuing the utopian aspiration that wars would never take place, international law has been directed to minimise the harm that armed conflict inflicts on human beings. The law of occupation, as part of the laws of armed conflict, serves the same purpose in a discrete situation: originally intended to regulate a brief period from the end of hostilities until the establishment of a new sovereign order or reversion to the old one, today it mitigates the impermissibility of unilateral, forcible assertion of control over territory and change of political status or structure. Yet throughout its history, the law of occupation has been more honoured in the avoidance, breach and disregard than in the observance. This was the consequence of resistance by regimes which expressly engaged in bringing about political change, in a complete anathema to the original purpose of the law of occupation, namely the preservation of the domestic political *status quo ante*. But it was also the result of the obsolescence of the law against the social and economic phenomena against which it was formulated.

These shortcomings of the law of occupation have not been overlooked. In the early years after World War II, more than one scholar and critic have suggested a

103 On the relations between the *erga omnes* and the peremptory character of norms see Tams 2005, pp. 139–145.

104 ILC, Draft Articles on Responsibility of States for Internationally Wrongful Acts, with commentaries, UN Doc A/56/10 (2001) Article 40(2); for the consequences of unlawfulness see Ronen 2008, pp. 201–45.

105 Zemach 2015.

106 Benvenisti 2012, p. 245; Ben-Naftali et al. 2012, pp. 551–614.

revision of the law of occupation to bring it in line with realities.[107] Indeed, the last century has therefore seen far-reaching changes in the law of occupation, although those were hardly the consequence of any intellectual fashion or progressive legal development. Rather, they were the consequence of inescapably complex and varied character of military and political events.[108] Through time, the definition of occupation has been interpreted expansively so as to prevent loopholes through which military and other non-sovereign forms of governance escape international legal regulations. On the other hand, the constraints on the powers and authority of the occupant have been loosened, allowing legitimisation of policies otherwise viewed as excesses of the occupant.[109] Together these developments enable the law of occupation to be more inclusive, and to enable legal scrutiny—and control—of a wider array of situations.

At the same time, the fact remains that the law of occupation is rarely applied in practice, notwithstanding the frequent incidence of situations which fall within its ambit. In such situations, bodies of law other than the law of occupation, particularly international human right law, may offer a practical alternative ground for engaging with an occupant which does not consider itself bound by the law of occupation. But the applicability of the law of occupation, although it has proven largely nominal, is not redundant.[110] It continues to convey a strong message by the international rule of law regarding the temporary character of the situation.

References

Allemés MF, Schuster EJ (1924) The legality or illegality of the Ruhr occupation. Trans Grotius Soc 10:61–87

Arndt A (1948) Status and development of constitutional law in Germany. Ann Am Acad Polit Soc Sci 260:1–9

Arai-Takahashi Y (2009) The law of occupation: continuity and change of international humanitarian law, and its interaction with international human rights law. Brill, Leiden

Ben-Naftali O et al (2012) Illegal occupation: framing the occupied Palestinian territory. Berkeley J Int Law 24:551–614

Benvenisti E (1993) The international law of occupation. Yale University Press, New Haven

Benvenisti E (2012) The international law of occupation, 2nd edn. Oxford University Press, Oxford

Bisschop WR (1918) German war legislation in the occupied territory of Belgium. Trans Grotius Soc 4:110–168

Blum Y (1968) The missing reversioner: reflections on the status of Judea and Samaria. Isr Law Rev 3:279–301

Boon KE (2008) The future of the law of occupation. Can Yearb Int Law 46:107–142

Braas, A (1918) Considérations sur l'occupation de guerre: section III du règlement annexé à la Convention de La Haye du 18 octobre 1907. Liège

---

107 E.g. Stone 1959, p. 732; von Glahn 1957, pp. 291–92.

108 Adam Roberts 1984, p. 299.

109 Von Glahn 1957, pp. 291–92.

110 For views to this effect see Boon 2008, pp. 111–14.

Colby E (1925) Occupation under the laws of war. Columbia Law Rev 25:904–922
Debbasch O, Maurice F (1962) L'occupation militaire: pouvoirs reconnus aux forces armées hors de leur territoire national. Librairie générale de droit et de jurisprudence, Paris
Dinstein Y (2009) The international law of belligerent occupation. Cambridge University Press, Cambridge
Fahy C (1948) Legal problems of German occupation. Mich Law Rev 47:11–22
Falk R (1989) Some legal reflections on prolonged Israeli occupation of Gaza and the West Bank. J Refugee Stud 2:40–51
Feilchenfeld EH (1971) The international economic law of belligerent occupation. Johnson Reprint Corporation, New York
Ferraro T (2012) Occupation and other forms of administration of foreign territory—expert meeting report. ICRC, Geneva
Friedmann W (1956) Some impacts of social organization on international law. Am J Int Law 50:475–513
Garner JW (1925) Recent developments in international law. The University of Calcutta, Kolkata
Graber DA (1949) The development of the law of belligerent occupation, 1863–1914: a historical survey. Columbia University Press, New York
Graziani J (1928) L'occupation temporaire. Thèse pour le doctorat en droit, sciences politiques et économiques. Université de Paris. Faculté de droit. Les Presses Universitaires de France, Paris
Hall WE (1895) A treatise on international law, 4th edn. Clarendon Press, London
Imsei A (2003) On the Fourth Geneva Convention and the occupied Palestinian territory. Harvard Int Law J 44:65–138
Jones FL (1923) Military occupation of alien territory in time of peace. Trans Grotius Soc 9:149–163
Judge Advocate General's School (1945) Law of belligerent occupation. JAGS Text No 11, 1945
Kautsky K (1922) Documents allemands relatifs à l'origine de la guerre. Collection complète des documents officiels 3
Kolb R, Vité S (2009) Le droit de l'occupation militaire: perspectives historiques et enjeux juridiques actuels. Bruylant, Bruxelles
Kunz JL (1950) The status of occupied Germany under international law: a legal dilemma. West Polit Q 3:538–565
Lemkin R (1944) Axis rule in occupied Europe. Carnegie endowment for international peace, Division of international law
Olivier EE (1913) De l'occupation d'un territoire ennemi d'après les résolutions des Conférences de La Haye. Rousseau, Paris
Oppenheim L (1917) Legal relations between an occupying power and the inhabitants. Law Q Rev 33:363–370
Orakhelashvili A (2007) Overlap and convergence: the interaction between jus ad bellum and jus in bello. J Conf Secur Law 12:157–196
Potter PB (1949) Legal bases and character of military occupation in Germany and Japan. Am J Int Law 43:323–325
Ratner SR (2005) Foreign occupation and international territorial administration: the challenges of convergence. Eur J Int Law 16:695–719
Roberts A (1984) What is a military occupation? Br Yearb Int Law 55:249–269
Roberts A (1987) The applicability of human rights law during military occupations. Review of International Studies 13:39–48
Roberts A (1990) Prolonged military occupation: the Israeli-occupied territories since 1967. Am J Int Law 84:44–103
Roberts A (1993) The laws of war in the 1990–91 Gulf conflict. Int Secur 18:134–181
Robin R (1913) Des occupations militaires en dehors des occupations de guerre (translated in to English by the division of international law of the Carnegie Endowment). Capricorn House Publishers, Paris

Ronen Y (2008) Illegal occupation and its consequences. Isr Law Rev 41:201–245
Ronen Y (2014) Post-occupation law. In: Stahn C et al (eds) Jus post bellum: mapping the normative foundations. Oxford University Press, Oxford, pp 429–446
Scheffer D (2003) Beyond occupation law. Am J Int Law 97:842–860
Schwenk EH (1945) Legislative power of the military occupant under Article 43, Hague Regulations. Yale Law J 54:393–416
Shamgar M (1982) Legal concepts and problems of the Israel military government—the initial stage. In: Shamgar M (ed) Military government in the territories administered by Israel 1967–1980: the legal aspects. Hebrew University, Jerusalem, pp 13–59
Stone J (1959) Legal controls of international conflict: a treatise on the dynamics of disputes-and war-law. Maitland Publications, Sydney
Tams CJ (2005) Enforcing obligations erga omnes in international law. Cambridge University Press, Cambridge
Von Glahn G (1957) The occupation of enemy territory: a commentary on the law and practice of belligerent occupation. The University of Minnesota Press, Minneapolis
Wilde R (2010) International territorial administration: how trusteeship and the civilizing mission never went away. Oxford University Press, Oxford
Wills S (2009) Protecting civilians: the obligations of peacekeepers. Oxford University Press, Oxford
Zemach A (2015) Can occupation resulting from a war of self-defense become illegal? Minnesota law review (forthcoming) 24

Other Consulted Source

Bowers P (2003) Iraq: law of occupation. House of Commons Library, London

Chapter 11
Casualties of Armed Conflict: Protecting Cultural Property

Kevin Chamberlain

Abstract The author stresses the importance of protecting cultural property from the effects of armed conflict as its damage or destruction destroys a community's identity and its links with its past, present and future, as well as diminishes the cultural heritage of humankind. The author draws attention to the recent destruction of cultural property in the civil war in Syria and the activities of the so-called Islamic State (ISIL) in Iraq. This chapter analyses the provisions of the principal legal instruments dealing with the protection of cultural property in armed conflict, namely the Convention on the Protection of Cultural Property in the Event of Armed Conflict (The 1954 Hague Convention), the 1954 Protocol for the Protection of Cultural Property in the Event of Armed Conflict and the 1999 Second Protocol to The Hague Convention for the Protection of Cultural Property in the Event of Armed Conflict, as well as other relevant instruments of international law. While the existing legal instruments may be adequate, the problem, as with international law generally, lies in their effective enforcement, particularly in situations of non-international armed conflict where the parties to the conflict have no regard for the dictates of international humanitarian law. But once hostilities have come to an end, it will be possible to bring offenders to justice, if necessary before the International Criminal Court. In the meantime, it is important that there should be widespread adherence to The 1954 Hague Convention and its two Protocols.

The author is a Barrister, former Deputy Legal Adviser Foreign and Commonwealth Office, author of *War and Cultural Heritage: A Commentary on the Hague Convention 1954 and Its Two Protocols* (Institute of Art and Law, Leicester).

K. Chamberlain (✉)
London, UK
e-mail: chamberlain594@btinternet.com

T.D. Gill et al. (eds.), *Yearbook of International Humanitarian Law 2014*,
Yearbook of International Humanitarian Law 17,
DOI 10.1007/978-94-6265-091-6_11

Keywords Cultural property · The 1954 hague convention for the protection of cultural property in the event of armed conflict, and its two protocols · Bringing offenders to justice

Contents

11.1 Introduction

Cultural property is particularly threatened by armed conflicts and, in some cases, by any resulting occupation. As cultural property reflects the life, history and identity of the community, its preservation helps to rebuild a broken community, re-establish its identity, and link its past with its present and future. In addition, the cultural property of any people contributes to the cultural heritage of humankind. Thus, loss of or damage to such property impoverishes humankind.[1]

The above quotation encapsulates in a few short sentences the essential reasons why the international community attaches importance to the protection of cultural property in times of armed conflict. It is a sad fact that in any armed conflict there will be casualties and the loss or destruction of property having no intrinsic military value. This includes the loss or destruction of cultural property. Often the loss

[1]UNESCO's website—www.unesco.org—Frequently asked questions on Armed Conflict and Heritage http://www.unesco.org/new/en/culture/themes/armed-conflict-and-heritage/frequently-asked-questions/.

or destruction is as a result of 'incidental' or 'collateral' damage. On other occasions the loss or destruction results from a cultural site being used, or being perceived to be used, in pursuit of a military objective. Unfortunately it is also the case that cultural sites are targeted for the purpose of demoralising the enemy by destroying its cultural heritage. Such was the case during the conflict in the former Yugoslavia, and the destruction and pillage of the adversary's non-renewable cultural resources became a tool to erase the manifestation of the adversary's identity.

Recent history provides numerous examples of the deliberate loss or destruction of cultural property, or its use to secure a military advantage. In the course of the war in the former Yugoslavia, there was widespread damage to cultural property. Churches and mosques, as well as symbols of ethnic diversity and cultural history were destroyed as part of a policy of ethnic cleansing. In March 2001, the Giant Buddhas of Bamiyan in Northern Afghanistan were destroyed by the Taliban armed forces. They were regarded as some of the finest examples of early Central Asian art. In the 2003 conflict in Iraq, there was evidence to suggest that Iraq was using antiquities in the same way that it used human shields and civilian centres like hospitals to inhibit coalition attacks.[2] In the Shi'ite shrine city of Karbala, there were scenes of Iraqi armed forces firing on coalition forces from within the ancient mosque of that city. It was also reported that at the time of the infamous looting of the Iraq National Museum in Baghdad, the museum was being used by the Iraqi military as a fortified military position.[3]

Unfortunately, as a result of the civil war in Syria, cultural sites in that country have suffered considerably. In fact, the fighting has damaged each of the six cultural sites inscribed on the UNESCO World Heritage List for Syria, including the Umayyad Mosque and Citadel in Aleppo. In 2013, all of Syria's designated cultural sites were placed on the List of World Heritage in Danger, as the armed conflicts are considered an imminent threat to their intrinsic cultural value.[4]

In 2013, a UNESCO-led expert mission to Mali evaluated the state of that nation's cultural heritage, which had been targeted by the non-state armed groups that occupied the region of Timbuktu through the beginning of the year. It emerged that parts of a Timbuktu's Mosque and other cultural monuments in the city were damaged or entirely destroyed, including some 14 of its mausolea, nine of which are inscribed on World Heritage List.[5] In addition to the damage caused to cultural

[2]Iraq accused of sheltering behind antiquities, *The Age*, 2 April 2003.

[3]'Lost and Found in Iraq', *The Times,* 16 June 2003.

[4]They include the ancient city of Damascus, the ancient city of Bosra, the site of Palmyra, the ancient city of Aleppo, the castles of Krac des Chevaliers and Qal-at Salah El-Din, and about 40 ancient villages situated in north-western Syria. See: http://whc.unesco.org/en/list/21. See also: Article 11(4), 1972 World Heritage Convention, which explicitly mentions 'the outbreak or threat of an armed conflict' as a serious and specific danger for cultural heritage.

[5]See the UNESCO press release of 7 June 2013, at: http://www.unesco.org/new/en/unesco/resources/unesco-expert-mission-evaluates-damage-to-malis-cultural-heritage/. See also the UN press release, at: http://www.un.org/apps/news/story.asp/html/story.asp?NewsID=45118&Cr=+mali+&Cr1. See further Zwaagstra 2013.

sites, it was estimated that more than 4,000 manuscripts were burnt, while thousands of others have been at risk of being illicitly trafficked.[6]

More recently there has been extensive destruction by the so-called Islamic State (ISIL) of Iraq's cultural heritage. Mosques and shrines (mainly Shi'ite) have been destroyed, as well as Christian churches, mainly in Mosul. On February 26, 2015, ISIL released a video showing the destruction of various ancient artefacts in the Mosul Museum. Men are seen toppling statues and using sledgehammers and drills to destroy the artefacts. On the same day, the Islamic State also reportedly destroyed the Mosul public library, which housed more than 8,000 rare books and manuscripts. At the request of UNESCO, the Security Council held an emergency meeting and a press statement was issued on 27 February by the President of the Security Council which *inter alia* reiterated the Security Council's condemnation of the destruction of cultural heritage in Iraq and Syria, particularly by ISIL, including targeted destruction of religious sites and objects,[7] On 5 March 2015, ISIL reportedly started the demolition of Nimrud, an Assyrian city from the thirteenth century BC. On the same day the UN Secretary General condemned the destruction of cultural sites in Iraq which he described as a 'war crime'.[8] The destruction was completed over the weekend of 11/12 April 2015 when the Islamic State posted a video showing the city reduced to dust by barrels filled with explosives. On 13 April 2015, the UNESCO Director-General said: "I condemn this mad, destructive act that accentuates the horror of the situation. It confirms that the terrorists are not only destroying representations of figures and bas-reliefs. With their hammers and explosives they are also obliterating the site itself, clearly determined to wipe out all traces of the history of Iraq's people." In addition to the destruction of cultural sites, there have been many reports that ISIL funds its activities by selling portable antiquities on the black market and that this trade is second only to oil as a source of revenue for the organisation.[9]

These examples, possibly some of the most egregious in recent history, serve to illustrate the continuing importance for international humanitarian law to provide clear and enforceable rules to ensure the adequate protection of the cultural heritage in time of armed conflict.

This article examines the principal legal instruments for the protection of cultural property in armed conflict and considers whether they are fit for purpose in the light of recent events.

---

[6]See UNESCO, 'Damage to Timbuktu's cultural heritage worse than first estimated reports UNESCO mission', Press release, 7 June 2013, at: http://tinyurl.com/m72fc26.

[7]http://www.un.org/press/en/2015/sc11804.doc.htm.

[8]http://www.un.org/press/en/2015/sgsm16570.doc.htm.

[9]http://news.usni.org/2014/10/27/isis-funds-terror-black-market-antiquities-trade. See also UN Security Council Resolution 2199 of 12 February 2015 (S/RES/2199 (2015) which condemned the looting and smuggling of Iraqi and Syrian Cultural Property by ISIL and others in order to fund their activities and extended the prohibition on trade in illegally removed Iraqi cultural property under UN Security/Council Resolution 1483 to trade in illegally removed Syrian cultural property (paras 16 and 17).

11.2 The Convention for the Protection of Cultural Property in the Event of Armed Conflict, Signed at The Hague 14 May 1954

Legal provisions specifically aimed at the protection of cultural property in armed conflict are not new. For example, the first modern provisions designed to protect cultural property can be found in the United States of America War Department's General Orders No. 100: *Instructions for the Governance of the Armies of the United States in the Field*, drafted by Francis Lieber and first published in April 1863. These provided that property belonging to churches, to hospitals or other establishments of an exclusively charitable nature, to establishments of education, or to foundations for the promotion of knowledge, such as musea of fine arts, shall not be considered public property.[10] The Instructions also provided that classical works of art, libraries, scientific collections or precious instruments must be secured against all avoidable injury, even when they are contained in fortified places whilst besieged or bombarded.[11] Convention II of the 1899 Hague Conference prohibited pillage and seizure by invading forces (Articles 23, 28 and 47) and required armies to take all necessary steps to spare edifices devoted to religion, art, science, and charitable purposes, hospitals and places where there were sick and wounded, provided these buildings were not used at the time for military purposes (Article 27). Article 27 also stipulated that the besieged ought to indicate these buildings or places by particular and visible signs to be notified in advance to the opposing side. The 1899 Hague Conference was followed by the 1907 Hague Conference which drew up a number of Conventions, the most important of which were Convention No. IV on the Law and Customs of War on Land and Convention No. IX Respecting Bombardment by Naval Forces in Time of War. Convention No. IV annexed a set of Regulations containing a number of provisions relating specifically to the protection of cultural property.[12] Convention No. IX protected hospitals, buildings devoted to religion, charitable purposes, art and science and historic monuments. Such property was to be marked with a distinctive symbol sufficiently large as to be visible from sea.[13]

The years between the two world wars saw a number of measures for the protection of cultural property. The Washington Conference of 1922 on the Limitation of Armaments appointed a Commission of Jurists charged with the preparation of rules relating to aerial warfare and rules concerning the use of radio in time of war. It prepared rules for the control of radio in time of war (part I of the report of the Commission) and rules of air warfare (part II). To a great extent, they

[10]Article 34.

[11]Article 35.

[12]See Articles 27 and 56.

[13]The symbol consisted of a large stiff rectangular panel divided diagonally into two coloured portions, the upper portion black and the lower portion white.

corresponded to the customary rules and general principles underlying treaties on the law of war on land and at sea. They refined the concept of military objective. And for the first time a distinction was drawn between general protection and special protection to be given to monuments of great historic value.[14]

The Treaty of Washington of 1935 (also known as the Roerich Pact)[15] provided that 'the historic monuments, museums, scientific, artistic, educational and cultural institutions shall be considered as neutral and as such respected and protected by belligerents'. The Treaty also provided for cultural property to be marked with a distinctive symbol.[16] Signed by 21 American Governments, the treaty is still in force in most parts of North, Central and South America.

The massive loss of life, the extensive damage to the towns and cities of Europe and the destruction and looting of cultural property during the Second World War prompted a firm resolve on the part of states to avoid such horrors in the future. The adoption of the Charter of the United Nations outlawing armed conflict was rapidly followed by the adoption of the Universal Declaration of Human Rights of 1948, the Genocide Convention of 1948 and the four Geneva Conventions of 1949. These instruments illustrated the determination of the international community to place humanitarian issues at the top of the agenda. As a result of the massive destruction of cultural heritage during the Second World War, a concerted international effort was also made to draw up new legal provisions to secure protection to cultural property in armed hostilities. The result of this effort was the drafting, under the auspices of UNESCO, of the Convention for the Protection of Cultural Property in the Event of Armed Conflict which was opened for signature at The Hague in 1954.

The 1954 Hague Convention needs to be seen in the context of the historical background. The 1949 Geneva Conventions, in particular the Fourth Convention relative to the protection of civilian persons in time of war reinforced existing provisions of customary international law, in particular, Article 53 of the Fourth Convention prohibited the destruction by an Occupying Power of private property, property belonging to the State, or to other public authorities, or to social or co-operative organisations, except where such destruction is rendered absolutely necessary by military operations.

The 1949 Geneva Conventions exercised a fundamental influence on the drafting of The Hague Convention. Many of its provisions have been inspired by the equivalent provisions in the Geneva Conventions. Furthermore, the distinctive blue and white shield, devised by the Contracting Parties as the symbol for the protection of cultural property, was intended to perform the same role for cultural

---

[14]Rules concerning the Control of Wireless Telegraphy in Time of War and Air Warfare. Drafted by a Commission of Jurists at The Hague, December 1922—February 1923, Part II Articles 25 and 26.

[15]Article I.

[16]Article III.

property as did the Red Cross and Red Crescent for persons protected by the Geneva Conventions.[17]

The Hague Convention attempts to strike a balance between humanitarian and military requirements. Whether the balance that has been struck is the right one is a matter for debate. Nevertheless, at the time the Convention represented considerable progress. The Convention consolidated the law relating to the protection of cultural property and it remains the most important legal instruments for the protection of cultural property in time of armed conflict. Although some 126 States are parties to the Convention, it is now generally accepted that the provisions of the Convention dealing with the treatment of cultural property during hostilities reflect customary international law and the principles of the Convention have achieved widespread acceptance, even among those States that are not formally parties to it.[18]

The Convention takes as its starting point the principle that the preservation of the cultural heritage is not solely a matter for the State in whose territory it is located but is a matter of international concern. The loss of cultural heritage, wherever situated, is a loss suffered by humanity as a whole. Its protection must therefore be assured by both national and international measures that operate both in times of peace and conflict.[19]

The Convention requires Contracting States to take a number of measures in peacetime to protect cultural property.[20] In time of conflict, its scope of application mirrors that of common Article 2 of the 1949 Geneva Conventions. In other words, it applies to situations of declared war or of any other armed conflict between two or more Contracting Parties, even if the state of war is not recognised by one or more of them. It also applies to all cases of total or partial occupation of the territory of a Contracting Party, even if the occupation meets with no armed resistance.[21] Like common Article 3 of the 1949 Geneva Conventions, it also applies to conflicts that are not of an international character. In such conflicts, the Contracting Parties are obligated to apply as a minimum those provisions of the Convention that relate to 'respect for' cultural property.[22]

It should be noted that the Convention applies only to situations involving the use of conventional weapons. Although not expressly stated in the Convention

[17]The use of a distinctive symbol to protect cultural property is not new. See Convention No. IX respecting bombardment by naval forces in time of war 1907, The Rules concerning the Control of Wireless Telegraphy in Time of War and Air Warfare. Drafted by a Commission of Jurists at The Hague, December 1922—February 1923, Part II Article 26 and the Treaty of Washington 1935 referred to above. But neither symbols attracted as widespread acceptance as the blue and white shield.

[18]See for example Rules 38–40 of the ICRC Study on Customary International Humanitarian Law: Henckaerts and Doswald-Beck 2005 pp. 127–135.

[19]See preamble.

[20]Article 3.

[21]Article 18.

[22]Article 19.

itself, the Conference which adopted the Convention followed the approach adopted by other conferences on international humanitarian law where the issue of weapons of mass destruction, such as nuclear weapons, was left to one side.[23]

11.2.1 Definition of Cultural Property

Neither The Hague Convention of 1907 nor the Roerich Pact of 1935 contained definitions of cultural property. Article 27 of The Hague Regulations of 1907 referred to the need to spare as far as possible 'buildings dedicated to religion, art science, or charitable purposes, historic monuments, hospitals and places where the sick or wounded were collected, provided they were not being used at the time for military purposes'. Article 1 of the Roerich Pact provided that 'historic monuments, museums, scientific, artistic, educational and cultural institutions…shall be respected and protected'. Both these instruments accorded protection to the buildings themselves and the protected property is listed in terms of its purpose. For the first time, the 1954 Convention defines 'cultural property' by moving away from these earlier definitions and defining cultural property in terms of its cultural importance. Thus to qualify for protection under the Convention, the cultural property must be 'of great importance to the cultural heritage of every people' (Article 1). The term 'cultural property' includes not only movable and immovable property, but also buildings designed to preserve or house movable cultural property and centres containing large amounts of cultural property.

11.2.2 Obligations of the Parties in Peacetime

In peacetime, the Parties undertake to prepare for the safeguarding of cultural property situated within their territory against the foreseeable effects of armed conflict by taking the 'appropriate measures' (Article 3). They undertake to introduce in their military regulations and instructions provisions to ensure observance of the Convention and respect for cultural property as well as to establish specialist personnel in their armed forces to secure respect for cultural property and co-operate with the civilian authorities responsible for safeguarding it (Article 7), and to disseminate the text of the Convention and the Regulations for its execution as widely as possible in their respective countries and provide training of their military personnel (Article 25).

[23]See Toman 1996, pp. 23–24. See also Henckaerts and Doswald-Beck 2005, p. 255. When ratifying the Convention in 2009 the US also expressed its understanding that the Convention only applied to situations involving the use of conventional weapons.

11.2.3 Obligations of the Parties in Armed Conflict

In time of armed conflict, the Parties undertake to respect cultural property within their territory and within the territory of other Parties by refraining from the use of cultural property or its immediate surroundings which would expose it to the risk of damage or destruction and to refrain from any act of hostility against cultural property (Article 4). However, this obligation to 'respect' cultural property can be waived 'where military necessity imperatively requires such a waiver'. The notion of 'imperative military necessity' was intended to reconcile the tension that existed at the Diplomatic Conference between those who favoured the removal of the military necessity exception and those representing the interests of the military who favoured its retention. A major difficulty with the term is that it is not defined and potentially open to abuse. It had to be left to the 1999 Protocol to provide some clearer guidance as to the circumstances in which the military necessity exception could be invoked by linking it to the concept of 'military objective' as defined in Additional Protocol I to the 1949 Geneva Conventions.

The Convention also required the Parties to prevent, prohibit and put a stop to any form of theft, pillage, misappropriation or acts of vandalism against cultural property and to refrain from requisitioning moveable cultural property on the territory of another Party. Here there is no exception for military necessity (Article 4). Where a Party is occupying part or the whole of the territory of another Party, it must support the competent authorities of the occupied territory to safeguard and preserve its cultural property. Where it is necessary to preserve cultural property damaged by military operations and the competent national authorities are unable to do so, the occupying power must take those measures itself in co-operation with the competent national authorities (Article 5).

11.2.4 Special Protection

Provision was made for the granting of 'special protection' to a limited number of refuges for the protection of movable cultural property and for centres containing monuments and other immovable cultural property 'of very great importance'. To qualify such sites had to be situated an adequate distance from large industrial centres or important military objectives and were not to be used for military purposes (Article 8). Immunity from attack was guaranteed by entry in the International Register maintained by UNESCO and immunity could only be withdrawn where the site is used for military purposes or in 'exceptional cases of unavoidable military necessity'. For a variety of reasons, the number of sites subject to special protection has been meagre. There is only one centre containing monuments (Vatican City) and four refuges on the International Register; the last addition to the Register was in 1978.[24] The system of special protection has now been replaced by that of 'enhanced protection' introduced by the 1999 Protocol.[25]

11.2.5 The Distinctive Emblem

The Convention introduced the use of a distinctive emblem (illustrated), the purpose of which was to identify cultural property to which general or special protection has been accorded, as well as to refuges, transport, personnel and identity cards. The use of a distinctive emblem to protect cultural property is not new. Article 27 of the 1907 Hague Regulations imposed an obligation on a besieged Party to mark buildings dedicated to religion, art, science or charitable purposes, historic monuments, hospitals and places where the sick and wounded are collected by 'distinctive and visible signs', which must be communicated to the enemy beforehand. However, the design of the sign was not specified. Article 5 of the Ninth Hague Convention concerning Bombardment by Naval Forces in Time of War did introduce a special sign designed to protect buildings of this kind. This consisted of a large stiff rectangular panel divided diagonally into two coloured portions, the upper portion black and the lower portion white. The Treaty on the Protection of Artistic and Scientific Institutions and Historic Monuments (the Roerich Pact) also provided for a distinguishing symbol (a red circle with a triple red sphere in the circle on a white background). The 1954 Convention specifically provides that as between the parties to the Convention who are parties to the earlier Conventions, the distinctive emblem in the Convention replaces the emblems in the earlier Conventions. As a result, the emblem in the 1954 Convention has gained universal acceptance. It should be noted that the use of the distinctive emblem to identify cultural property protected by the Convention is not compulsory (except for property under special protection). There may be a number of reasons why a State might not wish to mark cultural property under general protection. For example, it might not wish to do so because it considers that the property might be at greater risk of attack from terrorists or irregular forces. A State is free to

---

[24]International Register of Property under Special Protection UNESCO Doc. 13 April 2014 CLT/CEM/CHP.

[25]See Chamberlain 2013, pp. 37–38 and 139.

decide whether to mark such property, bearing in mind that failure to display the distinctive emblem could increase the risk of the property being attacked inadvertently by opposing forces. During an armed conflict, the Parties must forbid the use of the distinctive emblem except where provided under the Convention and prevent the use for any purpose whatever of a sign resembling the distinctive emblem.

11.2.6 Sanctions

One weakness of the Convention was the lack of clear provisions to repress breaches of the Convention. The only provision is Article 28 under the heading of 'Sanctions' which obligated the Parties to 'take within the framework of their ordinary criminal jurisdiction, all necessary steps to prosecute and impose penal or disciplinary sanctions upon those persons, of whatever nationality, who commit or order to be committed a breach of the present Convention'.

The 1949 Geneva Conventions contained detailed provisions regarding the prosecution or extradition of persons suspected of committing 'grave breaches' of the Conventions. The Contracting Parties are obliged to search for persons alleged to have committed grave breaches and to bring such persons, regardless of their nationality before their own courts or extradite them to another Contracting Party, provided that Party has made a *prima facie* case.[26] To commit a grave breach, an offender must have committed the offence 'wilfully' or 'wantonly'. As regards acts contrary to the provisions of the Conventions other than grave breaches, Contracting Parties are obliged to 'take the measures necessary for the suppression' of such acts.

The Geneva Conventions must be contrasted with the vaguer provisions in Article 28 of The Hague Convention. This gives rise to a number of problems of interpretation. What offences are covered by Article 28? Under what conditions can the offences be committed, in particular what *mens rea* (mental element) is required (i.e. does the offence have to be committed 'wilfully' or 'wantonly')? On what basis would Contracting Parties exercise jurisdiction over the offences? Nor is it clear in what circumstances it would be appropriate to impose a disciplinary sanction as opposed to a penal sanction.

The position has now been considerably improved under the Second Protocol, Chap. 4 of which contains detailed provisions on criminal responsibility and jurisdiction.

11.2.7 Application of the Convention to Non-international Armed Conflicts (Article 19)

As mentioned above, the Convention mirrors common Articles 2 and 3 of the 1949 Geneva Conventions and applies to international armed conflicts (including cases

[26]See Articles 49, 50, 129, 146 of Geneva Convention I, II, III and IV respectively.

of occupation) and to non-international armed conflicts. As to what constitutes a non-international armed conflict, one must assume that the drafters of the 1954 Convention intended it to have the same meaning as in the 1949 Geneva Conventions. The Conventions do not define the expression, although para 2 of Article 1 of Additional Protocol II defines what is not an armed conflict falling within the scope of the Protocol. Thus, the Protocol does not apply to 'situations of internal disturbance and tensions, such as riots, isolated and sporadic acts of violence and other acts of a similar nature, as not being armed conflicts'.[27] A conflict must therefore achieve a certain level of intensity before falling within the ambit of common Article 3. The Commentary on the Geneva Conventions has drawn up a list of criteria against which the question of whether that level of intensity has been reached can be judged. These include whether the party in revolt possesses an organised military force, an authority responsible for its acts and the means of ensuring respect for the Convention; whether the legal government is obliged to use its regular military forces against insurgents organised as military and in possession of part of the national territory; whether the *de jure* government has recognised the insurgents as belligerents or has claimed belligerent rights; whether the dispute has been admitted to the agenda of the Security Council or the General Assembly as a threat to peace, a breach of the peace, or an act of aggression; whether the insurgents have an organisation having the characteristics of a State, or whether they exercise de facto authority over part of the national territory.[28] However, these criteria are not intended to be exhaustive. It should also be borne in mind that the authors of this provision intended that there should be the maximum extension of protection to armed conflicts that were not of an international character. Accordingly, it would be consistent with the object and purpose of the Geneva Conventions to interpret the scope of common Article 3 as widely as possible. The same would apply to the interpretation of Article 19 of the 1954 Convention, in light of the object and purpose of the Convention to secure the maximum protection for cultural property in the event of armed conflict. This would also be consistent with Article 31 of the 1969 Vienna Convention on the Law of Treaties according to which 'a treaty shall be interpreted in good faith in accordance to the ordinary meaning to be given to the terms of the treaty in their context and in the light of its object and purpose'.

Unfortunately, Article 19 is not entirely clear as to precisely what the obligations of the parties to a non-international armed conflict are under the Convention. The Article merely states that they are to 'apply as a minimum the provisions of the present Convention which relate to respect for cultural property'. In view of the fact that in recent times the conflicts that have given rise to the most damage to cultural property are conflicts of a non-international character, it is all the more

[27]This wording has been carried forward to Article 22(2) of the Second Protocol to the 1954 Convention.

[28]See Pictet 1958, pp. 35–36.

important that there should be clarity on the extent to which the Convention applies to such conflicts. Article 4 of the Convention is entitled 'Respect for Cultural Property' but it would be a perverse interpretation of Article 19 to say that the sole obligation of the parties to the conflict in the case of a non-international conflict is to comply with the provisions of Article 4. This would mean that all the other provisions of the Convention, such as the regime of special protection, the distinctive emblem, provisions on transport etc., only apply in cases of international armed conflict. This cannot have been the intention of the drafters of the Convention. If it were, then why not refer specifically to Article 4? Given that the purpose of the Convention is to protect cultural property in the event of armed conflict then it is immaterial whether the conflict is international or internal. Again applying the principles of interpretation in Article 31 of the Vienna Convention on the law of Treaties, it would be consistent with the object and purpose of the Convention to interpret 'respect for cultural property' in the widest sense. This means that the parties to an internal conflict remain bound by all the provisions of the Convention that relate directly to the protection of cultural property with the exception of those that expressly or by necessary implication are only applicable in conflicts to which Article 18 applies (international armed conflicts).[29]

The obligation to apply the provisions of the Convention as they relate to respect for cultural property applies to 'each party' to the conflict. This obligation extends not only to the Contracting Party in whose territory the conflicts is taking place, who may be the *de jure* government, but also to insurgents engaged in conflict either with the *de jure* government or among themselves. (It should be noted that unlike other Articles, in Article 19 the word 'party' is spelt with a small 'p'). Accordingly, when a government becomes a Party to the Convention, the obligations of Article 19 are imposed not simply on the State and its organs but on individuals.

In case of an internal conflict, a Contracting State may be powerless to prevent violations of the Convention by insurgent forces. But this does not mean that the State is absolved of any responsibility for what has happened. Once the State has assumed control, the State has a duty to prevent further violations and bring to justice those responsible for the violations of the Convention. Furthermore, in the event that the State where the offences may have been committed is either unable or unwilling to take action, the Second Protocol to the 1954 Convention now contains provisions which enable those committing the most serious offences against cultural property to be brought to justice irrespective of where the offences may have been committed and offenders can also be brought to trial before the International Criminal Court.[30]

[29]See Toman 1996, pp. 213–215. The Second Protocol now makes no distinction between international and non-international armed conflicts (see Article 3(1)).

[30]See Articles 8, 13 and 14 of the Statute of the International Criminal Court.

11.3 The Protocol for the Protection of Cultural Property in the Event of Armed Conflict, Signed at The Hague 14 May 1954

The Second World War saw not only the destruction of cultural property, but also the systematic pillage of works of art from the occupied territories. Often transactions were cloaked with a veneer of legality with owners forced to agree to part with their possessions and paid only a fraction of their market value. In the Inter-Allied Declaration against Acts of Dispossession Committed in Territories under Enemy Occupation or Control of 5 January 1943 (the 1943 Joint Declaration) the 18 Allied Powers included the following provision:

> The Governments of...
>
> Hereby issue a formal warning to all concerned, and in particular to persons in neutral countries, that they intend to do their utmost to defeat the methods of dispossession practised by governments with which they are at war against the countries and peoples who have been so wantonly assaulted and despoiled.
>
> Accordingly the governments making this Declaration and the French National Committee reserve all their rights to declare invalid any transfers of, or dealings with, property, rights and interests of any description whatsoever, which are, or have been, situated in the territories which have come under the occupation or control, direct or indirect, of the governments with which they are at war, or which belong, or have belonged, to persons (including juridical persons) resident in such territories. This warning applies whether such transfers or dealings have taken the form of open looting or plunder, or of transactions apparently legal in form, even when they purport to be voluntarily effected.

The contents of the Declaration were commonly accepted as an unequivocal agreement to undertake restitution on a wide scale. To facilitate its implementation, the Declaration reserved the right to invalidate all changes concerning property rights introduced in the occupied territories. Publishing the Declaration with such contents and provisions indicated a disavowal of the principle of protecting person acquiring looted works of art in good faith.

It was against this background that the 1954 Intergovernmental Conference that drew up The Hague Convention wanted to include provision in the Convention itself to prohibit trafficking of moveable cultural property from occupied territories. For various reasons, this was not acceptable and the Conference decided instead to draw up a separate Protocol that could be ratified independently of the Convention. The Protocol, as adopted by the Conference, is in three parts. Part I deals with the return of property exported from a territory under occupation, Part II deals with the return of property coming from the territory of one Contracting Party and deposited in the territory of another Contracting party for the purpose of protecting such property from the dangers of an armed conflict and Part III contains the final provisions. On becoming Parties to the Protocol States have the option of accepting the Protocol in its entirety, or opting to accept either Part I or

Part II. There are currently 103 States parties to the Protocol and all have accepted both Parts of the Protocol.[31]

Under Part I of the Protocol, each Contracting Party is under an obligation to prevent the exportation from a territory occupied by it during an armed conflict of cultural property as defined in Article 1 of the Convention. The obligation extends to all cultural property, whether movable or detached from immovable cultural property and irrespective of its origin or ownership. It is not clear from this whether this obligation extends to all exports, including exports that may be perfectly legal under the law in force in the territory under occupation and not resulting from any kind of duress. It is perhaps understandable that the Protocol at the time did not exclude exports that may have been legal, given that the Joint Declaration referred to above extended to 'transactions apparently legal in form, even when they purport to be voluntarily effected'.[32] The obligation of a contracting Party to prevent export of cultural property from territory occupied by it would apply irrespective of whether the territory occupied belongs to another Contracting Party or not.

In addition to preventing the export of cultural property from territory occupied by a Contracting Party, the Protocol requires any Contracting Party to seize cultural property imported into its territory either directly or indirectly from any occupied territory, irrespective of whether the occupier or the State whose territory is under occupation are Contracting Parties. Such seizure should be taken either automatically or at the request of the competent authorities of the occupied territory. Any property seized must be returned to the 'competent authorities' of the territory previously occupied at the close of hostilities. Such property must never be retained as war reparations.

Provision is also made to compensate holders in good faith of any seized cultural property. However, the obligation to do so rests not on the Contracting Party that seized the cultural property but on the Contracting Party in occupation whose obligation it was to prevent the export of the cultural property in the first place. The obligation to take the property into custody and return it is not dependent on compensation being paid. It is for the good faith holder, or the country returning the property, or the country of nationality of the holder to seek to obtain compensation from the occupying Contracting Party. This may not be easy, particularly if the State to whom the property being returned is not the former occupying Power.

[31]Japan qualified its acceptance of the Protocol with the following reservation, 'In applying the provisions of para 3 of I of the Protocol, Japan will fulfil the obligation under those provisions in a manner consistent with its domestic laws including the civil code. Japan will be, therefore, bound by the provisions of Section I of the Protocol to the extent that their fulfilment is compatible with the above-mentioned domestic laws.'

[32]This provision should be compared with Article 11 of the 1970 UNESCO Convention on the Means of Prohibiting and Preventing the Illicit Import, Export and Transfer of Ownership of Cultural Property which states, 'The export and transfer of ownership of cultural property under compulsion arsing directly or indirectly from the occupation of a country by a foreign power shall be regarded as illicit'.

And as noted, the obligation to return property applies irrespective of whether the occupying Power is a Party to the Protocol. Where the occupying Power is not a Party to the Protocol then it cannot be bound by any obligation under the Protocol to pay compensation to holders in good faith.

Part II deals with the case of cultural property coming from the territory of one Contracting Party and deposited in the territory of another Contracting Party for the purpose of protecting the property from the dangers of armed conflict. Such property must be returned by the latter Contracting party to the competent authorities of the territory from which it came at the end of hostilities.[33] Unlike Part I, which applies to property exported in the course of occupation by a State of the territory of another which would constitute an international armed conflict, Part II applies to both international and non-international armed conflicts. It would also apply to property sent to another country for safe keeping before the outbreak of hostilities. Property transferred under this provision must be returned from the competent authorities of the territory from where it came at the close of hostilities.

It has to be said that the 1954 Protocol has not been a great success. In his review of the 1954 Convention, Patrick J Boylan states with regard to the Protocol:

> Unfortunately all the evidence suggests that the provisions are almost totally ineffective in practice. The haemorrhage of cultural property of all kinds from areas both international and civil war zones has been on an enormous scale for decades. Obvious examples have included much of Indo-China through the 1960s and 1970s, and the 'leakage' of archaeological material, antiquities of art from occupied north Cyprus. There are also persistent reports of large-scale losses from both public collections and protected monuments during the Iran-Iraq war of the 1980s, and in the Shiite cultural regions of southern Iraq in the internal offensive of 1991 and still continuing. Few identifiable items have appeared in the international art markets so far, but this may simply due to stock-piling in intermediate countries with short statute of limitation periods, after which the rightful owner can no longer reclaim their stolen or smuggled property.[34]

Despite this, it can be said that the principle that an occupying power must prevent the illicit export of cultural property from the territory it occupies is established as a norm of customary international law. Rule 41 of the ICRC's Rules of Customary International Humanitarian Law states:

---

[33]There have in fact been very few examples of the operation of para 5 in practice. At the commencement of World War II a number of objects of cultural importance were removed from Wawel Castle in Cracow Poland and eventually found their way to Canada. Just before the end of the war St Stephen's Crown and coronation regalia were sent from Hungary to the United States for safekeeping. With the advent of the Cold War there was a reluctance on the part of both Governments to return these objects. Canada argued that it had never accepted responsibility for these objects in the first place and informed the Polish Government that if it wanted these objects back then it could bring proceedings in the Canadian courts. After lengthy negotiations the last of these objects were returned in 1961. It was not until 1978 that the United States and Hungarian Governments reached agreement on the return of St Stephen's Crown and coronation regalia but even then an unsuccessful attempt was made to block their return through proceedings in the US courts (see O'Keefe 2004, pp. 111–112).

[34]Boylan 1993, p. 100. For further discussion of the inadequacies of the 1954 Protocol the reader is referred to the article by O'Keefe 2004, p. 99.

> The occupying power must prevent the illicit export of cultural property from occupied territory and must return illicitly exported property to the competent authorities of the occupied territories.

The commentary on this rule observes that state practice establishes this rule as a norm of customary international law applicable in international armed conflicts.[35]

Part I of the 1954 Protocol has largely been superseded by Article 9(1) of the Second Protocol which *inter alia* obliges a Party in occupation of the whole or part of the territory of another Party to prohibit and prevent in relation to the occupied territory 'any illicit export, or other removal or transfer of ownership of cultural property'.

11.4 The Second Protocol to The Hague Convention of 1954 for the Protection of Cultural Property in the Event of Armed Conflict, Signed at The Hague 26 March 1999

The effectiveness of the 1954 Convention became a subject of general concern in the early 1990s, during the first Gulf War and the war in the former Yugoslavia. A further development was the adoption in 1977 of the Additional Protocols to the 1949 Geneva Conventions which reaffirmed the existing rules of customary international law prohibiting attacks on civilian targets and specifically prohibited acts of hostility against historic monuments, works of art or places of worship which constitute the cultural or spiritual heritage of peoples and for such attacks in certain circumstances to constitute grave breaches.

The Second Protocol is additional to the 1954 Convention, which remains the basic text. A State can only become a party to the Second Protocol if it is a party to the 1954 Convention.[36] The Protocol applies to armed conflicts of an international character and to conflicts not of an international character occurring in the territory of one of the Parties (but not to situations of internal disturbances and tensions such as riots). It therefore gives greater precision to the rather vague application of the 1954 Convention to internal conflicts. The principal features of the Protocol are:

- Enhanced provisions for the safeguarding of cultural property in peacetime.
- The establishment of more stringent conditions for invoking imperative military necessity.
- The establishment of detailed precautions to be taken in attack and against the effects of hostilities.

[35] See Henckaerts and Doswald-Beck 2005, pp. 135–137.

[36] Articles 40, 41 and 42 of the Protocol restrict signature, ratification, acceptance or approval and accession to 'High Contracting Parties' defined in Article 1 as States Parties to the 1954 Convention.

- Provisions for the protection of cultural property in occupied territory, in particular, a prohibition on the illicit export, removal or transfer of ownership of cultural property, a prohibition on archaeological excavations, and a prohibition on any alteration to, or change of use of cultural property which is intended to conceal or destroy cultural, historic or scientific evidence.
- The establishment of a new regime of 'enhanced protection' to replace the 'special protection' regime in the 1954 Convention.
- Provisions for the establishment of jurisdiction over, and the prosecution and extradition of, persons committing serious violations of the Protocol.
- The establishment of a Committee for the Protection of Cultural Property in the Event of Armed Conflict, as well as a Fund for the Protection of Cultural Property in the Event of Armed Conflict..
- Provisions on dissemination and international co-operation and assistance.
- The establishment of a conciliation procedure to deal in particular with disputes between the Parties to a conflict over the interpretation and application of the Protocol.[37]

There are currently 68 States Parties to the Protocol.

11.4.1 Imperative Military Necessity Under the Second Protocol

The establishment of more stringent conditions for invoking imperative military necessity and more detailed precautions to be taken in attack and against the effects of hostilities so far as they affect cultural property were major achievements of the Second Protocol. They codified the existing rules set out in Article 57 of Additional Protocol I to the 1949 Geneva Conventions limiting attacks to military objectives as defined in Article 57, thus laying down how Article 4(2) of the 1954 Convention is to be interpreted and applied. Article 6 of the Protocol sets out two conditions that must be present cumulatively before the waiver of 'imperative military necessity' under Article 4(2) of the Convention can be invoked to direct an act of hostility against cultural property. First, the property has by its function been made into a 'military objective' This is defined in the Protocol in identical terms to the definition in Article 52(2) of Additional Protocol I to the 1949 Geneva Conventions, namely 'an object which by its nature, location, purpose, or use makes an effective contribution to military action and whose total or partial destruction, capture or neutralisation, in the circumstances ruling at the time, offers a definite military advantage' and; second, there is no feasible alternative available to obtain a similar military advantage to that offered by directing an act of hostility against that objective.

[37]For a detailed analysis of the improvements introduced by the Second Protocol see Toman 2009.

As regards the first condition, the property must 'by its function' have been made into a military objective. Thus it is the *function* to which the cultural property is put in the circumstances prevailing at the time, rather than the inherent nature of the property that determines whether it has been made into a military objective. Thus the mere location of cultural property could never turn it into a military objective. Some positive action should be required from the holder of the property before it could become a military objective. The second condition is that there is no feasible alternative available to obtain a similar military advantage to that offered by directing an act of hostility against that military objective. This condition in effect clarifies the requirement of the 1954 Convention that the military necessity has to be 'imperative', namely, that no other feasible alternative is available. This means that when there is a choice between several military objectives whose total or partial destruction, capture or neutralisation, in the circumstances ruling at the time, would offer a definite military advantage but one of them is cultural property, the latter must not be attacked.

Similar considerations apply where imperative military necessity can be invoked to justify the use of cultural property for purposes which are likely to expose it to destruction or damage in the event of armed conflict. Such use is only permitted when and for as long as no choice is possible between such use of the cultural property and another feasible method for obtaining a similar military advantage. In other words, where a choice exists between a number of measures to secure a similar military advantage, the choice that favours the least risk of damage or destruction to cultural property should be preferred.

Finally, the Protocol requires any decision to invoke military necessity to be taken sufficiently high up in the chain of command, at least at the level of the officer commanding a battalion or larger. However, the decision can be taken at a lower level of command 'where circumstances do not permit otherwise'. Although this provides some flexibility, it is important to recall that the purpose of requiring that the decision be taken at a sufficiently high level is to ensure that the decision is taken responsibly and with a degree of objectivity. It would therefore be rare for the decision to be taken at the level of the officer actually leading the attack since it is unlikely that he (or she) would be in a position to exercise the necessary degree of objectivity.[38]

11.4.2 Precautions to Be Taken in an Attack

Article 57 of Additional Protocol I to the 1949 Geneva Conventions contained detailed provisions on the precautions to be observed in the conduct of military operations to spare the civilian population, civilians and civilian objects. These are now reflected in Article 7 of the Protocol. This requires Parties to the conflict,

[38]See Van Woudenberg and Lijnzaad 2010, pp. 45–47.

(a) to do everything feasible to verify that the objects to be attacked are not cultural property protected under Article 4 of the Convention, (b) to take all feasible precautions in the choice of means and methods of attack to avoid, and in any event minimise, incidental damage to cultural property, (c) to refrain from launching an attack which may be expected to cause incidental damage to cultural property which would be excessive in relation to the concrete and direct military advantage anticipated and (d) to cancel an attack if it becomes apparent that the objective is cultural property protected under the Convention, or if the attack may be expected to cause incidental damage which would be excessive in relation to the concrete and direct military advantage anticipated.

11.4.3 Enhanced Protection

The Protocol introduced the system of Enhanced Protection to replace to largely discredited system of Special Protection under the Convention. To qualify for enhanced protection cultural property must be 'cultural heritage of the greatest importance to humanity'[39] Decisions for inclusion in the List of Property under Enhanced Protection are taken by the Committee for the Protection of cultural Property in the Event of Armed Conflict established under Article 24 of the Protocol. The Committee acts impartially and on the basis of objective criteria. The Parties to a conflict are required to ensure that property under enhanced protection has immunity by refraining from making the property the object of an attack or from using the property or its immediate surroundings in support of military action. Enhanced protection may only be lost if the protection is suspended or cancelled by the Committee or the property has, by its use, become a military objective. In the latter event, the property may only be attacked if the attack is the only feasible means of terminating its use as a military objective and all feasible precautions are taken to minimise damage to the property. In addition, the attack must be ordered at the highest operational level of command, effective warning must be given to the opposing forces requiring the termination of its use to secure a military advantage and a reasonable time be given to the opposing forces to redress the situation (subject to circumstances permitting). As of 2014 there were ten sites in the UNESCO List of Property under Enhanced Protection all of which are also World Heritage sites.[40]

11.4.4 Criminal Responsibility and Jurisdiction

The Second Protocol builds on Article 28 of the 1954 Convention and Article 15 sets out a number of crimes which constitute 'serious violations' of the Protocol. These are:

[39] Article 10.

[40] UNESCO List of Cultural Property under Enhanced Protection 20/03/2014.

(a) making cultural property under enhanced protection the object of attack;
(b) using cultural property under enhanced protection to its immediate surroundings in support of military action;
(c) extensive destruction or appropriation of cultural property protected under the Convention and the Protocol
(d) making cultural property protected under the Convention and the Protocol the object of attack, and;
(e) theft, pillage or misappropriation of, or acts of vandalism directed against cultural property protected under the Convention.

Under Article 16, each Party to the Protocol is obliged to establish jurisdiction over these offences when committed on its territory or by its nationals. Furthermore, with respect to the offences listed in sub-paragraphs (a)–(c) above, each Party must establish jurisdiction over the offences where the alleged offender is present within its territory. However, the exercise of so-called universal jurisdiction in these cases is subject to the limitation that members of the armed forces or nationals of a State that is not a Party to the Protocol incur no criminal responsibility under the Protocol, and the Protocol does not impose any obligation on a State Party to the Protocol to establish jurisdiction over such persons or to extradite them (except in the case where a State that is not a Party to the Protocol accepts the obligations of the Protocol under Article 3(2), or where a national of a state that is not a Party to the Protocol commits an offence while serving in the armed forces of a State Party to the Protocol).[41] This limitation is modified by the proviso that the Protocol does not preclude the incurring of criminal responsibility or the exercise of jurisdiction under national or international law, or affect the exercise of jurisdiction under customary international law.[42] This would open the door to criminal responsibility and the exercise of jurisdiction under other instruments such as Article 85.4 (d) of Additional Protocol I to the 1949 Geneva Convention[43] and Article 8 of the statute of the International Criminal Court.[44]

[41] Article 16.2(b).

[42] Article 16.2(a).

[43] Article 85.4(d) defines as a 'grave breach' of the Protocol when committed wilfully and in violation of the Conventions and Protocol, 'making the clearly recognised historic monuments, works of art or places of worship which constitute the cultural or spiritual heritage of peoples and to which special protection has been given by special arrangement, for example, within the framework of a competent international organisation, the object of attack, causing as a result extensive destruction thereof, where there is no evidence of the violation by the adverse Party of article 53, subparagraph (b) (using such objects in support of the military effort), and when such historic monuments, works of art and places of worship are not located in the immediate proximity of military objectives'.

[44] Article 8 confers jurisdiction on the International Criminal Court for 'War Crimes'. This includes under Article 8(2)(b)(ix) (international armed conflicts) and under Article 8(2)(e)(iv) (non-international armed conflicts) 'intentionally directing attacks against buildings dedicated to religion, education, arts, science or charitable purposes, historic monuments, hospitals and places where the sick and wounded are collected provided they are military objectives'.

11.5 Conclusion

Recent events in Syria and Iraq involving the deliberate and wide-scale destruction of cultural property have led one to question the adequacy of the existing legal instruments designed to protect cultural property in times of armed conflict. The nature of armed conflict has changed in recent times: such conflicts are likely to be non-international armed conflicts with those involved in the conflict having scant regard for the dictates of international humanitarian law, including those relating to the protection of cultural property. The recent activities of ISIL referred to in the introduction to this chapter are an example of this. The deterrence of such wanton acts of vandalism presents one of the greatest challenges to the international community in the twenty-first century. As seen from the foregoing, there is no lack of legal provision, but the weakness with international law in general is the difficulty of enforcing it. In many situations, therefore, particularly where international humanitarian law is at stake, the existence of international restrictions does not necessarily result in preventing the harm that the law is intended to prevent. However, international humanitarian law does often provide effective punishment after-the-fact, for example, as in the cases of the Nuremberg Trials following World War II and the International Criminal Tribunal for the former Yugoslavia, which has prosecuted many of the former Serbian leaders who perpetrated crimes against humanity during the Balkan Wars of the 1990s, including offences against cultural property.

The entry into force of the Rome Statute of the International Criminal Court opens up new possibilities to bring offenders to justice. There can surely be little doubt that the wanton destruction of cultural property that we have witnessed recently constitutes a 'war crime' within the meaning of Article 8 of the Rome Statute.[45] Although neither Syria nor Iraq is party to the Rome Statute, the Court is able to exercise jurisdiction if the case is referred to the Prosecutor by the Security Council acting under Chapter VII of the UN Charter.[46] In addition, a State Party to the Statute can refer a case to the Prosecutor where the alleged crime has been committed by a national of a State Party.[47]

In the meantime, it is important that there be widespread adherence to the 1954 Convention and its two Protocols, particularly the Second Protocol of which there are only 68 States Parties so far.[48] Unfortunately, the United Kingdom has not set

[45]See Note 44 above.

[46]See Article 13 of the Rome Statute. As already noted (see note 9 above) the Security Council in Resolution 2199 of 12 February 2015 has already taken some action by condemning the destruction of Iraqi and Syrian cultural heritage and prohibiting trade in illegally removed Iraqi and Syrian cultural objects (Articles 15–17).

[47]See Article 14 of the Rome Statute.

[48]Although both Iraq and Syria are Parties to the 1954 Convention and the First Protocol, neither are Parties to the Second Protocol.

a good example in this respect. Having announced in 2004 its intention to ratify the 1954 Convention and accede to its two Protocols, The UK Government published in 2008 a draft bill, the Draft Cultural Property (Armed Conflicts) Bill,[49] which would make the necessary changes to UK law to enable the United Kingdom to ratify the 1964 Convention and its Protocols. So far, the UK Government has not presented the bill to the UK Parliament. The United Kingdom is now the most significant military power not to have become a party to the 1954 Convention and its Protocols.

References

Boylan PJ (1993) Review of the convention for the protection of cultural property in the event of armed conflict. UNESCO Doc. CLT-93/W5/12

Chamberlain K (2013) War and cultural heritage: Commentary on the Hague Convention 1954 and Its Two Protocols. Institute of Art and Law, Leicester

Henckaerts J-M, Doswald-Beck L (2005) ICRC: customary international humanitarian law vol 1: rules. Cambridge University Press, Cambridge

O'Keefe P (2004) The first protocol to the Hague Convention fifty years on Art, Antiquity and Law 9(2):99–116

Pictet JS (1958) Commentary vol IV Geneva Convention relative to the Protection of Civilian Persons in Time of War. ICRC, Geneva

Toman J (1996) The protection of cultural property in the event of armed conflict. Dartmouth Publishing/UNESCO Publishing, Paris

Toman J (2009) Cultural property in war: improvement in protection. UNESCO Publishing, Paris

Van Woudenberg N, Lijnzaad L (2010) Protecting cultural property in armed conflict. Martinus Nijhoff, Leiden

Zwaagstra D (2013) Crimes against cultural property in Mali. Peace Palace Library Blog. http://www.peacepalacelibrary.nl/2013/01/crimes-against-cultural-property-in-mali/

[49] Cm 7298.

Part VI
Other Articles

Chapter 12
Year in Review 2014

Frédérique van Oijen and Jessica Dorsey

Abstract 2014 was marked with several noteworthy events with particular relevance to international humanitarian law, such as the continuation of the conflict in Syria and the incidents related to the use of chemical weapons in that conflict; several key decisions in international and hybrid courts related to the adjudication of war crimes, crimes against humanity and genocide; the entry into force of the Arms Trade Treaty; release of the US Report on Torture and a Global Summit to End Sexual Violence in Armed Conflict. This chapter addresses a number of these issues among other events of note.

Keywords International humanitarian law · International criminal law · Armed conflict · Chemical weapons · War crimes · Torture · Sexual violence

Contents

F van Ooijen, LL.M., International Law and Security, LL.M., International and European Law.
The authors would like to especially thank Alina Balta for her assistance in the preparation of this Year In Review.

F. van Oijen (✉) · J. Dorsey
T.M.C. Asser Instituut, The Hague, The Netherlands
e-mail: F.D.C.vanOijen@gmail.com

J. Dorsey
e-mail: j.dorsey@asser.nl

T.D. Gill et al. (eds.), *Yearbook of International Humanitarian Law 2014*,
Yearbook of International Humanitarian Law 17,
DOI 10.1007/978-94-6265-091-6_12

12.1 Situations and Phenomena

12.1.1 Afghanistan

There has been an ongoing conflict since October of 2001 (begun as a response to the attacks on the United States on September 11, 2001),[1] and it continued throughout the duration of 2014. In December of 2014, NATO made a formal end to 13 years of conflict in Afghanistan, though some 12,500 foreign troops will remain in the country to train Afghanis.[2] The country, starting in 2015, will be solely in the hands of the country's 350,000 soldiers and police.[3] Looking back 4 years of the conflict (2009–2013), Amnesty International released a report[4] that included allegations that US military has failed to hold its soldiers accountable for

[1]See 'History, the War in Afghanistan', BBC News, http://www.bbc.co.uk/history/the_war_in_afghanistan (accessed 6 May 2015).

[2]See C. Mallick, 'NATO formally ends 13 year conflict in Afghanistan', Jurist (29 December 2014), http://jurist.org/paperchase/2014/12/nato-holds-ceremony-to-formally-end-13-year-conflict-in-afghanistan---dnp.php (accessed 6 May 2015).

[3]See North American Treaty Organization (NATO), 'NATO Secretary General's statement on a new chapter in Afghanistan', NATO website (28 December 2014) http://www.nato.int/cps/en/natohq/news_116341.htm?selectedLocale=en (accessed 6 May 2015).

[4]See Amnesty International, 2014 'Afghanistan: No justice for thousands of civilians killed in US/NATO operations', (11 August 2014) https://www.amnesty.org/en/articles/news/2014/08/afghanistan-no-justice-thousands-civilians-killed-usnato-operations/ (accessed 6 May 2015).

various abuses in Afghanistan, including unlawful civilian killings, torture, and other potential crimes. In July, the UN released its own report detailing the sharp increase in civilian casualties as the conflict between government forces and insurgents had moved closer to densely populated areas. The report stated "[b]etween 1 January and 30 June 2014, UNAMA documented 4,853 civilian casualties, (1,564 civilian deaths and 3,289 injured) recording a 17 per cent increase in civilian deaths, and a 28 per cent increase in civilians injured for a 24 per cent overall increase in civilian casualties compared to the first 6 months of 2013."[5]

12.1.2 Central African Republic

The ongoing conflict in the Central African Republic between the Séléka rebels and the governmental forces began at the end of 2012 due to accusations of the Séléka rebels against President François Bozizé of failure to follow peace agreements from 2007 and 2011.[6] Despite previous ceasefire agreements, efforts by the UN Security Council to curb the violence (through the MISCA peacekeeping force), the conflict continued into 2014. In January, the UN Security Council adopted Resolution 2134, to extend the mandate of the BINUCA (UN Integrated Peacebuilding Office in the Central African Republic) and imposed travel bans as well as asset freezes on those suspected of committing war crimes.[7] In March, the Security Council established the International Commission of Inquiry on the Central African Republic in order to investigate allegations of some of the worst crimes with the aim of preventing an escalation, possibly, to genocide.[8]

In June, as fighting continued, the UN found "ample evidence" that both sides of the conflict were committing war crimes as well as crimes against humanity, but at that point there was not enough evidence to show the conflict had led to genocide or ethnic cleansing.[9] Amnesty International, however, objected to this last finding, saying that displacement of the Muslim population was not just an effect of the violence,

---

[5]See United Nations Assistance Mission in Afghanistan (UNAMA), 2014 p. 1. http://unama.unmissions.org/LinkClick.aspx?fileticket=OhsZ29Dgeyw%3D&tabid=12254&mid=15756&language=en-US (accessed 3 June 2015).

[6]See Uppsàla University UCDP Conflict Encyclopedia 'Central African Republic', http://www.ucdp.uu.se/gpdatabase/gpcountry.php?id=31&regionSelect=2-Southern_Africa# (accessed 6 May 2014).

[7]See S/Res/2134 http://www.un.org/en/ga/search/view_doc.asp?symbol=S/RES/2134(2014) (accessed 6 May 2015).

[8]See 'Central African Republic: UN probe set to investigate reports of rights violations', UN News Centre (10 March 2014), http://www.un.org/apps/news/story.asp?NewsID=47314&Cr=central+african+republic&Cr1=%20-%212.UyF5-l81iAx#.VUnxEU0cRHg (accessed 6 May 2015).

[9]See 'UN report disputes genocide claims in CAR' Al Jazeera (6 June 2014) http://www.aljazeera.com/news/africa/2014/06/un-report-disputes-genocide-claims-car-20146610611138683.html (accessed 15 June 2015).

but rather its goal.[10] Later that month, the African Union came out in support of a UN Report[11] recommending the creation of a special war crimes tribunal[12] and the government of the Central African Republic submitted a request to the International Criminal Court to begin investigation of crimes under the jurisdiction of the Court since August 2012,[13] which was accepted on September 24 by the Prosecutor.[14]

Several human rights organizations, such as the International Federation for Human Rights, Human Rights Watch,[15] and Amnesty International, released statements detailing alleged crimes committed, many of which amounted to international crimes, war crimes, and crimes against humanity. In December, Amnesty also reported that the "failure of the Central African Republic authorities and the United Nations to effectively investigate war crimes is perpetuating the cycle of violence and fear in the country."[16] At the time of this publication, the conflict was still ongoing.

12.1.3 Colombia

The conflict in Colombia, categorized by most as a non-international armed conflict,[17] continued between government forces and FARC (*Fuerzas Armadas Revolucionarias de Colombia*) rebels. As a result of this conflict, ongoing since

---

[10]Ibid.

[11]See 'Central African Republican Crisis: war crimes committed,' BBC News (6 June 2014) http://www.bbc.com/news/world-africa-27727465 (accessed 15 June 2015).

[12]See 'AU backs call for war crimes tribunal in CAR,' Al Jazeera (7 June 2014) http://www.aljazeera.com/news/africa/2014/06/au-backs-call-war-crimes-tribunal-car-20146781117534173.html (accessed 17 June 2015).

[13]See ' Central African Republic president requests ICC investigation,' Jurist (13 June 2014) http://jurist.org/paperchase/2014/06/central-african-republic-president-requests-icc-investigation.php (accessed 18 June 2015).

[14]See ICC Office of the Prosecutor 'Statement of the Prosecutor of the International Criminal Court, Fatou Bensouda, on opening a second investigation in the Central African Republic' (24 September 2014) http://www.icc-cpi.int/EN_Menus/icc/press%20and%20media/press%20releases/pages/pr1043.aspx (accessed 10 June 2015).

[15]See Human Rights Watch: "Central African Republic: ICC Investigation Needed," (26 June 2014) http://www.hrw.org/news/2014/06/26/central-african-republic-icc-investigation-needed (accessed 15 June 2015).

[16]See Amnesty International: "CAR: Failure to effectively investigate war crimes fuels further atrocities and fear," (11 December 2014) https://www.amnesty.org/en/latest/news/2014/12/car-failure-effectively-investigate-war-crimes-fuels-further-atrocities-and-fear/ (accessed 1 July 2015).

[17]See 'Colombia: the challenges of a continuing armed conflict', Interview with Christophe Beney, Head of the ICRC Delegation in Colombia (29 September 2011), http://www.icrc.org/eng/resources/documents/interview/2011/colombia-interview-2011-09-29.htm (accessed 28 May 2014). See also S. Sivakumaran, Law of Non-International Armed Conflict, Oxford University Press, Oxford, p. 230: "Despite their very real cross-border elements, the non-international character of the Colombia/FARC armed conflict…is not seriously challenged."

1964, figures cited by Human Rights Watch show more than four million Colombians have been displaced and more than 100,000 are displaced each year that the conflict continues.[18] The year 2014 was marked with several attempts at continued peace negotiations between government representatives and members of FARC. In November of 2012, the first peace talks in approximately a decade between the FARC and Colombian government officials began in Norway.[19] They subsequently moved to Cuba in 2013.[20] In April 2014, the Colombian ICRC stated that peace talks might help solve the mystery behind tens of thousands of deaths in the 50-year conflict.[21]

In June, prior to the reelection of President Juan Manuel Santos, FARC declared a three-week ceasefire and backed Santos in his continued efforts for peace.[22] For the first time, victims joined peace discussions in Cuba in August, a moved praised by UNHCHR Commissioner Navi Pillay, who called it "unprecedented and a potential model for other countries dealing with issues of justice, peace and reconciliation."[23] Despite this progress, in November, President Santos suspended peace negotiations following the kidnapping of an army general and four other individuals by the FARC rebels.[24] A few days later, FARC agreed to release the hostages[25] and shortly thereafter, peace negotiations resumed.[26] On

[18]See Human Rights Watch, World Report 2013, p. 214: www.hrw.org/sites/default/files/wr2013_web.pdf (accessed 3 June 2015). Amnesty International said that figures were very difficult to verify, but at least tens of thousands of people per year are displaced due to the conflict, see Amnesty International Report 2013, p. 65: The State of The World's Human Rights, http://files.amnesty.org/air13/AmnestyInternational_AnnualReport2013_complete_en.pdf. (accessed 5 June 2015).

[19]See 'Colombia's FARC peace talks resume in Cuba', BBC News (5 December 2012), http://www.bbc.co.uk/news/world-latin-america-20618131 (accessed 28 May 2015).

[20]See 'Q&A: Colombia peace talks', BBC News (2 September 2013), http://www.bbc.co.uk/news/world-latin-america-19875363 (accessed 9 June 2015).

[21]See Julia Symmes Cobb: 'Colombia ICRC says peace may solve mystery of disappeared,' Reuters (23 April 2014) http://www.reuters.com/article/2014/04/23/us-colombia-rebels-idUSBREA3M23M20140423 (accessed 1 July 2015).

[22]See Peter Murphy: 'Colombia's FARC declare poll ceasefire, take swipe at Zuluaga,' Reuters (7 June 2014) http://www.reuters.com/article/2014/06/08/us-colombia-elections-farc-idUSKBN0EI0XB20140608 (accessed 1 July 2015).

[23]See 'Colombia conflict victims join Farc peace talks in Cuba,' BBC News (17 August 2014) http://www.bbc.com/news/world-latin-america-28822683 (accessed 3 July 2015).

[24]See 'Colombia's government suspends FARC peace talks,' EuroNews, (17 November 2014) http://www.euronews.com/2014/11/17/colombia-government-suspends-farc-peace-talks/ (accessed 2 July 2015).

[25]See 'Colombia's FARC to release captured general,' Al Jazeera (21 November 2014) http://www.aljazeera.com/news/americas/2014/11/farc-agrees-release-captured-general-2014111923152242381l.html (accessed 3 July 2015).

[26]See Andrew Willis and Nathan Gill, "Colombian Peace Talks to Resume After FARC Frees Hostages," Bloomberg News (1 December 2014) http://www.bloomberg.com/news/articles/2014-12-01/colombian-peace-talks-to-resume-after-farc-frees-hostages (accessed 3 July 2015).

December 17, FARC representatives declared an indefinite unilateral ceasefire, stating: "We have resolved to declare a unilateral ceasefire and end hostilities for an indefinite period of time, which should be transformed into an armistice."[27] At the time of publication, the situation is still ongoing.

12.1.4 Democratic Republic of the Congo

In 2014, following the end of a period of general hostilities between 2003 and 2013,[28] several developments can be noted in post-conflict justice mechanisms in the Democratic Republic of the Congo, though it should be noted that numerous armed groups remained active, carrying out attacks against civilians, and allegations of governmental abuse of civilians still were made. In February, The Office of the Prosecutor for the ICC alleged that Congolese war crimes suspect Bosco Ntaganda was instrumental in organizing and ordering militias of "child soldiers" to attack civilians,[29] 18 charges which were confirmed unanimously by the Pre-Trial Chamber in June.[30] The ICC found Germain Katanga guilty of war crimes and crimes against humanity in his involvement with murders and civilian attacks in Bogoro, Ituri, in February. The Court sentenced him in May to 12 years in prison, after which Katanga did not appeal the ruling and issued an apology to victims of the crimes.[31]

Early in 2014, Human Rights Watch urged the DRC to adopt new mechanisms—including the establishment of specialized mixed chambers[32] and the adoption of legislation implementing the Rome Statute of the ICC—to prosecute war crimes, which was adopted by the Council of Ministers on April 22 and presented to the National Assembly on May 2.[33]

---

[27]See 'Colombia Farc rebels declare indefinite unilateral truce,' BBC News (17 December 2014) http://www.bbc.com/news/world-latin-america-30525871 (accessed 3 July 2015).

[28]See 'Democratic Republic of Congo profile', BBC News (11 March 2014), http://www.bbc.co.uk/news/world-africa-13286306 (accessed 1 July 2015).

[29]See 'ICC prosecutors allege Congo war crimes suspect used child soldiers,' Jurist (10 February 2014) http://jurist.org/paperchase/2014/02/icc-prosecutors-allege-congo-war-crimes-suspect-used-child-soldiers.php (accessed 2 July 2015).

[30]See 'ICC ready to put Congolese warlord on trial,' Reuters (9 June 2014) http://www.reuters.com/article/2014/06/09/uk-icc-congodemocratic-warlord-idUSKBN0EK1I320140609 (accessed 1 July 2015).

[31]See Human Rights Watch World Report 2015, http://www.hrw.org/world-report/2015/country-chapters/democratic-republic-congo (accessed 3 July 2015).

[32]See Human Rights Watch: 'Accountability for Atrocities Committed in the Democratic Republic of the Congo,' (1 April 2014) http://www.hrw.org/news/2014/04/01/accountability-atrocities-committed-democratic-republic-congo (accessed 3 July 2015).

[33]See Human Rights Watch World Report 2015, http://www.hrw.org/world-report/2015/country-chapters/democratic-republic-congo (accessed 3 July 2015).

In May, two of the 39 soldiers on trial for mass rape carried out in 2013, were found guilty and sentenced to life in prison in a DRC military court.[34] At least 97 women and 33 girls, some as young as six, were reported to have been raped in the eastern town of Minova over 2 days as thousands of civilians fled fighting between Congo's ill-disciplined army and the M23 rebel group.[35] Following the June Global Summit to End Sexual Violence in Conflict, held in London,[36] DRC's President Kabila appointed a presidential adviser on sexual violence and child recruitment in the DRC. Additionally, a comprehensive action plan was launched in August to take on the issue of sexual violence committed by soldiers.[37]

In November, a military court handed down a 10-year sentence for the Congolese General Jérôme Kakwaku,[38] finding him guilty of committing war crimes. The head of the UN peacekeeping mission in the Democratic Republic of the Congo (DRC) stated that this decision is a step toward reinforcing the rule of law in this country.[39] In December, a military court convicted Lieutenant Colonel Bedi Mobuli Engangela on several counts of crimes against humanity.[40] He received life sentence for murder, 20-year sentence for rape, two 15-year terms for "sexual slavery and 'other inhuman actions,'" such as torture and abduction, and 10 years for "imprisonment and other forms of grave deprivation of physical liberty."[41]

---

[34]See 'Two soldiers jailed for life over Congo mass-rape case,' Reuters (5 May 2015) http://www.reuters.com/article/2014/05/05/us-congodemocratic-rape-idUSBREA440N820140505?feedType=RSS&feedName=worldNews&rpc=69 (accessed 3 July 2015).

[35]See Al Jazeera Inside Story: 'War rape: Is justice being done?' (5 May 2014) http://www.aljazeera.com/programmes/insidestory/2014/05/war-rape-justice-being-done-201455163130173.html (accessed 3 July 2015).

[36]See Global Summit to End Sexual Violence, 10–13 June 2014 https://www.gov.uk/government/topical-events/sexual-violence-in-conflict (accessed 3 July 2015).

[37]See Human Rights Watch World Report 2015, http://www.hrw.org/world-report/2015/country-chapters/democratic-republic-congo (accessed 3 July 2015).

[38]See 'DR Congo court gives rebel turned general 10 years for war crimes,' New Vision (8 November 2014) http://www.newvision.co.ug/news/661614-dr-congo-court-gives-rebel-turned-general-10-years-for-war-crimes.html (accessed 3 July 2015).

[39]See 'DR Congo: UN official applauds sentencing of militia leader for war crimes,' UN News Centre (9 November 2014) http://www.un.org/apps/news/story.asp?NewsID=49291#.VZOXbGcw9Hh (accessed 3 July 2015).

[40]See 'Congolese colonel gets life for crimes against humanity,' The New Age Online, (15 December 2015) http://www.thenewage.co.za/146272-1019-53-Congolese_colonel_gets_life_for_crimes_against_humanity (accessed 3 July 2015).

[41]Ibid.

12.1.5 Drones (Unmanned Aerial Vehicles) and Targeted Killing

In February, the former High Representative of the Union for Foreign Affairs and Security Policy and Vice President of the Commission (HRVP) Catherine Ashton stated: "The EU raises these matters in its regular consultations with the US on human rights, and will continue to do so in forthcoming consultations, including as regards information on facts and legal basis and on possible investigations. The EU stresses that the use of drones has to conform to international law, including the law of armed conflict when applicable. The international legal framework regarding the use of drones is also addressed in the informal dialogue among EU and US legal advisers."[42]

Likewise, on February 26, 2014, Dimitrios Kourkoulas, President-in-Office of the European Council, made a statement during the European Parliament's Plenary Session in Strasbourg on behalf of Catherine Ashton and remarked: "The use of drones has raised some concerns on respect for human rights and international law. Their use in countering terrorism has already been raised and questioned by the UN Special Rapporteur on the Promotion and Protection of Human Rights and Fundamental Freedoms. Our position is very clear: we have to ensure that any use will be consistent with both European and international law. It is not the technology, but rather its use, that is key."[43]

EU Counter-Terrorism Coordinator Gilles De Kerchove and his advisor Christiane Höhn therefore concluded that "[t]he EU's position is that RPAS, or drones, have to be used in full respect of international law, but there is no EU position on the interpretation of international law related to RPAS."[44]

Later in February, the European Parliament passed a resolution[45] and held a debate in Strasbourg on the use of armed drones. The resolution called for opposition to and banning of extrajudicial targeted killings; ensuring that Member States do not carry out unlawful targeted killings or assist other states in carrying these out; the inclusion of armed drones in relevant disarmament and arms control regimes (international and European); banning of development of fully autonomous weapons enabling strikes to be carried out without a human in the loop; a

---

[42]See European Parliament, Parliamentary questions, "Answer given by High Representative/ Vice-President Ashton on behalf of the Commissions", 4 February 2014, http://www.europarl.europa.eu/sides/getAllAnswers.do?reference=E-2013-012201&language=EN.

[43]European Parliament, Debates, Wednesday, 26 February 2014, Strasbourg, 15. Use of armed drones (debate), Dimitrios Kourkoulas, http://www.europarl.europa.eu/sides/getDoc.do?pubRef=-//EP//TEXT+CRE+20140226+ITEM-015+DOC+XML+V0//EN.

[44]G. De Kerchove and C. Höhn, "Counter-Terrorism and International Law Since 9/11, Including in the EU-US Context", in: T.D. Gill, T. McCormack, R. Geiβ, R. Heinsch, Ch. Paulussen and J. Dorsey (eds.), Yearbook of International Humanitarian Law, Vol. 2013, T.M.C. Asser Press: The Hague, 2015, p. 291.

[45]European Parliament, Debates, Wednesday, 26 February 2014, Strasbourg, 15. Use of armed drones (debate), Dimitrios Kourkoulas, http://www.europarl.europa.eu/sides/getDoc.do?pubRef=-//EP//TEXT+CRE+20140226+ITEM-015+DOC+XML+V0//EN.

commitment to take measures, when reasonable grounds for believing an individual or entity falling under Member States' jurisdiction may have carried out unlawful targeted killings abroad, in accordance with legal obligations (domestic and international); and support for the work of both UN Special Rapporteurs Heyns and Emmerson (respectively, on extrajudicial, summary or arbitrary execution and on the promotion and protection of human rights and fundamental freedoms while countering terrorism) and a follow-up on their recommendations.

In March, Special Rapporteur Emmerson's final report was published.[46] Additionally, On March 28, 2014, the UN Human Rights Council voted to approve a Pakistan-sponsored resolution (A/HRC/25/L.32) entitled, "Ensuring use of remotely piloted aircraft or armed drones in counterterrorism and military operations in accordance with international law, including international human rights and humanitarian law."[47] It passed with 27 states in favor, six against, and fourteen abstentions.[48] In response, Human Rights Watch urged the EU to press the United States on its secrecy surrounding the drone program, stating: "EU states often deplore legally questionable actions by foreign governments. Yet they have hesitated to do the same when it comes to their close ally, the United States."[49]

Prior to the UN Human Rights Council's discussion on the use of armed drones in counterterrorism and military operations in September, several NGOs and civil society organizations submitted a joint letter outlining their concerns of state practice in the use of such drones and urging the Council to support states in, *inter alia,* ensuring that lethal targeting operations comply with international law and in ensuring transparency on the use of armed drones.[50] The UN Human Rights

[46]The Special Rapporteur's final report can be found on the Human Rights Council's website: "Report of the Special Rapporteur on the promotion and protection of human rights and fundamental freedoms while countering terrorism, Ben Emmerson", A/HRC/25/59, 11 March 2014, http://www.ohchr.org/EN/HRBodies/HRC/RegularSessions/Session25/Pages/ListReports.aspx (accessed 3 July 2015).

[47]The resolution (A/HRC/25/L.32, 24 March 2014) is available at: http://www.un.org/ga/search/view_doc.asp?symbol=A/HRC/25/L.32 (accessed 3 July 2015).

[48]States voting in favor (27): Algeria, Argentina, Botswana, Brazil, Chile, China, Congo, Costa Rica, Cuba, Gabon, Indonesia, Ireland, Kazakhstan, Kenya, Kuwait, Maldives, Mexico, Morocco, Pakistan, Peru, Philippines, Russian Federation, Saudi Arabia, Sierra Leone, South Africa, Venezuela and Vietnam. States voting against (6): France, Japan, Republic of Korea, The former Yugoslav Republic of Macedonia, United Kingdom, and United States of America. States abstaining (14): Austria, Benin, Burkina Faso, Côte d'Ivoire, Czech Republic, Estonia, Ethiopia, Germany, India, Italy, Montenegro, Namibia, Romania, and United Arab Emirates.

[49]See Letta Tayler, 'EU should press Obama on drone secrecy,' Human Rights Watch (27 March 2014) http://www.hrw.org/news/2014/03/27/eu-should-press-obama-drone-secrecy (accessed 3 July 2015).

[50]See e.g., American Civil Liberties Union, Amnesty International, Center for Human Rights & Global Justice, and the Global Justice Clinic, NYU School of Law, Center for Civilians in Conflict, Center for Constitutional Rights, Human Rights Clinic, Columbia Law School, Human Rights First, Human Rights Watch, International Commission of Jurists, Open Society Foundations, "Joint Letter to the UN Human Rights Council on Targeted Killings and the Use of Armed Drones", 18 September 2014, http://www.hrw.org/news/2014/09/18/joint-letter-un-human-rights-council-targeted-killings-and-use-armed-drones (accessed 3 July 2015).

Council discussed the use of armed drones in counterterrorism and military operations to ensure that their use is in accordance with international law—including international humanitarian and human rights law—as unlawful killings may amount to war crimes.[51]

The Parliamentary Assembly of the Council of Europe's Committee on Legal Affairs and Human Rights also held a discussion in September regarding "Drones and targeted killings: the need to uphold human rights" and heard from Special Rapporteur Ben Emmerson, Head of Strategic Litigation Programme, Polish Helsinki Foundation for Human Rights, Warsaw, Irmina Pacho; and Associate Professor, School of Law, University of Miami, Florida, USA, Markus Wagner.[52]

12.1.6 Israel/Palestine

The conflict in Israel/Palestine continued throughout 2014, with new hostilities launched in July. Operation Protective Edge was a seven-week Israeli military operation launched in order to stop rockets from being fired from Gaza (allegedly being done by Hamas to increase the pressure lift the blockade of the Gaza Strip).[53] The hostilities escalated through July and August, and ultimately 2,100 Palestinians and 66 Israeli soldiers and seven civilians perished during the fighting.[54]

The UN Human Rights Council passed Resolution S-21/1 in a special session calling for a commission of inquiry into possible war crimes commissions by all parties to the ongoing conflict,[55] a move welcomed by Amnesty

[51]See OHCHR, 'Human Rights Council holds panel on remotely piloted aircraft or armed drones in counterterrorism and military operations' (22 September 2014) http://www.ohchr.org/EN/NewsEvents/Pages/DisplayNews.aspx?NewsID=15080&LangID=E (accessed 3 July 2015). The draft report from 15 December 2014 is available at: http://www.ohchr.org/EN/HRBodies/HRC/RegularSessions/Session28/Documents/A_HRC_28_38_ENG.doc (accessed 2 July 2015).

[52]Parliamentary Assembly of the Council of Europe, Committee on Legal Affairs and Human Rights, Declassified Minutes of the hearing on "Drones and targeted killings: the need to uphold human rights", held in Strasbourg (Palais de l'Europe) on 30 September 2014 http://www.assembly.coe.int/CommitteeDocs/2014/ajpv06-2014.pdf (accessed 3 July 2015).

[53]See 'Hamas and Israel cling to their war aims,' DeutscheWelle (23 July 2014) http://www.dw.com/en/hamas-and-israel-cling-to-their-war-aims/a-17801137 (accessed 3 July 2015).

[54]See 'Gaza Crisis: Toll of operations in Gaza,' BBC News (1 September 2014) http://www.bbc.co.uk/news/world-middle-east-28439404 (accessed 2 July 2015).

[55]See HRC/RES/S-21/1 'Ensuring respect for international law in the Occupied Palestinian Territory, including East Jerusalem' (24 July 2014) http://www.ohchr.org/Documents/HRBodies/HRCouncil/SpecialSession/Session21/A-HRC-RES-S-21-1_en.doc (accessed 3 July 2015).

International.[56] UN Secretary-General Ban Ki-moon strongly condemned the Israeli attack on a UN school in Gaza sheltering civilians, and said it demands justice and accountability.[57] Amnesty International urged the UN Security Council to refer the ongoing situation in Israel and the Occupied Palestinian Territories to the ICC to bring those responsible for committing serious violations of international humanitarian law to justice. Amnesty International said it documented compelling evidence that since Israel began its offensive in Gaza on July 8, Israel, Hamas, and other Palestinian armed groups have carried out indiscriminate attacks in densely populated areas and direct attacks on civilian homes which may amount to war crimes. Furthermore, it emphasized that an ICC investigation is crucial to end impunity for the perpetrators of these serious crimes.[58]

In August, representatives from Hamas said it would support the Palestinian effort to join the ICC in order to pursue Israel for war crimes committed in Gaza, even though this would mean that Hamas itself could be subjected to the jurisdiction of the ICC.[59] Despite this pledge, in September, Hamas hampered efforts of an ICC formal investigation into alleged war crimes committed.[60] In December, however, Palestine was officially granted observer status by the ICC to participate in the Assembly of States Parties 13th session in New York[61] and looked toward 2015 for full membership of the Court.

12.1.7 IS (Islamic State)

The Islamic State in Iraq and Syria (ISIS), the Islamic State (IS), Daesh, or the Islamic State in Iraq and the Levant (ISIL), started as a splinter group of al-Qaeda with the aim to create an Islamic state (caliphate) across areas in mainly Sunni

[56]See Amnesty International, 'Israel/Gaza Conflict: Questions and Answers,' (25 July 2014) https://www.amnesty.org/en/latest/news/2014/07/israelgaza-conflict-questions-and-answers/ (accessed 3 July 2015).

[57]See 'Gaza: deadly shelling of another UN school draws condemnation, calls for ceasefire,' UN News Center (30 July 2014) http://www.un.org/apps/news/story.asp?NewsID=48369#.VZTsstOqqkp (accessed 3 July 2015).

[58]See Amnesty International: 'Israel/OPT: The International Criminal Court must investigate war crimes' (1 August 2014) https://www.amnesty.org.uk/sites/default/files/mde150192014en.pdf (accessed 3 July 2015).

[59]See 'Hamas declares support for Palestinian bid to join international criminal court,' The Guardian (23 August 2014). http://www.theguardian.com/world/2014/aug/23/hamas-back-palestinian-bid-international-criminal-court (accessed 3 July 2015).

[60]See 'Is the PA stalling Gaza war crimes probe?' *Al Jazeera* (12 September 2014) http://www.aljazeera.com/news/middleeast/2014/09/pa-leadership-speaking-with-two-voices-201491110113l329372.html (accessed 12 June 2015).

[61]See 'Palestine officially granted ICC observer status,' *RT* (9 December 2014) http://rt.com/news/212663-palestine-icc-observer-status/ (accessed 3 July 2015).

areas of Iraq and Syria. The group, led by Abu Bakr al-Baghdadi (also known as Al-Khalifah Ibrahim) currently has control over hundreds of square kilometers, without regard for international borders and ruling by Sharia law. In addition to carrying out brutal executions and kidnappings and IS has also destroyed valuable antiquities. In February, al-Qaeda renounced ties to IS after several months of hostilities between al-Nusra Front and IS.[62]

A few months later, in May, 140 Kurdish schoolboys were kidnapped and then forced to take lessons in Islamic theology.[63] The cities of Mosul and Tikrit fell into the control of IS in June, in addition to al-Qaim and three other Iraqi towns.[64] The UN announced that because of the violence, somewhere around 1.2 million Iraqis have been forced to flee.[65] Syrian cities and a major oil field had been taken over by IS by July. In Homs province, IS claimed to have killed 270 people in order to take over another oil field.[66] Jonah's Tomb, a holy site located in Mosul, was destroyed by IS militants in July as well.[67] In August, IS fighters raid Sinjar, home to the Yazidi minority group, where thousands of Yazidi women and girls are raped and captured before being sold into slavery; hundreds of men are executed, and more than 40,000 Yazidi become stranded in the mountains outside Sinjar.[68]

In response, in August, US President Barack Obama authorized air strikes of Sunni extremists in Iraq in order to protect US personnel from IS fighters or to prevent a genocide of minorities by IS.[69] The bombing is focused on the ISIS stronghold of Raqqa, a city in northern Syria. In November, a team of independent

---

[62]See CNN, 'ISIS Fast Facts' (last updated 4 July 2015 http://edition.cnn.com/2014/08/08/world/isis-fast-facts/ (accessed 6 July 2015).

[63]See Salma Abdelaziz, 'Syrian radicals "brainwash" kidnapped Kurdish schoolchildren,' *CNN* (26 June 2014) http://www.cnn.com/2014/06/25/world/meast/syria-isis-schoolboys/index.html?hpt=hp_t2 (accessed 3 July 2015).

[64]See Michael Martinez et al., '4 western Iraqi towns fall to advancing ISIS militants,' *CNN* (22 June 2014) http://www.cnn.com/2014/06/21/world/meast/iraq-crisis/index.html?iref=allsearch (accessed 3 July 2015).

[65]See 'Number of people fleeing ongoing crisis in Iraq increasing rapidly,' *United Nations Radio*, (30 June 2014) http://www.unmultimedia.org/radio/english/2014/06/number-of-people-fleeing-ongoing-crisis-in-iraq-increasing-rapidly/#.VZUD99Oqqkp (accessed 3 July 2015).

[66]See Salma Abdelaziz, 'Group: ISIS takes major oilfield,' *CNN* (3 July 2014) http://www.cnn.com/2014/07/03/world/meast/syria-isis-oil-field/index.html?iref=allsearch (accessed 3 July 2015).

[67]See Dana Ford and Mohammed Tawfeeq, 'Extremists destroy Jonah's tomb, officials say,' *CNN* 25 July 2014) http://edition.cnn.com/2014/07/24/world/iraq-violence/index.html (accessed 3 July 2015).

[68]See Ivan Watson, "Treated like cattle," Yazidi women sold, raped, enslaved by IS,' *CNN* (30 October 2014) http://edition.cnn.com/2014/10/30/world/meast/isis-female-slaves/index.html (accessed 1 July 2015).

[69]See Chelsea Carter, et al., 'U.S. jet fighters, drones strike ISIS fighters, convoys in Iraq,' *CNN* (9 August 2014) http://edition.cnn.com/2014/08/08/world/iraq-options/index.html?hpt=hp_t1 (accessed 3 July 2015).

UN investigators asserted that the commanders of the Islamic State of Iraq and Syria (ISIS) are responsible for war crimes and crimes against humanity on a "massive scale" in areas under their control, from northeast Syria, where they spread terror by beheading, stoning, and shooting civilians and captured fighters.[70]

Furthermore, a report released by Amnesty International revealed that IS fighters use rape as a weapon in attacks amounting to war crimes and crimes against humanity. According to the report, girls as young as 14, 15, and 16 have been kidnapped, subjected to torture and ill treatment, including rape and other forms of sexual violence, and have likewise been pressured into converting to Islam.[71] Additionally, information released by the UK-based Syrian Observatory for Human Rights revealed that the IS executed 1,878 people in Syria over the last 6 months of 2014. Of those killed, the majority were civilians, while 120 were foreign fighters, members of IS, trying the leave the ranks and head home. It has been reported that many civilians were executed for actions that were seen as violating Islamic law, such as stealing, blasphemy, adultery, and homosexuality.[72] At the time of publication, the conflict was still ongoing.

12.1.8 Mali

Beginning in January 2012, several insurgent groups started a campaign for independence or autonomy for northern Mali in the Azawad area against the Malian government.[73] The National Movement for the Liberation of Azawad (MNLA), initially backed by the Ansar Dine Islamist group, led the campaign with the aim of creating an independent homeland for the Tuareg people. Despite a peace

---

[70]See Stephanie Nebehay 'Islamic State commanders liable for massive war crimes: UN,' *Reuters* (14 November 2014) http://www.reuters.com/article/2014/11/14/us-mideast-crisis-un-warcrimes-idUSKCN0IY1CV20141114 .

[71]See Amnesty International, 'Iraq: Yezidi women and girls face harrowing sexual violence,' (23 December 2014) https://www.amnesty.org/en/latest/news/2014/12/iraq-yezidi-women-and-girls-face-harrowing-sexual-violence/ (accessed 6 July 2015).

[72]See 'About 2000 people killed by Islamic State since establishment of "Caliphate,"' *Syrian Observatory for Human Rights*, 28 December 2014) http://www.syriahr.com/en/2014/12/about-2000-people-killed-by-islamic-state-since-the-establishment-of-caliphate/ (accessed 3 July 2015).

[73]See ICC, Office of the Prosecutor , Report on Preliminary Examination Activities 2012 (November 2012), http://www.icc-cpi.int/NR/rdonlyres/C433C462-7C4E-4358-8A72-8D99FD00E8CD/285209/OTP2012ReportonPreliminaryExaminations22Nov2012.pdf (accessed 5 July 2015), para 168: "Since 17 January 2012, there is an ongoing non-international armed conflict in the territory of Mali between the government forces and different organized armed groups particularly Mouvement National de Libération de l'Azawad (MNLA), Al-Qaeda in the Islamic Maghreb (AQIM), Ansar Dine and Mouvement pour l'Unicité et le Jihad en Afrique de l'Ouest (MUJAO) and 'Arab militias,' as well as between these armed groups without the involvement of government forces".

agreement in June 2013 fighting continued, particularly in the north, through 2013 and into 2014.

In June, Human Rights Watch called for a special investigation cell to be established to start investigations into serious crimes committed during the country's 2012–2013 armed conflict.[74] The fighting continued as nine United Nations peacekeepers were killed in Mali in an ambush characterized by the deputy head of the United Nations mission as a "cowardly act of terrorism."[75]

12.1.9 Nigeria/Boko Haram

Boko Haram is a Salafi Islamist group based in northern Nigeria that seeks to establish "pure" Sharia law in the country. Boko Haram, which forbids Western influence including education, began in 2001 by Mohammed Yusuf and in its quest to implement Sharia law, schools, mosques, and churches as well as bars and beer gardens have been bombed or attacked. This situation has been ongoing since 2009. Hostilities continued into 2014. In May, the UN Security Council added Boko Haram to the terrorism list of al-Qaeda sanctions list. In May, several West African leaders agreed to work together to wage "total war" on Boko Haram, saying the Nigerian Islamist group had become a regional al-Qaeda that threatened all of them.[76]

Human Rights Watch released a report in July detailing approximately 2,053 civilian deaths at the hands of Boko Haram in the first 6 months of 2014.[77] Additionally, Amnesty International also detailed that Nigerian military forces were carrying out war crimes also, including extrajudicial executions, torture, and other serious human rights violations.[78] At the time of publication, the conflict was still ongoing.

---

[74]See Human Rights Watch, 'Mali: Establish Special Investigation Cell,' (25 June 2014) http://www.hrw.org/news/2014/06/25/mali-establish-special-investigation-cell (accessed 1 July 2015).

[75]See Adama Diarra and David Lewis, 'Nine U.N. troops killed on worst attack yet on Mali force,' *Reuters* (3 October 2014) http://www.reuters.com/article/2014/10/03/us-mali-un-peacekeepers-idUSKCN0HS0ZH20141003 (accessed 5 July 2015).

[76]See John Irish and Elizabeth Pineau, 'West Africa leaders vow to wage 'total war' on Boko Haram,' *Reuters* (18 May 2014) http://www.reuters.com/article/2014/05/18/us-nigerian-violence-summit-idUSBREA4G06120140518?feedType=RSS&feedName=worldNews&rpc=69 (accessed 3 July 2015).

[77]See Human Rights Watch, 'Nigeria: Boko Haram Kills 2053 Civilians in 6 Months,' (15 June 2014) http://www.hrw.org/news/2014/07/15/nigeria-boko-haram-kills-2053-civilians-6-months (accessed 5 July 2015).

[78]See Amnesty International, 'Nigeria: Gruesome footage implicates military in war crimes,' (5 August 2014) https://www.amnesty.org/en/latest/news/2014/08/nigeria-gruesome-footage-implicates-military-war-crimes/ (accessed 3 July 2015).

12.1.10 Sudan and South Sudan

The current situation between Sudan and South Sudan can be traced back many years through two separate civil wars. Much of the current conflict stems from the disputed region of Abyei as well as the disagreement regarding the Greater Nile Oil Pipeline.[79] In February, Human Rights Watch called for an investigation into the alleged use of cluster bomb after UN experts "found remnants of the weapons, including intact unexploded submunitions or 'bomblets,' in the week of February 7, 2014, near the town of Bor in an area not known to be contaminated by remnants prior to mid-December 2013."[80] UN Secretary-General Ban Ki-Moon called for a special tribunal to investigate crimes against humanity committed in South Sudan in May,[81] after UN officials urged the UN Security Council to take action or risk that the fighting could spiral into genocide.[82]

In August, Human Rights Watch said that both opposition forces and South Sudan's army have recruited and used child soldiers during the country's current armed conflict that began in December 2013. The government used child soldiers in renewed fighting in mid-August and reportedly deployed them at their front lines around Bentiu for weeks.[83] In November, reports of a mass rape of more than 200 women, allegedly perpetrated by Sudanese soldiers surfaced. It has been reported that of 200 women, 80 were minors, including basic school children. The community where the incident occurred called on the UN and ICC to save the village and bring the perpetrators to justice.[84] At the time of publication, the conflict was still ongoing.

---

[79]See 'Sudan and South Sudan in fierce border clashes', BBC News (27 March 2012), http://www.bbc.co.uk/news/world-africa-17515209 (accessed 3 July 2015).

[80]See Human Rights Watch, 'South Sudan: Investigate New Cluster Bomb Use,' (14 February 2014) http://www.hrw.org/news/2014/02/14/south-sudan-investigate-new-cluster-bomb-use (accessed 2 July 2015).

[81]See 'UN chief calls for tribunal on South Sudan crimes,' *Al Jazeera* (13 May 2014) http://www.aljazeera.com/news/africa/2014/05/un-chief-calls-tribunal-s-sudan-crimes-20145134362250668.html (accessed 6 July 2015).

[82]See Michelle Nichols, 'Genocide risk in South Sudan amid personal power struggle,' *Reuters* (2 May 2014) http://www.reuters.com/article/2014/05/02/us-southsudan-unrest-un-genocide-idUSBREA410XW20140502 (accessed 3 July 2015).

[83]See Human Rights Watch, 'South Sudan: Child Soldiers Thrust into Battle,' (20 August 2014) http://www.hrw.org/news/2014/08/20/south-sudan-child-soldiers-thrust-battle (accessed 5 July 2014).

[84]See 'Sudan: Mass Rape of 200 in North Darfur,' *All Africa News* (2 November 2014) http://allafrica.com/stories/201411031903.html (accessed 1 July 2015).

12.1.11 Syria

The armed conflict in Syria—which began as protests from those opposed to the Syrian's Ba'athist regime in response to the Syrian government's attempts to quell an uprising in 2010s Arab Spring and has now developed into an armed rebellion—has taken a massive civilian casualty toll. In January, UN High Commissioner for Human Rights Navi Pillay warned Syrian opposition groups that recent mass executions are in violation of international human rights law and may also constitute war crimes.[85] Furthermore in January, smuggled Syrian regime documents and photographs provided evidence show evidence of large-scale and/or systematic killing of up to 11,000 detainees; Syrian government officials could face war crimes charges.[86] Human Rights Watch reported that Syrian authorities deliberately demolished residential neighborhoods with explosives and bulldozers in Damascus and Hama over the last year, urged Syrian government to halt the wanton destruction of property, and urged UN Security Council to refer the situation to the ICC.[87] In February, UN OHCHR reported that all parties in Syrian conflict are committing war crimes and crimes against humanity, including executions and shelling of civilians.[88] In March, UN Independent International Commission of Inquiry on Syrian Arab Republic reports mass killings by jihadist rebels against Syrian civilians and use of barrel bomb attacks by government forces into residential neighborhoods of Aleppo city.[89]

The UN warned in June that UN investigators warned that the Syrian civil war and the current upsurge in killing by jihadist militants in Iraq might spillover into other countries resulting in a regional war in the Middle East.[90] Human Rights Watch published a report stating that rebel groups in Syria have recruited 15-year-old children to fight against Bashar al-Assad's troops, and children as young as 14

[85]See Addison Morris, 'UN rights chief: Syria executions may be war crimes,' *Jurist* (17 January 2014) http://jurist.org/paperchase/2014/01/un-rights-chief-syria-executions-may-be-war-crimes.php (accessed 5 July 2015).

[86]See Ian Black, 'Syrian regime document trove shows evidence of "industrial scale" killing of detainees,' *The Guardian* (21 January 2014) http://www.theguardian.com/world/2014/jan/20/evidence-industrial-scale-killing-syria-war-crimes (accessed 1 July 2015).

[87]Ibid.

[88]See UNHCHR, "Deprival of food, water, shelter and medical care—a method of war in Syria, and a crime against humanity" (6 February 2014) http://www.ohchr.org/EN/NewsEvents/Pages/DisplayNews.aspx?NewsID=14224&LangID=E (accessed 3 July 2015).

[89]See Bradley McAllister, 'UN: Syria rebels committed mass executions of civilians,' *Jurist* (18 March 2014) http://jurist.org/paperchase/2014/03/un-syria-rebels-committed-mass-executions-of-civilians.php (accessed 1 July 2015).

[90]See Stephanie Nebehay and Tom Miles, 'U.N. investigators warn of wider sectarian war across Iraq, Syria,' *Reuters* (17 June 2014) http://www.reuters.com/article/2014/06/17/us-syria-crisis-warcrimes-idUSKBN0ES10S20140617 (accessed 3 July 2015).

for support roles.[91] In August, UN High Commissioner for Human Rights Navi Pillay said that at least 191,369 people have been killed in the Syrian conflict up to April 2014, and repeated her call for referring alleged war crimes and crimes against humanity committed by all sides in the conflict to the ICC.[92]

In December, at the initiative of the Permanent Mission of Liechtenstein to the UN, in cooperation with the Liechtenstein Institute on Self-Determination, some 25 diplomats and experts assembled to discuss accountability options for Syria. They opined, *inter alia*, that the ICC remained the preferred option, while there was no expectation that it will succeed in the near future and that national trials would be the best way to ensure accountability. They also proposed the setting up of a hybrid court, which could involve international, Arab judges, prosecutors, and lawyers alongside Syrians.[93] At the time of publication, the conflict was still ongoing.

12.2 Tribunals and Courts[94]

12.2.1 International Tribunals

12.2.1.1 International Criminal Tribunal for the Former Yugoslavia

Although the target date of December 31, 2014 set for completion of the judicial work of the International Criminal Tribunal for the former Yugoslavia (ICTY) was not reached due to numerous factors including, among others, the health of some of the accused and the size and complexity of some cases, the Tribunal is close to ending most of its trials. As of the beginning of 2015, only four trials and five appeal cases were remaining. Four outstanding appeal cases and three of the four cases at trial stage will most probably be concluded in 2015. The judgment in the *Mladić* case is expected to be delivered in March 2017 or even later, and appeal proceedings originating from the trial judgments will be concluded by the Mechanism for International Criminal Tribunals (MICT).

---

[91]See Human Rights Watch, 'Syria: Armed Groups Send Children into Battle,' (22 June 2014) http://www.hrw.org/news/2014/06/22/syria-armed-groups-send-children-battle (accessed 3 July 2015).

[92]See Stephanie Nebehay, 'U.N. says Syria death toll tops 190,000, rights envoy raps world powers,' *Reuters* (22 August 2014) http://www.reuters.com/article/2014/08/22/us-syria-crisis-deaths-idUSKBN0GM0KH20140822 (accessed 3 July 2015).

[93]See Liechtenstein Institute on Self-Determination, 'Accountability in Syria: Meeting at Princeton University,' (17 November 2014) http://www.regierung.li/files/medienarchiv/voelkerrecht/2014-11-17_Accountability_in_Syria_summary_final.pdf?t=635530491389745970 (accessed 3 July 2015).

[94]In this year's Year in Review, we do not handle domestic tribunal developments. For developments concerning domestic tribunals, please see www.internationalcrimesdatabase.org.

In 2014, the Appeals Chamber delivered two judgments. First, on January 23, 2014, when the Appeals Chamber issued its 810-pages judgment in the *Šainović et al.* case,[95] one of the largest and most complex cases dealt with by the Chamber.[96] This case involved four high-ranking Serbian officials who were convicted by Trial Chamber III in February 2009 for crimes committed by Serbian forces in Kosovo against Kosovo Albanian civilians between March and May 1999.[97] The Appeals Chamber, by majority, affirmed the Trial Chamber's ruling that Nikola Šainović, Nebojša Pavković and Sreten Lukić participated in a joint criminal enterprise (JCE) with the common purpose to forcibly displace Kosovo Albanians both within and outside Kosovo,[98] and which was implemented through the crimes of murder, deportation, other inhumane acts (forcible transfer), and persecutions. The JCE eventually led to the killings of hundreds and the expulsion of hundreds of thousands of Kosovo Albanians. The Appeals Chamber also upheld the decision of the Trial Chamber that Vladimir Lazarević could be held individually criminally responsible for aiding and abetting the deportation and forcible transfer of Kosovo Albanians from Kosovo by forces of the Former Republic of Yugoslavia (FRY) and Serbia as crimes against humanity. After having analyzed ICTY case law and case law of the International Criminal Tribunal for Rwanda (ICTR), national legislation and jurisprudence, as well as customary international law,[99] the Appeals Chamber came "to the *compelling* conclusion that 'specific direction' is not an element of aiding and abetting liability under customary international law".[100] Thereby, the Appeals Chamber "unequivocally" rejected the approach adopted in the *Perišić* appeal judgment of February 2013 (discussed in last year's *Year in Review*) in which the majority of the Chamber, although in a different setting, ruled that Momčilo Perišić, former Chief of Staff of the Yugoslav Army (VJ), could not be held liable for aiding and abetting crimes against humanity and war crimes committed by the Army of the Republika Srpska (VRS) in Sarajevo and Srebrenica between 1993 and 1995 because it was not proven beyond a reasonable doubt that he specifically directed assistance toward the

[95]See ICTY, Appeals Chamber, Prosecutor v. Nikola Šainović, Nebojša Pavković, Vladimir Lazarević and Sreten Lukić, 'Judgement', Case No. IT-05-87-A (5 February 2014), http://www.icty.org/x/cases/milutinovic/acjug/en/140123.pdf (accessed 2 February 2015).

[96]See ICTY, Press Release, 'Convictions for Kosovo crimes upheld for four senior Serbian officials' (23 January 2014), http://www.icty.org/sid/11443 (accessed 2 February 2015).

[97]See ICTY, Trial Chamber I, Prosecutor v. Milan Milutinović, Nikola Šainović, Dragoljub Ojdanić, Nebojša Pavkovi, Vladimir Lazarević and Sreten Lukić, 'Judgement', Case No. IT-05-87-T (26 February 2009), http://www.icty.org/x/cases/milutinovic/tjug/en/jud090226-e1of4.pdf (accessed 2 February 2015).

[98]See ICTY, Appeals Chamber, Prosecutor v. Nikola Šainović, Nebojša Pavković, Vladimir Lazarević and Sreten Lukić, 'Judgement', Case No. IT-05-87-A (23 January 2014), http://www.icty.org/x/cases/milutinovic/acjug/en/140123.pdf (accessed 2 February 2015), para 664.

[99]Ibid., paras 1623–1648.

[100]Ibid., para 1649 (emphasis added).

commission of the crimes.[101] In other words, while the Appeals Chamber in *Perišić* found that "specific direction" is an essential element of the *actus reus* of aiding and abetting liability and must be established beyond a reasonable doubt, the Appeals Chamber in the *Šainović* case took the exact opposite stance by ruling that in order to be held liable for aiding and abetting it is not required that an accused's conduct was specifically directed at the perpetration of the crimes committed.[102] Although the Appeals Chamber ruled that the accused could indeed be held individually criminally responsible for crimes against humanity and war crimes, it found that a limited reduction in the sentences imposed upon Šainović, Lazarević and Lukić was justified after taking into account the proportionality principle, as well as such factors as the circumstances of the case and the gravity of the crimes for which the three accused were held responsible. Pavković's sentence was confirmed as he remained convicted of very serious crimes.[103] In the dissenting opinion appended by Judge Bakhtiyar Tuzmukhamedov, he did not take a position on whether or not "specific direction" is an element of aiding and abetting,[104] but argued that the Appeals Chamber should not have addressed the issue of specific direction in order "to preserve as much as possible, judicial harmony in the case law that impacts the development of international criminal law and international humanitarian law, as well as legal certainty, stability and predictability (…)".[105] Moreover, Judge Tuzmukhamedov noted that "in order to ensure the fair trial rights of an accused to have 'like cases treated alike', the Appeals Chamber should follow its previous decisions unless there are cogent reasons to depart from them in the interests of justice".[106] In response to the Appeals Chamber's decision issued in the *Šainović* case, the Office of the Prosecutor (OTP) filed a motion before the Appeals Chamber, requesting it to reconsider the acquittal of Perišić for aiding and abetting crimes committed in Sarajevo and Srebrenica between 1993 and 1995.[107] However, on March 20, 2014, the Appeals Chamber rejected the

[101]Ibid., para 1650; See also ICTY, Appeals Chamber, Prosecutor v. Momčilo Perišić, 'Judgement', Case No. IT-04-81-A (28 February 2013), http://www.icty.org/x/cases/perisic/acjug/en/130228_judgement.pdf (accessed 2 February 2015), para 73.

[102]See ICTY, Appeals Chamber, Prosecutor v. Nikola Šainović, Nebojša Pavković, Vladimir Lazarević and Sreten Lukić, 'Judgement', Case No. IT-05-87-A (23 January 2014), http://www.icty.org/x/cases/milutinovic/acjug/en/140123.pdf (accessed 2 February 2015), paras 1650 and 1651.

[103]Ibid, paras 1842–1846.

[104]See, 'Dissenting Opinion of Judge Tuzmukhamedov' (23 January 2014), http://www.icty.org/x/cases/milutinovic/acjug/en/140123.pdf (accessed 2 February 2015), para 412.

[105]Ibid., para 45.

[106]Ibid., para 47.

[107]See ICTY, Press Release, 'Statement of Prosecutor Serge Brammertz in relation to the motion for reconsideration submitted by the Prosecution in the Perišić case' (3 February 2014), http://www.icty.org/sid/11447 (accessed 2 February 2015).

Prosecution's motion noting that it lacks the power to reconsider its final judgments.[108]

Only a few days later, on January 27, 2014, the Appeals Chamber issued its second appeal judgment of 2014 in the case against Vlastimir Đorđević, who was originally indicted with Pavković, Lazarević and Lukić before their case was joined with the case against Milan Milutinović, Šainović and Dragoljub Ojdanić. However, the case against Đorđević was severed because he was still at large when the proceedings began. The Appeals Chamber upheld the Trial Chamber's decision of February 2011 that Đorđević could be held guilty for crimes against humanity and war crimes committed against Kosovo Albanians in Kosovo in the period between January and June 1999. However, although the Appeals Chamber agreed that Đorđević could be held guilty for committing these crimes through his participation in the JCE in which Šainović, Lukić, Pavković, and Lazarević also participated, it reversed his conviction for aiding and abetting the crimes as requested by the Defense. The Appeals Chamber recalled that an accused can be convicted on the basis of more than one mode of liability,[109] but that in this case "the totality of Đorđević's criminal conduct [was] fully reflected in a conviction based solely on his participation in the JCE".[110] Đorđević's sentence was reduced from 27 to 18 years' imprisonment and thereby brought in line with the sentences imposed on JCE members Šainović, Lukić, Pavković, and Lazarević. This judgment marks the ICTY's final judgment with regard to persons who have been indicted for crimes committed in Kosovo.[111]

On February 20, 2014, Trial Chamber II delivered its Rule 98*bis* decision in the case against Goran Hadžić, former President of the self-proclaimed Republic of Serbian Krajina during the Croatian War of Independence.[112] According to Rule 98*bis* of the Tribunal's Rules of Procedure and Evidence (RPE), the Trial Chamber shall pronounce the acquittal of the accused on any count of the indictment at the end of the Prosecution's case when the evidence presented by the Prosecution is insufficient to support a conviction on challenged charges. The Defense did not request an acquittal on any count in its entirety but instead on charges within a count, arguing that Rule 98*bis* RPE "allows the Chamber to look within counts in the Indictment to examine whether an accused may be acquitted on a portion of a

[108] See ICTY, Appeals Chamber, Prosecutor v. Momčilo Perišić, 'Decision on Motion for Reconsideration', Case No. IT-04-81-A (20 March 2014), http://www.icty.org/x/cases/perisic/acdec/en/1403212.pdf (accessed 2 February 2015).

[109] See ICTY, Appeals Chamber, Prosecutor v. Vlastimir Đorđević, 'Judgement', Case No. IT-05-87/1-A (27 January 2014), http://www.icty.org/x/cases/djordjevic/acjug/en/140127.pdf (accessed 6 February 2015), para 831.

[110] Ibid., para 833.

[111] See ICTY, Press Release, 'Vlastimir Đorđević's responsibility for crimes in Kosovo confirmed on appeal' (27 January 2014), http://www.icty.org/sid/11445 (accessed 6 February 2015).

[112] See ICTY, Trial Chamber, 'Oral Decision on Defense Motion for Acquittal Pursuant to Rule 98 bis' (20 February 2014), http://www.icty.org/x/cases/hadzic/tdec/en/1402212.pdf (accessed 9 February 2015).

count".[113] However, after analyzing the approaches taken by other ICTY Trial Chambers on motions for acquittal and by taking into account the legislative history of Rule 98*bis*, Trial Chamber II concluded that such motions could only be considered with regard to entire counts. Accordingly, the Defense's motion for a judgment of acquittal on various charges contained in separate counts of Hadžić's indictment was dismissed. As to the presentation of evidence, the Prosecution concluded its case in October 2013. However, in early April 2014, the Trial Chamber nevertheless permitted the Prosecution to call on Borislav Bogunović as final prosecution witness because he was serving a 20-year prison sentence in Serbia at the time the Prosecution's case took place. The Defense began its case on July 3, 2014, starting with Hadžić's testimony. The trial was adjourned on October 20, 2014 for reasons related to Hadžić's health.

A few months later, on June 6, 2014, the Appeals Chamber affirmed Trial Chamber III's decision ordering the continuation of proceedings against Vojislav Šešelj from the close of the hearings as soon as Judge Mandiaye Niang, who was appointed to replace Judge Frederik Harhoff following his disqualification,[114] has fully familiarized himself with the case file containing 97 witness testimonies and 1,399 pieces of evidence.[115] Since Judge Niang had indicated that he needed more time to review the case file, the proceedings against Šešelj were prolonged. Since Šešelj already spent more than 11 years in custody and still no date was set for pronouncement of the judgment, Presiding Judge Jean-Claude Antonetti issued an invitation on June 13, 2014, requesting both the Defense and Prosecution to submit their opinion on whether or not Šešelj should be provisionally released pending his trial judgment.[116] On November 6, 2014, the Appeals Chamber, Judge Niang dissenting,[117] ordered *proprio motu* the provisional release of Šešelj on humanitarian grounds so that he could travel to Serbia for medical treatment as he was diagnosed with cancer in 2013.[118]

---

[113]Ibid.

[114]See ICTY, Press Release, 'Judge Harhoff disqualified from Šešelj case' (29 August 2013), http://www.icty.org/sid/11357 (accessed 12 February 2015).

[115]See ICTY, Appeals Chamber, The Prosecutor v. Vojislav Šešelj, 'Decision on Appeal against Decision on Continuation of Proceedings', Case No. IT-03-67-AR15bis (6 June 2014), http://www.icty.org/x/cases/seselj/acdec/en/140606.pdf (accessed 12 February 2015).

[116]See ICTY, Trial Chamber III, The Prosecutor v. Vojislav Šešelj, 'Order inviting the Parties to make submissions on possible provisional release of the accused proprio motu', Case No. IT-03-67-T (13 June 2014), http://www.icty.org/x/cases/seselj/tord/en/140613.pdf (accessed 12 February 2015).

[117]See ICTY, Trial Chamber II, The Prosecutor v. Vojislav Šešelj, 'Dissenting Opinion of Judge Mandiaye Niang to the order on provisional release of the accused proprio motu', Case No. IT-03-67-T (11 November 2014), http://www.icty.org/x/cases/seselj/tord/en/141111.pdf (accessed 12 February 2015).

[118]See ICTY, Trial Chamber III, The Prosecutor v. Vojislav Šešelj, 'Order on the provisional release of the Accused Propio Motu', Case No. IT-03-67-T (6 November 2014), http://www.icty.org/x/cases/seselj/tord/en/141106.pdf (accessed 12 February 2015).

The ICTY is also close to the end of the trials involving Ratko Mladić and Radovan Karadžić. In the *Prosecutor v Ratko Mladić* case, the Defense confidentially submitted a motion for acquittal under Rule 98*bis* of the Tribunal's RPE on February 26, 2014 following the Prosecution's closure of its case 2 days earlier. The Defense asked for acquittal on the two counts of genocide as well as on charges within other counts of the indictment, arguing that the Prosecution did not provide enough evidence to support the charges. After carefully having considered the oral submissions from both the Defense and Prosecution, Trial Chamber I rejected the Defense's motion for acquittal.[119] With regard to the scope of Rule 98*bis*, the Trial Chamber referred to the Rule 98*bis* decision in the *Hadžić* case when it held that motions for acquittal cannot be considered with regard to charges within a count. Furthermore, the Trial Chamber noted that there was sufficient evidence to establish that acts of genocide took place in the municipalities and during the period covered in the indictment. In addition, the Chamber found that Mladić participated in and made a significant contribution to a JCE with the goal "to permanently remove the Bosnian Muslims and Bosnian Croats from Bosnian-Serb claimed territory in Bosnia and Herzegovina through the commission of crimes charged in the Indictment. [Mladić] shared the intent of the other members of the overarching JCE to carry out its objective through the commission of crimes".[120] On July 24, 2014, the Appeals Chamber dismissed the interlocutory appeal confidentially filed by the Defense, appealing the Trial Chamber's Rule 98*bis* decision in relation to the two genocide counts. The Appeals Chamber opined that on the basis of the evidence available, "the Trial Chamber did not err in finding that a reasonable trier of fact could have concluded that, taken at its highest, there was sufficient evidence to infer that Mladić possessed genocidal intent".[121] On October 23, 2014, Presiding Judge Alphons Orie of Trial Chamber I granted a request issued by the Prosecution to reopen its case in order to present evidence from the mass grave discovered in September 2013 in the village of Tomašica in northwestern Bosnia and Herzegovina to support the genocide charges.[122] The Chamber found that the newly discovered evidence was related to the case and agreed that the Prosecution could not have presented it during its case because "the necessary analysis of the grave, as well as the compiling of witness statements and expert

---

[119]See ICTY, Trial Chamber I, 'Rule 98 bis Judgement summary in the case of Ratko Mladic' (15 April 2014), http://icty.org/x/cases/mladic/tjug/en/140415-summary.pdf (accessed 17 February 2015).

[120]Ibid.

[121]See ICTY, Appeals Chamber, Prosecutor v. Ratko Mladić, 'Public Redacted Version of Decision on Defence Interlocutory Appeal from the Trial Chamber Rule 98 bis decision', Case No. IT-09-92-AR73.4 (24 July 2014), http://www.icty.org/x/cases/mladic/acdec/en/140724.pdf (accessed 17 February 2015), para 18.

[122]See ICTY, Trial Chamber I, Prosecutor v. Ratko Mladić, 'Decision on Prosecution Motion to Re-Open its Case-in-Chief'. Case No. IT-09-92-T (23 October 2014), http://www.icty.org/x/cases/mladic/tdec/en/141023.pdf (accessed 17 February 2015).

reports continued up until August 2014".[123] Moreover, since the Prosecution's request was made at an early stage in the Defense case, namely on August 26, 2014, a reopening would not cause prejudice to the Defense's case, nor would it unduly prolong the trial.[124] A similar request issued in the *Karadžić* case was rejected in March 2014 because the trial reached its final stage and reopening of the Prosecution's case would therefore not be in the interests of justice.[125]

In the *Karadžić* case, which continued on January 16, 2014, Mladić appeared before the Court on January 28, 2014 following the approval of Karadžić's request to subpoena *Mladić* as a witness in his trial.[126] However, Mladić refused to answer questions posed by Karadžić's Defense, citing poor health and arguing that his testimony could have a negative impact on his own trial. The Defense case was closed in early March 2014 when a final witness was heard. After resting his case, Karadžić filed a motion for bifurcated judgment on May 5, 2014, requesting his verdict to be determined in a separate sentencing hearing in case of conviction. The Trial Chamber denied this motion on May 22, 2014.[127] Another motion was filed by Karadžić on May 19, 2014, requesting the President of the Mechanism for International Criminal Tribunals (MICT), Judge Theodor Meron, to appoint a Single Judge to determine "whether members of the [ICTY] Office of the Prosecutor have wilfully interfered with the administration of justice at this Tribunal in violation of Rule 90(A) by failing to disclose all exculpatory evidence and falsely testifying that they had done so".[128] According to Karadžić, various documents were not disclosed to the Defense throughout the trial, including witness statements and other documents necessary for the preparation of the Defense's case. On June 19, 2014, President Meron approved Karadžić's request and appointed Judge Vagn Joensen to investigate whether contempt of court

[123]Ibid., para 9.

[124]Ibid., para 112.

[125]See ICTY, Trial Chamber, Prosecutor v. Radovan Karadžić, 'Decision on Prosecution Motion to Re-Open its Case and Prosecution Motion for Protective Measures for Witness KDZ614', Case No. IT-95-5/18-T (20 March 2014), http://www.icty.org/x/cases/karadzic/tdec/en/1403212.pdf (accessed 17 February 2015).

[126]See ICTY, Trial Chamber, Prosecutor v. Radovan Karadžić, 'Decision on Accused's motion to subpoena Ratko Mladić', Case No. IT-95-5/18-T (11 December 2013), http://www.icty.org/x/cases/karadzic/tdec/en/131211a.pdf (accessed 20 February 2015).

[127]See ICTY, Trial Chamber, Prosecutor v. Radovan Karadžić', 'Decision on Accused's Motion for Bifurcated Judgement', Case No. IT-95-5/18-T (22 May 2014), http://icty.org/x/cases/karadzic/tdec/en/140522.pdf (accessed 20 February 2015).

[128]See UNMICT, The President of the Mechanism, The Prosecutor v. Radovan Karadzic, 'Request for designation of single judge to consider appointment of amicus curiae prosecutor to investigate contempt by Office of the Prosecutor'. Case No. MICT-13-55-R912.3 (19 May 2014), http://www.unmict.org/sites/default/files/casedocuments/mict-13-55/miscellaneous-documents/en/140519.pdf (accessed 2o February 2015), para 1.

proceedings could be instigated against the Prosecution.[129] However, Judge Joensen found that the Karadžić Trial Chamber retained jurisdiction to decide on the issue and therefore invited it to make a determination.[130] The Trial Chamber found that the Prosecution indeed violated its disclosure obligations several times, but that it could not be concluded that "such violations were indicative of a lack of good faith on the part of the Prosecution".[131] Therefore, there was no reason to believe that contempt had been committed by members of the ICTY's OTP. Accordingly, Karadžić's motion was dismissed by Judge Joensen.[132] Closing arguments were presented by the Prosecution and Defense from September 29 to October 2, 2014, after which the hearings were declared closed.

12.2.1.2 International Criminal Tribunal for Rwanda

Since the ICTR already concluded all trials at first instance, the remaining judicial work of the ICTR in 2014 had been focused on the Appeals Chamber. Ahead of the Tribunal's closure at the end of 2015, the Appeals Chamber completed almost all of its work by issuing judgments in several cases. The *Nyiramasuhuko* et al. ("Butare") case is the only outstanding case. The Appeals Chamber delivered its first judgment in 2014 in *The Prosecutor v. Augustin Ndindiliyimana, Augustin Bizimungu, Françoise-Xavier Nzuwonemeye, and Innocent Sagahutu* case, also known as the *"Military II"* case.[133] Before pronouncing the judgment on February 11, 2014, the Appeals Chamber ordered the severance of the appeals concerning Bizimungu, a former general of the Rwandan Army who was tried along with

---

[129]See UNMICT, The President of the Mechanism, Prosecutor v. Radovan Karadžić, 'Decision on Prosecution Motion to Strike and Assigning a Single Judge', Case No. MICT-13-55-R912.3 (5 June 2014), http://www.unmict.org/sites/default/files/casedocuments/mict-13-55/president%E2%80%99s-decisions/en/140605.pdf (accessed 20 February 2015).

[130]See UNMICT, Single Judge, Prosecutor v. Radovan Karadžić, 'Decision to invite the ICTY Trial Chamber in the Karadzic case to determine whether there is "reason to believe" that contempt has been committed by members of the Office of the Prosecutor', Case No. MICT-13-55-R912.3 (21 July 2014), http://www.unmict.org/sites/default/files/casedocuments/mict-13-55/trial-decisions/en/140721.pdf (accessed 20 February 2015).

[131]See ICTY, Trial Chamber, Prosecutor v. Radovan Karadžić, 'Decision on Invitation from the Single Judge of the Mechanism for International Criminal Tribunals', Case No. IT-95-5/18-T (6 August 2014), http://icty.org/x/cases/karadzic/tdec/en/140806.pdf (accessed 20 February 2015).

[132]See UNMICT, Single Judge, Prosecutor v. Radovan Karadžić, Decision on Request for Designation of Single Judge to Consider Appointment of Amicus Curiae Prosecutor to Investigate Contempt by Office of the Prosecutor', Case No. MICT-13-55-R912.3 (22 August 2014), http://www.unmict.org/sites/default/files/casedocuments/mict-13-55/trial-decisions/en/140822.pdf (accessed 20 February 2015).

[133]See ICTR, Appeals Chamber, Augustin Ndindiliyimana, François-Xavier Nzuwonemeye and Innocent Sagahutu v. The Prosecutor, 'Judgement', Case No. ICTR-00-56-A (11 February 2014), http://www.unictr.org/sites/unictr.org/files/case-documents/ictr-00-56/appeals-chamber-judgements/en/140211.pdf (accessed 23 February 2015).

Ndindiliyimana, Nzuwonemeye, and Sagahutu.[134] The Appeals Chamber, among other things, opined that Ndindiliyimana, who was a major general and subsequently Chief of Staff of the Rwandan Gendarmerie during the 1994 Rwandan genocide, could not be held responsible as a superior for crimes committed by gendarmes during the attack on Kansi Parish on April 21, 1994 because there was not sufficient evidence for the Trial Chamber to come to the conclusion that he had effective control over the gendarmes subordinated to the Rwandan Army after April 7, 1994.[135] Nzuwonemeye and Sagahutu, both former Commander of the Reconnaissance Battalion of the Rwandan Army, were held responsible as a superior for crimes against humanity. With respect to Nzuwonemeye, the Appeals Chamber concluded that the Trial Chamber erred in determining that Nzuwonemeye exercised "de facto authority" over the gendarmes that participated in an attack on Tutsi refugees at Saint André College on April 13, 1994.[136] Also the Trial Chamber's finding that Nzuwonemeye, together with Sagahutu, could be held responsible for aiding and abetting the killing of Prime Minister Agathe Uwilingiyimana was overruled.[137] However, the Appeals Chamber found that Sagahutu could indeed be held criminally responsible as a superior for aiding and abetting the killing of two UNAMIR peacekeepers on April 7, 1994.[138] Accordingly, the convictions of both Ndindiliyimana and Nzuwonemeye were reversed in its entirety, and the sentence of Innocent Sagahutu was reduced from 20 to 15 years' imprisonment following the reversal of some of his convictions.[139]

In late June, the Appeals Chamber issued its judgment in the *Augustin Bizimungu v. The Prosecutor* case. The Chamber had ordered the severance of the appeals concerning Bizimungu because the Trial Chamber failed to provide a reasoned opinion by not making any legal findings with regard to Bizimungu's conviction on some events concerning genocide and crimes against humanity.[140] The Appeals Chamber recalled that "a trial chamber's failure to provide a reasoned opinion constitutes an error of law which allows the Appeals Chamber to consider

[134]See ICTR, Press Release, 'Appeals Chamber Delivers Judgement in Military II Case' (11 February 2014), http://www.unictr.org/en/news/appeals-chamber-delivers-judgement-military-II-case (accessed 23 February 2015).

[135]See ICTR, Appeals Chamber, Augustin Ndindiliyimana, François-Xavier Nzuwonemeye and Innocent Sagahutu v. The Prosecutor, 'Judgement', Case No. ICTR-00-56-A (11 February 2014), http://www.unictr.org/sites/unictr.org/files/case-documents/ictr-00-56/appeals-chamber-judgements/en/140211.pdf (accessed 23 February 2015), para 61.

[136]Ibid., para 75.

[137]Ibid., para 254.

[138]Ibid., para 253.

[139]Ibid., para 448.

[140]See ICTR, Appeals Chamber, Augustin Bizimungu v. The Prosecutor, 'Judgement', Case No. ICTR-00-56B-A (30 June 2014), http://www.unictr.org/sites/unictr.org/files/case-documents/ictr-00-56/appeals-chamber-judgements/en/1406312.pdf (accessed 25 February 2015), paras 19–212.

the relevant evidence and factual findings (…)".[141] Therefore, it assessed "the findings and evidence relevant to each incident supporting Bizimungu's genocide conviction and [some events] related to Bizimungu's convictions for murder and rape as crimes against humanity to determine whether the elements of these crimes are established beyond reasonable doubt".[142] Bizimungu's conviction for some of the rape and murder charges confirmed against him were reversed, as well as the Trial Chamber's finding that Bizimungu could be held criminally responsible as a superior for exercising authority and effective control over the *Interahamwe* who participated in numerous attacks.[143] On June 30, 2014, the Appeals Chamber partially confirmed the conviction of Augustin Bizimungu for crimes against humanity, genocide, and serious violations of Common Article 3 to the Geneva Conventions and of Additional Protocol II. Despite the reversal of some of Bizimungu's convictions, the 30-year sentence imposed upon Bizimungu was affirmed because of the serious nature of the crimes for which he remained convicted.[144]

On September 29, 2014, the Appeals Chamber issued judgments in the *Édouard Karemera and Matthieu Ngirumpatse v. The Prosecutor* case,[145] *The Prosecutor v. Callixte Nzabonimana* case,[146] and in *The Prosecutor v. Ildélphonse Nizeyimana* case.[147] The convictions of the accused for the crimes of genocide, war crimes and crimes against humanity, including, *inter alia*, rape and murder, were affirmed by the Appeals Chamber. In the case of Karemera and Ngirumpatse, former Vice President and President, respectively, of the ruling MRND political party at the time of the Rwandan genocide, both accused argued that the Trial Chamber committed errors of law and fact and therefore asked for an acquittal, or alternatively, a sentence reduction. Although the Appeals Chamber reversed some of the Trial Chamber's findings, it upheld the convictions of Karemera and Ngirumpatse. Accordingly, their sentences of life imprisonment were affirmed. Also in the case of Nzabonimana, who was Minister of Youth and member of the MRND in 1994, the Appeals Chamber affirmed the sentence of life imprisonment

[141] Ibid., para 23.

[142] Ibid., para 24.

[143] Ibid., para 139.

[144] Ibid., para 408.

[145] See ICTR, Appeals Chamber, Édouard Karemera and Matthieu Ngirumpatse v. The Prosecutor, 'Judgement', Case No. ICTR-98-44-A (29 September 2014), http://www.unictr.org/sites/unictr.org/files/case-documents/ictr-98-44/appeals-chamber-judgements/en/140929.pdf (accessed 27 February 2015).

[146] See ICTR, Appeals Chamber, Callixte Nzabonimana v. The Prosecutor, 'Judgement', Case No. ICTR-98-44D-A (29 September 2014), http://www.unictr.org/sites/unictr.org/files/case-documents/ictr-98-44d/appeals-chamber-judgements/en/140929.pdf (accessed 27 February 2015).

[147] See ICTR, Appeals Chamber, Ildéphonse Nizeyimana v. The Prosecutor, 'Judgement', Case No. ICTR-00-55C-A (29 September 2014), http://www.unictr.org/sites/unictr.org/files/case-documents/ictr-00-55c/appeals-chamber-judgements/en/140929.pdf (accessed 27 February 2015).

handed down by Trial Chamber III for instigating genocide and extermination as a crime against humanity, and for conspiracy and direct and public incitement to commit genocide.[148] In the third appeal judgment issued in September 2014, the Appeals Chamber reduced the sentence of life imprisonment imposed on Ildélphonse Nizeyimana, former Captain in the Rwandan Army, to 35 years of imprisonment due to the reversal of some of the Trial Chamber's convictions.

April 2014 marked the 20th anniversary of the 1994 Rwandan genocide in which an estimated 800,000 people were killed over a period of approximately 100 days. On April 6, 2014, ICTR and MICT Prosecutor Hassan B. Jallow issued a statement marking the 20th anniversary of the Rwandan genocide. In his statement, Jallow expressed his "gratitude to the thousands of survivors who have, despite numerous challenges, testified at the ICTR and assisted the tribunal with the indispensable material for the execution of its mandate to render justice".[149] Jallow also emphasized that even 20 years after the Rwandan genocide there is still important work to be done. In this regard, he addressed the issue of fugitives since nine individuals originally indicted by the ICTR are still at large. As the ICTR will close its doors in 2015, the MICT retains jurisdiction over three of the fugitives (Augustin Bizimana, Félicien Kabuga, Protais Mpiranya), while six of them (Fulgence Kayishema, Charles Sikubwabo, Ladislas Ntaganzwa, Aloys Ndimbati, Charles Ryandikayo, and Phénéas Munyarugarama) will be tried in Rwandan courts. In honor of the 20th anniversary of the 1994 Rwandan genocide, the ICTR, in cooperation with the MICT, hosted a commemoration ceremony on April 10, 2014 at the Arusha Branch (Tanzania).

With regard to the ICTR's completion strategy, ICTR President Judge Joensen presented its six-monthly report on the completion strategy to the UN Security Council on June 5, 2014.[150] President Joensen briefed the Security Council, among other things, on the progress made in the transition from the ICTR to the MICT. The MICT, in particular the Arusha Branch, has already been tasked with several responsibilities from the ICTR since July 2012, including, *inter alia*, the tracking and prosecution of fugitives and the monitoring of cases that have been transferred to Rwanda. Moreover, also appeals filed with respect to judgments issued by the ICTR after July 1, 2012, fall under the MICT's responsibility. As a

---

[148]See ICTR, Trial Chamber III, The Prosecutor v. Callixte Nzabonimana, 'Judgement and Sentence', Case No. ICTR-98-44D-T (31 May 2012), http://www.unictr.org/sites/unictr.org/files/case-documents/ictr-98-44d/trial-judgements/en/120531.pdf (accessed 27 February 2015).

[149]See ICTR, Statement, 'Statement by Justice Hassan B. Jallow Chief Prosecutor, ICTR and MICT on the occasion of the 20th anniversary of the Rwandan genocide' (6 April 2014), http://www.unictr.org/sites/default/files/statements-and-speeches/140406_prosecutor_jallow_20th_anniversary_en.pdf (accessed 27 February 2015).

[150]See ICTR, Statement, 'Address to the United Nations Security Council: Six- Monthly Report On The Completion Strategy Of The International Criminal Tribunal For Rwanda (ICTR) By Judge Vagn Joensen, President' (5 June 2014), http://www.unictr.org/en/news/address-united-nations-security-council-six-monthly-report-completion-strategy-international (accessed 27 February 2015).

result, the Augustin Ngirabatware appeals case has been transferred to the MICT. Moreover, when presenting the ICTR's 19th Annual Report to the UN General Assembly in October 2014, President Joensen noted that despite the complexity of the outstanding "Butare" case, its completion remains on track.[151]

Furthermore, a highlight in the context of the ICTR is the publication of the OTP's Best Practices Manual for the Investigation and Prosecution of Sexual Violence Crimes in Post-Conflict Regions on January 30, 2014.[152] The Manual is based on the 20-year experience of the OTP in prosecuting sexual violence crimes committed during the 1994 Rwandan genocide and serves as a guideline for prosecutors at both the national and international level involved in the investigation and prosecution of sexual violence crimes committed in post-conflict regions.[153]

12.2.1.3 Mechanism for International Criminal Tribunals

The workload of the OTP of the MICT, which was established by the Security Council as a successor to the ICTY and ICTR, has gradually increased now both Tribunals are in the final phase of concluding their work in accordance with their respective completion strategies.

On February 6, 2014, the Mechanism's Appeals Chamber was seized with a request for review filed by Milan Lukić, former leader of a group of local Bosnian Serb paramilitaries in the Bosnian town of Višegrad during the 1992–1995 conflict. Lukić requested a review of a decision issued in July 2009 by Trial Chamber III of the ICTY, convicting him for crimes against humanity and violations of the laws and customs of war, and sentencing him to life imprisonment.[154] While his request was pending, Lukić was transferred to Estonia on February 10, 2014 in order to serve his life sentence.

Furthermore, on March 12–13, 2014, respectively, the President of the MICT, Judge Meron, dismissed without prejudice requests for revocation of the order

---

[151] See ICTR, Statement, 'Address to the United Nations General Assembly—19th Annual Report of the International Criminal Tribunal for Rwanda by judge Vagn Joensen, President' (13 October 2014), http://www.unictr.org/en/news/address-united-nations-general-assembly-19th-annual-report-international-criminal-tribunal (accessed 27 February 2015).

[152] The Best Practices Manual for the Investigation and Prosecution of Sexual Violence Crimes in Post-Conflict Regions can be found here: http://www.unictr.org/sites/unictr.org/files/publications/ICTR-Prosecution-of-Sexual-Violence.pdf (accessed 27 February 2015).

[153] See ICTR, Press Release, 'ICTR Office of the Prosecutor releases best practices manual on The Prosecution of Sexual Violence Crimes in Post-Conflict Regions and hosts an International workshop in Kampala Uganda' (30 January 2014), http://www.unictr.org/en/news/ictr-office-prosecutor-releases-best-practices-manual-prosecution-sexual-violence-crimes-post (accessed 27 February 2015).

[154] See ICTY, Trial Chamber III, Prosecutor v. Milan Lukić and Sredoje Lukić, 'Judgement', Case No. IT-98-32/1-T (20 July 2009), http://www.icty.org/x/cases/milan_lukic_sredoje_lukic/tjug/en/090720_j.pdf (accessed 4 March 2015).

referring the *Uwinkindi* and *Munyagishari* cases to Rwanda for prosecution.[155] Jean Uwinkindi and Bernard Munyagishari requested a revocation of the referral order so that they could be tried before the Mechanism instead in a Rwandan court. The MICT is nevertheless responsible for monitoring those cases pursuant to Article 6(5) of its Statute.

On June 5, 2014, MICT President Judge Meron presented a six-monthly progress report to the Security Council and briefed it on the work of the Mechanism. Meron addressed, among other things, the importance of cooperation among the Member States in order to arrest the nine ICTR indictees who are still at large, including three of them who fall under the MICT's jurisdiction. That same day, MICT Prosecutor Jallow also addressed the Security Council.[156]

On June 30, 2014, the Appeals Chamber of the MICT heard oral arguments in the appeal filed by Augustin Ngirabatware against a judgment delivered by Trial Chamber II of the ICTR on December 20, 2012.[157] Ngirabatware, a Rwandan Minister during the 1994 Rwandan genocide, was held criminally responsible by the Trial Chamber for committing direct and public incitement to commit genocide, and of instigating and aiding and abetting genocide by distributing weapons and by issuing statements. The Trial Chamber sentenced Ngirabatware to 35 years' imprisonment. In his appeal, Ngirabatware argued that the Trial Chamber committed a number of errors of law and fact, and requested the Appeals Chamber to overturn his convictions and to subsequently acquit him or, alternatively, reduce the sentence imposed on him. On December 18, 2014, the Appeals Chamber of the MICT issued its first-ever appeal judgment in the appeal case lodged by Ngirabatware.[158] The Chamber unanimously affirmed Ngirabatware's conviction

[155]See UNMICT, The President of the Mechanism, Prosecutor v. Jean Uwinkindi, 'Decision on request for revocation of an order referring a case to the Republic of Rwanda', Case No. MICT-12-25 (12 March 2014), http://www.unmict.org/sites/default/files/casedocuments/mict-12-25/president's-decisions/en/140312.pdf (accessed 4 March 2015); UNMICT, The President of the Mechanism, Prosecutor v. Bernard Munyagishari, 'Decision on request for revocation of an order referring a case to the Republic of Rwanda', Case No. MICT-12-20 (13 March 2014), http://www.unmict.org/sites/default/files/casedocuments/mict-12-20/president's-decisions/en/140313-1.pdf (accessed 4 March 2015).

[156]See UNMICT, Press Release, 'Prosecutor Jallow addresses UN Security Council' (5 June 2014), http://www.unmict.org/en/news/prosecutor-jallow-addresses-un-security-council (accessed 4 March 2015); The report can be found here: http://www.unmict.org/sites/default/files/attachments/articles/050614%20report.pdf (accessed 4 March 2015).

[157]See ICTR, Trial Chamber II, The Prosecutor v. Augustin Ngirabatware, 'Judgement and Sentence', Case No. ICTR-99-54-T (20 December 2012), http://www.unictr.org/sites/unictr.org/files/case-documents/ictr-99-54/trial-judgements/en/1212212.pdf (accessed 4 March 2015).

[158]See UNMICT, Appeals Chamber, Augustin Ngirabatware v. The Prosecutor, 'Judgement', Case No. MICT-12-29-A (18 December 2014), http://www.unmict.org/sites/default/files/casedocuments/mict-12-29/appeals-chamber-judgements/en/141218.pdf (accessed 4 March 2015).

for direct and public incitement to commit genocide, as well as his conviction for instigating and aiding and abetting genocide.[159] However, because it was not proven by the Prosecution that Ngirabatware contributed to a JCE's common purpose of exterminating the Tutsis pleaded under the count of extermination, the Chamber held that Ngirabatware's conviction for rape pursuant to the extended form of JCE could not be sustained. Therefore, the Chamber reversed his conviction for rape as a crime against humanity under the extended form of joint criminal enterprise.[160] As a result of the reversal of Ngirabatware's conviction for rape as a crime against humanity, the Appeals Chamber reduced his sentence to 30 years' imprisonment.

On October 13, 2014, President Meron presented the second Annual Report of the MICT to the UN General Assembly,[161] addressing, *inter alia*, the two major challenges faced by the MICT: the apprehension of the nine remaining ICTR indictees and the relocation of persons who are acquitted or fully served their sentence. Meron emphasized the importance of enhanced cooperation between all Member States in order to assist the Prosecutor to arrest and prosecute the nine remaining fugitives.

12.2.1.4 International Criminal Court

The International Criminal Court (ICC) achieved some relative success in 2014, particularly in *The Prosecutor v. Germain Katanga* case concerning the February 24, 2003 attack on the village of Bogoro, located in the Ituri district in northeastern Democratic Republic of the Congo (DRC).[162] At the time, Katanga was the alleged commander of the *Force de Résistance Patriotique en Ituri (*FRPI, Patriotic Resistance Forces in Ituri*)*, an armed militia group comprised of ethnic Ngiti that took part in the attack on Bogoro. Trial Chamber II issued its 711-pages judgment in this case on March 7, 2014. While Katanga was initially charged with committing, as principal perpetrator within the meaning of Article 25(3)(a) of the Rome Statute, seven counts of war crimes (rape; sexual slavery; wilful killing; directing an attack against civilians; destruction of property; pillaging; and using children

[159] See UNMICT, Appeals Chamber, 'Appeal Judgement Summary for Augustin Ngirabatware' (18 December 2014), http://www.unmict.org/sites/default/files/casedocuments/mict-12-29/appeals-chamber-judgements/en/141218_12.pdf (accessed 4 March 2015), paras 9 and 14–15.

[160] Ibid., para 23.

[161] See UNMICT, Press Release, 'President Meron Presents Second Annual Report to the United Nations General Assembly' (14 October 2014), http://www.unmict.org/en/news/president-meron-presents-second-annual-report-united-nations-general-assembly (accessed 4 March 2015); The report can be found here: http://www.unmict.org/sites/default/files/documents/140801-annual-report_en.pdf (accessed 4 March 2015).

[162] See ICC, La Chambre de Première Instance II, Situation en République Démocratique du Congo, Affaire Le Procureur c. Germain Katanga, 'Jugement rendu en application de l'article 74 du Statut', Case No. ICC-01/04-01/07 (7 March 2014), http://www.icc-cpi.int/iccdocs/doc/doc1744366.pdf (accessed 6 March 2015).

under the age of 15 years to participate actively in the hostilities) and three counts of crimes against humanity (murder; rape; and sexual slavery), the Trial Chamber dismissed the mode of liability because it could not be proven beyond reasonable doubt that Katanga "had the material ability to issue and ensure compliance with orders or, furthermore, that he had the power to punish commanders from various camps".[163] Therefore, a majority of the Judges decided to use regulation 55 of the Regulations of the Court to change the characterisation of the mode of liability and convicted Katanga of being an accessory within the meaning of Article 25(3)(d) of the Rome Statute to four counts of war crimes (murder; attacking a civilian population; destruction of property; and pillaging) and one count of crimes against humanity (murder).[164] According to the Trial Chamber, it had been established beyond reasonable doubt that Katanga significantly contributed to the commission of the crimes of murder, attacking a civilian population, destruction of property and pillaging by the Ngiti militia, in particular because he had collected and distributed arms and ammunition to local combatants. However, the Trial Chamber unanimously acquitted Katanga of all charges concerning rape and sexual slavery. Although the Chamber found that primarily on the basis of testimonies given by direct victims it was proven that these crimes were committed, the evidence presented at trial was insufficient to held Katanga responsible for these crimes.[165] With regard to the charge concerning the use of child soldiers, the Trial Chamber found that there were children younger than 15 years within the Ngiti militia and among the combatants who were in Bogoro on the day of the attack, but that it could not be established that Katanga used them to participate actively in the attack.[166] Although Judge Christine Van den Wyngaert agreed that Katanga could not be held guilty as a principal perpetrator pursuant to Article 25(3)(a) of the

[163]See ICC, Trial Chamber II, Situation in the Democratic Republic of the Congo, In the case of The Prosecutor v. Germain Katanga, 'Summary of Trial Chamber II's Judgment of 7 March 2014, pursuant to article 74 of the Statute in the case of the Prosecutor v. Germain Katanga', http://www.icc-cpi.int/en_menus/icc/press%20and%20media?press%20release/Documents/986/14_0259_ENG_summary_judgment.pdf (accessed 6 March 2015), para 52.

[164]See ICC, Press Release, 'Germain Katanga found guilty of four counts of war crimes and one count of crime against humanity committed in Ituri, DRC' (7 March 2014), http://www.icc-cpi.int/en_menus/icc/press%20and%20media/press%20releases/Pages/pr986.aspx (accessed 6 March 2015).

[165]See ICC, Trial Chamber II, Situation in the Democratic Republic of the Congo, In the case of The Prosecutor v. Germain Katanga, 'Summary of Trial Chamber II's Judgment of 7 March 2014, pursuant to article 74 of the Statute in the case of the Prosecutor v. Germain Katanga', http://www.icc-cpi.int/en_menus/icc/press%20and%20media?press%20release/Documents/986/14_0259_ENG_summary_judgment.pdf (accessed 6 March 2015), paras 35–36.

[166]See ICC, Trial Chamber II, Situation in the Democratic Republic of the Congo, In the case of The Prosecutor v. Germain Katanga, 'Summary of Trial Chamber II's Judgment of 7 March 2014, pursuant to article 74 of the Statute in the case of the Prosecutor v. Germain Katanga', http://www.icc-cpi.int/en_menus/icc/press%20and%20media/press%20releases/Documents/986/14_0259_ENG_summary_judgment.pdf (accessed 6 March 2015), paras 41–43.

Rome Statute, she strongly dissented from the majority's decision, particularly regarding the use of regulation 55.[167] Judge Van den Wyngaert argued that the mode of liability could not be changed from "principle" liability to "accessory" liability without substantially transforming the charges, and, moreover, that the recharacterisation violated several of Katanga's most fundamental rights enshrined in Article 67 of the Rome Statute, especially since the Defense was not properly notified of the new charges and therefore had no chance to prepare its Defense against the charges.[168] Judge Van den Wyngaert stated that the majority of the Appeals Chamber, by activating regulation 55, "exceeded the scope of the facts and circumstances as confirmed by the Pre-Trial Chamber".[169] With respect to the charges under Article 25(3)(d) of the Statute, Judge Van den Wyngaert found that Katanga could not be held guilty beyond a reasonable doubt on the basis of the evidence provided as it did not support the charges against him.[170] On May 23, 2014, Trial Chamber II, Judge Van den Wyngaert dissenting, sentenced Katanga to 12 years' imprisonment.[171] The Defense appealed against the Appeals Chamber's judgment seeking reversion of Katanga's conviction on each charge,[172] and the Prosecution appealed against the acquittal of Katanga on the charges of rape and sexual slavery.[173] However, on June 25, 2014, Katanga withdrew its appeal and issued a declaration accepting the findings made against him and expressed his "sincere regret" to all those who suffered because of his conduct, including the

[167]See ICC, 'Minority Opinion of Judge Christine Van den Wyngaert' (7 March 2014), http://www.icc-cpi.int/iccdocs/doc/doc1744372.pdf (accessed 6 March 2015).

[168]Ibid., para 9.

[169]Ibid., para 12.

[170]See ICC, Trial Chamber II, Situation in the Democratic Republic of the Congo, In the case of The Prosecutor v. Germain Katanga, 'Summary of Trial Chamber II's Judgment of 7 March 2014, pursuant to article 74 of the Statute in the case of the Prosecutor v. Germain Katanga', http://www.icc-cpi.int/en_menus/icc/press%20and%20media?press%20release/Documents/986/14_0259_ENG_summary_judgment.pdf (accessed 6 March 2015), para 58.

[171]See ICC, La Chambre de Première Instance II, Situation en République Démocratique du Congo, Affaire Le Procureur c. Germain Katanga, 'Décision relative à la peine (article 76 du Statut) ', Case No. ICC-01/04-01/07 (23 mai 2014), http://www.icc-cpi.int/iccdocs/doc/doc1771079.pdf (accessed 6 March 2015).

[172]See ICC, The Appeals Chamber, Situation in the Democratic Republic of Congo, In the case of The Prosecutor v. Germain Katanga, 'Defence Notice of Appeal against the decision of conviction 'Jugement rendu en application de l'article 74 du Statut' rendered by Trial Chamber II, 7th March 2014', Case No. ICC-01/04-01/07 (9 April 2014), http://www.icc-cpi.int/iccdocs/doc/doc1759481.pdf (accessed 6 March 2015).

[173]See ICC, The Appeals Chamber, Situation in the Democratic Republic of Congo, In the case of The Proseuctor v. Germain Katanga, 'Prosecution's Appeal against Trial Chamber II's "Jugement rendu en application de l'article 74 du Statut', Case No. ICC-01/04-01/07 (9 April 2014), http://www.icc-cpi.int/iccdocs/doc/doc1759535.pdf (accessed 6 March 2015).

Bogoro victims.[174] As a response to Katanga's withdrawal of appeal, the Prosecution also dropped its appeal.[175] The judgment in the case of *The Prosecutor v. Germain Katanga* marks the Court's first final judgment.

Another conviction in the situation involving the DRC was reached in the appeal case of Thomas Lubanga Dyilo, marking the Court's first concluded appeal trial. The case was concluded on December 1, 2014 when the Appeals Chamber delivered its judgments on both Trial Chamber I's conviction and sentencing decision.[176] The Appeals Chamber, by majority, upheld Lubanga's conviction for committing as a co-perpetrator the war crimes of conscripting and enlisting children under the age of 15 and using them to participate actively in the hostilities that took place in northeastern DRC between September 2002 and August 2003. All seven grounds of appeal filed by Lubanga against the verdict were dismissed. With respect to the sentence, the Appeals Chamber opined that the Trial Chamber stayed within the broad discretion it enjoys in determining an appropriate sentence, and concluded that Lubanga's sentence is not disproportionate to the gravity of the crimes committed by him. Accordingly, the Appeals Chamber dismissed both the Defense's and Prosecution's appeal against the sentence and confirmed Lubanga's 14-year prison sentence. Judge Anita Ušacka issued a strongly worded dissenting opinion, arguing that she would have reversed the conviction and acquitted Lubanga of the crimes.[177] First, Judge Ušacka held that Lubanga's right to a fair trial was breached because he was not able to adequately prepare his defense since the charges of which he was convicted lacked specificity. Second, Judge Ušacka argued that because of the weakness of the Prosecution's evidence, it was not established beyond reasonable doubt that the children conscripted, enlisted or used in the hostilities that took place between September 2002 and August 2003, were under the age of fifteen. Judge Sang-Hyun Song adopted a partly dissenting opinion, agreeing with the Chamber's decision to dismiss all

---

[174]See ICC, The Appeals Chamber, Situation in the Democratic Republic of Congo, In the case of The Proseuctor v. Germain Katanga, 'Defence Notice of Discontinuance of Appeal against the 'Jugement rendu en application de l'article 74 du Statut' rendered by Trial chamber II on 7 April 2014', Case No. ICC-01/04-01/07 (25 June 2014), http://www.icc-cpi.int/iccdocs/doc/doc1794409.pdf (accessed 6 March 2015).

[175]ICC, Appeals Chamber, Situation in the Democratic Republic of Congo, In the case of The Prosecutor v. Germain Katanga, 'Notice of Discontinuance of the Prosecution's Appeal against the Article 74 Judgment of Conviction of Trial Chamber II dated 7 March 2014 in relation to Germain Katanga', Case No. ICC-01/04-01/07 (25 June 2014), http://www.icc-cpi.int/iccdocs/doc/doc1794475.pdf (accessed 6 March 2015).

[176]See ICC, Appeals Chamber, Situation in the Democratic Republic of the Congo, In the case of The Prosecutor v. Thomas Lubanga Dyilo, 'Judgment on the appeal of Mr Thomas Lubanga Dyilo against his conviction', Case No. ICC-01/04-01/06 A 5 (1 December 2014), http://www.icc-cpi.int/iccdocs/doc/doc1876833.pdf (accessed 9 March 2015).

[177]See 'Dissenting Opinion of Judge Anita Ušacka' (1 December 2014), http://www.icc-cpi.int/iccdocs/doc/doc1877188.pdf (accessed 9 March 2015).

appeals filed by Lubanga but partly disagreeing with the majority's determination that the enlistment, conscription, and the use of children under the age of fifteen to actively participate in the hostilities, could be considered as three separate crimes.[178] Therefore, with regard to the sentence, Judge Song found that the Trial Chamber should have imposed just one sentence for the crime of child soldiering in general.

In the case against Bosco Ntaganda, who was initially indicted together with Lubanga but who had only just voluntarily surrendered himself in March 2013, the confirmation of charges hearing took place from February 10–14, 2014. Having considered about 69,000 pages of evidence,[179] Pre-Trial Chamber II issued its decision on the confirmation of charges on June 9, 2014. The Chamber unanimously confirmed 13 counts of war crimes, and five counts of crimes against humanity allegedly committed by troops of the Patriotic Front for the Liberation of Congo (FPLC) between July 2002 and December 2003 in the Ituri province in northeastern DRC.[180] The confirmed charges included, *inter alia*, murder, destruction of property, and rape and sexual slavery of civilians. It was the first time since the establishment of the Court in 2002 that a Pre-Trial Chamber unanimously confirmed all sexual- and gender-based crimes charged by the Prosecution. The Chamber found that there was sufficient evidence to establish substantial grounds to believe that Ntaganda could be held criminally responsible for the alleged crimes under different modes of liability, namely as direct perpetrator and indirect co-perpetrator pursuant to Article 25(3)(a), for ordering or inducing the crimes pursuant to Article 25(3)(b) or for any other contribution to the commission or attempted commission of the crimes pursuant to Article 25(3)(d), and as a military commander for the crimes committed by his subordinates pursuant to Article 28(a) of the Rome Statute. On June 16, 2014, the Defense sought leave to appeal the confirmation of charges decision, arguing that the Pre-Trial Chamber's decision was based on indirect or anonymous witness statements and on statements of deceased witnesses.[181] However, on July 4, 2014, the Defense's request for leave

---

[178]See 'Partly Dissenting Opinion of Judge Sang-Hyun Song' (1 December 2014), http://www.icc-cpi.int/iccdocs/doc/doc1876833.pdf (accessed 9 March 2015).

[179]See ICC, Press Release, 'Pre-Trial Chamber II commits Bosco Ntaganda to trial' (9 June 2014), http://www.icc-cpi.int/en_menus/icc/press%20and%20media/press%20releases/Pages/pr1013.aspx (accessed 11 March 2015).

[180]See ICC, Pre-Trial Chamber II, Situation in the Democratic Republic of the Congo, In the case of The Prosecutor v. Bosco Ntaganda, 'Decision Pursuant to Article 61(7)(a) and (b) of the Rome Statute on the Charges of the Prosecutor Against Bosco Ntaganda', Case No. ICC-01/04-02/06 (9 June 2014), http://www.icc-cpi.int/iccdocs/doc/doc1783301.pdf (accessed 11 March 2015).

[181]See ICC, La Chambre Préliminaire II, Situation en République Démocratique du Congo, Affaire Le Procureur C/ Bosco Ntaganda, 'Requête de la Défense sollicitant l'autorisation d'interjeter appel de la Décision sur la confirmation des charges datée du 9 juin 2014', Case No. ICC-01/04-02/06 (16 June 2014), http://www.icc-cpi.int/iccdocs/doc/doc17834512.pdf (accessed 11 March 2015).

to appeal was not granted by Single Judge Ekaterina Trendafilova of Pre-Trial Chamber II, because she found that there were no appealable issues arising from the decision that did meet the requirements of Article 82(1)(d) of the Rome Statute.[182] Trial Chamber VI is in charge of the case against Ntaganda.

Other developments in 2014 stemmed from the situation in Côte d'Ivoire, in particular in the case against Laurent Gbagbo, the former President of Côte d'Ivoire. Gbagbo is the first former head of state brought before the Court since its establishment and also the first one tried for crimes committed during the period of violence that followed Côte d'Ivoire's 2010 presidential election. Gbagbo, together with members of his alleged inner circle, allegedly adopted a policy and common plan in order for Gbagbo to stay in power after being defeated by Alassane Ouattara in the presidential election. Pro-Gbagbo forces, allegedly under the control and authority of Gbagbo and his inner circle, made a substantial contribution to the common plan by carrying out widespread and systematic attacks against civilians perceived to support Ouattara. Following a decision issued in early June 2013 to adjourn the confirmation of charges hearing due to insufficient evidence,[183] the Prosecutor submitted the amended document containing the charges against Gbagbo as well as the amended list of evidence on January 13, 2014.[184] In response, the Defense filed its list of evidence, and disputed the reliability of certain parts of the evidence presented by the Prosecutor. After having carefully analyzed the facts of the case as well as the evidence presented by both the Prosecution and Defense, on June 12, 2014, a majority of Pre-Trial Chamber I confirmed four charges against Gbagbo for crimes against humanity allegedly committed between December 2010 and April 2011. The majority of the Judges, Judge Van den Wyngaert dissenting,[185] found that there are substantial grounds to believe that Gbagbo bears individual criminal responsibility pursuant to three modes of liability under Article 25 of the Rome Statute for the alleged crimes

[182]See ICC, Pre-Trial Chamber II, Situation in the Democratic Republic of the Congo, In the case of The Prosecutor v. Bosco Ntaganda, 'Decision on the "Requête de la Défense sollicitant l'authorisation d'interjeter appel de la Décision sur la confirmation des charges datée du 9 juin 2014"', Case No. ICC-01/04-02/06 (4 July 2014), http://www.icc-cpi.int/iccdocs/doc/doc1796795.pdf (accessed 13 March 2015), paras 20 and 29.

[183]See ICC, Pre-Trial Chamber I, Situation in the Republic of Côte d'Ivoire, In the case of The Prosecutor v. Laurent Gbagbo, 'Decision adjourning the hearing on the confirmation of charges pursuant to article 61(7)(c)(i) of the Rome Statute', Case No. ICC-02/11-01/11 (3 June 2013), http://www.icc-cpi.int/iccdocs/doc/doc1599831.pdf (accessed 16 March 2015).

[184]See ICC, Pre-Trial Chamber I, Situation in the Republic of Côte d'Ivoire, In the case of The Prosecutor v. Laurent Gbagbo, 'Prosecution's Submission of Document amendé de notification des charges, l'inventaire amendé des éléments de preuve à charge, and le Tableau amendé des éléments constitutifs des crimes, and Response to issues raised by Pre-Trial Chamber I', Case No. ICC-02/11-01/11 (13 January 2014), http://www.icc-cpi.int/iccdocs/doc/doc17104712.pdf (accessed 16 March 2015).

[185]See 'Dissenting Opinion of Judge Christine Van den Wyngaert' (12 June 2014), http://www.icc-cpi.int/iccdocs/doc/doc1783397.pdf (accessed 16 March 2015).

against humanity, including murder, rape, other inhumane acts or, in the alternative, attempted murder, and persecution.[186] Specifically, Pre-Trial Chamber I concluded that Gbagbo could be held responsible "under article 25(3)(a) of the Statute for committing these crimes, jointly with members of his inner circle and through members of the pro-Gbagbo forces, or, in the alternative, under article 25(3)(b) of the Statute or, in the alternative, under article 25(3)(d) of the Statute for contributing in any other way to the commission of these crimes".[187] However, the Chamber, also by majority, did not confirm the charges for superior responsibility under Article 28(a) and (b) of the Rome Statute because it was "not persuaded that the narrative of the facts, as established by the evidence, points to Laurent Gbagbo's criminal responsibility based on his mere failure to prevent or repress the crimes committed by others pursuant to article 28 of the Statute".[188] Instead, the majority held that Gbagbo's failure to prevent the crimes or to punish those who committed them "was an *inherent* component of the deliberate effort to achieve the purpose of retaining power at any cost, including through the commission of crimes".[189] Judge Van den Wyngaert issued a dissenting opinion in which she argued that despite "a considerable quantitative increase in evidence submitted by the Prosecutor since the adjournment on 3 June [2013]",[190] there was still insufficient evidence to confirm the charges for the modes of liability under Article 25 of the Rome Statute, thereby taking into consideration the applicable evidentiary threshold set forth in Article 61(7) of the Statute.[191] Judge Van den Wyngaert was not convinced that Gbagbo and his alleged inner circle had the plan to commit crimes or that Gbagbo, alone or in cooperation with members of his inner circle, instigated the forces at his disposal to commit crimes against supporters of Ouattara.[192] Similarly, Van den Wyngaert found that there was not enough evidence to prove the existence of a group acting with a common purpose.[193] However, Judge Van den Wyngaert argued that she would have confirmed the charges under Article 28 of the Rome Statute in part, namely for the crimes allegedly committed by the Defense and Security Forces (FDS). According to Judge Van den Wyngaert, members of the FDS could be considered as Gbagbo's

[186]See ICC, Pre-Trial Chamber I, Situation in the Republic of Côte d'Ivoire, In the case of The Prosecutor v. Laurent Gbagbo, 'Decision on the confirmation of charges against Laurent Gbagbo', Case No. ICC-02/11-01/11 (12 June 2014), http://www.icc-cpi.int/iccdocs/doc/doc1783399.pdf (accessed 16 March 2015).

[187]Ibid., para 266.

[188]Ibid., para 263.

[189]Ibid., para 264 (emphasis added).

[190]See 'Dissenting Opinion of Judge Christine Van den Wyngaert' (12 June 2014), http://www.icc-cpi.int/iccdocs/doc/doc1783397.pdf (accessed 16 March 2015), para 2.

[191]Ibid., para 4.

[192]Ibid., paras 5–7.

[193]Ibid., paras 8–9.

subordinates because they were acting under his effective authority and control as required by Article 28(b) of the Rome Statute.[194] On September 11, 2014, Pre-Trial Chamber I did not grant a request filed confidentially by the Defense for leave to appeal the decision on the confirmation of charges, thereby confirming that Gbagbo will face trial on four counts of crimes against humanity.[195] Trial Chamber I is in charge of the trial.

Laurent Gbagbo's wife, Simone Gbagbo, has also been indicted by the ICC for her alleged role as indirect co-perpetrator for the crimes against humanity of murder, rape and other forms of sexual violence, persecution, and other inhumane acts committed during the 2010 postelection violence. More specifically, Simone Gbagbo was allegedly involved in the implementation of the common plan by instructing pro-Gbagbo forces to use violence against individuals who were perceived to constitute a threat to Gbagbo's power after his refusal to step down following his election defeat. Despite the warrant of arrest issued for Simone Gbagbo in February 2012,[196] Côte d'Ivoire has refused to hand her over and already challenged the admissibility of the case on September 30, 2013. In the challenge, it was argued by Côte d'Ivoire that, pursuant to Article 17(1)(a) of the Rome Statute, it is under no obligation to surrender Simone Gbagbo to the Court because it is willing and able to try her, and that proceedings on similar charges were already instituted against her before a national court.[197] In support of its admissibility challenge, Côte d'Ivoire submitted additional information at two different moments. First, on February 25, 2014, after being granted authorisation by Judge Silvia Fernández de Gurmendi, acting as Single Judge.[198] Second, on October 10,

---

[194]Ibid., para 11.

[195]See ICC, Pre-Trial Chamber I, Situation in the Republic of Côte d'Ivoire, In the case of The Prosecutor v. Laurent Gbagbo, 'Decision on the Defence request for leave to appeal the "Decision on the Confirmation of Charges against Laurent Gbagbo"', Case No. ICC-02/11-01/11 (11 September 2014), http://www.icc-cpi.int/iccdocs/doc/doc1814133.pdf (accessed 16 March 2015).

[196]See ICC, Pre-Trial Chamber III, Situation in the Republic of Côte d'Ivoire, In the case of The Prosecutor v. Simone Gbagbo, 'Warrant of Arrest for Simone Gbagbo', Case No. ICC-02/11-01/12 (29 February 2012), http://www.icc-cpi.int/iccdocs/doc/doc1344439.pdf (accessed 18 March 2015).

[197]See ICC, La Chambre Préliminaire I, Situation en Republique de Cote D'ivoire, Affaire Le Procureur c. Simone Gbagbo, 'Requête de la République de Côte d'Ivoire sur la recevabilité de l'affaire le procureur c. Simone Gbagbo, et demande de sursis à exécution en vertu des Articles 17, 19 et 95 du Statut de Rome', Case No. ICC-02/11-01/12 (30 September 2013), http://www.icc-cpi.int/iccdocs/doc/doc1653132.pdf (accessed 18 March 2015).

[198]See ICC, La Chambre Préliminaire I, Situation en Republique de Cote D'ivoire, Affaire Le Procureur c. Simone Gbagbo, 'Depot de documents complementaires a l'appui de la requête de la République de Côte d'Ivoire sur la recevabilité de l'affaire le procureur c. Simone Gbagbo, et demande de sursis à exécution en vertu des articles 17, 19 et 95 du Statut de Rome', Case No. ICC-02/11-01/12 (25 February 2014), http://www.icc-cpi.int/iccdocs/doc/doc1738578.pdf (accessed 18 March 2015).

2014,[199] as requested by Pre-Trial Chamber I "in order to perform a meaningful assessment as to whether the case against Simone Gbagbo allegedly subject to national proceedings sufficiently mirrors the case before the Court".[200] In response to Côte d'Ivoire's first submission, the Prosecutor advanced, in particular, that "it remains unclear whether the national offences described in the Applicant's submissions and the supporting materials cover all aspects of the offences which are the subject of the case before the Court, such that there continues to be insufficient information and evidence to demonstrate the actual contours of the case at the national level".[201] In addition, the Prosecutor advanced that although national proceedings are initiated against Simone Gbagbo, it cannot be established that, in light of Article 17(1)(a) of the Rome Statute, "concrete and progressive investigative steps" have been undertaken in order to determine whether she can be held responsible for the alleged offenses.[202] On December 11, 2014, following a thorough examination of all the documentation submitted by Côte d'Ivoire, Pre-Trial Chamber I rejected the admissibility challenge.[203] The Pre-Trial Chamber found that it has not been demonstrated that "concrete, tangible and progressive investigative steps are being undertaken by the domestic authorities of Côte d'Ivoire in order to ascertain Simone Gbagbo's criminal responsibility for the same conduct as that alleged in the proceedings before the Court. Nor does this documentation indicate that Simone Gbagbo is currently being prosecuted by Côte d'Ivoire for the same conduct attributed to her in the case before the Court".[204] Accordingly, the Pre-Trial Chamber found the case admissible before the Court and, therefore, reminded Côte d'Ivoire of its obligation to transfer Simone Gbagbo to The Hague without delay.

---

[199]See ICC, La Chambre Préliminaire I, Situation en Republique de Cote D'ivoire, Affaire Le Procureur c. Simone Gbagbo, 'Second dépôt de documents complémentaires à l'appui de la requête de la république de Côte d'Ivoire sur la recevabilité de l'affaire le procureur c. Simone Gbagbo, et demande de sursis à exécution en vertu des articles 17, 19 et 95 du Statut de Rome', Case No. ICC-02/11-01/12 (10 October 2014), http://www.icc-cpi.int/iccdocs/doc/doc1847551.pdf (accessed 18 March 2015).

[200]See ICC, Pre-Trial Chamber I, Situation in the Republic of Côte d'Ivoire, In the case of The Prosecutor v. Simone Gbagbo, 'Decision on further submissions on issues related to the admissibility of the case against Simone Gbagbo', Case No. ICC-02/11-01/12 (28 August 2014), http://www.icc-cpi.int/iccdocs/doc/doc1813945.pdf (accessed 18 March 2015).

[201]See ICC, Pre-Trial Chamber I, Situation in the Republic of Côte d'Ivoire, In the case of The Prosecutor v. Simone Gbagbo, 'Public redacted version of "Prosecution's Response to Côte d'Ivoire's Challenge to the admissibility of the case against Simone Gbagbo", IC-02/11-01/12-41-Conf, 9 April 2014', Case No. ICC-02/11-01/12 (24 June 2014), http://www.icc-cpi.int/iccdocs/doc/doc1792827.pdf (accessed 18 March 2015), para 47.

[202]Ibid., para 55.

[203]See ICC, Pre-Trial Chamber I, Situation in the Republic of Côte d'Ivoire, In the case of The Prosecutor v. Simone Gbagbo, 'Decision on Côte d'Ivoire's challenge to the admissibility of the case against Simone Gbagbo', Case No. ICC-02/11-01/12 (11 December 2014), http://www.icc-cpi.int/iccdocs/doc/doc1882718.pdf (accessed 18 March 2015).

[204]Ibid., para 78.

Another case that arose from the postelection violence in Côte d'Ivoire, is the case against Charles Blé Goudé, former Minister in Gbagbo's government and member of Gbagbo's alleged inner circle. Blé Goudé first appeared before Court on March 27, 2014 after the national authorities of Côte d'Ivoire surrendered him to the ICC's custody 5 days earlier. The Defense filed a request for state party cooperation on April 10, 2014, because Blé Goudé wanted to challenge the legality of the circumstances surrounding his arrest and, in addition, considered a challenge to the admissibility of the proceedings initiated against him.[205] The Single Judge of Pre-Trial Chamber I, Judge Fernández de Gurmendi, was asked to order the authorities of Ghana and Côte d'Ivoire to disclose all documents within their possession relevant to all legal proceedings instigated in their country against Blé Goudé and which are related to and proceed from the period of the postelection violence.[206] According to Article 57(3)(b) of the Rome Statute, the Defense is permitted to file a request with the Pre-Trial Chamber seeking the cooperation of States Parties when this is necessary for the preparation of its case. However, Judge Fernández de Gurmendi dismissed this request, arguing that the Defense should first request the Prosecutor access to documents in its possession which are relevant for the preparation of the Defense's case or, when necessary, requesting the documents directly from the States concerned.[207] Following this dismissal, the Defense unsuccessfully sought to obtain the relevant documents from the Prosecutor and Côte d'Ivoire directly as not all the documents were in the Prosecutor's possession, and Côte d'Ivoire rejected the request arguing that, according to its national law, it is not obliged to provide suspects access to the required documents.[208] Therefore, on May 23, 2014, the Defense filed a second request for state party cooperation.[209] Despite the Defense's attempts, Judge Fernández de Gurmendi also rejected the second request because she was of the opinion that the Chamber should not intervene at this stage because "[i]t appears that the information sought is either not relevant or may be otherwise provided by the Ivorian authorities, without necessarily transmitting the judicial file as

[205]See ICC, Pre-Trial Chamber I, Situation in the Republic of Côte d'Ivoire, In the case of The Prosecutor v. Charles Ble Goude, 'Defence Request for State Party Cooperation', Case No. ICC-02/11-02/11 (10 April 2014), http://www.icc-cpi.int/iccdocs/doc/doc1760552.pdf (accessed 20 March 2015), para 6.

[206]Ibid., para 13.

[207]See ICC, Pre-Trial Chamber I, Situation in the Republic of Côte d'Ivoire, In the case of The Prosecutor v. Charles Blé Goudé, 'Decision on the Defence Request for State Party Cooperation', Case No. ICC-02/11-02/11 (17 April 2014), http://www.icc-cpi.int/iccdocs/doc/doc1757021.pdf (accessed 20 March 2015), para 8.

[208]See ICC, Pre-Trial Chamber I, Situation in the Republic of Côte d'Ivoire, In the case of The Prosecutor v. Charles Blé Goudé, 'Second Request for State Party Cooperation', Case No. ICC-02/11-02/11 (23 May 2014), http://www.icc-cpi.int/iccdocs/doc/doc1780663.pdf (accessed 20 March 2015), paras 35 and 37.

[209]Ibid., para 43.

such".[210] On April 16–22, 2014,[211] the Office of Public Counsel for Victims (OPCV) filed requests for victim participation, seeking the admission of 199 victims permitted to participate in the case *The Prosecutor v. Laurent Gbagbo* as participants in the proceedings against Blé Goudé. Judge Fernández de Gurmendi granted the requests on June 11, 2014 and authorized the 199 victims already participating in the case against Laurent Gbagbo to also participate as victims in the underlying case, arguing that "the subject-matter of the present case appears to be the same of that of the Gbagbo Case as the same crimes are alleged in both cases and the same four incidents support the charges against the two suspects".[212] In addition, on August 1, 2014, 272 other individuals were admitted as victims and thereby allowed to participate in the proceedings with the OPCV as their common legal representative.[213] On December 11, 2014, Pre-Trial Chamber I, Judge Van den Wyngaert partially dissenting,[214] confirmed four charges of crimes against humanity against Blé Goudé.[215] After analyzing more than 40,000 pages of evidence and more than 1200 items of audio and video material,[216] the Chamber concluded that there were substantial grounds to believe that Blé Goudé committed the alleged crimes against humanity of murder, rape, and other inhumane acts or, in the alternative, attempted murder, and persecution committed during the violence that followed the 2010 presidential election in Côte d'Ivoire. Pre-Trial

[210]See ICC, Pre-Trial Chamber I, Situation in the Republic of Côte d'Ivoire, The Prosecutor v. Charles Blé Goudé, Decision on Second Defence Request for State Party Cooperation', Case No. ICC-02/11-02/11 (17 June 2014), http://www.icc-cpi.int/iccdocs/doc/doc1783486.pdf (accessed 20 March 2015), para 8.

[211]See ICC, Pre-Trial Chamber I, Situation in the Republic of Côte d'Ivoire, In the case of The Prosecutor v. Charles Blé Goudé, 'Transmission of a submission by the OPCV', Case No. ICC-02/11-02/11 (16 April 2014), http://www.icc-cpi.int/iccdocs/doc/doc1757011.pdf (accessed 20 March 2015); See also ICC, Situation in the Republic of Côte d'Ivoire, In the case of The Prosecutor v. Charles Blé Goudé, 'Registry transmission of the second submission by the OPCV', Case No. ICC-02/11-02/11 (23 March 2014), http://www.icc-cpi.int/iccdocs/doc/doc1757054.pdf (accessed 20 March 2015).

[212]See ICC, Pre-Trial Chamber I, Situation in the Republic of Côte d'Ivoire, In the case of The Prosecutor v. Charles Blé Goudé, 'Decision on victims' participation in the pre-trial proceedings and related issues', Case No. ICC-02/11-02/11 (11 June 2014), http://www.icc-cpi.int/iccdocs/doc/doc1783345.pdf (accessed 20 March 2015).

[213]See ICC, Pre-Trial Chamber I, Situation in the Republic of Côte d'Ivoire, In the case of The Prosecutor v. Charles Blé Goudé, 'Second Decision on victims' participation in the pre-trial proceedings and related issues', Case No. ICC-02/11-02/11 (1 August 2014), http://www.icc-cpi.int/iccdocs/doc/doc1802045.pdf (accessed 20 March 2015).

[214]See ICC, 'Partly Dissenting Opinion of Judge Christine Van den Wyngaert' (11 December 2014), http://www.icc-cpi.int/iccdocs/doc/doc1879934.pdf (accessed 20 March 2015).

[215]See ICC, Pre-Trial Chamber I, Situation in the Republic of Côte d'Ivoire, In the case of The Prosecutor v. Charles Blé Goudé, 'Decision on the confirmation of charges against Charles Blé Goudé', Case No. ICC-02/11-02/11 (11 December 2014), http://www.icc-cpi.int/iccdocs/doc/doc1879935.pdf (accessed 20 March 2015).

[216]See ICC, Press Release, 'ICC Pre-Trial Chamber I commits Charles Blé Goudé to trial' (11 December 2014), http://www.icc-cpi.int/en_menus/icc/press%20and%20media/press%20releases/Pages/pr1076.aspx (accessed 20 March 2015).

Chamber I was convinced that Blé Goudé can be held individually criminally responsible for the alleged crimes, alternatively, as indirect co-perpetrator pursuant to Article 25(3)(a), or for ordering, soliciting or inducing the crimes pursuant to Article 25(3)(b), or for aiding, abetting or otherwise assisting pursuant to Article 25(3)(c), or for contributing in any other way to the commission of these crimes pursuant to Article 25(3)(d) of the Rome Statute. On December 16, 2014, the Prosecution filed a request to join the cases of *The Prosecutor v. Laurent Gbagbo* and *The Prosecutor v. Charles Blé Goudé*, submitting, *inter alia*, "that a joinder serves the interests of justice by minimising the impact of the upcoming trial proceedings on victims and witnesses".[217]

With regard to the situation in Libya, on May 21, 2014, the Appeals Chamber dismissed Libya's appeal against the decision of Pre-Trial Chamber I declaring the case against Saif Al Islam Gaddafi admissible.[218] The majority of the Judges concluded that Pre-Trial Chamber I had not erred in finding that Libya has failed to prove that domestic investigations cover the alleged crimes ('same conduct') as in the case against Gaddafi which was already before the Court. Judge Song issued a separate concurring opinion.[219] Although he agreed that the case against Gaddafi was admissible before the Court because Libya was unable to obtain custody of Gaddafi, he was of the view that Libya was investigating the same case.[220] In a dissenting opinion adopted by Judge Ušacka,[221] she disagreed with the majority by arguing that the test which was established by the Pre-Trial Chamber in order to determine whether Libya was indeed investigating the same case was erroneous and too demanding. Judge Ušacka held that the Pre-Trial Chamber, by requiring that "Libya's investigation had to cover more of the conduct or even entirely the same conduct as what is considered to be the essence of the warrant of arrest against Mr Gaddafi", wrongly interpreted Article 17(1)(a) of the Statute which provides that the Court must declare a case inadmissible when the same case is being investigated or prosecuted by a State which has jurisdiction over it, unless the State is unwilling or unable genuinely to carry out the investigation or

---

[217]See ICC, Trial Chamber I, Situation in the Republic of Côte d'Ivoire, In the case of The Prosecutor v. Charles Blé Goudé, 'Prosecution's Request to join the cases of The Prosecutor v. Laurent Gbagbo and The Prosecutor v. Charles Blé Goudé', Case No. ICC-02/11-02/11 (22 December 2014), http://www.icc-cpi.int/iccdocs/doc/doc1892019.pdf (accessed 20 March 2015), para 17.

[218]See ICC, Appeals Chamber, Situation in Libya, In the case of The Prosecutor v. Saif Al-Islam Gaddafi and Abdullah Al-Senussi, 'Judgment on the appeal of Libya against the decision of Pre-Trial Chamber I of 31 May 2013 entitled "Decision on the admissibility of the case against Saif Al-Islam Gaddafi"', Case No. ICC-01/11-01/11 OA4 (21 May 2014), http://www.icc-cpi.int/iccdocs/doc/doc1779877.pdf (accessed 23 March 2015).

[219]See 'Separate Opinion of Judge Sang-Hyun Song' (21 May 2014), http://www.icc-cpi.int/iccdocs/doc/doc1779878.pdf (accessed 23 March 2015).

[220]Ibid., para 1.

[221]See 'Dissenting Opinion of Judge Anita Ušacka' (21 May 2014), http://www.icc-cpi.int/iccdocs/doc/doc1779879.pdf (accessed 23 March 2015).

prosecution.[222] Judge Ušacka was of the view that "article 17 (1) (a) of the Statute, applied in accordance with the principle of complementarity, does not require domestic authorities to investigate '(substantially) the same' conduct as the conduct that forms the basis of the 'case before the Court'".[223]

The Court's proceedings against Abdullah Al-Senussi, who was charged alongside Gaddafi, came to an end on July 24, 2014 when the Appeals Chamber unanimously confirmed Pre-Trial Chamber I's decision of October 2013, according to which the case is inadmissible before the Court.[224] Al-Senussi's Defense had requested the Appeals Chamber to declare the case admissible,[225] but as provided by Article 17(1)(a) of the Rome Statute, a case will be declared inadmissible before the Court when the same case is being investigated or prosecuted by a State which has jurisdiction over it. The Appeals Chamber agreed with Pre-Trial Chamber I that the case against Al-Senussi was subject to domestic proceedings conducted by competent Libyan authorities, and accordingly held that the Defense had failed to prove that the Libyan authorities were unwilling and unable to genuinely prosecute Al-Senussi.[226] Therefore, the Appeals Chamber concluded that Al-Senussi's trial could take place in Libya. Judges Ušacka and Song agreed with the judgment of the Court finding that the Pre-Trial Chamber did not err when it concluded that Libya was investigating the same case, but nevertheless issued separate opinions mainly presenting their own view on how the complementarity requirements contained in Article 17(1)(a) of the Rome Statute should be interpreted.[227]

In the Kenya situation, in the case of *The Prosecutor v. William Samoei Ruto and Joshua Arap Sang,* on January 15, 2014, Trial Chamber V(a) granted Deputy Kenyan President Ruto conditional permission not to be continuously present at

---

[222]Ibid., para 46.

[223]Ibid., para 51.

[224]See ICC, Pre-Trial Chamber I, Situation in Libya, In the case of The Prosecutor v. Saif Al-Islam Gaddafi and Abdullah Al-Senussi, 'Decision on the admissibility of the case against Abdullah Al-Senussi', Case No. ICC-01/11-01/11 (11 October 2013), http://www.icc-cpi.int/iccdocs/doc/doc1663102.pdf (accessed 23 March 2015).

[225]See ICC, Appeals Chamber, Situation in Libya, In the case of The Prosecutor v. Saif Al-Islam Gaddafi and Abdullah Al-Senussi, 'Appeal on behalf of Abdullah Al-Senussi against Pre-Trial Chamber I's 'Decision on the admissibility of the case against Abdullah Al-Senussi", and Request for Suspensive Effect', Case No. ICC-01/11-01/11 (17 October 2013), http://www.icc-cpi.int/iccdocs/doc/doc1666694.pdf (accessed 23 March 2015).

[226]See ICC, Appeals Chamber, Situation in Libya, In the case of The Prosecutor v. Saif Al-Islam Gaddafi and Abdullah Al-Senussi, 'Judgment on the appeal of Mr Abdullah Al-Senussi against the decision of Pre-Trial Chamber I of 11 October 2013 entitled "Decision on the admissibility of the case against Abdullah Al-Senussi"', Case No. ICC-01/11-01/11 OA 6 (24 July 2014), http://www.icc-cpi.int/iccdocs/doc/doc1807073.pdf (accessed 23 March 2015).

[227]See 'Separate Opinion of Judge Anita Ušacka' (24 July 2014), http://www.icc-cpi.int/iccdocs/doc/doc1807108.pdf (accessed 25 March 2015); See also 'Separate Opinion of Judge Sang-Hyun Song' (24 July 2014), http://www.icc-cpi.int/iccdocs/doc/doc1807074.pdf (accessed 23 March 2015).

trial pursuant to Rule 134*quater* of the ICC RPE.[228] On February 18, 2014, Trial Chamber V(a) provided the reasons for the decision to conditionally excuse Ruto from presence at trial, and also provided the two conditions to be fulfilled.[229] First, the submission of a signed waiver authorizing Ruto's trial to proceed in his absence. Second, Ruto's physical presence in court (1) when victims present their views and concerns in person; (2) when the judgment will be delivered; (3) during the entirety of the sentencing hearing; (4) during the actual sentencing hearing; (5) during the victim impact hearings; (6) during the reparation hearings; (7) for the first 5 days of hearing starting after judicial recess; and (8) for any other attendance directed by the Chamber *proprio motu* or as requested by a party or participant. According to the Trial Chamber, Ruto could not be granted continuous excusal because this would be incompatible with the interests of justice, in particular because of the active participation of victims in the proceedings. On April 17, 2014, a majority of Trial Chamber V(a) summoned eight prosecution witnesses to appear before Court in the trial against Ruto and Sang.[230] Trial Chamber V(a) decided to grant the Prosecution's request to subpoena these witnesses because they were no longer cooperating or willing to testify following the disclosure of their identities to the Defense.[231] The Trial Chamber found that it could compel these witnesses to testify pursuant to Article 64(6)(b) of the Rome Statute, and that it, pursuant to Article 93(1)(d) and (l) of the Rome Statute, can issue a binding cooperation request obliging the Kenyan Government both to serve summonses and to assist in compelling the appearance of the witnesses summonsed. Moreover, the Chamber noted that Kenyan domestic law permits it to issue such a cooperation request.[232] Accordingly, all eight prosecution witnesses were ordered

---

[228]See ICC, Trial Chamber V(A), Situation in the Republic of Kenya, In the case of The Prosecutor v. William Samoei Ruto and Joshua Arap Sang, 'Status Conference', Case No. ICC-01/09-01/11 (15 January 2014), http://www.icc-cpi.int/iccdocs/doc/doc17115912.pdf (accessed 25 March 2015).

[229]See ICC, Trial Chamber V(A), Situation in the Republic of Kenya, In the case of The Prosecutor v. William Samoei Ruto and Joshua Arap Sang, 'Reasons for the Decision on Excusal from Presence at Trial under Rule 134quater', Case No. ICC-01/09-01/11 (18 February 2014), http://www.icc-cpi.int/iccdocs/doc/doc1734492.pdf (accessed 25 March 2015).

[230]See ICC, Trial Chamber V(A), Situation in the Republic of Kenya, In the case of The Prosecutor v. William Samoei Ruto and Joshua Arap Sang, 'Decision on Prosecutor's Application for Witness Summonses and resulting request for State Party Cooperation', Case No. ICC-01/09-01/11 (17 April 2014), http://www.icc-cpi.int/iccdocs/doc/doc1771401.pdf (accessed 25 March 2015).

[231]See ICC, Trial Chamber V(A), Situation in the Republic of Kenya, In the case of The Prosecutor v. William Samoei Ruto and Joshua Arap Sang, 'Dissenting Opinion of Judge Herrera Carbuccia on the 'Decision on Prosecutor's Application for Witness Summonses and resulting Request for State Party Cooperation'', Case No. ICC-01/09-01/11 (29 April 2014), http://www.icc-cpi.int/iccdocs/doc/doc1757148.pdf (accessed 25 March 2015), paras 12–18.

[232]See ICC, Trial Chamber V(A), Situation in the Republic of Kenya, In the case of The Prosecutor v. William Samoei Ruto and Joshua Arap Sang, 'Decision on Prosecutor's Application for Witness Summonses and resulting request for State Party Cooperation', Case No. ICC-01/09-01/11 (17 April 2014), http://www.icc-cpi.int/iccdocs/doc/doc1771401.pdf (accessed 25 March 2015), para 193.

to appear before court to testify via video link from a location in Kenya. Judge Olga Herrera Carbuccia issued a dissenting opinion on April 29, 2014.[233] Although Judge Carbuccia agreed that Trial Chamber V(a) has the power to summon witnesses who are unwilling to testify voluntarily, she disagreed with the majority's finding that the Kenyan Government is obliged to compel the eight unwilling witnesses to appear before the Court. Judge Carbuccia argued that, pursuant to Article 93(1)(e) of the Rome Statute, there would only be a legal obligation for the Kenyan Government to ensure the witnesses' appearance when they voluntarily agreed to appear before the Court.[234] On June 5, 2014, both Defense teams appealed Trial Chamber V(a)'s decision, and in its documents supporting the appeal, Ruto's Defense made a request for suspensive effect to the extent that the decision requested the Kenyan Government to compel the attendance of the eight witnesses.[235] However, without prejudice to the Appeals Chamber's decision on the merits, the Appeals Chamber rejected the request for suspensive effect on June 17, 2014.[236] The Appeals Chamber found that the submissions in support of the request failed to prove how the implementation of Trial Chamber V(a)'s decision "(i) would lead to an irreversible situation that could not be corrected; (ii) would lead to consequences that would be very difficult to correct and may be irreversible; or (iii) could potentially defeat the purpose of the appeal", if the Appeals Chamber would eventually decide the case in favor of Ruto and Sang.[237] Moreover, the Appeals Chamber was not convinced that if the Trial Chamber's decision would be overturned after the witnesses have provided testimony, this would have irreparable consequences on the trial itself. In the meantime, on June 9, 2014, a new Prosecution request to summon a ninth witness who also refused to cooperate, was granted. The first witness summoned to appear attended a hearing before Trial Chamber V(a) on September 17, 2014. On October 9, 2014, the Appeals Chamber dismissed the appeals against the April 17, 2014 decision and

[233]See ICC, Trial Chamber V (A), Situation in the Republic of Kenya, In the case of The Prosecutor v. William Samoei Ruto and Joshua Arap Sang, 'Dissenting Opinion of Judge Herrera Carbuccia on the 'Decision on Prosecutor's Application for Witness Summonses and resulting Request for State Party Cooperation'', Case No. ICC-01/09-01/11 (29 April 2014), http://www.icc-cpi.int/iccdocs/doc/doc1757148.pdf (accessed 25 March 2015), para 8.

[234]Ibid., paras 12–18.

[235]See ICC, Appeals Chamber, Situation in the Republic of Kenya, In the case of the Prosecutor v. William Samoei Ruto and Joshua Arap Sang, 'Defence appeal against the "Decision on Prosecutor's Application for Witness Summonses and resulting Request for State Party Cooperation"', Case No. ICC-01/09-01/11 (5 June 2014), http://www.icc-cpi.int/iccdocs/doc/doc1785733.pdf (accessed 25 March 2015).

[236]See ICC, Appeals Chamber, Situation in the Republic of Kenya, In the case of The Prosecutor v. William Samoei Ruto and Joshua Arap Sang, 'Decision on Mr William Samoei Ruto's request for suspensive effect', Case No. ICC-01/09-01/11 OA 7 OA 8 (17 June 2014), http://www.icc-cpi.int/iccdocs/doc/doc1789628.pdf (accessed 25 March 2015).

[237]Ibid., para 8.

unanimously upheld Trial Chamber V(a)'s decision.[238] In its decision on the merits, the Appeals Chamber held that the Trial Chamber had the power to summon and compel the attendance of the eight witnesses who were reluctant to testify in the trial of Ruto and Sang. In addition, the Appeals Chamber found that the Kenyan Government was indeed obliged to provide assistance, when necessary, to ensure the witnesses' appearance before the Trial Chamber, either by sitting in situ or via video link. However, the Appeals Chamber found that Article 93(1)(b) provided the legal obligation for the Kenyan Government to compel the witnesses to appear.[239]

Interesting developments also took place in the case against Kenyan President Uhuru Muigai Kenyatta, who is the first sitting head of state that appeared before the Court. On January 13, 2014, following the Prosecution's request to adjourn the start of the trial against Kenyatta for 3 months due to a lack of sufficient evidence partly resulting from the withdrawal of two key witnesses,[240] the Defense requested Trial Chamber V(b) to terminate the proceedings, citing insufficiency of evidence.[241] After receiving these requests, Trial Chamber V(b) decided to postpone the opening of the trial which was scheduled for February 5, 2014,[242] and instead held a status conference on this day to discuss the issues raised by both the Prosecution and Defense in relation to their requests. During a status conference held on February 13, 2014, the alleged noncooperation by the Kenyan Government was discussed. The Prosecution alleged that the Kenyan Government was withholding Kenyatta's financial and other records of which it was believed to hold key evidence in the case, but the Attorney General of Kenya argued that conforming to Kenyan law the requested records could only be provided after having received an

[238]See ICC, Appeals Chamber, Situation in the Republic of Kenya, In the case of The Prosecutor v. William Samoei Ruto and Joshua Arap Sang, 'Judgment on the appeals of William Ruto and Mr Joshua Arap Sang against the decision of Trial Chamber V (A) of 17 April 2014 entitled "Decision on Prosecutor's Application for Witness Summonses and resulting Request for State Party Cooperation"', Case No. ICC-01/09-01/11 OA 7 OA 8 (9 October 2014), http://www.icc-cpi.int/iccdocs/doc/doc1847142.pdf (accessed 25 March 2015).

[239]Ibid., para 128.

[240]See ICC, Trial Chamber V(B), Situation in the Republic of Kenya, In the case of The Prosecutor v. Uhuru Muigai Kenyatta, 'Notification of the removal of a witness from the Prosecution's witness list and application for an adjournment of the provisional trial date', Case No. ICC-01/09-02/11 (19 December 2013), http://www.icc-cpi.int/iccdocs/doc/doc1703998.pdf (accessed 27 March 2015).

[241]See ICC, Trial Chamber V(B), Situation in the Republic of Kenya, In the case of The Prosecutor v. Uhuru Muigai Kenyatta, 'Public redacted version of the 13 January 2014 'Defence Response to the Prosecution's "Notification of the removal of a witness from the Prosecution's witness list and application for an adjournment of the provisional trial date" (ICC-01/09-02/11-878-Conf)', Case No. ICC-01/09-02/11 (24 January 2014), http://www.icc-cpi.int/iccdocs/doc/doc1716851.pdf (accessed 27 March 2015).

[242]See ICC, Trial Chamber V(B), Situation in the Republic of Kenya, In the case of The Prosecutor v. Uhuru Muigai Kenyatta, 'Order vacating trial date of 5 February 2014, convening a status conference, and addressing other procedural matters', Case No. ICC-01/09-02/11 (23 January 2014), http://www.icc-cpi.int/iccdocs/doc/doc17166212.pdf (accessed 27 March 2015).

order from the Trial Chamber and not from the OTP. On January 31, 2014, after reconsidering its previous request for an adjournment of 3 months, the Prosecutor requested Trial Chamber V(b) to indefinitely adjourn the proceedings against Kenyatta until the Kenyan Government would have provided the Prosecution with the requested records.[243] After carefully considering all submissions made and the potential impact a further adjournment might have on Kenyatta's rights, on March 31, 2014, Trial Chamber V(b) decided to adjourn the trial until October 7, 2014.[244] The Prosecution was requested to submit a revised request to the Kenyan Government to provide financial and other records relating to Kenyatta, and the Kenyan Government was ordered to comply with this request. However, on September 19, 2014, Trial Chamber V(b) vacated the trial commencement date of 7 October and instead held status conferences on both October 7–8, 2014. During the latter status conference, the Prosecution as well as the Legal Representative of Victims (LRV) requested for indefinite adjournment of the trial, while the Defense again issued a request for termination of the proceedings. On December 3, 2014, Trial Chamber V(b) dismissed the requests for indefinite adjournment of the case because this would be contrary to the interests of justice or of the victims, and ordered it to either proceed to trial or to withdraw the charges against Kenyatta.[245] The Defense's request to terminate the proceedings against Kenyatta was also rejected. On December 5, 2014, the Prosecutor filed a notice of withdrawal of charges against Kenyatta.[246] In a statement given later that day, the Prosecutor noted that "given the state of the evidence in this case, [she had] no alternative but to withdraw the charges against Mr. Kenyatta". However, the Prosecutor held that this was "without prejudice to the possibility of bringing a new case should additional evidence become available".[247]

---

[243]See ICC, Trial Chamber V(B), Situation in the Republic of Kenya, In the case of The Prosecutor v. Uhuru Muigai Kenyatta, 'Prosecution opposition to the Defence request for the termination of the Kenyatta case', Case No. ICC-01/09-02/11 (31 January 2014), http://www.icc-cpi.int/iccdocs/doc/doc1720686.pdf (accessed 27 March 2015).

[244]See ICC, Trial Chamber V(B), Situation in the Republic of Kenya, In the case of The Prosecutor v. Uhuru Muigai Kenyatta, 'Decision on Prosecution's applications for a finding of non-compliance pursuant to Article 87(7) and for an adjournment of the provisional trial date', Case No. ICC-01/09-02/11 (31 March 2014), http://www.icc-cpi.int/iccdocs/doc/doc17551912.pdf (accessed 27 March 2015).

[245]See ICC, Trial Chamber V(B), Situation in the Republic of Kenya, In the case of The Prosecutor v. Uhuru Muigai Kenyatta, 'Decision on Prosecution's application for a further adjournment', Case No. ICC-01/09-02/11 (3 December 2014), http://www.icc-cpi.int/iccdocs/doc/doc1878156.pdf (accessed 27 March 2015).

[246]See ICC, Trial Chamber V(B), Situation in the Republic of Kenya, In the case of The Prosecutor v. Uhuru Muigai Kenyatta, 'Notice of withdrawal of the charges against Uhuru Muigai Kenyatta', Case No. ICC-01-09/02/11 (5 December 2014), http://www.icc-cpi.int/iccdocs/doc/doc1879204.pdf (accessed 6 February 2015).

[247]See ICC, Press Release, 'Statement of the Prosecutor of the International Criminal Court, Fatou Bensouda, on the withdrawal of charges against Mr. Uhuru Muigai Kenyatta' (5 December 2014), http://www.icc-cpi.int/en_menus/icc/press%20and%20media/press%20releases/Pages/otp-statement-05-12-2014-2.aspx (accessed 27 March 2015).

The ICC also moved forward with *The Prosecutor v. Jean-Pierre Bemba Gombo* case, the Court's first command responsibility case. In October 2014, Trial Chamber III reopened the presentation of evidence and recalled a prosecution witness, 'Witness 169', with regard to allegations of collusion between prosecution witnesses and payments made to some of them by the OTP in exchange for their testimonies.[248] Although the reopening of a case in order to submit new evidence is not expressly provided for by the Rome Statute, the Judges agreed that there were exceptional circumstances permitting the reopening of the presentation of evidence and the recall of Witness P-169.[249] Accordingly, on October 22, 2014, Witness 169 reappeared in Court and gave testimony in closed session. The oral closing arguments in Bemba's trial were heard on November 12–13, 2014. The Prosecution asked Trial Chamber III to hold Bemba responsible for the murder, rape, and pillaging committed by his Movement for the Liberation of Congo (MLC) troops during the hostilities in the Central African Republic (CAR) in 2002 and 2003. The Defense requested for the acquittal of Bemba, arguing that the Prosecution failed to prove its allegations against him. On December 23, 2014, Trial Chamber III denied a request issued by the Defense to grant Bemba provisional release until the rendering of the judgment.[250] It is for the first time that the Court must decide whether an accused can be held responsible on the basis of command responsibility.

In connection with the trial against Bemba, the Prosecutor brought a second case in November 2013 against Bemba and two of his former lawyers, Aimé Kilolo Musamba and Jean-Jacques Mangenda Kabongo, and two aides, Fidèle Babala Wandu and Narcisse Arido, for committing offenses against the administration of justice and presenting false evidence at Bemba's trial. Following the transfer of Kilolo, Kabongo and Babala to The Hague, Arido was surrendered to the Court by French authorities on March 18, 2014 after his appeal against extradition was rejected by a French Appellate Court. Arido first appeared before Court on March 20, 2014. On July 11, 2014, the Appeals Chamber, by majority, affirmed a March 2014 decision of Pre-Trial Chamber II rejecting a request for interim release of Kilolo, Babala and Mangenda because it did not find any appealable error in the Pre-Trial Chamber's decision.[251] Judges Erkki Kourula and Ušacka

[248]See ICC, Trial Chamber III, Situation in the Central African Republic, In the case of The Prosecutor v. Jean-Pierre Bemba Gombo, 'Redacted version of "Decision on 'Prosecution's Information to Trial Chamber III on issues involving witness CAR-OTP-PPPP-0169' (ICC-01/05-01/08-3138-Conf-Red) and 'Defence Urgent Submissions on the 5 August Letter (ICC-01/05-01/08-3139-Conf)" of 2 October 2014', Case No. ICC-01/05-01/08 (10 October 2014), http://www.icc-cpi.int/iccdocs/doc/doc1847668.pdf (accessed 30 March 2015).

[249]Ibid., para 29.

[250]See ICC, Trial Chamber III, Situation in the Central African Republic, In the case of The Prosecutor v. Jean-Pierre Bemba Gombo, 'Decision on "Defence Urgent Motion for Provisional Release"', Case No. ICC-01/05-01/08 (23 December 2014), http://www.icc-cpi.int/iccdocs/doc/doc1889061.pdf (accessed 30 March 2015).

[251]See ICC, Press Release, 'Bemba, Kilolo et al. case: Appeals Chamber dismisses the appeals of Messrs. Kilolo, Babala and Mangenda' (11 July 2014), http://www.icc-cpi.int/en_menus/icc/press%20and%20media/press%20releases/Pages/pr1027.aspx (accessed 30 March 2015).

dissented, arguing that their continued detention could not be justified since the alleged offenses do not meet the same degree of gravity as the core crimes under the Rome Statute. However, in order to ensure that the length of the suspects' pre-trial detention would not be excessive, Pre-Trial Chamber II *motu proprio* reviewed their detention on October 21, 2014. The Chamber came to the conclusion that the suspects' release was needed to avoid that the length of pre-trial detention would become disproportionate because the case concerned offenses against the administration of justice for which in case of conviction a fine or a term of imprisonment not exceeding 5 years can be imposed. Therefore, on October 21, 2014, the Single Judge of Pre-Trial Chamber II, Judge Cuno Tarfusser, granted interim release to the four co-accused of Bemba on the basis of Article 60(4) of the Rome Statute.[252] Kilolo, Mangenda, Babala and Arido would be released to Belgium, the United Kingdom, the DRC, and France respectively. The Prosecutor appealed this decision but the Appeals Chamber rejected its request for suspensive effect.[253] Bemba remained in custody because the separate trial against him was still ongoing. On November 11, 2014, Pre-Trial Chamber II partially confirmed the charges against the five suspects and committed them to trial.[254] The Chamber found that there were substantial grounds to believe that all suspects committed offenses against the administration of justice by bribing witnesses to give false testimonies in the case of *The Prosecutor v. Jean-Pierre Bemba Gombo*. However, due to a lack of evidence, Pre-Trial Chamber II declined to confirm the charge that Bemba, Kilolo, Mangenda and Arido knowingly presented false or forged documents as evidence during the trial, which was also charged by the Prosecution.[255] Trial Chamber VII is in charge of the case of *The Prosecutor v. Jean-Pierre Bemba Gombo, Aimé Kilolo Musamba, Jean-Jacques Mangenda Kabongo, Fidèle Babala Wandu and Narcisse Arido.*

---

[252]See ICC, Pre-Trial Chamber II, Situation in the Central African Republic, In the case of The Prosecutor v. Jean-Pierre Bemba Gombo, Aimé Kilolo Musamba, Jean-Jacques Mangenda Kabongo, Fidèle Babala Wandu and Narcisse Arido, 'Decision ordering the release of Aimé Kilolo Musamba, Jean-Jacques Mangenda Kabongo, Fidèle Babala Wandu and Narcisse Arido', Case No. ICC-01/05-01/13 (21 October 2014), http://www.icc-cpi.int/iccdocs/doc/doc1845009.pdf (accessed 30 March 2015).

[253]See ICC, Appeals Chamber, Situation in the Central African Republic, In the case of The Prosecutor v. Jean-Pierre Bemba Gombo, Aimé Kilolo Musamba, Jean-Jacques Mangenda Kabongo, Fidèle Babala Wandu and Narcisse Arido, 'Decision on the Prosecutor's urgent request for suspensive effect of the 'Decision ordering the release of Aimé Kilolo Musamba, Jean-Jacques Mangenda Kabongo, Fidèle Babala Wandu and Narcisse Arido" of 21 October 2014', Case No. ICC-01/05-01/13 OA 9 (22 October 2014), http://www.icc-cpi.int/iccdocs/doc/doc1854382.pdf (accessed 30 March 2015).

[254]See ICC, Pre-Trial Chamber II, Situation in the Central African Republic, In the case of The Prosecutor v. Jean-Pierre Bemba Gombo, Aimé Kilolo Musamba, Jean-Jacques Mangenda Kabongo, Fidèle Babala Wandu and Narcisse Arido, 'Decision pursuant to Article 61(7)(a) and (b) of the Rome Statute', Case No. ICC-01/05-01/13 (11 November 2014), http://www.icc-cpi.int/iccdocs/doc/doc1857534.pdf (accessed 30 March 2015).

[255]Ibid., para 512.

With regards to ICC investigations, the Court became involved in various conflict areas around the world as the global security situation has changed greatly in 2014. The Court's focus was shifted away from Africa when the ICC OTP opened a preliminary examination into the situation in Ukraine. On April 17, 2014, the Ukrainian Government issued a declaration under Article 12(3) of the Rome Statute, accepting the jurisdiction of the Court over alleged crimes committed on its territory from November 21, 2013 to February 22, 2014.[256] According to Article 12(3) of the Rome Statute, States are allowed to accept the jurisdiction of the Court on an ad hoc basis without having fully ratified the Statute. One week later, the ICC Prosecutor, Fatou Bensouda, decided to open a preliminary investigation into the situation in Ukraine in order to determine whether the statutory criteria for the opening of an investigation are met.[257] On September 24, 2014, the Prosecutor also decided to open a second investigation into crimes allegedly committed in the CAR since 2012.[258] After carefully having analyzed relevant and reliable information, Bensouda found that an investigation was justified since the information "provides a reasonable basis to believe that both the Séléka and the anti-balaka groups have committed crimes against humanity and war crimes including murder, rape, forced displacement, persecution, pillaging, attacks against humanitarian missions and the use of children under fifteen in combat".[259] However, in December, the Prosecutor decided to suspend the Court's investigation into alleged war crimes committed in Sudan's Darfur region due to a lack of support by the UN Security Council that itself referred the situation in Darfur to the Court in March 2005 in a response to the death of approximately 400,000 people.[260] Up until then, none of the individuals alleged of having committed crimes in Darfur, including Sudanese President Ohmar Al Bashir, was brought to justice. Despite a warrant of arrest issued against Al Bashir for his alleged responsibility for crimes against humanity, war crimes, and genocide, he was able to travel to multiple African countries in 2014 without being arrested. On April 9, 2014, Pre-Trial Chamber II already found that the DRC failed to cooperate with the Court by

[256]See ICC, Press Release, 'Ukraine accepts ICC jurisdiction over alleged crimes committed between 21 November 2013 and 22 February 2014' (17 April 2014), http://www.icc-cpi.int/en_menus/icc/press%20and%20media/press%20releases/Pages/pr997.aspx (accessed 31 March 2015).

[257]See ICC, Press Release, 'The Prosecutor of the International Criminal Court, Fatou Bensouda, opens a preliminary examination in Ukraine' (25 April 2014), http://www.icc-cpi.int/en_menus/icc/press%20and%20media/press%20releases/Pages/pr999.aspx (accessed 31 March 2015).

[258]See ICC, Press Release, 'Statement of the Prosecutor of the International Criminal Court, Fatou Bensouda, on opening a second investigation in the Central African Republic' (24 September 2014), http://www.icc-cpi.int/en_menus/icc/press%20and%20media/press%20releases/Pages/pr1043.aspx (accessed 31 March 2015).

[259]Ibid.

[260]The Prosecutor's Statement to the United Nations Security Council on the Situation in Darfur can be found here: http://www.icc-cpi.int/iccdocs/otp/stmt-20threport-darfur.pdf (accessed 31 March 2015).

not arresting him during his visit to the country in late February 2014.[261] The matter was referred to the UN Security Council and to the Assembly of States Parties (ASP).

Another remarkable moment in the context of the ICC occurred on 5 June 2014, when the Prosecutor published a Policy Paper on Sexual- and Gender-Based Crimes,[262] which "will guide the Office of the Prosecutor in its work in fighting against impunity for sexual and gender-based crimes, and promote transparency and clarity, as well as predictability in the application of the legal framework of the Rome Statute to such crimes. In turn, the policy will contribute to ensuring not only the effective investigation and prosecution of sexual and gender-based crimes, but also to enhancing access to justice for victims of these crimes, through the ICC".[263] The Policy Paper will also serve as a reference guide for States and other actors on how to prosecute sexual- and gender-based crimes.

Furthermore, in December 2014, the thirteenth annual session of the ASP took place at the UN headquarters in New York. During the session, six new ICC judges were elected and Justice Minister Sidiki Kaba of Senegal was appointed the first African President of the ASP. When addressing the ASP, Kaba emphasized that he was committed "[to reconcile] the ICC with all regions of the world, including Africa", "to develop cooperation between the ICC and States", to focus on "strengthening complementarity", and, finally, "to work toward the universality of the ICC".[264] With respect to the allegation that the Court is unfairly targeting African States, officials from various countries, including, *inter alia*, Côte d'Ivoire, Sierra Leone and the DRC, reaffirmed their commitment to the Court. In that regard, a statement was delivered on behalf of African States Parties to the Rome Statute, stating that the creation of the ICC was "a major milestone in international criminal justice", and emphasizing that "African States have the highest regard for the Rome Statute because of the protection and promotion of the rule of law".[265] However, in the statement, the African States also reiterated the African Union's call for an amendment of the Rome Statute providing immunity before the court for sitting leaders.

---

[261]See ICC, Pre-Trial Chamber II, Situation in Darfur, Sudan, In the case of The Prosecutor v. Omar Hassan Ahmad Al Bashir, 'Decision on the Cooperation of the Democratic Republic of the Congo Regarding Omar Al Bashir's Arrest and Surrender to the Court', Case No. ICC-02/05-01/09 (9 April 2014), http://www.icc-cpi.int/iccdocs/doc/doc1759849.pdf (accessed 31 March 2015).

[262]The Policy Paper on Sexual and Gender-Based Crimes can be found here: http://www.icc-cpi.int/iccdocs/otp/OTP-Policy-Paper-on-Sexual-and-Gender-Based-Crimes--June-2014.pdf (accessed 31 March 2015).

[263]See ICC, Press Release, 'The Prosecutor of the International Criminal Court, Fatou Bensouda, publishes comprehensive Policy Paper on Sexual and Gender-Based Crimes' (5 June 2014), http://www.icc-cpi.int/en_menus/icc/press%20and%20media/press%20releases/Pages/pr1011.aspx (accessed 31 March 2015).

[264]The statement can be found here: http://www.icc-cpi.int/iccdocs/asp_docs/ASP13/ASP13-OP-Statement-PASP-ENG.pdf (accessed 31 March 2015).

[265]The statement can be found here: http://www.icc-cpi.int/iccdocs/asp_docs/ASP13/GenDeba/ICC-ASP13-GenDeba-Lesotho-AfricanStatesParties-ENG.pdf (accessed 31 March 2015).

12.2.2 *Hybrid Tribunals*

12.2.2.1 EULEX Kosovo

On February 5, 2014, the Pristina Court of Appeals confirmed the decision issued by a Pre-Trial Judge from the Mitrovica Basic Court regarding the detention on remand for Serb politician Oliver Ivanović, who allegedly committed war crimes and aggravated murder during the 1998–1999 armed conflict in Kosovo.[266] The Court of Appeals found that a one-month detention could be imposed on Ivanović because there was a substantial risk that he would flee or intimidate witnesses if released. Moreover, the detention period was extended with 2 months at the end of February 2014. On March 11, 2014, Ivanović's request to be transferred from the detention center in Pristina to the detention center in Mitrovica, was granted by the Court of Appeals after the Prosecution unsuccessfully appealed the transfer request. In April 27, 2014, Ivanović's detention was extended for the period of 2 months by a Pre-Trial Judge, arguing that both the flight risk and the risk of influencing witnesses was still present.[267] On August 26, 2014, his detention was extended for another 2 months.

Furthermore, on February 4, 2014, Dragoljub (aka Dragan) Delibašić was arrested upon an order issued by a Prosecutor of the Kosovo Special Prosecution Office (SPRK).[268] Delibašić acted as a Police Commander in Mitrovica in the period 1999–2000 and was charged with incitement to commit aggravated murder and incitement to commit attempted aggravated murder, all committed in co-perpetration with Oliver Ivanović.[269] Delibašić pleaded not guilty to all charges.

In the same month, Ivan Radivojević was convicted of war crimes against the civilian population for offenses committed in Kosovo on March 26, 1999 pursuant to Articles 22 and 142 of the Criminal Code of the Socialist Federal Republic of Yugoslavia (CC SFRY), in conjunction with Common Article 3 of the 1949 Geneva Conventions and Articles 4 and 5(1) of Additional Protocol II. Radivojević was sentenced to 8 years' imprisonment.[270]

On May 27, 2014, the Court of Appeals of Kosovo annulled the acquittal of two persons, "J.D." and "Dj.B.", for war crimes against civilians under Article 142 of the CC SFRY. However, the Court convicted them again for the same crime and sentenced them to 12 and 10 years' imprisonment, respectively. J.D. was found

---

[266] See EULEX, Press Release, 'Appeals Court confirms Ivanovic's detention' (5 February 2014), http://www.eulex-kosovo.eu/en/pressreleases/0553.php (accessed 4 April 2015).

[267] See EULEX, Press Release, 'Detention on remand extended for Oliver Ivanovic' (26 April 2014), http://www.eulex-kosovo.eu/en/pressreleases/0598.php (accessed 4 April 2015).

[268] See EULEX, Press Release, 'SPRK arrests suspect in Lesak/Leshak' (5 February 2014), http://www.eulex-kosovo.eu/en/pressreleases/0552.php (accessed 4 April 2015).

[269] Ibid.

[270] See EULEX, Press Release, 'Verdict in war crime case' (13 February 2014), http://www.eulex-kosovo.eu/en/pressreleases/0559.php (accessed 4 April 2015).

guilty of abduction and rape of an Albanian woman and Dj.B. was found guilty for the rape of the same woman, by forcing her to have (various types) of sexual intercourse.[271]

12.2.2.2 Extraordinary Chambers in the Courts of Cambodia

2014 was an important year for the Extraordinary Chambers in the Courts of Cambodia (ECCC) as it delivered its second trial judgment. On August 7, 2014, the Court announced the judgment in the first trial of Case 002, "Case 002/01", the case against Chea Nuon, former Chairman of the Democratic Kampuchea National Assembly and Deputy Secretary of the Communist Party of Kampuchea, and Samphan Khieu, former Head of State of Democratic Kampuchea (for the procedural overview, see last year's *Year in Review*). Case 002/01 is limited to the crimes of forced evacuation of the entire population from Phnom Penh into the countryside in April 1975 ("first population movement"), to further forced evacuation of the population from, to and within the Central, Southwest, West and East Zones which took place between September 1975 and December 1977 ("second population movement"), and to the executions of former Khmer Republic officials committed at Tuol Po Chrey in April 1975. All other crimes committed between 1975 and 1979 during the Khmer Rouge regime will be dealt with in future trials. On August 7, 2014, the Trial Chamber found both Chea Nuon and Samphan Khieu guilty for committing crimes against humanity regarding the first population movement, the second population movement, as well as for the executions of Khmer Republic officials at Tuol Po Chrey, all committed between April 17, 1975 and December 1977.[272] More specifically, with regard to the first population movement during which approximately two million people were forcibly transferred by Khmer Rouge soldiers from cities and towns to rural areas, resulting in the death of many of them due to exhaustion, malnutrition and diseases, the Chamber found that the defendants could be held guilty of the crimes against humanity of murder, political persecution and other inhumane acts including forced transfers and attacks against human dignity.[273] Chea Nuon and Samphan Khieu were also found guilty of crimes against humanity (political persecution and other inhumane acts including forced transfers and attacks against human dignity) because of the death and starvation of civilians which resulted from the second population movement,

[271]See EULEX, Court of Appeals, 'Judgment', http://www.eulex-kosovo.eu/eul/repository/docs/(2014.05.27)_JUD_-_J.D._&_Dj.B._(CoA)_Eng.pdf (accessed 4 April 2015).

[272]See ECCC, Trial Chamber, 'Case 002/01 Judgement', Case No. 002/19-09-2007/ECCC/TC (7 August 2014), http://www.eccc.gov.kh/sites/default/files/documents/courtdoc/2014-08-07%2017:04/E313_Trial%20Chamber%20Judgement%20Case%20002_01_ENG.pdf (accessed 18 April 2015).

[273]See ECCC, Press Release, 'Nuon Chea and Khieu Samphan Sentenced to Life Imprisonment for Crimes against Humanity' (7 August 2014), http://www.eccc.gov.kh/en/articles/nuon-chea-and-khieu-samphan-sentenced-life-imprisonment-crimes-against-humanity (accessed 18 April 2015).

the phase during which about 430,000 persons were forcibly displaced throughout Cambodia.[274] Finally, both defendants were also found guilty for murder and extermination of at least 250 former Khmer Republic and Lon Nol government officials at Tuol Po Chrey by implementing the common purpose of a JCE in which they participated through a policy to target those officials.[275] In its 623-pages judgment, the Trial Chamber found that the defendants in their capacities committed the crimes by actively participating in a JCE that had the common purpose of implementing a socialist revolution in Cambodia by whatever means necessary. The common purpose of the JCE was implemented by both defendants by developing the (above-discussed) policies of the Communist Party of Kampuchea (CPK, also known as the Khmer Rouge) to forcibly displace people from cities and towns (the first population movement), to transfer people from various locations throughout Cambodia (the second population movement), and to target former Khmer Republic officials. The Trial Chamber also held Nuon Chea criminally responsible for all the crimes on the basis of superior responsibility because he "exercised ultimate decision-making power" in his function as Pol Pot's second in command.[276] Nuon Chea played a vital role in ordering particular attacks and had a de facto superior-subordinate relationship with the zone commanders as well as the military.[277] The Trial Chamber dismissed the superior responsibility charges in relation to Samphan Khieu, arguing that he had no authority to issue orders, that "substantial influence alone does not establish effective control within a command structure", and that there was insufficient evidence to establish that he exercised effective control over the perpetrators of the crimes.[278]

The Trial Chamber held that the two accused in their respective positions had access to reports and other information on the situations at hand, such as the forcible movements and the poor travel and living conditions of the population due to these movements. In his position as Chairman of the Democratic Kampuchea National Assembly, Chea Nuon had knowledge of the occurring events and also actively participated to achieve the policies of the Khmer Rouge.[279] Furthermore, in the field of propaganda-related matters, he gave various speeches, gathered cadres and conducted training sessions, knowing that this indoctrination would lead to violence.[280] In this regard, Chea Nuon participated in meetings on forced movements of the population,[281] such as the forcible transfer of the population of

[274]Ibid.

[275]Ibid.

[276]See ECCC, Trial Chamber, 'Case 002/01 Judgement', Case No. 002/19-09-2007/ECCC/TC (7 August 2014), http://www.eccc.gov.kh/sites/default/files/documents/courtdoc/2014-08-07%2017:04/E313_Trial%20Chamber%20Judgement%20Case%20002_01_ENG.pdf (accessed 18 April 2015), para 893.

[277]Ibid., para 894.

[278]Ibid., paras 1007 and 1021.

[279]Ibid., paras 318 and 321–323.

[280]Ibid., para 8412.

[281]Ibid., para 843.

Phnom Penh.[282] Chea Nuon admitted that he participated in the first population movement,[283] and that he had knowledge of the second population movement.[284] More importantly, he was well aware of the deaths resulting from those movements of the civilian population.[285] With regard to the execution of former Khmer Republic officials, the Chamber held that Chea Nuon was strongly involved in military and security matters by receiving regular reports and by giving advice and instructions on these matters, either directly or indirectly.[286] Moreover, as being one of the main authors of the CPKs' *Revolutionary Flag* magazine through which the Khmer Rouge's policy on enemies was spread, and as a participant and speaker during various meetings where this policy was indoctrinated, Chea Nuon had knowledge of the Khmer Rouge's policy of targeting former Khmer Republic officials, including the executions at Tuol Po Chrey.[287] The Trial Chamber found that Samphan Khieu not only had knowledge about the movements of the population, such as the forcible transfer of the population of Phnom Penh, but that he also supported whatever means in order to achieve the objectives of the Khmer Rouge's policies. In addition, he assisted in the planning of the forcible transfer of the population from urban areas.[288] Moreover, Samphan Khieu was also aware of the fact that crimes were being committed by and for the CPK, and knowingly withheld this information from the inhabitants of Cambodia, which he tried to persuade and indoctrinate during speeches and trainings he provided.[289]

The Trial Chamber sentenced both senior leaders to life imprisonment and awarded reparations to the 3,866 victims that participated in the trial. In determining the sentence, the Chamber took various circumstances into account: the gravity of the crimes, the fact that the crimes were committed against a very high number of victims, the impact of the crimes upon the victims and the Cambodian population in general, both defendants enjoyed a good education and therefore could have been aware of the consequences of their acts, etcetera.[290]

The second trial of Case 002, Case 002/02, dealing with, amongst others, the crimes of genocide, forced marriages, and rape, was scheduled for October 17, 2014. However, due to the appeal in Case 002/01, the Defense for Samphan Khieu refused to participate in the proceedings in order to have more time to devote to

[282]Ibid., para 845.

[283]Ibid., para 849.

[284]Ibid., para 8512.

[285]Ibid., para 851.

[286]Ibid., para 347.

[287]Ibid., paras 853–854.

[288]Ibid., para 948.

[289]Ibid., para 945.

[290]See ECCC, Press Release, 'Nuon Chea and Khieu Samphan Sentenced to Life Imprisonment for Crimes against Humanity' (7 August 2014), http://www.eccc.gov.kh/en/articles/nuon-chea-and-khieu-samphan-sentenced-life-imprisonment-crimes-against-humanity (accessed 18 April 2015).

the appeal since the deadline for appeal was set for December 29, 2014. Therefore, the Chamber decided to postpone the hearings in Case 002/02 to January 2015.[291]

12.2.2.3 Special Tribunal for Lebanon

In the context of the Special Tribunal for Lebanon (STL), the most interesting development that transpired in 2014 was the start of the trial against Salim Jamil Ayyash, Mustafa Amine Badreddine, Assad Hassan Sabra, and Hussein Hassan Oneissi (the *Ayyash et al.* case), all indicted under Article 2 of the STL Statute and the Lebanese Criminal Code for their alleged roles as coconspirators in the February 14, 2005 attack in Beirut that killed former Lebanese Prime Minister Rafik Hariri as well as 21 other persons, and which injured 226 others. The four defendants are being tried in absentia because they are still at large. The Prosecution began presenting evidence in the *Ayyash* et al. case before the Trial Chamber on January 22, 2014, following the opening statements made by the Prosecution, the LRV participating in the trial, and the Defense.[292] On February 11, 2014, the case was joined with the case against Hassan Habib Merhi whose indictment containing five counts for involvement in the February 14, 2005 attack was confirmed by the Pre-Trial Judge on July 31, 2013 (see last year's *Year in Review*).[293] The Trial Chamber held that the Prosecution's request for joinder of the cases could be granted because "joining the two proceedings (Ayyash and Merhi) would better protect the rights of all five Accused to a fair and expeditious trial, provided that certain measures were taken". Therefore, a joinder was "ordered on the basis that the Trial Chamber would take—and will continue to take, as necessary—all the measures required to ensure a fair trial for all five Accused".[294] As a result of the joinder, the Defense for Merhi requested adjournment of the proceedings for 5–6 months so it would have enough time to adequately prepare for trial. A few days later, Merhi's Defense submitted additional arguments substantiating justification for delay: "(1) the exceptional volume of the Ayyash et al. case; (2) the particular character of the Defense for the Accused, Mr Merhi, which cannot be likened to the defenses of the other Accused; (3) the effective date when the Merhi Defense team was formed; (4) the expedited pre-trial phase of the case which has occupied the Defense, and continues to occupy it,

[291]See ECCC, Press Release, 'Hearing in case 002/02 adjourned until January 2014' (24 November 2014), http://www.eccc.gov.kh/sites/default/files/media/ECCC%20PR%2024%20Nov%202014%20Eng.pdf (accessed 18 April 2015).

[292]See STL, Press Release, 'The Prosecution starts presenting evidence in the Ayyash et al. case' (22 January 2014), http://www.stl-tsl.org/en/news-and-press/press-releases/2828-22-01-2014-the-prosecution-starts-presenting-evidence-in-the-ayyash-et-al-case (accessed 25 April 2015).

[293]See STL, Press Release, 'Merhi case joined with the Ayyash et al. case' (11 February 2014), http://www.stl-tsl.org/en/news-and-press/press-releases/2922-merhi-case-joined-with-the-ayyash-et-al-case (accessed 25 April 2015).

[294]Ibid.

instead of allowing it to concentrate on preparing the case on the merits; and (5) the need to determine a line of defense, conduct investigations and obtain relevant expert advice in order to contest the Prosecution evidence".[295] On February 25, 2014, the Trial Chamber ordered the adjournment of the proceedings with at least 3 months in order to ensure that Merhi's Defense had enough time to adequately prepare its defense.[296] The trial of *Ayyash et al.* eventually resumed on June 18, 2014.[297] In the first part of its case, the Prosecution presented evidence directly related to the crime scene of the February 14, 2005 attack. The second part of the Prosecution's case involved the acts undertaken by the accused and their coconspirators in 2004 and 2005 to prepare for the killing of former Lebanese Prime Minister Hariri. It is expected that the Prosecution will close its case by the end of 2015.

With regard to the contempt charges before the Tribunal, an amicus curiae, Stéphane Bourgon, was appointed by the Registrar to investigate "three incidents which could potentially be considered interference with the administration of justice through publication of alleged witness identities".[298] Following the presentation of the results of an investigation conducted by the amicus curiae, the initial Contempt Judge, Judge Baragwanath, held that proceedings for contempt were justified and accordingly summoned two Lebanese journalists and two Lebanese media organizations charged with counts of contempt and obstruction of justice to appear before the Tribunal pursuant to Rule 60*bis* of the Tribunal's RPE.[299] Journalist Ibrahim Mohamed Ali Al Amin and company Akhbar Beirut S.A.L. (case STL-14-06) both faced one count: knowingly and wilfully interfering with the administration of justice by publishing information on purported confidential

[295]See STL, Trial Chamber, The Prosecutor v. Salim Jamil Ayyash, Mustafa Amine Badreddine, Hussein Hassan Oneissi and Assad Hassan Sabra, 'Additional observations regarding the time needed to prepare the defence of the interests of Mr Merhi', Case No. STL-11-01/PT/TC (17 February 2014), http://www.stl-tsl.org/en/the-cases/stl-11-01/filings/main-case/other/2933-f1409 (accessed 25 April 2015), para 13.

[296]See STL, Press Release, 'STL Trial Chamber adjourns hearings in the Ayyash et al. trial' (26 February 2014), http://www.stl-tsl.org/en/news-and-press/press-releases/2950-stl-trial-chamber-adjourns-hearings-in-the-ayyash-et-al-trial (accessed 25 April 2015).

[297]See STL, Press Release, 'Prosecution's opening statement' (19 June 2014), http://www.stl-tsl.org/en/news-and-press/press-releases/3340-19-06-2014-prosecutions-opening-statement (accessed 25 April 2015).

[298]See STL, Press Release, 'STL Appoints New Investigator to Deal with Contempt Charges' (10 April 2014), http://www.stl-tsl.org/en/news-and-press/press-releases/3054-10-04-2014-still-appoints-new-investigator-to-deal-with-contempt-charges (accessed 27 April 2014); See also STL, Press Release, 'Tribunal to launch investigation in alleged witness intimidation' (29 April 2013), http://www.stl-tsl.org/en/media/press-releases/29-04-2013-tribunal-to-launch-investigation-in-alleged-witness-intimidation (accessed 25 April 2015).

[299]See STL, 'About the Contempt Cases', http://www.stl-tls.org/en/the-cases/about-the-contempt-cases (accessed 25 April 2015).

witnesses in the *Ayyash et al.* case.[300] Journalist Karma Mohamed Tahsin Al Khayat and media organization New TV S.A.L. (case STL-14-05) faced the same count, but also a second one: knowingly and wilfully interfering with the administration of justice by failing to remove from Al Jadeed TV's website and Al Jadeed TV's YouTube channel information on purported confidential witnesses. In his decision to summon the accused, Judge Baragwanath recalled that "publishing purported names of witnesses may amount to interference with the administration of justice, because it reduced the confidence of both actual witnesses and the public, in the ability and the will of the Tribunal to protect its witnesses".[301] Judge Nicola Lettieri became in charge of the cases and a new amicus curiae was appointed to prosecute the accused journalists and media organizations. Following a motion issued by the Defense in case STL-14-05, challenging the jurisdiction of the Tribunal regarding cases concerning contempt in relation to legal persons, the Contempt Judge Lettieri ruled on July 24, 2014 that the Tribunal cannot hear cases involving charges brought against legal persons for alleged contempt and obstruction of justice under Rule 60*bis* of the Tribunal's RPE. However, the Contempt Judge Lettieri confirmed that the Tribunal has jurisdiction to hear cases for offenses related to the administration of justice against natural persons pursuant to Rule 60*bis* of the Tribunal's RPE. On July 31, 2014, the amicus curiae Prosecutor appealed the decision issued by the Contempt Judge Lettieri to a three-Judge Appeals Panel. The majority of the Judges of the Appeals Panel concluded that the Tribunal does have jurisdiction to hear cases involving obstruction of justice charges brought against legal persons and, therefore, on October 2, 2014, ruled that the case against New TV S.A.L. could proceed, just like the case against Karma Al Khayat.[302] The trial in case STL-14-05 was scheduled to begin in April 2015. In the case STL-14-06, Ibrahim Al Amin represented himself and Akhbar Beirut S.A.L. and appeared in court on May 29, 2014.[303] The defendants in this case had also challenged the Tribunal's jurisdiction to hear the case brought against them. However, despite the Appeals Panel's ruling in case STL-14-05, the

---

[300] See STL, Press Release, 'Special Tribunal for Lebanon issues summons to appear in contempt cases' (24 April 2014), http://www.stl-tls.org/en/special-tribunal-for-lebanon-issues-summons-to-appear-in-contempt-cases-stl-press-release (accessed 25 April 2015).

[301] Ibid.

[302] See STL, Appeals Panel, In the case against New TV S.A.L. and Karma Mohamed Tahsin Al Khayat, 'Decision on interlocutory appeal concerning personal jurisdiction in contempt proceedings', Case No, STL-14-05/PT/AP/AR126.1 (2 October 2014), http://www.stl-tsl.org/en/decision-on-interlocutory-appeal-concerning-personal-jurisdiction-in-contempt-proceedings (accessed 25 April 2015); See also STL, Press Release, 'Appeals Panel decides on jurisdiction in Case STL-14-05' (2 October 2014), http://www.stl-tsl.org/en/news-and-press/press-releases/3514-judicial-panel-decides-on-jurisdiction-in-case-stl-14-05 (accessed 25 April 2015).

[303] See STL, Press Release, 'Written Decision on the Assignment of Counsel in the Case against Akhbar Beirut S.A.L. and Ibrahim Al Amin' (5 June 2014), http://www.stl-tsl.org/en/news-and-press/press-releases/3219-05-06-2014-written-decision-on-the-assignment-of-counsel-in-the-case-against-akhbar-beirut-s-a-l-and-ibrahim-al-amin (accessed 25 April 2015).

Contempt Judge Lettieri held that the Tribunal only has jurisdiction to hear the case against natural person Ibrahim Al Amin.[304]

In the first week of March 2014, the Tribunal submitted its fifth annual report to the UN Secretary-General and to the Lebanese President and Prime Minister, addressing the Tribunal's achievements, challenges and overall progress for the period March 1, 2013 to September 28, 2014.[305] In the report, the President of the Tribunal, Judge Sir David Baragwanath, highlighted, among other things, the (joinder of the) *Ayyash et al.* and *Mehri* case. President Baragwanath emphasized in his introduction note that "[o]f vital importance to its judicial work is the Tribunal's commitment to informing the Lebanese people and broader international public about that work, and supporting Lebanon's wide-reaching efforts to promote the rule of law".[306]

12.3 Arms Control and Disarmament

12.3.1 Conventional Weapons

12.3.1.1 Arms Trade Treaty

After more than 50 ratifications, United Nations officials welcomed the entry into force of the Arms Trade Treaty (ATT) on December 24, 2014, hailing it as a new chapter in collective efforts to bring responsibility, accountability and transparency to the global arms trade. "From now on, the States Parties to this important treaty will have a legal obligation to apply the highest common standards to their international transfers of weapons and ammunition," Secretary-General Ban Ki-moon said.[307]

---

[304] See STL, Contempt Judge, In the case against Akhbar Beirut S.A.L. and Ibrahim Mohamed Ali Al Amin, 'Decision on motion challenging jurisdiction', Case No. STL-14-06/PT/CJ (6 November 2014), http://www.stl-tsl.org/en/the-cases/contempt-cases/stl-14-06/filings-stl-14-06/3593 (accessed 25 April 2015); See also STL, Press Release, 'Contempt Judge Lettieri decides on jurisdiction in the case against Akhbar Beirut S.A.L. and Mr Ibrahim Mohamed Ali Al Amin (STL-14-06)' (6 November 2014), http://www.stl-tsl.org/en/news-and-press/press-releases/3594-06-11-2014-contempt-judge-lettieri-decideds-on-jurisdiction-in-the-case-against-akhbar-beirut-s-a-l-and-mr-ibrahim-mohamed-ali-al-amin-stl-14-06 (accessed 25 April 2015).

[305] See STL, Press Release, 'STL publishes its fifth annual report' (10 March 2014), http://www.stl-tsl.org.en/news-and-press/press-releases/2985-10-03-2014-stl-publishes-its-fifth-annual-report (accessed 25 April 2015); The report can be found here: http://www.stl-tsl.org/en/documents/stl-documents/presidents-reports-and-memoranda/2984-fifth-annual-report-2013-2014 (accessed 25 April 2015).

[306] Ibid.

[307] http://www.un.org/apps/news/story.asp?NewsID=49668#.VZZjltOqqko.

12.3.2 Chemical Weapons

Based on the latest report of the OPCW Fact-Finding Mission (FFM), the OPCW's Executive Council concluded: "chlorine was used as a weapon systematically and repeatedly" against villages in northern Syria.[308] The finding does not attribute the attacks to any of the parties to the conflict in Syria. The brief of the FFM reports the use of chlorine gas as a weapon. The OPCW Director-General calls it a "tragic irony that a 100 years after chlorine was first used on the battlefield, its misuses to kill and terrorize unarmed civilians has again raised its ugly head."

12.4 Miscellaneous

12.4.1 Torture in 2014—30 Years of Broken Promises

Amnesty International releases torture report that details the persistence and growth of torture worldwide.[309]

12.4.2 Global Summit to End Sexual Violence in Conflict

The four-day Global Summit to End Sexual Violence in Conflict,[310] which aimed to create "irreversible momentum against sexual violence in conflict and practical action that impacts those on the ground," took place in June. High-level officials of the International Criminal Court, the Assembly of States Parties to the Rome Statute, and the Trust fund for Victims took part.[311] In November, The Protocol on

---

[308]See Organization for the Prevention of Chemical Weapons, 'Executive Council Discusses Findings of Fact-Finding Mission,' (26 September 2014) http://www.opcw.org/news/article/executive-council-discusses-findings-of-fact-finding-mission/ (accessed 1 July 2015).

[309]See Amnesty International, 'Torture in 2014: 30 Years of Broken Promises,' (12 May 2014) http://www.amnestyusa.org/research/reports/torture-in-2014-30-years-of-broken-promises (accessed 3 July 2015).

[310]See United Kingdom Government, 'About the Global Summit to End Sexual Violence,' (10 June 2014) https://www.gov.uk/government/topical-events/sexual-violence-in-conflict/about (accessed 3 July 2015).

[311]See International Criminal Court: 'ICC, ASP and TFV join in Global Summit to End Sexual Violence in Conflict,' (11 June 2014)
http://www.icc-cpi.int/en_menus/icc/press and media/press releases/Pages/pr1014.aspx (accessed 3 July 2015).

investigating and documenting sexual violence in wartime, released in June during the Global Summit to End Sexual Violence in Conflict, was welcomed in Sarajevo.[312] It contains guidelines and best practices for the recognition and documentation of cases involving sexual violence.

12.4.3 Children and Armed Conflict

In July, the UN Secretary-General released[313] his annual report on children and armed conflicts,[314] which lists parties to armed conflict that committed serious violations of international humanitarian law against children—including crimes of sexual violence and the recruitment and use of children as soldiers. Against a background of 15 million children affected by violent conflicts in the Central African Republic, Iraq, South Sudan, the State of Palestine, Syria and Ukraine, UNICEF declared 2014 "a devastating year for children" in December.[315] As the Executive Director of UNICEF acknowledged, "children have been killed while studying in the classroom and while sleeping in their beds; they have been orphaned, kidnapped, tortured, recruited, raped and even sold as slaves. Never in recent memory have so many children been subjected to such unspeakable brutality."

[312] See 'Protocol on Sexual Violence Greeted in Bosnia,' *Balkan Insight*, (20 November 2014) http://www.balkaninsight.com/en/article/time-to-act-against-sexual-violence?utm_source=Balkan+Transitional+Justice+Daily+Newsletter&utm_campaign=4b2bf05973-RSS_EMAIL_CAMPAIGN&utm_medium=email&utm_term=0_561b9a25c3-4b2bf05973-319688785#.VG3mAWgPm58.twitter (accessed 3 July 2015).

[313] See UN News Center, 'Child rights being violated in conflict situations with total impunity, says UN official,' (1 July 2014) http://www.un.org/apps/news/story.asp?NewsID=48180#.U7PFtWeKCih (accessed 3 July 2015).

[314] See A/68/878 S/2014/339 'Children and Armed Conflict, Report of the Secretary General,' (15 May 2014) http://www.un.org/ga/search/view_doc.asp?symbol=a/68/878&referer http://childrenandarmedconflict.un.org/press-release/secretary-generals-annual-report-on-children-and-armed-conflict-documents-continued-child-suffering-in-23-conflict-situations/&Lang=E (accessed 5 July 2015).

[315] See UNICEF Press Release, 'With 15 million children caught up in major conflicts, UNICEF declares 2014 a devastating year for children,' http://www.unicef.org/media/media_78058.html (accessed 3 July 2015).

12.4.4 UN Secretary-General's 2014 Report on the Responsibility To Protect (R2P)

The UN Secretary-General's 2014 report on the Responsibility to Protect (R2P) was released in August.[316] This report is entitled "Fulfilling our collective responsibility: international assistance and the responsibility to protect" and outlines the ways in which national, regional and international actors can assist states in fulfilling their responsibility to protect populations from genocide, war crimes, ethnic cleansing and crimes against humanity.

12.4.5 UN SC Resolution 2171 on Conflict Prevention

In a meeting opened by UN Secretary-General Ban Ki-moon and UN High Commissioner for Human Rights Navi Pillay, the UN Security Council unanimously adopted Resolution 2171[317] on conflict prevention.[318] The Security Council expressed its commitment to prevent armed conflict as part of its primary responsibility to maintain international peace and security, and reaffirmed that each state has the responsibility to protect its population from genocide, war crimes, ethnic cleansing, and crimes against humanity.

12.4.6 The US Report on Torture

In December, the US Senate Select Committee on Intelligence released a summary report documenting the crimes of torture and enforced disappearances of terrorist suspects by the "Bush-era CIA".[319] Drawing on millions of internal CIA docu-

[316] UN Secretary General Report on 'Fulfilling our Collective Responsibility: International Assistance and the Responsibility to Protect,' (12 August 2014) http://www.responsibilitytoprotect.org/index.php/component/content/article/35-r2pcs-topics/5497-2014-report-of-the-un-secretary-general-on-rtop-fulfilling-our-collective-responsibility (accessed 3 July 2015).

[317] See United Nations, 'Security Council, Adopting Resolution 2171 (2014), Pledges Better Use of System-Wide Approach to Conflict Prevention,' (21 August 2014) http://www.un.org/press/en/2014/sc11528.doc.htm (accessed 2 July 2015).

[318] See UN News Centre, 'Briefing Security Council, senior officials urge UN system-wide approach to early warning, conflict prevention' (21 August 2014) http://www.un.org/apps/news/story.asp?NewsID=48531#.U_cE12eKCih (accessed 3 July 2015).

[319] See Senate Select Committee on Intelligence, 'Committee Study of the Central Intelligence Agency's Detention and Interrogation Program,' (declassified 3 December 2014) https://web.archive.org/web/20141209165504/http://www.intelligence.senate.gov/study2014/sscistudy1.pdf (accessed 1 July 2015).

ments, the report concluded that the CIA deliberately misled Congress and the White House about information obtained by means of "enhanced interrogations techniques", which were more "brutal" and "ineffective" than the public was led to believe.[320] Following the release of the torture report by the US Senate Select Committee on Intelligence, legal experts said that the US has an obligation under international law to investigate its citizens suspected of engaging in torture.[321] The experts also identified that the ICC could prosecute Americans who ordered or carried out torture, on the basis that the court can prosecute the most serious crimes in countries that have signed the Rome Statute, like Afghanistan, where torture has allegedly taken place.

[320]Jaclyn Belczyk, 'Senate report: enhanced interrogation techniques "ineffective,"' *Jurist* (9 December 2014) http://jurist.org/paperchase/2014/12/senate-report-enhanced-interrogation-techniques-ineffective.php (accessed 3 July 2015).

[321]See Somini Sengupta, 'Americans Involved in Torture Can be Prosecuted Abroad, Analysts Say,' *New York Times*, (10 December 2014) http://www.nytimes.com/2014/12/11/us/politics/americans-involved-in-torture-can-be-prosecuted-abroad-analysts-say.html?emc=edit_tnt_20141210&nlid=67995904&tntemail0=y&_r=1 (accessed 3 July 2015) .

Chapter 13
Military Advantage: A Matter of "Value", Strategy, and Tactics

Kenneth Watkin

> *If, then, civilized nations do not put their prisoners to death or devastate cities and countries, it is because intelligence plays a larger part in their methods of warfare and has taught them more effective ways of using force than the crude expression of instinct (Von Clausewitz 1976, p. 76).*
>
> Carl Von Clausewitz

Abstract The concept of "military advantage" is an underexplored, but essential aspect of the humanitarian law governing targeting. The precise meaning of military advantage has proven difficult to articulate, although in general terms it has a particular resonance with "military necessity". The analysis of military advantage has often centered on two almost polar opposite interpretations: one focused on tactical gains, and the other more strategically on "the advantage anticipated from the attack considered as a whole and not from isolated or particular parts of the attack." Considered together these two approaches only begin to scratch the surface of the complexity of the issue. Separately, they appear to significantly under-represent the challenge facing practitioners, legal analysts and courts when dealing with targeting issues arising from complex contemporary security operations. Practical considerations of military advantage are often masked by the use of terms such as "high-value target", and assessing the "effects" of an attack to achieve a particular objective. The focus of this article is on adding "flesh" to the textual "bones" provided under

Brigadier-General (Ret'd) Kenneth Watkin, QC, is Former Judge Advocate General of the Canadian Forces and from 2001 to 2012 was the Charles H. Stockton Professor of International Law at the United States Naval War College.

K. Watkin (✉)
Kingston, Ontario, Canada
e-mail: kenwatkin@hotmail.com

T.D. Gill et al. (eds.), *Yearbook of International Humanitarian Law 2014*,
Yearbook of International Humanitarian Law 17,
DOI 10.1007/978-94-6265-091-6_13

Additional Protocol I. The term "military advantage" plays a critical role in identifying the wide range of objects that may be targeted as military objectives, and further acts as the counterweight to collateral civilian effects when assessing the proportionality of an attack. Military advantage is a "value" based concept, with the anticipated advantage being interpreted as an indication of the importance of the target to the military effort. While a particular focus has been placed on "high-value targets" there are targets, which by virtue of their status (e.g., people) or remoteness from the war effort that might justify only limited, or even no collateral civilian effects. It is also evident from the 2011 bin Laden raid that determining a target is particularly important will not automatically lead to a large number of collateral civilian casualties. The military advantage requires a broader assessment of factors than simply the importance of the target and the potential collateral damage (i.e., the need to confirm the target is killed). To date the courts have not dealt in a comprehensive manner with the concept of military advantage. The frequent use of science based analytical approaches for assessing both that advantage, and the related concept of proportionality requires close scrutiny. Like strategy, the assessment of anticipated military advantage designed to attain conflict goals does not lend itself to precision, or an entirely scientific resolution. This is evident in the conclusion that proportionality, which requires the weighing of military advantage against the collateral effects of an attack, cannot be measured to a "standard of precision". Understanding the context within which military advantage is assessed is an essential aspect of applying that legal standard. In this respect the conduct of a strategic air campaign; the concurrent impact of jus ad bellum principles when acting in self-defense; and participation in a counterinsurgency can all influence how military advantage is assessed.

Keywords Military advantage · Targeting · Proportionality · Levels of war · Counterinsurgency · Accountability

Contents

13.1 Introduction

The concept of "military advantage" is an underexplored, but essential, aspect of the humanitarian law governing targeting. From a simple "black letter" perspective it is, as is set out in Article 52(2) of *Additional Protocol I*, a foundational element of what constitutes a "military objective."[1] It is also part of the test for determining if an attack is indiscriminate,[2] one of the precautionary criteria to be applied in the assessment of targeting proportionality[3] and part of the determination of when an attack shall be canceled or suspended.[4] Nor is its use limited to targeting. International legal experts have identified the term military advantage as an essential part of the test for determining whether a naval or aerial blockade has a disproportionate impact on the civilian population of the affected territory.[5]

In terms of the attention paid to military advantage it is like another term introduced in the 1977 *Additional Protocol I*: "direct participation in hostilities." That latter term did not receive serious consideration regarding its meaning until after the attacks of 9/11. The same pressures that forced an analysis of direct participation in hostilities are also applicable to military advantage. A combination of state involvement in a more individualized targeting process associated with counterinsurgency and counterterrorism; the availability of more technologically advanced weapons systems, which lead to expectations of more precise targeting; and a greater focus on accountability for the use of force is increasing the scrutiny placed on all the targeting criteria found in humanitarian law. As the international legal community continues to focus on the legal rules governing targeting, it is anticipated that greater attention will be paid over the next few years to the meaning of military advantage and how that term is applied when justifying the use of force.

As has been fairly noted, in the context of determining what constitutes a military objective, "the notion of 'military advantage' is not singularly helpful."[6] The precise meaning of military advantage has proven difficult to articulate. The use of

[1]Protocol Additional to the Geneva Conventions of 12 August 1949, and Relating to the Protection of Victims of International Armed Conflicts, opened for signature December 12, 1977 1125 UNTS 3 (*Additional Protocol I—AP I*).

[2]AP I, Article 51 (5)(b).

[3]AP I, Article 57(2)(a)(iii).

[4]AP I, Article 57(b).

[5]San Remo Manual 1995, p. 179, Rule 102(b), and Air and Missile Warfare Commentary 2009, p. 297, Rule 157(b). See also Turkel Commission (2011), paras 87–97 (where this proportionality standard was applied in assessing whether the Israeli blockade of Gaza was lawful).

[6]Dinstein 2004, p. 86.

that term in the definition of military objective, and as a part of targeting proportionality test creates a situation that has the potential for misunderstanding and misapplication. This occurs because both legal concepts can be relevant to the assessment of the same targeting mission. In general terms, it has a particular resonance with "military necessity," which confusingly, after the forced split of just war theory into its *jus ad bellum* and *jus in bello* categories, is found in both bodies of law. However, unlike its *jus ad bellum* use, which focuses on the justification to go to war, under humanitarian law, military advantage has been interpreted to mean "any consequence of an attack which directly enhances friendly military operations or hinders those of the enemy."[7]

The potential for uncertainty as to what military advantage means and how it is applied is not aided by a general avoidance of the term in everyday discussion about targeting. It has also not been the subject of concerted academic analysis. Rather, the contemporary dialog about targeting focuses on collateral civilian casualties and damage. Practical considerations of the military advantage are often masked by the use of terms such as "high-value target,"[8] and assessing the "effects" of an attack to achieve a particular objective.[9] This has meant that from a legal perspective, what actually constitutes a military advantage is often glossed over or sometimes not addressed at all.

Perhaps the clearest example of the degree to which the term military advantage represents an underdeveloped concept, and one about which there has been little consensus, is found in the different ways it is said to be applicable. The analysis of military advantage has centered on two almost polar opposite interpretations. On the one hand is the reference in the *ICRC Commentary* that "[a] military advantage *can only* consist of ground gained and in annihilating or weakening the enemy armed forces."[10] This statement deals primarily with tactical gains, although it is also noted: "it goes without saying that an attack carried out in a concerted manner in numerous places can only be judged in its entirety."[11] Contrasting the *Commentary* approach is the reservation made by a number of countries when signing *Additional Protocol I* that "the military advantage anticipated from an attack is intended to refer to the advantage anticipated from the attack *considered as a whole* and not from isolated or particular parts of the

[7]Air and Missile Warfare Commentary 2009, para 3. Similarly, see Crawford 2013, p. 167 ("military necessity has come to mean having a military objective, doing something that is useful to win the war"). See also Canadian Law of Armed Conflict Manual 2001, para 202(2) ("Military necessity is related to the primary aim of armed conflict—the complete submission of the enemy at the earliest possible moment with the least possible expenditure of personnel and resources. The concept of military necessity justifies the application of force not forbidden by International Law, to the extent necessary, for the realization of the purpose of armed conflict").

[8]DOD Dictionary 2015.

[9]Schmitt 2006, p. 274.

[10]ICRC Additional Protocol I Commentary 1987, Article 57, para 2218.

[11]Ibid.

attack."[12] This broader interpretation has been reinforced by reference in Article 8(2)(b)(iv) of the Rome Statute to the "overall" military advantage that is anticipated.

States generally adopt a more strategic approach in relying on assessments of the military advantage to be gained. This does not mean that the tactical effects of targeting are not a central part of the consideration of military advantage from a state perspective. However, consistent with a broader interpretation of that term, states such as the United States, Australia, and New Zealand view military advantage as extending to the security of attacking forces.[13] Further, the advantage to be gained can apply to allied or Coalition partners.[14] As will be discussed, taken together, the tactical interpretation found in the *Commentary* and the strategic focus applied by states only scratch the surface of the full scope of military operations and warfare. Separately, they appear to significantly under-represent the challenge facing practitioners, legal analysts, and courts when dealing with targeting issues arising from complex contemporary security operations.

The goal of this article is to consider the role that "military advantage" plays in regulating conflict and violence under humanitarian law. The focus will be on adding "flesh" to the textual "bones" provided under *Additional Protocol I*. This will be done in four parts. First, there is an assessment of how military advantage is situated within the overall legal targeting framework. This will establish the critical role that term plays in identifying the wide range of objects that may be targeted as military objectives. Consideration is also given to the application of military advantage as the counterweight to collateral civilian effects when assessing the proportionality of an attack. This analysis highlights that military advantage does not have a different meaning when looked at as part of the definition of an objective, as compared to being a factor considered when assessing proportionality.

Second, the meaning of military advantage is assessed as a "value"-based concept, with the anticipated advantage being interpreted as an indication of the importance of the target. It becomes evident that military advantage is a broad concept, and cannot be limited solely to consideration of the relative importance of the objective being targeted. As will be highlighted, the existing doctrinal focus is on "high value" targets, which can mask the requirement to consider a wider range of factors affect the assessment of military advantage. This is followed by consideration of military advantage in terms of targeting people and objects, and the impact that lower value targets can have on consideration of the advantages to be gained from an attack, the manner in which attacks may be carried out, and any assessment of excessive collateral civilian casualties and damage. The issue of context is then explored to establish it as an essential requirement when making decisions about military advantage. This includes consideration of a broader strategic perspective of where that target fits within the overall military campaign.

---

[12] Henckaerts and Doswald-Beck 2005, p. 49.

[13] Dinstein 2010, para 228.

[14] Ibid.

The third area of analysis looks at the judicial treatment of military advantage and its relationship with proportionality. What becomes evident is that courts are just beginning to deal with these complicated targeting issues. This analysis highlights the complexity of the issues involved, and some of the challenges facing courts as they are asked to interpret this area of humanitarian law. What becomes evident is that the judiciary will have to consider not only scientific evidence regarding the efficacy of targeting, but also issues of morality and the exercise of professional military judgment when considering how military advantage works within the humanitarian law targeting framework. Ultimately, the proportionality assessment, which involves the weighing of anticipated military advantage and collateral effects, will be seen to lack the precision often claimed to be associated with science-based efforts to resolve this difficult issue. It is also suggested that courts will have to consider the operational context within which targeting decisions are made, with the result that there remains in certain situations the potential for significantly higher collateral civilian casualties and damage when protecting particularly important military, political, or commercial interests.

Finally, the relationship between military advantage and the manner in which warfare is actually conducted from a strategic, operational, and tactical perspective is explored. The assessment of military advantage requires knowledge not only of the technical aspects of humanitarian law, but also the operational context within which that law is applied. Therefore, understanding how wars are fought, and in particular the impact of the levels of war on how hostilities are conducted is critical to assessing military advantage in contemporary conflict. From a strategic perspective the unique role performed by air power will be explored. This includes considering efforts to strategically influence a civilian population and its leadership, which is subject to the overriding prohibition on terrorizing that same population. The issues that arise from assessing military advantage in the context of a strategic targeting campaign are also identified. Finally, the unique manner in which the military advantage during counterinsurgency and counterterrorism operations will be considered. The result will normally be significantly more limited attacks and less justifiable collateral injury and damage. Fighting among the population forces consideration of the negative strategic impact on the civilian population of many attacks, which alters the assessment of military advantage. This leads to an operational approach that prioritizes the protection of the civilians who are not taking a direct part in hostilities.

13.2 Military Advantage and the Targeting Framework

In assessing military advantage, it is helpful to first situate the term in the regulatory framework governing targeting. Military advantage is referred to in two articles of *Additional Protocol I* that are particularly integral to the targeting process: the identification of military objects and the test for excessive collateral damage (i.e., proportionality).[15] The definition of a military object in Article 52(2) of the *Protocol* provides that:

> In so far as objects are concerned, military objectives are limited to those objects which by their nature, location, purpose or use make an effective contribution to military action and whose total or partial destruction, capture or neutralization, in the circumstances ruling at the time, offers a definite military advantage.

The term "definite" has been noted to have no apparent dissonance with the use of "obvious" found in an earlier articulation of military objective in the 1923 *Hague Rules of Air Warfare*, which never became binding at law.[16] It has been suggested "[t]he thrust is that of 'a concrete and perceptible advantage rather than a hypothetical and speculative one.'"[17]

Military advantage is not one of the criteria specifically set out in *Additional Protocol I* for ascertaining whether persons are lawful targets. People become "targetable" due to their direct participation in hostilities, either as members of armed forces, organized armed groups, or as civilians undertaking such activity.[18] In this respect, it is too limiting, and overly formalistic to think of membership in armed forces as simply being a "status" issue. There is also a real danger of conflating status in terms of attaining prisoner of war protection with the issue of whether members of the armed forces take a direct part in hostilities. In assessing membership in regular armed forces, as well as organized armed groups, consideration must be given to the function those persons perform. It is not simply a question of whether domestic criteria for enrollment in the armed forces are met or whether a uniform is worn.[19] Members in both regular armed forces, and organized armed groups carry out combat, combat support, or combat support functions, which reflect a "combat function" related to direct participation in hostilities.[20] Although Article 3 of the *1907 Hague Land Warfare Regulations* reflects a nineteenth century notion that there can be both combatant and noncombatant members of armed forces it is a concept that has narrowed considerably over course of the twentieth

---

[15]The term "military advantage" is also found in AP I, Article 51(5)(b) in the examples of indiscriminate attacks, and Article 57(2)(b) regarding when an attack should be canceled or suspended. However, these references are substantially the same as that found in the test for excessive collateral damage found in Article 57(2)(a)(iii) and will be dealt with in that context.

[16]Dinstein 2010, para 226.

[17]Ibid [Professor Dinstein quotes Solf 1982, p. 326.].

[18]AP I, arts. 43(2) and 51(3). See also AP II, Article 1(1) (For reference to "organized armed groups").

[19]ICRC Interpretive Guidance 2009, p. 25. For a critique of this domestic law approach see Watkin 2010, pp. 651–52.

[20]Watkin 2010, pp. 690–93 and Pomper 2012, p. 189 (for a discussion of the combat support and combat service support functions common to regular armed forces and organized armed groups). See also Watkin 2010, pp. 683–86 (for a discussion of "combat function," in contrast to "continuous combat function"). Note that even the ICRC Interpretive Guidance 2009, p. 16 links membership to "continuous combat function" and ultimately a direct part in hostilities.

century, as is reflected in Article 43 of *Additional Protocol I*.[21] All members of regular armed forces and organized armed groups (other than medical personnel and chaplains) perform functions that involve direct participation in hostilities.[22]

It has been suggested "the core criteria for the assessment of military necessity [in *Additional Protocol I*, Article 52(2)], namely military action must be reasonably expected to lead to a 'definite military advantage,' can be generalized and applied also to action against persons."[23] It is not clear why this suggested blending of criteria is necessary, or even desirable. As will be discussed, the range of valid military objects is considerably broader than it is for persons. The "object" unique limiting criterion of "military action" is not easily divorced from its nature, purpose, location, and use; effective contribution; destruction, capture, or neutralization; and "circumstances ruling at the time" factors. Importantly, the suggested introduction of the military object focused criteria into an assessment of targeting people could have the unintended and highly undesirable consequences of watering down the protection available to persons. The danger is that people will come to be treated as "objects." *Additional Protocol I* incorporates a significantly more limiting criterion in the form of requiring persons being targeted to be taking a direct part in hostilities either as members of armed forces and organized armed groups or as individual civilians. Such participation inherently contributes to military action.

It is Article 57(2)(a)(iii) of *Additional Protocol I* that sets out the test for assessing if an attack, either against military objects or persons, may be expected to cause collateral casualties or damage "which would be excessive in relation to the *concrete and direct* military advantage to be gained." The meaning of the term "concrete and direct" has proven difficult to decipher. For the ICRC it is suggested to show:

> That the advantage concerned should be substantial and relatively close, and that advantages which are hardly perceptible and those which should appear in the long term should be disregarded.[24]

However, as Yoram Dinstein rightly indicates, this paraphrasing is problematic since "substantial" is not synonymous with "concrete."[25]

---

[21]Baxter 1988, p. 104, quoted in Watkin 2005, p. 4 n 7 [where it is noted the term "combatant" was not a technical treaty term and had been used "in a general sense to describe any member of the "fighting" armed forces, (other than medical personnel and chaplains and service and support personnel), or any civilian who engages in combat"]. However, see now, AP I, Article 43 ["Members of the armed forces of a Party to a conflict (other than medical personnel and chaplains…) are combatants, that is to say, they have the right to participate directly in hostilities." Unlike the historical approach, under this definition combat service support and combat support personnel would be included as combatants].

[22]Watkin 2010, pp. 691 ("Such a [combat] function would involve combat, combat support, and combat service support functions, carrying arms openly, exercising command over the armed group, carrying out planning related to the conduct of hostilities, or other activities indicative of membership in an armed group").

[23]Melzer 2008, p. 292.

[24]ICRC Additional Protocol I Commentary 1987, Article 57, para 2209. See also Tallin Manual 2013, pp. 161–62 (where this test was adopted.).

[25]Dinstein 2010, p. 134, para 328. See also Melzer 2008, p. 293.

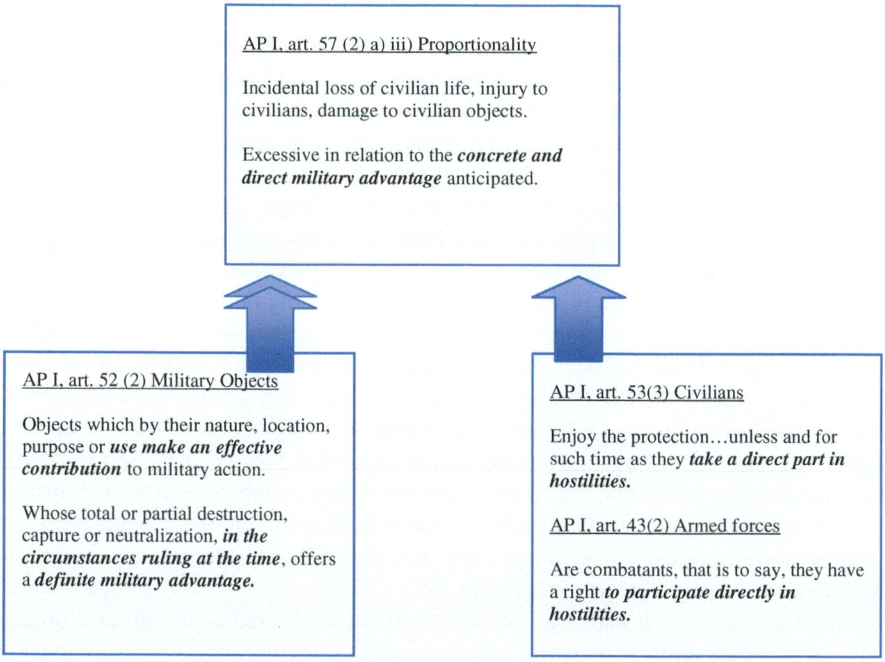

Fig. 13.1 Main factors relevant to an *Additional Protocol I* targeting assignment

A plain reading of the text of the *Protocol* highlights that military advantage is ordinarily assessed twice when considering an attack on military objects and once for attacks on persons. Figure 13.1 sets out the main factors relevant to such an *Additional Protocol I* targeting assessment.

As has been noted, the lack of a specific reference to military advantage in *Additional Protocol I* when identifying which "persons" may be targeted highlights the different nature of the two types of military objectives. The targeting of persons is restricted to those taking a direct part in hostilities. While attempts to definitively interpret what is meant by direct participation in hostilities have proven controversial[26] It is clear that persons only providing indirect support cannot be targeted, although the test for participation is not as narrow as the *ICRC Interpretive Guidance* seeks to suggest.[27] This can be contrasted with the targeting of military objects. These targets include a broad set of objects that both directly and indirectly support military action. A key aspect of the test for establishing an object as a military objective is whether the potential target makes an effective contribution to military action.

---

[26] ICRC Interpretive Guidance 2009 (for the ICRC interpretation of what direct participation means). For a critique of its findings see Watkin 2010, p. 641, Schmitt 2010, p. 697, Boothby 2010, p. 741 and Parks 2010, p. 769. See also the reply in Melzer 2010, p. 831.

[27] Watkin 2010, pp. 683–86.

A civilian object can lose his or her immunity from attack "through use that is only indirectly related to combat action, but which nevertheless makes an effective contribution to the military part of the overall war-fighting capability."[28] This includes "activities providing administrative and logistical support to military operations such as transportation and communications systems, railroads, airfields and port facilities and industries of fundamental importance for the conduct of armed conflict."[29] The targeting of industries and similar war supporting targets highlights the economic aspect of traditional interstate conflict. As Leslie Green noted, military objectives can include "economic targets that indirectly but effectively support enemy operations."[30] The conduct of economic warfare is also evident in the authority under international humanitarian law for a state to conduct naval[31] and aerial blockades,[32] the visit and search of ships[33] and the inspection and interception of aircraft.[34] Indeed it would appear out of step to suggest that there is no ability to conduct economic coercion during armed conflict, when a significant tool for forcing states to comply with United Nations direction has been the imposition of economic sanctions applicable even during peacetime.[35] Further, reference to blockade is specifically found in Article 42 of the *United Nations Charter* setting out the enforcement measures that may be authorized to maintain or restore international peace or security.[36]

The potential for a broader set of objects to be considered to be military objectives, in comparison to a narrower category of persons, is reflected in the general effort following World War II to cease the consideration of factory workers being legitimate targets as a form of quasi-combatant.[37] These workers are civilians and

---

[28]San Remo Manual 1995, p. 117, para 40.12.

[29]Ibid, p. 117, para 40.11.

[30]Green 2008, pp. 218–219.

[31]San Remo Manual 1995, pp. 176–180. For an outline of the legal requirements of blockade see the Turkel Commission (2011), pp. 38–45, paras 29–36.

[32]Air and Missile Warfare Commentary 2009, pp. 287–300.

[33]San Remo Manual 1995, pp. 195–205.

[34]Air and Missile Warfare Commentary 2009, pp. 272–86.

[35]Cortright and Lopez (2002), p. 1 ("...in a relatively brief time and in diverse and numerous ways, sanctions have become integral, if not indispensable, instruments of multilateral action, designed to preserve regional security or enhance the prospects for effective regional peacekeeping."). See also Allen 2006, p. 122 n. 16 (for reference to "maritime interdiction operations" being the term applied to naval operations used to enforce United Nations imposed embargos and lawfully imposed sanctions).

[36]*United Nations Charter*, Article 42 ("Such action may include demonstrations, *blockade*, and other operations by air, sea, or land forces of Members of the United Nations.") (Emphasis added).

[37]Spaight 1947, pp. 44–47 (outlining the approach suggested prior to World War II that men and women who worked as munitions factories were quasi-combatants. In this 1947 analysis the author criticizes the trend to treat such workers as noncombatants).

can no longer be targeted.[38] However, there has been no similar restriction on treating the factories or industries in which they work as lawful objectives. Having identified this broader set of targets the question then turns to what military advantage accrues to attacks on objects that may only indirectly support the overall war-fighting capability of an enemy. Because a similar assessment of military advantage is not required at this stage in respect of persons taking a direct part in hostilities, this may suggest that the need to consider the military advantage of targeting objects arises particularly from the indirect nature of their impact on war-fighting capability. The result is that in respect of objects the military advantage is assessed both in the military objective identification phase and during the proportionality assessment.

This raises a question as to whether military advantage is to be interpreted in the same manner in both situations. It has been suggested that "the words 'concrete and direct' impose stricter conditions on the attacker than those implied by the criteria defining military objectives in Article 52."[39] However, the *ICRC Commentary* also acknowledges that there is no historical record why the various expressions were used, but that all the conditions must be fulfilled.[40] The strict narrower view of Article 52 might be interpreted as establishing a two-step assessment of the military advantage to be gained from an attack. A broader test for military advantage would apply to what constitutes a military object, while a narrower "concrete and direct" test would then modify the application of the same term during an assessment of whether there are excessive collateral casualties or damage. However, in practical terms if the modifying words "concrete and direct" found in Article 57(2)(a)(iii) of *Additional Protocol I* were intended to narrow the meaning of military advantage it is likely that would have been clearly stated. In addition, as is reflected in interpretations of the meaning of "definite"[41] and "concrete and direct."[42] These terms appear to be focused on the same goal, ensuring clarity and avoiding speculative or hypothetical claims of military advantage to be gained from an attack. The *Oxford English Dictionary* definitions of definite ("clearly stated or decided; not vague or doubtful"), concrete ("existing in a material or physical form; not abstract"), and direct ("extending or moving from one place to another without changing direction or stopping") support this conclusion.[43]

---

[38]Bothe et al. 1982, p. 303 and ICRC Additional Protocol I Commentary 1987, Article 51, para 1945 ("There should be a clear distinction between direct participation in hostilities and participation in the war effort.").

[39]ICRC Additional Protocol I Commentary 1987, Article 57, para 2218.

[40]ICRC Additional Protocol I Commentary 1987, Article 52, paras 2027–2028.

[41]Dinstein 2010, pp. 92–93, para 226 ("[t]he thrust is that of 'a concrete and perceptible advantage rather than a hypothetical and speculative one'").

[42]ICRC Additional Protocol I Commentary 1987, Article 57, para 2209 ("That the advantage concerned should be substantial and relatively close, and that advantages which are hardly perceptible and those which should appear in the long term should be disregarded").

[43]Oxford English Dictionary. However, see Boivin and Sandoz 2006, p. 21 (where it is acknowledged the term "definite" is similar to the "concrete and direct" wording used in relation to military advantage in the proportionality assessment, but still suggests the "latter wording appears to introduce an additional element of specificity").

In addition, in practical terms it is the proportionality version of the test that would ordinarily become determinative if it was given a more narrow meaning. The targeting precautions must always be applied. Given the increased likelihood that conflicts will occur in urban settings, the predominance of counterinsurgency and counterterrorism, and the increased use of civilian contractors to support state armed forces, the circumstances under which fighting will take place in an environment where there is no likelihood of civilian casualties or damage are increasingly limited. Trying to employ a two-stage test would not only be administratively wasteful and confusing in application, it could in a variety of circumstances be unrealistic given the time constrained situations under which many targeting decisions have to be made. Further, the test applied for interpreting military advantage has to work not only when considering the deliberate prosecution of targets during a strategic air campaign, which may number daily in their thousands, but also has to be relied on by individual soldiers deciding whether to fire on a tactical objective situated immediately before them. In any event, notwithstanding an evident willingness under international law to apply different meaning to terms such as proportionality the same should not be the case in respect of military advantage.[44] Given the repeated use of "military advantage" in the context of the same activity: targeting, that term would most likely retain the same meaning independent of any modifying words, which themselves do not substantively distinguish its application.

Greater insight into what military advantage means can be gained by looking at the definition of military objective. While the concepts of military action and military advantage found in that definition are invariably linked, the former relates to a concrete "military engagement,"[45] while an advantage pertains to "a condition or circumstance that puts one in a favourable or superior position."[46] After first determining that an object provides an effective contribution to military action, the analysis turns to the advantage gained from its "total or partial destruction, capture or neutralization."[47] The gain is observed in the "effect" arising from any attack. Therefore, buried in the definition of military objective is the very theoretical framework that has been a hallmark of contemporary military doctrinal approaches toward targeting. That is "effects-based" targeting. Under the effects-based theory, the goal is to create a desired effect from the prosecution of a target that accomplishes targeting-related tasks and objectives for the military force involved.[48] The assessment of the effects of an attack inevitably leads to consideration of the "value" that a particular target provides in advancing the war effort. As William Boothby suggests, effects-based targeting represents both something old and new.[49] The old aspect of the theory is perhaps best represented by

---

[44]Barak 2012, p. 202 ("Proportionality is a general concept of international law. It serves several functions."). See Franck 2008, p. 715.

[45]Oxford English Dictionary (from the definition of the noun "action" as it pertains to armed conflict).

[46]Ibid (definition of "advantage").

[47]AP I, Article 52(2).

[48]Joint Targeting 2013, para 4. A.

[49]Boothby 2012, pp. 497–498.

Clausewitz's approach to war, regarding it "as an act of violence intended to compel our opponent to fulfill our will."[50] The new twist in its application seeks to "deliver a tangible measured, and focused message or stimulus to the enemy with the purpose that message or stimulus will produce a particular effect that has been identified in advance."[51] It is a message focused on the destruction of systemic capabilities.

13.3 Military Advantage and the "Value" of Targets

13.3.1 High-Value Targets

While the determination of what constitutes a valid military object involves an assessment of both military action and military advantage, it is the later part of the test that is relevant to the consideration of excessive collateral civilian casualties and damage. Because military advantage is also a factor to be considered under Article 57(2)(a)(iii) of *Additional Protocol I*, an analysis of the meaning of the term in that context can also aid in consideration of its application in Article 52 of that same *Protocol*. It is in the context of the proportionality assessment where the idea that military advantage is linked to the value to be gained from an attack becomes particularly evident. This is perhaps most evident in the widespread use of the term "high-value target."[52] The value-laden nature of the test is reflected in the fact that what is often referred to colloquially as a proportionality assessment is actually derived from the medieval moral doctrine of "double effect."[53] It is a moral doctrine that has been codified as a legal rule in *Additional Protocol I*.[54] That rule has ultimately provided the basis for a war crime, albeit with an additional element being added that the collateral civilian casualties and damage must be "clearly" excessive.[55]

The Israeli case *Public Committee Against Torture in Israel v. Gov't of Israel* (widely referred to as the *Targeted Killings Case*), the judicial decision that has most comprehensively dealt with targeting, confirmed that the proportionality assessment is a "values[-]based test" focused on "a balancing between conflicting values and interests," where "the benefit stemming from the attainment of the proper military objective is proportionate to the damage caused to innocent

[50]Von Clausewitz 1976, p. 75.

[51]Boothby 2012, p. 498.

[52]DOD Dictionary 2015.

[53]Walzer 2000, pp. 151–153.

[54]AP I, Article 57(2)(a)(iii).

[55]*Rome Statute Of The International Criminal Court*, 2187 U.N.T.S. 90, *Entered Into Force* July 1, 2002, Article 8(2)(b)(iv).

civilians harmed by it."[56] The reference to value does not mean it is exclusively connected to "morality." This can be seen by the use of terms such as "benefit" and "interest" by the Israeli court. One of the challenges in using the term "value" is that it can have so many meanings. Value in terms of military advantage is primarily applied as a question of the importance, worth, or usefulness gained from attacking a target, rather than a principle or standard of behavior, or a numerical amount.[57] This does not mean the requirement to consider the value of a human life, which engages significant issues of morality, is not relevant to military advantage. For example, the right to life of a soldier is an important humanitarian and human rights law consideration.[58] Value judgments about the right to life arise most often in the context of weighing the military advantage to be gained against the collateral civilian effects of an attack.[59] Value may also have a numerical component. As will be discussed, the use of science and mathematical indicators (e.g., percentages) as objective indicators for assessing attacks is a significant part of the contemporary dialogue about targeting. However, in respect of military advantage, "value" appears to be used most often as a form of shorthand providing some indication of the relative benefit to be gained from an attack in order to meet the objectives of a military operation.

While the term "value" gained broad use, the linking of military advantage solely to that concept is too limiting. The advantage to be gained may not simply be a question of the importance of a target, but can also flow from the purpose of the attack, or manner in which it is carried out. A classic example of the effect of the purpose of the attack is seen in Yoram Dinstein's reference to a raid not having any perceptible military advantage on its own, however, "it is justified by misleading the enemy to shift its strategic gaze to the wrong sector of the front…."[60] In terms of the manner of an attack, there is an advantage in limiting risk to your own forces in order to maintain your fighting strength, saving precision munitions for other attacks, or, as will be seen in the case of the Osama bin Laden raid, conducting an operation in a way that enables you to prove the identify of a target.

The fact that the proportionality test ultimately involves an assessment of the advantage gained in destroying, capturing or neutralizing military forces, or "things" in comparison to the loss of civilian life is what makes this area of law so

[56]*Public Committee Against Torture in Israel v. Israel*, Israel Supreme Court [16 December 2006], 46 ILM 375, para 45. See Roach 2011, pp. 124–28 (for a discussion of the *Targeted Killings Case*).

[57]Oxford Dictionary (the meaning of "value" includes: "[t]he regard that something is held to deserve; the importance, worth, or usefulness of something," "[p]rinciples or standards of behaviour; one's judgement of what is important in life," or "[t]he numerical amount denoted by an algebraic term; a magnitude, quantity, or number").

[58]Meron 2000, pp. 266–67 (Human rights and humanitarian law "share a common 'core' of fundamental standards which are applicable at all times, in all circumstances and to all parties, and from which no derogation is permitted").

[59]AP I, Article 57(2)(iii).

[60]Dinstein 2010, para 232.

challenging. The problem created is that "[s]ince the quantities being measured, civilian losses and military advantage, are dissimilar, it is not possible to establish any reasonably exact proportionality equation between them."[61] As Thomas Franck has noted, the assessment of proportionality is "likely to require the awkward balancing of apples and oranges."[62] However, there has been a tendency to try and "concretize" the inevitable disparity in factors that have to be considered by turning to "scientific" analysis.[63] This reliance on science can be seen in efforts to reduce the quandaries to ones that might be solvable by the use of computer programs, such as the insensitively entitled "Bugsplat,"[64] which was later to be called the Fast Assessment Strike Tool-Collateral Damage (FAST-CD).[65] The FAST-CD program was used "for estimating collateral damage for 'time-sensitive targets' in both Afghanistan and Iraq because it could take a little as 5 min to run the estimate."[66] Such tools represent a concentrated effort since the 1991 Gulf War to apply computer modeling to assess both collateral casualties and damage anticipated from an attack.[67]

The use of scientific tools for determining the collateral effects of air campaigns was almost inevitable since there can be hundreds of planned sorties per day,[68] as well as a large proportion of unplanned targets.[69] Both the terminology (e.g., Bugsplat) and the search for a scientific answer to the value-laden issues that arise from the assessment of collateral casualties and damage provide some indication of the overall objectification of these aspects of the targeting process. Accepting that computer models can provide helpful guidance, there are inevitably limits to the application of such analytical approaches. Even high-tech "digital"

[61] Fenrick 1982, p. 92.

[62] Franck 2008, p. 716.

[63] Oxford Dictionary (where "science" is defined as "the intellectual and practical activity encompassing the systematic study of the structure and behavior of the physical and natural world through observation and experiment…").

[64] Meilinger 2013, p. 17 (for a description of the software targeting program called "Bugsplat"). See also Boothby 2012, p. 478 [for an outline of the operation of a computerized assessment of damage taken from Roblyer 2003, p. 18].

[65] Crawford 2013, p. 351.

[66] Ibid.

[67] Ibid, pp. 350–51. (where it is explained engineering estimates were computed for collateral damage assessments in respect of each individual target during the first Gulf War. This led to the development of programs such as the Conventional Casualty Estimation Tool (CCET) and Collateral Damage Estimation Tool (CDET) for the 1999 Kosovo campaign. A requirement to speed up collateral damage estimates led to the development of FAST CD and ultimately Advanced CDET and FAST-CD 2.0).

[68] Boyne 2005, p. 379 (In Iraq between March 19 to 20 and April 25, 2003 the Coalition forces flew nearly 50,000 fixed wing missions. Thirty-six percent were strike sorties that dropped 28,820 munitions).

[69] Murray and Scales 2003, pp. 170–171 (During that same war 1,500 to 2,000 sorties were launched per day over a two-day period. However, of these attacks just 500 targets were preplanned in each 24-hour period).

solutions are not particularly well suited to dealing with time sensitive targets, or action taken in self-defense by troops in contact with the enemy where the pilot of an aircraft may only be provided GPS coordinates and a general description of a building or location to be attacked.[70] A reliance on scientifically tangible criteria, rather than wrestling with the importance of human life, can be seen in the use of numbers of persons killed or injured to establish the different command levels at which authority must be given to conduct certain types of strikes.[71] Science may make it easier to conclude the identified advantage appears to be "concrete and direct."[72] However, this approach does not reflect the breadth of the factors that have to be considered in successfully conducting military operations, or considering the advantage to be gained from an attack.

The "values" issue, and therefore assessing what constitutes a military advantage, can be a complex one. Even within a theoretical construct where all life is considered to be of equal value, the discussion sometimes shifts to consideration of factors such as gender and age. Therefore "military-age males" might more readily be considered targets,[73] and special weight is given the loss of life involving women and children.[74] There have also periodically been suggestions that military personnel give up their right to life,[75] although the *Targeted Killings Case* clearly identified that risk to the life of soldiers is a factor to be considered when assessing whether a terrorist had to be captured or a targeted killing could be carried out.[76] However, in trying to make sense of the military advantage standard the assigning of a different value to targets in terms of their relative importance, even when dealing with "humans" who have a right to life, is almost inevitable.

---

[70]Meilinger 2013.

[71]D Jehl and E Schmitt, "Errors Are Seen in Early Attacks on Iraqi Leaders," *NY Times* (13 June 2004), http://www.nytimes.com/2004/06/13/world/struggle-for-iraq-intelligence-errors-are-seen-early-attacks-iraqi-leaders.html?pagewanted=allandsrc=pm (accessed 26 March 2015) (where it is indicated that during the 2003 Iraq invasion United States commanders "were required to obtain advance approval from Mr. Rumsfeld if any planned airstrike was likely to result in the deaths of 30 more civilians. More than 50 such raids were proposed, and all were approved." Time sensitive attacks were not subject to that constraint.). See also Crawford 2013, p. 355.

[72]AP I, Article 57 (2) (iii).

[73]The Civilian Impact Of Drones 2012, p. 32. See also Montalvo 2013, p. 17 n 25 (where it is suggested "[t]his term was eliminated from the military vernacular because it was applied too broadly by service members, which led to unnecessary detentions and the unsupportable use of deadly force").

[74]"*U.S. drone strike kills 20 people in Pakistan," Reuters* (23August 2010), http://www.reuters.com/article/2010/08/23/us-pakistan-drone-idUSTRE67M44U20100823 (accessed 25 March 2015) ("They said the missiles were fired at a militant hideout. Most of the militants killed were members of the Afghan Taliban. Four women and three children were among the dead, said the officials").

[75]Abresch 2005, p. 757 ("the combatant trades his right to life for the right to kill") and McKeogh 2002, p164 (where it is suggested soldiers are to be treated as "instruments").

[76]*Public Committee Against Torture in Israel v. Israel*, Israel Supreme Court [16 December 2006], 46 ILM 375, para 40.

Given the exceptionally complex nature of armed conflict, and the potential for a broad range of targets, there is significant scope for the prioritization of military advantage. The United States has one of the best developed and most sophisticated targeting doctrines. That doctrine requires the prioritization of targets, as is reflected in terms such as "target priority"[77] and "Joint Integrated Prioritized Target List" (JIPTL).[78] Further, in the conduct of targeting, such as during an air campaign, attacks are planned in a systemic way involving "[a]n all-source examination of potential target systems to determine relevance to stated objectives, military importance, and priority of attack."[79] The concept of priority is particularly relevant to the sequencing of attacks as part of the effort to conduct the military operation in the most efficient and effective manner. It is not that the importance of a target from a military perspective is not relevant. For example, a target may be identified as being of particular importance to the accomplishment of a mission, or such a threat to friendly forces and allies that it is considered to be time sensitive thereby warranting priority attention.[80] Further, it is clear that attacks must be conducted in accordance with humanitarian law.[81] As part of that assessment, the value of the target may be considered such as when assessing the purpose or use made of an object by an enemy.[82]

However, this process does not clearly indicate what makes one target more important than another such that it receives priority attention. Unfortunately, the relative value of a target and the impact a lower value target might have on the proportionality assessment does not appear to be fully explored. The absence of a focus on lower value targets is represented in the fact that the *DOD Dictionary* only provides a definition for "high-value targets" (HVT) and "High Payoff Targets" (HPT), but not those of lesser importance. An HVT is defined in a rather anodyne fashion as, "[a] target the *enemy commander* requires for the successful completion of the mission," while a HPT is "[a] target whose *loss to the enemy* will *significantly contribute* to the success of the friendly course of action."[83] Reference can also be found to "High Value Individuals" (HVI).[84] It is states themselves that have developed this HVT terminology. On one level, the doctrine appears to act as a time/resource allocation guide. However, what the doctrine does not appear to concretely address is the value of a target if its destruction contributes, but not in a significant way, to friendly action or does not provide as advantageous an outcome as other targets.

[77]DOD Dictionary (2015)("A grouping of targets with the indicated sequence of attack").

[78]Ibid ("A prioritized list of targets approved and maintained by the joint force commander").

[79]Ibid (the definition of "Target System Analysis"). See also Joint Targeting 2013, p xi (where target system analysis is identified as part of Phase 2 Target identification and prioritization).

[80]Joint Targeting 2013, p xi.

[81]Ibid, Appendix A ("Legal Considerations in Targeting").

[82]Ibid, A-4, para 4.b.(4).

[83]DOD Dictionary (2015)(emphasis added).

[84]Joint Targeting 2013, pp. I-27 and I-28.

An HPT is derived from the list of HVTs and can include time sensitive targets.[85] It appears that a high value is defined in respect of the enemy's reliance on the target (HVT) and the impact of its loss to the enemy (HPT). In both cases the focus is on mission success, in one case the enemy's, and in the other, the friendly forces. The value of a target may be considered in terms of its "relative military, economic, political, psychological, informational, environmental, cultural, or geographic importance."[86] What is not clear is how a target that is not a high-value one is defined. Consistent with its being a targeting doctrine developed with an interstate conventional conflict in mind, it appears the prioritization of targets is anticipated to take place in a "target-rich" environment where there will be a need to prioritize among a large number of HVTs. Overall, the doctrinal focus on HVTs with a definition that is expansively worded is not particularly helpful in ascertaining what might constitute a medium- or low value target. In this respect, there is a danger that widespread reference to high-value in a targeting context can undermine the significance of the term. The degree to which the term has entered common military parlance and may be losing some of its impact is reflected in the unit infiltrating Fallujah in November 2004 ahead of the main assault calling itself "Task Force HVT."[87]

The HVT definition is also not particularly helpful in dealing with contemporary counterinsurgency and counterterrorism operations. The post-9/11 focus on kinetically dismantling terrorist and insurgent organizations reflects a different and more layered assessment of the value of targets. This appears particularly evident when the value of a target is assessed in terms of the position held, or function performed within a terrorist organization. This has included referring to terrorist groups being organized in "tiers," although it has also been suggested with respect to Al Qaeda in Iraq, "this was entirely a feature of the American analytical approach rather than a description of the genuine levels within the jihadist organization."[88] Targets having a high value clearly do exist. Even with the existence of terrorist groups that take on networked, horizontal, or cellular organizational structures, there will be leaders, or members with special technical skills, who perform particularly important functions. The term "high-value target" has also been used to identify other priority targets. For example, direction was provided for the April 2004 assault on Fallujah that "[r]aids will be conducted against regimental high-value targets," which included the killers of four Blackwater security contractors.[89] The March 2004 Blackwater incident, which became the subject of newscasts throughout the United States and the Middle-East, had at the same time

[85]Ibid, para 5 c.

[86]Ibid, para 3.d.(4)(b)1.a.

[87]Camp 2009, p. 197.

[88]Urban 2010, p. 152 (for al-Qaeda in Iraq, Tier 1 terrorists where those in direct contact with its leader, Zarqawi; Tier 2 were leaders in local or regional areas; and Tier 3 were ordinary fighters).

[89]Camp 2009, p. 63.

emboldened the insurgency,[90] and heightened American resolve to hunt down the criminals involved and pacify Fallujah.[91]

What is not entirely evident is when or how a relative value is assigned to a target in the context within which targeting takes place. In a counterterrorism context, a "high-value target" is a term that has gained greater prominence through its use to justify targeted killing, particularly through the use of drones to strike at leaders of terrorist groups such as Al Qaeda. It appears to be the perceived strategic value of removing a terrorist leader that elevates the relative importance of such a target. It seems inevitable that the use of a term like "high-value," or "Tier-1" to describe the target, and therefore the military benefit to be gained from a successful strike, carries with it the connotation of an acceptance of greater collateral injury or death.[92] In this regard the family, friends, and close associates of higher value targets can often be at greater risk than their counterparts found in the proximity of "medium"- or "low"-value targets. However, this may not always be the case. Precision munitions can often be employed to lessen collateral effects.

When targeting terrorists and insurgents, there is usually a correlation between the value of the target and where the person stands in the leadership hierarchy. This conclusion is consistent with the participation in armed conflict and terrorism being fundamentally a group activity. There can be little doubt that leaders such as Osama bin Laden, Abu Musab al-Zarqawi and Hakimullah Meshud qualified as high-value targets. However, the value from an organizational perspective may also arise from the function the targeted person performs. In this context individuals possessing particular technical abilities, such as in the realm of bomb making, would logically elevate their status in terms of an opponent wanting to neutralize them and as result the threat they pose. This could have included a former member of the Iraqi intelligence service, Mohammad Khudair al-Dulaimi, "an expert in sabotage, assassinations and setting up remote-controlled explosions," who is reported to have joined the insurgency following the 2003 invasion.[93] How valuable a target might be logically could relate to their span of control within the group and their influence over the conduct of operations and terrorist acts. Paying particular attention to leaders and technical experts of the terrorist organizations that they face appears to occur in an Israeli context.[94]

---

[90]Ibid, pp. 1–7

[91]Ibid, p. 7 (where the United States deputy operations officer for the Joint Task Force in Iraq is quoted as stating "We will hunt down the criminals. We will kill or we will capture them…and we will pacify Fallujah").

[92]Gardam 2004, p. 100.

[93]Hashim 2006, pp. 158–160.

[94]H Sherwood, "Hamas says 'gates of hell opened' as Israel kills military leader in Gaza," *The Guardian* (15 November 2012, http://www.theguardian.com/world/2012/nov/14/israel-assassinates-hamas-military-chief (outlining that the leader of the Hamas militant wing, Ahmed al-Jabari, was targeted in a drone strike at the outset of Operation Pillar of Defence.). Byman 2011, pp. 307–323.

Clearly if there are high-value targets then there are other targets of lesser value, and presumably in the terminology of the doctrine that have less relative military importance. However, a challenge from a practical perspective is that attacks on most militarily relevant objects are generally considered important and ultimately necessary to defeat the enemy. Combined with an approach adopted by a number of countries that acknowledges an inherent right of self-defense,[95] and broad defensive concepts such as "force protection" there is the potential to make all targets appear important.[96] Such a perception appears to be evident in the objections made by an Afghan Senator to the entry into homes by foreign military forces in Afghanistan. She is reported as stating that "[e]very situation is serious for them…[a]ll those people who have been killed by American soldiers were exceptions."[97] This generalization appears harsh given the challenges of conducting a war among the people; however, it also reflects sensitivity by the population to the use of force during counterinsurgency operations.[98] This raises the question of how the use of force is assessed across the spectrum of conflict when not all targets may be of high value. In other words, how is the military advantage calculated for medium or lower value objects or people, and more importantly what impact does a lesser advantage have on a subsequent proportionality assessment?

13.3.2 Targeting People and "Value"

The military advantage standard referred to in Article 57(2)(a)(iii) applies equally to targets that are persons as it does to objects. The targeting of a low-level terrorist found in a house in a built up urban area with a high density civilian population provides a contemporary example of how a more limited military advantage to be gained from the attack can affect targeting. The limited advantage gained from killing or capturing a "low-value" target, such as an ordinary fighter or "foot soldier" of an organized armed group could directly affect how an operation is conducted. If a high-value target justifies greater collateral effects than when a low value is assigned to a target, the use of force could carry with it, under many circumstances, a lower tolerance for collateral damage when the proportionality assessment is done. In a scenario involving a "low-level" terrorist, a determination

---

[95]Rules Of Engagement Handbook 2009, para 8. ("International law and the domestic laws of all nations recognise a ***right*** of *self-defence,* which is the use of force to defend against *attack* or imminent *attack. Self-defence* is available in all situations, including armed conflict. National laws differ on the definition and content of the right of self-defence.") (emphasis added in bold type).

[96]Gale and Pickering 2007, p. 35.

[97]E Graham-Harrison, "Hamid Karzai urges Afghans to let US forces stay another decade," *The Guardian* (21 November 2013), http://www.theguardian.com/world/2013/nov/21/hamid-karzai-afghans-us-forces-decade (accessed 26 March 2015).

[98]Smith 2007, pp. 3–5 (for reference to the term "war amongst the people.").

may be made that weapons posing a significantly reduced risk of collateral damage should be used. In this respect, the limited advantage to be gained from killing the terrorist could mean that the use of most aerial delivered ordnance, or indirect fire weapons would likely not justify the potential collateral effects to be caused by these weapons systems.

The type of analysis of the method and means used in such an attack is captured in the United Kingdom's *The Joint Service Manual Of The Law Of Armed Conflict* where the impact of the types of weapons chosen and the means adopted is discussed as follows:

> Automatic fire is by its nature less discriminating than single aimed rounds; automatic fire loosed off in the general direction of the enemy may increase the risks to civilians if there are any in the vicinity. Sometimes, especially during fighting in towns, the tactics employed can make a great difference to the control of incidental damage. Artillery fire can cause a lot of incidental damage without any appreciable military advantage. The same military advantage might be just as well achieved by manoeuvre, outflanking or by-passing the objective, rather than direct assault.[99]

This does not mean that airpower and artillery can never be justified in an urban area. In some cases, it may be the weapon of choice, particularly where low yield munitions involving precision technology are available.[100] Much depends upon the tactical situation and the precision with which force is applied. In this regard, the use of airpower and artillery in Fallujah in 2004[101] and airpower in Tripoli in 2011[102] can be contrasted with the Russian assault on Grozny in 1995, which reportedly devastated that city predominately with artillery fire, but also with the use of aerial attacks.[103]

Depending upon the circumstances, the conclusion might also be reached that a capture operation would be appropriate in order to limit adverse collateral effects to the greatest extent possible. However, it is also clear efforts to capture a terrorist or fighter hiding in a house or compound that does not want to be taken alive will

---

[99]The Joint Service Manual Of The Law Of Armed Conflict (2004), para 5.32.4 (2004).

[100]"Security cameras allegedly record IAF strike on Gaza terrorists," *Jerusalem Post* (26 June 2014), http://www.jpost.com/Middle-East/VIDEO-Security-cameras-allegedly-record-IAF-strike-on-Gaza-terrorists-360852 (accessed 25 March 2015)(for a video depicting a highly accurate and low collateral damage use of missiles to strike at terrorist targets in an urban environment).

[101]Ricks 2007, pp. 398–99 (indicating that careful preparation prevented the assault on Fallujah from becoming a bloodbath. That preparation included a warning to the inhabitants of the city prompting a large-scale evacuation.). See also West 2005, pp. 315–16 (while considerable effort was made to limit collateral casualties and damage in Fallujah it is reported that during the November 2004 phase of the battle "[t]here were 540 air strikes and 14,000 artillery and mortar shells fired, as well as 2,500 tank main gun rounds. Eighteen thousand of Fallujah's 39,000 buildings were damaged or destroyed."). However, see Crawford 2013, pp. 283–294 (for a critical assessment of the Fallujah battle).

[102]"Nato air strikes hit Tripoli in heaviest bombing yet," *The Guardian* (24 May 2011), http://www.theguardian.com/world/2011/may/24/nato-airstrikes-tripoli-heaviest-bombing-libya (accessed 26 March 2015).

[103]Joes 2007, pp. 145–146, Shultz and Dew 2006, pp. 124–26, and DiMarco 2012, pp. 166–67.

not necessarily be non-violent.[104] Where the risk is too great to the surrounding population, an attack or an operation to capture the terrorist may have to be delayed altogether if the advantage gained from the attack is limited. The effect of applying the process of analyzing attack precautions in this scenario, including the tactical options, the military advantage to be gained, as well as the risk to civilians and soldiers generally results in a more narrow scope for acceptable civilian collateral death, injury, or damage. It is within this narrower range of proportionality that the military commander exercises discretion, whether framed as a policy decision, or simply professional judgment on how the particular operation is to be conducted.

As has been noted, the military advantage gained in targeting a higher value target may result in justifiably elevated levels of collateral death, injury, and damage. However, that may not always be the case. The planning for and conduct of the 2011 attack on the bin Laden compound in Abbottabad, Pakistan provides an excellent example of the interaction of factors that may be taken into consideration when targeting the most valuable of targets. As was demonstrated in that case, the result was an operation with a lower likelihood of collateral civilian effects despite the high value assigned to the target. The planning for the operation, which involved targeting one of the world's most notorious terrorists, is reported to have continually looked for ways to minimize risk.[105]

A number of attack options were considered. In the final analysis concerns over potential collateral damage in the case of a potential B-52 strike with 2,000-pound bombs,[106] the possibility that a drone strike would not kill the target,[107] a desire to confirm bin Laden's identity,[108] apprehension concerning possible security breaches regarding a joint operation with Pakistani security forces[109] and the preferred outcome of being able to conduct sensitive site exploitation, led to the decision to carryout a raid by Special Forces units.[110] Powerful factors influencing the choice of a raid appears to have been the desire to avoid collateral civilian casualties[111] and "to know for certain that they had killed bin Laden."[112] This is because the military advantage to be gained resulted not only from killing a target that was

[104]Cohen Century 2008, p. 199. See also Murray and Scales 2003, pp. 234–35 (outlining the violence used in the unsuccessful attempt to capture the sons of Saddam Hussein following the Iraq invasion).

[105]Klaidman 2012, p. 243.

[106]Bergen 2012, p. 178 and Schmitt and Shanker 2011, p. 261.

[107]Bergen 2012, p. 200, and Schmitt and Shanker 2011, p. 260.

[108]Bergen 2012, p. 178, and Schmitt and Shanker 2011, p. 261.

[109]Klaidman 2012, p. 235, and Schmitt and Shanker 2011, p. 261.

[110]Bergen 2012, p. 178.

[111]*Ibid.* Schmitt and Shanker 2011, p. 261 and Klaidman 2012, p. 242.

[112]Sanger 2012, p. 86.

of high value, but also by being able to prove it. The requirement for such proof in this instance appears to have significantly affected the means and methods chosen for the raid. It also resulted in the choice of an attack option that offered a lower potential for collateral casualties.

Proof of death is not always necessary or may be established by other means. This in turn could affect the assessment of the military advantage to be gained when considering the available methods and means for other attacks leading to the use of air strikes with no ground incursion. Obtaining proof of death may occur where there has been an aerial strike. For example, in 2008, Colombian armed forces launched an aerial strike from inside Colombian airspace against a senior FARC commander located at a camp inside Ecuador. This attack also involved Colombian forces who "rushed across the border into Ecuador to retrieve [Raul] Reyes's remains and also scooped up a large treasure trove of computer equipment that would turn out to be the most valuable FARC intelligence find ever."[113] In the bin Laden case, it was the exceptionally high value of the target and the apparent likelihood there would be no remains to collect because of the type of air strike required, which resulted in extra steps being taken to prove his death.[114] The daring "boots on the ground" bin Laden operation also highlights the degree to which, under the right tactical situation, the surreptitious entry of compounds has become a routine event for United States Special Forces in the decade following 9/11.[115] The question of whether the proposed dropping of up to thirty-two 2,000-pound bombs to destroy a one-acre compound in an urban area actually would have led to excessive collateral casualties or damage was avoided.[116]

In any event, even before the impact of dropping bombs or using a drone strike needed consideration, there was the question of whether any such attack should even be carried out. It is reported there was only a 50–50 chance the target was bin Laden.[117] As Article 50(3) *Additional Protocol I* states in cases of doubt a person "shall be considered a civilian." The *Customary Law Study* indicates that the United States has not accepted the "doubt" rule as a reflection of customary law in

[113]D Priest, "Covert Action in Columbia," *Washington Post* (21 December 2013) http://www.washingtonpost.com/sf/investigative/2013/12/21/covert-action-in-colombia/ (accessed 26 March 2015). See also M Huwais, "Drone kills three Qaeda suspects in Yemen," *Al Ahkbar* (21 April 2014), http://english.al-akhbar.com/content/us-drone-kills-another-three-yemen (accessed 26 March 2015)(where it is reported that a helicopter retrieved the bodies of three suspected Al Qaeda terrorists killed in a drone strike in Yemen).

[114]Schmitt and Shanker 2011, p. 261 ("How could American officials be certain that bin Laden had been there if his remains were obliterated?").

[115]Owen 2012, p. 174 ("[t]his target wasn't any more complicated than hundreds of others we'd assaulted over the years.") and Bergen 2012, p. 183.

[116]Schmitt and Shanker 2011, p. 261 and Bergen 2012, p. 174.

[117]Klaidman 2012, p. 243 and Bergen 2012, p. 198.

respect of military objects [Article 52(3)].[118] However, it is also evident that the principle of distinction places an obligation on the attacker to separate lawful targets from unlawful ones, thereby meaning that some standard has to be applied. Further, the first precaution under Article 57(2)(i) of that *Protocol* requires that everything be done to verify "the objectives to be attacked are neither civilians nor civilian objects." Assuming a standard of reasonableness, it is difficult to see how a 50 percent chance of certainty would suffice to justify a strike even with the reported availability of especially small drone-fired munitions that could result in limited collateral effect.[119] This fact could also have influenced the choice of a raid over an aerial attack.

The bin Laden operation represents an almost textbook example of the application of precautions in the attack. It was also unique in a number of other respects, not the least of which was the ability of the United States to carry out a covert raid so far within Pakistani territory. The conduct of that raid rather than the use of aerial delivered strikes substantially reduced concerns that the target had not been definitively identified.[120] Had this option not been available, and assuming the target could not have been identified with the certainty necessary to meet the requirement of distinction, greater consideration might have had to be given to an aerial attack. However, the problem of confirmation of success would still have remained. It is in this situation that the very high value of the target, and the significant military advantage to be gained by killing bin Laden, would have had to be assessed against the potentially significant collateral effects. A concern over those collateral effects is reported to have weighed heavily on the planners and the President of the United States, who was the ultimate decision maker.[121] The tactics employed on the raid were such that questions were even raised in the aftermath of the assault as to whether Osama bin Laden could have been captured, although his status as the leader of Al Qaeda, an organized armed group engaged in hostilities with the United States, meant he was lawfully targetable under humanitarian law.[122] A helicopter assault under these circumstances was not without considerable risk. However, the method of attack selected significantly reduced the likelihood of collateral casualties and injury even though planning for these types of operations "always entailed options for massive support for the special forces should they become trapped."[123]

[118]Henckaerts and Doswald-Beck 2005, para 752.

[119]Bergen 2012, p. 200 and Klaidman 2012, p. 243.

[120]Bergen 2012, p. 203.

[121]Ibid, p. 178, Schmitt and Shanker 2011, p. 261 and Klaidman 2012, p. 242.

[122]M Lander and H Cooper, "*New U.S. Account Says Bin Laden Was Unarmed During Raid,*" *NY Times* (3 May 2011), http://www.nytimes.com/2011/05/04/world/asia/04raid.html (accessed 26 March 2015).

[123]Hull 2011, p. 79.

13.3.3 Targeting Objects and "Value"

The assessment of the relative anticipated military advantage is not limited to attacks on persons taking a direct part in hostilities. In targeting objects the question also arises as to what constitutes a high-value target. In some respects the answer may be straightforward. For example, a particular weapons system may pose a unique threat in terms of destructive power or range. During the 1991 Gulf War Saddam Hussein's use of scud missiles to target Israel represented a strategic threat that could have undermined the coalition of states against fighting against Iraq. This resulted in particular attention being paid by Coalition Forces to targeting those missiles in order to avoid a defensive response by Israel, although the threat was never completely neutralized.[124] Similarly, during the 2006 Israel/Hezbollah conflict, the threat posed by intermediate-range rockets,[125] hidden by Hezbollah within the civilian infrastructure in Southern Lebanon, prompted air strikes at the beginning of that conflict that significantly reduced the ability of Hezbollah to attack deep into Israel.[126] Countering the impression that striking high-value targets inevitably leads to excessive collateral damage these attacks are reported to have resulted in 20 Lebanese civilians being killed,[127] even though it was apparently initially estimated by the Israeli Air Force research branch that 100 to 400 civilians could be killed.[128] Successful missions against longer range Hezbollah missiles located in the Beirut area followed these attacks.[129]

However, assessing the relative value of military objects that are not readily associated with military weapons or equipment may not be as straightforward. As has been noted, potential targets can include a broader range of objects extending to what is normally civilian industry and infrastructure being used to indirectly support the war effort. A challenging issue is what the military advantage is to destroying targets that could, as was seen in the 1991 Gulf Conflict, be as diverse as a state's transportation system, oil production and distribution facilities, the electrical power system, and facilities used for nuclear and for Iraq facilities related to chemical and biological weapons production.[130] Targeting decisions are further complicated by the complexity of modern society and interaction between various potential target sets. For example, the electrical grid may provide power to the railroad system, which is a crucial part of the enemy logistic system.[131]

---

[124]Clancy and Stiner 2002, pp. 443–441.

[125]Harel and Issacharoff 2008, pp. 48–49 (for an outline of the missile threat posed by Hezbollah prior to the 2006 conflict). See also Cordesman et al. 2007, pp. 99–105 and Blanford 2011, pp. 337–41.

[126]Harel and Issacharoff 2008, p. 91.

[127]Ibid.

[128]Ibid, p. 80.

[129]Ibid, p. 92.

[130]Lewis 2003, pp. 489–496.

[131]Joint Targeting 2013, p. para 3.d.(2)(a).

Further, even within these target sets, there can be factors that impact on the relative importance of targeting their component parts. The targeting process recognizes that attacking certain parts or "nodes" of a system is critical to changing how a target operates.[132]

Recognition that the destruction of targets can provide different advantages obviously means that not all objects being targeted will be high value. An example of a situation where a military objective may be considered of more limited military value occurs when assessing the targeting of sources of financing for a terrorist or insurgent group. This issue is of particular relevance to contemporary armed conflict since "terrorist groups around the world have been known to use all forms of criminal activity to raise money, including drug trafficking, extortion, kidnapping, human trafficking, all forms of fraudulent schemes and counterfeiting."[133] Such targeting raises two issues. First, there is the question of whether it is even lawful to target income-producing activity such as a drug-smuggling operation. Second, if targeting takes place then what is the military advantage to be gained from such action. In Afghanistan, the Taliban have obtained funds through taxation of production and trade of the drug crop, the levying of a road tax, providing security at drug laboratories, guarding shipments and working in the poppy fields.[134] This resulted in consideration within NATO as to whether the drug production facilities and drug traffickers with links to the insurgency could be targeted as lawful military objectives.[135] As a 2009 Report to the Committee on Foreign Relations in the United States Senate noted, the authorization to use lethal force in this context in Afghanistan "caused some countries to question whether the killing of traffickers and destroying drug labs complied with international law."[136]

The targeting of the drug traffickers themselves is inevitably limited by the requirement that they be members of an organized armed group, or otherwise taking a direct part in hostilities. In other words, members of the Taliban "armed forces." Being a member of the Taliban armed group would mean they remain targetable during the entire time they have that status.[137] Outside that membership, simply participating in the drug trade would not constitute direct participation in hostilities.[138] There are also very strong arguments against including drug-related facilities and infrastructure within the definition of military objects. However, one way it might

[132]Ibid, para 3 (c).

[133]Zarate 2013, p. 23. See also Levitt 2013, p. 272 ("One area in which groups affiliated with both Hezbollah and al-Qaeda are now active is smuggling drugs through Africa").

[134]Schmitt 2009, p. 6.

[135]Geraghty 2010, p. 347.

[136]Ibid, p. 348.

[137]Watkin 2010, pp. 690–93 (for an outline of a suggested approach for determining membership in an organized armed group).

[138]ICRC Interpretive Guidance 2009, pp. 33–35, and Watkin 2010, pp. 683–686 (this is a result that occurs whether the narrower criteria of the "continuous combat function" test found in DPH Study is used, or the "combat function" test used by others including the author is applied).

be considered is on the basis of a "war sustaining" argument. In this regard the United States has uniquely claimed the right to attack objects on that basis. This approach is usually linked to the historical Civil War example of destroying raw cotton within Confederate territory because its sale provided funds for the purchase of arms and ammunition.[139] The international response to this approach has largely been a negative one. It has been suggested that the connection between "crops for export and military action is 'too remote.' "[140] It has also been stated that to allow war-sustaining effort as a criterion for targeting is going too far "as this might easily be interpreted to encompass virtually every activity in the enemy country."[141] The issue of remoteness is particularly germane to the assessment of the military advantage to be gained in attacking an object since, unlike people; those potential targets only need to indirectly support the war-fighting capability of the enemy. However, there is continuing reliance on the "war sustaining" theory, as can be seen in the United States, and limited number of other countries, targeting of Islamic State controlled oil production facilities in Syria in 2014.[142]

Given the connection between the use of profits from the drug trade and the conduct of the insurgency in Afghanistan, it has been suggested by one commentator "the targeting of drug-related objects would generally be permissible under IHL for those who characterize "war-sustaining" entities as military objectives."[143] However, it seems likely that if strikes could be justified on that basis, a relatively low value would need to be assigned to the target when considering the military advantage gained from attacks on drug-related infrastructure. Those facilities only tangentially provide support to an opponent. This in turn would make the collateral killing or injury of civilians much more difficult to justify. Here the remoteness of the connection between the drug infrastructure and the use of funds that arises from activities such as a tax being levied on its participants by the Taliban has a particular impact. It is not that financing is not ultimately important to the conduct of an insurgent or terrorist campaign. However, in this case the objects themselves do not provide as definite a military advantage due to that tangential relationship. A similar issue of the remoteness between the facilities being attacked, and their relationship to military action (e.g., proceeds of sales used for the war effort) arise in respect of the bombing of Islamic State facilities.[144]

As a result, a strike against such infrastructure justified under a "war-sustaining" argument might best parallel the efforts made during 15 May 2012 European

---

[139]Dinstein 2010, para 233. In making this statement reliance is placed on the San Remo Manual 1995, p. 161. See also The Commander's Handbook On The Law Of Naval Operations 2007, para 5.3.1 [for reference to war fighting/war sustaining as criteria for targeting objects as military objectives. War fighting can be equated to "military action" as found in AP I, Article 52(2)].

[140]Dinstein 2010, para 233. See also San Remo Manual 1995, para 67.27, and the Missile Warfare Commentary 2009, Rule 24, para 2.

[141]Kalshoven 1991, p. 310.

[142]Watkin 2014b.

[143]Schmitt 2009, p. 19.

[144]Watkin 2014b, p. 507

Union Naval Force aerial attack against a pirate infrastructure in Somalia.[145] That use of force, which appears to have been carried out under a human rights-based law enforcement mandate, was conducted in a manner that avoided any civilian casualties.[146] Adopting similarly stringent requirements in the Afghanistan drug production and smuggling context means a strike conducted under humanitarian law would have to avoid killing or injuring participants in the drug trade who were not members of the Taliban organized armed group, since those participants would have civilians status. While limited circumstances might arise where such a strike is possible, the potential for collateral casualties and damage means that addressing the drug problem is likely more amenable to traditional law enforcement even if the war-sustaining approach to targeting is believed to apply.[147]

The issue of remoteness is also relevant to attacks on other targets, such as economic ones, that indirectly but remotely provide support to military action. The degree to which the object is removed from military action and hostilities could impact on how the value of those targets is assessed in terms of military advantage to be gained from an attack on that object and what collateral civilian impact is justified. This does not mean that the acceptable collateral damage would necessarily be reduced to zero. The conduct of hostilities is not law enforcement. However, neither do all military objects offer the same military advantage or value to the war effort such that collateral civilian casualties and damage is always warranted. Not all objects are of high value. For targets of lesser importance, alternative approaches to neutralizing them might be considered. For example, depending upon the military capability of the state involved and the operational situation there remains other methods of economic warfare such as visit and search,[148] the inspection and interception of aircraft,[149] or the establishment of a blockade.[150]

In terms of accountability, the degree of military advantage to be gained from an attack needs to be fully articulated in order to justify what may appear to be elevated collateral effects. However, consideration of the relative importance of targets seems generally to have been missing from legal discussions about targeting. However, doctrinally state militaries have embraced the concept of HVTs,

[145]"EU Naval Force delivers blow against Somali Pirates on Shoreline," European Naval Force Somalia, Media and Public Information (15 May 2012), http://www.eunavfor.eu/2012/05/eu-naval-force-delivers-blow-against-somali-pirates-on-shoreline/ (accessed 26 March 2015).

[146]Lieblich 2014, p. 104 ("The operation implies a law enforcement approach since, as emphasized by EU NAVFOR, it was careful not to target the pirates themselves, thereby safeguarding their right to life").

[147]However, see ibid, pp. 150–155 (for an analysis that suggests air strikes against objects could be justified under human rights law on the basis of derogations from property and due process rights in public emergencies, but only after ensuring the right to life of suspected criminals or innocent bystanders is not jeopardized).

[148]San Remo Manual 1995, pp. 195–205.

[149]Missile Warfare Commentary 2009, pp. 272–286.

[150]San Remo Manual 1995, p. 176–180, and Air and Missile Warfare Commentary 2009, pp. 287–300.

tiers and target value generally, thereby opening the door to that discussion. It is an aspect of targeting that should be considered to a greater degree regarding attacks on military objects. It is not enough that "a" military advantage is identified in establishing under Article 52(2) of *Additional Protocol I* that an object is a military objective. That process should also consider the relative value to be obtained from the destruction, capture or neutralization of the object from a military perspective, and its remoteness in terms of aiding the war effort in order to complete the next part of the targeting process, the assessment of whether excessive collateral casualties or damage is likely to result from an attack. The more remote that connection, the more challenging that explanation may be.[151]

13.3.4 Assessing Value and Perspective

Assessing military advantage inevitability raises a fundamental question about the perspective from which the value of the target is to be considered. Is the importance of a target assessed from the viewpoint of the higher level commander (i.e., the strategic level) or the individual soldier (i.e., the tactical level)? The almost obsessive attention given to the deliberate targeting of high-level targets with drone strikes, such as Osama bin Laden and other Al Qaeda or Taliban leaders has masked the reality that such attacks occur in a unique and quite limited context. Very little of contemporary targeting can involve the same multi-agency effort and the highest levels of Government preparing "kill lists."[152] The killing of the enemy is most likely to involve low ranking soldiers engaged in intimate combat with an enemy equally dedicated to ending their lives. The same law that applies to strategic level targeting also applies to the use of force at the lowest level of operations.[153]

Referring back to the example of the low-level foot soldier hiding in an urban area, that person may present a much more serious threat to soldiers operating at the tactical level than the "high-value" leader. This situation brings back memories of General Norman Schwarzkopf's comment about minefields during the 1991 Gulf Conflict and the threat soldiers faced, "[a]ll there's got to be is one mine, and that's intense."[154] For that soldier a lone potential sniper can be an extremely

[151]Franck 2008, p. 734 (referring to a United States air force assessment of the 2006 Lebanon War that indicated "Israel had lost the war for public opinion by bombing too many targets of questionable importance to its aims, and by not explaining, in convincing terms of military necessity, why it had bombed what it had").

[152]Scahill 2013, p. 351 (where it is indicated by early 2010 there were "at least three entities within the US government that were maintaining kill lists: the National Security Council…the CIA; and the US military").

[153]Rogers 2004, pp. 111–13 (where it is suggested those who plan or decide on an attack "have more responsibilities than those who carry them out").

[154]T Wilkinson, "Schwarzkopf Revels in a Moment of Glory: Strategy: The allied commander tells a media briefing how he and the allies pulled off what shapes up to be the biggest victory of his career," *Los Angeles Times* (21 February 1991), http://articles.latimes.com/1991-02-28/news/mn-2875_1_biggest-victory (accessed 26 March 2015).

important target, and the use of force to remove that threat might be seen to justify significant collateral effects. This understandable personal reaction points to one of the problems of looking at targets solely through a tactical lens. To help avoid a situation where the infliction of broader collateral civilian casualties might be claimed in the routine violence of war, the assessment of military advantage must be put in a context that is consistent with the way war is fought. This involves consideration of the broader operational and strategic environment within which that target is situated when assessing value. That means that the assessment of the importance of the target must be considered not only at the tactical level, but also within the context of the overall military operations (i.e., the strategic level).

However, simply because a target is seen as being of lower importance does not mean it cannot be targeted. The low-level member of an organized armed group found in an urban setting, where collateral civilian impact may significantly outweigh the limited military advantage gained from an air strike, might still be attacked. However, the method and means employed may be significantly altered. That same target can be more readily targeted when located in a rural area with a much less dense population. While the killing of individual low-level terrorists or insurgents may not, in certain circumstances, appear to provide an increased military advantage that will not always be the case. For example, the targeting of insurgents participating in a group attack on a military unit, terrorists conducting a suicide mission, or participating in the construction of explosives as part of an IED cell may not only offer greater military advantage, it will likely also alter the priority assigned to that operation by the state military forces involved. The assessment of value requires consideration of the operational context within which the target is presented, and also a broader perspective of where that target fits within the overall military campaign.

13.4 The Courts, Military Advantage, and Proportionality

13.4.1 An (Over-)Reliance on Science

The challenge in ascertaining what "military advantage" means, both in its own right and as part of the proportionality assessment is evident in two cases: *Prosecutor v Gotovina*[155] and the *Targeted Killings Case*.[156] Each case, in its own way, addresses issues of science and precision. The *Targeted Killings Case*

[155] *Prosecutor v Gotovina*, ICTY Case No IT-06-90-T, Vol. I, Trial Chamber, 15 April 2011, http://www.icty.org/x/cases/gotovina/tjug/en/110415_judgement_vol1.pdf, *Prosecutor v Gotovina*, ICTY Case No IT-06-90-T, Vol. II, Trial Chamber, 15 April 2011, http://www.icty.org/x/cases/gotovina/tjug/en/110415_judgement_vol2.pdf, and *Prosecutor v Gotovina*, ICTY Case No IT-06-90-A, Appeal Chamber, 16 November 2012, http://www.icty.org/x/cases/gotovina/acjug/en/121116_judgement.pdf (collectively the *Gotovina Case*, or separately as the *Gotovina Case Trial Decision*, or *Gotovina Case, Appeal Decision*).

[156] *Public Committee Against Torture in Israel v. Israel*, Israel Supreme Court [16 December 2006], 46 ILM 375.

highlights the lack of precision with which the outer limits of justifiable collateral effects arising from an attack can be identified, while the *Gotovina Case* stands out because of the focus exhibited by the trial and appellate levels of the International Criminal Tribunal for the Former Yugoslavia on the exact scientific parameters of the "range of error" for attacks when assessing criminal culpability.

Dealing first with the *Gotovina Case*, that decision included allegations of war crimes arising from Operation Storm, which involved Croatian military action in 1995 to take control of the Krajina region of Croatia. Among the allegations was the shelling of civilians and unlawful attacks on civilians and civilian objects.[157] It was alleged that artillery fire was used indiscriminately in attacks on towns resulting in 20,000 Krajina Serbs being forced from their homes.[158] Particular emphasis was placed on the analysis of artillery impact sites, with the court adopting the position that "sites located more than 200 metres from a target it deemed legitimate served as evidence of an unlawful artillery attack."[159] The military advantage of the targeted objectives was discussed, including passing reference to some sites such as the main military headquarters being "the main and highest pay-off targets."[160] However, the case focused on the simple issue as to whether the targets struck were military ones. There was an assessment of proportionality in respect of attacks on an enemy commander's residence. The court determined that:

> Firing twelve shells of 130 mm at Martic's apartment [and shells of unknown calibre at other areas]...*created a significant risk* of a high number of civilian casualties and injuries, as well as damage to civilian objects. The Trial Chamber considers that *this risk was excessive in relation to the anticipated military advantage* of firing at the two locations where the HV believed Martić to have been present. This disproportionate attack shows that the HV paid little or no regard to the risk of civilian casualties and injuries and damage to civilian objects when firing artillery at a military target on at least three occasions.[161]

This finding was made on the basis of a "risk" of excessive collateral effects without any reference to actual civilian casualties, or damage.

---

[157] *Prosecutor v Gotovina*, ICTY Case No IT-06-90-A, Appeal Chamber, 16 November 2012, http://www.icty.org/x/cases/gotovina/acjug/en/121116_judgement.pdf, para 2.

[158] Ibid, para 24.

[159] Ibid, para 25. See also *Prosecutor v Gotovina*, ICTY Case No IT-06-90-T, Vol I, Trial Chamber, 15 April 2011, http://www.icty.org/x/cases/gotovina/tjug/en/110415_judgement_vol1.pdf, para 1375 n1539 ("In light of the evidence received from witnesses Konings, Corn, Rajčić, and Lesli.e., regarding the accuracy of the artillery weapons the HV had at its disposal during Operation Storm, the Trial Chamber has generally not further specified in its factual findings the locations of impacts within a 200 metre range of relevant objects").

[160] *Prosecutor v Gotovina*, ICTY Case No IT-06-90-T, Vol I, Trial Chamber, 15 April 2011, http://www.icty.org/x/cases/gotovina/tjug/en/110415_judgement_vol1.pdf, para 1191.

[161] *Prosecutor v Gotovina*, ICTY Case No IT-06-90-T, Trial Chamber, 15 April 2011, Vol II, http://www.icty.org/x/cases/gotovina/tjug/en/110415_judgement_vol2.pdf, para 1910 (emphasis added).

The comment by the Appeal Chamber that the lower court's analysis "was not based on a concrete assessment of comparative military advantage, and did not make any findings on resulting damages or casualties" is an apt one.[162] With the attacks having been carried out the issue was not the "risk" of excessive collateral effects, but whether there actually were any. Exploring the actual effects of the attacks could have provided concrete evidence upon which to base a decision. However, what really caught the attention of the appellate court was the reliance by the trial court on the impact analysis of the artillery strikes. The Appeals Chamber ruled that court erred in using a 200 metre "range of error"[163] to determine artillery shells fired in civilian inhabited areas was evidence of indiscriminate attacks.[164] The lower court was held not to have taken into consideration variable factors such as wind speed,[165] or evidence the range of error was actually 400 meters.[166] The trial court had also looked at other evidence on the record as ambiguous,[167] "and considered it indicative of unlawful artillery attacks only when viewed through the prism of the Impact Analysis."[168] The result was an acquittal of the accused.[169] By placing such overwhelming reliance on the "range of error" evidence, the trial court created the appearance of being far more comfortable with assessing scientific criteria that assessing other criteria that should have been given greater consideration.

As is reflected in the *Gotovina Case* there is a tendency to want to quantify the assessment of military advantage and risk of collateral damage in mathematic terms in almost all aspects of target analysis (e.g., indiscriminate attacks, military advantage, excessive collateral civilian effects). However, the reliance of science analysis, percentages, or probabilities has its limits.[170] That said, defaulting to a scientific approach is not a unique occurrence. The focus on scientific solutions is seen in the suggestion that to justify effects-based targeting there needs to be an understanding "*in the scientific sense* as to which stimuli in terms of attack may be anticipated to produce which military effects in the battle-space…."[171] This extends to demonstrating the causal relationships between the attack, its psychological effect and military advantage.[172] The invocation of such a scientific basis

[162]*Prosecutor v Gotovina*, ICTY Case No IT-06-90-A, Appeal Chamber, 16 November 2012, http://www.icty.org/x/cases/gotovina/acjug/en/121116_judgement.pdf, para 82.

[163]Ibid, para 57.

[164]Ibid, para 64.

[165]Ibid, para 60.

[166]Ibid, para 59.

[167]Ibid, paras 77–82.

[168]Ibid, para 82.

[169]Ibid, paras 156–57.

[170]Joint Targeting 2013, para 3a. (where an example of the application of assessment metrics is provided as "Destruction of Critical Node 1 will degrade Target A by at least 50 percent").

[171]Boothby 2012, p. 505 (emphasis added).

[172]Ibid, p. 507.

to assess military advantage raises the challenging question of whether "hard" science[173] is to be preferred over "soft" science, an issue that is fraught with its own challenges.[174]

A question posed by Michael Walzer when discussing the protection of civilians highlights the challenge of relying on a "percentages" approach. He asked whether "imposing a one-in-ten chance of death on them is justified, while imposing a three-in-ten chance is unjustifiable?"[175] In the end he concluded "the degree of risk that is permissible is going to vary with the nature of the target, the urgency of the moment, the available technology, and so on."[176] The use of "numbers" to explain targeting action can be an extremely helpful tool for establishing, particularly to an external audience, that an effort was made to be objective in making a decision to use force. Significantly, the ability to do so is often limited to particular types of targeting missions where there is time to plan and calculate with greater certainty what effects are desired and likely to occur. However, a reliance on computer programs, mathematical equations, or even the social sciences cannot on their own solve the fundamental moral challenges associated with taking human life under a double effect doctrine. As William Fenrick notes "since the quantities being measured, civilian losses and military advantage, are dissimilar, it is not possible to establish any reasonably exact proportionality equation between them."[177]

The result is that the relative anticipated military advantage to be gained from an attack, or the collateral effect likely to occur is not likely to be calculated with scientific precision. It requires consideration of a much broader set of factors than scientific ones. This conclusion is consistent with the reality that the exercise of command is both an art and a science, and requires above all the exercise of good judgment.[178] What this means for Commanders is ensuring there is not an overreliance on computerized projections of the collateral effects of an attack, even in circumstances such as large-scale interstate conflict where warfare may expand to include thousands of potential targets. The process put in place to assess targeting must provide for consideration of broader factors than science based projections. The inability to solely rely on such calculations is also an indication that the "concrete and direct" modifiers associated with military advantage do not involve the degree of precision that reliance on science criteria might suggest. The process established to assess targeting choices must still make room for professional

---

[173]Cambridge Dictionaries Online ("hard science" is defined as "science, or a branch of science, in which facts and theories can be firmly and exactly measured, tested or proved").

[174]T Wilson, "Stop bullying the 'soft' sciences," *Los Angeles Times* (12 July 2012), http://articles.latimes.com/2012/jul/12/opinion/la-oe-wilson-social-sciences-20120712 (accessed 27 March 2015)(where hard science is identified with physics, chemistry and biology, and soft science is identified as sociology and psychology).

[175]Walzer 2000, p. 156.

[176]Ibid.

[177]Fenrick 1982, pp. 91, 102.

[178]Freedman 2013, p. 75 (for reference to strategy being both a science and an art).

judgment. The assessment of proportionality must also include consideration of variables such as morality and professional judgment, which do not lend themselves readily to scientific analysis. In effect, targeting is not just a science.

13.4.2 The "Zone of Proportionality"

There is even less reference to military advantage in the 2006 *Targeted Killings Case* than in the 2011 *Gotovina Case*. This may arise in part from the Israeli court's handling of the targeting issue in a theoretical fashion without dealing with specific attacks, or targets. What reference is made to military advantage is in the context of the framework to be used when assessing the collateral effects of an attack. In this respect the Israeli court notes an "attack is proportionate if *the benefit stemming from the attainment of the proper military objective* is proportionate to the damage caused to innocent civilians harmed by it."[179] It is the issue of proportionality that takes up much of the court's attention. In this context, the court is addressing a far broader issue of general application than the narrower question of whether there is a duty to consider capture before killing, which is often assessed on the facts of that case in terms of threats arising in occupied territory. A particularly important aspect of the Israeli court's handling of the proportionality involves the issue of "precision." As will be discussed this becomes evident when the court assesses the outer limits of justifiable collateral casualties or damage arising from an attack.

A unique feature of the *Targeted Killings Case* is that it provides the most detailed and considered judicial interpretation to date of proportionality in a targeting context. In doing so it introduced the concept of a "zone of proportionality" when assessing the respective roles of the court (i.e., accountability) and the military commander (i.e., the targeting assessment). As the Israel High Court of Justice stated:

> Proportionality is not a standard of precision. At times there are a number of ways to fulfill its conditions. A zone of proportionality is created. It is the borders of that zone that the Court guards. The decision within the borders is the executive branch's decision. That is its margin of appreciation....[180]

It is within this concept of a "zone of proportionality" that an assessment must be made of military advantage and its application to determine justifiable collateral effects resulting from an attack.

In assessing this zone of proportionality concept consideration will first be given to the impact of there being a relatively limited degree of precision with which

[179] *Public Committee Against Torture in Israel v. Israel*, Israel Supreme Court [16 December 2006], 46 ILM 375, para 45 (emphasis added).

[180] Ibid, para 58.

proportionality can be assessed. Next, the manner in which military advantage is applied when assessing precautions in the attack will be explored in order to establish that the process is not necessarily as sequential as the regulatory framework set out in AP I, Article 57 implies. This is particularly evident where there are multiple possible courses of action available to a decision maker (i.e., "there are a number of ways to fulfill its conditions"[181]). Finally, notwithstanding the requirement to limit or avoid civilian casualties, the continuing scope for broad collateral effects related to the nature of the military advantage being sought will be discussed in the context of identifying the outer boundaries of a zone of proportionality.

Turning first to the issue of precision, one of the challenges in assessing what constitutes excessive collateral casualties or damage is that there is limited judicial consideration of this area of the law. The reference in the *Targeted Killings Case* to proportionality not being a standard of precision is important for a number of reasons. It captures the potential complexity of military operations, and the reality that in certain circumstances there may be a number of courses of action available to military commanders. These courses of action can raise a variety of different anticipated military advantages. The concept of a zone of proportionality also highlights that, unlike human rights-based law enforcement, there is a more ready acknowledgement that collateral civilian casualties and damage can result from military operations. This theoretical construct also reflects the challenging interface between the military commanders and the courts. When exercising their professional judgment, military commanders will inevitably need to have considerable discretion in determining how an operation is to be conducted. However, courts have an essential role in carrying out legal oversight over the targeting decisions that are made during armed conflict.

The proportionality assessment concerns "attacks that are being planned and the stage at which the decision is taken whether to launch an attack."[182] As has been stated "[o]nce that minimum collateral damage method has been identified it is then assessed to establish its proportionality."[183] It is the final proportionality assessment set out in Article 57(2)(a)(iii) of *Additional Protocol I* that appears to have attracted the most legal and public attention in terms of the critical analysis of targeting. A focus on this final precautionary stage is unfortunate to the extent it masks the importance of the role of other such measures found in the *Protocol*. It also often presents a picture of having to make difficult moral issues associated with the determination of what are the "excessive" collateral effects of targeting without giving adequate weight to the mitigating effect of the prior analysis in Article 57(2)(a).

It might be attractive to conclude from the use of the term "zone of proportionality" that the establishment of legal boundaries and the exercise of executive decision-making occur independently up to that stage. That, in effect, the law sets the

[181]Ibid.

[182]Boothby 2012, p. 125.

[183]Ibid.

boundaries and any decisions made by military commanders occur uniquely within those boundaries as a matter of discretion, policy, or as the Court stated as a "margin of appreciation." However, a proportionate attack is the product of a process that identifies the most appropriate course of action in relation to its collateral effects. This raises the issue of the degree to which the precautions in Articles 57(2)(a) of *Additional Protocol I* must be considered as distinct steps separate from the final proportionality determination. As has been noted "Article 57 recognizes that targeting is undertaken by applying a process in which there is a sequence of activities starting with the planning, progressing to the decision to attack, and culminating in the attack itself."[184]

While the precautions in Article 57(2) of *Additional Protocol I* are listed sequentially their fulfillment in practice may require a near simultaneous comparison of multiple attack options, where they exist, in determining the appropriate form of attack. Importantly, it is the precautionary requirements of Article 57(2)(a)(ii) that potentially can have the greatest impact in protecting civilians since it forces consideration of the practical military options available to avoid or limit collateral casualties and damage. Given the inherently difficult moral nature of the decision that can arise in weighing military advantage against likely collateral civilian casualties or damage, it is the process of following these precautions that places the decision maker in a position of being able to state a reasonable result has occurred. It is in this context that the second area of analysis is introduced: the impact of the legal criterion of "military advantage" in the planning of an attack.

The establishment of the boundaries of the zone of proportionality is directly linked to the requirement to apply the precaution set out in Article 57(2)(a)(ii) of *Additional Protocol I*. That provision necessitates that those planning or deciding upon an attack shall take "all feasible precautions in the *choice* of means and methods of attack with a view to avoiding, and in any event to minimizing, incidental loss of civilian life, injury to civilians and damage to civilian objects."[185] While military advantage is not specifically addressed in that precaution, the "choice" set out in Article 57(2)(a)(ii) refers not only to an executive decision, but also the potential that more than one option may have to be considered. This means the advantage to be gained from a number of potential choices will be compared to one another when reaching a decision on the ultimate course of action to be applied to the proportionality assessment. The result is that the precautionary process can be much more interactive and interrelated than the sequential listing of the steps in Article 57(2) may suggest.

The dialogue about the choice of methods and means of attack engages commanders on subjects about which they are most comfortable and knowledgeable. It is military commanders who identify and assess a chosen form of attack as to whether it leads to the desired outcome designed to gain a military advantage while limiting collateral effects. However, when there is more than one available

---

[184]Ibid, p. 120.

[185]AP I, Article 57(2)(a)(ii)(emphasis added).

option for attacking a target the decision maker must identify and take into account the military advantage to be gained from that approach, as well as the incidental collateral effects resulting from the means and method chosen. It is in this context that the application of the second precaution in Article 57(2)(a)(ii) can result in a comparative assessment of a number of courses of action. For example, in assessing options for bombing a target factors such as the direction of attack, altitude, ordnance used, timing, weather, and anticipated anti-aircraft defenses (i.e., risk to aircrew and aircraft) could lead to the consideration of three or four ways of attacking an objective, each with varying collateral damage predictions and anticipated military advantage to be gained. These precautions are carried out prior to the ultimate assessment of proportionality and help define the reasonableness of the potential boundaries of collateral casualties and damage. The assessment of proportionality is intimately linked to means and methods chosen for the attack.[186] In the final analysis it is the operation of this precaution that may have the greatest humanitarian impact in the targeting process.

During that assessment, consideration may be given to a course of action that is rejected because it does not sufficiently minimize or avoid civilian casualties or damage. Similarly, a course of action resulting in relatively low collateral effects may also have to be rejected because it may elevate the risk to attacking forces to an unacceptable level, or is an option that is less likely to adequately neutralize a target. In other words, it results in a relatively lower anticipated military advantage than other options. In addition, while there may be more than one course of action practically available to the commander for reducing collateral casualties or damage it may not always be clear which will be the least problematic. For example, a decision to attempt to capture a target may ultimately result in a greater number of incidental civilian casualties or collateral damage if the military forces do not adequately control the territory where that person is located. Any requirement for a military force to fight its way into or out of the location of the operation, particularly in an urban setting, can result in significant violence and with it the potential for elevated civilian and military casualties.[187] This leaves a commander deciding between kill or capture missions with difficult assessments having to be made about the potential outcomes of each in terms of military advantage and collateral effects.

Other factors may also have to be considered by the decision maker. The ultimate military goal of the overall campaign may be an important factor in assessing a choice of method or means of a potential attack. That factor can affect a commander's allocation of resources and the assessment of the military advantage to

[186]Boivin and Sandoz 2006, p. 38 (where it is noted "[t]o be sure, the two principles are linked: proportionality cannot be evaluated in the abstract because what is deemed excessive is contingent upon the means and methods available to the attacking Party. If it can be established that a target could have been attacked causing less or no collateral damage, then it is not sufficient to argue that the loss of any life is proportionate to the military advantage gained").

[187]Urban 2010, pp. 153–156 (outlining a difficult 2006 raid by United States Special Forces in Iraq to detain insurgent suspects that was carried out in daylight).

be gained from the available means and methods employed. In making that assessment the person planning or deciding on the attack will consider the impact of the use of certain means and methods on the campaign more broadly (i.e., where the limited number of precision weapons may be required for other attacks[188]) and the risk to soldiers and civilians not taking a direct part in hostilities.[189] The assessment of proportionality may also have to look at different aspects or phases of an attack. Consideration may be given to using certain levels of force for an assault, but retain the ability to use more destructive, and possibly even more accurate means should military forces have to act in self-defense. For example, while an operation may be focused on the capture of a suspected insurgent the fact an aircraft is on call for a defensive mission means consideration must also be given to the circumstances under which its ordnance might be used, as well as the collateral damage that use might cause. However, this does not mean that defensive uses of force will permit greater levels of collateral civilian casualties and damage. In this respect concern over the use of close air support has led to ISAF direction to limit the use of such force in the proximity of residential compounds during the counterinsurgency in Afghanistan.[190]

It is finding the right balance between the concrete and direct military advantage anticipated and the limitation or avoidance of collateral civilian impact in consideration of the various options for attack that leads to a justifiable course of action. It is a balance that can only be struck by comparing both desired anticipated outcomes and their possible effects among the available options. As was noted in the *Targeted Killings Case* "[t]he question is whether the decision of the military commander falls within the zone of reasonable activity on the part of the military commander."[191] The legal issue is "whether the decision which the military commander made is a decision that a reasonable military commander was permitted to make."[192] In making targeting decisions different commanders may not come to exactly the same conclusion on the means and methods to be employed, or on the military advantage anticipated from a successful attack. However, the chosen course of action is likely to be considered a reasonable one particularly when it can be assessed against other available options.

It must be stressed that not all targeting decisions will be made in the context of a multiplicity of courses of action. Further, while the targeting process is sequential in terms of the planning, decision, and conduct of an attack it is a process that may be considerably truncated when soldiers are required to use force in self-defense or against fleeting targets. Many uses of force will be made by soldiers

[188]Boothby 2012, pp. 124–125 (for a discussion of the use of precision munitions).

[189]Ibid, p. 124 (for an outline of various factors that may have to be considered by planners and decision makers).

[190]NOTA/ISAF 2009, Tactical Directive.

[191]*Public Committee Against Torture in Israel v. Israel*, Israel Supreme Court [16 December 2006], 46 ILM 375, para 57.

[192]Ibid. See also Rogers 2004, pp. 110–11 (for a discussion of the reasonableness of decision making by a commander).

acting in extremis, without the benefit of well developed intelligence, or the time to consider options beyond pulling the trigger or not. However, for many attacks the reasonableness of a course of action can be measured not only in the circumstances of the individual proposed attack, but also in comparison to other feasible attacks that might have been undertaken.

The third area of inquiry pertains to how broadly the boundaries of proportionality might be set. As has been noted, the *Targeted Killings Case* did not deal with specific incidents of targeting. However, in terms of the analysis of proportionality by that court a particularly important incident was likely a 2002 Israeli air strike in Gaza. In that incident a single 2,000-pound bomb was used to kill the Hamas leader, Saleh Shehada. That attack destroyed the apartment building where the target was located. It also killed 13 civilians not directly involved in terrorist activities including Shehada's wife, daughter, and nine other children and wounding dozens in the vicinity.[193] A Special Investigatory Commission ordered by the Israeli Government subsequently concluded that the target was a lawful one,[194] although there had been failures in intelligence,[195] particularly relating to the presence of civilians in adjacent buildings.[196] It was determined that in hindsight this made the attack a disproportionate one.[197]

The circumstances of the Shehada strike appear to have been in the mind of the court. It was indicated that when seeking to identify the boundaries of the zone of proportionality shooting at a sniper could be proportionate, even if a civilian neighbor or passer-by is harmed.[198] However, the court noted "[t]hat is not the case if the building is bombed from the air and *scores of its residents and passersby are harmed*."[199] Clearly, an attack where one neighbor or passer-by was killed, or injured could be justifiable. This lower boundary is consistent with much of the contemporary dialog about targeting and proportionality. There is also a discussion increasingly focused on capturing suspects[200] and adopting the approach that "causing civilian casualties and civilian property damage is neither 'by chance' nor 'minor.'"[201] As will be discussed, this dialog has a particular relevance

[193]Salah Shehadeh-Special Investigatory Commission 2011, para 1, and Byman 2011, pp. 307–310.

[194]Salah Shehadeh-Special Investigatory Commission 2011, para 9.

[195]Ibid, para 10.

[196]Ibid, para 11.

[197]Ibid, para 10.

[198]Raviv and Melman 2012, p. 322 (where it is reported that in 2008 a Syrian general was killed while eating dinner at a coastline villa by a sniper located on an Israeli naval vessel. There were no collateral injuries).

[199]*Public Committee Against Torture in Israel v. Israel*, Israel Supreme Court [16 December 2006], 46 ILM 375, para 46 (emphasis added).

[200]For a discussion of the capture versus kill issue see Goodman 2013a, p. 819, Schmitt 2013, p. 855, and Goodman 2013b, p. 863.

[201]Beran 2010, p. 8.

to counterinsurgency campaigns; however, it is not applicable to all forms of conflict, including those involving transnational terrorist groups.

What is noteworthy in the *Targeted Killings Case* is the identification of the outer limits of proportionality as being "scores" of collateral casualties, even when a residential building is bombed and its inhabitants are collateral casualties.[202] This analysis highlights the challenge of attempting to identify with any precision the borders of the zone of proportionality, even if many of the weapons now used are themselves considered to be precise in terms of their ability to strike the target. It also serves as an indication that the resulting collateral damage can very much depend upon the choice of means or method of attack. That choice, which is made by a commander or other decision maker, can be directly related to an assessment of the military advantage to be gained from the means employed. It is that assessment, made during the Article 57(2)(a)(ii) precaution stage, that is likely to be determinative of the collateral casualties and damages that are to result. While this analysis may be surprising to those who seek to limit the collateral effects of warfare, the tactical circumstances and a sufficiently important advantage to be gained in striking a target may justify casualties even beyond the scores noted above. This is evident in an example that also highlights that the assessment of military advantage is not limited to attacks that are offensive in nature:[203] a repeat of the 9/11-style attacks with hijacked aircraft. In that situation the nature of the target being defended may justify significant collateral casualties or damage in response to such an attack.

The 9/11 attacks, which involved crashing hijacked aircraft into selected targets were acts that precipitated an armed conflict. They constituted an "armed attack" under Article 51 of the United Nations Charter. The resulting conflict, which commenced with those attacks continued in Afghanistan and elsewhere, and has lasted over a decade. The existence of an armed conflict created by such an attack means that humanitarian law can govern the state response. During the 9/11 attacks, two planes struck the World Trade office towers in New York City[204] resulting in 2,753 persons being killed.[205] Had military aircraft been able to respond in time, the assessment of the military advantage to be gained in defending those buildings would have included consideration not only of the lives of the persons at risk in the buildings, on the plane and elsewhere on the ground, but also the physical damage to the buildings struck and the potential economic impact arising from the destruction of those centers of commerce. A third plane struck the Pentagon,[206] while the fourth had intended to strike the Capitol Building or the White House.[207]

---

[202] *Public Committee Against Torture in Israel v. Israel*, Israel Supreme Court [16 December 2006], 46 ILM 375, para 46.

[203] AP I, Article 49(1)(where it is indicated attacks "means acts of violence against the adversary, whether in offence or in defence").

[204] The National commission on terrorist attacks upon the United States 2004, pp. 7, 8.

[205] "September 11 Anniversary Fast Facts," *CNN* (11 September 2013), http://www.cnn.com/2013/07/27/us/september-11-anniversary-fast-facts/ (accessed 26 March 2015)

[206] The National commission on terrorist attacks upon the United States 2004, p. 10.

[207] Ibid, p. 14.

These third and fourth attacks were clearly directed at the military and political power of the United States and also involved the considerable loss of life.[208] As with the attacks on the commercial enterprises, the political and military impact of those strikes would have had to be considered, in addition to the lives at risk, when assessing the military advantage of attempting to shoot down the hijacked planes. These are all factors related to national defense and security.

A decision to shoot down a civilian passenger aircraft could result in hundreds of civilians being killed, not only on the plane, but also on the ground.[209] While there are a defined number of people on the plane who would likely be killed, that same level of certainty would not be available regarding civilians at the terrorist's point of attack (i.e., the persons ultimately being protected), or any place where a damaged plane might crash. In such a situation it is also evident the assessment of military advantage would require consideration not only of the lives at risk, but also of the importance of protecting commercial, political, and military objects. Such an analysis reflects the complex balancing of conflicting values and interests required to assess proportionality that is referred to by the Israeli High Court of Justice.[210]

The consideration of these complex military advantage factors also highlights the difference between humanitarian law and human rights law. A human rights law assessment, which focuses on the right to life, is unlikely to provide much assistance in resolving the challenge facing state security personnel unless that body of law is prepared to deal with the requirement to weigh the potential for collateral casualties and damages against the consequences of mission failure (i.e., the military advantage related to the military, political, or commercial impact). An example indicating that a human rights-based analysis may not be well suited to deal with this challenge can be seen in *Dr. H. et al. v. s.14.3 of the Aviation Security Act of 11 January 2005* (2006).[211] In that case, the German Constitutional Court assessed the shoot down question under the law enforcement rather than a *jus ad bellum* self-defence framework. The court struggled with the whole idea of shooting down hijacked aircraft from a policing perspective.[212] This included

[208]"September 11 Anniversary Fast Facts," *CNN* (11 September 2013), http://www.cnn.com/2013/07/27/us/september-11-anniversary-fast-facts/ (accessed 26 March 2015)(where it is reported 184 people were killing in the Pentagon attack and 40 passengers and crew died when Flight 93 crashed in a field near Shanksville, Pennsylvania).

[209]Raviv and Melman 2012, pp. 137–38 (In February 1973 the Israeli air force tragically shot down a Libyan civilian airliner that refused to respond to radio calls or internationally recognized signals such as the flapping of wings by the fighters. In total 105 out of 122 passengers and crew were killed).

[210]*Public Committee Against Torture in Israel v. Israel*, Israel Supreme Court [16 December 2006], 46 ILM 375, para 45.

[211]*Dr. H.* et al. *v. s.14.3 of the Aviation Security Act of 11 January 2005* (2006) www.bundesverfassungsgericht.de/en/decisions/rs20060215_1bvr035705en.html.

[212]See also Naske and Nolte 2007, p. 466 [for an overview of *Dr. H.* et al. *v. s.14.3 of the Aviation Security Act of 11 January 2005* (2006)]

coming to grips with the reality that people may be killed on the ground by aircraft wreckage,[213] the assessment and motivation of the hijackers is often difficult to establish,[214] the possibility there will be poor communications,[215] the small air space and multi-tiered decision making process could lead to enormous time pressures and premature decisions,[216] and that the facts upon which a shoot down decision would have to be based could not be determined with certainty.[217]

A particular emphasis was placed on the passengers' being innocent victims. The Court determined their rights and human dignity must be considered, and "the weighing up of lives against lives according to the standard of how many people are possibly affected on the one side and how many on the other side is impermissible."[218] Finally, the discussion of the consequences of not acting in terms of the "value" of the objects potentially being targeted was not addressed. The focus of the court was on human life.

The issues that the German court struggled with are the very life and death ones that military personnel are required to assess and make decisions about, often under severe time constraints and in the "fog of war." They are at the heart of the comparison between military advantage and collateral effects. This is not to suggest that a human rights analysis will never accept a large number of collateral deaths and injury. This has already occurred in the *Case of Finogenov and Others v. Russia*.[219] In that case, the European Court of Human Rights accepted that the death of 129 hostages at a Moscow theater during a hostage rescue operation "was not in the circumstances a disproportionate measure."[220] It is estimated that 730 hostages were rescued.[221] However, in making a distinction between the use of gas in a controlled hostage rescue situation, and "bombs or air missiles" in other Russian anti-terrorist operations the German court indicates it may not be prepared to fully address the challenges arises from the broader use of force during armed conflict.[222]

As the 9/11 example demonstrates, the issues at stake during armed attacks, or in the context of other violence occurring in armed conflict, may prompt

---

[213] *Dr. H.* et al. *v. s.14.3 of the Aviation Security Act of 11 January 2005* (2006), para 151, www.bundesverfassungsgericht.de/en/decisions/rs20060215_1bvr035705en.html.

[214] Ibid, para 123.

[215] Ibid, para 126.

[216] Ibid, para 127.

[217] Ibid, para 123.

[218] Ibid, para 35. See also ibid, para 14

[219] *Finogenov v. Russia*, VI Eur. Ct. H. R. 2011.

[220] Ibid, para 236 (where it is indicated over 900 people were held hostage).

[221] Ibid, para 24 ("As a result of the operation the majority of hostages were released (over 730 people). The exact number is unknown…").

[222] Ibid, para 232. See also Lieblich 2014, pp. 113–114 (for a discussion of the limited impact of the *Moscow Theatre Case* from a human rights/law enforcement perspective).

consideration of collateral effects of a scale that defies exact precision. As has been noted "[the military decision maker] cannot operate on the basis of absolute certainty." The term definite does not mean it is "certain or bound to happen."[223] In these circumstances not making a decision can also have a significant impact on the operational situation, the conduct of the war and the lives of civilians and military personnel. Given that the context within which targeting decisions are made can vary so widely even during armed conflict the Court in the *Targeted Killings Case* wisely did not definitively set the outer boundaries of proportionality.

As can be seen from the analysis of both the *Gotovina Cases* and *Targeted Killings Case,* courts are just beginning to be asked to deal with targeting-related issues. Their handling of the cases brought before them has highlighted the complexity of the issues that arise and the challenges they will face in seeking to interpret this area of humanitarian law. That complexity is largely not evident in the legal framework itself, which is generally well articulated in Article 57(2) of the *Additional Protocol I.* Rather the complexity arises from the uncertain nature of warfare itself, the scope and scale of violence, and the requirement to consider not simply the technical capabilities of weapons, but also difficult moral issues associated with the incidental killing of civilians during armed conflict. This is an area of law that does not lend itself to precise calculations or definitive conclusions, except in the most obvious of situations of excessive collateral effects.[224] Ultimately the military advantage to be gained, and collateral effects that can be justified will be highly context dependent. For any court embarking on the legal analysis of targeting a crucial element must be the consideration of how wars are fought. Such consideration highlights both the strategic and tactical nature of warfare. It is to that issue that the analysis now turns.

13.5 Military Advantage and How Wars Are Fought

13.5.1 The Levels of War: Strategy, Operational, and Tactical

The problem with focusing on military advantage at either the tactical or strategic levels of war is that it does not fully reflect how wars are fought.[225] An indication that the conduct of hostilities involves targeting at multiple levels of war can be

[223] Boothby 2012, p. 101.

[224] Schmitt 2005, p. 51 ("It is impossible to relate objectively the value of military advantage to collateral damage and incidental injury; they are dissimilar values that cannot be compared meaningfully except in extreme cases").

[225] For a discussion of the impact of airpower theory on air targeting generally see Watkin 2014, p. 1.

seen in the *Gotovina Case* where reference is made to both operational[226] and tactical level targets having been identified for artillery engagement.[227] However, this reference does not reflect the full scope of armed conflict with hostilities inevitably being planned and conducted at the strategic, operational, and tactical levels of war. Understanding this reality will be a crucial requirement for any court seeking to assess targeting during armed conflict, and in particular the manner in which the military advantage sought to be gained, impacts on the identification of military objectives and the assessment of the proportionality of military action. As will be discussed it is the interaction between the various levels of war that affects the scope of the conflict, impacts on what targets are struck to influence an opponent to quite the fight, and assists in the identification of which targets should be struck to degrade an enemy's ability to conduct military operations.

The multiplicity of levels upon which warfare is conducted is particularly evident in interstate conflict. A hallmark of the rise of the state has been the industrialization of war, the conduct of economic warfare, and ultimately the prosecution of strategic air campaigns. In this regard, the exceptional destructive power of the state can be linked directly to the ability of that entity to marshal vast resources to conduct hostilities. While much depends upon the nature and scope of a conflict, degrading the overall ability of an opposing state to wage war by targeting the resources used to engage in warfare took on a high profile in the twentieth century. The technological advancement of warfare witnessed the development of an aerial strike capability, which enabled states to attack these resources on the "home front." This not only broadened the geographic area over which war was fought, it also expanded the range of possible targets and increased the adverse impact on civilian populations.[228] As a result, interstate warfare became not only a clash of military forces, but also attacks on the state infrastructure contributing to the warfighting capability of the antagonists.

As a result, the strategic, operational, and tactical levels of war are an important aspect of modern warfare and the military doctrine with which such warfare is conducted. A key to understanding armed conflict is the acknowledgment that warfare between organized armed entities ultimately involves fighting for a political purpose. As Clausewitz most famously noted "war is not merely an act of policy

---

[226]*Prosecutor v Gotovina*, ICTY Case No IT-06-90-T, Vol. I, Trial Chamber, 15 April 2011, para 1189, http://www.icty.org/x/cases/gotovina/tjug/en/110415_judgement_vol1.pdf (The tactical level targets "were command posts of brigades; firing positions of the artillery; communication centres and relay nodes; depots for military equipment, combat reserves and troops; roads and bridges; fortified combat features and enemy defence trenches; and any targets that would emerge during combat").

[227]Ibid ("On the operational level, the firing targets were the SVK Main Staff, the Ministry of Defence headquarters, the SVK communications centre, the bridges and the railway station, all in Knin; the police stations in Knin and Gračac; the military barracks facilities in Knin and other towns; and cross-roads in the towns of Knin, Drvar, Benkovac, and Gračac").

[228]Braudy 2003, p. 459 (In this regard "[w]ith advanced technology playing a greater and greater role in warfare, the strategy of attacking the enemy's industrial based (and civilian workforce) became at least as important as attacking his soldiers").

but a true political instrument, a continuation of political intercourse, carried on by other means."[229] Perhaps of equal import was Clausewitz's reference to the violence of war intended to compel an opponent to do one's will.[230] Similarly, it has been said that war is fought "to bring about a change in the mind in another state."[231] Nor is war only viewed as a political instrument in the context of inter-state conflict. Insurgencies and other conflict involving non-state actors also serve such as purpose.[232] Simply attacking the armed forces of the enemy will generally not achieve the desired end state. As a result war is not just fought at the tactical level. Rather there is a conceptual framework of levels of war that more fully reflects that broader nature of conflict. These levels of war have had a profound impact not only on the way fighting takes place, but also how it is regulated. Understanding how wars are fought requires a more nuanced assessment of all the levels of war, including what has come to be described as the operational level, given that the conduct and analysis of modern conflict is not limited to the binary construct of strategy and tactics.

This raises the question of how these strategic, operational and tactical levels of war are distinguished. This is because a military advantage is not sought solely at the tactical level. The use of the word "strategy" predated the nineteenth century, but came into general use at that time reflecting "the Enlightenment's growing confidence in empirical and the application of reason."[233] It appears to be no coincidence that the emergency of the concept of strategy is linked to the same period that saw the growth in influence of science on society. The general field of study was "first known as *tactics*, a word that had for some time referred to the orderly administration and maneuver of troops."[234] However, Clausewitz had considerable impact with his reliance on the two levels of war: strategy and tactics. Consistent with the idea of military action being grounded in targeting of military forces he stated tactics involve "the use of armed forces in the engagement."[235] In contrast, strategy was described as "the use of engagements for the object of the war."[236]

The British historian, Hew Strachan, suggests that Clausewitz's use of strategy is actually related to what now is considered the operational level of war, which is situated between modern strategy and tactics.[237] Strategy has come to have a

[229]Von Clausewitz 1976, p. 87.

[230]Ibid, p. 75.

[231]Spaight 1947, p. 250.

[232]Galula 1964, pp. 3–4. See also Mao Tse-Tung 2000, pp. 71–72 ("Without a political goal guerrilla, warfare must fail…") and Kolenda 2012, p.xv ("The political aspect [of counterinsurgency] is paramount").

[233]Freedman 2013, p. 72. See also Strachan 2013, p. 28.

[234]Ibid.

[235]Von Clausewitz 1976, p. 128.

[236]Ibid.

[237]Strachan 2013, p. 57.

greater connection to the interface between politics and higher level military planning and direction. This is reflected in the approach that the strategic level is divided into the higher (grand strategy) and lower (strategy) planes. Grand strategy has been called "policy in execution."[238] Its role is "to co-ordinate and direct all the resources of a nation, or band of nations, toward the attainment of the political object of the war—the goal defined by fundamental policy."[239] Strategy, on the other hand, is referred to as the "art of the general."[240]

High or grand strategy, "which so integrates the policies and armaments of the nation that the resort to war is either rendered unnecessary or is undertaken with the maximum chance of victory,"[241] is the level at which a state, or other political entity, is likely to be influenced. This level of war operates on a broader plane than simply that of the armed forces. It "calculates and develops the economic and man-power resources" of the state, "fosters the people's willing spirit" and regulates "the distribution of power between the several services, and between the services and industry."[242] In addition to fighting power, grand strategy "should take into account of and apply the power of financial pressure, of diplomatic pressure, of commercial pressure, and, not the least of ethical pressure, to weaken the opponent's will."[243] It is here that the conduct of strategic military campaigns have historically been directed in seeking to influence the "mind" of the state, as well as attack the broader resources allocated for war. The lower strategic level is concerned with "distributing and applying military means to fulfill the ends of policy."[244] The distinction between the two levels of strategy is that "while the horizon of strategy is bounded by the war, grand strategy looks beyond the war to subsequent peace."[245] It is at the lower level of strategy that the political objectives are translated into military ones, which are then executed at the tactical level to meet those policy goals. The outstanding issue is how the military advantage associated with the identification of military objectives and the resolution of the proportionality assessment is related to such strategic objectives.

Between the levels of strategy and tactics, there has developed the intervening operational level of war wherein "campaigns and major operations are planned, conducted, and sustained to achieve strategic objectives within theaters or other

---

[238]Liddell Hart 1991, p. 322. See also Strachan 2013, pp. 31–33 (where it is suggested this division of strategy into two levels is based on the work of J.F.C Fuller and the maritime warfare strategist, Julian Corbett. Julian Corbett used "major strategy" and "minor strategy." The former dealt with the whole resources of the nation, while the latter operational planning).

[239]Ibid. See also Earle 1971, p viii.

[240]Liddell Hart 1991, p. 322.

[241]Earle 1971, p vii.

[242]Liddell Hart 1991, p. 322.

[243]Ibid.

[244]Ibid, p. 321.

[245]Ibid, p. 322.

operational areas."[246] Previously referred to as "grand tactics," this level of warfare was closely tied to maneuver warfare. That form of warfare is a doctrinal approach embedded in Western military thought that advocated a military focus where "forces should be directed against the opponent's center of gravity."[247] The ISAF headquarters in Kabul, Afghanistan, established in the aftermath of the post-9/11 Coalition invasion of that country, is an example of an operational level headquarters. A principle role for such a headquarters is setting conditions for success at the tactical level as it "links strategic direction with traditional tactical activity."[248] Neither the tactical level, nor the military advantage to be gained from military action, exists in isolation.

The operational level of war is said to have developed in part because during the Cold War the threat of nuclear war caused strategic thought to focus on deterrence and less on actual fighting. The result was that "deterrence theory, strategic thought's principle output of the 1960s, was largely shaped by civilian strategists."[249] This change has been linked to the development of the operational level of war in order to insulate commanders from meddling politicians. In effect a "politics free zone."[250] However, in reality there can be no zone free from political, or legal influence for that matter. The challenge is to ensure that the political and military leaders remain constantly in a dialog. As Lawrence Freedman has noted:

> Political ends could not be discussed without regard for military risks. Whether or not to offer diplomatic concessions, seek resources or bases from third parties, or construct alliances, depended upon military assessments. These assessments in turn led to assumptions on the shape of the rival coalition and their ability to withstand long wars or extend their reach through bases. The idea of a military strategy separate from a political strategy was not only misleading but also dangerous.[251]

Therefore, what is required for the proper conduct of warfare is a much more dynamic interaction between the levels of war, and with it an appreciation of the military advantage to be gained from adopting a particular course of action. The result is that the strategic, operational, and tactical levels of war are focused on the broader military objectives of a campaign. The plans and methods of warfare that are designed to achieve politically directed ends originating from the level of high strategy.

---

[246]DOD Dictionary (2015)(the definition of the "operational level of war").

[247]Freedman 2013, p. 205.

[248]Connaughton 2008, p. 349.

[249]Strachan 2013, p. 212.

[250]Freedman 2013, p. 202.

[251]Ibid, p. 242.

13.5.2 The Strategic Impact of Airpower

In terms of targeting, the relationship between the use of airpower and the four levels of war is a powerful one that has strongly influenced targeting doctrine and consideration of the advantage to be gained from military action. At times it seems there is an inordinate focus on air warfare. It has been suggested, "air war in general, whether by helicopter gunship or remote aircraft carrier, tends to give the impression of disproportionality and indiscrimination, whether in Gaza, Baghdad, or Mogadishu."[252] This can be seen in the attention paid to the damage caused by aerial attacks during the 2006 Israeli-Hezbollah Conflict. During that conflict it is reported that in 34 days 15,500 sorties were flown (of which 10,000 were fighter sorties) and 7,000 targets were struck.[253]

This focus on airpower is all the more interesting given the increased capabilities of artillery forces. For example, during the 2006 Lebanon war, artillery batteries were reported to have fired close to 180,000 shells,[254] and the navy "conducted over 2,500 bombardments off the Lebanese coast...."[255] The identification of artillery fire as forming a significant threat to the civilian population is not a new issue[256] and is one that will likely attract increasing attention because of the expanded use of long-range ground-to-ground missiles by both non-state[257] and state actors.[258] It was clearly the subject of analysis in the *Gotovina Case*.[259] The

[252]Carmola 2005, p. 103.

[253]Cordesman et al. 2007, p. 121.

[254]Harel and Issacharoff 2008, p. 236.

[255]Catignani 2008, p. 189.

[256]Nurick 1945, pp. 683–685 (this article provides insightful 1945 review of the a variety of methods of warfare including artillery and the long-range "robot bomb" that the Germans used against London during World War II).

[257]Katz and Hendel 2012, p. 25 ("Israel estimated that Hezbollah in 2012 had somewhere between 50,000 and 60,000 rockets of various ranges that could reach almost anywhere within the State of Israel...").

[258]For example, see G Cohen, "IDF sets up battalion to launch rockets into populated areas," *Ha'aretz* (3 April 2012), http://www.haaretz.com/news/diplomacy-defense/idf-sets-up-battalion-to-launch-rockets-into-populated-areas-1.422226 (where it is indicated that the original range of the rockets would be from 30 to 40 km, but this would be increased to 160 km. It was further reported that "[a]ir force officers voiced reservations in discussions about the long-range rockets, saying their use would overlap some of the air force's missions").

[259]*Prosecutor v Gotovina*, ICTY Case No IT-06-90-T, Vol. I, Trial Chamber, 15 April 2011, http://www.icty.org/x/cases/gotovina/tjug/en/110415_judgement_vol1.pdf, *Prosecutor v Gotovina*, ICTY Case No IT-06-90-T, Vol. II, Trial Chamber, 15 April 2011, http://www.icty.org/x/cases/gotovina/tjug/en/110415_judgement_vol2.pdf, and *Prosecutor v Gotovina*, ICTY Case No IT-06-90-A, Appeal Chamber, 16 November 2012, http://www.icty.org/x/cases/gotovina/acjug/en/121116_judgement.pdf

increased capability of artillery munitions, particularly because of the development of more precise munitions, presents a scenario where they can be used to conduct many missions presently carried out by air forces.[260] It should also be noted that this focus on strategic effects is not limited to air or land warfare. Historically, creating such effects has also been an important part of conflict at sea.[261] It has been said that the object of maritime warfare is broader than that of the land environment since activities associated with economic warfare (i.e., blockade and the interdiction of commerce) extend to interrupting the "life of the nation."[262] In this regard "[t]he vital question for strategy was not how to win a battle but how to exert pressure on the enemy's society and government."[263] This aspect of warfare has not changed with time.

However, notwithstanding the need to look at other means and methods of warfare, it is airpower and its theorists that have had a particular influence on how wars are fought by states. In part, this may be because of the critical role that airpower has taken on in armed conflict starting in the early twentieth century.[264] The view of early airpower theorists following World War I was that airpower would decisively dominate future wars. Attacks would be made on "the enemy's great industrial and governing centers. All these attacks would be made against the civil population in order to compel it to accept the will of the attacker."[265] While efforts were made to regulate aerial warfare through the development of the *1923 Hague Rules of Air Warfare* the norm against bombing civilians prior to World War II was a weak one.[266] The result was that "the first seemingly indiscriminate attacks on capital cities began a spiral that quickly led to the loss of almost all restraint in the

---

[260] G Cohen, "IDF sets up battalion to launch rockets into populated areas," *Ha'aretz* (3 April 2012), http://www.haaretz.com/news/diplomacy-defense/idf-sets-up-battalion-to-launch-rockets-into-populated-areas-1.422226 (The Israeli rockets would at first be guided with a GPS guidance system, however, that would be replaced with more precise munitions.). See also D Lamothe, "Long shot: Artillery battery sets lethal record," *Marine Corps Times* (30 June 2013), http://www.marinecorpstimes.com/news/2012/06/marine-record-setting-long-shot-artillery-strike-m777-063012w/ [where it is reported the GPS guided 155 mm Excalibur round was fired 36 km (22 miles) in Helmand Province, Afghanistan. It is also indicated "Army officials said it provided 'unmatched precision and lethality for artillery projectiles critical to urban warfare'"].

[261] Corbett 2004.

[262] Ibid, pp. 90–100. Freedman 2013, p. 119 ["This argued for consideration of blockade and attacks on commerce ('guerre de course') as much as seeking out the enemy fleet."]. Strachan 2013, pp. 147–148 (The Royal Air Force interwar bombing strategy is linked to an interpretation the World War I blockade that viewed its effects as having forced the German population to seek peace.

[263] Freedman 2013, p. 119.

[264] Murray and Scales 2003, pp. 180 (It has meant, "U.S. ground forces have rarely had to deal with enemy aircraft overhead, and that air superiority has allowed U.S. ground forces the freedom to maneuver audaciously…").

[265] Spaight 1947, p. 14 [quoting from Fuller 1920, pp. 314–315].

[266] Thomas 2001, p. 125.

conduct of bombing."[267] The conduct of air campaigns came to be associated with wars of attrition.[268] However, bombing by both Britain and Germany "resulted in terrible civilian pain but had limited political effect. Their main effect was on the ability to prosecute the war by disrupting production and fuel supplies."[269] This did not necessarily degrade faith by theorists in airpower as a means to force an opponent to cease participation in a conflict. It was stated at the end of World War II that air power "will set itself to the task—a political rather than a strictly military one—of bringing pressure to bear upon the principals whose agents hitherto had to be destroyed…."[270]Although the effectiveness of the strategic bombing campaigns in Europe and elsewhere has been called into question,[271] belief in this approach as an effective war-winning weapon has remained strong.

Importantly, in respect of the normative restrictions on the use of airpower existing at that time it was noted in 1952 by a leading jurist, Hersch Lauterpacht, "[t]he fact is that in the matter of aerial bombardment there is no rule firmly grounded in the past on which we can place reliance—for aerial bombardment is a new weapon which raises new problems."[272] That was to begin to change in 1977 with the development of *Additional Protocol I.* As has been noted that *Protocol* placed emphasis on distinguishing between civilians and those who take a direct part in hostilities, thereby removing the civilians working in war industry or otherwise indirectly supporting military forces (i.e., the factory worker/quasi-combatant) as a target, established criteria for the identification of objects as military objectives, and prohibited attacks which would result in excessive collateral civilian casualties and damage. It was in this context that the criterion of military advantage was introduced as part of the legal framework intended to restrict the broad use of force. However, what the introduction of this normative framework did not do is alter the nature of warfare, or the importance of the high strategy and lower strategic levels of war.

In the direct aftermath of World War II, the focus from an airpower perspective was less on conventional warfare and more on nuclear capabilities.[273] Further, engagement in conflicts involving opponents waging guerrilla warfare led to the greater consideration of non-lethal roles performed by air forces, such as reconnaissance and air mobility.[274] However, airpower theory did not remain stagnant, even as the normative framework under which it would be assessed began to gain

---

[267]Ibid at 131.

[268]Liddell Hart 1991, pp. 350–351.

[269]Freedman 2013, p. 158.

[270]Spaight 1947, p. 3.

[271]Keegan 1993, p. 377 ("Strategic bombing had not defeated Germany"). However, see also Overy 2005, p. 151 (where it is noted the effects of World War II bombing degraded German capacity to sustain and expand the war, although it did not force a capitulation).

[272]Lauterpacht 1952, pp. 365–366.

[273]MacIssac 1984, p. 644.

[274]Ibid.

currency. In the late 1980s and early 1990s, an American theorist, Colonel John Warden, outlined an influential theory in *The Air Campaign: Planning for Combat*[275] and *The Enemy As a System*.[276] John Warden's theory placed more emphasis on attacking the enemy leadership (both political and military) than on economic warfare.[277] Under this theory "command" was targeted as a "true center of gravity."[278] His analytical construct sought to translate political and strategic objectives into operational plans by relating political ends to strategic ways to reach those ends and the identification of targets as the means by which to carry out that strategy.[279] The enemy was viewed as a "system" with five centers of gravity: leadership, organic essentials (i.e., electricity, oil, food, money), infrastructure (i.e., roads, transmission lines), civilian population (i.e., the people) and fielded forces (e.g., military, police and firemen)[280] that should be subjected to "parallel" attack "striking blows everywhere at the same time."[281] It was noted that a direct attack on a civilian population is "morally reprehensible and militarily difficult."[282] Instead the theory advocated an indirect approach like that followed by the North Vietnamese in the Vietnam war of influencing public resistance to the war in the United States "by raising American military casualty levels higher than the American people would tolerate."[283]

The Warden theory is noteworthy for its heavy reliance on examples and analogies that have a scientific connotation, such as equations (i.e., Physical x Moral = Outcome); the enemy system as a human body, or solar system; reference to electrons and atoms; reliance of architectural metaphors; and the use of the concept of centers of gravity. This theory was not the first time in history that such reference had been made.[284] For example, Clausewitz's theories of "friction in war" and "centers of gravity" were identified as being borrowed from the physics of the day.[285] Airpower theory, and the targeting assessments that it spawned, have long had an association, however, tenuous, with scientific terminology.

However, none of these theories about warfare reflects an enterprise that truly attracts the precision normally associated with the hard sciences of physics,

---

[275]Warden 1988.

[276]Warden 1995.

[277]Ibid (Where it is suggested "[t]he most critical ring is the command ring because it is the enemy command structure"). See also Holley 1997, p. 593.

[278]Warden 1988, p. 54.

[279]Holley 1997, p. 593.

[280]Warden 1995.

[281]Ibid.

[282]Ibid.

[283]Ibid.

[284]Boyne 2005, p. 355 (discussing that Douhet, Mitchell and Trenchard had emphasized vital centers and Clausewitz's reference to centers of gravity.), Liddell Hart 1991, p. 212 (talking in terms of paralyzing the enemy.) and Freedman 2013, pp. 130–31 (referring to John Fuller's advocacy of "brain warfare" and the analogy of an army as a "body").

[285]Freedman 2013, p. 91.

biology, or mathematics.[286] While biology and physics can act as helpful metaphors, they do not provide precise answers on either the utility of the use of force, or its actual effects. The scientific language appears to mask a more complex and less certain theoretical framework for the application of force. Further, undermining this reliance on scientific terminology to give an objective aura to this form of warfare is the long-standing view that strategy is both an art form and a science.[287] While it has also been suggested that strategy might be purely an art, due to the uncertainty of the situations within which it must operate,[288] the perspective it has some scientific basis in the planning stages has been said to give way at some point to the art of war as the conflict unfolds.[289] This is because "[w]hen battle is joined, the theory could say little because of the many variables in play."[290] Given the lack of precision associated with a fundamental theoretical construct for the conduct of warfare (e.g., strategy) it should come as no surprise that one of the outcomes of military operations: targeting proportionality, would be viewed in the *Targeted Killings Case* to not be a "standard of precision."[291] In this context there is a fundamental problem if the law demands more precision than the activity it regulates can deliver.

The version of airpower theory developed at the end of the twentieth century is noteworthy in that it marked a shift away from industrial attrition to "effects based" operations.[292] It was this theory that underpinned the 1991 air campaign conducted against Iraq.[293] It is an approach that has proven controversial even within the military. In what has been referred to as an ideological struggle,[294] there has been disagreement over whether air forces should be used primarily in a strategic campaign, or in a support role for ground or maritime forces.[295] During the 2003 Iraq War, the use of an independent strategic air campaign was rejected although strategic air attack was still conducted as part of an integrated air campaign.[296] Treating the enemy as a system, or a "system of systems," has continued to be a key aspect of air doctrine as part of what has become known as "Effects

[286] *Public Committee Against Torture in Israel v. Israel*, Israel Supreme Court [16 December 2006], 46 ILM 375, para 58.

[287] Freedman 2013, pp. 74–75 (where it is noted historically strategy was viewed as both a science and an art form with the former becoming equated with planning and once battle was joined it became an art form).

[288] Ibid, p. 612.

[289] Ibid, p. 75.

[290] Ibid.

[291] *Public Committee Against Torture in Israel v. Israel*, Israel Supreme Court [16 December 2006], 46 ILM 375, para 58.

[292] Schmitt 2004, p. 60.

[293] Lewis 2003, p. 481.

[294] Ibid, pp. 484–485.

[295] Ibid, p. 484.

[296] Grant 2003, pp. 36–38.

Based Operations" (EBO).[297] A systemic approach was also a part of a unique Israeli theory called "Systemic Operational Design" (SOD).[298] It provided an alternative approach to the traditional operational planning process that had been criticized for being cumbersome, rigid, time-consuming, and best suited for "large-scale, state-versus-state, mechanized warfare against a known enemy."[299] The SOD theory, which formed the basis of a military doctrine developed and adopted just prior to the 2006 Second Lebanon War, was particularly controversial. This new approach, designed to deal with asymmetric threats,[300] is indicated to have been abandoned after the conflict and replaced with the more broadly accepted effects-based warfare approach.

Criticism about a systemic approach for the conduct of warfare has not been limited to SOD. The theory of EBO has also been criticized within the United States military with airpower proponents remaining its most ardent champion.[301] At the heart of this dispute appears to be the different approach to warfare adopted by the air force in comparison to the other services. One scathing academic assessment of aerial bombing has suggested that strategic bombing persists because "it served the bureaucratic interests of air forces," "both civilian and military leaders want cheap and easy solutions to difficult international confrontations," "ignorance allows strategic bombing enthusiasts to sway public decisions with unsupported assumptions" and there has been "deliberate obfuscation of the brutality of strategic-bombing campaign."[302] Notwithstanding these disagreements about the efficacy of aerial bombing, the essence of the conduct of warfare remains based on achieving a political goal through the use of force applied at all levels of war across the conflict spectrum. In other words: creating an impact in order to influence an opponent's conduct of the war. It also means that effects-based targeting remains at the heart of targeting doctrine. The result is that the linear connection between the various levels of war (i.e., planning to use means and methods of warfare to meet strategic political and military objectives) and seeking to attain various effects when carrying out targeting continues to be an integral and important part of the targeting theory.[303] It is within this multi-level approach to war that military advantage also has to be considered.

---

[297]Deptula 2001, p. 5 ("Any political entity can be thought of as a system consisting of a number of subsystems, or to borrow a term coined in the former Air Force Systems Command—a system of systems").

[298]Lauder 2009, p. 44 (for a description of SOD).

[299]Ibid, p. 44.

[300]Harel and Issacharoff 2008, p. 59–61.

[301]Correll 2013, p. 50. See also Strachan 2013, p. 252 (where it is prematurely suggested effects-based operations are "now discredited and largely abandoned").

[302]Pape 1996, pp. 326–327.

[303]For example, see Joint Targeting 2013, p viii ("Targeting links the desired effects to actions and tasks"). See also Corn and Corn 2012, p. 337 (for a discussion of targeting including the use of indirect artillery fire in populated areas).

While conduct of warfare cannot simply be reduced to mathematical equations or scientific theories,[304] it is also clear that targeting cannot be guided by the "crude expression of instinct."[305] Consideration needs to be given to the legal framework that states themselves have developed to limit the conduct of warfare. However, that body of law has to regulate the full spectrum of conflict. It cannot be limited to one level or war (e.g., tactical), a particular type of conflict (e.g., interstate), or even a specific method or means of warfare (e.g., air warfare). Clausewitz wrote about warfare in physical terms without limitations associated with moral force.[306] To the extent the development of strategy was rooted in the Enlightenment, so were other schools of thought that saw the recognition and development of humanitarianism and human rights.[307] In this regard it is not only science that shapes strategy, or the manner in which war is conducted, but also morality and the law. Ultimately, assessing military advantage requires consideration of a wide variety of factors occurring at the different levels of war, including the strategic level. The goal of armed conflict is not just to destroy the armed forces of an enemy. It is also to influence that entity's decision makers to cease the conflict, and destroy the supporting infrastructure that enables the conduct of hostilities. However, the question remains as to how that theory is applied within a legal framework that requires the advantage being sought to be a military one.

13.5.3 Military Advantage and the Enemy Population

What is evident is that warfare is not just about tactics, or limited to assessing "ground gained and in annihilating or weakening the enemy armed forces."[308] A particularly challenging issue for any court will be determining whether a strategic targeting campaign is focused on attacking legitimate military objectives with a goal of creating an effect that forces the enemy population and their leaders to desist from participation in conflict, or in reality constitutes the terrorization of the civilian population. It is this issue that highlights the limits of what is considered to be the legitimate direct "military" advantage that can be anticipated from an attack, or series of attacks.

While exerting influence on an enemy might, on its face, appear to be an overly indirect goal it should be reinforced that seeking to impact decision makers through coercive action also occurs outside the context of an armed conflict. It has

[304] Kraska 2011, p. 19 (where it is noted "successfully prosecuting military operations at the operational level of war is both a science and an art") and Freedman 2013, p xii (where the realm of strategy is described as the "art of creating power").

[305] Von Clausewitz 1976, p. 76.

[306] Ibid, p. 75.

[307] Hunt 2007, pp. 76–82 (for a discussion of the impact of the spread of Enlightenment humanitarianism on judicially imposed torture and punishment).

[308] ICRC Additional Protocol I Commentary 1987, Article 57, para 2218.

been an inherent part of sanctions regimes that may be put in place by the United Nations to force a state to conform to its international obligations.[309] However, an issue that has resonance for strategic bombing is that the theoretical underpinnings of conventional approaches toward broad-based sanctions (e.g., a "pain-gain" formula designed to pressure populations to bring pressure on their political leaders) has been called into question on theoretical, empirical and ethical grounds.[310] Interestingly, the result has been the development of more "targeted" sanctions against the political leadership of a state or non-state actor focused on arms embargoes, financial sanctions and travel sanctions.[311] An area of caution for airpower advocates seeking a swift cessation of conflict is that states under threat through the use of sanctions have tended to change their behavior to endure rather than alter its policies.[312] Finally, there remains a crucial difference between the sanctions regime and strategic warfare. The sanctions regime does not seek to exert its influence through kinetic means.

The particular difference between sanctions and kinetic targeting is found in the emphasis placed in *Additional Protocol I* on there being a military advantage to carrying out an attack. In this respect, the most significant restrictions in the legal framework governing targeting are not the modifiers, "definite,"[313] or "concrete or direct" applied to the term military advantage.[314] It is that the advantage must be "military." While changing the mind of an opponent is an essential goal of warfare it is clear that hostilities cannot be conducted through attacks on purely political targets, or for purely political reasons.[315] Attacks can only be made against lawful military objectives, including both objects and persons. Influence can be attempted through the exercise of a strategically focused campaign by means of indirect effects arising from the successful prosecution of those targets. This includes the broader target set of objects that contribute to the war-fighting capacity of an opponent. Therefore, there are two effects that may result from an attack. First, by attacking the supporting infrastructure and resources (i.e., the electrical system, oil production capacity, transportation system), the direct goal is to deny the enemy the use of these objects. It is difficult to argue; particularly in terms of technologically advanced military forces that commodities such as oil, electricity, armaments and other outputs from that infrastructure will not make an effective contribution to military action.[316] The military advantage of denying such outputs to enemy

[309] Tostensen and Bull 2002, p. 373.

[310] Ibid, p. 375.

[311] Ibid, p. 382. See also "Security Council authorizes EU force, new sanctions regime in Central African Republic," *UN News Centre* (28 January 2014) http://www.un.org/apps/news/story.asp?NewsID=47027andCr=central+african+republicandCr1=#.Uuo8E3mBDIY (accessed 27 March 2015) (where the UN "added travel bans and asset freezes to an arms embargo already in place").

[312] Geiss 2005, p. 188.

[313] AP I, Article 52(2).

[314] AP I, Article 57(2)(a)(iii).

[315] Dinstein 2010, para 229.

[316] AP I, Article 52(2).

forces appears self-evident. Humanitarian law permits the targeting of the actual supplies, and the infrastructure that produces them. What may be at issue is the degree of importance, or value of the military advantage being sought in attacking those objects and of course the humanitarian impact of those attacks.

Secondly, the successful degradation of the capacity of an enemy to fight may also influence the political and military decision makers, as well as the population of the opposing state, or other entity, to adopt or refrain from following a particular course of military action. This inevitably raises the issue of deterrence, which has been noted "is based on the Latin *deterre*—to frighten from or away."[317] A strategy of deterrence, which involves "deliberate, purposive threats," was a concept that "developed prior to the Second World War in contemplation of strategic air raids."[318] This strategy still influences the writings of contemporary air power theorists seeking to shape the choices made by states and non-state actors. Deterrence is a concept commonly referred to in the Israeli context,[319] even having acquired a title "named after Beirut's southern suburbs where Hezbollah's leadership resides,"[320] the "Dahiyah doctrine." That neighborhood, which also housed Hezbollah's headquarters and its television station, Al Manar, was heavily damaged by strikes which was bombed extensively during the 2006 Israel/Hezbollah conflict.[321]

To the extent a deterrence theory relies on threatening a painful response to any attack, there remains the issue of proportionality, and whether a deterrent response can be exercised within the confines of humanitarian law targeting rules.[322] David Kretzmer suggests the "[u]se of force that seems to be largely punitive, the primary motive of which is deterrence or which has wide political aims will be regarded as disproportionate."[323] Deterrence is a concept that raises the issue of how the civilian population, including the political leadership, can be lawfully

---

[317]Freedman 2013, p. 157.

[318]Ibid.

[319]Y Lappin, "*Deterring Hezbollah: The ex-IDF deputy chief of staff shares his vision for Israeli security,*" The Jerusalem Post (28 March 2015), http://www.jpost.com/International/Deterring-Hezbollah-395275. (Accessed 28 March 2015).

[320]Blanford 2011, pp. 455–454.

[321]Harel and Issacharoff 2008, pp. 99–102 (It is reported that "[t]he area was transformed into a sea of rubble." These attacks were said to be controversial even within the Israeli Government. Criticism centered on the strikes constituting an expansion of the conflict away from southern Lebanon, where most of Hezbollah's military strength was concentrated; the potential harm to civilians; and a view that "[t]he military benefits of the bombing were marginal." See ibid, p. 100). However, see also Harel and Issacharoff 2008, p. 260 and Byman 2011, p. 203. In addition see Catignani 2008, p. 193 (where Israel initially was reported to have been seen to exude weakness) and Byman 2011, pp. 264–265 (for reference to discussion having turned to Hezbollah not firing rockets during the 2008–2009 Israel/Hamas conflict (Operation Cast Lead) and relative quiet along the border with Lebanon as an indication of its deterrent effect).

[322]Shapiro 2013, p. 57 (where reference is made to deterrence theory relying on an unpredictable reaction).

[323]Kretzmer 2013, p. 281.

influenced. Perhaps one of the most problematic aspects of airpower theory and, as a result, effects-based targeting is the idea that kinetic operations can motivate the civilian population, or a political leadership to bring about the end of a conflict. The question to be answered is whether such action offers a military advantage.

The non-legal challenges of carrying out a targeting campaign to influence a civilian population is reflected in John Warden's theory where he states, "let us reiterate that we hold direct attacks on civilians to be morally reprehensible and militarily difficult."[324] Further, he indicates "[a]s part of an overall effort to alter the enemy system, an *indirect* approach to the population is *probably* worthwhile; *one should not, however, count on it*."[325] This is less than robust theoretical support for such use of airpower, although in practice there continues to be reference by some military commanders to influencing the population by striking at targets such as electrical grids.[326] This raises the complex issue of identifying the true purpose of an attack and what constitutes appropriate direct and indirect effects arising from that attack.

Legally, it is not permitted to target the civilian population, or to carry out bombing for the purpose solely of demoralizing the population. For example, William Boothby has indicated, "it would be unlawful to make the civilian aspect of the electricity supply the object of the attack."[327] The same holds true for the civilian political leadership. That is established in Article 51(2) of *Additional Protocol I*, which states:

> The civilian population as such, as well as individual civilians, shall not be the object of attack. Acts or threats of violence *the primary purpose of which is to spread terror* among the civilian population are prohibited.[328]

This prohibition is linked to the idea of directly bombing the civilians, which was a prevalent part of the discussion about the use of airpower prior to World War II.[329] Although criticism of the Allied bombing of population centers was voiced during that conflict,[330] it was not until 1977 that the movement to legally limit the impact of aerial bombing found success in the creation of the *Additional Protocol I* provisions on targeting.[331]

---

[324] Warden 1995.

[325] Ibid (emphasis added).

[326] Boothby 2012, p. 499 [referring to comments made by Lieutenant-General Short regarding the 1999 Kosovo air campaign, as reported in C Whitney, "Air wars won't stay risk-free, general says," *NY Times* (18 June 1999).], and Harel and Issacharoff 2008, p. 184 (regarding attacking the Lebanese electrical grid).

[327] Boothby 2012, p. 503.

[328] AP I, Article 51(2) (emphasis added).

[329] Spaight 1947, pp. 10–15.

[330] Ibid, p. 250 (for reference to the Bishop of Gloucester having written in 1943 that "'The real work of the Air Force is to support troops in battle' and that anything else was 'a barbaric war'"). See also Lindqvist 2001, p. 99.

[331] Baxter 2013, p. 241 (setting out the post-World War II efforts to address aerial bombing prior to the Diplomatic Conferences leading to the creation of the *Additional Protocols*).

One impact of Article 51(2) is that the prohibition on spreading terror among the civilian population substantively returns the focus of the "terror" debate to the actions of a state, which was the original genesis of the term.[332] It has been noted that the use of "primary" in that article to describe the prohibited purpose of that attack "may give rise to difficulties."[333] However, that term has also been suggested to be a better alternative to an "exclusive" purpose test, as that approach "sets the standard too high."[334] The focus on the "primary" purpose raises questions regarding there being multiple purposes for an attack. It has been suggested that given an overall reading of *Additional Protocol I* a secondary purpose of the attack is to spread terror among the civilian population would also be unlawful.[335] That view should be extended to the position that no purpose of an attack, primary, secondary or tertiary can be to directly or indirectly terrorize the civilian population. At law, there can be no military advantage derived from terrorizing civilians.

More often, the debate will center on the question of whether the purpose of an attack is to terrorize, or simply indirectly influence a population. There is a very subtle difference between these two outcomes that comes into play in assessing the lawfulness of an air campaign. The *ICRC Commentary* notes in respect of the ban on terrorizing the civilian population: "there is no doubt that acts of violence related to a state of war almost always give rise to some degree of terror among the population and sometimes also among the armed forces.... This is not the sort of terror envisaged here."[336] This unfortunate wording could be read to suggest that some level of terror is permitted. This issue might have been better addressed by indicating that the violence associated with armed conflict not directed at the civilian population, but which inevitably causes them anxiety and fear, is not prohibited. Setting aside the issue of excessive collateral casualties prohibited under other provisions of the *Protocol*, humanitarian law does not preclude the civilian population from being adversely impacted as the result of an attack on lawful objectives as long as the primary purpose of the attack was not to terrorize the population.

What this reflects is that while the civilian population is protected to a significant degree from physical and psychological harm the protection is not absolute. This humanitarian rule highlights the unique position the opposing civilian population occupies in an interstate conflict. Unlike counterinsurgency operations and situations of occupation, gaining the support of a civilian population in a foreign territory is not ordinarily a strategic priority during international armed conflict.[337]

---

[332]Townshend 2002, p. 37 (noting that the eighteenth century French "Reign of Terror," "was informed by the Enlightenment assumption that the social order can be changed by human agency").

[333]Saul 2008, p. 294.

[334]Ibid, p. 295.

[335]Boothby 2012, p. 503.

[336]ICRC Additional Protocol I Commentary 1987, Article 57, para 1940.

[337]Watkin 2012, pp. 286–287.

Rather the intent is to influence the population to withdraw their support for the activities of their own government and hopefully apply pressure on the political leadership to cease the hostilities. The same goal applies in attempts to influence the enemy civilian politicians. However, the relationship between the civilian population and their political leaders can be a complicating factor in the ability to influence the course of the conflict. This is particularly so if the political leaders do not care what the population thinks, or can effectively manipulate the attacks to demonize the enemy.[338] Further, the political leadership may not be susceptible to the influence exerted by kinetic attacks, given that the capitulation of hostilities may mean not just a loss of power, but also imprisonment or even death.

It is the very subtlety of how a civilian population may be influenced that affects the approach for conducting attacks in order to force a change in the mind of the state. At law any object being targeted must be a military one in that it makes an effective contribution to military action. Further, that action must result a sufficiently important military advantage in its own right to warrant an attack separate from any ancillary effect its capture, destruction, or neutralization might have on the population. While it is clearly advantageous to cause an opponent to cease hostilities, whether as a result of pressure from the population or by influencing the political leadership, the advantage arising in that context is a derivative outcome, and one that is likely cumulative in nature arising from the prosecution of a number of lawful attacks. At some point the population comes to believe that further participation in the conflict is not to their advantage because the state is losing militarily. However, this does not appear to be the sort of advantage contemplated by *Additional Protocol I*, and certainly not one that would justify targeting people or objects that did not make a contribution to a military outcome.

It is on this point that airpower theory and the law seems to take different paths. As John Warden's theory suggests:

> It is imperative to remember that all actions are aimed against the mind of the enemy command or against the enemy system as a whole. Thus, an attack against industry or infrastructure is not primarily conducted because of the effect it might or might not have on fielded forces. Rather, it is undertaken for its direct effect on the enemy system, including its effect on national leaders and commanders who must assess the cost of rebuilding, the effect on the state's economic position in the postwar period, the internal political effect on their own survival, and whether the cost is worth the potential gain from continuing the war.[339]

This theory suggests that not all targets will be purely military in nature. It appears to be ambivalent regarding the impact on "fielded forces." However, in warfare, where an attack may have both military and political outcomes, there must be, in order to protect the civilian population, a tipping point at which the political purpose is seen to be dominant, and any possible military advantage fades

338 Tostensen and Bull 2002, p. 376 (outlining how Iraq did this with respect to the UN sanctions regime)

339 Warden 1995.

into the background. This is particularly so when the targeting of industry and infrastructure is said to be for the purpose of the impact it will have on a population, or national leaders. When that happens the prosecution of the target becomes problematic. As soon as military commanders and airpower theorists place emphasis on that impact, rather than on the military advantage to be gained from targeting the objects themselves because of their direct or indirect contribution to military action, this appears to make the attack an impermissible political rather than a lawful military one.

A particular challenge for proponents who advocate targeting for the purpose of impacting the will of the people is that they appear particularly hard pressed to present examples where this theory has actually worked. In this regard it has been indicated that the "shock and awe" campaign during the 2003 Iraq invasion had little effect on Saddam Hussein's hold on power.[340] John Warden's previously noted Vietnam example does not address the reality that the loss of small wars by democracies occurs for much broader societal concerns than a state's own casualties. It extends to the "brutality" of war, including the use of torture and elevated enemy civilian casualties.[341] Certainly, the acceptance of such "influence" operations by law abiding states is not particularly well supported by a reference to it having succeeded in the case of Iraqi terror attacks on Iran.[342] Attempts to influence a population, or a political leadership also appears to be a far more extended and uncertain process than airpower advocates suggest when claiming an ability to bring about a quick end to hostilities. Air campaigns do not appear to succeed as war-winning strategies on their own and certainly not in the time period often suggested. For example, with respect to the 1999 Kosovo Conflict, which has been suggested to be a war won by airpower,[343] there has been recognition that aerial bombing alone did not yield success.[344] Further, even after the fact it is difficult to know what factors are decisive in bring about victory. As has been noted "it may never be possible finally to decide why Slobodan Milosevic decided to yield to NATO towards the end of the Kosovo conflict."[345]

The inherent uncertainty in airpower theory is perhaps best reflected in its unsubstantiated claim that it has a uniquely, or particularly strong scientific basis. In this respect, it would be interesting to see how well the metaphors relied on by airpower theorists to underpin their approach stand up to the scrutiny of an accountability framework that may demand scientific proof of the anticipated

[340] Murray and Scales 2003, pp. 74.

[341] Merom 2003, p. 230 ("This book, then, argues that what fails democracies in small wars is the interaction of sensitivity to casualties, repugnance to brutal military behaviour, and commitment to democratic life").

[342] Warden 1995 (it is here John Warden notes such attacks are "morally reprehensible and militarily difficult").

[343] Lewis 2003, p. 486 n 40.

[344] Gray 2005, p. 101, and Boyne 2005, p. 363.

[345] Boothby 2012, p. 501.

psychological effect resulting from the conduct of such a campaign.[346] Ultimately, the challenge is that the influencing of a population, like strategy in general, is not amenable to a purely scientific analysis. However, in a context in which any strategic bombing may have a negative psychological or other effect on the civilians, Article 51(2) *Protocol* does preserve space for attacks that will have indirect systemic impact on the decision makers, or the population of the state.

13.5.4 Military Advantage and the Accumulation of "Effects"

A second area where the courts will likely have to consider the strategic nature of warfare is in assessing military advantage in the context of a cumulative targeting effort to degrade the infrastructure that supports participation in armed conflict. The nature of a strategic targeting campaign is that, depending upon the strategic goals and the effect to be achieved, a large number of targets may have to be prosecuted to achieve the desired effect. When that occurs there is also an elevated likelihood of collateral civilian casualties and damage since many of objects that indirectly, but effectively support enemy operations are often located in civilian inhabited areas. However, the number of targets actually struck to obtain the desired effect will be context dependent. In a strategic targeting campaign, a sophisticated target development process is applied that seeks to look at the relationship between targets and the ultimate "military advantage" to be achieved from an attack, or series of attacks. Campaign objectives are broadly developed at the strategic level, and the planning process proceeds down to the operational and then the tactical level of war where targets are prosecuted. The result is that there is a link between the targets that are tasked and the overall strategic objectives that are being sought. Those links mean strategic goals help define the militarily valid (i.e., necessary or advantageous) target that is ultimately attacked at the tactical level. It also means that tactical level action can have strategic impact. This phenomenon is not unique to aerial bombing campaigns as is represented by the 1990s concept of the "strategic corporal," which identified that the outcome of operations can hinge on decisions made at the lowest levels of command.[347]

It is this same linear relationship that facilitates political direction of the conflict. It is this relationship that makes the idea of an operational level of war completely free from political/policy interference so problematic.[348] In this respect, civilians "needed to consider whether the way a war was being fought was consistent with the purposes for which it was being fought, and look beyond

[346] Ibid, p. 507.

[347] Krulak 1999.

[348] Freedman 2013, p. 242.

upcoming battles to the following peace."[349] This theory has often proven difficult to put in practice, particularly with the military preferring to avoid what it often sees as political interference with the conduct of operations.[350] However, the military advantage gained from an attack, or from a series of attacks not only has strategic impact, it is conducted for a strategic military purpose. The purpose for which an attack is prosecuted and the advantage to be gained from such targeting must align with the strategic goals for the conflict. It is those strategic goals that also influence the type and scope of the military campaign. Ambitious political goals inevitably result in a more expansive strategy and the potential for a broader conflict.[351] In addition, the failure by commanders to consider the strategic impact of the humanitarian effects of operations, such as collateral civilian casualties can adversely impact the overall campaign.[352] Given the links between various levels of war, it is difficult to see how the legal framework governing targeting, a fundamental aspect of the conduct of hostilities, can be relegated to assessing attacks solely at the tactical, or some intermediate level.

One result of looking beyond the tactical level is that the overall number of attacks may be reduced in order to achieve the desired military outcome/advantage. Although numerous targets may be identified, this does not mean that all possible targets have to be hit to obtain the desired effect. This has been suggested to be a particular strength of EBO with the example given of attacks on the Iraqi electrical grid during the 1991 campaign that resulted in the shut down of the system even though all targets had not been prosecuted.[353] It is not a system of attack that is slavishly tied to the numbers of targets struck. An issue that does arise when multiple targets are struck is whether proportionality assessments should be carried out on a cumulative basis and what collateral impact is legally acceptable in seeking to attain a strategic targeting goal. It has been argued, using the example of the United States defoliation campaign in Vietnam, that military advantage cannot be assessed on a long-term cumulative basis since this would justify excessive collateral impact. This is because "each defoliating mission achieved little in itself but resulted in civilian casualties and widespread damage to civilian objects." [354] This raises the question of how the assessment is to be carried out of an "attack as a whole," which is the approach favored by a number of states.

[349] Ibid.

[350] Gray 2005, p. 364 (where it is noted "it is the American habit is to fight tactically, and now operationally as well, not to fight strategically. That is to say force is applied with scant political direction"). See also Catignani 2008, pp. 159–169 (suggesting Israel has lacked a sufficiently strategic approach toward terrorism and counterinsurgency).

[351] Gray 2005, p. 364 ("In support of an expansive, ambitious policy, strategy too must be expansive and ambitious. Strategy should always control the course of warfare").

[352] Catignani 2008, pp. 166–167.

[353] Deptula 2001, pp. 11–12. ("During the war some Iraqi power plant managers shut down their electric plants to avoid targeting thereby creating our desired effect without exposing Coalition members to danger, and freeing up air resources for another task…").

[354] Gardam 2004, p. 101.

Contrary to what is argued in the defoliation example, where a strategic effect is being sought the assessment may need to consider the "attack as a whole." This will not occur for all attacks. Calling in air support in respect of the defense of a unit in contact with the enemy does not ordinarily raise broader strategic issues. However, if the goal is to disrupt the electrical grid, or stop the production and transport of oil supplies then consideration of the advantage to be gained and when the collateral civilian impact may become excessive needs to be carried out within that systemic framework. This broader assessment is required because, consistent with the defoliation analysis, a relatively small likelihood of collateral death or injury for each of a large number of targets may add up to a significant number of casualties and elevated levels of damage that are hard to justify even on a systemic level.[355] However, in other cases, important, but less numerous "nodes" may be identified and struck as part of a systemic effort to degrade the ability of an opponent to fight reducing the overall collateral effect. The importance of these nodes can only be determined by looking at how the target functions within the system that it operates. An attack on the important node may carry with it a greater potential for collateral impact than a strike on another part of the system. However, overall such an attack may have a more limited collateral impact than if the more numerous targets providing less of a military advantage were prosecuted to gain the same effect.

A significant element of assessing military advantage will involve the tactical and operational effects of targeting. However, reflecting how warfare is conducted, the military advantage being sought is not necessarily limited to an individual attack, or those levels of war. It is the goal of attaining certain accumulated effects that often prompts the conduct of the mission in the first place. It would also be inconsistent to assess casualties on a cumulative basis, as often occurs, but not similarly consider the purpose for which a number of attacks are conducted. This does not mean that there is not a requirement for a case-by-case assessment of an attack. It is through the mandatory process of carrying out the targeting precautions for each individual attack and, in particular, seeking to avoid or minimize the collateral effects where some of the most effective protection is provided to civilians.[356]

Adopting this "attack as a whole" interpretation does not mean that a larger number of casualties would automatically be justified. Each claim of a military advantage being anticipated, whether at the tactical, operational, or strategic level must be justified in its own right. What the "attack as a whole" criterion does not extend to is assessing operation in relation to the "armed conflict as a whole."[357] It cannot be a situation of the ultimate victory justifies any level of death or damage. The result is that all attacks must be subjected to a case-by-case analysis of the

[355] Hitchens 2006 (for critical reporting on tragic humanitarian consequences linked to the use of Agent Orange during the Vietnam conflict).

[356] AP I, Article 52(2)(ii).

[357] Dinstein 2010, para 232.

military advantage to be gained and likely collateral effects. In carrying out that assessment in respect of some attacks both the advantage gained, as well as the potential for increased collateral impact needs to be scrutinized in terms of any broader operational, or strategic effects being sought.

13.5.5 Normative Frameworks, Military Advantage and the Type of Conflict

13.5.5.1 The *Jus Ad Bellum* Framework and Its Strategic Impact

Gaining an understanding of the operation of the targeting provisions of the *Additional Protocols*, and in particular the concept of military advantage requires consideration of not only the role humanitarian law plays in limiting the effects of warfare in the post-World War II period, but also how that law interfaces with the other great body of law influencing the state use of force: the *jus ad bellum*. The conduct of a strategic targeting campaign can broaden the scope of conflict, and with it an attendant risk of elevated collateral casualties and damage. However, there are strong normative forces that act to limit what targets can be prosecuted. As will be discussed these limiting factors have a strategic impact on targeting. First, there is the self-defense framework found in Article 51 of the *United Nations Charter* and under customary law that restricts the recourse to war and with it the response to an armed attack. Secondly, there is the regulatory framework governing the identification of military objectives, and prosecution of those targets found in *Additional Protocol I* and customary international humanitarian law. This is a regulatory framework that acts to restrict state action independently of the *jus ad bellum*.

There are two schools of thought regarding the application of *jus ad bellum* principles that the use of force in self-defense must be necessary, proportionate and in response to an imminent threat. One broad interpretation suggests that framework applies both leading up to and during armed conflict.[358] The second more traditional approach, suggested by Yoram Dinstein, is a more limited one. It accepts the continuing influence of the *jus ad bellum* principles only with respect to certain, albeit frequently occurring, types of hostilities.[359] Under this approach where a "war" is launched in self-defense the *jus ad bellum* principles do not apply.[360] Therefore, in a conflict between two states "[o]nce war is raging, the

---

[358]Greenwood 1989, p. 274 and Gardam 2004, p. 156.

[359]The *jus ad bellum* principles apply to defensive action taken by States that Yoram Dinstein calls "on-the-spot reactions," "defensive armed reprisals," "protection of nationals abroad," and "extra-territorial law enforcement." See Dinstein 2011, para 644; para 656; para 676; and para 728, respectively. See also Kretzmer 2013, pp. 258–259 (for a discussion of Yoram Dinstein's theory).

[360]Dinstein 2011, para 697.

exercise of self-defence may bring about 'the destruction of the enemy's army, regardless of the condition of [the *jus ad bellum* concept] of proportionality.'"[361]

Under the first, broader "overarching" theory, the determination of what constitutes a military objective remains based on the criteria of Article 52 of *Additional Protocol I*, including the requirement to assess the military advantage to be gained from an attack. Similarly, humanitarian law governs the assessment of proportionality. However, the application of *jus ad bellum* principles, which occurs at the strategic level, affects the temporal and geographic scope of a conflict, the choice of legitimate military targets to be prosecuted and possibly the weapons used.[362] For example, it has been suggested, "[a] target such as an electricity grid may meet the definition of a legitimate military target in IHL, but may be excessive in terms of achieving the aims of self-defence."[363] Under this approach the number and type of military objectives for which an attack is undertaken appears to be framed by principles of self-defense. As a result, there may be more or fewer military objectives that can be attacked depending upon the scope and scale of the permitted defensive action. There would also be a similar adjustment in the permissible accumulative collateral impact of those attacks.

Consistent with a reliance on concrete measures to establish the limits on the use of force during conflict the collateral impact of attacks is relevant to the *jus ad bellum* principle of proportionality, as well as being a subject for consideration under humanitarian law. Key practical indicators that have been suggested for assessing *jus ad bellum* proportionality are "consideration of the anticipated overall scale of civilian casualties, the level of destruction of the enemy forces, and finally damage to territory, the infrastructure of the target State and the environment generally."[364] While this theory has been discussed in the context of an interstate conflict the acknowledgement of a majority of international lawyers that right self-defense can be exercised against non-state actors would appear to make it applicable in that context as well.[365]

In respect of those conflicts for which the *jus ad bellum* continues to have application (i.e., including some responses under the more limited approach) the

[361] Ibid, para 697 [referring to Alland 1987, p. 183.]. See also Kunz 1947, pp. 876–877. See Kretzmer 2013, p. 259 (for a critique of this approach where "the armed attack is indeed fairly large-scale, but is isolated and has been completed before the victim state has had the chance to respond" and where "the attack was carried out by a group of non-state actors").

[362] Greenwood 1989, p. 275. See also Gardam 2004, p. 168 ("The requirements of proportionality in the exercise of self-defence also regulate the choice and methods of warfare and targets that are available to States in the exercise of this right").

[363] Gardam 2004, p. 169.

[364] Ibid, p. 168.

[365] Kretzmer 2013, p. 246 ("The view that an attack by non-state actors that is not imputable to a state cannot constitute an 'armed attack' has been rejected by the vast majority of publicists…"). See also Greenwood 1989, p. 274 (who would extend the application of self-defence principles to operations such as protection of nationals abroad, humanitarian intervention and the protection of national vital national or international interests if they were viewed as occurring outside the context of self-defence).

interaction between the recourse to war principle of proportionality and action permitted under humanitarian law must be reconciled. Here, the influence of the self-defense principles is properly situated at the strategic level where the assessment is focused on the overall impact of the use of force.[366] To permit the *jus ad bellum* principles to operate at the tactical level would erode the influence of humanitarian law and possibly with it the "equal application principle," which has been fundamental to its operation.[367] While during the deliberations regarding the *San Remo Manual* it was suggested that the self-defense "principles of necessity and proportionality could affect hostilities at all levels of the conflict," the better view is that they "cannot affect tactical behaviour once an action in self-defence has commenced and that these principles rather affect only strategic decisions on how to achieve the needs of self-defence."[368] It is after humanitarian based assessments of the anticipated military advantage to be gained, and the resulting likely collateral civilian effects are determined that the *jus ad bellum* proportionality assessment can be carried out. However, given the number of potential targets this too, like the application of targeting precautions, may be an interactive process.

The impact of the cumulative effect of a targeting campaign cannot be dismissed too lightly as it can be an important factor in the *jus ad bellum* proportionality assessment, which applies to most of contemporary conflict. It also has a direct impact on public perceptions of the legitimacy of the defensive response. An example of where allegations of excessive collateral casualties and damage were used as the basis to claim there was a disproportionate response in self-defence was in respect of Israel's 2006 operations in Lebanon.[369] Arguments used to support the claim that Israel's response was disproportionate were the scale of the Israeli attack, the destruction of military and civilian infrastructures located hundreds of miles from the area attacked, as well as the harm to civilians.[370] As Thomas Franck noted, "[w]hatever the technical legal position, proportionality has become an undeniable part of the public assessment of state conduct."[371]

In contrast to the broad theory of *jus ad bellum* application, the more limited approach focuses on the traditionally more violent and potentially broader state responses to attacks by other states that reach the level of a "war."[372] This approach prompts two observations. First, because war is narrowly defined as only

[366]Greenwood 1989, pp. 278–79 [where a distinction is made between the *jus ad bellum* operating at the strategic level ("strategic proportionality") and the *jus in bello* being relevant to a discussion of "tactical proportionality") See also Kretzmer 2013, p. 278 ("[w]hile the question in *jus in bello* relates to attacks on specific targets, in *jus ad bellum* the question relates to the whole picture").

[367]Roberts 2008, p. 932 (for a discussion of the equal application principle).

[368]San Remo Manual 1995, para 4.5.

[369]Cannizzaro 2006, p. 784.

[370]Ibid.

[371]Franck 2008, p. 734.

[372]Dinstein 2011, para 698 (It is stated that such conflict is, by its very nature, "virtually bound to be disproportionate to any measure 'short of war' that triggered it").

occurring between states, this means that a significant portion of contemporary conflict remains subject to *jus ad bellum* principles during the course of the conflict even under the more restricted approach. This would appear to include operations conducted against non-state actors such as Hezbollah and Hamas (although their rise to power and the degree of political control they exercise is different), since neither of those two groups is recognized as the lawful government in respect of the territory they control and over which a form of governance is exercised. Second, with the *jus ad bellum* concept of proportionality being limited to assessing the critical character of the initial attack it is humanitarian law that must provide the restrictive normative framework necessary to avoid the repeat of the widespread civilian casualties and destruction that occurred during World War II. It is to that body of law that the analysis now turns.

13.5.5.2 The Humanitarian Law Framework

13.5.5.2.1 Introduction

What is not sufficiently discussed is that at the strategic level the normative restraint on targeting does not come solely from an application of *jus ad bellum* principles. Humanitarian law treaties are strategic documents. In this respect, humanitarian law (both treaty and customary law) operates at the strategic level to restrain the use of force during armed conflict. It was suggested in 1911 that "[t]he separation of armies and peaceful inhabitants into two distinct classes is perhaps the greatest triumph of International Law."[373] Added to this fundamental "triumph" is the tremendous advance realized by the development of the targeting provisions found in the 1977 *Additional Protocol I* and recognized under customary law. While, as Professor Lauterpacht noted, there may not have been rules upon which to base the conduct of air warfare in 1952, they now clearly exist.[374]

These humanitarian law rules have fundamentally changed the dialog about targeting to one centered on distinction and the avoidance of collateral casualties and damage. The result is that even in the case of a total war, during which the normative restrictions of the *jus ad bellum* may be viewed as either non-existent or of limited effect, humanitarian law imposes a strategic framework on targeting that requires a justification of both the targets selected and the humanitarian impact of the execution of an attack. When assessing military advantage in a legal context a number of key issues must be addressed. First, there is the relationship between military advantage and military necessity. Second, the potential impact that the scope and type of the conflict has on what military advantage can be claimed from attacking military objects needs to be addressed. Finally, there is the issue of which authority is responsible for deciding what constitutes an appropriate "military advantage:" military decision maker or the courts.

---

[373] Spaight 1911, p. 37.

[374] Lauterpacht 1952, pp. 365–366.

13.5.5.2.2 Military Advantage and Necessity

There is ongoing debate regarding the degree to which military necessity, a fundamental principle of humanitarian law, is to be interpreted in a broad or restrictive fashion.[375] Given the link between military necessity and military advantage that debate has a particular resonance with the breadth of available targets under humanitarian law. At the heart of this debate is whether military necessity is to be interpreted in a fashion where it is "a synonym for military utility and functions as a license to override prohibitions on harm to noncombatants when doing so would be useful,"[376] or "that force is the only way to achieve a particular objective and one only uses so much force as is required."[377] This restrictive approach seeks to find a legal response to the long-standing moral problem identified by Michael Walzer as to whether a naked soldier taking a bath can be shot. The restrictive analysis would not permit his being killed.[378] The difficulty in adopting this approach is reflected in Nils Melzer's acknowledgement that it is "contrary to what powerful States and many authors appear to believe."[379]

One analysis of military necessity suggests, "since World War II and Korea, the United States' understanding of the balance between military necessity, force protection, and noncombatant immunity has evolved."[380] Neta Crawford identifies the different approaches taken toward military necessity during the Vietnam War, the 1991 Gulf War, Kosovo, Afghanistan and the 2003 Iraq invasion[381] indicating that the introduction of effects-based targeting on infrastructure at the beginning of the 1990s as the starting point of a trend to define "military necessity more broadly and permissively."[382] In contrast, it is also noted that United States military views became more restrictive during the more recent Afghanistan and Iraq conflicts to the point where "[c]ivilian protection became a priority when it was understood as a strategic necessity for the counterinsurgency strategy."[383] However, rather than being indicative of evolving trends toward less or more restrictive interpretations of military necessity, the differing approaches adopted for these conflicts could simply be representative of the significant impact that the nature of a conflict and the decisions taken at the strategic level in conducting a war have on the application of the humanitarian law based targeting framework.

13.5.5.2.3 Wide-scale InterState Conflict

The nature of the hostilities provides the context within which strategic objectives (both high strategy and military strategy) are developed and the legal targeting

[375] Melzer 2008, pp. 286–291.

[376] Crawford 2013, p. 175.

[377] Ibid, p. 174.

[378] Walzer 2000, pp. 138–143.

[379] Melzer 2008, p. 288.

[380] Crawford 2013, p. 186.

[381] Ibid, pp. 187–206.

[382] Ibid, p. 202.

[383] Ibid, p. 205.

precautions have to be applied. A wide-scale interstate conflict has a significant impact on the range of possible targets and the military advantage to be gained from attacks. Given the collective industrial capacity of states and the issues at stake (i.e., control over territory and resources) conflicts between them tend to have greater potential for violence, as well as the targeting of a broad range of targets. In some cases that targeting will occur during hostilities that are geographically broad and highly destructive. In this regard, interstate conflict is unique in its mobilization of the resources of the state leading to what can be viewed as an industrialized form of warfare. The military objects that are targeted may not only offer indirect support to the ability of a state to engage in hostilities, those targets may be numerous and interconnected.

Of necessity such conflict often includes the broad-based targeting of objects that are ordinarily civilian in nature, but which may directly or indirectly support the war effort. It is in this context that attacks on economic targets are most likely to occur. It is also an environment that lends itself to the conduct of a strategic air campaign that has an ancillary goal of degrading the willingness of a state to fight. Regarding the breadth of these targets available under widely accepted interpretations of humanitarian law it should be noted the difference between the *Additional Protocol I* standard of "military action" for identifying military objects and the United States standard of "war sustaining effort" may not be that great. The primary difference "being in respect to attacks on exports that may be the sole or principal source of financial resources for a belligerent's continuation of its war effort."[384] As evidence of the wide scope of lawful targets, ships sailing into enemy or enemy controlled territory carrying fuel or other supplies for their armed forces "would not differ from vessels carrying troops."[385] The military advantage to be gained is not simply the destruction of military forces. It extends to attacks on the supporting infrastructure of a warring party. This fact undermines a focus that is exclusively tactical in nature. A total war is more likely to involve consideration of military advantage in respect of strategic level targets and result in a broader target set.

13.5.5.2.4 Military Advantage in Conflicts of More Limited Scope

Not all conflict between states takes on a scope that involves targeting all, or even most, state resources allocated to advancing military operations. A conflict of very limited scope would not necessarily require a long term, or broad scale attack on the infrastructure of another state. States that have used force in the twenty-first century in support of policy goals have usually done so within geographic, temporal and military constraints.[386] The military advantage to be gained from an attack in these circumstances will ultimately be connected to the type of conflict, the strategic goals and its participants. In this respect not all states, or their armed forces are the same. States that have technologically highly developed military forces are

[384]Robertson 1998, pp. 210–211.

[385]San Remo Manual 1995, para 60.9.

[386]Strachan 2013, p. 275 (the examples provided are Russia in South Ossetia in 2008, Israel in Gaza in 2008–2009, and the United States in Iraq and Afghanistan in 2001 and 2003").

likely to have a larger infrastructure, both military and civilian, to support it. For example, one of the challenges in the application of airpower during the 2001 Afghanistan conflict was that with the Taliban being non-conventionally structured the normal supporting infrastructure did not exist.[387] The result was there was little supporting infrastructure that would provide a military advantage by striking it. Given the debate over the Taliban's status as the government of Afghanistan at that time it is clear this issue is not necessarily limited to interstate conflict.[388]

The limited strategic objectives identified for a conflict can impact on what targets may be lawfully struck. For example, the goal of an operation may be simply to remove enemy forces that have crossed the border. In this situation the question can be asked whether would it be justified to embark on a strategic aerial bombing campaign against the oil production infrastructure of another state, which could carry with it an increased potential for collateral civilian casualties and damage. Would the attack on that infrastructure in the circumstances of a more limited conflict put the attacker in a favorable or superior position militarily? Such an inquiry is particularly relevant in situations where attaining the desired effect, the reduction of the fuel supply to opposing military forces, may require a considerable length of time in order for that impact to be realized. Given the disparity that may exist in the military strength of the protagonists the conflict itself may not be anticipated to be of long duration. Cutting off the oil supply to military forces may at some point be advantageous, however, not necessarily "in the circumstances ruling at the time."[389] As the *ICRC Commentary* indicates, "it is not legitimate to launch an attack which only offers potential or indeterminate advantages."[390]

The idea that limited wars result in the targeting rules being applied more restrictively is reflected in the 1994 *San Remo Manual* where it was "agreed that the legal rules should remain the same in both general and limited war situations but that the application of these rules to the facts should result in a more restrictive approach to targeting in limited conflicts."[391] Similarly, William Fenrick noted in an article about the 1999 NATO bombing campaign in Kosovo that while certain core objects will be military objectives in any conflict, the classification of objects having both civilian and military uses is "situation-dependent" based "upon various factors, including the strategic objectives of the parties to the conflict and the degree to which the conflict approaches total war."[392] The military advantage anticipated from an attack must be justified separately prior to being applied to assess the lawfulness of any collateral impact it might have on the civilian

[387] Schroen 2005, p. 146.

[388] Parks 2009, pp. 258–61 (arguing that the Taliban was neither the de facto, nor de jure government at the time of the 9/11 attacks.) and Aldrich 2002, pp. 893–894 (states Taliban was the government of Afghanistan even if the United States and most other countries did not recognize it as such).

[389] AP I, Article 52(2).

[390] ICRC Additional Protocol I Commentary 1987, Article 52(2), para 2024.

[391] San Remo Manual 1995, para 40.8.

[392] Fenrick 2001, p. 494.

population. It is the linkage between conflict goals, the effects being sought and the justification of the military advantage based on the prevailing circumstances that helps ensures restraint on the conduct of hostilities even when other normative influences such as the *jus ad bellum* principles are not viewed as being operable.

However, this is an area of inquiry that must be approached with considerable caution. While a conflict may initially have limited objectives circumstances can change throughout its course.[393] As has been noted, the terrorist attacks of 9/11 in the United States resulted in an international armed conflict in Afghanistan, which in turn developed into a lengthy ongoing counterinsurgency. Hezbollah, which emerged following the 1982 Israeli invasion of Lebanon heavily supported by Iran and Syria, grew from a small militia organization to a political and military organization reportedly armed with 100,000 missiles.[394] Predicting the scale of violence, time period of a conflict, or its geographic scope is an exercise fraught with difficulty. Strategies are neither developed nor carried out in a controlled environment.[395] As the legitimate military strategic objectives expand and contract so can the list of potential lawful targets.

Armed conflict is an exceedingly non-static environment within which to impose limits. Those seeking definitive boundaries in order to enforce bright lines for accountability purposes will, as with the concepts of targeting proportionality discussed in the *Targeted Killings Case*, find themselves disappointed.[396] It is the examples of excess that will attract greater legal scrutiny. Returning to the United States decision to strike at Iraqi oil production during the 1991 Gulf War the question to be asked is whether it was reasonable to prosecute that strategic objective given the overall uncertainty that a conflict will come to a quick termination. It is fairly straightforward to conclude that it was. Applying such a standard of reasonableness is an approach that has been recognized as part of both international humanitarian law and human rights-based law enforcement regarding the use of force.[397] However, the key point is the need for a contextual justification of the military advantage to be gained from an attack.

---

[393]Dinstein 2010, para 224 ("The circumstances of warfare change swiftly, and with them the use of an object by the enemy").

[394]Levitt 2013, p. 11–16 (for an outline of the birth and development of Hezbollah) and D Williams, "Hoping to deter Hezbollah, Israel threatens Lebanese civilians," *Reuters* (29 January 2014), http://www.reuters.com/article/2014/01/29/us-israel-lebanon-hezbollah-idUSBREA0S1PS20140129 (accessed 27 March 2015)(where the Israeli defence minister is reported to have provided an update assessment of Hezbollah's missile capacity).

[395]Freedman 2013, p. 609.

[396]*Public Committee Against Torture in Israel v. Israel*, Israel Supreme Court [16 December 2006], 46 ILM 375, para 58.

[397]*Prosecutor v. Galić*, Case No. IT-98-29-T, Judgement, Trial Chamber (2003), paras 50–51, 55, http://www.icty.org/x/cases/galic/tjug/en/gal-tj031205e.pdf, and *McCann v. United Kingdom*, Application no. 18984/91, Eur. Ct H. R. (1995), para 200, http://hudoc.echr.coe.int/sites/eng/pages/search.aspx?i=001-57943#{"itemid":["001-57943"]}. See Tallin Manual 2013, para 10, and Air and Missile Warfare Commentary 2009, Rule 14, para 6.

13.5.5.2.5 Accountability: The Legal, Political and Operational Interface

There remains the issue of who decides on what is a proper military advantage, and how that advantage affects the identification of objects as military objectives and any proportionality assessment. The resolution of this issue at the tactical level ultimately hinges on the assessment of whether military advantage is seen as being a matter that is solely the purview of the commander as an executive decision, or as a legal issue to be resolved by a court. As has been indicated all warfare is fought for a political reason. Executive decisions regarding the conduct of hostilities are made for political, policy, or what can be described in military terms as command reasons. The types of armed conflict through which the political goals are attained are diverse, including total, or lesser forms of interstate warfare, transnational conflict with non-state actors, counterinsurgency and counterterrorism. In this respect, a conflict involving an insurgency is significantly different than a conventional interstate conflict.[398] Ultimately, warfare is context based and as a mechanism of oversight the law must be applied in a manner that is consistent with the type of armed conflict being fought. However, given their diversity, armed conflicts cannot all justify the same degree and type of military response.

There may be those who view the identification of strategic objectives and the resulting choices made in the conduct hostilities to be exclusively matters of politics, policy or command prerogative, depending upon the level at which they are assessed. However, it is a reality that decisions made at the strategic level inevitably involve a mixture of law and politics. If "[w]ar, therefore is an act of policy,"[399] it is also, for "civilized" countries, an activity that is bounded by the laws put in place to govern their relations.[400] This interaction between law and politics/policy is seen in the *Nuclear Weapons Case* where the International Court of Justice made reference to their close interrelationship when determining that it had jurisdiction to hear the matter.[401]. The interplay between law and policy is also referred to in legal commentary concerning the application of the *jus ad bellum* during conflict.[402] Similarly, since the humanitarian law regulation of the conduct of hostilities and targeting applies at all levels of warfare there is a similar

[398]Kolenda 2012, p xiv ("Counterinsurgency is not a strategy. Insurgency-counterinsurgency, like conventional war, is a type of conflict").

[399]Von Clausewitz 1976, p. 87.

[400]Ibid. p. 76 (for reference to the social conditions of the States and their relations to one another circumscribing and moderating war).

[401]*Advisory Opinion on the Legality of the Threat or Use of Nuclear Weapons*, [1996] I.C.J. Rep. 226, 234, para 13 (hereinafter the *Nuclear Weapons Case*) (where the International Court of Justice states: The fact that this question also has political aspects, as, in the nature of things, is the case with so many questions which arise in international life, does not suffice to deprive it of its character as a "legal question" and to "deprive the Court of a competence expressly conferred on it by its Statute").

[402]Greenwood 1989, p. 277 and Gardam 2004, p. 155 (for references to the interplay between law and politics at the strategic level).

requirement to resolve the political/policy/command/legal interface associated with those activities at all levels of planning and decision making.

This legal and command interface was assessed in the *Targeted Killings Case* where the Court explained its role, and that of the executive in resolving the issue of proportionality under humanitarian law. As that court noted "the question of the fulfillment of the conditions determined in customary international law for performing military operations is a legal question, the expertise in which is the Court's."[403] However, this is just one of the legal questions that arise in the context of targeting. While the determination of the strategic objectives of a military campaign and how the war is to be conducted might be viewed solely as policy matter, or a prerogative of command, the assessment of the "military advantage" being sought to pursue those strategic goals is an integral part of the legal accountability process for targeting. Military commanders may be called upon to justify the military advantage claimed as part of the process for establishing that objects were validly assessed as military objectives when attacked, or when a court assesses whether an attack was proportionate. Undoubtedly considerable discretion, or a "margin of appreciation" will be left to the military decision maker; however, their actions cannot take place in a zone with no legal oversight.

While to date there has been little adjudication concerning targeting, the military advantage claimed by those who plan or decide upon an attack is subject to legal inquiry and judicial scrutiny. Considering the manner in which states conduct warfare, this would extend to assessing that advantage from the strategic to the tactical level. Neither the decisions made by commanders, nor the law affecting targeting decisions is applied independently of one another, or in a contextual vacuum. From a strategic perspective the military advantage gained from an attack must be linked to objectives that are consistent with the limits of these legal frameworks and nature of the conflict being waged. During a post-strike accountability review, it is possible a person who planned or decided on the form of attack could be asked not only to justify why a particular means or method of attack was chosen, but also the rationale behind preferring it over any of the other feasible options that were rejected. This does not mean that only one approach may be justified since, depending on the circumstances, there can be more than one option available to a commander to fulfill the legal parameters of Article 57(2)(a) of *Additional Protocol I*. As has been noted proportionality is not a standard of precision and targeting is an uncertain business. In choosing between possible options "it is unrealistic to require absolute certainty concerning the military importance of a specific object before it can be lawfully attacked. However, not requiring absolute certainty is not the same as permitting disregard of the facts."[404]

Among the challenges for investigators and courts reviewing the outcome of an attack could be that many scenarios in which force is used (i.e., time sensitive targets, acting in self-defense) may only involve one feasible option for attack;

---

[403]*Public Committee Against Torture in Israel v. Israel*, Israel Supreme Court [16 December 2006], 46 ILM 375, para 58.

[404]Bothe 2002, p. 183.

provide little opportunity by the decision maker for a detailed assessment of various options, where they exist; and result in no record of all the options actually considered. Notwithstanding, these challenges the ultimate decision of whether an attack undertaken at the discretion of the military commander is proportionate is a legal question that may be ruled on by a court by reference to the information reasonably available to the decision maker at the relevant time.[405] This information must include an indication of the anticipated military advantage to be gained. As demands for accountability increase a particular challenge for military commanders and their legal advisors will be ensuring the rationale for an attack, including the military advantage to be gained, and the context within which the decision is made is adequately explained.

13.5.5.3 Counterinsurgency and Counterterrorism: Re-Thinking Military Advantage

In the analysis of the concept of a "zone of proportionality" it was indicated the potential exists, such as in the case of 9/11-style transnational attacks by non-state actors, for military advantage to justify large-scale collateral civilian casualties and damage. However, for much of contemporary conflict the debate is centered on there being significantly greater limitations of what collateral effects can be justified when states are engaged in counterinsurgency and counterterrorist operations. It is to this issue that the analysis now turns since the unique context within which such operations are conducted is having a profound influence on public perceptions of the acceptable impact of contemporary military operations.

The influence of strategic goals on the assessment of military advantage is not limited to interstate conflict. The context within which those goals are developed has a significant impact on how wars are fought. At a time where there are a declining number of interstate conflicts greater attention is now being paid to non-international armed conflict. Some of these armed conflicts (i.e., civil wars or those falling under the authority of Additional Protocol II[406]) by their nature can raise issues somewhat similar to international ones to the extent the non-state actors involved control territory, develop a political governance structure and organize their armed forces along the lines of their state counterparts. This is evident in respect of the conflict between Israel and the non-state actors controlling southern Lebanon and Gaza: Hezbollah and Hamas, respectively.

However, most conflict with non-state actors occurs in the context of states conducting operations internal to states, in occupied territories, or to counter transnational terrorism. Those activities are not a strategy, but rather an operational method.[407] As a result they are the means by which strategic objectives are

---

[405] Ibid.

[406] AP II, Article 1(1).

[407] Strachan 2013, p. 220.

obtained. Counterterrorism has grown in prominence since the attacks of 9/11 and the development of a capacity to utilize drones for targeted killing. For these conflicts there is significantly less opportunity to utilize a strategically focused targeting campaign because the supporting infrastructure of the organized armed groups is limited and inevitably hidden "amongst the people." This extends to the use of ground attack aircraft, unless "insurgents concentrate in large forces and aspire to conventional or positional warfare."[408]

This does not mean that strategic issues are not relevant. Rather than having an increase in the potential target set, and with it the likelihood for collateral impact, such as occurs in large-scale interstate conflict, attaining the strategic goals of a counterinsurgency or counterterrorism campaign can have the opposite effect. The factors most commonly associated with those operations, including during occupation, will normally cause military forces to use less force with a specific goal of creating more limited collateral casualties and damage. This is because a hard learned lesson of counterinsurgency, which unfortunately often has to be re-internalized periodically within state armed forces, is that "[a]n insurgent movement is a war for the people."[409] The recognition of an insurgency/counterinsurgency conflict as a type of warfare separate from total or limited war has been increasingly solidified in military doctrine.[410] As the United States joint doctrine on counterinsurgency indicates, this form of warfare "differs in many respects from a traditional military force-on-force operation and requires a special mindset. It is the population-centric nature of COIN that distinguishes it from most traditional military force-on-force operations."[411]

Maintaining the support of the people is a key aspect not only of counterinsurgency, but of counterterrorism as well.[412] For example, the sensitivity over the potential collateral impact of a bombing operation against Osama bin Laden was heightened due to the need to avoid alienating the population and government of Pakistan.[413] It is a sensitivity that can particularly arise in a conflict with a non-

---

[408]Corum and Johnson 2003, p. 428 (where it is noted the use of air strikes has a relatively small role in an insurgency when combat operations are "characterized by acts of terrorism and small hit-and-run raids..." and it is the heavy weapons, logistical bases, lines of communications, and headquarters elements that "are excellent targets for airpower"), and Towle 1989, p. 209 ("Air power on its own cannot defeat an insurgency which has the support of the majority of the population. The use of massive firepower against such an insurrection will only cause great bloodshed").

[409]Thompson 1966, p. 51. See also Galula 1964, pp. 89–90.

[410]For example see the Marine Corps Counterinsurgency Manual 2006. See also Beran 2010, pp. 4–5.

[411]Pouw 2013, para 2.

[412]Hull 2011, p. 15 (where a former United States Ambassador to Yemen indicates that counterterrorism "[i]n many ways resembled counterinsurgency, success of which depended primarily on winning the hearts and minds of the population").

[413]Schmitt and Shanker 2011, p. 261 ("And dropping that much ordinance [thirty-two, 2,000 lb. bombs] in a well-to-do community of a nation with which America was not at war risked a high civilian death toll and severe diplomatic damage").

state actor operating within another state when there is an advantage to maintaining the support of the host state and its population. In other words, when the conflict is with the non-state actor and not that state. These types of conflicts can be contrasted with conventional interstate conflict where gaining the support of the civilian population is not usually a strategic goal. Given the animosities that can develop between the populations of opposing states it may be, as Hugo Slim has noted, the best that can be obtained in conventional interstate conflict "if deeper compassion is not possible" is a level of toleration that includes respecting the basic rights of enemy civilians in that situation.[414] Clearly civilians must be protected "against dangers arising from military operations."[415] However, that is a different goal than trying to avoid alienating them, or actively seeking their support as occurs during counterinsurgency operations.

There may be limits with what can be achieved in terms of seeking not to alienate a population among which a non-State actor is operating. For example, it has been suggested that in the Israel/Palestinian context "[t]ruly winning over Palestinian 'hearts and minds' will be impossible…[g]iven the long decades of suffering and dispossession and the bitterness of the Second Intifada…."[416] However, particularly when performing a governance role, such as during an occupation, something more is required than mere toleration. In addition, the requirement to maintain support of the broader international community is an increasingly important factor in both counterinsurgency and counterterrorism operations. Significantly, sensitivity to the impact of operations on a local population is normally in the security interests of the military force involved. One way to limit risk to your own soldiers arising from the alienation of the local population is to avoid collateral civilian deaths and damage through the application of a more restrained use of force. This includes when targeting members of the organizational structure of a non-state actor armed group. The introduction of human rights-based norms into the *Targeted Killings Case* assessment of targeting reflects the goal of seeking a more restrained use of force.[417] In this regard the legal and political goals can blend together. As Daniel Byman has noted, "counterterrorism's political effects must be weighed with a particular emphasis on how they affect moderate forces in the Palestinian community."[418]

An armed conflict involving an insurgency/counterinsurgency is not the same type of conflict as an interstate one. Counterinsurgency and counterterrorism are operations that have different strategic objectives than most interstate conflict. It has been noted that "[i]n counterinsurgency the distinctions between levels of war, tactical, operational, strategic and political are much less clear than in

[414]Slim 2008, p. 278.

[415]AP I, Article 51(1).

[416]Byman 2011, p. 377.

[417]*Public Committee Against Torture in Israel v. Israel*, Israel Supreme Court [16 December 2006], 46 ILM 375, para 40. ("if a terrorist taking a direct part in hostilities can be arrested, interrogated, and tried, those are the means which should be employed…").

[418]Byman 2011, p. 378.

major war."[419] A key difference appears to be that "[p]olitical effects are therefore part of the immediate framework of military action."[420] As a result "political effects are disproportionately more important in wars of lower intensity."[421] The difference between major interstate conflict, and counterinsurgency or counterterrorism has an impact on what military advantage to is to be gained from an attack. In fighting an insurgency maintaining the support of the population is a crucial strategic military goal that normally overshadows the importance of an exclusive military victory. In this respect "[t]he heavy-handed application of military force might lead to a short-term military advantage yet prove to be counterproductive in the long run if military action turns popular sentiment against the government."[422] A key aspect of maintaining the support of the population is the avoidance of collateral civilian casualties and damage. Significant civilian collateral damage at the tactical level can have a negative impact on the strategic conduct of a conflict, even if the action taken is effective in terms of killing insurgents.[423]

Again the issue is not solely what advantage will be gained at the tactical level. The requirement to connect operational planning and the conduct of hostilities to strategic objectives will inevitably alter what targets provide the desired military advantage such that they are considered as lawful military objectives during a counterinsurgency. Without such a framework in place states would be unfettered in their expansion of the conflict and the use of force. This latter approach harkens back to the notion of strategic air campaigns for which it has been acknowledged that the normative constraints broke down during World War II.[424] Requiring that there is a framework within which the link between the nature of the conflict, the protagonists' strategic goals and the targets struck are assessed avoids each belligerent getting to be "the judge in its own cause with regard to whether its choice of targets, weapons, and rules of engagement protect noncombatants and do not cause excessive harm."[425] Given the crucial strategic requirement to maintain or gain the support of the population it can be to the military advantage of the state to restrict how operations are conducted and targets are neutralized. Not only may fewer targets be attacked, but direction may also be given to limit the types of weapons and weapons systems employed. Greater consideration might also be given to attempting capture missions as a means of neutralizing a threat.

---

419 Strachan 2013, p. 219.

420 Ibid.

421 Strachan 2013.

422 Corum and Johnson 2003, p. 426.

423 Catignani 2008, pp. 166–167.

424 Thomas 2001, p. 146 (where it is noted the pre-World War II bombing norm initially exerted influence, but as a weak and poorly developed norm "it soon cleared the stage for military and organizational pressures").

425 Crawford 2013, p. 174.

An issue that is inevitably raised is whether this altered and more restrictive approach toward the conduct of operations is simply a matter of policy, or command decision-making rather than a legal requirement. It has been suggested that winning the hearts and minds cannot constitute a military advantage any more than destroying enemy civilian morale.[426] When focusing on a military advantage, a "[p]olitical, economic or social advantage does not suffice."[427] An analysis of this approach, which is consistent with the ICRC view that the legal assessment of military advantage should be limited to tactical gains, suggests this means "the proportionality-calculus in counterinsurgency is strictly policy-based and powered by strategic imperatives, and results in restrictions on causing collateral damage not required by the LOAC-based principle of proportionality."[428] However, in contrast to the ICRC approach, it is states themselves that have demanded that military advantage under humanitarian law be assessed above the tactical level.

The killing of civilians and local insurgents often leads to broader strategic impact, such as insurgent recruiting and resistance to counterinsurgent forces.[429] It is difficult to see how conducting operations in a manner designed not to alienate the population is not on both utilitarian and legal grounds directly linked to the assessment of military advantage at the operational and strategic levels of war. Perhaps unsurprisingly given the propensity to look for objective measures, this reality has attracted its own aura of scientific "certainty." Reference in colloquial terms is made to the increased support for the insurgency being the product of counterinsurgency "math"[430] where the killing of two insurgents can create twenty or more new recruits.[431]

With regard to military advantage being a stand-alone principle, separate from it being weighed against the collateral humanitarian impact, its existence on that basis is reflected in the straightforward acknowledgement that if a commander fails to win the battle for the support of the population the counterinsurgency campaign is set up for failure. The alienation of that population simply does not place the state in a militarily more favorable or superior position. It offers no military advantage. The strategic goal is to maintain or gain the support of the civilian population. Avoiding civilian casualties is one of the obvious means by which that goal is achieved. As a result "[c]ounterinsurgents must therefore be strategic in applying force and sensitive to its second-order political and military effects."[432]

---

[426]Schmitt 2009, p. 321.

[427]Ibid.

[428]Pouw 2013, p. 297.

[429]C Savage, "Drone Strikes Turn Allies Into Enemies, Yemeni Says," *NY Times* (23 April 2013), http://www.nytimes.com/2013/04/24/world/middleeast/judiciary-panel-hears-testimony-on-use-of-drones.html?ref=middleeastand_r=0 (accessed 27 March 2015) See also Owen and Kiernan 2006, p. 67.

[430]Kolenda 2012, p. 19 (for reference to COIN or counterinsurgency math) and ISAF Commander's Counterinsurgency Guidance 2009, p. 2 (for reference to "attritional math" being turned on its head).

[431]ISAF Commander's Counterinsurgency Guidance 2009, p. 2.

[432]Sewall 2006, p xxv.

Further, the effects are felt at all levels of war. Alienation of the population can lead directly to greater casualties being inflicted on the counterinsurgent force, which in turn reduces their military efficiency and capacity.

What is key is that the assessment of what constitutes such an advantage has to be carried out in the context of the conflict that is being fought, rather than rely on interpretations originally developed for more conventional warfare.[433] The result is that humanitarian concerns can affect targeting twice: first, more broadly and strategically in terms of how operations are planned and conducted and then, second, more directly as part of any precautionary proportionality assessment. Commanders plan their campaigns to ensure the support of the population. The targeting conducted during those operations is subsequently conducted in a fashion that brings about a military advantage by avoiding alienation of that population.

The number and type of targets struck, as well as the methods and means applied are largely restricted to meet strategic goals since collectively elevated collateral casualties and damage can have an adverse impact on the conduct of the overall military campaign. It is not that the potential for collateral death, injury, and damage will to be reduced to zero. There will still remain a "zone of proportionality" that arises in the context of military commanders applying the law based precautionary measures of targeting. Further, the amount of force used will still be dependent upon the operational environment within which security forces must operate. For example, as was evidenced in the 2004 Fallujah operation conducted to remove insurgents seeking to hold that city, there will be instances in a counterinsurgency context when battles approximate conventional conflict and during which airpower, artillery, and direct fire weapons need to be employed.[434] However, during that operation the use of force by the United States military forces was restrained by Rules of Engagement that focused on "conduct" based rather than "status" targeting (i.e., exhibitions of hostile act or hostile intent, instead of forces being declared hostile), sought to minimize collateral damage and required consideration of escalation of force procedures to terminate a threat.[435]

When alternative action to a strike is considered, such as seeking to capture an insurgent leader, this does not necessarily mean the potential for civilian casualties will automatically be lowered. Further, where it is considered there is a greater military advantage in capturing rather than killing that leader greater collateral casualties or damage might even be justified than if a kinetic strike were

---

[433]See Beran 2010, p. 10 (where it is even suggested that the proportionality test should be fundamentally altered in a counterinsurgency context by removing the reference to the collateral civilian effects of an attack as being "incidental." Such a change to the treaty and customary law is unlikely to occur, and it is not clear the implementation of humanitarian law will be assisted by the creation of a multiplicity of tests).

[434]West 2005, pp. 315–16 (during the November 2004 battle for Fallujah there were 540 air strikes, 14,000 artillery and mortar shells fired, as well as 2,500 tank main gun rounds. It is reported 18,000 of Fallujah's 39,000 buildings were damaged or destroyed).

[435]Camp 2009, pp. 149–53.

attempted. An insurgency fundamentally remains an armed conflict, although clearly government forces are required to apply human rights-based law enforcement norms when using of force against uninvolved civilians, regardless of whether the operation is conducted under humanitarian law.[436] However, overall the pressure exerted at the strategic level in terms of the military advantage to be gained acts to narrow the zone of acceptable collateral effects in much of contemporary conflict.

There is, in effect, a form of rebuttable presumption where the military advantage to be gained in counterinsurgency and counterterrorism is predominately geared toward creating less collateral effects and the type of advantage associated with more conventional conflict is the exception. Even within that more restricted zone of proportionality states may make a choice to adopt methods of operation that more closely resemble the exercise of law enforcement. Such an approach appears to have been applied by the United States in the 2013 announcement of a revised approach toward the use of drone strikes in its conflict with Al Qaeda and associated armed groups. As President Obama announced "before any strike is taken, there must be a near-certainty that no civilians will be killed or injured—the highest standard we can set."[437]

13.6 Conclusions

While military advantage is an essential element of the humanitarian law targeting framework it has, unlike the term "direct participation in hostilities," received relatively little attention regarding its meaning, or how it is to be applied in the complex operating environment of twenty-first century warfare. Adding to the lack of certainty about the assessment of military advantage is a dispute between those who see it operating solely at the tactical level focused on military engagement, and states that argue it has a strategic application. In assessing the advantage to be gained from attacking either people or objects states appear to have linked targeting doctrine to the concept of "value." With a focus on high-value targets, military advantage is usually assessed in terms of the importance, worth or usefulness of the objective being attacked.

However, from a humanitarian perspective, there is considerable room for a deeper discussion about the degree of military advantage to be gained in targeting medium and lower value targets in term of both people and objects. In this respect there are targets, which by virtue of their status (i.e., people) or remoteness from the war effort (i.e., objects), that might justify only limited, or even no collateral

[436]Corn 2010, p. 61 and Watkin 2012, p. 311.

[437]"Obama's Speech on Drone Policy," *NY Times* (23 May 23 2013), http://www.nytimes.com/2013/05/24/us/politics/transcript-of-obamas-speech-on-drone-policy.html (accessed 27 March 2015). See also Human Rights Watch, The Wedding that became A Funeral 2014, p. 21 (where the President Obama's May 2013 statement on drones is described as a policy approach).

civilian effects. It is also evident from the bin Laden raid example that determining a target to be particularly important will not automatically lead to a large number of collateral civilian casualties. Military advantage requires a much broader assessment of factors than simply the importance assigned to a target. In the case of Osama bin Laden the analysis of the attack led to a discussion of other benefits that would be gained from proving he had been eliminated as a threat. In the end-result, that desire led to a method of attack that significantly minimized collateral civilian casualties.

To date the courts have not dealt in a comprehensive manner with the concept of military advantage. However, it is evident from the *Gotovina Cases*, and the *Targeted Killings Case* that the application of science-based analytical approaches for assessing both advantage and the related concept of proportionality will require close scrutiny. As with theories on war, and more specifically the conduct of aerial warfare, the use of scientific metaphors appears to mask the reality that engagement in armed conflict is an exceptionally uncertain enterprise. Like strategy, the assessment of anticipated military advantage designed to attain conflict goals does not lend itself to precision, or an entirely scientific resolution. This is evident in the conclusion that proportionality, which requires the weighing of military advantage against the collateral effects of an attack, cannot be measured to a "standard of precision." That lack of precision provides an indication why the standard for criminal liability regarding the attacks causing collateral civilian effects is framed in terms of their being "clearly" excessive in relation to the concrete and direct "overall" military advantage anticipated.[438]

Finally, even when a legal advisor or a court is comfortable with the technical aspects of targeting law, and what is meant by military advantage, there remains the requirement to consider the way in which wars are fought. How war is planned and executed at strategic, operational and tactical levels has a profound affect on manner in which hostilities are conducted and the results of military operations. Understanding the context within which military advantage is assessed is an essential aspect of applying that legal standard. In this respect there are aspects of contemporary warfare that appear to have a particular impact on targeting and the concept of military advantage. First, there is the use of air and other state power to influence an enemy population and its leaders. However, this can only be done indirectly by targeting military objectives that provide a military advantage, with the terrorization of a civilian population being prohibited under humanitarian law. Secondly, airpower provides the capacity to systemically attack the economic and supporting infrastructure of an opponent with a goal of degrading their capacity to wage war. This leads to consideration of targeting not only at tactical level, but also the conduct of war at the operational, strategic, and high strategic levels as well.

There is also often a requirement to assess military advantage when a state is conducting targeting while exercising a right to self-defense. In this situation the strategic impact of *jus ad bellum* based principles, such as proportionality, will

---

[438] *Rome Statute Of The International Criminal Court*, 2187 U.N.T.S. 90, *Entered Into Force* July 1, 2002, Article 8(2)(b)(iv).

have to be reconciled with decisions to carry out attacks against particular targets. In situations where the *jus ad bellum* framework is viewed as not being applicable the restrictive role, which humanitarian law performs in reining in potential state excess must also be considered. This occurs particularly when assessing the military advantage to be gained in attacks during military campaigns with limited objectives. Finally, there is a requirement to re-consider how military advantage is assessed in the context of counterinsurgency and counterterrorism, where a key goal is usually to maintain the support of the population within which an opponent is operating. Ultimately, the protection of that population is a strategic goal, which impacts on the assessment of the military advantage to be gained in respect of the identification of military objectives and the assessment of the collateral effects of an attack. This ultimately affects how operations are conducted, and generally narrows the zone of justifiable collateral civilian casualties and damage.

References

Abresch W (2005) A human rights law of internal armed conflict: The European Court of Human Rights in Chechnya. Eur J Int Law 16:740–767

Alland D (1987) International responsibility and sanctions: self-defence and countermeasures. In: Spinedi M, Simma B (eds) ILC codification of rules governing international responsibility, United Nations codification of State responsibility. Oceana Publications, New York, pp 143–195

Aldrich G (2002) The Taliban, Al Qaeda, and the determination of illegal combatants. Am J Int Law 96:891–898

Allen C (2006) Limits on the use of force in maritime operations in support of WMD counter-proliferation initiatives. Int Law Stud 81:77–139

Barak A (2012) Proportionality: constitutional rights and their limitations. Cambridge University Press, Cambridge

Baxter R (1988) The duties of combatants and the conduct of hostilities. In: Henry Dunant Institute and UNESCO (ed) International dimensions of humanitarian law. Martinus Nijhoff Publishers, The Hague, pp 93–133

Baxter R (2013) The law of war. In: Vagts D F et al (eds) Humanizing the laws of war: selected writings of Richard Baxter. Oxford University Press, Oxford, pp 241–247

Beran M (2010) The proportionality balancing test revisited: how counterinsurgency changes “military advantage”. The Army Lawyer 27-50-447:4–11

Bergen P (2012) Manhunt: the ten-year search for Bin Laden from 9/11 to Abbottabad. Doubleday Canada

Blanford N (2011) Warriors of God: inside Hezbollah’s thirty-year struggle against Israel. Random House, New York

Boivin A, Sandoz Y (2006) The legal regime applicable to targeting military objectives in the context of contemporary warfare. Research papers series, No. 2. Geneva University Centre for International Humanitarian Law. http://www.geneva-academy.ch/docs/publications/collection-research-projects/CTR_objectif_militaire.pdf. Accessed 24 March 2015

Boothby B (2010) “And for such time as”: the time dimension to direct participation in hostilities. NYU J Int Law Polit 42:741–768

Boothby W (2012) The law of targeting. Oxford University Press, Oxford

Bothe M (2002) Targeting. Int Law Stud 78:173–187

Bothe M et al (eds) (1982) New rules for victims of armed conflicts: commentary on the two 1977 Protocols Additional to the Geneva Conventions of 1949. Martinus Nijhoff Publishers, The Hague
Boyne W (2005) The influence of airpower upon history. Pen and Sword Aviation, South Yorkshire
Braudy L (2003) From chivalry to terrorism: war and the changing nature of masculinity. Vintage books, New York
Byman D (2011) A high price: the triumphs and failures of Israeli counterterrorism. Oxford University Press, Oxford
Camp D (2009) Operation phantom fury: the assault and capture of Fallujah, Iraq. Zenith Press, Minneapolis
Carmola K (2005) The concept of proportionality: old questions and new ambiguities. In: Evans Mark (ed) Just war theory: a reappraisal. Edinburgh University Press Ltd, Edinburgh, pp 93–113
Cannizzaro E (2006) Contextualizing proportionality: jus ad bellum and jus in bello in the Lebanese war. Int Rev Red Cross 88:779–792
Catignani S (2008) Israeli counter-insurgency and the Intifadas: dilemmas of a conventional army. Routledge, Abingdon
Clancy T, Stiner C (2002) Shadow warriors: inside the special forces. GP Putnam's Sons, New York
Cohen A, Century D (2008) Brotherhood of warriors. Harper Collins Publishers, New York
Connaughton R (2008) Modern warfare: the true story of conflict from the Falklands to Afghanistan. Constable and Robinson Ltd, London
Cordesman A et al (2007) Lessons of the 2006 Israeli-Hezbollah war. Center for strategic and international studies, Washington DC
Cortright D, Lopez G (2002) Sanctions and the search for security: challenges to U.N. action. Lynne Rienner Publishers Inc, Boulder
Corum J, Johnson W (2003) Airpower in small wars: fighting insurgents and terrorists. University Press of Kansas, Lawrence
Corn G (2010) Mixing apples and hand grenades: the logical limit of applying human rights norms to armed conflict. J Int Hum Leg Stud 1:52–94
Corn G, Corn G (2012) The law of operational targeting: viewing the LOAC through an operational lens. Tex Int Law J 47:337–380
Correll J (2013) The assault on EBO. Air Force Magazine 50–54
Crawford N (2013) Accountability for killing. Oxford University Press, Oxford
Deptula D (2001) Effects based operations: change in the nature of warfare. Aerospace education foundation, Arlington. http://www.ausairpower.net/PDF-A/AEF-AFA-Effect-Based-Operations-D.A.Deptula-2001.pdf. Accessed 25 March 2015
DiMarco L (2012) Concrete hell: urban warfare from Stalingrad to Iraq. Osprey Publishing, Oxford
Dinstein Y (2004) The conduct of hostilities under the law of international armed conflict. Cambridge University, Cambridge
Dinstein Y (2010) The conduct of hostilities under the law of international armed conflict, 2nd edn. Cambridge University, Cambridge
Dinstein Y (2011) War, aggression and self-defence, 5th edn. Cambridge University Press, Cambridge
Earle E (ed) (1971) Makers of modern strategy: military thought from Machiavelli to Hitler. Princeton University Press, Princeton, pp vii–xi
Franck T (2008) On proportionality of countermeasures in international law. Am J Int Law 102:715–767
Fenrick W (1982) The rule of proportionality and Protocol I in conventional warfare. Mil Law Rev 98:91–127
Fenrick W (2001) Targeting and proportionality during the NATO bombing campaign against Yugoslavia. Eur J Int Law 12:489–502

Freedman L (2013) Strategy: a history. Oxford University Press, Oxford
Fuller J (1920) Tanks in the Great War 1914–1918, E. P. Dutton and Company, New York
Gale A, Pickering W (2007) Force protection. Can Mil J http://www.journal.forces.gc.ca/vo8/no2/pick-eng.asp. Accessed 25 March 2015
Galula D (1964) Counterinsurgency warfare: theory and practice. Frederick A Praeger, New York
Gardam J (2004) Necessity, proportionality and the use of force by States. Cambridge University Press, Cambridge
Geraghty T (2010) Black ops: the rise of special forces in the C.I.A., the S.A.S., and Mossad. Pegasus Books, New York
Geiss R (2005) Humanitarian safeguards in economic sanctions regimes: a call for automatic suspension clauses, periodic monitoring, and follow-up assessment of long-term-effects. Harv H R J 18:167–199
Goodman R (2013a) The power to kill or capture enemy combatants. Eur J Int Law 24:819–853
Goodman R (2013b) The power to kill or capture enemy combatants: a rejoinder to Michael N. Schmitt. Eur J Int Law 24:863–866
Grant R (2003) The redefinition of airpower. 86 Air Force: J of the Air Force Association 86:32–38
Gray C (2005) Another bloody century: future war. Weidenfeld & Nicolson, London
Green L (2008) The contemporary law of armed conflict, 3rd edn. Manchester University Press, Manchester
Greenwood C (1989) Self-defense and the conduct of international armed conflict. In: Dinstein Y (ed) International law at a time of perplexity: essays in honour of Shabtai Rosenne. Martinus Nijhof Publishers, Dordrecht, pp 273–288
Harel A, Issacharoff A (2008) 34 Days: Israel, Hezbollah and the war in Lebanon. Palgrave MacMillan, New York
Hashim A (2006) Insurgency and counter-insurgency in Iraq. Cornell University Press, Ithaca
Henckaerts J-M, Doswald-Beck L (2005) Customary international humanitarian law study, vol 1. Cambridge University Press, Cambridge
Holley I Jr (1997) Reflections on the search for airpower theory. In: Meilinger P (ed) The paths of heaven: the evolution of airpower theory. Air University Press, Maxwell Air Force Base, pp 579–599
Hull E (2011) High-value target: countering Al Qaeda in Yemen. Potomac Books, Washington DC
Hunt L (2007) Inventing human rights: a history. WW Norton & Co, New York
ICRC (2009) Interpretive guidance on the notion of direct participation in hostilities under international humanitarian law https://www.icrc.org/eng/assets/files/other/icrc-002-0990.pdf. Accessed 24 March 2015
ISAF (2009) ISAF commander's counterinsurgency guidance, http://www.nato.int/isaf/docu/official_texts/counterinsurgency_guidance.pdf. Accessed 27 March 2015
Joes A (2007) Urban guerrilla warfare. The University Press of Kentucky, Lexington
Kalshoven F (1991) A comment to chapter 11 of the commander's handbook on the law of naval operations. Int Law Stud 64:300–330
Katz Y, Hendel Y (2012) Israel vs. Iran: the shadow war. Potomac Books, Washington DC
Keegan J (1993) The history of warfare. Vintage Books, New York
Klaidman D (2012) Kill or capture. Houghton Mifflin Harcourt, New York
Kraska J (2011) Maritime power and the law of the sea. Oxford University Press, Oxford
Kretzmer D (2013) The inherent right to self- defence and proportionality in jus ad bellum. Eur J Int Law 24:235–282
Kolenda C (2012) The counterinsurgency challenge: a parable of leadership and decision making in modern conflict. Stackpole Books, Mechanicsburg
Krulak C (1999) The strategic corporal: leadership in the three block war. Marines Mag http://www.au.af.mil/au/awc/awcgate/usmc/strategic_corporal.htm. Accessed 24 March 2015

Kunz K (1947) Individual and collective self-defense in Article 51 of the charter of the United Nations. Am J Int Law 41:872–879

Lauder M (2009) Systemic operational design: freeing operational planning from the shackles of linearity. Can Mil J http://www.journal.forces.gc.ca/vo9/no4/08-lauder-eng.asp. Accessed 24 March 2015

Lauterpacht H (1952) The problem of the revision of the law of war. Br Yearb Int Law 29:360–382

Lewis M (2003) The law of aerial bombardment in the 1991 Gulf War. Am J Int Law 97:481–509

Levitt M (2013) Hezbollah: the global footprint of Lebanon's Party of God. Georgetown University Press, Washington DC

Lieblich E (2014) Quasi-hostile acts: the limits on forcible disruption operations under international law. Bos U Int Law J 32:101-

Lindqvist S (2001) A history of bombing. The New Press, New York

MacIssac D (1984) Voices from the central blue: the airpower theorists. In: Paret Peter (ed) Makers of modern strategy. Princeton University Press, Princeton, pp 624–647

McKeogh C (2002) Innocent civilians: the morality of killing in war. Palgrave MacMillan, New York

Meilinger P (2013) Airpower and collateral damage: theory, practice and challenges. Air power Australia essay on military ethics and culture http://www.ausairpower.net/APA-EMEAC-2013-02.html. Accessed 15 Mar 2015

Melzer N (2008) Targeted killing in international law. Oxford University Press, Oxford

Melzer N (2010) Keeping the balance between military necessity and humanity: a response to four critiques of the ICRC's interpretive guidance on the notion of direct participation in hostilities. NYU J Int Law Politics 42:831–916

Merom G (2003) Why democracies lose small wars. Cambridge University Press, Cambridge

Meron M (2000) The humanization of humanitarian law. Am J Int Law 94:239–278

Montalvo E (2013) When did imminent stop meaning immediate?Jus in bello hostile intent, imminence, and self-defense in counterinsurgency. The Army Lawyer 9:24–35

Murray W, Scales R Jr (2003) The Iraq War. Harvard University Press, Cambridge

Naske N, Nolte G (2007) Aerial security law. Case No. 1 BvR 357/05. 115 BVerfGE 118. Am J Int Law 101:466–471

National commission on terrorist attacks upon the United States (2004) The 9/11 commission report. W.W. Norton & Co., New York

Nurick L (1945) The distinction between combatant and noncombatant in the law of war. Am J Int Law 39:680–697

Overy R (2005) Air warfare. In: Townsend Charles (ed) The Oxford history of modern war. Oxford University Press, Oxford, pp 262–279

Owen M (2012) No easy day: the autobiography of a Navy Seal. Dutton, New York

Owen T, Kiernan B (2006) Bombs over Cambodia. The Walrus pp 62–69. http://www.yale.edu/cgp/Walrus_CambodiaBombing_OCT06.pdf. Accessed 25 March 2015

Pape R (1996) Bombing to win. Cornell University Press, Ithaca

Parks WH (2009) Combatants. Int Law Stud 85:247–306

Parks WH (2010) Part IX of the ICRC "Direct Participation in Hostilities" study: no mandate, no expertise, and legally incorrect. NYU J Int Law Politics 42:769–830

Pomper S (2012) Toward a limited consensus on the loss of civilian immunity in non-international armed conflict: making progress through practice. Int Law Stud 88:181–193

Pouw E (2013) International human rights law and the law of armed conflict in the context of counterinsurgency. PhD dissertation, University of Amsterdam, on file with the author

Raviv D, Melman Y (2012) Spies against Armageddon: inside Israel's secret wars. Levant Books, Sea Cliff

Ricks T (2007) Fiasco: the American military adventure in Iraq. Penguin Books, New York

Roach K (2011) The 9/11 effect: comparative counter-terrorism. Cambridge University Press, Cambridge

Roberts A (2008) The equal application of the laws of war: a principle under pressure. Int Rev Red Cross 90:931–962
Roblyer DA (2003) Beyond precision: issues of morality and decision making in minimizing collateral casualties. Paper submitted to the Program in arms control, disarmament and international security, University of Illinois, Urbana-Champaign
Rogers A (2004) Law on the battlefield, 2nd edn. Manchester University Press, Manchester
Saul B (2008) Defining terrorism in international law. Oxford University Press, Oxford
Sanger David E (2012) Confront and conceal: Obama's secret wars and surprising use of American power. Broadway Paperbacks, New York
Scahill J (2013) Dirty wars: the world is a battlefield. Nation Books, New York
Schmitt E, Shanker T (2011) Counterstrike: the untold story of America's secret campaign against Al Qaeda. Times Books, New York
Schmitt M (2004) Targeting and humanitarian law: current issues. Isr Yearb H R 34:59–104
Schmitt M (2005) War, technology, and international humanitarian law. 4 occasional paper series http://www.hpcr.org/pdfs/OccasionalPaper4.pdf. Accessed 25 March 2015
Schmitt M (2010) Deconstructing direct participation in hostilities. NYU J Int Law Pol 42:697–739
Schmitt M (2013b) Wound, capture, or kill: a reply to Ryan Goodman's 'The Power to Kill or Capture Enemy Combatants". Eur J Int Law 24:855–861
Schroen G (2005) First in: an insider's account of how the CIA spearheaded the war on terror in Afghanistan. Ballantine Books, New York
Shapiro J (2013) The terrorist's dilemma: managing violent covert organizations. Princeton University Press, Princeton
Shultz R, Dew A (2006) Insurgents, terrorists and militias: warriors of contemporary combat. Columbia University Press, New York
Slim H (2008) Killing civilians: method, madness, and morality in war. Columbia University Press, New York
Smith R (2006) The utility of force: the art of war in the modern world. Penguin Books, London
Spaight J (1911) War rights on land. MacMillan and Co Ltd, London
Spaight J (1947) Air power and war rights, 3rd edn. Longmans, Green and Co Ltd, London
Strachan H (2013) The direction of war: contemporary strategy in historical perspective. Cambridge University Press, Cambridge
Thomas W (2001) The ethics of destruction. Cornell University Press, Ithaca
Thompson R (1966) Defeating communist insurgency. Hailer Publishing, St Petersburg
Tostensen A, Bull B (2002) Are smart sanctions feasible? World Polit 54(3):373–403
Towle P (1989) Pilots and rebels: the use of aircraft in unconventional warfare 1918–1988. Brassey's (UK) Ltd, London
Townshend C (2002) Terrorism: a very short introduction. Oxford University Press, Oxford
Turkel Commission (2011) Public commission to examine the maritime incident of 31 May 2010: Report part 1 https://www.jewishvirtuallibrary.org/jsource/Society_&_Culture/Turkel Commission.pdf. Accessed 25 March 2015
Urban M (2010) Task force black. St Martin's Griffin, New York
Von Clausewitz C (1976) On war. Princeton University Press, Princeton
Walzer M (2000) Just and unjust wars, 3rd edn. Basic Books, New York
Warden J (1988) The air campaign: planning for combat. National Defense University Press http://www.au.af.mil/au/awc/awcgate/warden/ward-toc.htm. Accessed 25 March 2015
Warden J (1995) The enemy as a system, Airpower Journal. http://www.airpower.maxwell.af.mil/airchronicles/apj/apj95/spr95_files/warden.htm. Accessed 25 March 2015
Watkin K (2005) Warriors without rights? Combatants, unprivileged belligerents, and the struggle over legitimacy. Program on humanitarian policy and conflict research Harvard University, Occasional paper series. http://www.hpcrresearch.org/sites/default/files/publications/OccasionalPaper2.pdf. Accessed 25 March 2015

Watkin K (2010) Opportunity lost: organized armed groups and the ICRC "Direct Participation in Hostilities" interpretive guidance. NYU J Int Law Politics 42:641–695

Watkin K (2012) Use of force during occupation: law enforcement and conduct of hostilities. Int Rev Red Cross 94:267–315

West B (2005) No true glory: a frontline account of the battle of Fallujah. Bantam Dell, New York

Other Consulted Sources

Canadian National Defence (2001) Law of armed conflict at the tactical and operational levels. Joint Doctrine manual, B-GJ-005-104/FP-021

Center for Civilians in Conflict/Columbia Law School (2012) The civilian impact of drones: unexamined costs, unanswered questions. http://web.law.columbia.edu/sites/default/files/microsites/human-rights-institute/files/The%20Civilian%20Impact%20of%20Drones.pdf. Accessed 24 March 2015

Corbett J (1911) Some Principles of maritime strategy. Republished in 2004. Dover Publications Inc, London

Doswald-Beck L (ed) (1995) San Remo manual on international law applicable to armed conflicts at sea. Cambridge University Press, Cambridge

Harvard Program on Humanitarian Policy and Conflict Research (2009) Commentary on the HPCR manual on international law applicable to air and missile warfare http://ihlresearch.org/amw/Commentary%20on%20the%20HPCR%20Manual.pdf. Accessed 24 March 2015

Howard M, Paret P (trans and eds) (1976) Carl Von Clausewitz—on war, Princeton University Press, Princeton

Human Rights Watch (2004) The wedding that became a funeral: US drone attack on marriage procession in Yemen http://www.hrw.org/reports/2014/02/19/wedding-became-funeral. Accessed 24 March 2015

International institute of humanitarian law (2009) Rules of engagement handbook https://www.usnwc.edu/getattachment/7b0d0f70-bb07-48f2-af0a-7474e92d0bb0/San-Remo-ROE-Handbook. Accessed 25 March 2015

Joint Chiefs of Staff (2010) Department of defense dictionary of military and associated terms (2010) (as amended through 15 January 2010) http://www.dtic.mil/doctrine/dod_dictionary/index.html. Accessed 24 March 2015

Joint Chiefs of Staff—US (2013) Joint Targeting, Joint Publication 3-60

Joint Doctrine and Concepts Centre (2004) The joint service manual of the law of armed conflict. Joint Service Publication 383 Ministry of Defence, Shrivenham

Liddell B (1991) Strategy, 2nd edn. A Meridan Book, New York

Mao T-T (1937) On guerrilla warfare. Samuel B Griffith trs (2000). University of Illinois Press, Urbana

NATO/ISAF (2009) Tactical directive, ISAF headquarters http://www.nato.int/isaf/docu/official_texts/Tactical_Directive_090706.pdf. Accessed 25 March 2015

Robertson HB Jr (1997) The principle of the military objective in the law of armed conflict. US Air Force Acad J Law Stud 8:35–70

Sandoz Y et al (eds) (1987), Commentary on the Additional Protocols of 8 June 1977 to the Geneva Conventions of 12 August 1949 (1987) http://www.cicr.org/ihl.nsf/COM/470-750073?OpenDocument. Accessed 24 March 2015

Schmitt M (2009a) Targeting narcoinsurgents in Afghanistan: the limits of international humanitarian law. Yearb Int Hum Law 12:1–20

Schmitt M (2009b) Targeting and international humanitarian law in Afghanistan. Int Law Stud 85:307–333

Schmitt M (ed) (2013a) Tallin manual on the international law applicable to cyber warfare. Cambridge University Press, Cambridge
Schmitt M (2006) Effects based operations and the law of aerial warfare. Wash Univ Glob Stud Law Rev 5(2):265–293
U.S. Army (2006), Marine corps counterinsurgency field manual. Marine corps Warfighting publication No. 3–33.5
U.S. Navy, Marine Corps and Coast Guard (2007) The commander's handbook on the law of naval operations. NWP 1-14 M https://www.usnwc.edu/getattachment/a9b8e92d-2c8d-4779-9925-0defea93325c/. Accessed 24 March 2015
Watkin K (2014a) Targeting in air warfare. Isr Yearb Hum Rights 44:1–67
Watkin K (2014b) Targeting "Islamic State" oil facilities. Int Law Stud 99:499
Zarate J (2011) Treasury's war: unleashing of a new era of financial warfare. Public Affairs, New York

Table of Cases[1]

International

[1]The Table of Cases was compiled by Ms C.C. Diepeveen, Middelburg, The Netherlands, e-mail: cdiep@zeelandnet.nl

T.D. Gill et al. (eds.), *Yearbook of International Humanitarian Law 2014*,
Yearbook of International Humanitarian Law 17,
DOI 10.1007/978-94-6265-091-6

International Criminal Court

International Criminal Tribunal for the Former Yugoslavia

International Criminal Tribunal for Rwanda

Index[2]

[2]The Index was compiled by Ms C.C. Diepeveen, Middelburg, The Netherlands, e-mail: cdiep@zeelandnet.nl

T.D. Gill et al. (eds.), *Yearbook of International Humanitarian Law 2014*,
Yearbook of International Humanitarian Law 17,
DOI 10.1007/978-94-6265-091-6

I

The manufacturer's authorised representative in the EU is Springer Nature Customer Service Centre GmbH, Europaplatz 3, 69115 Heidelberg, Germany. If you have any concerns regarding our products, please contact ProductSafety@springernature.com

Printed and bound by CPI Group (UK) Ltd, Croydon, CR0 4YY
30/09/2026
02225440-0013